One-Stop Internet Resources

Log on to taj.glencoe.com

ONLINE STUDY TOOLS

- Chapter Overviews
- Interactive Tutor
- Self-Check Quizzes
- E-Flashcards

ONLINE RESEARCH

- Student Web Activities
- Web Resources
- Current Events
- State Resources
- Beyond the Textbook Features

ONLINE STUDENT EDITION

- Complete Interactive Student Edition
- Textbook Updates

FOR TEACHERS

- Teacher Forum
- Web Activity Lesson Plans
- Literature Connections

Honoring America

For Americans, the flag has always had a special meaning.
It is a symbol of our nation's freedom and democracy.

Flag Etiquette

Over the years, Americans have developed rules and customs concerning the use and display of the flag. One of the most important things every American should remember is to treat the flag with respect.

- The flag should be raised and lowered by hand and displayed only from sunrise to sunset. On special occasions, the flag may be displayed at night, but it should be illuminated.

- The flag may be displayed on all days, weather permitting, particularly on national and state holidays and on historic and special occasions.

- No flag may be flown above the American flag or to the right of it at the same height.

- The flag should never touch the ground or floor beneath it.

- The flag may be flown at half-staff by order of the president, usually to mourn the death of a public official.

- The flag may be flown upside down only to signal distress.

- The flag should never be carried flat or horizontally, but always carried aloft and free.

- When the flag becomes old and tattered, it should be destroyed by burning. According to an approved custom, the Union (stars on blue field) is first cut from the flag; then the two pieces, which no longer form a flag, are burned.

The American's Creed

I believe in the United States of America as a Government of the people, by the people, for the people, whose just powers are derived from the consent of the governed; a democracy in a republic; a sovereign Nation of many sovereign States; a perfect union, one and inseparable; established upon those principles of freedom, equality, justice, and humanity for which American patriots sacrificed their lives and fortunes.

I therefore believe it is my duty to my Country to love it; to support its Constitution; to obey its laws; to respect its flag, and to defend it against all enemies.

The Pledge of Allegiance

I pledge allegiance to the Flag of the United States of America and to the Republic for which it stands, one Nation under God, indivisible, with liberty and justice for all.

The American Journey

Reconstruction to the Present

Joyce Appleby, Ph.D.

Alan Brinkley, Ph.D.

James M. McPherson, Ph.D.

NATIONAL GEOGRAPHIC

McGraw Hill Glencoe

New York, New York   Columbus, Ohio   Chicago, Illinois   Peoria, Illinois   Woodland Hills, California

Authors

Joyce Appleby, Ph.D. is Professor of History at UCLA. Dr. Appleby's published works include *Inheriting the Revolution: The First Generation of Americans; Capitalism and a New Social Order: The Jeffersonian Vision of the 1790s;* and *Ideology and Economic Thought in Seventeenth-Century England,* which won the Berkshire Prize. She served as president of both the Organization of American Historians and the American Historical Association, and chaired the Council of the Institute of Early American History and Culture at Williamsburg. Dr. Appleby has been elected to the American Philosophical Society and the American Academy of Arts and Sciences, and is a Corresponding Fellow of the British Academy.

Alan Brinkley, Ph.D. is Allan Nevins Professor of American History at Columbia University. His published works include *Voices of Protest: Huey Long, Father Coughlin, and the Great Depression,* which won the 1983 National Book Award; *The End of Reform: New Deal Liberalism in Recession and War; The Unfinished Nation: A Concise History of the American People;* and *Liberalism and its Discontents.* He received the Levenson Memorial Teaching Prize at Harvard University.

James M. McPherson, Ph.D. is George Henry Davis Professor of American History at Princeton University. Dr. McPherson is the author of 11 books about the Civil War era. These include *Battle Cry of Freedom: The Civil War Era,* for which he won the Pulitzer Prize in 1989, and *For Cause and Comrades: Why Men Fought in the Civil War,* for which he won the 1998 Lincoln Prize. He is a member of many professional historical associations, including the the Civil War Preservation Trust.

The National Geographic Society, founded in 1888 for the increase and diffusion of geographic knowledge, is the world's largest nonprofit scientific and educational organization. Since its earliest days, the Society has used sophisticated communication technologies, from color photography to holography, to convey knowledge to a worldwide membership. The School Publishing Division supports the Society's mission by developing innovative educational programs—ranging from traditional print materials to multimedia programs including CD-ROMs, videodiscs, and software. "National Geographic Geography & History," featured in each unit of this textbook, was designed and developed by the National Geographic Society's School Publishing Division.

About the Cover The images on the cover are: *Apollo* astronaut saluting U.S. flag on the moon, Statue of Liberty, Abraham Lincoln, Rosa Parks, Benjamin Franklin, and Colin Powell.

Send all inquiries to:
Glencoe/McGraw-Hill, 8787 Orion Place, Columbus, Ohio 43240-4027

ISBN 0-07-865399-1 (Student Edition) ISBN 0-07-865400-9 (Teacher Wraparound Edition)
Printed in the United States of America.
5 6   027/043   08 07 06

Consultants & Reviewers

Academic Consultants

Richard G. Boehm, Ph.D.
Professor of Geography
Southwest Texas State University
San Marcos, Texas

Margo J. Byerly, Ph.D.
Assistant Professor of Social
   Studies Methods
Ball State University
Muncie, Indiana

Maureen D. Danner
Project CRISS
National Training Consultant
Kalispell, MT

Frank de Varona
Visiting Associate Professor
Department of Curriculum and
   Instruction
Florida International University
Miami, Florida

William E. Nelson, Jr., Ph.D.
Research Professor of Black Studies
   and Professor of Political Science
The Ohio State University
Columbus, Ohio

Bernard Reich, Ph.D.
Professor of Political Science
   and International Affairs
George Washington University
Washington, D.C.

Donald A. Ritchie, Ph.D.
Associate Historian of the United
   States Senate Historical Office
Washington, D.C.

Carol Santa, Ph.D.
CRISS Project Developer
Kalispell, MT

Elmer Whitcraft
Project CRISS Master Trainer
Kalispell, MT

FOLDABLES Dinah Zike
Educational Consultant
Dinah–Might Activities, Inc.
San Antonio, Texas

Teacher Reviewers

John R. Doyle
Director, Division of Social Sciences
Dade County Public Schools
Miami, Florida

David J. Engstrom
American History Teacher
Discovery Junior High School
Fargo, North Dakota

Harry J. Hancock
Social Studies Teacher
Theodore Roosevelt
   Middle School
Kenner, Louisiana

**Elysa E. Toler Robinson,
   Ed.D.**
Program Supervisor
Detroit Public Schools
Detroit, Michigan

Kay R. Selah
Social Studies Teacher
Landmark Middle School
Jacksonville, Florida

Deborah N. Smith
Social Studies Teacher
New Albany Middle School
New Albany, Ohio

Larry John Smith
United States History Teacher
Mt. Savage School
Mt. Savage, Maryland

Cheryl Summers
Clinical Supervisor
Albuquerque Public Schools
Albuquerque, New Mexico

Renée Marie Trufant
Social Studies and
   Communications Skills
   Teacher
Brevard Middle School
Brevard, North Carolina

Sonya Lou Weaver
Social Studies Teacher
Greencastle–Antrim
   Middle School
Greencastle, Pennsylvania

Carol Davenport Wood
Social Studies Teacher
Lusher Extension
New Orleans, Louisiana

Contents

Features

What If...

Causes and Effects

TIME NOTEBOOK

Why It Matters

SKILLBUILDER

Critical Thinking

Social Studies

Study & Writing

Technology

People In History

Fact Fiction Folklore

Primary Source Quotes

A variety of quotations and excerpts throughout the text express the thoughts, feelings, and life experiences of people, past and present.

Primary Source Quotes

Charts & Graphs

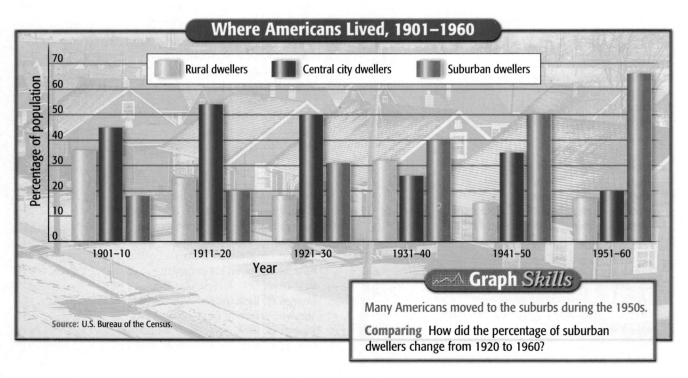

Where Americans Lived, 1901–1960

Rural dwellers   Central city dwellers   Suburban dwellers

Percentage of population

Year

Source: U.S. Bureau of the Census.

Graph Skills

Many Americans moved to the suburbs during the 1950s.

Comparing How did the percentage of suburban dwellers change from 1920 to 1960?

Previewing Your Textbook

Your textbook has been organized to help you learn about the significant events and people that make up American history. Before you start reading, though, here is a road map to help you understand what you will encounter in the pages of this textbook. Follow this road map before you read so that you can understand how this textbook works.

Units

Your textbook is divided into 5 units. Each unit begins with two pages of information to help you begin your study of the topics.

WHY IT MATTERS
Each unit begins with *Why It Matters.* This is a short summary about what you will study in the unit and the important topics in the unit.

QUOTATION
A short quotation gives a glimpse of the idea of a key figure from the era.

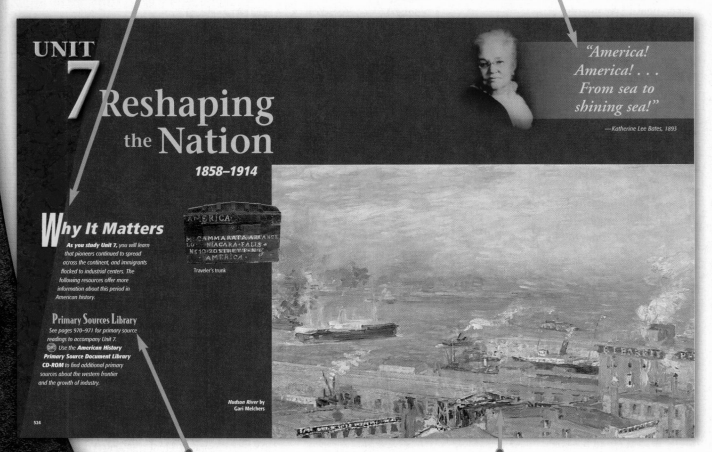

UNIT

7 Reshaping the Nation

1858–1914

Why It Matters

As you study Unit 7, you will learn that pioneers continued to spread across the continent, and immigrants flocked to industrial centers. The following resources offer more information about this period in American history.

Primary Sources Library
See pages 970–971 for primary source readings to accompany Unit 7. Use the *American History Primary Source Document Library* **CD-ROM** to find additional primary sources about the western frontier and the growth of industry.

Traveler's trunk

Hudson River by
Gari Melchers

524

"America! America! . . . From sea to shining sea!"

—Katherine Lee Bates, 1893

PRIMARY SOURCE LIBRARY
This tells you where to find the *Primary Sources Library* readings that accompany the unit.

VISUALS
A photograph or painting shows you what life was like during the time period.

Previewing Your Textbook

Chapters

Each unit in *The American Journey: Reconstruction to the Present* is made up of chapters. Each chapter starts by providing you with background information to help you get the most out of the chapter.

CHAPTER TITLE
The chapter title tells you the main topic you will be reading about.

WHY IT MATTERS
Why It Matters tells you why events you will study are important.

THE IMPACT TODAY
The Impact Today explains how these events changed the way we live today.

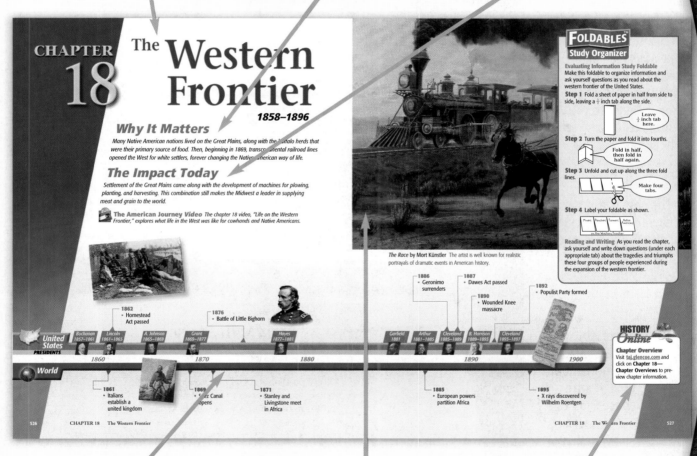

TIME LINE
The time line shows you when and where events happened during the period of time covered in the chapter.

VISUALS
A photograph or painting shows how people of the time lived.

WEB SITE
History Online directs you to the Internet where you can find more information, activities, and quizzes.

Previewing Your Textbook

Sections

A section is a division, or part, of the chapter. The first page of the section, the section opener, helps you set a purpose for reading.

READING STRATEGY
Completing the *Reading Strategy* activity will help you organize the information as you read the section.

READ TO LEARN
Keep the *Read to Learn* statements in mind as you read the section.

SECTION THEMES
Your textbook organizes the events of your nation's past and present around themes. You can read about the themes on pages xviii-xix.

MAIN IDEA
The *Main Idea* of this section is introduced here. Below it are important terms you will encounter as you read the section.

TIME LINE
The time line identifies important events you will study in the section.

AN AMERICAN STORY
Think of *An American Story* as a moment in time. It introduces you to an important event that you will read about.

SECTION 1 **The Mining Booms**

Guide to Reading

Main Idea
Discoveries of gold and silver drew thousands of fortune seekers to the West.

Key Terms
lode, ore, vigilante, ghost town, subsidy, transcontinental

Reading Strategy
Analyzing Information As you read the section, re-create the diagram below and explain why these places were significant to the mining boom.

	Significance
Pikes Peak	
Comstock Lode	
Promontory Point	

Read to Learn
• how the rush to find gold and silver led to the growth of new communities in the West.
• how development of the railroads affected the nation.

Section Theme
Geography and History Rail lines and mining speeded the flow of settlers to the West.

Preview of Events

1855 — 1865 — 1875 — 1885

1858 Gold is discovered at Pikes Peak
1869 Transcontinental railroad links East and West
1876 Colorado joins the Union
1883 Nation is divided into four time zones

AN American Story

*"We'll cross the bold Missouri, and we'll steer for the West,
And we'll take the road we think is the shortest and the best,
We'll travel over plains where the wind is blowing bleak,
And the sandy wastes shall echo with—Hurrah for Pikes Peak."*
—"The Gold Seeker's Song"

Miners sang this hopeful song in 1859 as they headed for Pikes Peak, Colorado, where gold had been discovered.

Mining Is Big Business

By the mid-1850s the California Gold Rush had ended. Disappointed miners, still hoping to strike it rich, began prospecting in other parts of the West.

In 1858 a mining expedition found gold on the slopes of **Pikes Peak** in the Colorado Rockies. Newspapers claimed that miners were making $20 a day panning for gold—a large sum at a time when servants made less than a dollar

528 CHAPTER 18 The Western Frontier

xiv

Previewing Your Textbook

Reading Roadmap

You will get more out of your textbook if you recognize the different elements that help you to understand what you read.

MAPS

Easy-to-read maps provide a link between geography and history. Questions test your understanding of the map's information.

PHOTOGRAPHS

Photographs show you important people, places, and events of the time. Questions help you interpret the photographs and relate them to content.

READING CHECKS

This *Reading Check* helps you check yourself. Did you understand the main ideas?

OUTLINE

Think of the headings as forming an outline. The blue titles are the main heading. The red titles that follow are the subsections.

VOCABULARY

The terms in blue are the key terms. The definition is also included here.

SECTION ASSESSMENT

The *Section Assessment* is the last item in every section. Completing the assessment can help evaluate how well you understand the material covered in this section.

NATIONAL GEOGRAPHIC
Western Native Americ...

Geography Skills

During the late 1800s, Native Americans and the United Sta... Army fought many battles over land.
1. **Location** In what state did the Battle of Little Bighor... take place?
2. **Analyzing Information** Which Native American nations resettled in present-day Oklahoma?

One large reservation was in **Oklahom**... "Indian Territory" that Congress had cre... the 1830s for Native Americans relocate... the Southeast. Another one, meant for th... people, was in the **Dakota Territory.** Ma... the reservations would be the job of the... Bureau of Indian Affairs.

Government agents often used tri... persuade Native American nations to... the reservations. Many reservation... located on poor land. In addition the... ment often failed to deliver promised...

544   CHAPTER 18   The Western Frontier

Analyzing *Political Cartoons*
This cartoon shows President Theodore Roosevelt in the role of the world's policeman. Roosevelt was given the title because of his "big stick" diplomacy. Do you think the cartoonist agrees with Roosevelt acting as an international policeman? Why or why not?

Colonel **William Gorgas,** an army doctor who had helped eliminate yellow fever in Cuba, went to Panama to fight the diseases. Gorgas instructed workers to drain swamps, spray insecticides, spread oil on stagnant pools of water, and cut grassy marshes in order to destroy mosquito breeding places. By 1906 these measures had eliminated yellow fever and greatly reduced the number of malaria cases. Without controlling disease, the United States could not have built the canal.

The Panama Canal was regarded as one of the great engineering feats of the time. Thousands of workers struggled to carve a path through the dense jungle and over mountains. They dug out huge amounts of earth and rock and used them to build a dam. They created a large lake and constructed giant locks to raise and lower ships from sea level over the mountains and then back to sea level again on the other side of the isthmus.

The Grand Opening
The Panama Canal opened on August 15, 1914, and a cargo ship, the *Ancon,* made the first trip through the canal. A great success from the start, the canal reduced shipping costs by cutting more than 7,000 miles off the voyage from New York City to San Francisco. The canal also helped extend American naval power by allowing the United States fleet to move freely between the Atlantic and Pacific Oceans.

In the long run, the canal guaranteed a strong American presence in Latin America, where the United States now had a valuable

658   CHAPTER 22   Overseas Expansion

property it intended to protect. Yet many Latin Americans remained bitter over how the Canal Zone was acquired. This resentment soured relations between the United States and Latin America for years.

✔ **Reading Check** **Analyzing** Why was Panama chosen as the site for a canal connecting the Atlantic and Pacific Oceans?

Policing the Western Hemisphere
President Roosevelt often quoted an African proverb, "Speak softly and carry a big stick." He believed the United States should respond to foreign crises not by threats but by military action. Roosevelt became known for his "big stick" approach to foreign affairs. America must exercise "an international police power," he maintained, to preserve order and prevent the world from falling into anarchy—disorder and lawlessness.

Roosevelt Corollary
Roosevelt worried that instability in the Caribbean region would lead European powers to intervene. Two incidents confirmed his fears. In 1902, when Venezuela failed to meet payments on its loans, European nations imposed a blockade. The following year a revolution in the Dominican Republic toppled the government, causing concern that European powers would step in to protect their financial interests there.

United States, he delivered a farewell... Congress. "Old soldiers never die," he said, "they just fade away."

✔ **Reading Check** **Comparing** How did Truman's view on the Korean War differ from General MacArthur's view?

SECTION 3 ASSESSMENT

Checking for Understanding
1. **Key Terms** Define the following terms: stalemate, demilitarized zone.
2. **Reviewing Facts** How did the Korean War begin?

Reviewing Themes
3. **Global Connections** How did American goals change during the course of the Korean War?

Critical Thinking
4. **Identifying Central Issues** Do you think Truman should have allowed MacArthur to attack China? Why or why not?
5. **Organizing Information** Re-create the diagram below and provide two reasons for the Korean War ending in a stalemate.

◯ → ◯ → ◯ (Stalemate)

Analyzing Visuals
6. **Geography Skills** Examine the map on page 803. When did UN forces make their farthest advance?

Interdisciplinary Activity
Persuasive Writing Write a one-page editorial in which you argue whether a U.S. military leader should or should not be able to override a president's decision.

CHAPTER 27   The Cold War Era   805

xv

Previewing Your Textbook

Special Features

A variety of special features will help you as you study *The American Journey: Reconstruction to the Present.*

PEOPLE IN HISTORY

People in History tells you the story of individuals that influenced American history.

People In History

Edward Rickenbacker 1890–1973

The son of Swiss immigrants who settled in Ohio, Edward Rickenbacker was the leading American combat pilot of World War I. "Captain Eddie" recorded 26 official victories against German aircraft during World War I and was awarded

automobile engines, then struck out on his own as a race car driver; he won many championships and set a world record for speed driving.

When the United States entered the war, Rickenbacker volunteered. After less than

American squadron and won more victories than any other squadron.

After the war, Rickenbacker was associated with several automotive and aviation companies. He purchased and managed the Indianapolis Motor Speedway. He also built Eastern Airlines

SKILLBUILDERS

Skillbuilders teach valuable skills that will be useful throughout the book.

Study & Writing SKILLBUILDER

Outlining

Why Learn This Skill?

To sketch a scene, you first draw the rough shape, or outline, of the picture. Then you fill in this rough shape with details. Outlining written material is a similar process. You begin with the rough shape of

Outline of Chapter 2
I. European Allies
    A. Allied armies
        1. Trench war

TWO VIEWPOINTS

Two Viewpoints compares the opposing viewpoints of two historic figures on a particular issue.

TWO VIEWPOINTS

Should We Welcome or Prevent Immigration to Our Country?

Immigrants struggled to find their place in American society. They changed American society with customs from their cultures. Many Americans resisted these changes and warned against further immigration.

San Francisco Real Estate Circular, September 1874

The Chinese come for a season only; and, while they give their labor, they do not [spend the money they earn] in the country. They do not come to settle or make homes . . . To compare the Chinese with even the lowest white laborers is, therefore, absurd.

Our best interests are suffering of these Asiatic slaves; we are trying to make them live decently while here, and to discourage their arrival in such numbers as to drive white laborers out of the country. . . .

Chinese immigrants

Attorney Louis Marshall Speaks Out Against Limiting Immigration, 1924

In common with all other immigrants, those who have come from the countries sought to be tabooed [forbidden] have been industrious, and law-abiding and have made valuable contributions to our industrial, commercial and social development. . . .

To say that they are not assimilable argues ignorance. The facts show that they adopt American standards of living and that they are permeated [filled] with the spirit of our institutions. It is said that they speak foreign languages, but in those foreign languages they are taught to love our Government. . . .

Louis Marshall

Learning From History

1. What did the writer from San Francisco seem to fear?
2. What did Louis Marshall claim about the immigrants' contributions?
3. What facts does Marshall use to support his view that the newcomers are "assimilable"?

communitihoods of Je
nese, and
developed
San Franci

The imr
some of th
The comr
revolved
tional in
were the
churches
worship
were cele
their hor
often act

The in
papers
opened
organize
munitie
immigra
heritage

Read

assim

Nativ

Assi
the at
Americ
happy
low
worke
These
immigr
jobs
wage

Eth
ence
Amer
Some Americans argued that the new immigrants—with their foreign languages, unfamiliar religions, and distinctive customs—did not fit into American society.

AMERICA'S LITERATURE

America's Literature analyzes excerpts from famous pieces of American fiction and describes its historical lessons.

America's LITERATURE

Maya Angelou (1928–)

Maya Angelou, born in 1928, has written poetry, fiction, and plays. Born Marguerite Johnson, Angelou and her brother, Bailey, were raised by their grandmother, Annie Henderson, the owner of a general store in Stamps, Arkansas.

READ TO DISCOVER

In the following excerpt from Angelou's autobiography, she is about 10 years old. Bright but painfully self-conscious, she has become withdrawn and refuses to speak to anyone. As you read, pay attention to the actions of the characters.

READER'S DICTIONARY

familiar: close friend or associate

Her World by Philip Evergood

I Know Why the Caged Bird Sing

Mrs. Bertha Flowers was the aristocrat of Black Stamps. She had the grace of control to appear warm in the coldest weather, and on the Arkansas summer days it seemed she had a private breeze which swirled around, cooling her. . . .

She was one of the few gentlewomen I have ever known, and has remained throughout my life the measure of what a human being can be.

Momma had a strange relationship with her. Most often when she passed on the road in front of the Store, she spoke to Momma in that soft yet carrying voice, "Good day, Mrs. Henderson." Momma responded with "How you, Sister Flowers?"

Mrs. Flowers didn't belong to our church, nor was she Momma's **familiar.** Why on earth did she insist on calling her Sister Flowers? Shame made me want to hide my face. Mrs. Flowers deserved better than to be called Sister. Then, Momma left out the verb. Why not ask, "How *are* you, Mrs. Flowers?" With the unbalanced passion of the young, I hated her for showing her ignorance to Mrs. Flowers. It didn't occur to me for many years that they were as alike as sisters, separated only by formal education. . . .

Occasionally, though, Mrs. Flowers would drift off the road and down to the Store and Momma would say to me, "Sister, you go on and play." As I left I would hear the beginning of an intimate conversation. Momma persistently using the wrong verb, or none at all. . . .

I heard the soft-voiced Mrs. Flowers and the textured voice of my grandmother merging and melting. They were interrupted from time to time by giggles that must have come from Mrs. Flowers. . . .

She acted just as refined as whitefolks in the movies and books and she was more beautiful, for none of them could have come near that warm color without looking gray by comparison.

From *I Know Why the Caged Bird Sings,* by Maya Angelou. Copyright © 1969 by Maya Angelou. Reprinted by permission of Random House, Inc.

ANALYZING LITERATURE

1. **Recall and Interpret** Describe the relationship between Momma and Mrs. Flowers.

2. **Evaluate and Connect** Do you think you would like Mrs. Flowers? Explain.

Interdisciplinary Activity

Informative Writing Write a one-page sketch describing an encounter you had with a person who influenced your life in a positive way.

Reviewing Themes

3. **Culture and Traditions** What were some of the cultural differences that immigrants had to adjust to in the United States?

Anti-immigrant feelings

Scavenger Hunt

The American Journey contains a wealth of information. The trick is to know where to look to access all the information in the book. If you run through this scavenger hunt exercise with your teachers or parents, you will see how the textbook is organized, and how to get the most out of your reading and study time. Let's get started!

1. How many chapters and how many units are in the book?

2. What time period does Unit 7 cover?

3. How many chapters are there in Unit 9? What is this unit about?

4. What is the title of Chapter 29, Section 1?

5. On what page of Chapter 18 can you find the *Foldables* Activity? What does the Activity help you do?

6. What is the skill you practice when you do the Chapter 19 Skillbuilder?

7. There are 3 Web sites in Chapter 25. The first previews the chapter and the second summarizes it. What does the third one do?

8. You want to quickly find all the maps in the book on World War II? Where do you look?

9. Most sections of a chapter open with an excerpt from a primary source—a document or other testimony dating from the period. Where else can you find extended primary sources in the textbook?

10. Where can you learn the definition of a physical map, a political map, and a special-purpose map?

How Do I Study History?

As you read *The American Journey: Reconstruction to the Present*, you will be given help in sorting out all the information you encounter. This textbook organizes the events of your nation's past and present around 10 themes. A theme is a concept, or main idea that happens again and again throughout history. By recognizing these themes, you will better understand events of the past and how they affect you today.

Themes in *The American Journey: Reconstruction to the Present*

Culture and Traditions
Being aware of cultural differences helps us understand ourselves and others. People from around the world for generations have sung of the "land of the Pilgrims' pride, land where our fathers died" even though their ancestors arrived on these shores long after these events occurred.

Continuity and Change
Recognizing our historic roots helps us understand why things are the way they are today. This theme includes political, social, religious, and economic changes that have influenced the way Americans think and act.

Geography and History
Understanding geography helps us understand how humans interact with their environment. The United States succeeded in part because of its rich natural resources and its vast open spaces. In many regions, the people changed the natural landscape to fulfill their wants and needs.

Individual Action

Responsible individuals have often stepped forward to help lead the nation. America's strong family values helped create such individuals. These values spring in part from earlier times when the home was the center of many activities, including work, education, and daily worship.

Groups and Institutions

Identifying how political and social groups and institutions work helps us work together. From the beginning, Americans formed groups and institutions to act in support of their economic, political, and religious beliefs.

Government and Democracy

Understanding the workings of government helps us become good citizens. Abraham Lincoln explained the meaning of democracy as "government of the people, by the people, for the people." Democracy, at its best, is "among" the people.

Science and Technology

Americans have always been quick to adopt innovations. The nation was settled and built by people who blended their old ways with new ways. Americans' lives are deeply influenced by technology, the use of science and machines. Perhaps no machine has so shaped modern life as the automobile. Understanding the roles of science and technology helps us see their impact on our society and the roles they will play in the future.

Economic Factors

The free enterprise economy of the United States is consistent with the nation's history of rights and freedoms. Freedom of choice in economic decisions supports other freedoms. Understanding the concept of free enterprise is basic to studying American history.

Global Connections

The world seems smaller than it did only 50 years ago. Modern transportation and communication have brought people around the globe closer together. As a result, countries today are more dependent on one another. As citizens of the United States and members of the global community, we have a responsibility to keep informed about developments in other nations and the world. Being aware of global interdependence helps us make decisions and deal with the difficult issues we will encounter.

Civic Rights and Responsibilities

For a democratic system to survive, its citizens must take an active role in government. The foundation of democracy is the right of every person to take part in government and to voice one's views on issues. An appreciation for the struggle to preserve these freedoms is vital to the understanding of democracy.

Using the Themes

You will find Section Themes at the beginning of every section of your text. You are asked questions that help you put it all together to better understand how ideas and themes are connected across time—and to see why history is important to you today.

READING TO LEARN

This handbook focuses on skills and strategies that can help you understand the words you read. The strategies you use to understand whole texts depend on the kind of text you are reading. In other words, you don't read a textbook the way you read a novel. You read a textbook mainly for information; you read a novel mainly for fun. To get the most out of your reading, you need to choose the right strategy to fit the reason you're reading.

USE THIS HANDBOOK TO HELP YOU LEARN

- how to identify new words and build your vocabulary
- how to adjust the way you read to fit your reason for reading
- how to use specific reading strategies to better understand what you read
- how to use critical thinking strategies to think more deeply about what you read

You will also learn about

- text structures
- reading for research

TABLE OF CONTENTS

Identifying Words and Building Vocabulary

What do you do when you come across a word you do not know as you read? Do you skip over the word and keep reading? If you are reading for fun or entertainment, you might. But if you are reading for information, an unfamiliar word may get in the way of your understanding. When that happens, try the following strategies to figure out how to say the word and what the word means.

Reading Unfamiliar Words

Sounding out the word One way to figure out how to say a new word is to sound it out, syllable by syllable. Look carefully at the word's beginning, middle, and ending. Inside the word, do you see a word you already know how to pronounce? What vowels are in the syllables? Use the following tips when sounding out new words.

- **Roots and base words** The main part of a word is called its root. When the root is a complete word, it may be called the base word. When you come across a new word, check whether you recognize its root or base word. It can help you pronounce the word and figure out the word's meaning.

ASK YOURSELF

- What letters make up the beginning sound or beginning syllable of the word?

  Example: In the word *coagulate, co* rhymes with *so.*

- What sounds do the letters in the middle part of the word make?

  Example: In the word *coagulate,* the syllable *ag* has the same sound as the

  ag in *bag,* and the syllable *u* is pronounced like the letter *u.*

- What letters make up the ending sound or syllable?

  Example: In the word *coagulate, late* is a familiar word you already know how to pronounce.

- Now try pronouncing the whole word:

  co ag u late.

- **Prefixes** A prefix is a word part that can be added to the beginning of a root or base word. For example, the prefix *pre-* means "before," so *prehistory* means "before history." Prefixes can change, or even reverse, the meaning of a word. For example, *un-* means "not," so *unconstitutional* means "not constitutional."

- **Suffixes** A suffix is a word part that can be added to the end of a root or base word to change the word's meaning. Adding a suffix to a word can also change that word from one part of speech to another. For example, the word *joy,* which is a noun, becomes an adjective when the suffix *-ful* (meaning "full of") is added. *Joyful* means "full of joy."

Determining a Word's Meaning

Using syntax Like all languages, the English language has rules and patterns for the way words are arranged in sentences. The way a sentence is organized is called the **syntax** of the sentence. If English is your first language, you have known this pattern since you started talking in sentences. If you're learning English now, you may find the syntax is different from the patterns you know in your first language.

In a simple sentence in English, someone or something (the *subject*) does something (the *predicate* or *verb*) to or with another person or thing (the *object*): The *soldiers attacked* the *enemy.*

Sometimes adjectives, adverbs, and phrases are added to add details to the sentence: The *courageous young* soldiers *fearlessly* attacked the *well-entrenched* enemy *shortly after dawn.*

CHECK IT OUT

Knowing about syntax can help you figure out the meaning of an unfamiliar word. Just look at how syntax can help you figure out the following nonsense sentence.

The blizzy kwarkles sminched the flerky fleans.

Your experience with English syntax tells you that the action word, or verb, in this sentence is *sminched.* Who did the *sminching? The kwarkles.* What kind of kwarkles were they? *Blizzy.* Whom did they *sminch?* The fleans. What kind of fleans were they? *Flerky.* Even though you don't know the meaning of the words in the nonsense sentence, you can make some sense of the entire sentence by studying its syntax.

Using context clues You can often figure out the meaning of an unfamiliar word by looking at its context, the words and sentences that surround it. To learn new words as you read, follow these steps for using context clues.

1. Look before and after the unfamiliar word for:
   • a definition or a synonym, another word that means the same as the unfamiliar word.
   • a general topic associated with the word.
   • a clue to what the word is similar to or different from.
   • an action or a description that has something to do with the word.
2. Connect what you already know with what the author has written.
3. Predict a possible meaning.
4. Use the meaning in the sentence.
5. Try again if your guess does not make sense.

Using reference materials Dictionaries and other reference sources can help you learn new words. Check out these reference sources:

• A **dictionary** gives the pronunciation and the meaning or meanings of words. Some dictionaries also give other forms of words, their parts of speech, and synonyms. You might also find the historical background of a word, such as its Greek, Latin, or Anglo-Saxon origins.

• A **glossary** is a word list that appears at the end—or Appendix—of a book or other written work and includes only words that are in that work. Like dictionaries, glossaries have the pronunciation and definitions of words.

• A **thesaurus** lists groups of words that have the same, or almost the same, meaning. Words with similar meanings are called *synonyms.* Seeing the synonyms of words can help you build your vocabulary.

Recognizing Word Meanings Across Subjects

Have you ever learned a new word in one class and then noticed it in your reading for other subjects? The word probably will not mean exactly the same thing in each class. But you can use what you know about the word's meaning to help you understand what it means in a different subject area.

CHECK IT OUT

Look at the following example from three subjects:

Social studies: One major **product** manufactured in the South is cotton cloth.

Math: After you multiply those two numbers, explain how you arrived at the **product.**

Science: One **product** of photosynthesis is oxygen.

Reading for a Reason

Why are you reading that paperback mystery? What do you hope to get from your geography textbook? And are you going to read either of these books in the same way that you read a restaurant menu? The point is, you read for different reasons. The reason you are reading something helps you decide on the reading strategies you use with a text. In other words, how you read will depend on **why** you're reading.

Knowing Your Reason for Reading

In school and in life, you will have many reasons for reading, and those reasons will lead you to a wide range of materials. For example,

- **to learn and understand new information,** you might read news magazines, textbooks, news on the Internet, books about your favorite pastime, encyclopedia articles, primary and secondary sources for a school report, instructions on how to use a calling card, or directions for a standardized test.

- **to find specific information,** you might look at the sports section for the score of last night's game, a notice on where to register for a field trip, weather reports, bank statements, or television listings.

- **to be entertained,** you might read your favorite magazine, e-mails or letters from friends, the Sunday comics, or even novels, short stories, plays, or poems!

Adjusting How Fast You Read

How quickly or how carefully you should read a text depends on your purpose for reading it. Because there are many reasons and ways to read, think about your purpose and choose a strategy that works best. Try out these strategies:

- **Scanning** means quickly running your eyes over the material, looking for *key words or phrases* that point to the information you're looking for. Scan when you need to find a particular piece or type of information. For example, you might scan a newspaper for movie show times.

- **Skimming** means quickly reading a piece of writing *to find its main idea* or to *get a general overview* of it. For example, you might skim the sports section of the daily newspaper to find out how your favorite teams are doing. Or you might skim a chapter in your textbook to prepare for a test.

- **Careful reading** involves *reading slowly and paying attention* with a purpose in mind. Read carefully when you're learning new concepts, following complicated directions, or preparing to explain information to someone else.

Understanding What You Read

Reading without understanding is like trying to drive a car on an empty gas tank. Fortunately, there are techniques you can use to help you concentrate on and understand what you read. Skilled readers adopt a number of strategies before, during, and after reading to make sure they understand what they read.

Previewing

If you were making a preview for a movie, you would want to let your audience know what the movie is like. When you preview a piece of writing, you are trying to get an idea about that piece of writing. If you know what to expect before reading, you will have an easier time understanding ideas and relationships. Follow these steps to preview your reading assignments.

DO IT!

1. Look at the title and any illustrations that are included.
2. Read the headings, subheadings, and anything in bold letters.
3. Skim over the passage to see how it is organized. Is it divided into many parts?

Is it a long poem or short story? Don't forget to look at the graphics—pictures, maps, or diagrams.

4. Set a purpose for your reading. Are you reading to learn something new? Are you reading to find specific information?

Using What You Know

Believe it or not, you already know quite a bit about what you are going to read. You bring knowledge and personal experience to a selection. Drawing on your own background is called *activating prior knowledge,* and it can help you create meaning in what you read. Ask yourself, *What do I already know about this topic?*

Predicting

You do not need any special knowledge to make *predictions* when you read. The predictions do not even have to be accurate. Take educated guesses before and during your reading about what might happen in the story or article you are reading.

Visualizing

Creating pictures in your mind as you read—called *visualizing*—is a powerful aid to understanding. As you read, set up a movie theater in your imagination. Picture the setting—city streets, the desert, or the surface of the moon. If you can visualize what you read, selections will be more vivid, and you will recall them better later on.

Identifying Sequence

When you discover the logical order of events or ideas, you are identifying *sequence.* Do you need to understand step-by-step directions? Are you reading a persuasive speech with the reasons listed in order of importance? Look for clues and signal words that will help you find the way information is organized.

Determining the Main Idea

When you look for the *main idea* of a selection, you look for the most important idea. The examples, reasons, and details that further explain the main idea are called *supporting details.* Some main ideas are clearly stated within a passage—often in the first sentence of a paragraph, or sometimes in the last sentence of a passage. Other times, an author does not directly state the main idea but provides details that help readers figure out what the main idea is.

ASK YOURSELF

- What is each sentence about?
- Is there one sentence that tells about the whole passage or that is more important

than any of the other sentences?
- What main idea do the supporting details point out?

Questioning

Keep up a conversation with yourself as you read by *asking questions* about the text. Ask about the importance of the information you are reading. Ask how one event relates to another. Ask yourself if you understand what you just read. As you answer your questions, you are making sure that you understand what is going on.

Clarifying

Clear up, or *clarify,* confusing or difficult passages as you read. When you realize you do not understand something, try these techniques to help you clarify the ideas.
- *Reread* the confusing parts slowly and carefully.
- *Look up* unfamiliar words.
- Simply *"talk out"* the part to yourself.

Reread the passage. The second time is often easier and more informative.

Reviewing

You probably *review* in school what you learned the day before so the ideas are firm in your mind. Reviewing when you read does the same thing. Take time now and then to pause and review what you have read. Think about the main ideas and reorganize them for yourself so you can recall them later. Filling in study aids such as graphic organizers, notes, or outlines can help you review.

Monitoring Your Comprehension

As you read, check your understanding by using the following strategies.

- **Summarize** what you read by pausing from time to time and telling yourself the main ideas of what you have just read. Answer the questions *Who? What?*

Where? When? Why? and *How?* Summarizing tests your comprehension by encouraging you to clarify key points in your own words.

- **Paraphrase** Sometimes you read something that you "sort of" understand, but not quite. Use paraphrasing as a test to see whether you really got the point. *Paraphrasing* is retelling something in your own words. So shut the book and try putting what you have just read into your own words. If you cannot explain it clearly, you should probably have another look at the text.

Thinking About Your Reading

Sometimes it is important to think more deeply about what you have read so you can get the most out of what the author says. These critical thinking skills will help you go beyond what the words say and get at the important messages of your reading.

Interpreting

When you listen to your best friend talk, you do not just hear the words he or she says. You also watch your friend, listen to the tone of voice, and use what you already know about that person to put meaning to the words. In doing so, you are interpreting what your friend says. Readers do the same thing when they interpret as they read. *Interpreting* is asking yourself, *What is the writer really saying here?* and then using what you know about the world to help answer that question.

Inferring

You may not realize it, but you infer, or make inferences, every day. Here is an example: You run to the bus stop a little later than usual. There is no one there. "I have missed the bus," you say to yourself. You may be wrong, but that is the way our minds work. You look at the evidence (you are late; no one is there) and come to a conclusion (you have missed the bus).

When you read, you go though exactly the same process because writers don't always directly state what they want you to understand. By providing clues and interesting details, they suggest certain information. Whenever you combine those clues with your own background and knowledge, you are making an inference.

An *inference* involves using your thinking and experience to come up with an idea based on what an author implies or suggests. In reading, you *infer* when you use context clues and your own knowledge to figure out the author's meaning.

Drawing Conclusions

Skillful readers are always *drawing conclusions,* or figuring out much more than an author says directly. The process is like a detective solving a mystery. You combine information and evidence that the author provides to come up with a statement about the topic. Drawing conclusions helps you find connections between ideas and events and gives you a better understanding of what you are reading.

Analyzing

Analyzing, or looking at separate parts of something to understand the entire piece, is a way to think critically about written work.

- In analyzing persuasive *nonfiction,* you might look at the writer's reasons to see if they actually support the main point of the argument.

- In analyzing *informational text,* you might look at how the ideas are organized to see what is most important.

Distinguishing Fact From Opinion

Distinguishing between fact and opinion is one of the most important reading skills you can learn. A *fact* is a statement that can be proved with supporting information. An *opinion,* on the other hand, is what a writer believes, on the basis of his or her personal viewpoint. Writers can support their opinions with facts, but an opinion is something that cannot be proved.

FOR EXAMPLE

Look at the following examples of fact and opinion.

Fact: George III was the British king during the American Revolution.

Opinion: King George III was an evil despot.

You could prove that George III was king during that period. It's a fact. However, not everyone might see that King George III was a despot. That's someone's opinion.

As you examine information, always ask yourself, "Is this a fact or an opinion?" Don't think that opinions are always bad. Very often they are just what you want. You read editorials and essays for their authors' opinions. Reviews of books, movies, plays, and CDs can help you decide whether to spend your time and money on something. It's when opinions are based on faulty reasoning or prejudice or when they are stated as facts that they become troublesome.

Evaluating

When you form an opinion or make a judgment about something you are reading, you are *evaluating.* If you are reading informational texts or something on the Internet, it is important to evaluate how qualified the author is to be writing about the topic and how reliable the information is that is presented. Ask yourself whether the author seems biased, whether the information is one-sided, and whether the argument presented is logical.

Synthesizing

When you *synthesize,* you combine ideas (maybe even from different sources) to come up with something new. It may be a new understanding of an important idea or a new way of combining and presenting information. For example, you might read a manual on coaching soccer, combine that information with your own experiences playing soccer, and come up with a winning plan for coaching your sister's team this spring.

Understanding Text Structure

Good writers do not just put together sentences and paragraphs in any order. They structure each piece of their writing in a specific way for a specific purpose. That pattern of organization is called *text structure.* When you know the text structure of a selection, you will find it easier to locate and recall an author's ideas. Here are four ways that writers organize text.

Comparison and Contrast

Comparison-and-contrast structure shows the similarities and differences between people, things, and ideas. Maybe you have overheard someone at school say something like "He is better at throwing the football, but I can run faster than he can." This student is using comparison-and-contrast structure. When writers use comparison-and-contrast structure, often they want to show you *how things that seem alike are different, or how things that seem different are alike.*

- **Signal words and phrases:** *similarly, on the one hand, on the other hand, in contrast to, but, however*

Cause and Effect

Just about everything that happens in life is the cause or the effect of some other event or action. Sometimes what happens is pretty minor: You do not look when you are pouring milk *(cause);* you spill milk on the table *(effect).* Sometimes it is a little more serious: You do not look at your math book before the big test *(cause);* you mess up on the test *(effect).*

Writers use cause-and-effect structure to explore the reasons for something happening and to examine the results of previous events. This structure helps answer the question that everybody is always asking: *Why?* A historian might tell us why an empire rose and fell. Cause-and-effect structure is all about explaining things.

- **Signal words and phrases:** *so, because, as a result, therefore, for the following reasons*

Problem and Solution

How did scientists overcome the difficulty of getting a person to the moon? How will I brush my teeth when I have forgotten my toothpaste? These questions may be very different in importance, but they have one thing in common: Each identifies a problem and asks how to solve it. *Problems* and *solutions* are part of what makes life interesting. Problems and solutions also occur in fiction and nonfiction writing.

- **Signal words and phrases:** *how, help, problem, obstruction, difficulty, need, attempt, have to, must*

Sequence

Take a look at three common forms of sequencing, *the order in which thoughts are arranged.*

- **Chronological order** refers to the order in which events take place. First you wake up; next you have breakfast; then you go to school. Those events don't make much sense in any other order.

    Signal words: *first, next, then, later,* and *finally.*

- **Spatial order** tells you the order in which to look at objects. For example, take a look at this description of an ice cream sundae: *At the bottom of the dish are two scoops of vanilla. The scoops are covered with fudge and topped with whipped cream and a cherry.* Your eyes follow the sundae from the bottom to the top. Spatial order is important in descriptive writing because it helps you as a reader to see an image the way the author does.

Signal words: *above, below, behind,* and *next to.*

- **Order of importance** is going from most important to least important or the other way around. For example, a typical news article has a most-to-least-important structure.

    Signal words: *principal, central, important,* and *fundamental.*

CHECK IT OUT

- **Tables of contents** Look at the table of contents first to see whether a resource offers information you need.
- **Indexes** An index is an alphabetical listing of significant topics covered in a book. It is found in the back of a book.
- **Headings and subheadings** Headings often tell you what information is going to follow in the text you're reading. Subheadings allow you to narrow your search for information even further.
- **Graphic features** Photos, diagrams, maps, charts, graphs, and other graphic features can communicate large amounts of information at a glance.

Reading for Research

An important part of doing research is knowing how to get information from a wide variety of sources. The following skills will help you when you have a research assignment for a class or when you want information about a topic outside of school.

Reading Text Features

Researching a topic is not only about asking questions; it is about finding answers. Textbooks, references, magazines, and other sources provide a variety of text features to help you find those answers quickly and efficiently.

Organizing Information

When researching a topic, you have to make sense of that information, organize it, and put it all together in ways that will help you explain it to someone else. Here are some ways of doing just that.

- **Record** information from your research and keep track of your resources on note cards.

- **Interpret graphic aids** carefully. These could include charts, graphs, maps and photographs.

- **Summarize** information before you write it on a note card. That way you will have the main ideas in your own words.

- **Outline** ideas so you can see how subtopics and supporting information will fit under the main ideas.

- **Make a table or graph** to compare items or categories of information.

REFERENCE ATLAS

NATIONAL GEOGRAPHIC

ATLAS KEY

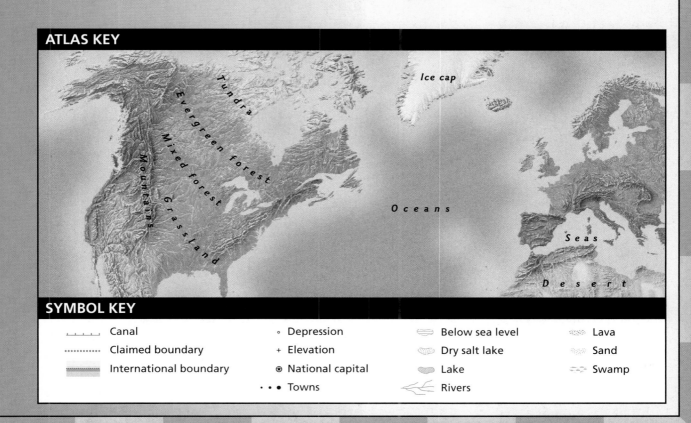

SYMBOL KEY

⊥⊥⊥⊥ Canal	○ Depression	〰 Below sea level	🗯 Lava
·········· Claimed boundary	+ Elevation	🗯 Dry salt lake	🗯 Sand
▓▓▓▓▓ International boundary	⊛ National capital	🗯 Lake	⊏⊐ Swamp
	· · ● Towns	⤙ Rivers	

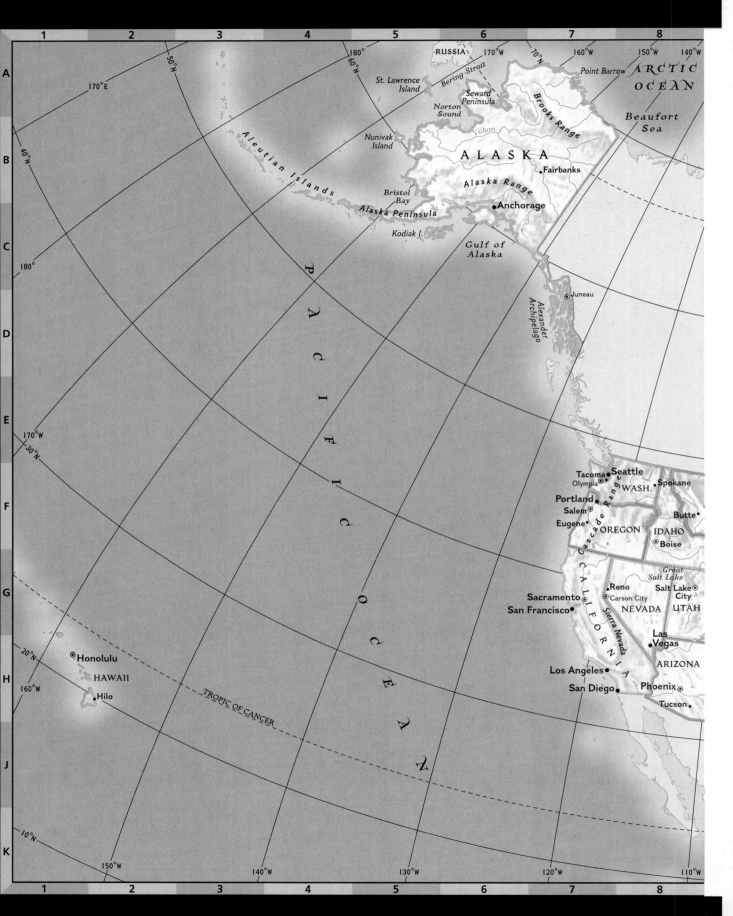

A
B
C
D
E
F
G
H
J
K

1 2 3 4 5 6 7 8

170°E
50°N
180°
60°N
170°W
RUSSIA
Bering Strait
70°N
160°W
150°W
140°W
Point Barrow
ARCTIC
OCEAN
St. Lawrence
Island
Seward
Peninsula
Norton
Sound
Brooks Range
Beaufort
Sea
40°N
Yukon
Nunivak
Island
ALASKA
•Fairbanks
Aleutian Islands
Alaska Range
Bristol
Bay
Alaska Peninsula
•Anchorage
180°
Kodiak I.
Gulf of
Alaska
Juneau
PACIFIC
Alexander
Archipelago
170°W
30°N
OCEAN
Tacoma• •Seattle
Olympia⊙   WASH. •Spokane
Portland•
Salem⊙
Eugene•
Cascade Range
OREGON
•Butte
IDAHO
⊙Boise
Great
Salt Lake
Reno•
⊙Carson City
Sacramento⊙•
San Francisco•
Salt Lake
City⊙
NEVADA   UTAH
160°W
Honolulu⊙
20°N
HAWAII
Hilo•
TROPIC OF CANCER
Sierra Nevada
CALIFORNIA
Las
•Vegas
ARIZONA
Los Angeles•
San Diego•
Phoenix⊙
Tucson•
10°N
150°W 140°W 130°W 120°W 110°W

130°W 120°W 110°W 100°W 90°W 80°W 70°W 60°W 50°W 40°W 30°W 70°N 30°W 60°N 20°W

A

GREENLAND
(KALAALLIT NUNAAT)
Den.

N

B

30°W

ARCTIC CIRCLE

50°N

C

UNITED STATES POLITICAL

0 mi   600

0 km   600

OBLIQUE AZIMUTHAL EQUIDISTANT PROJECTION

NATIONAL GEOGRAPHIC

40°W

D

C A N A D A

E

40°N

40°N

MAINE

Augusta

MONTANA

Helena

NORTH
DAKOTA

Bismarck

MINNESOTA

Lake Superior

MICHIGAN

Lake Huron

Montpelier

NEW
YORK

Portland
Concord, N.H.
Boston, MASS.
Providence, R.I.
Hartford, CONN.

50°N

F

Billings

SOUTH
DAKOTA

Pierre

WISCONSIN

Minneapolis St. Paul

Milwaukee
Madison

Lansing

Lake
Michigan

Detroit

Lake
Ontario

Buffalo

Albany

New York City

Casper

Sioux City

IOWA

Chicago

L. Michigan

Toledo

Cleveland

L. Erie

PA.

Harrisburg

Trenton, N.J.
Philadelphia

WYOMING

Cheyenne

Des Moines

ILLINOIS

IND.

Columbus

OHIO

Pittsburgh

Baltimore

Dover, DEL.

Annapolis, MD.

40°N

G

NEBRASKA

Omaha

Lincoln

Indianapolis

Cincinnati

Dayton W. VA.

Washington, D.C.

30°N

Denver

Kansas City

Springfield

Frankfort

Louisville

Richmond

Virginia Beach

COLORADO

Topeka

MISSOURI

St. Louis

KENTUCKY

Jefferson City

KANSAS

Bermuda Is.
U.K.

Santa Fe

Nashville

TENNESSEE

Raleigh

NORTH CAROLINA

Charlotte

30°N

H

Albuquerque

Oklahoma City

Tulsa

ARKANSAS

Memphis

SOUTH
CAROLINA

Columbia

NEW
MEXICO

OKLAHOMA

Little Rock

Atlanta

GEORGIA

Charleston

El Paso

Fort
Worth

Dallas

LOUISIANA

Birmingham

MISS.

ALABAMA

Montgomery

Savannah

Jackson

Austin

TEXAS

Baton Rouge

Tallahassee

Jacksonville

FLORIDA

San Antonio

Houston

New Orleans

Tampa

20°N

J

M E X I C O

Gulf of
Mexico

Miami

BAHAMAS

ATLANTIC OCEAN

ANTIGUA
& BARBUDA

Rio Grande

Straits of Florida

CUBA

ST. KITTS
& NEVIS

60°W

20°N

K

100°W

90°W

80°W

JAMAICA

Caribbean
Sea

HAITI

DOMINICAN
REPUBLIC

70°W

San Juan

PUERTO
RICO
U.S.

DOMINICA

Cape Flattery
Mt. Olympus
7,965 ft
2,428 m
Seattle
Columbia
CASCADE RANGE
COLUMBIA PLATEAU
Great Sandy
Desert
Blue Mts.
Clearwater
Mts.
Bitterroot Range
Salmon
River
Mts.
Snake
Snake River
Plain
Shoshone
Falls
Great Salt
Lake
Cape Mendocino
SIERRA NEVADA
Lake
Tahoe
Central Valley
GREAT
BASIN
Wasatch Range
Uinta Mts.
PACIFIC
OCEAN
San Francisco
Mt. Whitney
14,494 ft
4,418 m
Death Valley
-282 ft, -86 m
Lake
Mead
Lake
Powell
Colorado
Point Conception
RANGES
Mojave
Desert
Grand
Canyon
Colorado
Plateau
San Juan Mts.
Channel
Islands
Los Angeles
Salton
Sea
Colorado
San Diego
Phoenix
Sonoran
Desert
ROCKY
Absaroka Range
Wind River Range
Bighorn Mts.
Laramie Mts.
Missouri
Black
Hills
Missouri
Sand Hills
N. Platte
Platte
GREAT
Denver
14,433 ft
4,399 m
Mt. Elbert
Sangre de Cristo Mts.
Arkansas
MOUNTAINS
Sacramento Mts.
High
Plains
Llano
Estacado
Red
Rio Grande
Edwards
Plateau
Dallas
Brazos
C
A
N
C
A
N
A
D
A
MEXICO
TROPIC OF CANCER
Rio Grande
CO

ARCTIC OCEAN
Point Barrow
Chukchi
Sea
North Slope
Beaufort
Sea
Brooks Range
RUSSIA
Bering
Strait
ARCTIC CIRCLE
Seward
Pen.
ALASKA
St. Lawrence
Island
Yukon
CANADA
Nunivak
Island
Kuskokwim
Tanana
Alaska Range
Mt. McKinley (Denali)
20,320 ft, 6,194 m
Anchorage
Bering
Sea
Bristol
Bay
Gulf of
Alaska
Alexander
Archipelago
Alaska Peninsula
Kodiak I.
PACIFIC
OCEAN
ALASKA
0 mi   300
0 km   300

9   10   11   12   13   14   15   16

95°W   90°W   85°W   80°W   50°N   75°W   70°W   65°W   45°N

C A N A D A

Lake of
the Woods

Isle Royale
Lake Superior

Upper Peninsula

Lake
Champlain
Adirondack
Mts.

Green Mts.
White
Mts.

Gulf of
Maine

Minneapolis

Lake Michigan

Lower Peninsula

Lake Huron

Lake Ontario

Niagara
Falls

Hudson

Connecticut

Boston

Cape Cod

40°N

Milwaukee

Detroit

Lake Erie

Cleveland

Long Island
New York City

Chicago

Appalachian Plateau

A P P A L A C H I A N   M O U N T A I N S

Philadelphia

65°W

C E N T R A L

Pittsburgh

Allegheny Mts.

Baltimore

Delaware Bay

A T L A N T I C

L O W L A N D

Indianapolis

Washington

Chesapeake Bay

O C E A N

Ohio

St. Louis

Mississippi

Wabash

Cumberland Plateau

Blue Ridge

Piedmont

35°N

Flint
Hills

Cape Hatteras

Ozark Plateau

Cumberland

Mt. Mitchell
6,684 ft
2,037 m

Boston Mts.

Tennessee

Memphis

Ouachita Mts.

Atlanta

Savannah

65°W

Mississippi

Black Belt

A P P A L

Red

C O A S T A L

Jacksonville

30°N

Houston

New Orleans

Mississippi
River Delta

Cape Canaveral

Lake
Okeechobee

**UNITED
STATES**
PHYSICAL

G u l f   o f   M e x i c o

The
Everglades

Miami

0 mi   300
0 km   300

ALBERS CONIC EQUAL-AREA PROJECTION

70°W

90°W

Florida Keys

**NATIONAL
GEOGRAPHIC**

Straits of Florida

TROPIC OF CANCER

20°N

85°W

80°W

75°W

C U B A

159°W

156°W

Niihau

Kauai

Oahu

Honolulu

Molokai

Lanai

Maui — 21°N

Kahoolawe

Hawaii

P A C I F I C

O C E A N

Mauna Kea
13,796 ft
4,205 m

PRINCIPAL HAWAIIAN
ISLANDS

0 mi   100
0 km   100

95°W

90°W

85°W

80°W

75°W

9   10   11   12   13   14   15   16

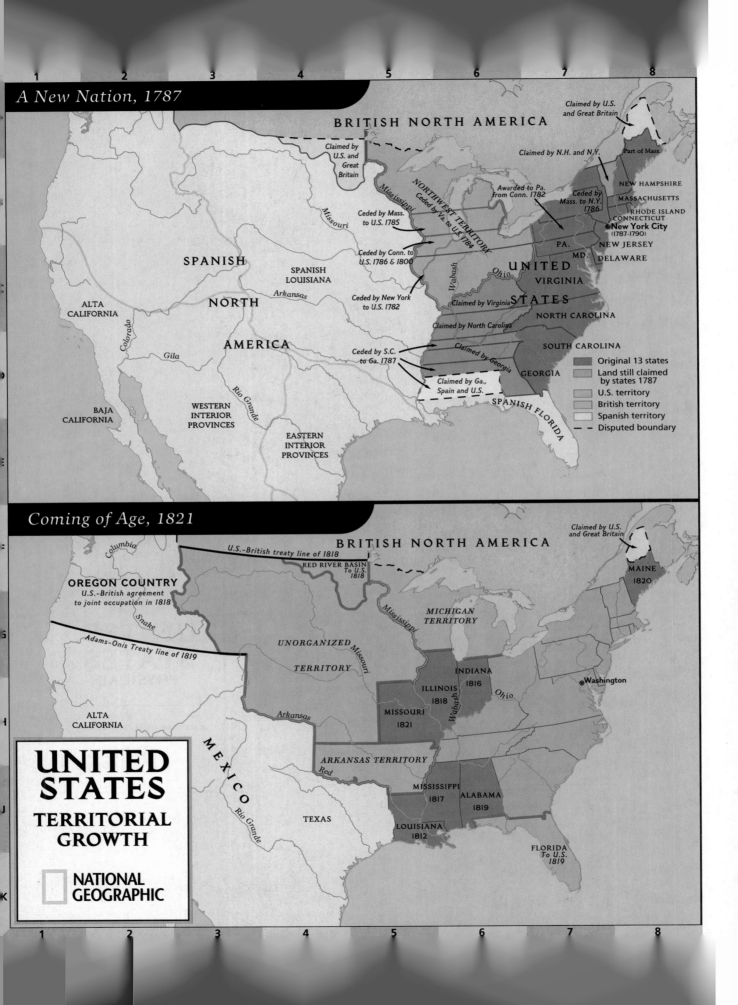

A New Nation, 1787

BRITISH NORTH AMERICA

Claimed by U.S. and Great Britain

Claimed by U.S. and Great Britain

Claimed by N.H. and N.Y.

Part of Mass.

NEW HAMPSHIRE

Awarded to Pa. from Conn. 1782

Ceded by Mass. to N.Y. 1786

MASSACHUSETTS

RHODE ISLAND

CONNECTICUT

NORTHWEST TERRITORY

Ceded by Va. to U.S. 1784

New York City (1787-1790)

Ceded by Mass. to U.S. 1785

Mississippi

Missouri

PA.

NEW JERSEY

MD.

DELAWARE

SPANISH

SPANISH LOUISIANA

Ceded by Conn. to U.S. 1786 & 1800

UNITED

VIRGINIA

Arkansas

NORTH

Ceded by New York to U.S. 1782

Wabash

Ohio

STATES

Claimed by Virginia

ALTA CALIFORNIA

Colorado

AMERICA

NORTH CAROLINA

Gila

Claimed by North Carolina

SOUTH CAROLINA

Ceded by S.C. to Ga. 1787

Claimed by Georgia

GEORGIA

Rio Grande

Claimed by Ga., Spain and U.S.

SPANISH FLORIDA

BAJA CALIFORNIA

WESTERN INTERIOR PROVINCES

EASTERN INTERIOR PROVINCES

Original 13 states
Land still claimed by states 1787
U.S. territory
British territory
Spanish territory
Disputed boundary

Coming of Age, 1821

Columbia

BRITISH NORTH AMERICA

U.S.-British treaty line of 1818

RED RIVER BASIN To U.S. 1818

Claimed by U.S. and Great Britain

OREGON COUNTRY
U.S.-British agreement to joint occupation in 1818

MAINE 1820

Snake

Adams-Onis Treaty line of 1819

UNORGANIZED

MICHIGAN TERRITORY

Mississippi

TERRITORY

Missouri

INDIANA 1816

Washington

ALTA CALIFORNIA

ILLINOIS 1818

Ohio

Wabash

Arkansas

MISSOURI 1821

M E X I C O

ARKANSAS TERRITORY

Red

MISSISSIPPI 1817

ALABAMA 1819

Rio Grande

TEXAS

LOUISIANA 1812

FLORIDA To U.S. 1819

UNITED STATES

TERRITORIAL GROWTH

NATIONAL GEOGRAPHIC

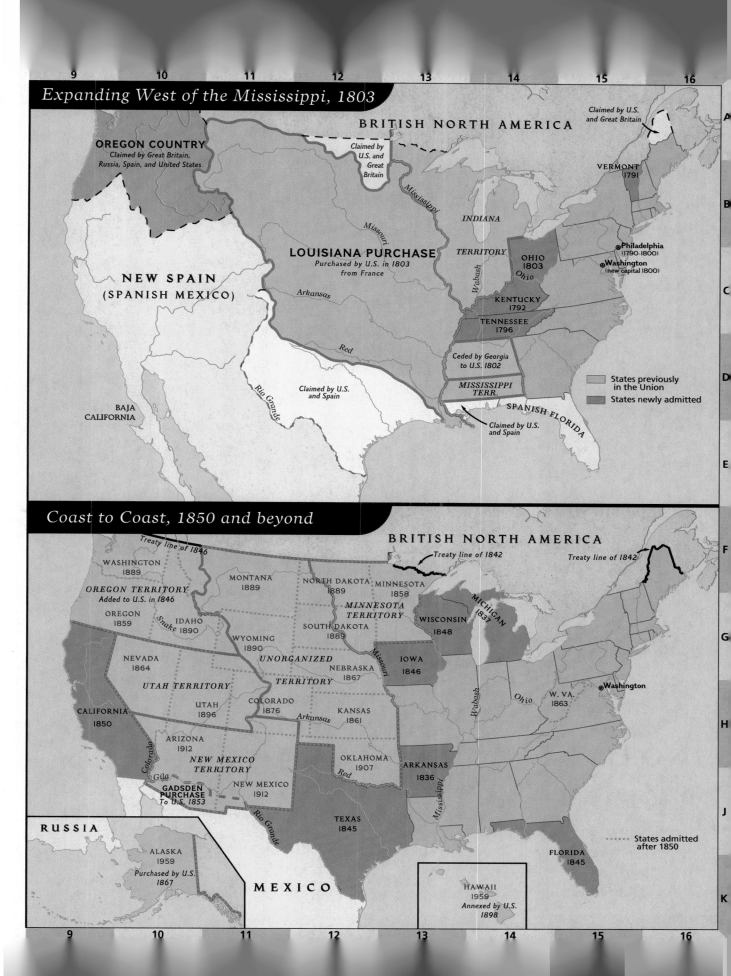

Expanding West of the Mississippi, 1803

BRITISH NORTH AMERICA

Claimed by U.S. and Great Britain

OREGON COUNTRY
Claimed by Great Britain, Russia, Spain, and United States

Claimed by U.S. and Great Britain

Mississippi

VERMONT 1791

Missouri

INDIANA

TERRITORY

LOUISIANA PURCHASE
Purchased by U.S. in 1803 from France

**NEW SPAIN
(SPANISH MEXICO)**

Arkansas

OHIO 1803

Ohio

● Philadelphia (1790-1800)

● Washington (new capital 1800)

Wabash

KENTUCKY 1792

TENNESSEE 1796

Red

Ceded by Georgia to U.S. 1802

Rio Grande

Claimed by U.S. and Spain

MISSISSIPPI TERR.

BAJA CALIFORNIA

SPANISH FLORIDA

Claimed by U.S. and Spain

☐ States previously in the Union
☐ States newly admitted

Coast to Coast, 1850 and beyond

BRITISH NORTH AMERICA

Treaty line of 1846

Treaty line of 1842

Treaty line of 1842

WASHINGTON 1889

MONTANA 1889

NORTH DAKOTA 1889

MINNESOTA 1858

MICHIGAN 1837

OREGON TERRITORY
Added to U.S. in 1846

MINNESOTA TERRITORY

OREGON 1859

Snake

IDAHO 1890

SOUTH DAKOTA 1889

WISCONSIN 1848

WYOMING 1890

NEVADA 1864

UNORGANIZED

Missouri

IOWA 1846

TERRITORY

NEBRASKA 1867

UTAH TERRITORY

Wabash

Ohio

● Washington

CALIFORNIA 1850

UTAH 1896

COLORADO 1876

Arkansas

KANSAS 1861

W. VA. 1863

ARIZONA 1912

Colorado

Gila

GADSDEN PURCHASE
To U.S. 1853

NEW MEXICO TERRITORY

OKLAHOMA 1907

Red

ARKANSAS 1836

NEW MEXICO 1912

Mississippi

RUSSIA

Rio Grande

TEXAS 1845

ALASKA 1959
Purchased by U.S. 1867

MEXICO

FLORIDA 1845

HAWAII 1959
Annexed by U.S. 1898

····· States admitted after 1850

ASIA

ARCTIC OCEAN

180°
170°W
160°W
150°W
140°W
130°W
90°N
80°N
70°N

Chukchi Sea

Bering Sea

St. Lawrence Island

Nunivak Island

Seward Peninsula

North Slope

Point Barrow

Brooks Range

Beaufort Sea

North Magnetic Pole

Oodaaq Island

Lincoln Sea

Queen Elizabeth Islands

GREENLAND

Greenland Sea

EUROPE

10°W
20°W
30°W
40°N
50°N
60°N

Hayes Peninsula

Gunnbjorn 12,139 ft 3,700 m

Arctic Circle

Bristol Bay

Aleutian Range

Kodiak I.

ALASKA

Kuskokwim

Alaska Range

Kenai Peninsula

Yukon

Mt. McKinley (Denali) 20,320 ft 6,194 m

Melville Island

Banks Island

Victoria Island

Prince of Wales I.

Boothia Peninsula

Devon I.

Somerset I.

Baffin Bay

Baffin Island

Melville Peninsula

Foxe Basin

Nuuk (Godthab)

Cape Farewell

Gulf of Alaska

Mt. Logan 19,551 ft 5,959 m

Yukon Plateau

Mackenzie Mts.

Great Bear Lake

CANADA

Southampton Island

Hudson Strait

Ungava Bay

Davis Strait

Labrador Sea

PACIFIC OCEAN

Alexander Archipelago

Queen Charlotte Islands

Vancouver Island

Olympic Peninsula

Coast Mountains

Fraser Plateau

Columbia Plateau

ROCKY

Peace

Athabasca

Slave

Great Slave Lake

Lake Athabasca

Saskatchewan

Churchill

Nelson

GREAT

Lake Winnipeg

Hudson Bay

CANADIAN

SHIELD

Belcher Islands

James Bay

LABRADOR

Laurentian Mountains

Island of Newfoundland

Avalon Peninsula

Cape Mendocino

Cascade Range

Sierra Nevada

Coast Ranges

Great Basin

Columbia Plateau

Snake

Great Salt Lake

Mt. Whitney 14,494 ft 4,418 m

Missouri

MOUNTAINS

Platte

Missouri

PLAINS

High Plains

CENTRAL LOWLAND

UNITED STATES

Lake Superior

L. Michigan

Lake Huron

L. Ontario

L. Erie

Ohio

Ottawa

St. Lawrence

Gaspe Pen.

Gulf of St. Lawrence

Cape Breton Island

Prince Edward Island

Nova Scotia

Bay of Fundy

Gulf of Maine

Cape Cod

Long Island

ATLANTIC OCEAN

Channel Islands

Death Valley 282 ft 86 m

Colorado Plateau

Grand Canyon

Sonoran Desert

Colorado

Arkansas

Red

Ozark Plateau

Mississippi

APPALACHIAN

Washington

Chesapeake Bay

Cape Hatteras

Bermuda Islands

TROPIC OF CANCER

20°N

Baja California

MEXICO

Sierra Madre Occidental

Gulf of California

Rio Grande

Sierra Madre Oriental

Gulf of Mexico

Orizaba 18,855 ft 5,747 m

Yucatan Peninsula

Cozumel Island

COASTAL PLAIN

Florida

Florida Keys

Havana

CUBA

BAHAMAS

Cayman Islands

WEST

Greater Antilles

JAMAICA

Kingston

Hispaniola

HAITI

DOMINICAN REPUBLIC

Puerto Rico

Virgin Islands

Guadeloupe

Martinique

INDIES

Lesser Antilles

Mexico City

Isthmus of Tehuantepec

Gulf of Tehuantepec

BELIZE

Belmopan

GUATEMALA

Guatemala City

San Salvador

EL SALVADOR

HONDURAS

Tegucigalpa

NICARAGUA

Managua

Lake Nicaragua

COSTA RICA

San Jose

CENTRAL

AMERICA

PANAMA

Isthmus of Panama

Panama City

Caribbean Sea

Trinidad

SOUTH AMERICA

10°N
0°

EQUATOR

100°W
90°W
80°W
70°W

NORTH AMERICA

PHYSICAL

0 mi 1000
0 km 1000

AZIMUTHAL EQUIDISTANT PROJECTION

NATIONAL GEOGRAPHIC

NORTH AMERICA
POLITICAL

0 mi   1000
0 km   1000

AZIMUTHAL EQUIDISTANT PROJECTION

NATIONAL GEOGRAPHIC

1. BAJA CALIFORNIA	
2. BAJA CALIFORNIA SUR	
3. SONORA	
4. CHIHUAHUA	
5. SINALOA	
6. DURANGO	
7. COAHUILA	
8. NUEVO LEON	
9. ZACATECAS	20. MEXICO
10. TAMAULIPAS	21. DISTRITO FEDERAL
11. NAYARIT	22. TLAXCALA
12. AGUASCALIENTES	23. MORELOS
13. SAN LUIS POTOSI	24. PUEBLA
14. JALISCO	25. VERACRUZ
15. GUANAJUATO	26. GUERRERO
16. QUERETARO	27. OAXACA
17. HIDALGO	28. TABASCO
18. COLIMA	29. CHIAPAS
19. MICHOACAN	30. CAMPECHE
	31. QUINTANA ROO
	32. YUCATAN

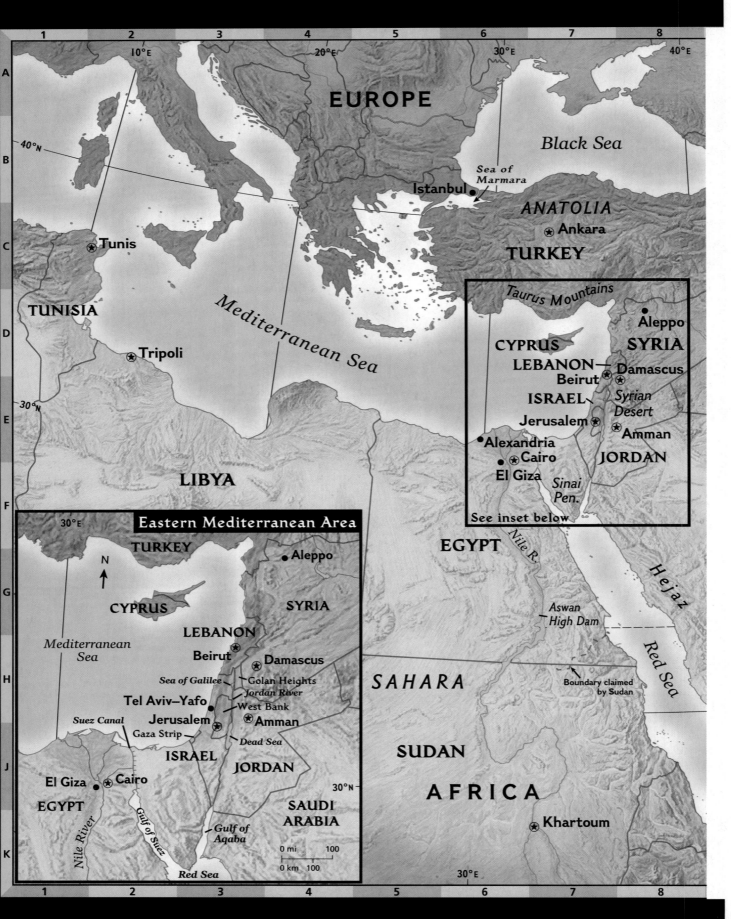

Map Labels

EUROPE

Black Sea

Sea of Marmara

Istanbul

ANATOLIA

Ankara

TURKEY

Taurus Mountains

Tunis

CYPRUS

SYRIA

Aleppo

TUNISIA

LEBANON

Damascus

Beirut

Syrian
Desert

ISRAEL

Tripoli

Jerusalem

Amman

Alexandria

Cairo

JORDAN

El Giza

Mediterranean Sea

LIBYA

Sinai
Pen.

See inset below

EGYPT

Nile R.

Hejaz

Aswan
High Dam

SAHARA

Red Sea

Boundary claimed
by Sudan

SUDAN

AFRICA

Khartoum

40°N

30°N

10°E

20°E

30°E

40°E

Eastern Mediterranean Area (inset):

Eastern Mediterranean Area

30°E

N

TURKEY

Aleppo

CYPRUS

SYRIA

Mediterranean
Sea

LEBANON

Beirut

Damascus

Sea of Galilee

Golan Heights

Jordan River

Tel Aviv–Yafo

West Bank

Suez Canal

Jerusalem

Amman

Gaza Strip

Dead Sea

ISRAEL

JORDAN

El Giza

Cairo

EGYPT

SAUDI
ARABIA

Nile River

Gulf of Suez

Gulf of
Aqaba

Red Sea

30°N

0 mi   100

0 km   100

9 10 11 12 13 14 15 16

50°E 60°E 70°E 40°N

A

Aral Sea UZBEKISTAN ⊛ Tashkent

Caucasus Mountains TAJIKISTAN B

GEORGIA *Caspian Sea* TURKMENISTAN ⊛ Dushanbe

Tbilisi ⊛

Baku ⊛ A S I A

Yerevan ⊛

ARMENIA ⊛ Ashkhabad Kabul ⊛ C

▲ Mashhad ●

Mt. Ararat (16,854 ft. 5,137 m) AFGHANISTAN

AZERBAIJAN *Elburz Mountains* 30°N

Tigris R. *Plateau of Iran* D

⊛ Tehran

IRAQ *Zagros Mountains*

Euphrates R. ⊛ Baghdad IRAN E

Al Basrah ● PAKISTAN

KUWAIT F

Kuwait ● *Persian Gulf*

Gulf of Oman TROPIC OF CANCER

Manama *Arabian Sea*

BAHRAIN ⊛ Abu

SAUDI QATAR ⊛ Dhabi ● Muscat ⊛ G

ARABIA ⊛ Riyadh Doha 20°N

UNITED OMAN

ARABIAN ARAB

A s i r *PENINSULA* EMIRATES H

Rub al Khali (Empty Quarter)

MIDDLE EAST J

PHYSICAL / POLITICAL

0 mi 500

Sanaa 0 km 500

⊛ YEMEN AZIMUTHAL EQUIDISTANT PROJECTION

N ↑ K

NATIONAL GEOGRAPHIC

40°E 50°E

Aden ● *Gulf of Aden*

9 10 11 12 13 14 15 16

1   **2**   **3**   **4**   **5**   **6**   **7**   **8**

150°W   120°W   90°W   60°W   30°W   0°

A R C T I C

Queen Elizabeth Islands

GREENLAND
(KALAALLIT NUNAAT)
Den.

Chukchi
Sea

Beaufort
Sea

Baffin
Bay

RUSSIA

Baffin
Island

Greenland Sea

ALASKA
U.S.

60°N

Bering
Sea

Anchorage

Gulf of
Alaska

Great Bear Lake

Great
Slave Lake

Nuuk

ARCTIC CIRCLE
⊛ Reykjavik
ICELAND

Aleutian Islands

Hudson
Bay

Labrador
Sea

Vancouver
Seattle

Calgary

C A N A D A

Island of
Newfoundland

UNITED
KINGDOM
Dublin ⊛
IRELAND

N O R T H

Missouri

Great Lakes

⊛ Ottawa

Toronto

London ⊛

San Francisco

UNITED STATES

Chicago

New York City

⊛ Washington

N O R T H

Madrid ⊛
PORTUGAL ⊛
SPAIN

P A C I F I C

Ohio

Azores
Port.

30°N

Los Angeles

Houston

Atlanta

A T L A N T I C

Madeira Is. Rabat ⊛
Port. MOROCCO

O C E A N

Rio Grande

Gulf of
Mexico

Mississippi

Canary Is.
Sp.

WESTERN
SAHARA
Morocco

TROPIC OF CANCER

Hawaiian
Islands
U.S.

MEXICO

Havana ⊛

CUBA

O C E A N

BAHAMAS

DOMINICAN REP.
Santo Domingo ⊛
PUERTO RICO U.S.

CAPE
VERDE

MAURITANIA

Guadalajara

BELIZE

Mexico City ⊛

HAITI

ST. KITTS & NEVIS
ANTIGUA & BARBUDA

MALI

GUATEMALA

JAMAICA

DOMINICA

SENEGAL

Guatemala City ⊛

HONDURAS

Caribbean Sea

BARBADOS

GAMBIA

EL SALVADOR

NICARAGUA

ST. LUCIA
GRENADA

ST. VINCENT &
THE GRENADINES
TRINIDAD & TOBAGO

GUINEA-
BISSAU

GUINEA

COSTA RICA

Caracas ⊛

BURKINA FASO

GHANA

PANAMA

VENEZUELA

FRENCH
GUIANA
Fr.

SIERRA LEONE

LIBERIA

CÔTE
D'IVOIRE

Medellin ⊛ Bogota

GUYANA

SURINAME

COLOMBIA

Christmas Island
Kiribati

0°

EQUATOR

Galapagos
Islands
Ecua.

Quito ⊛

ECUADOR

Manaus

Negro

Amazon

PERU

B R A Z I L

Recife

Marquesas
Islands
Fr.

Lima ⊛

Madeira

São Francisco

Salvador
(Bahia)

SAMOA

AMERICAN
SAMOA
U.S.

FRENCH POLYNESIA
Fr.

La Paz
BOLIVIA
Sucre ⊛

Brasilia ⊛

S O U T H

Rio de
Janeiro

A T L A N T I C

TONGA

TROPIC OF CAPRICORN

PARAGUAY

Sao Paulo

Paraná

S O U T H

Cordoba

Porto Alegre

O C E A N

30°S

Santiago ⊛

Asuncion ⊛

Buenos
Aires ⊛

URUGUAY
Montevideo ⊛

P A C I F I C

CHILE

ARGENTINA

O C E A N

Falkland Islands
U.K.

Tierra del Fuego

South
Georgia
U.K.

Strait of Magellan

Drake Passage

Antarctic
Peninsula

60°S

ANTARCTIC CIRCLE

Weddell
Sea

Ross
Sea

Berkner
Island

WORLD
POLITICAL

0 mi   2000

0 km   2000

WINKEL TRIPEL PROJECTION

**NATIONAL
GEOGRAPHIC**

MERIDIAN OF GREENWICH (LONDON)

1   **2**   **3**   **4**   **5**   **6**   **7**   **8**

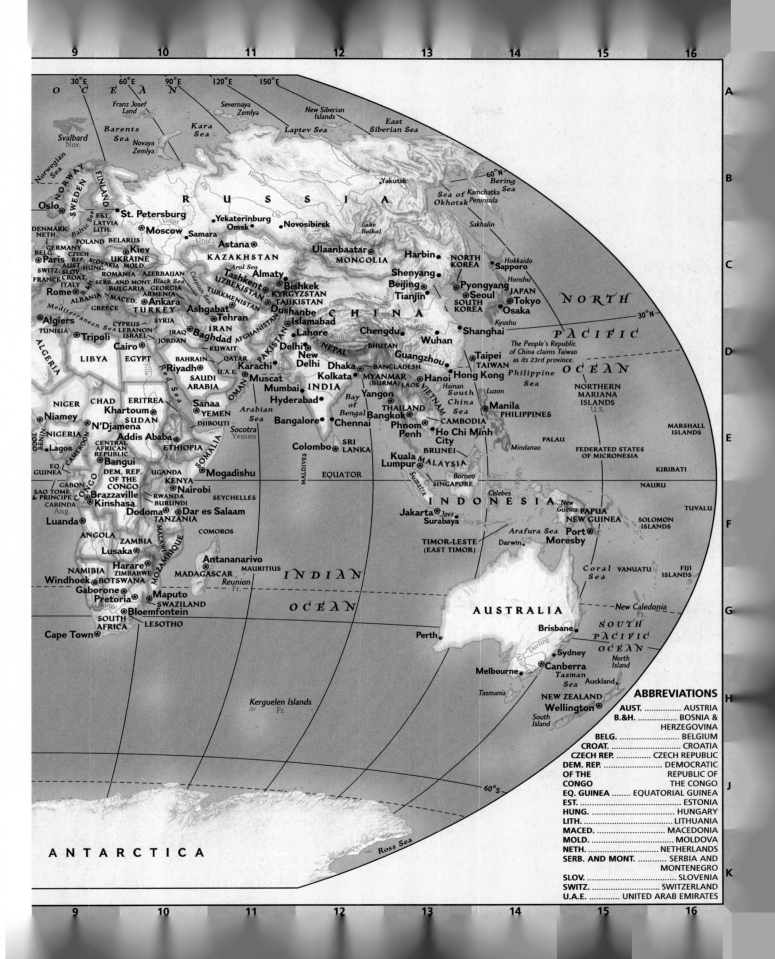

9 10 11 12 13 14 15 16

30°E 60°E 90°E 120°E 150°E

A

O C E A N

Svalbard
Nor.

Franz Josef
Land

Barents
Sea

Novaya
Zemlya

Severnaya
Zemlya

Kara
Sea

Laptev Sea

New Siberian
Islands

East
Siberian Sea

B

Norwegian Sea

SWEDEN
NORWAY
FINLAND

Oslo

EST.
LATVIA
LITH.

St. Petersburg
Moscow
Samara

Baltic Sea

Yekaterinburg
Omsk

Novosibirsk

Ob
Irtysh
Ural

Yenisey

R U S S I A

Lake
Baikal

Yakutsk

Amur

60°N

Sea of
Okhotsk

Bering
Sea

Kamchatka
Peninsula

Sakhalin

C

DENMARK
NETH.
GERMANY
BELG.
CZECH
Paris
SWITZ.
FRANCE
AUST. HUNG.
Rome
ITALY
SLOV.

POLAND BELARUS

Kiev
UKRAINE

ROMANIA AZERBAIJAN

SLOVAKIA MOLD.
SERB. AND MONT. Black Sea
BULGARIA GEORGIA
ALBANIA MACED. ARMENIA
GREECE TURKEY

Astana

KAZAKHSTAN

Aral Sea

Almaty

Tashkent
UZBEKISTAN
TURKMENISTAN

Bishkek
KYRGYZSTAN
TAJIKISTAN

Ulaanbaatar
MONGOLIA

Harbin

Shenyang

Beijing
Tianjin

NORTH
KOREA

Pyongyang
Seoul
SOUTH
KOREA

Hokkaido

Sapporo

Honshu

JAPAN

Tokyo
Osaka

N O R T H

P A C I F I C

O C E A N

30°N

Algiers
TUNISIA
Tripoli

CYPRUS
LEBANON
ISRAEL
JORDAN

SYRIA

Caspian Sea

Ankara
Ashgabat

IRAN
Tehran

Baghdad
IRAQ

Cairo

Dushanbe

AFGHANISTAN

Islamabad

Lahore

C H I N A

Chengdu

Wuhan

Shanghai

Kyushu

D

Mediterranean Sea

ALGERIA
LIBYA

EGYPT

Red Sea

Nile

KUWAIT
BAHRAIN
QATAR
Riyadh
U.A.E.
SAUDI
ARABIA
OMAN
Muscat

Karachi

PAKISTAN

Delhi
New
Delhi

NEPAL

Kolkata

Dhaka
BANGLADESH

BHUTAN

Brahmaputra

MYANMAR
(BURMA)

Guangzhou

Taipei
TAIWAN

Hanoi
LAOS

Hong Kong

Hainan

South
China
Sea

Philippine
Sea

Luzon

The People's Republic
of China claims Taiwan
as its 23rd province.

NORTHERN
MARIANA
ISLANDS
U.S.

NIGER
CHAD
ERITREA
Khartoum
SUDAN
N'Djamena
Niamey

Sanaa
YEMEN
DJIBOUTI

Arabian
Sea

Socotra
Yemen

Mumbai
I N D I A
Hyderabad

Bangalore

Chennai

Bay
of
Bengal

Yangon

THAILAND
Bangkok

VIETNAM

Phnom
Penh

CAMBODIA

Ho Chi Minh
City

Manila
PHILIPPINES

Mindanao

PALAU

FEDERATED STATES
OF MICRONESIA

MARSHALL
ISLANDS

E

NIGERIA
BENIN
TOGO
Lagos
CAMEROON
EQ.
GUINEA

CENTRAL
AFRICAN
REPUBLIC
Bangui

Addis Ababa

ETHIOPIA

SOMALIA

Colombo

SRI
LANKA

MALDIVES

EQUATOR

Kuala
Lumpur

BRUNEI

MALAYSIA

SINGAPORE

Borneo

KIRIBATI

NAURU

SAO TOME
& PRINCIPE
CABINDA
Ang.

GABON
CONGO
Brazzaville
Kinshasa

DEM. REP.
OF THE
CONGO

UGANDA
RWANDA
BURUNDI

KENYA
Nairobi

Dodoma
Dar es Salaam
TANZANIA

SEYCHELLES

Mogadishu

Sumatra

I N D O N E S I A

Jakarta
Surabaya
Java

Celebes

New
Guinea
PAPUA
NEW GUINEA

SOLOMON
ISLANDS

TUVALU

F

Luanda

ANGOLA
ZAMBIA
Lusaka

MALAWI
MOZAMBIQUE

COMOROS

Antananarivo

MADAGASCAR

MAURITIUS
Reunion
Fr.

I N D I A N

TIMOR-LESTE
(EAST TIMOR)

Arafura Sea

Darwin

Port
Moresby

Coral
Sea

VANUATU

New Caledonia
Fr.

FIJI
ISLANDS

NAMIBIA
Windhoek
Gaborone
Pretoria
SOUTH
AFRICA
Cape Town

Harare
ZIMBABWE
BOTSWANA

Maputo
SWAZILAND
Bloemfontein

LESOTHO

Orange

O C E A N

AUSTRALIA

Darling

Murray

Perth

Brisbane

Sydney
Canberra

S O U T H

P A C I F I C

O C E A N

North
Island

G

Kerguelen Islands
Fr.

Melbourne

Tasmania

Tasman
Sea

NEW ZEALAND
Wellington

South
Island

Auckland

H

J

60°S

A N T A R C T I C A

Ross Sea

K

9 10 11 12 13 14 15 16

United States Facts

Washington, D.C.
Population: 572,059
Land area: 61 sq. mi.

U.S. Territories

Puerto Rico
Population: 3,808,610
Land area: 3,425 sq. mi.

Guam
Population: 155,000 (est.)
Land area: 210 sq. mi.

U.S. Virgin Islands
Population: 121,000 (est.)
Land area: 134 sq. mi.

American Samoa
Population: 65,000 (est.)
Land area: 77 sq. mi.

The states are listed in the order they were admitted to the Union.

Population figures are based on U.S. Bureau of the Census for 2000. House of Representatives figures are from the Clerk of the House of Representatives. States are not drawn to scale.

1 Delaware
Year Admitted: 1787
Population: 783,600
Land area: 1,955 sq. mi.
Representatives: 1
Dover

2 Pennsylvania
Year Admitted: 1787
Population: 12,281,054
Land area: 44,820 sq. mi.
Representatives: 19
Harrisburg

3 New Jersey
Year Admitted: 1787
Population: 8,414,350
Land area: 7,419 sq. mi.
Representatives: 13
Trenton

9 New Hampshire
Year Admitted: 1788
Population: 1,235,786
Land area: 8,969 sq. mi.
Representatives: 2
Concord

10 Virginia
Year Admitted: 1788
Population: 7,078,515
Land area: 39,598 sq. mi.
Representatives: 11
Richmond

11 New York
Year Admitted: 1788
Population: 18,976,457
Land area: 47,224 sq. mi.
Representatives: 29
Albany

17 Ohio
Year Admitted: 1803
Population: 11,353,140
Land area: 40,953 sq. mi.
Representatives: 18
Columbus

18 Louisiana
Year Admitted: 1812
Population: 4,468,976
Land area: 43,566 sq. mi.
Representatives: 7
Baton Rouge

19 Indiana
Year Admitted: 1816
Population: 6,080,485
Land area: 35,870 sq. mi.
Representatives: 9
Indianapolis

25 Arkansas
Year Admitted: 1836
Population: 2,673,400
Land area: 52,075 sq. mi.
Representatives: 4
Little Rock

26 Michigan
Year Admitted: 1837
Population: 9,938,444
Land area: 56,809 sq. mi.
Representatives: 15
Lansing

27 Florida
Year Admitted: 1845
Population: 15,982,378
Land area: 53,997 sq. mi.
Representatives: 25
Tallahassee

33 Oregon
Year Admitted: 1859
Population: 3,421,399
Land area: 96,003 sq. mi.
Representatives: 5
Salem

34 Kansas
Year Admitted: 1861
Population: 2,688,418
Land area: 81,823 sq. mi.
Representatives: 4
Topeka

35 West Virginia
Year Admitted: 1863
Population: 1,808,344
Land area: 24,087 sq. mi.
Representatives: 3
Charleston

36 Nevada
Year Admitted: 1864
Population: 1,998,257
Land area: 109,806 sq. mi.
Representatives: 3
Carson City

42 Washington
Year Admitted: 1889
Population: 5,894,121
Land area: 66,582 sq. mi.
Representatives: 9
Olympia

43 Idaho
Year Admitted: 1890
Population: 1,293,953
Land area: 82,751 sq. mi.
Representatives: 2
Boise

44 Wyoming
Year Admitted: 1890
Population: 493,782
Land area: 97,105 sq. mi.
Representatives: 1
Cheyenne

45 Utah
Year Admitted: 1896
Population: 2,233,169
Land area: 82,168 sq. mi.
Representatives: 3
Salt Lake City

4 Georgia
Year Admitted: 1788
Population: 8,186,453
Land area: 57,919 sq. mi.
Representatives: 13

★ Atlanta

5 Connecticut
Year Admitted: 1788
Population: 3,405,565
Land area: 4,845 sq. mi.
Representatives: 5

★ Hartford

6 Massachusetts
Year Admitted: 1788
Population: 6,349,097
Land area: 7,838 sq. mi.
Representatives: 10

Boston ★

7 Maryland
Year Admitted: 1788
Population: 5,296,486
Land area: 9,775 sq. mi.
Representatives: 8

Annapolis ★

8 South Carolina
Year Admitted: 1788
Population: 4,012,012
Land area: 30,111 sq. mi.
Representatives: 6

Columbia ★

12 North Carolina
Year Admitted: 1789
Population: 8,049,313
Land area: 48,718 sq. mi.
Representatives: 13

★ Raleigh

13 Rhode Island
Year Admitted: 1790
Population: 1,048,319
Land area: 1,045 sq. mi.
Representatives: 2

★ Providence

14 Vermont
Year Admitted: 1791
Population: 608,827
Land area: 9,249 sq. mi.
Representatives: 1

★ Montpelier

15 Kentucky
Year Admitted: 1792
Population: 4,041,769
Land area: 39,732 sq. mi.
Representatives: 6

Frankfort ★

16 Tennessee
Year Admitted: 1796
Population: 5,689,283
Land area: 41,220 sq. mi.
Representatives: 9

★ Nashville

20 Mississippi
Year Admitted: 1817
Population: 2,844,658
Land area: 46,914 sq. mi.
Representatives: 4

★ Jackson

21 Illinois
Year Admitted: 1818
Population: 12,419,293
Land area: 55,593 sq. mi.
Representatives: 19

★ Springfield

22 Alabama
Year Admitted: 1819
Population: 4,447,100
Land area: 50,750 sq. mi.
Representatives: 7

Montgomery ★

23 Maine
Year Admitted: 1820
Population: 1,274,923
Land area: 30,865 sq. mi.
Representatives: 2

★ Augusta

24 Missouri
Year Admitted: 1821
Population: 5,595,211
Land area: 68,898 sq. mi.
Representatives: 9

Jefferson City ★

28 Texas
Year Admitted: 1845
Population: 20,851,820
Land area: 261,914 sq. mi.
Representatives: 32

Austin ★

29 Iowa
Year Admitted: 1846
Population: 2,926,324
Land area: 55,875 sq. mi.
Representatives: 5

Des Moines ★

30 Wisconsin
Year Admitted: 1848
Population: 5,363,675
Land area: 54,314 sq. mi.
Representatives: 8

Madison ★

31 California
Year Admitted: 1850
Population: 33,871,648
Land area: 155,973 sq. mi.
Representatives: 53

Sacramento ★

32 Minnesota
Year Admitted: 1858
Population: 4,919,479
Land area: 79,617 sq. mi.
Representatives: 8

Saint Paul ★

37 Nebraska
Year Admitted: 1867
Population: 1,711,263
Land area: 76,878 sq. mi.
Representatives: 3

Lincoln ★

38 Colorado
Year Admitted: 1876
Population: 4,301,261
Land area: 103,730 sq. mi.
Representatives: 7

Denver ★

39 North Dakota
Year Admitted: 1889
Population: 642,200
Land area: 68,994 sq. mi.
Representatives: 1

Bismarck ★

40 South Dakota
Year Admitted: 1889
Population: 754,844
Land area: 75,898 sq. mi.
Representatives: 1

Pierre ★

41 Montana
Year Admitted: 1889
Population: 902,195
Land area: 145,556 sq. mi.
Representatives: 1

★ Helena

46 Oklahoma
Year Admitted: 1907
Population: 3,450,654
Land area: 68,679 sq. mi.
Representatives: 5

Oklahoma City ★

47 New Mexico
Year Admitted: 1912
Population: 1,819,046
Land area: 121,365 sq. mi.
Representatives: 3

★ Santa Fe

48 Arizona
Year Admitted: 1912
Population: 5,130,632
Land area: 113,642 sq. mi.
Representatives: 8

Phoenix ★

49 Alaska
Year Admitted: 1959
Population: 626,932
Land area: 570,374 sq. mi.
Representatives: 1

Juneau ★

50 Hawaii
Year Admitted: 1959
Population: 1,211,537
Land area: 6,423 sq. mi.
Representatives: 2

Honolulu ★

GEOGRAPHIC
Geography Handbook

Acadia National ▶
Park, Maine

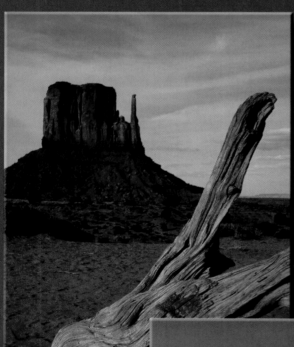

▲ Monument
Valley, Arizona

The Tongass National Forest in ▶
Southeastern Alaska, covering
nearly 17 million acres, is the
single largest national
forest in America.

What Is Geography?

The story of the United States begins with geography—the study of the earth in all of its variety. Geography describes the earth's land, water, and plant and animal life. It is the study of places and the complex relationships between people and their environments.

Geography of the United States

The United States is a land of startling physical differences. It is also a nation of diverse groups of people. A study of geography can help explain how the United States acquired its diversity.

The United States—with a total land area of 3,537,441 square miles (9,161,930 sq. km)—is the world's fourth-largest country in size.

The 50 States

Most of the United States—48 of the 50 states—spans the entire middle part of North America. This group of states touches three major bodies of water—the Atlantic Ocean, the Gulf of Mexico, and the Pacific Ocean. Two states—Alaska and Hawaii—lie apart from the 48 states.

Our Nation's Growth

Within the borders of the United States stretch a variety of landscapes—dense forests, hot deserts, rolling grasslands, and snow-capped mountains. Because of its large size and diverse regions, the United States throughout its history offered many opportunities. Over the centuries people from Europe, Africa, Asia, and other parts of the Americas have journeyed here. Today more than 281 million people make their homes in the United States.

NATIONAL GEOGRAPHIC

Physical Regions of the United States

Appalachian Highlands
Canadian Shield
Coastal Plains
Hawaii
Interior Plains
Intermountain
Pacific Coast
Rocky Mountains

CANADA

WASH.
OREG.
CASCADE RANGE
IDAHO
MONTANA
ROCKY MOUNTAINS
WYO.
N. DAK.
S. DAK.
NEBR.
MINN.
WIS.
IOWA
GREAT PLAINS
CENTRAL LOWLANDS
L. Superior
L. Michigan
L. Huron
L. Ontario
L. Erie
N.H.
VT.
MAINE
MASS.
N.Y.
R.I.
CONN.
MICH.
PA.
N.J.
IND. OHIO
W. VA. VA.
DEL.
MD.
SIERRA NEVADA
NEV.
UTAH
COLO.
KANSAS
MO.
ILL.
Ohio R.
KY.
N
W E
S
CALIF.
ARIZ.
N. MEX.
OKLA.
ARK.
TENN.
N.C.
S.C.
APPALACHIAN MOUNTAINS
ATLANTIC PLAIN
ATLANTIC OCEAN
PACIFIC OCEAN
MISS. ALA. GA.
Colorado R.
Missouri R.
Mississippi R.
TEXAS
LA.
GULF PLAIN
Rio Grande
Gulf of Mexico
FLA.

ALASKA
0 500 miles
0 500 kilometers
170°W 160°W 150°W

HAWAII
0 200 miles
0 200 kilometers
160°W 0 200 kilometers

MEXICO

0 500 miles
0 500 kilometers
Lambert Equal-Area projection
TROPIC OF CANCER
90°W
80°W
50°N
40°N
30°N
70°N
60°N
20°N

1

I Study Geography?

To understand how our world is connected, some geographers have broken down the study of geography into five themes. The **Five Themes of Geography** are (1) location, (2) place, (3) human/environment interaction, (4) movement, and (5) regions. You will see these themes highlighted in the Geography Skills accompanying the maps of *The American Journey: Reconstruction to the Present.*

Six Essential Elements

Recently, geographers have begun to look at geography in a different way. They break down the study of geography into **Six Essential Elements,** which are explained below. Being aware of these elements will help you sort out what you are learning about geography.

Element 1

The World in Spatial Terms

Geographers first take a look at where a place is located. **Location** serves as a starting point by asking "Where is it?" Knowing the location of places helps you develop an awareness of the world around you.

Element 2

Places and Regions

Place has a special meaning in geography. It means more than where a place is. It also describes what a place is like. These features may be physical characteristics such as landforms, climate, and plant or animal life. They may also be human characteristics, including language and way of life.

To help organize their study, geographers often group places or areas into regions. **Regions** are united by one or more common characteristics.

Element 3

Physical Systems

When studying places and regions, geographers analyze how **physical systems**—such as hurricanes, volcanoes, and glaciers—shape the earth's surface. They also look at communities of plants and animals that depend upon one another and their surroundings for survival.

Human Systems

Geographers also examine human systems, or how people have shaped our world. They look at how boundary lines are determined and analyze why people settle in certain places and not in others. A key theme in geography is the continual **movement** of people, ideas, and goods.

Environment and Society

"How does the relationship between people and their natural surroundings influence the way people live?" This is one of the questions that the theme of **human/ environment interaction** answers. This theme also shows how people use the environment and how their actions affect the environment.

The Uses of Geography

Knowledge of geography helps people understand the relationships among people, places, and environments over time. Understanding geography, and knowing how to use the tools and technology available to study it, prepares you for life in our modern society.

I Use Maps?

Maps of many different kinds are used in *The American Journey: Reconstruction to the Present* to help you see the connection between geography and the history of our nation.

Different Kinds of Maps

Physical Maps

A physical map shows the physical features of an area, such as its mountains and rivers. Physical maps use color and shadings to show **relief**—how flat or rugged the land surface is. Colors also may be used to show **elevation**—the height of an area above sea level.

Political Maps

Political maps generally show political, or human-made, divisions of countries or regions. The political map on pages RA2–RA3, for example, shows boundaries between the states that comprise the United States.

Special-Purpose Maps

Besides showing political or physical features, some maps have a special purpose. Human activities such as exploration routes, territorial expansion, or battle sites appear on special-purpose maps, also called **thematic maps.** The maps on pages RA6–RA7, for example, show territorial growth of the United States.

Latitude and Longitude

Maps have lines of latitude and longitude that form a grid. Lines of latitude circle the earth, either north or south of the Equator (0° latitude). Lines of longitude stretch from the North Pole to the South Pole, either east or west of the Prime Meridian (0° longitude). The distance between the lines is measured in degrees (°). Every place on the earth has a unique position or "address" on this grid.

Knowing this address makes it easier for you to locate cities and other places on a map. For example, the map on page RA5 shows you that the address of New Orleans is 30°N latitude, 90°W longitude.

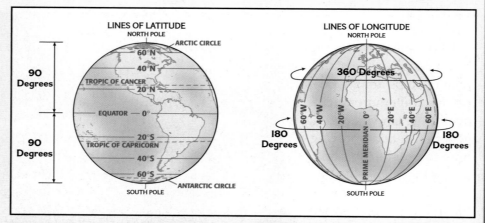

Parts of Maps

Map Key The map key explains the lines, symbols, and colors used on a map. For example, the map on this page shows the various climate regions of the United States. The key shows what climates the different colors represent. Map keys also may show structures created by people. Cities are usually symbolized by a solid circle (•). A star within a circle represents capitals (⊛). On this map, you can see the capital of Texas and the cities of New Orleans, Los Angeles, Seattle, and Chicago.

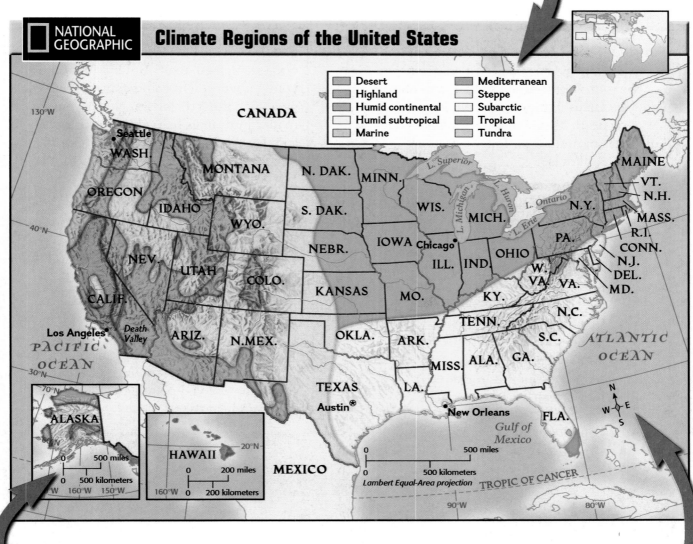

NATIONAL GEOGRAPHIC

Climate Regions of the United States

Key:
- Desert
- Highland
- Humid continental
- Humid subtropical
- Marine
- Mediterranean
- Steppe
- Subarctic
- Tropical
- Tundra

Lambert Equal-Area projection

Scale A measuring line, often called a **scale bar,** helps you determine distance on the map. The map scale tells you what distance on the earth is represented by the measurement on the scale bar.

Compass Rose An important first step in reading any map is to find the direction marker. A map has a symbol that tells you where the **cardinal directions**—north, south, east, and west—are positioned.

How Does Geography Influence History?

Geographic factors—landforms, waterways, natural resources—have shaped America's history. Here are some examples of geography's influences in history that are highlighted in *The American Journey: Reconstruction to the Present.*

Different Worlds Meet As settlement spread, Native Americans created distinctive civilizations appropriate to their climates and resources. For example, Native Americans in the Great Plains depended on herds of buffalo for food, clothing, shelter, and tools.

Colonial Settlement Beginning in the 1500s, Europeans came to North America seeking land, riches, and freedom. Groups from Spain, France, Great Britain, and other countries established colonies. The British colonies along the Atlantic coast were hemmed in by the Appalachian Mountains—the first physical barrier to the West.

Creating a Nation The hardships of the land shaped the colonial settlers' cultural identities. The colonists were isolated from much of the world and became more independent. Eventually they broke away from Great Britain and won their independence.

The New Republic When the United States was established, many doubted that the young government could control people over such great distances. New rivers, roads, and canals helped to open up the country. At the same time an Industrial Revolution had begun in New England.

The Growing Nation Through wars, treaties, and purchases, the United States gained control of the lands west of the Mississippi River. Settlers were drawn to Western territories by opportunities. Native Americans were forced onto reservations. Railroads enabled people to overcome geographic barriers.

Civil War and Reconstruction Demand for cotton by the textile industry increased the demand for labor provided by enslaved African Americans. In 1861 regional differences and a dispute over slavery sparked the Civil War between the North and South.

Reshaping the Nation After the Civil War, railroads transported goods from the East to the West and carried food products from the West to the East. The workers who advanced this industrial boom were immigrants and people who moved from farms to the cities. Pioneers changed the Great Plains from wilderness to farmland. (Unit 7)

Reform, Expansion, and War As industry grew in the United States, foreign trade became more important. America became more involved with other nations, expanded its empire around the world, and became involved in a world war. (Unit 8)

Turbulent Decades Environmental disasters during the first part of the 1900s affected the national economy. Due to poor farming methods, in the 1930s winds blew away so much of the soil in the Great Plains that the area became known as the Dust Bowl. (Unit 9)

Turning Points After World War II, the world's nations became much more connected and America became more involved in international affairs. Increased technology broke many long-standing geographic barriers. Americans were now able to travel greater distances in less time, leading to increased trade, travel, and opportunities. (Unit 10)

Modern America Americans take a leading role maintaining world peace. Many also are more aware of their impact on the surrounding environment. The government has begun to conserve and protect nature. Americans also face a new century with advanced technology. (Unit 11)

Geographic Dictionary

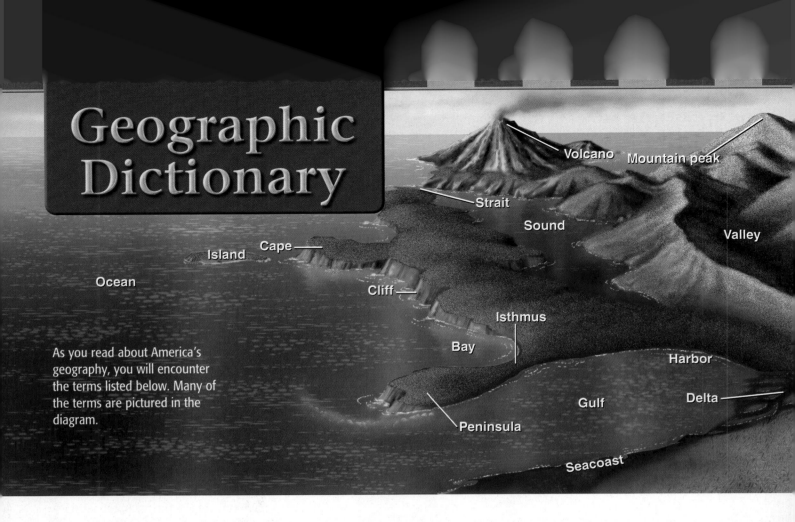

As you read about America's geography, you will encounter the terms listed below. Many of the terms are pictured in the diagram.

Labels in diagram: Volcano, Mountain peak, Strait, Sound, Valley, Island, Cape, Ocean, Cliff, Isthmus, Bay, Harbor, Peninsula, Gulf, Delta, Seacoast

absolute location exact location of a place on the earth described by global coordinates

basin area of land drained by a given river and its branches; area of land surrounded by lands of higher elevations

bay part of a large body of water that extends into a shoreline, generally smaller than a gulf

canyon deep and narrow valley with steep walls

cape point of land that extends into a river, lake, or ocean

channel wide strait or waterway between two land-masses that lie close to each other; deep part of a river or other waterway

cliff steep, high wall of rock, earth, or ice

continent one of the seven large landmasses on the earth

cultural feature characteristic that humans have created in a place, such as language, religion, housing, and settlement pattern

delta flat, low-lying land built up from soil carried downstream by a river and deposited at its mouth

divide stretch of high land that separates river systems

downstream direction in which a river or stream flows from its source to its mouth

elevation height of land above sea level

Equator imaginary line that runs around the earth halfway between the North and South Poles; used as the starting point to measure degrees of north and south latitude

glacier large, thick body of slowly moving ice

gulf part of a large body of water that extends into a shoreline, generally larger and more deeply indented than a bay

harbor a sheltered place along a shoreline where ships can anchor safely

highland elevated land area such as a hill, mountain, or plateau

hill elevated land with sloping sides and rounded summit; generally smaller than a mountain

island land area, smaller than a continent, completely surrounded by water

isthmus narrow stretch of land connecting two larger land areas

lake a sizable inland body of water

latitude distance north or south of the Equator, measured in degrees

longitude distance east or west of the Prime Meridian, measured in degrees

lowland land, usually level, at a low elevation

map drawing of the earth shown on a flat surface

meridian one of many lines on the global grid running from the North Pole to the South Pole; used to measure degrees of longitude

mesa broad, flat-topped landform with steep sides; smaller than a plateau

Mountain range

Source of river

Channel

Glacier

Highland

Plateau

Lake

Hills

Canyon

Desert

Mouth of river

River

Upstream

Downstream

Lowland

Plain

Basin

Tributary

mountain land with steep sides that rises sharply (1,000 feet or more) from surrounding land; generally larger and more rugged than a hill

mountain peak pointed top of a mountain

mountain range a series of connected mountains

mouth (of a river) place where a stream or river flows into a larger body of water

ocean one of the four major bodies of salt water that surround the continents

ocean current stream of either cold or warm water that moves in a definite direction through an ocean

parallel one of many lines on the global grid that circle the earth north or south of the Equator; used to measure degrees of latitude

peninsula body of land jutting into a lake or ocean, surrounded on three sides by water

physical feature characteristic of a place occurring naturally, such as a landform, body of water, climate pattern, or resource

plain area of level land, usually a low elevation and often covered with grasses

plateau area of flat or rolling land at a high elevation, about 300–3,000 feet high

Prime Meridian line of the global grid running from the North Pole to the South Pole through Greenwich, England; starting point for measuring degrees of east and west longitude

relief changes in elevation over a given area of land

river large natural stream of water that runs through the land

sea large body of water completely or partly surrounded by land

seacoast land lying next to a sea or ocean

sea level position on land level with surface of nearby ocean or sea

sound body of water between a coastline and one or more islands off the coast

source (of a river) place where a river or stream begins, often in highlands

strait narrow stretch of water joining two larger bodies of water

tributary small river or stream that flows into a large river or stream; a branch of the river

upstream direction opposite the flow of a river; toward the source of a river or stream

valley area of low land between hills or mountains

volcano mountain created as liquid rock or ash erupts from inside the earth

Be an Active Reader

Think about your textbook as a tool that helps you learn more about the world around you. It is an example of nonfiction writing—it describes real-life events, people, ideas, and places. Here is a menu of reading strategies that will help you become a better textbook reader. As you come to passages in your textbook that you don't understand, refer to these reading strategies for help.

✔ Before You Read

Set a purpose
- Why are you reading the textbook?
- How does the subject relate to your life?
- How might you be able to use what you learn in your own life?

Preview
- Read the chapter title to find what the topic will be.
- Read the subtitles to see what you will learn about the topic.
- Skim the photos, charts, graphs, or maps. How do they support the topic?
- Look for vocabulary words that are bold-faced. How are they defined?

Draw From Your Own Background
- What have you read or heard concerning new information on the topic?
- How is the new information different from what you already know?
- How will the information that you already know help you understand the new information?

Question
- What is the main idea?
- How do the photos, charts, graphs, and maps support the main idea?

Connect
- Think about people, places, and events in your own life. Are there any similarities with those in your textbook?
- Can you relate the textbook information to other areas of your life?

Predict
- Predict events or outcomes by using clues and information that you already know.
- Change your predictions as you read and gather new information.

Visualize
- Pay careful attention to details and descriptions.
- Create graphic organizers to show relationships that you find in the information.

Look For Clues As You Read

Comparison and Contrast Sentences
- Look for clue words and phrases that signal comparison, such as *similarly*, *just as*, *both*, *in common*, *also*, and *too*.
- Look for clue words and phrases that signal contrast, such as *on the other hand*, *in contrast to*, *however*, *different*, *instead of*, *rather than*, *but*, and *unlike*.

Cause-and-Effect Sentences
- Look for clue words and phrases such as *because*, *as a result*, *therefore*, *that is why*, *since*, *so*, *for this reason*, and *consequently*.

Chronological Sentences
- Look for clue words and phrases such as *after*, *before*, *first*, *next*, *last*, *during*, *finally*, *earlier*, *later*, *since*, and *then*.

✓ After You Read

Summarize
- Describe the main idea and how the details support it.
- Use your own words to explain what you have read.

Assess
- What was the main idea?
- Did the text clearly support the main idea?
- Did you learn anything new from the material?
- Can you use this new information in other school subjects or at home?
- What other sources could you use to find more information about the topic?

Prologue

Beginnings to 1877

Why It Matters

As you study the Prologue, you will learn that the first immigrants came to the Americas long before written history. Much later, Europeans settled on the continent and started down a path of events that would lead to the founding of the United States. Great examples of conflict and cooperation marked America's early history.

Primary Sources Library

See pages 958–969 for primary source readings to accompany the Prologue. Use the **American History Primary Source Document Library CD-ROM** to find additional primary sources about the formation and growth of the United States.

Daniel Boone Escorting Settlers Through the Cumberland Gap by George Caleb Bingham

"*Observe good faith and justice toward all nations.*"

—George Washington, 1796

A Nation is Born

Beginnings to 1791

Why It Matters

The Americas today consist of peoples and cultures from around the globe. Over hundreds of years, the United States became a country where people of different backgrounds and beliefs could live together. As the country grew and matured, it adapted to meet the changing needs of its people.

The Impact Today

Evidence of the earliest migration can be clearly seen in the United States today. The federal government officially recognizes 562 Native American tribes. European influence is easily seen throughout the country as well.

The Americas

c. 28,000 B.C.
• Asian hunters enter North America

c. A.D. 1300
• Hohokam civilization begins to decline

Prehistory   *1300*   *1500*

World

c. 10,000 B.C.
• Last Ice Age ends

A.D. 1295
• Italian traveler Marco Polo returns from China

1517
• Martin Luther promotes Church reform

George Washington Addressing the Constitutional Convention

1607
- Jamestown settled

1718
- French establish port of New Orleans

c. 1740
- Great Awakening peaks

1776
- Declaration of Independence signed

1788
- U.S. Constitution ratified

1600   *1700*

c. 1605
- Shakespeare writes *King Lear*

1689
- English Bill of Rights signed

1769
- Watt patents steam engine

1789
- French Revolution begins

HISTORY
Online

Chapter Overview
Visit taj.glencoe.com and click on **Prologue Chapter 1— Chapter Overviews** to review chapter information.

Different Worlds Meet

Guide to Reading

Main Idea
Millions of people lived in the Americas before Europeans arrived.

Key Terms
nomads, migration, maize, theocracy, federations, Renaissance, circumnavigate, conquistadors

Reading Strategy
Categorizing Information As you read the section, re-create the diagram below and describe the regions where each civilization existed.

Civilization	Region
Maya	
Aztec	
Inca	

Read to Learn
- how the first people arrived and lived in the Americas.
- how different factors led to European exploration.
- how the Aztec and Inca Empires came to an end.

Section Theme
Geography and History Various civilizations developed different cultures and societies depending on where they settled in the Americas.

Preview of Events

♦Prehistory ♦500 ♦1000 ♦1500

c. 10,000 B.C.
Last Ice Age ends

C. A.D. 300
Maya build large cities

1492
Columbus lands in the Americas

1535
Pizarro gains control of the Inca empire

AN American Story

No one knows for sure why the first people to settle in North America crossed the land bridge that once connected Asia and North America. With spears poised, small bands of hunters may have pursued a mammoth, a large game animal that is now extinct, or other large animals. Later settlers may have come by boat, hunting seals and whales. Over time, these "native Americans" would inhabit both North and South America.

The First Americans

When Europeans arrived in the Americas in the late 1400s, they found native peoples with advanced cultures already living there. The mixture of Native American and European cultures that occurred in the New World shaped the history of the Americas and the future of the United States.

Early Peoples

The early Americans were nomads, people who moved from place to place. Scientists believe the first Americans were people from Asia who crossed over a broad strip of land between Asia and North America that was exposed during the last Ice Age. These early peoples probably reached the Americas about 30,000 years ago.

The crossing of this land bridge, called Beringia, was a migration, a movement of a large number of people into a new homeland. Separate groups spread out across the Americas, going as far east as the Atlantic Ocean and as far south as the tip of South America.

These early people first hunted large mammals, but eventually shifted to small game such as deer and birds. About 9,000 years ago, people settled in what is today Mexico and began planting a form of corn called maize.

With dependable supplies of food, early Americans began developing permanent communities. Knowing they would harvest enough food, they began improving their lives with permanent dwellings, pottery, and new forms of government. Over time, the many different groups of people living in the Americas developed distinctive cultures.

Cities and Empires

In what is today Mexico and Central and South America, three large, advanced civilizations developed—the Maya, the Aztec, and the Inca. Each thrived for centuries.

The Maya

The Maya built their civilization in the rain forests of what is today Mexico, Guatemala, Honduras, and Belize. By A.D. 300 the Maya had built many large cities. Each city was dominated by at least one stone pyramid. The pyramids served as religious and political centers. The civilization of the Maya was a theocracy, a society ruled by religious leaders. Mayan priests performed religious ceremonies and studied the night sky from temples built on top of the pyramids. The priests developed an understanding of astronomy. They created a 365-day calendar to schedule plantings, harvests, and religious ceremonies. The Maya also traded up and down Mexico's eastern coast. No one knows why, but around A.D. 800 the Mayan civilization began to decline.

The Aztec

Centuries after the fall of the Maya, a group of hunters called the Aztec wandered through central Mexico. They settled on an island in

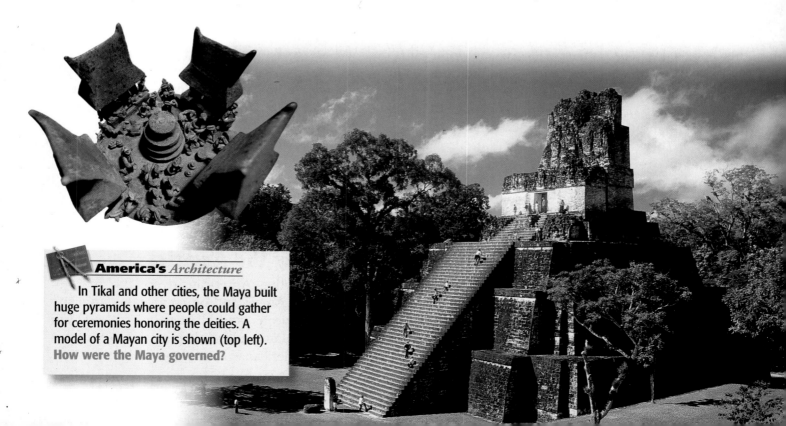

America's *Architecture*

In Tikal and other cities, the Maya built huge pyramids where people could gather for ceremonies honoring the deities. A model of a Mayan city is shown (top left). How were the Maya governed?

Lake Texcoco, today part of Mexico City. On this island the Aztec built one of the greatest cities in the Americas—Tenochtitlán (tay nawch teet LAHN). At its height, the city was the largest city in the Americas, perhaps the largest in the world. By A.D. 1500, nearly 200,000 people lived there.

The Inca

A third civilization, the Inca, founded their capital city of Cuzco (KOOS koh) around A.D. 1200. Through their power and military conquest, the Inca built an empire that stretched for more than 3,000 miles (4,800 km). It reached from what is today Colombia to northern Argentina and Chile.

At its height, the Inca Empire had a population of more than 6 million, including many conquered peoples. To control this empire, more than 10,000 miles (16,000 km) of stone-paved roads were constructed through jungles and over mountains.

North American Peoples

Besides the civilizations of South and Central America, many other cultures developed on the North American continent.

The Hohokam and the Anasazi lived in the desert Southwest between A.D. 200 and A.D. 1300. The Hohokam developed irrigation canals to carry water to their settlements along the Gila and Salt River Valleys. The Anasazi built cliff dwellings in what is today Utah, Colorado, Arizona, and New Mexico.

A group of many different peoples known as the Mound Builders lived in the American Midwest. The earthen mounds they built lifted temples above the towns and may have served those who studied the night sky. The largest settlement of the Mound Builders was Cahokia (kuh HOH kee uh) in what is today Illinois. This city, built between A.D. 900 and A.D. 1200 by a people called the Mississippians, may have had 30,000 or more residents.

People of the North

Although the civilizations of the Hohokam, the Anasazi, and the Mound Builders eventually faded away, other Native American cultures arose to take their place. The Inuit lived in the northern lands around the Arctic Ocean. They developed the ability to build homes made of blocks of snow and ice, and to craft clothing of sealskin and thick fur. They fished the coastal waters for seals, whales, and walruses.

People of the West

In western North America, groups like the Tlingit (TLIHNG kuht) and Chinook lived off of the forest and the sea. They made canoes and cloth from tree bark and lived mainly off the abundance of salmon along the coast and in the rivers. In the Southwest, groups such as the Hopi, the Acoma, and the Zuni descended from the Anasazi. They built their dwellings from sun-dried mud brick called adobe.

Nomadic peoples lived on the Great Plains, following the herds of antelope, deer, and buffalo. Every growing season the women grew squash, maize, and beans. The Apache and Dakota later learned how to ride the horses that were introduced to the Americas by the Spanish in the 1500s.

People of the East

The eastern woodlands of North America were home to the Iroquois and the Cherokee. They governed their peoples with complex law codes and federations, or governments that linked different groups.

Wherever they lived in North America, the first Americans developed ways of life that were well suited to their environments. In the 1500s, however, they would meet Europeans whose cultures, beliefs, and ways of life were different from anything they had known or ever seen.

Reading Check **Identifying** In what area did the Anasazi live?

Exploring the Americas

While Native Americans were the first to inhabit the American continents, the English, Spanish, Africans, and other peoples would all eventually play a role in shaping the culture we now call American.

NATIONAL GEOGRAPHIC   Native American Cultures Before 1500

1 Tepees were used by the Plains cultures.

2 Cultures in the Northeast Woodlands built longhouses.

3 Southwest cultures built pueblos.

Culture Groups

- Arctic
- Subarctic
- Northwest Coast
- Plateau
- Great Basin
- California
- Southwest
- Great Plains
- Northeast Woodlands
- Southeast

0 1,000 miles
0 1,000 kilometers
Azimuthal Equidistant projection

Geography *Skills*

1. **Region** To which culture group did the Apache and Hopi belong?
2. **Making Inferences** Based on the description of the dwellings, which cultures were nomadic?

A Changing World

A period of intellectual and artistic creativity known as the **Renaissance** (reh nuh SAHNTS) spread across western Europe between the thirteenth and fifteenth centuries. A spirit of discovery led to an age of exploration. Using more accurate maps and better navigational instruments, Europeans set sail. Their goal was to explore and develop trading routes to the rich eastern cultures of China and India.

While searching for better routes from Europe to Asia, Europeans encountered powerful African kingdoms south of the Sahara. The empires of Ghana, Mali, and Songhai had grown rich trading gold, copper, and iron ore.

Early Exploration

Determined rulers hoped to find a more direct trade route to China, India, and West Africa. Dri-

ven by this economic goal, Portuguese explorers began learning more about the sea and the African coast. In 1488 a Portuguese expedition led by Bartholomeu Dias rounded the tip of Africa. Ten years later, another Portuguese expedition, headed by Vasco da Gama, crossed the Indian Ocean to Calicut on the coast of India. The sea routes that Portuguese sailors opened challenged other European nations to make their own explorations.

Columbus Crosses the Atlantic

Italian sailor Christopher Columbus believed that a better way to reach Asia was to sail west across the Atlantic Ocean. But Columbus needed a sponsor to finance his big project. After many failures he convinced King Ferdinand and Queen

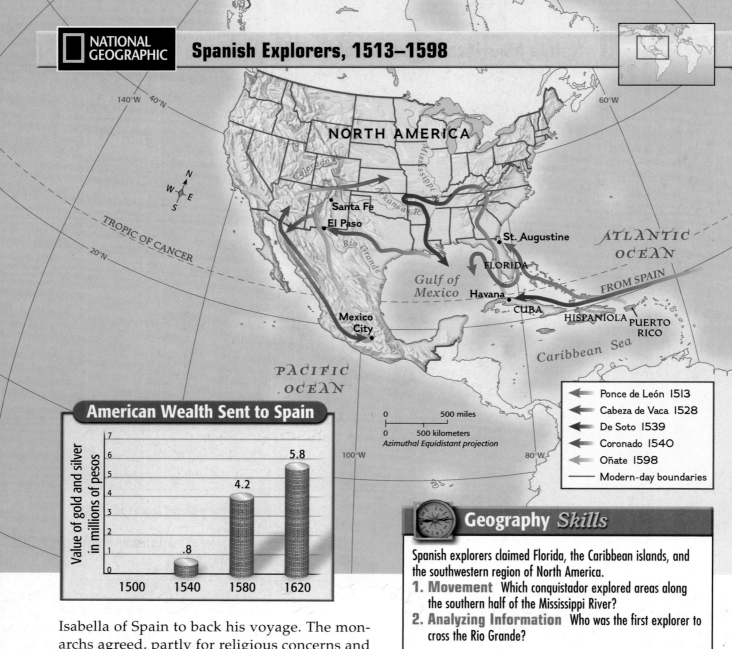

Spanish Explorers, 1513–1598

NORTH AMERICA

140°W 40°N

TROPIC OF CANCER

20°N

Colorado

Santa Fe

El Paso

Rio Grande

Arkansas R.

Mississippi

Gulf of Mexico

Mexico City

PACIFIC OCEAN

St. Augustine

FLORIDA

Havana

CUBA

HISPANIOLA

PUERTO RICO

Caribbean Sea

ATLANTIC OCEAN

FROM SPAIN

60°W

80°W

100°W

American Wealth Sent to Spain

Value of gold and silver in millions of pesos

7
6 — 5.8
5
4 — 4.2
3
2
1 — .8
0

1500   1540   1580   1620

0   500 miles
0   500 kilometers
Azimuthal Equidistant projection

← Ponce de León 1513
← Cabeza de Vaca 1528
← De Soto 1539
← Coronado 1540
← Oñate 1598
— Modern-day boundaries

Geography *Skills*

Spanish explorers claimed Florida, the Caribbean islands, and the southwestern region of North America.

1. **Movement** Which conquistador explored areas along the southern half of the Mississippi River?

2. **Analyzing Information** Who was the first explorer to cross the Rio Grande?

Isabella of Spain to back his voyage. The monarchs agreed, partly for religious concerns and partly to gain wealth.

On August 3, 1492, Columbus set out from Palos, Spain, expecting to reach Asia in about two months. He based his calculations on the work of ancient Greek astronomer Ptolemy, who had unfortunately underestimated the size of the world. Though his crew began to worry after a month at sea, Columbus maintained his faith. His confidence was soon rewarded. On October 12, 1492, a lookout shouted *"Tierra! Tierra!"*— "Land! Land!"

Columbus was convinced he had reached the East Indies—the islands off the coast of Asia. However, he was actually in the Atlantic Ocean, southeast of present-day Florida. Columbus also explored what is today areas of Haiti and the Dominican Republic, Cuba, Jamaica, and the coasts of Central America and northern South America in 1493, 1498, and 1502.

Sailing Around the World

In 1519 the Spanish sent Portuguese captain Ferdinand Magellan to lead a new expedition through or around South America to find a passage to Asia. In November 1520, Magellan finally found a twisting, narrow passage to the Pacific Ocean at the southern tip of South America.

He expected the remainder of the trip to Asia to last just a few weeks. Instead, the voyage across the Pacific lasted four months. Quickly out of food, the crew ate sawdust, rats, and pieces of leather to stay alive. Magellan was killed in a local war during a stop in the Philippines, but some of his crew returned to Spain. Only one of the five original ships and 18 of the 250 crew members completed the full journey. They were the first to circumnavigate, or sail around, the world.

Spanish Conquests

Spanish conquistadors (kahn KEES tuh dawrs) explored the Americas. These men used their own money to explore and establish settlements, agreeing to give the Spanish crown one-fifth of any gold or treasure discovered. This way, failure of the expedition hurt only the explorer. Success, however, provided wealth and glory for the explorer and Spain.

Cortés and Pizarro

Hernán Cortés came to Mexico in 1519 looking for gold and glory. Using his soldiers, cannons, and nearby enemies of the Aztec, he conquered the Aztec Empire.

When he marched on the capital of Tenochtitlán in November, the emperor, Montezuma (mahn tuh ZOO muh), welcomed the Spaniard. Cortés imprisoned the emperor and eventually killed him and other Aztec nobles to prevent any rebellion. The Aztec drove the Spanish out of the city in anger. Cortés retaliated with more troops in 1521 and destroyed the city.

In 1530 Francisco Pizarro sailed with 180 soldiers down the Pacific Coast of South America, searching for the fabled wealth of the Inca. In 1532, Pizarro captured the Inca ruler, Atahualpa (ah tah WAHL pah), along with much of the Incan army. When Atahualpa was killed a few months later, his army was unable to fight effectively without leadership. By 1535 Pizarro had gained control of most of the vast Inca Empire.

The Spanish were able to quickly conquer these Native American empires for several reasons. They used superior weapons. They were helped by other Native Americans who had been treated badly by the Aztec and Inca. The Spanish also brought diseases with them. Since Native Americans had no immunity to these diseases, illnesses killed large numbers of Inca and Aztec.

✓ **Reading Check** **Analyzing** Why was Portugal interested in exploration?

SECTION 1 ASSESSMENT

Checking for Understanding

1. **Key Terms** Use each of these terms in a complete sentence that will help explain its meaning: nomads, federations, migration, Renaissance, maize, circumnavigate, theocracy, conquistadors.
2. **Reviewing Facts** How did the development of farming 9,000 years ago change the lives of nomads?

Reviewing Themes

3. **Geography and History** Where did Columbus land on his first voyage?

Critical Thinking

4. **Making Generalizations** How did the Portuguese efforts to reach Asia differ from Columbus's efforts?
5. **Analyzing Information** Re-create the diagram below and describe why the Maya, Aztec, and Inca were advanced civilizations.

Advanced Civilizations		
Maya	Aztec	Inca

Analyzing Visuals

6. **Geography Skills** Study the map on page 7. What groups lived in present day California? What groups lived in the Southeast? What groups lived in or near the area in which you live?

Interdisciplinary Activity

Art Draw a map of the world as you think Christopher Columbus might have mapped it in 1492. Remember Columbus' error in calculations.

Colonial America

Guide to Reading

Main Idea
Europeans settled in North America and established a wide variety of colonies.

Key Terms
Northwest Passage, joint-stock company, Separatists, Mayflower Compact, Puritans, proprietary colony

Reading Strategy
Comparing As you read the section, re-create the diagram below and describe economic activities in the three kinds of North American colonies.

Colonies	Economic Activities
New England Colonies	
Middle Colonies	
Southern Colonies	

Read to Learn
• how exploration influenced cultures around the world.
• why colonial America was made up of a diverse population.

Section Theme
Culture and Traditions Each colony was culturally different, depending on who settled there.

Preview of Events

1500 — 1600 — 1700

1565 Spanish build fort in St. Augustine, Florida

1619 Colonists establish House of Burgesses

1681 William Penn founds Pennsylvania

1733 First settlers arrive in Georgia

★★★★★★★★★★
AN American Story

In the summer of 1588, Spanish warships sailed toward the coast of England. King Philip of Spain had sent an armada, or war fleet, of 132 ships to invade England. With 30,000 troops and 2,400 guns, the Spanish Armada was the mightiest naval force the world had ever seen. Yet the smaller, swifter English ships quickly gained the upper hand. The Spanish Armada fled north to Scotland, where violent storms destroyed and scattered the fleet. Only about one-half of the Spanish ships straggled home. Though Spain lost its naval battle with England, it led the way in exploring the North American continent.

North American Developments

Spain was the first European nation to explore North America, but it would not be the only one. The French and the English would begin their own explorations of the Americas, eventually setting up their own colonial outposts.

Spanish Explorations

Spanish exploration of North America was led by Juan Ponce de León. He landed on the east coast of what is today Florida in 1513. Ponce de León's exploration led to the first Spanish settlement in what is now the United States.

In 1565, the Spanish established a fort at St. Augustine, Florida. Francisco Vásquez de Coronado traveled through northern Mexico and what is today Arizona and New Mexico in early summer 1540. Juan de Oñate (day ohn•YAH•tay) was sent from Mexico to gain control over lands to the north and to convert the natives. In 1598 Oñate founded the province of New Mexico and introduced cattle and horses to the Pueblo people.

Hernando de Soto led an expedition through Florida and the Southeast that lasted three years. He traced the southern portion of the Mississippi River. Other expeditions led further west and established Spanish colonies in what is today the southwestern United States.

A Northwest Passage

In 1497 England sent the Italian John Cabot to find a Northwest Passage to Asia—a more direct water route through the Americas. France hired another Italian, Giovanni da Verrazano, in 1524 for the same purpose. Cabot probably landed in what is today Newfoundland. Verrazano explored from Nova Scotia to the Carolinas.

The Dutch and French Explore

In 1609 the Dutch hired Henry Hudson, who charted the river that bears his name. The following year, this time sailing for the English, he discovered a huge inlet in eastern Canada, now called Hudson Bay.

The French sent explorers to North America who were more interested in establishing trading rights than building empires. Beginning with the settlement of Quebec, French traders spread through what is today Canada, and started trading posts to collect furs from Native Americans.

NATIONAL GEOGRAPHIC

The First English Settlements

80°W

MASSACHUSETTS
Plymouth • Cape Cod
Wampanoag
Narraganset

Plymouth, 1620
Adults 70%
Children 30%
1620

40°N

APPALACHIAN MOUNTAINS
Hudson R.
Delaware R.
Susquehanna
Leni-Lenape
Potomac R.

ATLANTIC OCEAN

VIRGINIA
Powhatan — Nanticoke
James R. — Chesapeake Bay
Jamestown 1607

Jamestown, 1607
Adults 96%
Children 4%

1585, 1587

Roanoke R.
Tuscarora
Roanoke Island

0   100 miles
0   100 kilometers
Lambert Equal-Area projection

N W E S

70°W

Geography Skills

Many Native American groups lived near the first English settlements in the late 1500s and early 1600s.
1. **Location** Which colony was located farthest north?
2. **Location** Which Native American groups lived nearest to the Jamestown colonists?

Reading Check **Analyzing** Why was the idea of a Northwest Passage important?

America Develops

In 1585, Sir Walter Raleigh sent about 100 men to settle on Roanoke Island, off the coast of what is today North Carolina. After a difficult winter, the unhappy colonists returned to England. Two years later Raleigh tried again, sending 91 men, 17 women, and 9 children to Roanoke. John White returned to England for supplies and to recruit more settlers. When he returned, after a three-year delay, the settlement was deserted. The Roanoke colonists were never seen again.

Jamestown Settlement

In December 1606, a group of merchants known as the Virginia Company of London sent 144 settlers to America. The colony was organized as a joint-stock company, which provided investors in the company partial ownership and a share in its future profits.

The colonists entered Chesapeake Bay and settled Jamestown in April 1607. They faced difficulty, as disease and hunger devastated the colonists. By January 1608, when ships arrived with additional men and supplies, only 38 of the colonists remained alive.

The colony survived when Captain John Smith managed to get corn from the Powhatan people. They also discovered they could make money for the investors by growing tobacco. Planters were soon raising the crop, and the colony of Virginia began to prosper and grow.

Representative Government

As the colony grew, the settlers complained about taking orders from the Virginia Company in London. In 1619 two important events occurred. First, the company agreed to let the colonists have some say in their government. Governor George Yeardley allowed the men of the colony to elect representatives, called burgesses, to a legislative assembly known as the House of Burgesses. Second, Dutch traders brought 20 Africans to work in the tobacco fields. They were the first of many Africans to come to America.

Until about 1640 some African laborers in Jamestown were free and even owned property. In the years to follow, however, many more shiploads of Africans would arrive in North America, and those unwilling passengers would be sold as enslaved persons. Slavery was first recognized in Virginia law in 1661.

New England Colonies

Further to the north, another colony formed in what is today New England. A group of religious Separatists, Protestants who fled to the Netherlands to avoid religious persecution, made an arrangement with the Virginia Company to settle in Virginia. In September 1620, 35 Separatist Pilgrims and 102 other passengers began their journey to Virginia aboard the *Mayflower*.

The Pilgrims first sighted land well north of Virginia at Cape Cod. Due to the fast approach of winter, however, they settled in December at Plymouth. Because Plymouth was outside the control of the Virginia Company, the Pilgrims drew up a document called the Mayflower Compact to govern their new colony.

Massachusetts Bay

In 1628 another religious group, the Puritans, received a royal charter to establish the Massachusetts Bay Company north of Plymouth. In 1630, under the leadership of John Winthrop, 1,000 men, women, and children settled in a place they called Boston. The Puritans were unwilling to allow other religious groups freedom to practice their beliefs. This lack of tolerance led to the creation of new colonies on neighboring areas.

Connecticut and Rhode Island

In the 1630s colonists began settling in the Connecticut River valley. Some who were frustrated with the Puritan rule in Massachusetts migrated to Connecticut. The colony of Rhode Island was made up initially of colonists forced out of Massachusetts.

Roger Williams received a charter for the colony of Rhode Island in 1644. It became a safe harbor for religious dissenters and was the first place in America where people of all faiths—including Jews—could worship freely.

Middle Colonies

Between the two clusters of English settlement in Virginia and New England lay lands controlled by the Netherlands. The main Dutch settlement was New Amsterdam on Manhattan Island. In 1664 the English captured the valuable port of New Amsterdam.

King Charles II gave the colony to his brother, the Duke of York, who renamed it New York. It differed from the New England Colonies which were run by private corporations under a royal charter. New York was a proprietary colony, a colony in which the owner, or proprietor, owned all the land and controlled the government.

New Jersey and Pennsylvania

The southern part of the New York colony, between the Hudson and Delaware Rivers, was renamed New Jersey. The proprietors of New Jersey hoped to make a profit by charging the settlers rent for the tracts of land they settled on. The profits never met expectations, and by 1702 the colony had become a royal colony.

In 1680 William Penn asked King Charles to give him land in America rather than repay a large loan the king once received from his father. The new Pennsylvania colony became a "holy experiment" for another group of Protestant dissenters called the Society of Friends, or Quakers.

To encourage European settlers to come to his colony, Penn advertised throughout Europe. By 1683 more than 3,000 English, Welsh, Irish, Dutch, and German settlers had arrived. In 1701, in the Charter of Liberties, Penn granted the colonists the right to elect representatives to the legislative assembly. In 1703 the southernmost part of Pennsylvania was allowed to form its own legislature. It began to function as the separate colony of Delaware.

Southern Colonies

In 1634 two ships and 200 settlers sailed up the Potomac River north of Virginia and established the colony of Maryland as a safe place for Catholics. Knowing that tobacco had saved the Vir-

ginia colony, the colonists turned first to tobacco farming. Most Maryland tobacco farmers also produced wheat, fruit, vegetables, and livestock.

The organizers of Maryland also welcomed Protestants to settle in the colony. From the beginning, the Protestants outnumbered the Catholics. To ensure that Catholics could worship freely, the colony's government passed the Act of Toleration in 1649. It granted all Christians the right to worship freely. Religious freedom was becoming rooted in the colonies.

Northern and Southern Carolina

In two charters issued in 1663 and 1665, King Charles II created a large proprietary colony south of Virginia named Carolina. Farmers from Virginia's backcountry settled the northern part of Carolina. The southern part of Carolina was more prosperous, thanks to fertile farmland and a good harbor at the main city of Charles Town (later Charleston).

In the 1680s planters discovered that rice grew well in the wet coastal lowlands. Slaves brought by the settlers worked in the rice fields. By 1700 more than half the people who arrived in Charles

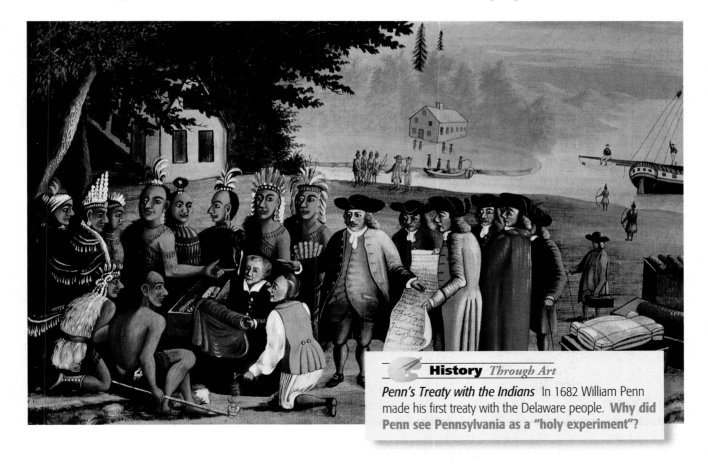

History *Through Art*

Penn's Treaty with the Indians In 1682 William Penn made his first treaty with the Delaware people. **Why did Penn see Pennsylvania as a "holy experiment"?**

Town were enslaved Africans. Tension grew between the people of northern and southern Carolina. In 1729 they split into two colonies— North and South Carolina.

Georgia

Georgia, the last of the British colonies in America to be established, was founded in 1733. General James Oglethorpe received a charter to create a colony where debtors and poor people could make a fresh start. The British government also wanted Georgia to serve as a military barrier between Spanish Florida and South Carolina. The first group of settlers built the town of Savannah, as well as forts to defend themselves from the Spanish. Oglethorpe initially limited the size of landholdings and banned slave labor. Frustrated with the slow growth of Georgia, however, he gave up altogether in 1751, turning the colony back over to the king.

Spanish and French Settlements

The British were not the only Europeans who were colonizing North America. The Spanish expanded from their colonial base of Mexico, the Caribbean, and Central and South America. They reached into the western and southern part of what would one day be the United States.

Spanish missionaries, soldiers, and settlers founded Santa Fe in present-day New Mexico in 1610. Other groups of missionaries and settlers expanded the Spanish presence into what is today Arizona, Texas, and California.

The French had founded Quebec in 1608. In 1663 New France became a royal colony whose main concern was the fish and fur trade in the interior of North America. In the 1670s, the French spread their explorations along the Mississippi River. They hoped to find gold, silver, other precious metals, and a water passage to the Pacific Ocean. Eventually the French followed the Mississippi River all the way to the Gulf of Mexico. Claiming this territory for France, Robert Cavelier Sieur de La Salle named it Louisiana in honor of King Louis XIV. In 1718 the French governor founded the port of New Orleans at the mouth of the Mississippi River.

France and Great Britain were great rivals during the colonial period. Both nations were expanding their settlements in North America. In the late 1700s and early 1800s, wars in Europe between the British and the French would shape events across the Atlantic even more decisively.

✔ **Reading Check** **Analyzing** Why was the House of Burgesses important?

SECTION 2 ASSESSMENT

Checking for Understanding

1. **Key Terms** Write a short paragraph in which you use all of the following terms: Northwest Passage, Mayflower Compact, joint-stock company, Puritans, Separatists, proprietary colony
2. **Reviewing Facts** Explain why Maryland passed the Act of Toleration.

Reviewing Themes

3. **Culture and Traditions** How did the need for workers contribute to cultural diversity in the Southern Colonies?

Critical Thinking

4. **Making Comparisons** How did the goals of the French in the Americas differ from the goals of other European countries?
5. **Organizing Information** Re-create the diagram below and describe how the three types of colonies were formed.

Formation of American Colonies		
New England Colonies	Middle Colonies	Southern Colonies

Analyzing Visuals

6. **Geography Skills** Study the map and graphs on page 11. What percentage of settlers in Plymouth were children? In what year did settlers arrive in Plymouth?

Interdisciplinary Activity

Geography Create a poster that might have attracted early colonists to the area where you live. Focus on the location as well as natural features in your area such as good farmland, forests, waterways, and mineral resources.

Critical Thinking
SKILLBUILDER

Understanding Cause and Effect

Why Learn This Skill?

You know that if you watch television instead of completing your homework you will receive poor grades. This is an example of a cause-and-effect relationship. The cause—watching television instead of doing homework—leads to an effect—poor grades.

Causes and Effects of the Slave Trade

Causes

- Colonists need to grow cash crops, such as tobacco and rice.
- European demand for tobacco and rice increases.
- Growing tobacco and rice requires large labor force.

Effects

- Africans are robbed of basic human rights.
- Population of enslaved Africans grows.
- Slavery creates feelings of injustice and plants seeds of regional conflict.

Learning the Skill

A *cause* is any person, event, or condition that makes something happen. What happens as a result is known as an *effect*. These guidelines will help you identify cause and effect.

- Identify two or more events.
- Ask questions about why events occur.
- Look for "clue words" that alert you to cause and effect, such as *because, led to, brought about, produced,* and *therefore.*
- Identify the outcome of events.

Practicing the Skill

Study the cause-and-effect chart about the slave trade on this page. Think about the guidelines listed above. Then answer the questions below.

1 What were some causes of the development of slavery in the colonies?

2 What were some of the short-term effects of enslaving Africans?

3 What was the long-term effect of the development of slavery?

Applying the Skill

Understanding Cause and Effect Read an account of a recent event or chain of events in your community newspaper. Determine at least one cause and one effect of that event. Show the cause-and-effect relationship in a chart.

 Glencoe's **Skillbuilder Interactive Workbook CD-ROM, Level 1,** provides instruction and practice in key social studies skills.

SECTION 3 Colonial Growth and Change

Guide to Reading

Main Idea
As the English colonies grew, they became more independent.

Key Terms
triangular trade, mercantilism, writs of assistance, boycott

Reading Strategy
Determining Cause and Effect As you read the section, re-create the diagram below and identify three factors that led the American colonies closer to independence.

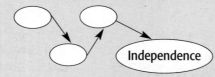

Independence

Read to Learn
• what economic factors spurred growth in the colonies.
• why conflict arose between the British and French in America.
• why resentment toward British rule grew among the American colonists.

Section Theme
Continuity and Change Change was inevitable in the colonies as Americans created wealth far from the authorities in England.

Preview of Events

♦1750   ♦1775

1754
French and Indian War begins

1765
Britain passes the Stamp Act

1770
Boston Massacre takes place

1773
Boston Tea Party occurs

AN American Story

In 1760 Englishman Andrew Burnaby traveled throughout the North American colonies, observing American life. He could not imagine that these colonies would ever join in union for they were as different from one another as "fire and water," and each colony was jealous of the other. "In short, such is the difference of character, of manners, of religion, of interest, of the different colonies, that I think . . . were they left to themselves, there would soon be a civil war, from one end of the continent to the other."

The English Colonies Grow

In the 1700s control of North America shifted dramatically in favor of the British. France was eliminated as a major colonial power in the area. Spain was weakened as well, though it retained its control in the American Southwest.

During the 1700s, the population of the English colonies grew a great deal. The number of people living in the colonies rose from about 250,000 in 1700 to 2.5 million in 1775.

Life in New England

Farming was the main economic activity in all the colonies, but in New England long winters and thin, rocky soil made large-scale farming difficult. New England also had many small businesses. Some people used the waterpower from the streams on their land to run grain mills. Skilled craftspeople set themselves up as blacksmiths, shoemakers, furniture makers, gunsmiths, metalsmiths, and printers.

Shipbuilding and fishing provided other important economic activities. New England ship merchants took fish, grain, meat, and lumber to the West Indies (the Caribbean islands). There the ship's captain traded for sugar, molasses, and fruit, which he then took back to New England. Rum, made from the molasses, along with manufactured goods, was then shipped to West Africa. There the goods were traded for enslaved Africans, who came to the Americas along what was called the Middle Passage. This complex web of shipping routes came to be called the triangular trade.

The Middle and Southern Colonies

Farmers in the Middle Colonies grew large quantities of wheat and livestock, but many home-based industries such as carpentry and flour making were also important. There were many mines and lumber mills as well.

The Southern Colonies developed plantations that produced large harvests of tobacco and rice. The rich soil and warm climate produced a profitable lifestyle based on agriculture. Consequently, the Southern Colonies had little need to develop commerce or industry. For the most part, London merchants rather than local merchants managed Southern trade.

Slavery was part of colonial life and one reason for the economic success of the Southern Colonies. Many Puritans, Quakers, and Mennonites—a German religious group—condemned slavery. Slavery, however, generated great wealth for plantation owners, who controlled the economic and political life of the South.

Store Room

Store Room

Slaves packed in a ship

Picturing **History**

A deck plan (above) reveals tightly packed ranks of slaves on a ship bound from Africa to the Americas. Once docked, the ship's human cargo was replaced with rum or molasses. **What does the term "Middle Passage" refer to?**

Triangular Trade Routes

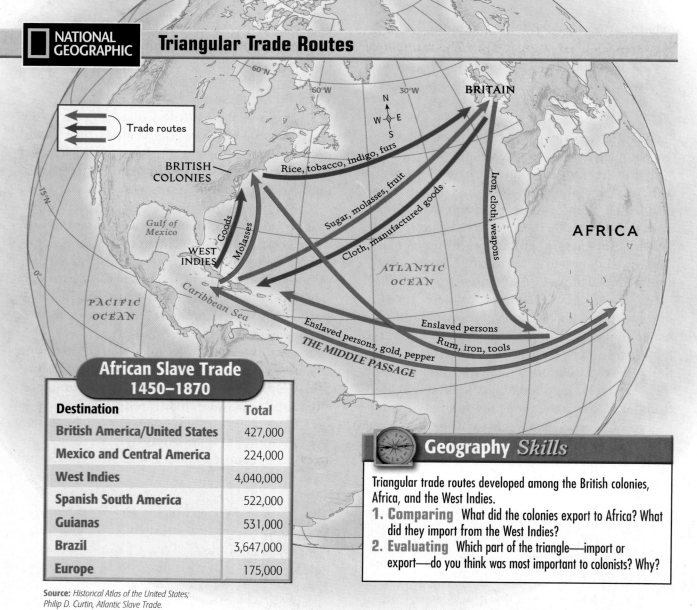

Trade routes

BRITISH COLONIES

Rice, tobacco, indigo, furs

Sugar, molasses, fruit

Cloth, manufactured goods

Iron, cloth, weapons

BRITAIN

AFRICA

Gulf of Mexico

WEST INDIES

Goods

Molasses

PACIFIC OCEAN

Caribbean Sea

ATLANTIC OCEAN

Enslaved persons, gold, pepper

THE MIDDLE PASSAGE

Enslaved persons

Rum, iron, tools

African Slave Trade 1450–1870	
Destination	**Total**
British America/United States	427,000
Mexico and Central America	224,000
West Indies	4,040,000
Spanish South America	522,000
Guianas	531,000
Brazil	3,647,000
Europe	175,000

Source: Historical Atlas of the United States; Philip D. Curtin, Atlantic Slave Trade.

Geography Skills

Triangular trade routes developed among the British colonies, Africa, and the West Indies.

1. **Comparing** What did the colonies export to Africa? What did they import from the West Indies?
2. **Evaluating** Which part of the triangle—import or export—do you think was most important to colonists? Why?

Colonial Government

England viewed its North American colonies as an economic resource. The colonies provided England with raw materials, which English manufacturers used to produce finished goods. These goods were then sold to the colonists. This process followed an economic theory called mercantilism. This theory stated that a nation's power depended on expanding its trade and earning profit from its colonies.

To make certain that only England benefited from trade with the colonies, Parliament passed a series of laws in the 1650s called the Navigation Acts. These laws forced colonists to send goods to England only on English ships and prevented products such as sugar or tobacco from being sent outside England's empire. Some colonists ignored these laws and began trading illegally with other nations.

As the colonies grew, they relied more and more on their own governments to make local laws. Colonial legislatures gave only white men who owned property the right to vote. Neither women, indentured servants, landless and poor people, nor enslaved Africans could vote.

France and Britain Clash in America

By 1700 Britain and France were the major powers in North America. The nations clashed over the fur trade and over rights to North

Atlantic fishing areas. The French discouraged British expansion into the Ohio Valley by building a string of forts along the rivers of the upper Ohio Valley.

France's attempt to control the Ohio Valley led to clashes with the English colonists. One of the first conflicts began when 21-year-old George Washington led a surveying mission into the Ohio Valley and demanded that the French leave. In the spring of 1754, Washington led his troops in battle against a group of French soldiers at the site of present-day Pittsburgh. The larger French forces quickly defeated him.

Representatives from the New England colonies, New York, Pennsylvania, and Maryland met in Albany, New York, to discuss the threat of war. The representatives adopted a plan suggested by Benjamin Franklin. His plan called for "one general government" for all the American colonies in which a single elected legislature would govern the colonies. Not one colonial assembly approved the Albany Plan of Union. The colonies were not yet ready to put aside their own concerns and agree to act in a united fashion.

☑ **Reading Check** **Examining** Under mercantilism, who controlled trade and who supplied raw materials?

The French and Indian War

Washington's defeat in the Ohio Valley, combined with reports of the French building forts in the valley, concerned the British government in London. It decided to support the colonists' struggle in America.

The British Government Takes Action

British General Edward Braddock was appointed commander in chief of all the British forces. His first action was to march 1,400 British regular soldiers and a number of colonial militiamen to Fort Duquesne, a French fort in western Pennsylvania. In June 1755, Washington helped guide the British into the Ohio Valley. He tried to tell Braddock that the formal marching style of the army made them open to ambush. There were French and Indian sharpshooters hidden in the dense forests. Braddock ignored Washington's advice.

Britain Declares War on France

On July 9, the British forces were ambushed just as Washington had warned. Braddock called for an orderly retreat, but panic overcame the British and nearly 1,000 soldiers were killed, including Braddock. Britain declared war on France as a result, and the Seven Years' War began. During this war, French, British, and Spanish forces clashed in Cuba, the West Indies, India, and the Philippines, as well as in North America and Europe.

In North America, the war was known as the French and Indian War. The first years of the war were disastrous for the British and their American colonies. Great Britain's fortunes improved, however, after William Pitt came to power as secretary of state and then as prime minister. He picked skilled military commanders and oversaw the war effort from London. Though Pitt ran up an enormous debt fighting the war, Great Britain finally defeated the French after capturing Quebec in the heart of New France in 1759.

The Continent Changes Hands

The Treaty of Paris of 1763, which formally ended the war, allowed France to keep its sugar-producing islands in the West Indies, but forced it to hand over Canada and its lands east of the Mississippi River to the British. France's ally, Spain, gave Florida to the British but received French lands west of the Mississippi—the Louisiana Territory—as well as the port of New Orleans.

The Treaty of Paris marked the end of France as a power in North America. Great Britain now controlled all the land east of the Mississippi River. Spain controlled large areas of the continent west of the Mississippi.

☑ **Reading Check** **Identifying** Who led England during the French and Indian War?

Road to Independence

The vast territory that the British gained after the war with France led to new conflicts with the Native Americans living in North America. A series of raids on British forts and villages along the western frontier led the British to take two measures to end these troubles.

Causes

- Colonists' tradition of self-government
- Americans' desire for a separate identity from Britain
- Proclamation of 1763
- Harsh British policies toward North America after 1763

Effects

- A long war with Great Britain
- Self-government for the United States
- World recognition of United States independence

Graphic Organizer → Skills

Relations between Britain and America worsened during the 1760s and the 1770s.

Analyzing Information Why did the colonists fight for self-government?

To prevent more fighting, King George III issued the Proclamation of 1763 to halt the settlers' westward expansion. This act set the Appalachian Mountains as the temporary western border between the colonies and Native American lands. The British also planned to station 10,000 soldiers in the colonies. Although the end of the French and Indian War brought peace for the first time in many years, King George III's proclamation created friction between Britain and the colonies.

Intended to settle growing problems between the expanding colonies and the Native American population, the Proclamation led to the first of many conflicts between the British government and the colonists in North America.

Taxation Without Representation

The measures taken by the British alarmed the colonists. Most colonists were satisfied with the government in London prior to 1763. Now many feared that the large number of British troops in North America might be used to interfere with their liberties. They saw the Proclamation of 1763 as a limit on their freedom.

In 1764 the British finance minister began a series of actions to make the colonists contribute more toward British expenses in North America. First, they took action against smuggling in the colonies, claiming that the smugglers kept money meant for the British Empire. To catch colonists involved in smuggling, customs officers were allowed to obtain general writs of assistance. These legal documents enabled the officers to search homes and warehouses for goods that might be smuggled. Many colonists considered this a terrible abuse of power. They were horrified that government officials could come into their homes without warning.

Second, in 1764 Parliament passed the Sugar Act to stop the smuggling between the colonies and the French West Indies. By lowering the tax on molasses imported by the colonists, the British hoped to encourage colonists to pay the duty on foreign molasses. The British could then collect the tax on molasses and increase their earnings.

Never before had colonial taxes been used to raise money for the British treasury. James Otis, a young Boston lawyer, argued that the colonists should not be taxed by Parliament because they could not vote for members of Parliament. Otis coined a slogan for colonial protesters:

❝Taxation without representation is tyranny.❞

The Stamp Act Rebellion

In 1765 Parliament passed an even more disturbing law. The Stamp Act placed a tax on almost all printed material in the colonies—everything from newspapers and pamphlets to wills and playing cards. All printed materials had to have a stamp, which was applied by British colonial officials. The Stamp Act was a terrible nuisance. Since it affected everyone in the colonial cities, however, it had the effect of convincing many colonists of the need for unified action.

Colonial protesters argued that Parliament had interfered in colonial affairs. It had taxed the colonies directly and violated the tradition of colonial self-government by not consulting with the colonies before the Act was passed. In Boston, Samuel Adams started a protest organization called the Sons of Liberty. Other cities soon formed their own Sons of Liberty organizations. Merchants began to boycott—refuse to buy—British and European goods. Patrick Henry persuaded the Virginia House of Burgesses to take action against the Stamp Act. When he was accused of treason, Henry replied,

❝If this be treason, make the most of it!❞

Building Colonial Unity

In October 1768 a fleet of British ships sailed into Boston Harbor with hundreds of soldiers ready to quell any further protest. Many colonists, especially those in Boston, felt that the British had pushed them too far. First they had passed a series of laws that violated colonial rights. Now they had sent an army to occupy colonial cities.

Throughout the next year, the tense atmosphere between the "redcoats"—the British soldiers—and the Boston colonists grew. On March 5, 1770, the tension finally reached a peak. A fight broke out between townspeople and soldiers. As the crowd grew, the soldiers grew increasingly nervous and several confused soldiers fired into the crowd, killing five colonists.

The colonists called the tragic encounter the Boston Massacre.

News spread describing the "massacre" which led many colonists to call for stronger boycotts on British goods. The only boycott to continue, however, was against the last remaining taxed product—tea. On December 16, 1773, members of the Boston Sons of Liberty disguised themselves as native Mohawks and threw 342 chests of British East India tea into Boston harbor.

Britain Reacts

When news of the "Boston Tea Party" reached London, King George III realized that Britain was losing control of the colonies. Lord North, the British prime minister, decided to make an example of Massachusetts. In 1774 very harsh laws called the Coercive Acts were enacted, designed to make Massachusetts pay for its resistance. Boston Harbor was closed, cutting off food and other supplies. Most town meetings were prohibited. The British hoped to isolate Boston, but other colonies sent food and clothing in support of Boston. Having a newfound unity, the colonies called these new laws the Intolerable Acts.

✓ **Reading Check** **Explaining** How did the Stamp Act collect money?

SECTION 3 ASSESSMENT

Checking for Understanding

1. **Key Terms** Use each of these terms in a complete sentence that will help explain its meaning: triangular trade, writs of assistance, mercantilism, boycott

2. **Reviewing Facts** List two reasons the French felt threatened by British interest in the Ohio River Valley.

Reviewing Themes

3. **Continuity and Change** Why did the Stamp Act anger the colonists?

Critical Thinking

4. **Making Inferences** How do you think plantation owners in the Southern Colonies justified their use of enslaved Africans?

5. **Organizing Information** Re-create the diagram below and provide three reasons why the colonists were becoming more and more upset with England.

Reasons for Opposing England		

Analyzing Visuals

6. **Geography Skills** Study the map on page 18. What goods were traded from the British Colonies to Great Britain? From the West Indies to the British Colonies?

Interdisciplinary Activity

Persuasive Writing Write a letter to the editor of a colonial newspaper in which you attempt to persuade fellow American colonists to boycott British goods. In wrting your letter, make sure you use standard grammar, spelling, sentence structure, and punctuation.

SECTION 4 Creating a Nation

AN American Story

At first few colonists wanted a complete break with Britain. One of the most popular songs at the time, "The Bold Americans," called for both liberty and continued loyalty to the British king:

We'll honor George, our sovereign, while he sits on the throne,
If he grants us liberty, no other king we'll own.
If he grants us liberty, so plainly shall you see,
We are the boys that fear no noise! Success to liberty.

Road to Independence

With the passage of the Intolerable Acts, the colonial leaders realized that they must be more vigorous in protesting the abuses from their British rulers. The outpouring of sympathy from other colonies for Bostonians showed that the people wanted them to continue resisting new taxes. Bostonians vowed to boycott all British goods, but something new was needed—a gathering of the colonial leaders. Word spread from Massachusetts to Virginia: the colonies must unite in protest or lose their liberties.

A Call to Arms

The colonies showed increased unity on September 1774, when 56 men, representing every colony except Georgia, gathered in Philadelphia. This new organization, called the Continental Congress, planned to establish a political body to represent the colonists' interests. Patrick Henry summed up the meaning of the gathering: "The distinctions between Virginians, Pennsylvanians, New Yorkers, and New Englanders are no more," he said. "I am not a Virginian, but an American."

The delegates passed a resolution to form militias, groups of citizen soldiers. If fighting broke out, the colonies would be ready with their own armed forces.

Militia companies in Massachusetts began frequent training sessions, made bullets, and stockpiled rifles and muskets. The British also prepared for conflict. British general Sir Thomas Gage ordered 700 troops to move to Concord, Massachusetts, where gunpowder was stored. It seemed war between the British and the colonists could not be avoided.

The First Battles

Paul Revere and William Dawes rode through the night on April 18, 1775, to warn the Concord and Lexington townspeople of the approaching British troops. After arriving, the British destroyed what gunpowder had not been removed from Concord, and began their march back to Boston.

All along the road from Concord to Boston, colonists fired on the troops from behind trees, rocks, and stone fences. By the time the redcoats reached Boston, more than 200 were wounded and 73 were dead. The battle for America's independence had begun.

Following the battles of Lexington and Concord, committees in the colonies sent out calls for volunteers to join the militias. On June 16, 1775, about 1,200 of the militiamen gathered in and around Boston at Bunker Hill and Breed's Hill.

The next day redcoats charged up Breed's Hill straight into deadly American gunfire. After running out of gunpowder the colonial forces

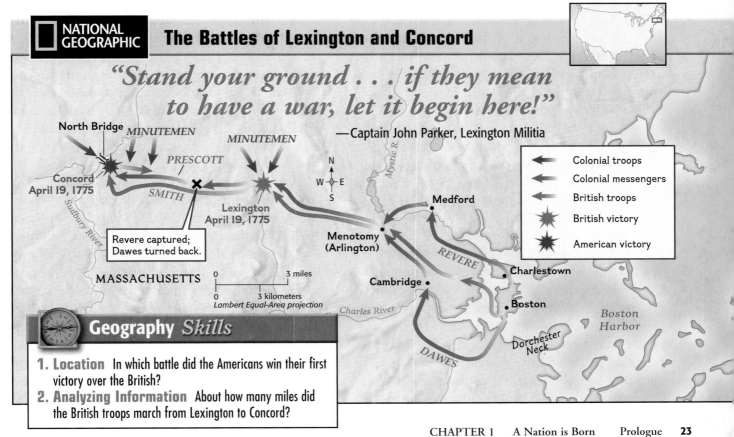

NATIONAL GEOGRAPHIC **The Battles of Lexington and Concord**

"*Stand your ground . . . if they mean to have a war, let it begin here!*"
—Captain John Parker, Lexington Militia

North Bridge MINUTEMEN
MINUTEMEN
PRESCOTT
Concord
April 19, 1775
SMITH
Lexington
April 19, 1775
Revere captured; Dawes turned back.
MASSACHUSETTS
Sudbury River
N W E S
Mystic R.
Medford
Menotomy (Arlington)
REVERE
Charlestown
Cambridge
Boston
DAWES
Dorchester Neck
Charles River
Boston Harbor

0   3 miles
0   3 kilometers
Lambert Equal-Area projection

Colonial troops
Colonial messengers
British troops
British victory
American victory

Geography *Skills*

1. **Location** In which battle did the Americans win their first victory over the British?
2. **Analyzing Information** About how many miles did the British troops march from Lexington to Concord?

withdrew. Heavy British losses indicated, however, that defeating the Americans on the battlefield would not be quick or easy.

As American colonists heard about these battles, they faced a major decision. The Loyalists—those who chose to remain loyal to Britain—did not consider unfair taxes and regulations enough cause for rebellion. The Patriots, on the other hand, were determined to fight the British to the end—until American independence was won.

Moving Toward Independence

Three weeks after the battles of Lexington and Concord, the Second Continental Congress met in Philadelphia. All 13 colonies sent delegates that included some of the greatest political leaders in America: John and Samuel Adams, Patrick Henry, George Washington, Benjamin Franklin, John Hancock, and Thomas Jefferson.

The Congress Becomes a Government

The Second Continental Congress began to govern the colonies. It created the Continental Army and chose George Washington to be the army's commander. He had military experience and the delegates admired and trusted him.

The delegates then offered Britain one last chance to avoid all-out war. A formal request called the Olive Branch Petition was sent to George III. It asked the king to protect the colonists' rights. George III refused to receive the petition and instead hired more than 30,000 German troops to add to the British forces in America.

Drafting the Declaration of Independence

While the delegates of the Second Continental Congress debated whether the colonies should declare themselves a separate nation, a committee was chosen to draft a Declaration of Independence. The committee included Jefferson, Franklin, John Adams, Roger Sherman of Connecticut, and Robert Livingston of New York. Jefferson was chosen to write the document.

After about two weeks, the draft was complete. On July 2, 1776, twelve colonies at the Congress voted for independence. While New York did not initially vote, it later announced its support. After making some changes to Jefferson's draft, the Declaration was approved on July 4, 1776.

Copies of the Declaration went out to the newly declared states. Washington had it read aloud to the militiamen he was training. In New York American soldiers tore down a statue of George III in celebration.

Reading Check **Explaining** What was the purpose of the Continental Congress?

The American Revolution

Both the British and the Americans expected the war to be short. The British planned to crush the rebellion by force. Most of the Patriots believed the British would give up after losing one or two major battles. Few believed John Adams when he predicted in April 1776: "We shall have a long, obstinate [stubborn], and bloody war to go through."

At first glance the British had an overwhelming advantage in the war. They had the strongest navy in the world, an experienced army, and the wealth of a worldwide empire. The colonists lacked a regular army and a strong navy, and weapons and ammunition were in short supply. The Americans did, however, possess some advantages. They were fighting on their own ground with a great determination to protect it.

The Early Years

Initially, neither side achieved victory. The Americans showed no lack of bravery, but ran short of supplies for the army. In the winter of 1776–1777 the Patriot cause was near collapse. The Continental Army dwindled as soldiers refused to reenlist after completing their term of service. Some states ignored a congressional ban barring the use of African American soldiers. By the end of the war, every state except South Carolina enlisted African Americans to fight.

Patriot author Thomas Paine wrote a pamphlet, *The American Crisis,* in which he reminded despondent Americans that "the harder the conflict, the more glorious the triumph." Washington had Paine's encouraging words read to his troops to inspire them to continue the fight.

Gaining Allies

In the face of this low point in American morale, there came a dramatic victory at Saratoga, New York, in October 1777. This success convinced France that America had a chance to win. In February 1778, France declared war on Britain and sent money, equipment, and troops to aid the Patriots. Spain and the Netherlands also contributed to the American effort.

Facing this development, the British stepped up efforts in the South to bring the war to an end. The British believed the many Loyalists in the South would help them. However, the British received less help than they expected from the southern Loyalists. Rather, the sudden hit-and-run guerrilla warfare of southern Patriots kept the British army off guard.

The War Is Won

Washington and his army camped north of New York City in the summer of 1781. Knowing that the British army under General Charles Cornwallis was surrounded by Patriot forces on the Yorktown peninsula in Virginia, and hearing that French troops were sailing towards Chesapeake Bay, Washington changed his plans. He decided to advance on the British at Yorktown rather than at New York City.

Washington's army marched south, gaining reinforcements from another group of French soldiers. He sent word to Patriot troops from the western territories to march to Virginia, while anxiously hoping the French troops disembarking Chesapeake Bay would arrive in time. By the end of September 1781, 17,000 American and French troops converged and trapped Cornwallis's 8,000 British and Hessian troops at Yorktown. Surrounded, under heavy cannon fire, and running low on supplies, Cornwallis surrendered on October 19.

The Treaty of Paris

While the victory at Yorktown did not end all the fighting, it convinced the British that the war was too costly to pursue. The Treaty of Paris of

America's *Architecture*

Independence Hall The Pennsylvania State House, later known as Independence Hall, was the site of the signing of the Declaration of Independence and of the Constitutional Convention. Independence Hall was restored in 1950 and is now maintained as a museum. **Why do you think this site was used for many important events?**

1783 recognized the United States as an independent nation and awarded to the new nation land from the Appalachian Mountains to the Mississippi River.

✓ Reading Check Summarizing What disadvantages did the Patriots face?

A More Perfect Union

While Americans were fighting for their independence on the battlefield, they were also creating new governments. After rejecting British rule, they needed to establish their own political institutions at both the state and national levels. Additionally, the new nation needed to demonstrate strength and the ability to command respect from the rest of the world.

The Articles of Confederation

Their experience with British rule made Americans cautious about strong governments. For that reason the states adopted constitutions that limited governmental power. They also divided government functions between the governor and the legislature.

Establishing separate state governments was a much easier task than creating a single national government. Americans agreed that their nation should be a republic, a government in which citizens ruled through elected representatives.

The Second Continental Congress designed America's first constitution—the Articles of Confederation. This national government had the authority to conduct foreign affairs, maintain armed forces, borrow money, and issue currency. Yet it could not regulate trade, force soldiers to join the army, or impose taxes.

If the Confederation Congress needed to raise money or troops, it had to ask the state legislatures—but the states were not required to contribute. In addition the new national government lacked a chief executive to enforce its laws. The Congress could not pass a law unless 9 states voted in favor of it. Any attempt to change the Articles required the consent of all 13 states.

Unfortunately the Confederation government had so little power, it could not deal with the nation's large war debt. Lacking the power to tax, the Confederation could not pay its debts to the American citizens and foreign nations that had financed the Revolutionary War effort.

Convention and Compromise

The American Revolution had led to a union of 13 states; it had not yet created a nation. Some leaders were satisfied with a system of independent state governments that resembled the old colonial governments. Others saw a strong national government as the solution to America's problems. They demanded a reform of the Articles of Confederation.

In September 1786, James Madison, a Virginia planter, proposed calling a convention in Philadelphia to discuss trade issues. He also suggested that this convention consider amending the Articles of Confederation.

Deciding to close their doors to the public and to keep the proceedings secret to create an atmosphere of free debate, the delegates began their discussions in May 1787. Madison quickly demonstrated the desire to build a strong but fair republican system that balanced the need to act quickly and decisively with the need to protect the people from misuse of power. His carefully thought out proposal became known as the Virginia Plan.

Compromise Wins Out

The plan called for a two-house legislature, a chief executive chosen by the legislature, and a court system. The members of the lower house of the legislature would be elected by the people. The members of the upper house would be chosen by the lower house. In both houses the number of representatives would correspond in size to the population of each state.

Delegates from small states were unhappy with this plan that centered power in states with large populations. An alternate New Jersey Plan modified the original Articles of Confederation. It kept the Confederation's one-house Congress with equal representation and gave the Congress expanded powers to tax and regulate trade.

Roger Sherman of Connecticut proposed a compromise that aimed at pleasing both large and small states. He suggested a bicameral legislature in which the lower house's size varied according to the state's population. The upper house gave each state equal representation—with two members each.

Sherman's plan also addressed another disagreement between Northern and Southern states. Enslaved persons were counted as three-fifths of a free person for both taxation and representation. This prevented over-representing the South's free population, while not inflating the South's tax burden. The delegates also agreed to leave the United States slave trade intact for the time being.

Ratifying the Constitution

Before this new government could go into effect, nine of the 13 states had to approve it. In late 1787, state legislatures set up special committees to debate the document. Those who supported the Constitution were called Federalists. They had enjoyed the support of most of the delegates who approved the document in Philadelphia, including the respected figures of Ben Franklin and George Washington.

The opponents of the new Constitution, called Antifederalists by the Federalist group, mainly argued that the new Constitution would take away the liberties fought for in the Revolu-

George Washington

tion. These opponents considered the strong powers of the federal government to be threatening to the states.

Most effectively, the Antifederalists criticized the lack of a bill of rights—common in state constitutions—to specifically protect individual freedoms. After vigorous and persuasive arguments by both sides, Delaware became the first state to approve the Constitution on December 7, 1787. Six months later, New Hampshire became the ninth state needed to approve the Constitution.

Though technically the new government was now in force, the nation's two largest states—New York and Virginia—had not yet voted. In order to move these important states to approval, the Federalists agreed to add a bill of rights amendment, an addition to the document. Finally, in May 1790, Rhode Island became the thirteenth state to approve the new document. The Bill of Rights would be added in 1791, after the new government took office. Now it was time for the nation to elect leaders and begin the work of government.

✓**Reading Check** **Explaining** Why did many see a new national government as necessary?

SECTION 4 ASSESSMENT

Checking for Understanding

1. **Key Terms** Use each of these terms in a complete sentence that will help explain its meaning: militias, republic, Loyalists, Federalists, Patriots, amendment, guerrilla warfare

2. **Reviewing Facts** Compare the strengths of the British and American military forces.

Reviewing Themes

3. **Groups and Institutions** Why was the Second Continental Congress

useful during the war?

Critical Thinking

4. **Identifying the Main Idea** Why was a powerful national government needed to unite the states after the war?

5. **Organizing Information** Re-create the diagram below and describe each individual's role in the movement towards self-government.

	role
Thomas Jefferson	
George Washington	
James Madison	

Analyzing Visuals

6. **Picturing History** Study the photo on page 25. Why would the modern city of Philadelphia want to preserve this building today?

Interdisciplinary Activity

Citizenship Refer to the Bill of Rights on pages 63–64 of your textbook. Collect photographs from newspapers or magazines that illustrate the freedoms guaranteed in the Bill of Rights. Put your photographs on a poster entitled "Pictures of Liberty."

Chapter Summary

A Nation is Born

c. 28,000 B.C.
- Asian hunters enter North America

A.D. 700
- Maya empire reaches peak

1492
- Christopher Columbus reaches America

1607
- English establish first permanent settlement at Jamestown

1620
- Puritans begin settling Massachusetts Bay

1754
- French and Indian War begins

1763
- Proclamation of 1763

1770
- Boston Massacre

1776
- Declaration of Independence signed

1777
- Articles of Confederation written

1781
- British surrender at Yorktown

1787
- U.S. Constitution signed

Reviewing Key Terms

On a sheet of paper, use all of the following terms to write several short, historically accurate paragraphs related to the information in the chapter.

1. migration
2. Renaissance
3. circumnavigate
4. joint-stock company
5. Separatists
6. Puritans
7. triangular trade
8. mercantilism
9. boycott
10. republic
11. Federalists

Reviewing Key Facts

12. Why did Asians cross the land bridge to the Americas?
13. Which country supported Columbus on his quest to find a water route to Asia?
14. Why did the Virginia Company create the House of Burgesses?
15. What was the purpose of the first Continental Congress?
16. Why did the Proclamation of 1763 create friction between Britain and the colonies?
17. What European nations supported the Americans during their struggle in the Revolutionary War?
18. Why did some states want a bill of rights added to the Constitution as it was originally written?

Critical Thinking

19. **Determining Cause and Effect** Why were European countries interested in exploring overseas?
20. **Analyzing Information** What economic factors led to the growth and success of the New England Colonies? The Southern Colonies?
21. **Analyzing Primary Sources** What did Patrick Henry mean when he said, "I am not a Virginian, but an American"?
22. **Comparing** Re-create the diagram below and compare Federalists and Antifederalists by providing qualities of each group.

Federalists	Antifederalists

NATIONAL GEOGRAPHIC

Missions in New Spain by the 1800s

0 300 miles
0 300 kilometers
Lambert Equal-Area projection

- City
- Mission
- Present-day boundary

PACIFIC OCEAN

MEXICO

Gulf of Mexico

San Francisco · NEV. · UTAH · COLO. · CALIF. · Los Angeles · San Diego · ARIZ. · Santa Fe · N. MEX. · El Paso · TEXAS · San Antonio · Mexico City

Geography and History Activity

Study the map above and answer the following questions.

23. Place In what present-day states were the Spanish missions located?

24. Location Near what city was the northernmost Spanish mission located?

Practicing Skills

25. Determining Cause and Effect The following sentence illustrates a cause-and-effect relationship. Identify the cause(s) and effect(s) in this sentence.

"During the 1700s the population of the English colonies grew dramatically as a result of high immigration."

Citizenship Cooperative Activity

26. When you become 18 years old, you can begin to exercise one of your most important rights—the right to vote. First, however you must register. Work with a partner to find out where you can obtain a voter registration card. Make a list of the information you will need for the card. Share your information with the class.

Economics Activity

27. Working with a partner, create a map showing a trade route that colonial merchants might use. To get started,

Self-Check Quiz
Visit taj.glencoe.com and click on **Prologue Chapter 1—Self-Check Quizzes** to prepare for the chapter test.

examine maps and information from your text and from encyclopedias and historical atlases. Include the physical features that the colonial merchants had to face, including rivers, mountains, lakes and so on.

Technology Activity

28. Using a Word Processor Search the library or Internet for information on boats and sailing. Using a word processor, prepare a report about a navigational instrument that is in use today. Include different instances where this instrument would be useful in modern navigation. Describe how it would have been helpful to an explorer such as Magellan.

Alternative Assessment

29. Review the chapter and make a list of the differences between the Federalists and Antifederalists. Based on your list, create a symbol to represent each of the groups.

Standardized Test Practice

Directions: Choose the *best* answer to the following question.

Which colony was founded to put Quaker ideas into practice?

A Plymouth
B Virginia
C Georgia
D Pennsylvania

Test-Taking Tip:

As you read the stem of each multiple-choice question, try to anticipate the answer before you look at the choices. If your answer is one of the choices, it is probably correct.

The Declaration of Independence

In Congress, July 4, 1776. The unanimous Declaration of the thirteen united States of America,

[Preamble]

When in the Course of human events, it becomes necessary for one people to dissolve the political bands which have connected them with another, and to assume among the Powers of the earth, the separate and equal station to which the Laws of Nature and of Nature's God entitle them, a decent respect to the opinions of mankind requires that they should declare the causes which **impel** them to the separation.

[Declaration of Natural Rights]

We hold these truths to be self-evident, that all men are created equal, that they are **endowed** by their Creator with certain unalienable Rights, that among these are Life, Liberty, and the pursuit of Happiness.

That to secure these rights, Governments are instituted among Men, deriving their just powers from the consent of the governed,

That whenever any Form of Government becomes destructive of these ends, it is the Right of the People to alter or to abolish it, and to institute new Government, laying its foundation on such principles and organizing its powers in such form, as to them shall seem most likely to effect their Safety and Happiness. Prudence, indeed, will dictate that Governments long established should not be changed for light and transient causes; and accordingly all experience hath shown, that mankind are more disposed to suffer, while evils are sufferable, than to right themselves by abolishing the forms to which they are accustomed. But when a long train of abuses and usurpations, pursuing invariably the same Object evinces a design to reduce them under absolute **Despotism,** it is their right, it is their duty, to throw off such Government, and to provide new Guards for their future security.

[List of Grievances]

Such has been the patient sufferance of these Colonies; and such is now the necessity which constrains them to alter their former Systems of Government. The history of the present King of Great Britain is a history of repeated injuries and **usurpations,** all having in direct object the establishment of an absolute Tyranny over these States. To prove this, let Facts be submitted to a candid world.

He has refused his Assent to Laws, the most wholesome and necessary for the public good.

What It Means
The Preamble The Declaration of Independence has four parts. The Preamble explains why the Continental Congress drew up the Declaration.

impel *force*

What It Means
Natural Rights The second part, the Declaration of Natural Rights, lists the rights of the citizens. It goes on to explain that, in a republic, people form a government to protect their rights. The Declaration refers to these rights as *unalienable rights.* The word unalienable means non-transferable. An unalienable right is a right that cannot be surrendered.

endowed *provided*

despotism *unlimited power*

What It Means
List of Grievances The third part of the Declaration lists the colonists' complaints against the British government. Notice that King George III is singled out for blame.

usurpations *unjust uses of power*

He has forbidden his Governors to pass Laws of immediate and pressing importance, unless suspended in their operation till his Assent should be obtained; and when so suspended, he has utterly neglected to attend to them.

He has refused to pass other Laws for the accommodation of large districts of people, unless those people would **relinquish** the right of Representation in the Legislature, a right **inestimable** to them and formidable to tyrants only.

relinquish *give up*
inestimable *priceless*

He has called together legislative bodies at places unusual, uncomfortable, and distant from the depository of their Public Records, for the sole purpose of fatiguing them into compliance with his measures.

He has dissolved Representative Houses repeatedly, for opposing with manly firmness his invasions on the rights of the people.

He has refused for a long time, after such dissolutions, to cause others to be elected; whereby the Legislative Powers, incapable of **Annihilation**, have returned to the People at large for their exercise; the State remaining in the mean time exposed to all the dangers of invasion from without, and **convulsions** within.

annihilation *destruction*

convulsions *violent disturbances*

He has endeavoured to prevent the population of these States; for that purpose obstructing the Laws for **Naturalization of Foreigners;** refusing to pass others to encourage their migrations hither, and raising the conditions of new Appropriations of Lands.

Naturalization of Foreigners *process by which foreign-born persons become citizens*

He has obstructed the Administration of Justice, by refusing his Assent to Laws for establishing Judiciary Powers.

He has made Judges dependent on his Will alone, for the **tenure** of their offices, and the amount and payment of their salaries.

tenure *term*

He has erected a multitude of New Offices, and sent hither swarms of Officers to harass our people, and eat out their substance.

He has kept among us, in times of peace, Standing Armies without the Consent of our legislature.

He has affected to render the Military independent of and superior to the Civil Power.

He has combined with others to subject us to a jurisdiction foreign to our constitution, and unacknowledged by our laws; giving his Assent to their acts of pretended legislation:

quartering *lodging*

For **quartering** large bodies of troops among us:

For protecting them, by a mock Trial, from Punishment for any Murders which they should commit on the Inhabitants of these States:

For cutting off our Trade with all parts of the world:

For imposing taxes on us without our Consent:

For depriving us in many cases, of the benefits of Trial by Jury:

For transporting us beyond Seas to be tried for pretended offences:

For abolishing the free System of English Laws in a neighbouring Province, establishing therein an Arbitrary government, and enlarging its

render *make*

Boundaries so as to **render** it at once an example and fit instrument for introducing the same absolute rule into these Colonies:

For taking away our Charters, abolishing our most valuable Laws, and altering fundamentally the Forms of our Governments:

For suspending our own Legislature, and declaring themselves invested with Power to legislate for us in all cases whatsoever.

abdicated *given up*

He has **abdicated** Government here, by declaring us out of his Protection and waging War against us.

He has plundered our seas, ravaged our Coasts, burnt our towns, and destroyed the lives of our people.

He is at this time transporting large armies of foreign mercenaries to compleat the works of death, desolation and tyranny, already begun with

perfidy *violation of trust*

circumstances of Cruelty & **perfidy** scarcely paralleled in the most barbarous ages, and totally unworthy the Head of a civilized nation.

He has constrained our fellow Citizens taken Captive on the high Seas to bear Arms against their Country, to become the executioners of their friends and Brethren, or to fall themselves by their Hands.

insurrections *rebellions*

He has excited domestic **insurrections** amongst us, and has endeavoured to bring on the inhabitants of our frontiers, the merciless Indian Savages, whose known rule of warfare, is an undistinguished destruction of all ages, sexes and conditions.

petitioned for redress *asked formally for a correction of wrongs*

In every stage of these Oppressions We have **Petitioned for Redress** in the most humble terms: Our repeated Petitions have been answered only by repeated injury. A Prince, whose character is thus marked by every act which may define a Tyrant, is unfit to be the ruler of a free People.

Nor have We been wanting in attention to our British brethren. We have warned them from time to time of attempts by their legislature to extend an

unwarrantable jurisdiction *unjustified authority*

unwarrantable jurisdiction over us. We have reminded them of the circumstances of our emigration and settlement here. We have appealed to their native justice and magnanimity, and we have conjured them by the ties of our common kindred to disavow these usurpations, which, would inevitably interrupt our connections and correspondence. They too have been deaf to the voice of justice and of **consanguinity**. We must, therefore,

consanguinity *originating from the same ancestor*

acquiesce in the necessity, which denounces our Separation, and hold them, as we hold the rest of mankind, Enemies in War, in Peace Friends.

[Resolution of Independence by the United States]

We, therefore, the Representatives of the united States of America, in General Congress, Assembled, appealing to the Supreme Judge of the world for the **rectitude** of our intentions, do, in the Name, and by Authority of the good People of these Colonies, solemnly publish and declare, That these United Colonies are, and of Right ought to be Free and Independent States; that they are Absolved from all Allegiance to the British Crown, and that all political connection between them and the State of Great Britain, is and ought to be totally dissolved; and that as Free and Independent States, they have full Power to levy War, conclude Peace, contract Alliances, establish Commerce, and to do all other Acts and Things which Independent States may of right do.

And for the support of this Declaration, with a firm reliance on the Protection of Divine Providence, we mutually pledge to each other our Lives, our Fortunes and our sacred Honor.

John Hancock
   President from
   Massachusetts

Georgia
Button Gwinnett
Lyman Hall
George Walton

North Carolina
William Hooper
Joseph Hewes
John Penn

South Carolina
Edward Rutledge
Thomas Heyward, Jr.
Thomas Lynch, Jr.
Arthur Middleton

Maryland
Samuel Chase
William Paca
Thomas Stone
Charles Carroll
   of Carrollton

Virginia
George Wythe
Richard Henry Lee
Thomas Jefferson
Benjamin Harrison
Thomas Nelson, Jr.
Francis Lightfoot Lee
Carter Braxton

Pennsylvania
Robert Morris
Benjamin Rush
Benjamin Franklin
John Morton
George Clymer
James Smith
George Taylor
James Wilson
George Ross

Delaware
Caesar Rodney
George Read
Thomas McKean

New York
William Floyd
Philip Livingston
Francis Lewis
Lewis Morris

New Jersey
Richard Stockton
John Witherspoon
Francis Hopkinson
John Hart
Abraham Clark

New Hampshire
Josiah Bartlett
William Whipple
Matthew Thornton

Massachusetts
Samuel Adams
John Adams
Robert Treat Paine
Elbridge Gerry

Rhode Island
Stephen Hopkins
William Ellery

Connecticut
Samuel Huntington
William Williams
Oliver Wolcott
Roger Sherman

What It Means
Resolution of Independence The Final section declares that the colonies are "Free and Independent States" with the full power to make war, to form alliances, and to trade with other countries.

rectitude *rightness*

What It Means
Signers of the Declaration The signers, as representatives of the American people, declared the colonies independent from Great Britain. Most members signed the document on August 2, 1776.

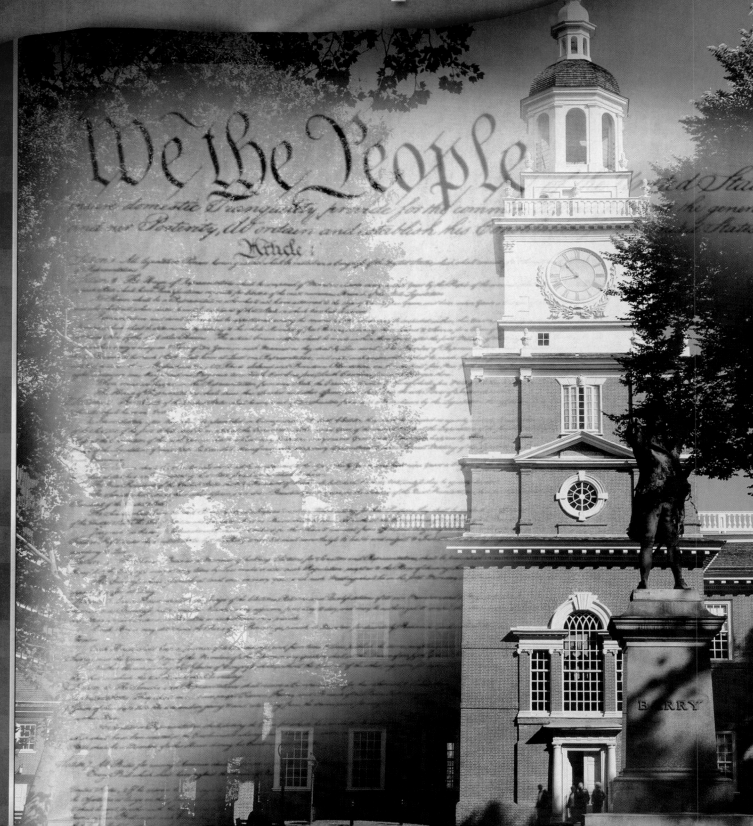

Civics in Action
A Citizenship Handbook

SECTION 1 The Constitution

Guide to Reading

Main Idea

For more than 200 years, the Constitution has provided the framework for the United States government and has helped preserve the basic rights of American citizens.

Key Terms

preamble, domestic tranquility, popular sovereignty, republicanism, federalism, enumerated powers, reserved powers, concurrent powers, amendment, implied powers, judicial review

Read to Learn

• why the Constitution is the nation's most important document.
• the goals of the Constitution.
• the principles that form the basis of the Constitution.

Goals of the Constitution

The Preamble, or introduction, to the Constitution reflects the basic principle of American government—the right of the people to govern themselves. It also lists six goals for the United States government:

❝. . .to form a more perfect Union, establish Justice, insure domestic Tranquility, provide for the common defence [defense], promote the general Welfare, and secure the Blessings of Liberty to ourselves and our Posterity.❞

These goals guided the Constitution's Framers as they created the new government. They remain as important today as they were when the Constitution was written.

To Form a More Perfect Union Under the Articles of Confederation, the states functioned almost like independent nations. For the most part, they did not work together on important matters such as defense and finances. This lack of unity could have been dangerous for the nation during times of crisis. To form "a more perfect Union" the Framers believed the states needed to agree to operate as a single country and cooperate on major issues.

To Establish Justice For the Framers, treating each citizen equally was one of the fundamental principles on which to build the new nation.

The Constitution provides a national system of courts to protect the people's rights, and to hear cases involving violations of federal law and disputes between the states.

To Insure Domestic Tranquility Shays's Rebellion began in 1786 and shocked Americans. The United States had become a self-governing nation, yet a group of people had resorted to violence to express their anger over government policies. The Constitution provides a strong central government to "insure domestic Tranquility"—that is, to keep peace among the people.

To Provide for the Common Defense The Articles of Confederation required nine states to approve any decision by the Confederation Congress to build an army or navy. The Constitution gives the federal government the power to maintain armed forces to protect the country and its citizens from attack.

To Promote the General Welfare The Declaration of Independence states that the purpose of government is to promote "Life, Liberty, and the pursuit of Happiness" for the people of the nation. The Constitution includes ways to "promote the general Welfare"—or well-being—of the people by maintaining order, protecting individual liberties, regulating commerce and bankruptcies, and promoting science and technology by granting patents.

To Secure the Blessings of Liberty The American colonists fought the Revolutionary War to gain their liberty. The Framers believed that preserving liberty should also be a major goal of the Constitution. The Constitution guarantees that no American's basic rights will be taken away now or for posterity (generations not yet born).

✔ **Reading Check** **Analyzing** What is the purpose of the Preamble?

Major Principles

The principles outlined in the Constitution were the Framers' solution to the problems of a representative government. The Constitution rests on seven major principles: (1) popular sovereignty, (2) republicanism, (3) limited govern-ment, (4) federalism, (5) separation of powers, (6) checks and balances, and (7) individual rights.

Popular Sovereignty The Declaration of Independence states that governments derive their powers from "the consent of the governed." The opening words of the Constitution, "We the people," reinforce this idea of popular sovereignty—or "authority of the people."

Republicanism Under republicanism, voters hold sovereign power. The people elect representatives and give them the responsibility to make laws and conduct government. For most Americans today, the terms *republic* and *representative democracy* mean the same thing: a system of limited government where the people are the ultimate source of governmental power.

Limited Government The Framers saw both benefits and risks in creating a powerful national government. They agreed that the nation needed strong central authority but feared misuse of power. They wanted to prevent the government from using its power to give one

Major Principles of the Constitution	
Popular Sovereignty	People are the source of the government's power.
Republicanism	People elect their political representatives.
Limited Government	The Constitution limits the actions of government by specifically listing powers it does and does not have.
Federalism	In this government system, power is divided between national and state governments.
Separation of Powers	Each of the three branches of government has its own responsibilities.
Checks and Balances	Each branch of government holds some control over the other two branches.
Individual Rights	Basic liberties and rights of all citizens are guaranteed in the Bill of Rights.

〰 Chart *Skills*

The Principles outlined in the Constitution were the Framers' solution to the complex problems presented by a representative government.

Analyzing Information What is the relationship between checks and balances and separation of powers?

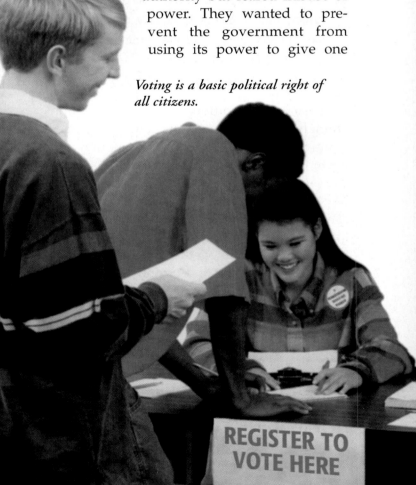

Voting is a basic political right of all citizens.

REGISTER TO VOTE HERE

The Federal System

National Government	National & State Governments	State Governments
Enumerated Powers	**Concurrent Powers**	**Reserved Powers**
• Regulate trade	• Enforce the laws	• Regulate trade within the state
• Coin Money	• Establish courts	• Establish local government systems
• Provide an army and navy	• Collect taxes	• Conduct elections
• Conduct Foreign affairs	• Borrow money	• Establish public school systems
• Set up federal courts	• Provide for the general welfare	

group special advantages or to deprive another group of its rights. By creating a limited government, they made certain the government would have only those powers granted by the people.

Article I of the Constitution states the powers that the government has and the powers that it does not have. Other limits on government appear in the Bill of Rights, which guarantees certain rights and liberties to the people.

Limited government can be described as the "rule of law." No people or groups are above the law. Government officials must obey the law.

Federalism When the states banded together under the Constitution, they gave up some independence. States could no longer print their own money or tax items imported from other states. Nevertheless, each state governed itself much as it had in the past.

This system, in which the power to govern is shared between the national government and the states, is called the federal system, or federalism. Our federal system allows the people of each state to deal with their needs in their own way. At the same time, it lets the states act together to deal with matters that affect all Americans.

The Constitution defines three types of government powers. Enumerated powers belong only to the federal government. These include the power to coin money, regulate interstate and foreign trade, maintain the armed forces, and create federal courts (Article I, Section 8).

The second kind of powers are those retained by the states, known as reserved powers. They include such rights as the power to establish schools, pass marriage and divorce laws, and regulate trade within a state. Although reserved powers are not listed specifically in the Constitution, the Tenth Amendment says that all powers not specifically granted to the federal government "are reserved to the States."

The third set of powers defined by the Constitution are concurrent powers—powers shared by the state and federal governments. Among these powers are the right to raise taxes, borrow money, provide for public welfare, and administer criminal justice.

When conflicts arise between state law and federal law, the Constitution declares that the Constitution is "the supreme Law of the Land." Conflicts between state law and federal law must be settled in a federal court.

Separation of Powers To prevent any single group or institution in government from gaining too much authority, the Framers divided the federal government into three branches: **legislative, executive,** and **judicial.** Each branch has its own functions and powers. The legislative branch, Congress, makes the laws. The executive branch, headed by the president, carries out the laws. The judicial branch, consisting of the Supreme Court and other federal courts, interprets and applies the laws.

Checks and Balances As an additional safeguard, the Framers established a system of **checks and balances** in which each branch of government can check, or limit, the power of the other branches. This system helps maintain a

How the Constitution is Amended

STEP 1: Amendment Proposed by:

A two-thirds vote of both houses of Congress

OR

A constitutional convention called by Congress on petition of two-thirds of the 50 states

STEP 2: Amendment Ratified by:

Three-fourths of the 50 state legislatures

OR

Three-fourths of special constitutional conventions called by the 50 states

New amendment to the Constitution

balance in the power of the three branches. For example, Congress can pass a law. Then the president can reject the law by vetoing it. However, Congress can override, or reverse, the president's veto if two-thirds of the members of both houses vote again to approve the law.

Over the years, the Supreme Court has acquired the power to determine the meaning of the Constitution and to declare that a law or a government policy goes against the Constitution. In doing so, the Court provides a check on the powers of Congress and the president. Judicial decisions—those made by the courts—can be overruled by amending the Constitution. The president and the Senate provide a check on the judicial branch through their power to appoint and approve federal judges. Congress can also change a law so that it no longer conflicts with the Constitution, or it can amend the Constitution. The Fourteenth Amendment, passed by Congress in 1866, overturned the Supreme Court's ruling in the *Dred Scott* decision, which had ruled that enslaved African Americans were not citizens.

Individual Rights The Bill of Rights became part of the Constitution in 1791. These first 10 amendments protect basic liberties and rights that you may take for granted—including freedom of speech, freedom of the press, freedom of assembly, freedom of religion, and the right to a trial by jury.

The 17 amendments that follow the Bill of Rights expand the rights of Americans and adjust certain provisions of the Constitution. Included among them are amendments that abolish slavery, define citizenship, guarantee the right to vote to all citizens, authorize an income tax, and set a two-term limit on the presidency.

Reading Check **Explaining** What is popular sovereignty?

A Living Constitution

Two years after the Constitutional Convention, Benjamin Franklin wrote, "Our Constitution is in actual operation; everything appears to promise that it will last; but in this world nothing is certain but death and taxes."

Despite Franklin's uncertainty about the Constitution's future, it is still very much alive today. The Constitution has survived because the Framers wrote a document that the nation could alter and adapt to meet changing needs. The result is a flexible document that can be interpreted in different ways in keeping with the conditions of a particular time. The Constitution's flexibility allows the government to deal with matters the Framers never anticipated—such as regulating nuclear power plants or developing a space program. In addition the Constitution contains a provision for amending—changing or adding to—the document.

Amending the Constitution The Framers intentionally made the amendment process difficult to discourage minor or frequent changes being made. Although thousands of amendments—changes to the Constitution—have been proposed since 1788, only 27 of them have actually become part of the Constitution.

An amendment may be proposed in two ways: by the vote of two-thirds of both houses of Congress or by two-thirds of the state legislatures asking for a special convention on the amendment. The second method has never been used. Ratification of an amendment requires approval by three-fourths of the states. The Constitution can be ratified by the approval of state legislatures or by special state conventions.

Only the Twenty-first Amendment—which repealed the Eighteenth Amendment, banning the sale of alcoholic beverages—was ratified by state conventions. Voters in each state chose the delegates to the special conventions.

Interpreting the Constitution The Constitution includes two provisions that give Congress the power to act as needed to meet changing conditions. The first of these provisions is what is known as the "elastic clause" (Article I, Section 8). It directs Congress to "make all Laws which shall be necessary and proper" for executing all the powers of government. Congress has interpreted this clause to mean that it has certain implied powers, powers not specifically defined in the Constitution. Over the years, Congress has drawn on its implied powers to pass laws to deal with the needs of society.

The second provision used to expand congressional authority, the "commerce clause" (Article I, Section 8), gives Congress the power to "regulate Commerce with foreign Nations, and among the several States." Congress has used this clause to expand its powers into a number of areas, such as regulation of the airline industry, radio and television, and nuclear energy.

Powers of the Presidency The Constitution describes the role and the powers of the president in general terms. This has allowed the executive branch to extend its powers. In 1803, for example, President Thomas Jefferson approved a treaty with France that enabled the United States to buy an enormous tract of land.

The Bill of Rights

1	Guarantees freedom of religion, speech, assembly, and press, and the right of people to petition the government
2	Protects the rights of states to maintain a militia and of citizens to bear arms
3	Restricts quartering of troops in private homes
4	Protects against "unreasonable searches and seizures"
5	Assures the right not to be deprived of "life, liberty, or property, without due process of law"
6	Guarantees the right to a speedy and public trial by an impartial jury
7	Assures the right to a jury trial in cases involving the common law (the law established by previous court decisions)
8	Protects against excessive bail, or cruel and unusual punishment
9	Provides that people's rights are not restricted to those specified in the first eight Amendments
10	Restates the Constitution's principle of federalism by providing that powers not granted to the national government nor prohibited to the states are reserved to the states and to the people

"I have finally been included in 'We the people.'"

—*Barbara Jordan, U.S. representative from Texas, 1972–1978*

The Courts The role of the judicial branch has also grown as powers implied in the Constitution have been put into practice. In 1803 Chief Justice John Marshall expanded the powers of the Supreme Court by striking down an act of Congress in the case of *Marbury* v. *Madison*. In that decision the Court defined its right to determine whether a law violates the Constitution. Although not mentioned in the Constitution, judicial review has become a major power of the judicial branch.

The process of amending the Constitution and applying its principles in new areas helps keep our government functioning well. In 1974 Barbara Jordan, an African American member of Congress and a constitutional scholar, spoke in ringing tones of her faith in the Constitution:

    ❝I felt somehow for many years that George Washington and Alexander Hamilton just left me out by mistake. But through the process of amendment, interpretation, and court decision I have finally been included in 'We the people.'❞

✓ **Reading Check** **Explaining** What are implied powers?

SECTION 1 ASSESSMENT

Checking for Understanding

1. **Key Terms** Write complete sentences using each group of terms below. Group 1: republicanism, federalism. Group 2: enumerated powers, concurrent powers. Group 3: preamble, amendment.
2. **Reviewing Facts** Explain the origin of judicial review.

Reviewing Themes

3. **Government and Democracy** What is the importance of federalism in the Constitution?

Critical Thinking

4. **Analyzing Information** Why was it so important for basic freedoms to be guaranteed in the Constitution?
5. **Comparing** Re-create the diagram below and describe how each branch of government has power over another branch.

Branch	Power
Legislative	
Executive	
Judicial	

Analyzing Visuals

6. **Reading a Table** Refer to the table on page 36. How are popular sovereignty and republicanism related?

Interdisciplinary Activity

Civics The Bill of Rights guarantees certain basic rights to all Americans. Select one of the 10 amendments that make up the Bill of Rights (see page 39) and research its history. Present your findings in a one-page essay.

SECTION 2
The Federal Government

Guide to Reading

Main Idea

The government of the United States has three branches: the legislative branch, the executive branch, and the judicial branch.

Key Terms

appropriate, impeach, constituents

Read to Learn

- the goals of the three branches of the government.
- the powers of the three branches of the government.

The Legislative Branch

Congress, the legislative branch of the government, makes the nation's laws. It also has the power to "lay and collect taxes" and to declare war. Congress has two houses, the House of Representatives and the Senate.

The House and Senate Today the House of Representatives has 435 voting members and five nonvoting delegates from the District of Columbia, Puerto Rico, Guam, American Samoa, and the Virgin Islands. The number of representatives from each state is determined by the state's population. Representatives, who must be at least 25 years old, serve two-year terms.

The Senate consists of 100 senators, two from each state. Senators, who must be at least 30 years old, serve six-year terms. The senators' terms are staggered, which means that one-third of the Senate seats come up for election every two years.

Seal of the U.S. Congress

The Role of Congress Congress has two primary functions: to make the nation's laws and to control government spending. The government cannot spend any money unless Congress **appropriates**, or sets aside, funds. All tax and spending bills must originate in the House of Representatives and gain approval in both the House and the Senate before moving on to the president for signature.

Congress also serves as a watchdog over the executive branch, monitoring its actions and investigating possible abuses of power. The House of Representatives can **impeach**, or bring formal charges against, any federal official it suspects of wrongdoing or misconduct. If an official is impeached, the Senate acts as a court and tries the accused official. Officials who are found guilty may be removed from office.

The Senate also holds certain special powers. Only the Senate can ratify treaties made by the president and confirm presidential appointments of federal officials, such as department heads, ambassadors, and federal judges.

All members of Congress have the responsibility of representing their **constituents**, the people of their home states and districts. As a constituent you can expect your senators and representatives to promote and protect your state's interests as well as those of the nation.

Congress at Work Thousands of **bills**, or proposed laws, are introduced in Congress every year. Because individual members of Congress

The American System of Checks and Balances

Appoints judges

Can declare acts of the
president unconstitutional

Executive Branch
Proposes policy
Carries out laws
Makes treaties

*"You must first enable the government
to control the governed; and in the next
place oblige it to control itself."*
—James Madison, 1787

Judicial Branch
Interprets laws

Can override veto

Can impeach judges

Can impeach president

Can reject appointment
of judges

Can reject presidential appointments
and refuse to approve treaties

Can veto legislation

Can declare laws
unconstitutional

Legislative Branch
Makes laws

cannot possibly study all these bills carefully, both houses use committees of selected members to evaluate proposed legislation.

Standing committees are permanent committees in both the House and the Senate that specialize in a particular topic, such as agriculture, commerce, or veterans' affairs. These committees usually are broken down into **subcommittees** that focus on a particular aspect of a problem or issue.

The House and the Senate sometimes form temporary **select committees** to deal with issues requiring special attention. These committees meet only until they complete their task.

Occasionally the House and the Senate form **joint committees** with members from both houses. These committees meet to consider specific issues, such as the system of federal taxation. One type of joint committee, a **conference committee,** has a special function. If the House

and the Senate pass different versions of the same bill, a conference committee tries to work out a compromise bill acceptable to both houses.

When it receives a bill, a committee can kill it by rejecting it outright, "pigeonhole" it by setting it aside without reviewing it, or prepare it for consideration by the full House or Senate. While preparing bills, committees hold public hearings at which citizens can present arguments and documents supporting or opposing the bills.

Once a bill is approved by a committee in either house of Congress, it is sent to the full Senate or House for debate. After debate the bill may be passed, rejected, or returned to committee for further changes.

When both houses pass a bill, the bill goes to the president. If the president approves the bill and signs it, it becomes law. If the president vetoes the bill, it does not become law, unless Congress **overrides** (cancels) the presidential veto by a vote of two-thirds of the members in each house.

✓ **Reading Check** **Sequencing** List the basic steps of how a bill becomes a law.

The Executive Branch

The executive branch of government includes the president, the vice president, and various executive offices, departments, and agencies. The executive branch carries out the laws that Congress passes.

Chief Executive The president plays a number of different roles in government, each of which has specific powers and responsibilities. These roles include the nation's chief executive, chief diplomat, commander in chief, chief of state, and legislative leader.

As chief executive, the president is responsible for carrying out the nation's laws. Many executive departments and agencies assist the president in this job.

Chief Diplomat As chief diplomat, the president directs foreign policy, appoints ambassadors, and negotiates treaties with other nations. Treaties must be approved by a two-thirds vote of the Senate before they go into effect.

Commander in Chief As commander in chief of the armed forces, the president can use the military to intervene or offer assistance in crises at home and around the world. The president cannot declare war; only Congress holds this power. The president can send troops to other parts of the world for up to 60 days but must notify Congress when doing so. The troops may remain longer only if Congress gives approval or declares war.

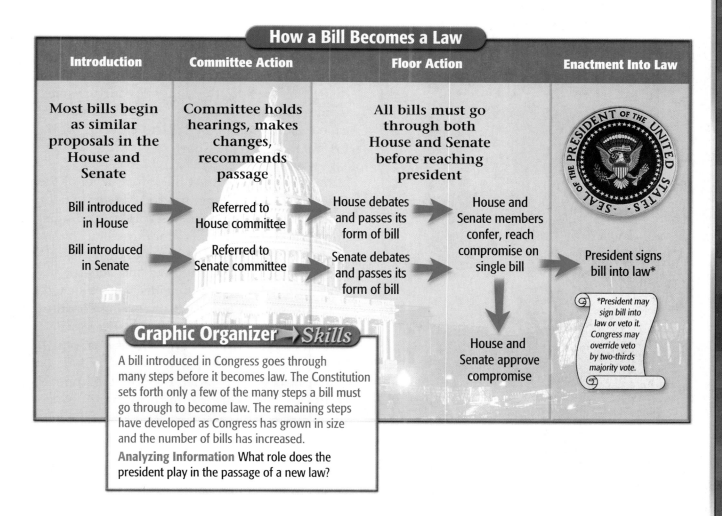

How a Bill Becomes a Law

Introduction	Committee Action	Floor Action	Enactment Into Law
Most bills begin as similar proposals in the House and Senate	Committee holds hearings, makes changes, recommends passage	All bills must go through both House and Senate before reaching president	
Bill introduced in House	Referred to House committee	House debates and passes its form of bill	House and Senate members confer, reach compromise on single bill	President signs bill into law*
Bill introduced in Senate	Referred to Senate committee	Senate debates and passes its form of bill	House and Senate approve compromise	

*President may sign bill into law or veto it. Congress may override veto by two-thirds majority vote.

Graphic Organizer → Skills

A bill introduced in Congress goes through many steps before it becomes law. The Constitution sets forth only a few of the many steps a bill must go through to become law. The remaining steps have developed as Congress has grown in size and the number of bills has increased.

Analyzing Information What role does the president play in the passage of a new law?

Chief of State As chief of state, the president serves a symbolic role as the representative of all Americans. The president fulfills this role when receiving foreign ambassadors or heads of state, visiting foreign nations, or bestowing honors on Americans.

Legislative Leader The president serves as a legislative leader by proposing laws to Congress and working to see that they are passed. In the annual State of the Union address, the president presents goals for legislation.

The Executive Branch at Work Many executive offices, departments, and independent agencies help the president carry out and enforce the nation's laws. The Executive Office of the President (EOP) is made up of individuals and agencies that directly assist the president. Presidents rely heavily on the EOP for advice and for gathering information.

The executive branch also includes 14 executive departments, each responsible for a different area of government. For example, the

Department of State plans and carries out foreign policy, and the Department of the Interior manages and protects the nation's public lands and natural resources. The heads, or secretaries, of these departments are members of the president's **cabinet,** a group that helps the president make decisions and set government policy.

The independent agencies manage federal programs in many fields. These include aeronautics and space, banking, communications, farm credit, and trade. Government corporations are government agencies that are run like privately owned businesses. One government corporation whose services you may often use is the United States Postal Service.

✓ **Reading Check** **Describing** What is the president's cabinet?

The Judicial Branch

Article III of the Constitution called for the creation of a Supreme Court and "such inferior [lower] courts as Congress may from time to time ordain and establish." In 1789 Congress passed a **Judiciary Act,** which added a series of district courts to the federal court system. Congress added appeals courts, sometimes called circuit courts, in 1891 to ease the workload of the Supreme Court.

Lower Federal Courts At the lowest level of the federal court system are the United States **district courts.** These courts consider criminal and civil cases that come under federal, rather than state, authority. The criminal cases include such offenses as kidnapping and federal tax evasion. Civil cases cover claims against the federal government and cases involving constitutional rights, such as free speech. There are 91 district courts in the nation, with at least one in every state.

The next level of federal courts, the **appeals courts,** reviews district court decisions in which the losing side has asked for a review of the verdict. If an appeals court disagrees with the lower court's decision, it can either overturn the verdict or order a retrial. There are 14 appeals courts in the United States.

Picturing **History**

President George W. Bush describes a legislative program in the annual State of the Union message to Congress. **What powers does the president hold in his role as commander in chief?**

The Supreme Court The **Supreme Court** stands at the top of the American legal system. Article III of the Constitution created the Supreme Court as one of three coequal branches of the national government, along with Congress and the president.

The Supreme Court is composed of nine justices: the chief justice of the United States and eight associate justices. Congress sets this number and has the power to change it. Over the years it has varied from 5 to 10, but it has been 9 since 1869.

The Constitution does not describe the duties of the justices. Instead, the duties have developed from laws, through tradition, and as the needs and circumstances of the nation have developed. The main duty of the justices is to hear and rule on cases. This duty involves them in three decision-making tasks: deciding which cases to hear from among the thousands appealed to the Court each year; deciding the case itself; and determining an explanation for the decision, called the Court's **opinion.**

Shaping Public Policy The Supreme Court is both a political and a legal institution. It is a legal institution because it is responsible for settling disputes and interpreting the meaning of laws. The Court is a political institution because when it applies the law to specific disputes, it often determines what national policy will be. For example, when the Court rules that certain parts of the Social Security Act must apply to men and women equally, it is determining government policy.

Judicial Review As you have read, the Supreme Court's power to examine the laws and actions of local, state, and national governments and to cancel them if they violate the Constitution is called judicial review. The Supreme Court first assumed the power of judicial review in the case of *Marbury* v. *Madison* (1803). Since then, the Court has invalidated, or canceled, nearly 200 provisions of federal law.

The Supreme Court may also review presidential policies. In the case of *Ex parte Milligan* (1866), the Court ruled President Lincoln's suspension of certain civil rights during the Civil War was unconstitutional.

Judicial review of state laws and actions may have as much significance as the Court's activities at the federal level. In *Brown* v. *Board of Education of Topeka* (1954), the Court held that laws requiring or permitting racially segregated schools in four states were unconstitutional. The *Brown* decision cleared the way for the end of segregated schools throughout the nation.

Reading Check **Describing** How was the court system set up?

SECTION 2 ASSESSMENT

Checking for Understanding

1. **Key Terms** Use each of these terms in a complete sentence that helps explain its meaning: appropriate, impeach, constituents.
2. **Reviewing Facts** List three responsibilities of the president.

Reviewing Themes

3. **Government and Democracy** Why is Congress's power to appropriate money important?

Critical Thinking

4. **Analyzing Information** Which branch of government do you think is most powerful? Explain why you think so.
5. **Analyzing Information** Re-create the diagram below and provide five different kinds of Congressional committees.

Analyzing Visuals

6. **Reading a Flowchart** Refer to the flowchart on page 43. What do committees do to a bill?

Interdisciplinary Activity

Current Events Research in newspapers and news magazines about bills that are being debated in Congress. Find out what the bill will do if it is passed. Write a one-page paper about the bill and what has happened to it as it has gone through Congress.

SECTION 3 Citizens' Rights and Responsibilities

Guide to Reading

Main Idea
Citizens of the United States have both rights and responsibilities.

Key Terms
due process of law, citizen, naturalization

Read to Learn
- where the rights of citizens come from.
- the rights and responsibilities of United States citizens.

The Rights of American Citizens

66We hold these truths to be self-evident, that all men are created equal, that they are endowed by their Creator with certain unalienable Rights, that among these are Life, Liberty, and the pursuit of Happiness.99

These words from the Declaration of Independence continue to inspire Americans. They have encouraged Americans to pursue the ideals expressed in the Declaration and to create a Constitution and a Bill of Rights that protect these rights. The rights of Americans fall into three broad categories: the right to be protected from unfair actions of the government, to have equal treatment under the law, and to have basic freedoms.

Due Process The Fifth Amendment states that no person shall "be deprived of life, liberty, or property, without due process of law." Due process of law means that the government must follow procedures established by law and guaranteed by the Constitution, treating all people according to these principles.

Equal Protection All Americans, regardless of race, religion, or political beliefs, have the right to be treated the same under the law. The Fourteenth Amendment requires every state to grant its citizens "equal protection of the laws."

Basic Freedoms The basic freedoms involve the liberties outlined in the First Amendment—freedom of speech, freedom of religion, freedom of the press, freedom of assembly, and the right to petition. In a democratic society, power exists in the hands of the people. Therefore, its citizens must be free to exchange ideas freely.

The First Amendment allows citizens to criticize the government, in speech or in the press, without fear of punishment. It also states that the government cannot endorse a religion, nor can it prohibit citizens from practicing a religion if they choose to do so. In addition, the Ninth Amendment states that the rights of Americans are not limited to those mentioned in the Constitution. This has allowed basic freedoms to expand over the years through the passage of other amendments and laws. The Twenty-sixth Amendment, for example, extends the right to vote to American citizens 18 years of age.

Limits on Rights Our rights are not unlimited. The government can establish laws or rules to restrict certain standards to protect the health, safety, security, and moral standards of a community. Moreover, rights may be limited to prevent one person's rights from interfering with the rights of others. The restrictions of rights, however, must be reasonable and must apply to everyone equally.

✔ **Reading Check** **Summarizing** What is due process of law?

Citizen Participation

A citizen is a person who owes loyalty to and is entitled to the protection of a state or nation. How do you become an American citizen? Generally, citizenship is granted to anyone born within the borders of the United States. Citizenship is also granted to anyone born outside the United States if one parent is a United States citizen. A person of foreign birth can also become a citizen through the process of naturalization.

To qualify, applicants must be at least 18 years old. They must have been lawfully admitted for permanent residence and have lived in the United States for at least five years. They must possess good moral character and accept the principles of the Constitution. Applicants must also understand English and demonstrate an understanding of the history and principles of the government of the United States. Before being admitted to citizenship, applicants must be willing to give up any foreign allegiance and must promise to obey the Constitution and the laws of the United States.

As citizens of the United States, we are expected to carry out certain duties and responsibilities. **Duties** are things we are required to do by law. **Responsibilities** are things we should do. Fulfilling both our duties and our responsibilities helps ensure that we have a good government and that we continue to enjoy our rights.

Duties One of the duties of all Americans is to obey the law. Laws serve three important functions. They help maintain order; they protect the health, safety, and property of all citizens; and they make it possible for people to live together peacefully. If you disobey laws, for example, you endanger others and interfere with the smooth functioning of society. If you believe a law needs to be changed, you can work through your elected representatives to improve it.

Americans also have a duty to pay taxes. The government uses tax money to defend the nation, provide health insurance for people over 65, and build roads and bridges. Americans benefit from services provided by the government.

Flag Etiquette

★ The flag should be raised and lowered by hand and displayed only from sunrise to sunset. On special occasions, it may be displayed at night.

★ The flag may be displayed on all days, weather permitting, particularly on national and state holidays and on historic and special occasions.

★ No flag should be flown above the American flag or to the right of it at the same height.

★ The flag may be flown at half-mast to mourn the death of public officials.

★ The flag should never touch the ground or floor beneath it.

★ The flag may be flown upside down only to signal distress.

★ When the flag becomes old and tattered, it should be destroyed by burning. According to an approved custom, the Union (the white stars on the blue field) is first cut from the flag; then the two pieces, which no longer form a flag, are burned.

Another duty of citizens is to defend the nation. All males aged 18 and older must register with the government in case they are needed for military service. The nation no longer has a **draft**, or required military service, but a war could make the draft necessary again.

The Constitution guarantees all Americans the right to a trial by a jury of their peers (equals). For this reason you should be prepared to serve on a jury when you become eligible at the age of 18. Having a large group of jurors on hand is necessary to guarantee the right to a fair and speedy trial. You also have a duty to serve as a witness at a trial if called to do so.

Responsibilities The responsibilities of citizens are not as clear-cut as their duties. Because responsibilities are voluntary, people are not arrested or punished if they do not fulfill these obligations. The quality of our government and of our lives will diminish, however, if our responsibilities are not carried out.

Keep in mind that government exists to serve you. Therefore, one of your responsibilities as a citizen is to know what the government is doing and to voice your opinion when you feel strongly about something the government has done or has failed to do. When the government learns that most people favor or oppose an action, it usually follows their wishes.

You also need to be informed about your rights and to exercise them when necessary. Knowing your rights helps preserve them. Other responsibilities include respecting diversity, accepting responsibility for your actions, and supporting your family.

Citizens taking part in a town meeting

Vote, Vote, Vote! Perhaps your most important responsibility as an American citizen will be to vote when you reach the age of 18. Voting allows you to participate in government and guide its direction. When you vote for people to represent you in government, you will be exercising your right of self-government. If you disapprove of the job your representatives are doing, it will be your responsibility to help elect other people in the next election. You can also let your representatives know how you feel about issues through letters, telephone calls, and petitions.

While not everyone holds public office, everyone can participate in government in other ways. Working on a political campaign, volunteering to help in a hospital or a library, and participating in a local park cleanup are all ways to take responsibility and to make a contribution to good government and a well-run community.

Respecting Others' Rights To enjoy your rights to the fullest, you must be prepared to respect the rights of others. Respecting the rights of others also means respecting the rights of people with whom you disagree. Respecting and accepting others regardless of race, religion, beliefs, or other differences is essential in a democracy. All Americans are entitled to the same respect and good treatment.

✓ **Reading Check** **Identifying** What is naturalization?

SECTION 3 ASSESSMENT

Checking for Understanding

1. **Key Terms** Use each of these terms in a complete sentence that helps explain its meaning: due process of law, citizen, naturalization.
2. **Reviewing Facts** Why are personal responsibilities important?

Reviewing Themes

3. **Government and Democracy** Summarize three of the freedoms granted in the First Amendment.

Critical Thinking

4. **Analyzing Information** The Fifth Amendment states that people have the right of "due process of law." Why is this phrase important?
5. **Analyzing Information** Re-create the diagram below and provide the three categories of American rights.

Analyzing Visuals

6. **Analyzing a Chart** Refer to the chart on page 47. For what reason may the flag be flown at half-mast?

Interdisciplinary Activity

Civics One responsibility of being an American citizen is to become involved in the democratic system. Make a poster showing how students can get involved in their community's democracy. Display your poster in a prominent place in school.

Handbook Assessment

✓ Reviewing Key Terms

Write the key term that completes each sentence. Then write a sentence for each term not chosen.

a. popular sovereignty   **d.** amendment

b. enumerated powers   **e.** implied powers

c. reserved powers   **f.** judicial review

1. A(n)_____ is a change to the Constitution.
2. Those powers that are suggested but not directly stated in the Constitution are called _____.
3. _____ is the Supreme Court's power to review all congressional acts and executive actions.
4. Those powers mentioned specifically in the Constitution are called _____.

✓ Reviewing Key Facts

5. List the six goals of government stated in the Preamble.
6. How does one become a naturalized citizen?
7. Explain why the amendment process is so difficult.
8. Explain why responsible citizenship is important. Provide examples of responsible citizenship.
9. How does the Constitution protect individual rights?
10. Summarize the basic freedoms outlined in the First Amendment.

✓ Critical Thinking

11. **Analyzing Information** Analyze how limited government, republicanism, and popular sovereignty are important parts of the Constitution.
12. **Identifying Options** Describe five possible ways a person can fulfill his or her responsibilities in society and at home.
13. **Comparing** Some people argue that there should be a limit on the number of terms a senator or representative can serve. What are some of the advantages of the present system, which does not limit these terms? What are some of the disadvantages?
14. **Predicting Consequences** Re-create the diagram below and predict what might have happened to the U.S. if the Framers had not provided for a system of checks and balances.

✓ Citizenship Cooperative Activity

15. **Examining Citizens' Rights** Working with a partner, choose one of the following rights and trace its historical development in the United States from the time the Constitution was ratified to the present:

    suffrage   freedom of speech

    freedom of religion   equal protection of law

16. **Civic Planning** Constitutions provide a plan for organizing and operating governments. What plan provides the rules for your local government? Contact a local government official to find out about the basic plan of your city or town. Share your findings with the class.

✓ Alternative Assessment

17. **Portfolio Writing Activity** Part of your responsibility as an American citizen is to be informed about what the government is doing and to voice your opinion about its actions. Compose a letter to the editor of your local newspaper. In your letter, express your opinion about an issue in your community.

Standardized Test Practice

Directions: Choose the *best* answer to the following question.

Under the Constitution, the president chooses judges to serve on the Supreme Court, but each choice must be approved by the Senate. This is an example of what principle of government?

A Checks and balances

B Federalism

C Separation of powers

D Judicial Review

Test-Taking Tip:

What do you think would happen if the president could choose all judges without anyone else's approval? The writers of the Constitution wanted to make sure that none of the three branches of government became too powerful. Which answer shows this idea?

The Constitution of the United States

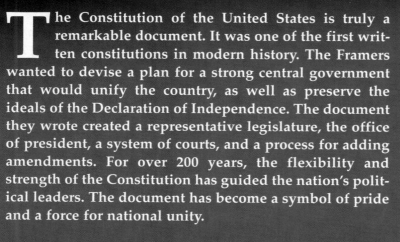

The Constitution of the United States is truly a remarkable document. It was one of the first written constitutions in modern history. The Framers wanted to devise a plan for a strong central government that would unify the country, as well as preserve the ideals of the Declaration of Independence. The document they wrote created a representative legislature, the office of president, a system of courts, and a process for adding amendments. For over 200 years, the flexibility and strength of the Constitution has guided the nation's political leaders. The document has become a symbol of pride and a force for national unity.

The entire text of the Constitution and its amendments follows. Those passages that have been set aside, outdated by the passage of time, or changed by the adoption of amendments are printed in blue. Also included are explanatory notes that will help clarify the meaning of each article and section.

James Madison, author of the Constitution

Preamble

We the People of the United States, in Order to form a more perfect Union, establish Justice, insure domestic Tranquility, provide for the common defence, promote the general Welfare, and secure the Blessings of Liberty to ourselves and our Posterity, do ordain and establish this Constitution for the United States of America.

The Preamble introduces the Constitution and sets forth the general purposes for which the government was established. The Preamble also declares that the power of the government comes from the people.

The printed text of the document shows the spelling and punctuation of the parchment original.

Article I

Section 1

All legislative Powers herein granted shall be vested in a Congress of the United States, which shall consist of a Senate and House of Representatives.

Section 2

[1.] The House of Representatives shall be composed of Members chosen every second Year by the People of the several States, and the Electors in each State shall have the Qualifications requisite for Electors of the most numerous Branch of the State Legislature.

[2.] No person shall be a Representative who shall not have attained to the Age of twenty five Years, and been seven Years a Citizen of the United States, and who shall not, when elected, be an Inhabitant of that State in which he shall be chosen.

[3.] Representatives and direct Taxes shall be apportioned among the several States which may be included within this Union, according to their respective Numbers, which shall be determined by adding to the whole Number of free Persons, including those bound to Service for a Term of Years, and excluding Indians not taxed, three fifths of all other Persons. The actual Enumeration shall be made within three Years after the first Meeting of the Congress of the United States, and within every subsequent Term of ten Years, in such Manner as they shall by Law direct. The Number of Representatives shall not exceed one for every thirty Thousand, but each State shall have at Least one Representative; and until such enumeration shall be made, the State of New Hampshire shall be entitled to chuse three; Massachusetts eight, Rhode-Island and Providence Plantations one, Connecticut five, New-York six, New Jersey four, Pennsylvania eight, Delaware one, Maryland six, Virginia ten, North Carolina five, South Carolina five, and Georgia three.

[4.] When vacancies happen in the Representation from any State, the Executive Authority thereof shall issue Writs of Election to fill such Vacancies.

[5.] The House of Representatives shall chuse their Speaker and other Officers; and shall have the sole Power of Impeachment.

Article I. The Legislative Branch

The Constitution contains seven divisions called articles. Each article covers a general topic. For example, Articles I, II, and III create the three branches of the national government—the legislative, executive, and judicial branches. Most of the articles are divided into sections.

Section 2. House of Representatives

Division of Representatives Among the States The number of representatives from each state is based on the size of the state's population. Each state is entitled to at least one representative. *What are the qualifications for members of the House of Representatives?*

Vocabulary

preamble: *introduction*
constitution: *principles and laws of a nation*
enumeration: *census or population count*
impeachment: *bringing charges against an official*

Section 3. The Senate

Number of Members, Terms of Office, and Voting Procedure Originally, senators were chosen by the state legislators of their own states. The Seventeenth Amendment changed this, so that senators are now elected by the people. There are 100 senators, 2 from each state. The vice president serves as president of the Senate.

John Adams, the first vice president

Section 3. The Senate

Trial of Impeachment One of Congress's powers is the power to impeach—to accuse government officials of wrongdoing, put them on trial, and if necessary remove them from office. *Which body has the power to decide the official's guilt or innocence?*

Vocabulary

president pro tempore: *presiding officer of Senate who serves when the vice president is absent*
indictment: *charging a person with an offense*
quorum: *minimum number of members that must be present to conduct sessions*
adjourn: *to suspend a session*
immunity privilege: *members cannot be sued or prosecuted for anything they say in Congress*
emoluments: *salaries*
bill: *draft of a proposed law*
revenue: *income raised by government*

Section 3

[1.] The Senate of the United States shall be composed of two Senators from each State, chosen by the Legislature thereof, for six Years; and each Senator shall have one Vote.

[2.] Immediately after they shall be assembled in Consequence of the first Election, they shall be divided as equally as may be into three Classes. The Seats of the Senators of the first Class shall be vacated at the Expiration of the second Year, of the second Class at the Expiration of the fourth Year, and of the third Class at the Expiration of the sixth Year, so that one third may be chosen every second Year; and if Vacancies happen by Resignation, or otherwise, during the Recess of the Legislature of any State, the Executive thereof may make temporary Appointments until the next Meeting of the Legislature, which shall then fill such Vacancies.

[3.] No Person shall be a Senator who shall not have attained to the Age of thirty Years, and been nine Years a Citizen of the United States, and who shall not, when elected, be an Inhabitant of that State for which he shall be chosen.

[4.] The Vice President of the United States shall be President of the Senate, but shall have no Vote, unless they be equally divided.

[5.] The Senate shall chuse their other Officers, and also a President pro tempore, in the Absence of the Vice President, or when he shall exercise the Office of the President of the United States.

[6.] The Senate shall have the sole Power to try all Impeachments. When sitting for that Purpose, they shall be on Oath or Affirmation. When the President of the United States is tried, the Chief Justice shall preside: And no Person shall be convicted without the Concurrence of two thirds of the Members present.

[7.] Judgment in Cases of Impeachment shall not extend further than to removal from Office, and disqualification to hold and enjoy any Office of honor, Trust or Profit under the United States: but the Party convicted shall nevertheless be liable and subject to Indictment, Trial, Judgment and Punishment, according to Law.

Section 4

[1.] The Times, Places and Manner of holding Elections for Senators and Representatives, shall be prescribed in each State by the Legislature thereof; but the Congress may at any time by Law make or alter such Regulations, except as to the Places of chusing Senators.

[2.] The Congress shall assemble at least once in every Year, and such Meeting shall be on the first Monday in December, unless they shall by Law appoint a different Day.

Section 5

[1.] Each House shall be the Judge of the Elections, Returns and Qualifications of its own Members, and a Majority of each shall constitute a Quorum to do Business; but a smaller Number may adjourn from day to day, and may be authorized to compel the Attendance of absent Members, in such Manner, and under such Penalties as each House may provide.

[2.] Each House may determine the Rules of its Proceedings, punish its Members for disorderly Behaviour, and, with the Concurrence of two thirds, expel a Member.

[3.] Each House shall keep a Journal of its Proceedings, and from time to time publish the same, excepting such Parts as may in their Judgment require Secrecy; and the Yeas and Nays of the Members of either House on any question shall, at the Desire of one fifth of those Present, be entered on the Journal.

[4.] Neither House, during the Session of Congress, shall, without the Consent of the other, adjourn for more than three days, nor to any other Place than that in which the two Houses shall be sitting.

Section 6

[1.] The Senators and Representatives shall receive a Compensation for their Services, to be ascertained by Law, and paid out of the Treasury of the United States. They shall in all Cases, except Treason, Felony and Breach of the Peace, be privileged from Arrest during their Attendance at the Session of their respective Houses, and in going to and returning from the same; and for any Speech or Debate in either House, they shall not be questioned in any other Place.

[2.] No Senator or Representative shall, during the Time for which he was elected, be appointed to any civil Office under the Authority of the United States, which shall have been created, or the Emoluments whereof shall have been encreased during such time; and no Person holding any Office under the United States, shall be a Member of either House during his Continuance in Office.

Section 7

[1.] All Bills for raising Revenue shall originate in the House of Representatives; but the Senate may propose or concur with Amendments as on other Bills.

[2.] Every Bill which shall have passed the House of Representatives and the Senate, shall, before it become a Law, be presented to the President of the United States; If he approve he shall sign it, but if not he shall return it, with his Objections to that House in which it shall have originated, who shall enter the Objections at large on their Journal, and proceed to reconsider it. If after such Reconsideration two thirds of that House shall agree to pass the Bill, it shall be sent, together with the Objections, to the other House, by which it shall likewise be reconsidered, and if approved by two thirds

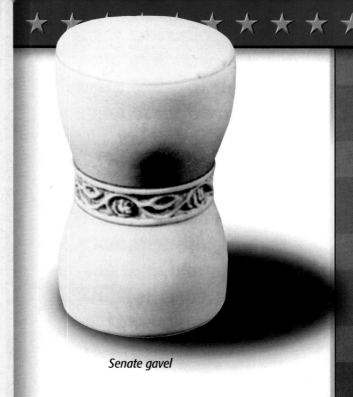

Senate gavel

Section 6. Privileges and Restrictions

Pay and Privileges To strengthen the federal government, the Founders set congressional salaries to be paid by the United States Treasury rather than by members' respective states. Originally, members were paid $6 per day. In 2002, all members of Congress received a base salary of $150,000.

Section 7. Passing Laws

Revenue Bills All tax laws must originate in the House of Representatives. This ensures that the branch of Congress that is elected by the people every two years has the major role in determining taxes.

Section 7. Passing Laws

How Bills Become Laws A bill may become a law only by passing both houses of Congress and by being signed by the president. The president can check Congress by rejecting—vetoing—its legislation. *How can Congress override the president's veto?*

of that House, it shall become a Law. But in all such Cases the Votes of both Houses shall be determined by yeas and Nays, and the Names of the Persons voting for and against the Bill shall be entered on the Journal of each House respectively. If any Bill shall not be returned by the President within ten Days (Sundays excepted) after it shall have been presented to him, the Same shall be a Law, in like Manner as if he had signed it, unless the Congress by their Adjournment prevent its Return, in which Case it shall not be a Law.

[3.] Every Order, Resolution, or Vote to which the Concurrence of the Senate and House of Representatives may be necessary (except on a question of Adjournment) shall be presented to the President of the United States; and before the Same shall take Effect, shall be approved by him, or being disapproved by him, shall be repassed by two thirds of the Senate and House of Representatives, according to the Rules and Limitations prescribed in the Case of a Bill.

Section 8

[1.] The Congress shall have the Power To lay and collect Taxes, Duties, Imposts and Excises, to pay the Debts and provide for the common Defence and general Welfare of the United States; but all Duties, Imposts and Excises shall be uniform throughout the United States;

[2.] To borrow Money on the credit of the United States;

[3.] To regulate Commerce with foreign Nations, and among the several States, and with the Indian Tribes;

[4.] To establish an uniform Rule of Naturalization, and uniform Laws on the subject of Bankruptcies throughout the United States;

[5.] To coin Money, regulate the Value thereof, and of foreign Coin, and fix the Standard of Weights and Measures;

[6.] To provide for the Punishment of counterfeiting the Securities and current Coin of the United States;

[7.] To establish Post Offices and post Roads;

[8.] To promote the Progress of Science and useful Arts, by securing for limited Times to Authors and Inventors the exclusive Right to their respective Writings and Discoveries;

[9.] To constitute Tribunals inferior to the supreme Court;

[10.] To define and punish Piracies and Felonies committed on the high Seas, and Offences against the Law of Nations;

[11.] To declare War, grant Letters of Marque and Reprisal, and make Rules concerning Captures on Land and Water;

Section 8. Powers Granted to Congress

Expressed Powers Expressed powers are those powers directly stated in the Constitution. Most of the expressed powers of Congress are listed in Article I, Section 8. These powers are also called enumerated powers because they are numbered 1–18. *Which clause gives Congress the power to declare war?*

Civil War money

Vocabulary

resolution: *legislature's formal expression of opinion*

naturalization: *procedure by which a citizen of a foreign nation becomes a citizen of the United States*

tribunal: *a court*

letter of marque: *authority given to a citizen to outfit an armed ship and use it to attack enemy ships in time of war*

reprisal: *taking by force property or territory belonging to another country or to its citizens*

insurrection: *rebellion*

[12.] To raise and support Armies, but no Appropriation of Money to that Use shall be for a longer Term than two Years;

[13.] To provide and maintain a Navy;

[14.] To make Rules for the Government and Regulation of the land and naval Forces;

[15.] To provide for calling forth the Militia to execute the Laws of the Union, suppress Insurrections and repel Invasions;

[16.] To provide for organizing, arming, and disciplining, the Militia, and for governing such Part of them as may be employed in the Service of the United States, reserving to the States respectively, the Appointment of the Officers, and the Authority of training the Militia according to the discipline prescribed by Congress;

[17.] To exercise exclusive Legislation in all Cases whatsoever, over such District (not exceeding ten Miles square) as may, by Cession of particular States, and the Acceptance of Congress, become the Seat of Government of the United States, and to exercise like Authority over all Places purchased by the Consent of the Legislature of the State in which the Same shall be, for the Erection of Forts, Magazines, Arsenals, dock-Yards, and other needful Buildings;—And

[18.] To make all Laws which shall be necessary and proper for carrying into Execution the foregoing Powers, and all other Powers vested by this Constitution in the Government of the United States, or in any Department or Officer thereof.

Section 9

[1]. The Migration or Importation of such Persons as any of the States now existing shall think proper to admit, shall not be prohibited by the Congress prior to the Year one thousand eight hundred and eight, but a Tax or duty may be imposed on such Importation, not exceeding ten dollars for each Person.

[2.] The Privilege of the Writ of Habeas Corpus shall not be suspended, unless when in Cases of Rebellion or Invasion the public Safety may require it.

[3.] No Bill of Attainder or ex post facto Law shall be passed.

[4.] No Capitation, or other direct, Tax shall be laid, unless in Proportion to the Census or Enumeration herein before directed to be taken.

[5.] No Tax or Duty shall be laid on Articles exported from any State.

[6.] No Preference shall be given by any Regulation of Commerce or Revenue to the Ports of one State over those of another: nor shall Vessels bound to, or from, one State, be obliged to enter, clear, or pay Duties in another.

Seal of the U.S. Navy

Section 8. Powers Granted to Congress

Elastic Clause The final enumerated power is often called the "elastic clause." This clause gives Congress the right to make all laws "necessary and proper" to carry out the powers expressed in the other clauses of Article I. It is called the elastic clause because it lets Congress "stretch" its powers to meet situations the Founders could never have anticipated.

What does the phrase "necessary and proper" in the elastic clause mean? Almost from the beginning, this phrase was a subject of dispute. The issue was whether a strict or a broad interpretation of the Constitution should be applied. The dispute was first addressed in 1819, in the case of *McCulloch* v. *Maryland*, when the Supreme Court ruled in favor of a broad interpretation.

Section 9. Powers Denied to the Federal Government

Habeas Corpus A writ of habeas corpus issued by a judge requires a law official to bring a prisoner to court and show cause for holding the prisoner. A bill of attainder is a bill that punished a person without a jury trial. An "ex post facto" law is one that makes an act a crime after the act has been committed. *What does the Constitution say about bills of attainder?*

[7.] No Money shall be drawn from the Treasury, but in Consequence of Appropriations made by Law; and a regular Statement and Account of the Receipts and Expenditures of all public Money shall be published from time to time.

[8.] No Title of Nobility shall be granted by the United States: And no Person holding any Office of Profit or Trust under them, shall, without the Consent of the Congress, accept of any present, Emolument, Office, or Title, of any kind whatever, from any King, Prince, or foreign State.

Section 10. Powers Denied to the States

Limitations on Power Section 10 lists limits on the states. These restrictions were designed, in part, to prevent an over-lapping in functions and authority with the federal government.

Section 10

[1.] No State shall enter into any Treaty, Alliance, or Confederation; grant Letters of Marque and Reprisal; coin Money; emit Bills of Credit; make any Thing but gold and silver Coin a Tender in Payment of Debts; pass any Bill of Attainder, ex post facto Law, or Law impair-ing the Obligation of Contracts, or grant any Title of Nobility.

[2.] No State shall, without the Consent of the Con-gress, lay any Imposts or Duties on Imports or Exports, except what may be absolutely necessary for executing it's inspection Laws: and the net Produce of all Duties and Imposts, laid by any State on Imports and Exports, shall be for the Use of the Treasury of the United States; and all such Laws shall be subject to the Revision and Controul of the Congress.

[3.] No State shall, without the Consent of Congress, lay any Duty of Tonnage, keep Troops, or Ships of War in time of Peace, enter into any Agreement or Compact with another State, or with a foreign Power, or engage in War, unless actually invaded, or in such imminent Danger as will not admit of delay.

United States coins

Article II. The Executive Branch

Article II creates an executive branch to carry out laws passed by Congress. Article II lists the powers and duties of the presidency, describes qualifications for office and procedures for electing the president, and provides for a vice president.

Article II

Section 1

[1.] The executive Power shall be vested in a President of the United States of America. He shall hold his Office during the Term of four Years, and, together with the Vice President, chosen for the same Term, be elected, as follows

[2.] Each State shall appoint, in such Manner as the Legislature thereof may direct, a Number of Electors, equal to the whole Number of Senators and Representa-tives to which the State may be entitled in the Congress: but no Senator or Representative, or Person holding an Office of Trust or Profit under the United States, shall be appointed an Elector.

[3.] The Electors shall meet in their respective States, and vote by Ballot for two Persons, of whom one at least shall not be an Inhabitant of the same State with

Vocabulary

appropriations: *funds set aside for a specific use*
emolument: *payment*
impost: *tax*
duty: *tax*

themselves. And they shall make a List of all the Persons voted for, and of the Number of Votes for each; which List they shall sign and certify, and transmit sealed to the Seat of the Government of the United States, directed to the President of the Senate. The President of the Senate shall, in the Presence of the Senate and House of Representatives, open all the Certificates, and the Votes shall then be counted. The Person having the greatest Number of Votes shall be the President, if such Number be a Majority of the whole Number of Electors appointed; and if there be more than one who have such Majority, and have an equal Number of Votes, then the House of Representatives shall immediately chuse by Ballot one of them for President; and if no person have a Majority, then from the five highest on the List the said House shall in like Manner chuse the President. But in chusing the President, the Votes shall be taken by States, the Representation from each State having one Vote; A quorum for this Purpose shall consist of a Member or Members from two thirds of the States, and a Majority of all the States shall be necessary to a Choice. In every Case, after the Choice of the President, the Person having the greatest Number of Votes of the Electors shall be the Vice President. But if there should remain two or more who have equal Votes, the Senate shall chuse from them by Ballot the Vice President.

[4.] The Congress may determine the Time of chusing the Electors, and the Day on which they shall give their Votes; which Day shall be the same throughout the United States.

[5.] No Person except a natural born Citizen, or a Citizen of the United States, at the time of the Adoption of this Constitution, shall be eligible to the Office of President; neither shall any Person be eligible to that Office who shall not have attained to the Age of thirty five Years, and been fourteen Years a Resident within the United States.

[6.] In Case of the Removal of the President from Office, or of his Death, Resignation, or Inability to discharge the Powers and Duties of the said Office, the Same shall devolve on the Vice President, and the Congress may by Law provide for the Case of Removal, Death, Resignation or Inability, both of the President and Vice President, declaring what Officer shall then act as President, and such Officer shall act accordingly, until the Disability be removed, or a President shall be elected.

[7.] The President shall, at stated Times, receive for his Services, a Compensation, which shall neither be encreased nor diminished during the Period for which he shall have been elected, and he shall not receive within that Period any other Emolument from the United States, or any of them.

[8.] Before he enter on the Execution of his Office, he shall take the following Oath or Affirmation:—"I do solemnly swear (or affirm) that I will faithfully execute the Office of President of the United States, and will to the best of my Ability, preserve, protect and defend the Constitution of the United States."

Section 1. President and Vice President
Former Method of Election The Twelfth Amendment, added in 1804, changed the method of electing the president stated in Article II, Section 1, paragraph 3. The Twelfth Amendment requires that the electors cast separate ballots for president and vice president.

George Washington, the first president

Section 1. President and Vice President
Qualifications The president must be a citizen of the United States by birth, at least 35 years of age, and a resident of the United States for 14 years.

Section 1. President and Vice President
Vacancies If the president dies, resigns, is removed from office by impeachment, or is unable to carry out the duties of the office, the vice president assumes the duties of the president. The Twenty-Fifth Amendment sets procedures for presidential succession.

Section 1. President and Vice President
Salary Originally, the president's salary was $25,000 per year. The president's current salary is $400,000 plus a $50,000 nontaxable expense account per year. The president also receives living accommodations in two residences—the White House and Camp David.

Section 2. Powers of the President

Military, Cabinet, Pardons Mention of "the principal officer in each of the executive departments" is the only suggestion of the president's cabinet to be found in the Constitution. The cabinet is an advisory body, and its power depends on the president. Section 2, Clause 1 also makes the president—a civilian—the head of the armed services. This established the principle of civilian control of the military.

Section 2. Powers of the President

Treaties and Appointments An executive order is a command issued by a president to exercise a power which he has been given by the U.S. Constitution or by a federal statute. In times of emergency, presidents sometimes have used the executive order to override the Constitution of the United States and the Congress. During the Civil War, President Lincoln suspended many fundamental rights guaranteed in the Constitution and the Bill of Rights. He closed down newspapers that opposed his policies and imprisoned some who disagreed with him. Lincoln said that these actions were justified to preserve the Union.

Impeachment ticket

Article III. The Judicial Branch

The term *judicial* refers to courts. The Constitution set up only the Supreme Court but provided for the establishment of other federal courts. The judiciary of the United States has two different systems of courts. One system consists of the federal courts, whose powers derive from the Constitution and federal laws. The other includes the courts of each of the 50 states, whose powers derive from state constitutions and laws.

Section 2

[1.] The President shall be Commander in Chief of the Army and Navy of the United States, and of the Militia of the several States, when called into the actual Service of the United States; he may require the Opinion, in writing, of the principal Officer in each of the executive Departments, upon any Subject relating to the Duties of their respective Offices, and he shall have Power to grant Reprieves and Pardons for Offences against the United States, except in Cases of Impeachment.

[2.] He shall have Power, by and with the Advice and Consent of the Senate, to make Treaties, provided two thirds of the Senators present concur; and he shall nominate, and by and with the Advice and Consent of the Senate, shall appoint Ambassadors, other public Ministers and Consuls, Judges of the supreme Court, and all other Officers of the United States, whose Appointments are not herein otherwise provided for, and which shall be established by Law: but the Congress may by Law vest the Appointment of such inferior Officers, as they think proper, in the President alone, in the Courts of Law, or in the Heads of Departments.

[3.] The President shall have Power to fill up all Vacancies that may happen during the Recess of the Senate, by granting Commissions which shall expire at the End of their next Session.

Section 3

He shall from time to time give to the Congress Information of the State of the Union, and recommend to their Consideration such Measures as he shall judge necessary and expedient; he may, on extraordinary Occasions, convene both Houses, or either of them, and in Case of Disagreement between them, with Respect to the Time of Adjournment, he may adjourn them to such Time as he shall think proper; he shall receive Ambassadors and other public Ministers; he shall take Care that the Laws be faithfully executed, and shall Commission all the Officers of the United States.

Section 4

The President, Vice President and all civil Officers of the United States, shall be removed from Office on Impeachment for, and Conviction of, Treason, Bribery, or other high Crimes and Misdemeanors.

Article III

Section 1

The judicial Power of the United States, shall be vested in one supreme Court, and in such inferior Courts as the Congress may from time to time ordain and establish. The Judges, both of the supreme and inferior Courts, shall hold their Offices during good Behaviour, and shall, at stated Times, receive for their Services, a Compensation, which shall not be diminished during their Continuance in Office.

Section 2

[1.] The judicial Power shall extend to all Cases, in Law and Equity, arising under this Constitution, the Laws of the United States, and Treaties made, or which shall be made, under their Authority;—to all Cases affecting Ambassadors, other public Ministers and Consuls;—to all Cases of admiralty and maritime Jurisdiction;—to Controversies to which the United States shall be a Party;—to Controversies between two or more States;—between a State and Citizens of another State;—between Citizens of different States,—between Citizens of the same State claiming Lands under Grants of different States, and between a State, or the Citizens thereof, and foreign States, Citizens or Subjects.

[2.] In all Cases affecting Ambassadors, other public Ministers and Consuls, and those in which a State shall be Party, the supreme Court shall have original Jurisdiction. In all the other Cases before mentioned, the supreme Court shall have appellate Jurisdiction, both as to Law and Fact, with such Exceptions, and under such Regulations as the Congress shall make.

[3.] The Trial of all Crimes, except in Cases of Impeachment, shall be by Jury; and such Trial shall be held in the State where the said Crimes shall have been committed; but when not committed within any State, the Trial shall be at such Place or Places as the Congress may by Law have directed.

Section 3

[1.] Treason against the United States, shall consist only in levying War against them, or in adhering to their Enemies, giving them Aid and Comfort. No Person shall be convicted of Treason unless on the Testimony of two Witnesses to the same overt Act, or on Confession in open Court.

[2.] The Congress shall have Power to declare the Punishment of Treason, but no Attainder of Treason shall work Corruption of Blood, or Forfeiture except during the Life of the Person attainted.

Article IV

Section 1

Full Faith and Credit shall be given in each State to the public Acts, Records, and judicial Proceedings of every other State. And the Congress may by general Laws prescribe the Manner in which such Acts, Records and Proceedings shall be proved, and the Effect thereof.

Section 2. Jurisdiction
Statute Law Federal courts deal mostly with "statute law," or laws passed by Congress, treaties, and cases involving the Constitution itself.

Section 2. Jurisdiction
The Supreme Court A Court with "original jurisdiction" has the authority to be the first court to hear a case. The Supreme Court primarily has "appellate jurisdiction" and mostly hears cases appealed from lower courts.

Article IV. Relations Among the States

Article IV explains the relationship of the states to one another and to the national government. This article requires each state to give citizens of other states the same rights as its own citizens, addresses admitting new states, and guarantees that the national government will protect the states.

Vocabulary

original jurisdiction: *authority to be the first court to hear a case*

appellate jurisdiction: *authority to hear cases that have been appealed from lower courts*

treason: *violation of the allegiance owed by a person to his or her own country, for example, by aiding an enemy*

Section 3. New States and Territories

New States Congress has the power to admit new states. It also determines the basic guidelines for applying for statehood. Two states, Maine and West Virginia, were created within the boundaries of another state. In the case of West Virginia, President Lincoln recognized the West Virginia government as the legal government of Virginia during the Civil War. This allowed West Virginia to secede from Virginia without obtaining approval from the Virginia legislature.

Section 4. Federal Protection for States

Republic Government can be classified in many different ways. The ancient Greek philosopher Aristotle classified government based on the question: Who governs? According to Aristotle, all governments belong to one of three major groups: (1) autocracy—rule by one person; (2) oligarchy—rule by a few persons; or (3) democracy—rule by many persons. A republic is a form of democracy in which the people elect representatives to make laws and conduct government.

Article V. The Amendment Process

Article V spells out the ways that the Constitution can be amended, or changed. All of the 27 amendments were proposed by a two-thirds vote of both houses of Congress. Only the Twenty-first Amendment was ratified by constitutional conventions of the states. All other amendments have been ratified by state legislatures. *What is an amendment?*

Vocabulary

extradition: *surrender of a criminal to another authority*
amendment: *a change to the Constitution*
ratification: *process by which an amendment is approved*

Section 2

[1.] The Citizens of each State shall be entitled to all Privileges and Immunities of Citizens in the several States.

[2.] A Person charged in any State with Treason, Felony, or other Crime, who shall flee from Justice, and be found in another State, shall on Demand of the executive Authority of the State from which he fled, be delivered up, to be removed to the State having Jurisdiction of the Crime.

[3.] No Person held to Service of Labour in one State, under the Laws thereof, escaping into another, shall, in Consequence of any Law or Regulation therein, be discharged from such Service or Labour, but shall be delivered up on Claim of the Party to whom such Service or Labour may be due.

Section 3

[1.] New States may be admitted by the Congress into this Union; but no new State shall be formed or erected within the Jurisdiction of any other State; nor any State be formed by the Junction of two or more States, or Parts of States, without the Consent of the Legislatures of the States concerned as well as of the Congress.

[2.] The Congress shall have Power to dispose of and make all needful Rules and Regulations respecting the Territory or other Property belonging to the United States; and nothing in this Constitution shall be so construed as to Prejudice any Claims of the United States, or of any particular State.

Section 4

The United States shall guarantee to every State in this Union a Republican Form of Government, and shall protect each of them against Invasion; and on Application of the Legislature, or of the Executive (when the Legislature cannot be convened) against domestic Violence.

Article V

The Congress, whenever two thirds of both Houses shall deem it necessary, shall propose Amendments to this Constitution, or, on the Application of the Legislatures of two thirds of the several States, shall call a Convention for proposing Amendments, which, in either Case, shall be valid to all Intents and Purposes, as Part of this Constitution, when ratified by the Legislatures of three fourths of the several States, or by Conventions in three fourths thereof, as the one or the other Mode of Ratification may be proposed by the Congress; Provided that no Amendment which may be made prior to the Year One thousand eight hundred and eight shall in any Manner affect the first and fourth Clauses in the Ninth Section of the first Article; and that no State, without its Consent, shall be deprived of its equal Suffrage in the Senate.

Article VI

[1.] All Debts contracted and Engagements entered into, before the Adoption of this Constitution, shall be as valid against the United States under this Constitution, as under the Confederation.

[2.] This Constitution, and the Laws of the United States which shall be made in Pursuance thereof; and all Treaties made, or which shall be made, under the Authority of the United States, shall be the supreme Law of the Land; and the Judges in every State shall be bound thereby, any Thing in the Constitution or Laws of any State to the Contrary notwithstanding.

[3.] The Senators and Representatives before mentioned, and the Members of the several State Legislatures, and all executive and judicial Officers, both of the United States and of the several States, shall be bound by Oath or Affirmation, to support this Constitution; but no religious Test shall ever be required as a Qualification to any Office or public Trust under the United States.

Article VII

The Ratification of the Conventions of nine States, shall be sufficient for the Establishment of this Constitution between the States so ratifying the Same.

Done in Convention by the Unanimous Consent of the States present the Seventeenth Day of September in the Year of our Lord one thousand seven hundred and Eighty seven and of the Independence of the United States of America the Twelfth. In witness whereof We have hereunto subscribed our Names,

Article VI. National Supremacy

Article VI contains the "supremacy clause." This clause establishes that the Constitution, laws passed by Congress, and treaties of the United States "shall be the supreme Law of the Land." The "supremacy clause" recognized the Constitution and federal laws as supreme when in conflict with those of the states.

Article VII. Ratification

Article VII addresses ratification and declares that the Constitution would take effect after it was ratified by nine states.

Signers

*George Washington, **President and Deputy from Virginia***

New Hampshire
John Langdon
Nicholas Gilman

Massachusetts
Nathaniel Gorham
Rufus King

Connecticut
William Samuel Johnson
Roger Sherman

New York
Alexander Hamilton

New Jersey
William Livingston
David Brearley
William Paterson
Jonathan Dayton

Pennsylvania
Benjamin Franklin
Thomas Mifflin
Robert Morris
George Clymer
Thomas FitzSimons
Jared Ingersoll
James Wilson
Gouverneur Morris

Delaware
George Read
Gunning Bedford, Jr.
John Dickinson
Richard Bassett
Jacob Broom

Maryland
James McHenry
Daniel of St. Thomas Jenifer
Daniel Carroll

Virginia
John Blair
James Madison, Jr.

North Carolina
William Blount
Richard Dobbs Spaight
Hugh Williamson

South Carolina
John Rutledge
Charles Cotesworth Pinckney
Charles Pinckney
Pierce Butler

Georgia
William Few
Abraham Baldwin

Attest: William Jackson,
Secretary

Bill of Rights

The first 10 amendments are known as the Bill of Rights (1791). These amendments limit the powers of government. The First Amendment protects the civil liberties of individuals in the United States. The amendment freedoms are not absolute, however. They are limited by the rights of other individuals. *What freedoms does the First Amendment protect?*

Amendment 2

Right to Bear Arms This amendment is often debated. Originally, it was intended to prevent the national government from repeating the actions of the British, who tried to take weapons away from the colonial militia, or armed forces of citizens. This amendment seems to support the right of citizens to own firearms, but the Supreme Court has ruled that it does not prevent Congress from regulating the interstate sale of weapons. *Why is the Second Amendment's meaning debated?*

Amendment 5

Rights of Accused Persons This amendment contains important protections for people accused of crimes. One of the protections is that government may not deprive any person of life, liberty, or property without due process of law. This means that the government must follow proper constitutional procedures in trials and in other actions it takes against individuals. *According to Amendment V, what is the function of a grand jury?*

Vocabulary

quarter: *to provide living accommodations*
probable cause: *police must have a reasonable basis to believe a person is linked to a crime*
warrant: *document that gives police particular rights or powers*
common law: *law established by previous court decisions*
bail: *money that an accused person provides to the court as a guarantee that he or she will be present for a trial*

Amendment I

Congress shall make no law respecting an establishment of religion, or prohibiting the free exercise thereof; or abridging the freedom of speech, or of the press; or the right of the people peaceably to assemble, and to petition the Government for a redress of grievances.

Amendment II

A well regulated Militia, being necessary to the security of a free State, the right of the people to keep and bear Arms, shall not be infringed.

Amendment III

No Soldier shall, in time of peace be quartered in any house, without the consent of the Owner, nor in time of war, but in a manner to be prescribed by law.

Amendment IV

The right of the people to be secure in their persons, houses, papers, and effects, against unreasonable searches and seizures, shall not be violated, and no Warrants shall issue, but upon probable cause, supported by Oath or affirmation, and particularly describing the place to be searched, and the persons or things to be seized.

Amendment V

No person shall be held to answer for a capital, or otherwise infamous crime, unless on a presentment or indictment of a Grand Jury, except in cases arising in the land or naval forces, or in the Militia, when in actual service in time of War or public danger; nor shall any person be subject for the same offence to be twice put in jeopardy of life or limb; nor shall be compelled in any criminal case to be a witness against himself, nor be deprived of life, liberty, or property, without due process of law; nor shall private property be taken for public use without just compensation.

Amendment VI

In all criminal prosecutions, the accused shall enjoy the right to a speedy and public trial, by an impartial jury of the State and district wherein the crime shall have been committed, which district shall have been previously ascertained by law, and to be informed of the nature and cause of the accusation; to be confronted with the witnesses against him; to have compulsory process for obtaining Witnesses in his favor, and to have the assistance of counsel for his defence.

Amendment 6
Right to a Speedy, Fair Trial A basic protection is the right to a speedy, public trial. The jury must hear witnesses and evidence on both sides before deciding the guilt or innocence of a person charged with a crime. This amendment also provides that legal counsel must be provided to a defendant. In 1963, the Supreme Court ruled, in *Gideon* v. *Wainwright*, that if a defendant cannot afford a lawyer, the government must provide one to defend him or her. *Why is the right to a "speedy" trial important?*

Amendment VII

In Suits at common law, where the value in controversy shall exceed twenty dollars, the right of trial by jury shall be preserved, and no fact tried by a jury, shall be otherwise reexamined in any Court of the United States, than according to the rules of common law.

Amendment VIII

Excessive bail shall not be required, nor excessive fines imposed, nor cruel and unusual punishments inflicted.

Amendment IX

The enumeration in the Constitution, of certain rights, shall not be construed to deny or disparage others retained by the people.

Amendment 9
Powers Reserved to the People This amendment prevents government from claiming that the only rights people have are those listed in the Bill of Rights.

Amendment X

The powers not delegated to the United States by the Constitution, nor prohibited by it to the States, are reserved to the States respectively, or to the people.

Amendment 10
Powers Reserved to the States The final amendment of the Bill of Rights protects the states and the people from an all-powerful federal government. It establishes that powers not given to the national government—or denied to the states—by the Constitution belong to the states or to the people.

Amendment XI

The Judicial power of the United States shall not be construed to extend to any suit in law or equity, commenced or prosecuted against one of the United States by Citizens of another State, or by Citizens or Subjects of any Foreign State.

Amendment 11
Suits Against States The Eleventh Amendment (1795) limits the jurisdiction of the federal courts. The Supreme Court had ruled that a federal court could try a lawsuit brought by citizens of South Carolina against the state of Georgia. This case, *Chisholm* v. *Georgia*, decided in 1793, raised a storm of protest, leading to passage of the Eleventh Amendment.

Amendment 12

Election of President and Vice President The Twelfth Amendment (1804) corrects a problem that had arisen in the method of electing the president and vice president. This amendment provides for the Electoral College to use separate ballots in voting for president and vice president. *If no candidate receives a majority of the electoral votes, who elects the president?*

Ballot and ballot marker

Amendment 13

Abolition of Slavery Amendments Thirteen (1865), Fourteen (1868), and Fifteen (1870) often are called the Civil War amendments because they grew out of that great conflict. The Thirteenth Amendment outlaws slavery.

Vocabulary

majority: *more than half*
devolve: *to pass on*
abridge: *to reduce*
insurrection: *rebellion against the government*
emancipation: *freedom from slavery*

Amendment XII

The electors shall meet in their respective states and vote by ballot for President and Vice-President, one of whom, at least, shall not be an inhabitant of the same state with themselves; they shall name in their ballots the person voted for as President, and in distinct ballots the person voted for as Vice-President, and they shall make distinct lists of all persons voted for as President, and of all persons voted for as Vice-President, and of the number of votes for each, which lists they shall sign and certify, and transmit sealed to the seat of the government of the United States, directed to the President of the Senate;—The President of the Senate shall, in the presence of the Senate and House of Representatives, open all the certificates and the votes shall then be counted;—The person having the greatest number of votes for President, shall be the President, if such number be a majority of the whole number of Electors appointed; and if no person have such majority, then from the persons having the highest numbers not exceeding three on the list of those voted for as President, the House of Representatives shall choose immediately, by ballot, the President. But in choosing the President, the votes shall be taken by states, the representation from each state having one vote; a quorum for this purpose shall consist of a member or members from two-thirds of the states, and a majority of all the states shall be necessary to a choice. And if the House of Representatives shall not choose a President whenever the right of choice shall devolve upon them, before the fourth day of March next following, then the Vice-President shall act as President, as in the case of the death or other constitutional disability of the President. The person having the greatest number of votes as Vice-President, shall be the Vice-President, if such number be a majority of the whole number of Electors appointed, and if no person have a majority, then from the two highest numbers on the list, the Senate shall choose the Vice-President; a quorum for the purpose shall consist of two-thirds of the whole number of Senators, and a majority of the whole number shall be necessary to a choice. But no person constitutionally ineligible to the office of President shall be eligible to that of Vice-President of the United States.

Amendment XIII

Section 1

Neither slavery nor involuntary servitude, except as a punishment for crime whereof the party shall have been duly convicted, shall exist within the United States, or any place subject to their jurisdiction.

Section 2

Congress shall have power to enforce this article by appropriate legislation.

Amendment XIV

Section 1

All persons born or naturalized in the United States, and subject to the jurisdiction thereof, are citizens of the United States and of the State wherein they reside. No State shall make or enforce any law which shall abridge the privileges or immunities of citizens of the United States; nor shall any State deprive any person of life, liberty, or property, without due process of law; nor deny to any person within its jurisdiction the equal protection of the laws.

> **Amendment 14**
> **Rights of Citizens** The Fourteenth Amendment (1868) originally was intended to protect the legal rights of the freed slaves. Today it protects the rights of citizenship in general by prohibiting a state from depriving any person of life, liberty, or property without "due process of law." In addition, it states that all citizens have the right to equal protection of the law in all states.

Section 2

Representatives shall be apportioned among the several States according to their respective numbers, counting the whole number of persons in each State, excluding Indians not taxed. But when the right to vote at any election for the choice of electors for President and Vice President of the United States, Representatives in Congress, the Executive and Judicial officers of a State, or the members of the Legislature thereof, is denied to any of the male inhabitants of such State, being twenty-one years of age, and citizens of the United States, or in any way abridged, except for participation in rebellion, or other crime, the basis of representation therein shall be reduced in the proportion which the number of such male citizens shall bear to the whole number of male citizens twenty-one years of age in such State.

> **Amendment 14. Section 2**
> **Representation in Congress** This section reduced the number of members a state had in the House of Representatives if it denied its citizens the right to vote. Later civil rights laws and the Twenty-Fourth Amendment guaranteed the vote to African Americans.

Section 3

No person shall be a Senator or Representative in Congress, or elector of President and Vice President, or hold any office, civil or military, under the United States, or under any State, who, having previously taken an oath, as a member of Congress, or as an officer of the United States, or as a member of any State legislature, or as an executive or judicial officer of any State, to support the Constitution of the United States, shall have engaged in insurrection or rebellion against the same, or given aid or comfort to the enemies thereof. But Congress may by a vote of two-thirds of each House, remove such disability.

> **Amendment 14. Section 3**
> **Penalty for Engaging in Insurrection** The leaders of the Confederacy were barred from state or federal offices unless Congress agreed to remove this ban. By the end of Reconstruction all but a few Confederate leaders were allowed to return to public life.

Section 4

The validity of the public debt of the United States, authorized by law, including debts incurred for payment of pensions and bounties for service in suppressing insurrection or rebellion, shall not be questioned. But neither the United States nor any State shall assume or pay any debt or obligation incurred in aid of insurrection or rebellion against the United States, or any claim for the loss or emancipation of any slave; but all such debts, obligations and claims shall be held illegal and void.

> **Amendment 14. Section 4**
> **Public Debt** The public debt acquired by the federal government during the Civil War was valid and could not be questioned by the South. However, the debts of the Confederacy were declared to be illegal. *Could former slaveholders collect payment for the loss of their slaves?*

Amendment 15

Right to Vote The Fifteenth Amendment (1870) prohibits the government from denying a person's right to vote on the basis of race. Despite the law, many states denied African Americans the right to vote by such means as poll taxes, literacy tests, and white primaries. During the 1950s and 1960s, Congress passed successively stronger laws to end racial discrimination in voting rights.

Internal Revenue Service

Amendment 17

Direct Election of Senators The Seventeenth Amendment (1913) states that the people, instead of state legislatures, elect United States senators. *How many years are in a Senate term?*

Vocabulary

apportionment: *distribution of seats in House based on population*
vacancy: *an office or position that is unfilled or unoccupied*

Section 5

The Congress shall have power to enforce, by appropriate legislation, the provisions of this article.

Amendment XV

Section 1

The right of citizens of the United States to vote shall not be denied or abridged by the United States or by any State on account of race, color, or previous condition of servitude.

Section 2

The Congress shall have power to enforce this article by appropriate legislation.

Amendment XVI

The Congress shall have power to lay and collect taxes on incomes, from whatever source derived, without apportionment among the several States and without regard to any census or enumeration.

Amendment XVII

Section 1

The Senate of the United States shall be composed of two Senators from each State, elected by the people thereof, for six years; and each Senator shall have one vote. The electors in each State shall have the qualifications requisite for electors of the most numerous branch of the State legislatures.

Section 2

When vacancies happen in the representation of any State in the Senate, the executive authority of such State shall issue writs of election to fill such vacancies: *Provided,* That the legislature of any State may empower the executive thereof to make temporary appointments until the people fill the vacancies by election as the legislature may direct.

Section 3

This amendment shall not be so construed as to affect the election or term of any Senator chosen before it becomes valid as part of the Constitution.

Amendment XVIII

Section 1
After one year from ratification of this article, the manufacture, sale, or transportation of intoxicating liquors within, the importation thereof into, or the exportation thereof from the United States and all territory subject to the jurisdiction thereof for beverage purposes is hereby prohibited.

Section 2
The Congress and the several States shall have concurrent power to enforce this article by appropriate legislation.

Section 3
This article shall be inoperative unless it shall have been ratified as an amendment to the Constitution by the legislatures of the several States, as provided in the Constitution, within seven years from the date of the submission hereof to the States by the Congress.

Amendment XIX

Section 1
The right of citizens of the United States to vote shall not be denied or abridged by the United States or by any State on account of sex.

Section 2
Congress shall have power by appropriate legislation to enforce the provisions of this article.

Amendment XX

Section 1
The terms of the President and Vice President shall end at noon on the 20th day of January, and the terms of the Senators and Representatives at noon on the 3d day of January, of the years in which such terms would have ended if this article had not been ratified; and the terms of their successors shall then begin.

Section 2
The Congress shall assemble at least once in every year, and such meeting shall begin at noon on the 3d day of January, unless they shall by law appoint a different day.

Amendment 18
Prohibition of Alcoholic Beverages The Eighteenth Amendment (1919) prohibited the production, sale, or transportation of alcoholic beverages in the United States. Prohibition proved to be difficult to enforce. This amendment was later repealed by the Twenty-first Amendment.

Amendment 19
Woman Suffrage The Nineteenth Amendment (1920) guaranteed women the right to vote. By then women had already won the right to vote in many state elections, but the amendment put their right to vote in all state and national elections on a constitutional basis.

Amendment 20
"Lame-Duck" Amendment The Twentieth Amendment (1933) sets new dates for Congress to begin its term and for the inauguration of the president and vice president. Under the original Constitution, elected officials who retired or who had been defeated remained in office for several months. For the outgoing president, this period ran from November until March. Such outgoing officials had little influence and accomplished little, and they were called lame ducks because they were so inactive. *What date was fixed as Inauguration Day?*

Amendment 20. Section 3
Succession of President and Vice President This section provides that if the president-elect dies before taking office, the vice president-elect becomes president.

John Tyler was the first vice president to become president when a chief executive died.

Amendment 21
Repeal of Prohibition Amendment The Twenty-first Amendment (1933) repeals the Eighteenth Amendment. It is the only amendment ever passed to overturn an earlier amendment. It is also the only amendment ratified by special state conventions instead of state legislatures.

Vocabulary

president-elect: *individual who is elected president but has not yet begun serving his or her term*
District of Columbia: *site of nation's capital, occupying an area between Maryland and Virginia*

Section 3
If, at the time fixed for the beginning of the term of the President, the President elect shall have died, the Vice President elect shall become President. If a President shall not have been chosen before the time fixed for the beginning of his term, or if the President elect shall have failed to qualify, then the Vice President elect shall act as President until a President shall have qualified; and the Congress may by law provide for the case wherein neither a President elect nor a Vice President elect shall have qualified, declaring who shall then act as President, or the manner in which one who is to act shall be selected, and such person shall act accordingly until a President or Vice President shall have qualified.

Section 4
The Congress may by law provide for the case of the death of any of the persons from whom the House of Representatives may choose a President whenever the right of choice shall have devolved upon them, and for the case of the death of any of the persons from whom the Senate may choose a Vice President whenever the right of choice shall have devolved upon them.

Section 5
Sections 1 and 2 shall take effect on the 15th day of October following the ratification of this article.

Section 6
This article shall be inoperative unless it shall have been ratified as an amendment to the Constitution by the legislatures of three-fourths of the several States within seven years from the date of its submission.

Amendment XXI

Section 1
The eighteenth article of amendment to the Constitution of the United States is hereby repealed.

Section 2
The transportation or importation into any State, Territory, or possession of the United States for delivery or use therein of intoxicating liquors, in violation of the laws thereof, is hereby prohibited.

Section 3
This article shall be inoperative unless it shall have been ratified as an amendment to the Constitution by conventions in the several States, as provided in the Constitution, within seven years from the date of the submission hereof to the States by the Congress.

Amendment XXII

Section 1

No person shall be elected to the office of the President more than twice, and no person who had held the office of President, or acted as President, for more than two years of a term to which some other person was elected President shall be elected to the office of the President more than once. But this Article shall not apply to any person holding the office of President when this Article was proposed by the Congress, and shall not prevent any person who may be holding the office of President, or acting as President, during the term within which this Article becomes operative from holding the office of President or acting as President during the remainder of such term.

Section 2

This article shall be inoperative unless it shall have been ratified as an amendment to the Constitution by the legislatures of three-fourths of the several States within seven years from the date of its submission to the States by the Congress.

Amendment XXIII

Section 1

The District constituting the seat of Government of the United States shall appoint in such manner as the Congress may direct:

A number of electors of President and Vice President equal to the whole number of Senators and Representatives in Congress to which the District would be entitled if it were a State, but in no event more than the least populous State; they shall be in addition to those appointed by the States, but they shall be considered, for the purposes of the election of President and Vice President, to be electors appointed by a State; and they shall meet in the District and perform such duties as provided by the twelfth article of amendment.

Section 2

The Congress shall have power to enforce this article by appropriate legislation.

Amendment 22

Limit on Presidential Terms The Twenty-second Amendment (1951) limits presidents to a maximum of two elected terms. It was passed largely as a reaction to Franklin D. Roosevelt's election to four terms between 1933 and 1945.

Presidential campaign buttons

Amendment 23

Presidential Electors for the District of Columbia The Twenty-third Amendment (1961) allows citizens living in Washington, D.C., to vote for president and vice president, a right previously denied residents of the nation's capital. The District of Columbia now has three presidential electors, the number to which it would be entitled if it were a state.

Amendment 24

Abolition of Poll Tax The Twenty-fourth Amendment (1964) prohibits poll taxes in federal elections. Prior to the passage of this amendment, some states had used such taxes to keep low-income African Americans from voting. In 1966 the Supreme Court banned poll taxes in state elections as well.

Amendment 25

Presidential Disability and Succession The Twenty-fifth Amendment (1967) established a process for the vice president to take over leadership of the nation when a president is disabled. It also set procedures for filling a vacancy in the office of vice president.

This amendment was used in 1973, when Vice President Spiro Agnew resigned from office after being charged with accepting bribes. President Richard Nixon then appointed Gerald R. Ford as vice president in accordance with the provisions of the 25th Amendment. A year later, President Nixon resigned during the Watergate scandal and Ford became president. President Ford then had to fill the vice presidency, which he had left vacant upon assuming the presidency. He named Nelson A. Rockefeller as vice president. Thus individuals who had not been elected held both the presidency and the vice presidency. *Whom does the president inform if he or she cannot carry out the duties of the office?*

President Gerald Ford

Amendment XXIV

Section 1

The right of citizens of the United States to vote in any primary or other election for President or Vice President, for electors for President or Vice President, or for Senator or Representative in Congress, shall not be denied or abridged by the United States or any State by reason of failure to pay any poll tax or other tax.

Section 2

The Congress shall have power to enforce this article by appropriate legislation.

Amendment XXV

Section 1

In case of the removal of the President from office or his death or resignation, the Vice President shall become President.

Section 2

Whenever there is a vacancy in the office of the Vice President, the President shall nominate a Vice President who shall take the office upon confirmation by a majority vote of both Houses of Congress.

Section 3

Whenever the President transmits to the President pro tempore of the Senate and the Speaker of the House of Representatives his written declaration that he is unable to discharge the powers and duties of his office, and until he transmits to them a written declaration to the contrary, such powers and duties shall be discharged by the Vice President as Acting President.

Section 4

Whenever the Vice President and a majority of either the principal officers of the executive departments or of such other body as Congress may by law provide, transmit to the President pro tempore of the Senate and the Speaker of the House of Representatives their written declaration that the President is unable to discharge the powers and duties of his office, the Vice President shall immediately assume the power and duties of the office of Acting President.

Thereafter, when the President transmits to the President pro tempore of the Senate and the Speaker of the House of Representatives his written declaration that no inability exists, he shall resume the powers and duties of his office unless the Vice President and a majority of either the principal officers of the executive department or of such other body as Congress may by law provide, transmit within four days to the President pro tempore of the Senate and the Speaker of the House of Representatives their written declaration that the President is unable to discharge the powers and duties of his office. Thereupon Congress shall decide the issue, assembling within forty-eight hours for that purpose if not in session. If the Congress, within twenty-one days after receipt of the latter written declaration, or, if Congress is not in session, within twenty-one days after Congress is required to assemble, determines by two-thirds vote of both Houses that the President is unable to discharge the powers and duties of his office, the Vice President shall continue to discharge the same as Acting President; otherwise, the President shall resume the power and duties of his office.

Amendment XXVI

Section 1

The right of citizens of the United States, who are eighteen years of age or older, to vote shall not be denied or abridged by the United States or by any State on account of age.

Section 2

The Congress shall have power to enforce this article by appropriate legislation.

Amendment XXVII

No law, varying the compensation for the services of Senators and Representatives, shall take effect, until an election of representatives shall have intervened.

Amendment 26
Eighteen-Year-Old Vote The Twenty-sixth Amendment (1971) guarantees the right to vote to all citizens 18 years of age and older.

Amendment 27
Restraint on Congressional Salaries The Twenty-seventh Amendment (1992) makes congressional pay raises effective during the term following their passage. James Madison offered the amendment in 1789, but it was never adopted. In 1982 Gregory Watson, then a student at the University of Texas, discovered the forgotten amendment while doing research for a school paper. Watson made the amendment's passage his crusade.

Joint meeting of Congress

A Growing Nation

1789–1877

Why It Matters

After the United States declared itself independent from British rule, many countries watched to see how the young country would survive on its own. In the years that followed, the nation grew stronger. Manufacturing took on a stronger role in the economy. People moved westward across the continent in greater and greater numbers. By the end of this period, however, the nation would be almost torn apart by a civil war.

The Impact Today

The rights that Americans fought for during this period remain with us today. Many of these rights can be seen in amendments to the Constitution.

1804
• Lewis and Clark begin expedition

1838
• Cherokee forced to move west

1789
• Washington becomes first president

1825
• Erie Canal completed

The Americas

1750

1800

World

1793
• Louvre opens as public museum in Paris

1812
• Napoleon invades Russia

1821
• Peru claims independence from Spain

Boston Harbor by Robert Salmon Salmon recorded the emerging cities and harbors of the young nation.

1848
• Seneca Falls convention

1852
• *Uncle Tom's Cabin* published

1861
• Civil War begins

1877
• Reconstruction ends

1850   *1900*

1843
• Charles Dickens writes "A Christmas Carol"

1848
• Marx publishes *The Communist Manifesto*

1863
• French troops occupy Mexico City

1882
• Beginning of British occupation of Egypt

HISTORY Online

Chapter Overview
Visit taj.glencoe.com and click on **Prologue Chapter 2— Chapter Overviews** to review chapter information.

The New Republic

Guide to Reading

Main Idea
The young government faced many challenges, but was successful in establishing peace and order.

Key Terms
precedent, cabinet, implied powers, judicial review

Reading Strategy
Comparing As you read the section, re-create the diagram below and compare the Federalists to the Democratic-Republicans by describing qualities of each party.

Federalists	Democratic-Republicans

Read to Learn
• what actions Washington and Congress took to launch the new government.
• what events defined the Jefferson Era.

Section Theme
Government and Democracy The Constitution assured that democracy would flower in the new United States.

Preview of Events

◆1775   ◆1800

1789
Washington takes oath of office

1795
Treaty of Greenville is signed

1797
John Adams becomes president

1803
Senate ratifies Louisiana Purchase treaty

AN American Story

Celebrations erupted in the streets of Philadelphia, New York, Boston, and Charleston in 1789. News about the Constitution's ratification was greeted with relief and enthusiasm. All that was needed now was a leader to guide the new nation.

On April 6 the new Senate counted the presidential ballots. To no one's surprise, the votes were unanimous. Senator John Langdon wrote to General George Washington: "Sir I have the honor to transmit to Your Excellency the information of your unanimous election to the office of President of the United States of America."

A New Nation

Washington and the new Congress made many important decisions about the structure of the government. For example, the Constitution gave Congress the power to establish departments. However, it did not specify whether the department heads would report to the president or to the Congress. These early politicians set the tone for the young republic's future. Washington knew that the precedents, or traditions, he established as the nation's first president would shape the future of the United States.

The First President

During the summer of 1789, Congress set up departments in the executive branch of government to assist the president. Washington chose the leaders of each department. The State Department handled relations with other nations, the Treasury Department dealt with financial matters, and the War Department provided for national defense.

In addition, the office of Attorney General was created by Congress to oversee the government's legal affairs, and the postmaster general ran the new postal service. Washington requested that the heads of each department and the attorney general meet with him regularly. This group of advisors became known as the cabinet.

The first Congress also created the nation's court system with the Judiciary Act of 1789. In this act, Congress established a federal court system with 13 district courts and three circuit courts. State laws would remain, but the federal courts had the power to reverse state decisions. The nation's Supreme Court served as the final authority on many issues.

Once the basic structures of the new government had been created and filled with individuals, Congress considered constitutional amendments for the promised bill of rights. Congress passed 12 amendments and the states agreed on 10 of them. In December 1791, these 10 amendments were added to the Constitution and became known as the **Bill of Rights.**

Early Challenges

Secretary of the Treasury Alexander Hamilton struggled with the nation's financial problems. Hamilton tried to find a way to strengthen the nation and improve the government's financial reputation. Hamilton called for

new national taxes. These taxes upset many Americans. In western Pennsylvania, farmers rebelled. The armed protest, called the Whiskey Rebellion, alarmed government leaders. President Washington sent 13,000 soldiers to put down the uprising.

The new government also faced other problems in the West. The Native Americans that lived between the Appalachian Mountains and the Mississippi River denied that the United States had any authority over them. On many occasions Native Americans turned to Britain and Spain for support. President Washington used negotiations with Britain and direct attacks on Native American groups to bring peace to the area.

Treaties and Neutrality

Twelve Native American nations in the Great Lakes region signed the Treaty of Greenville in 1795. The treaty opened most of Ohio to white settlement. These successes, in turn, convinced the Spanish to make peace with the United States. In Pinckney's Treaty, also signed in 1795, the Spanish gave the United States open access to the Mississippi River and promised to dismantle all Spanish forts in American territory.

Washington declined to seek a third term as president in the spring of 1796. In his farewell address Washington attacked the evils of the developing political parties in the United States and urged the nation to avoid alliances with any other nation.

Picturing **History**

Upon signing the Treaty of Greenville, 12 Native American nations received $20,000 worth of goods to share. **How did the treaty affect white settlement?**

Causes and Effects of Political Parties

Causes

- Different philosophies of government
- Conflicting interpretations of the Constitution
- Different economic and regional interests
- Disagreement over foreign affairs

Effects

- Federalists and Democratic-Republicans propose different solutions
- The two parties nominate candidates
- Political parties become a way of American life

Graphic Organizer → Skills

Thomas Jefferson and Alexander Hamilton emerged as the leaders of the two opposing parties.

Analyzing Information How did the first two political parties emerge?

The First Political Parties

Washington had criticized political parties and warned that they would divide the nation. Nevertheless, as various issues arose in the new republic, it was only natural that people would disagree about them and that people of similar views would band together.

In Washington's cabinet, Secretary of the Treasury Alexander Hamilton and Secretary of State Thomas Jefferson increasingly took opposing sides on issues.

Those who supported the policies of Hamilton wished for a vigorous federal government. These Americans, called **Federalists,** tended to support banking and shipping interests.

Jefferson's supporters began calling their party the Republicans, or the **Democratic-Republicans.** They wanted to leave as much power as possible to the state governments rather than giving more power to the national government.

One difference between Federalists and Democratic-Republicans concerned the basis of government power. Hamilton believed in implied powers, those not specifically mentioned in the Constitution. Jefferson and James Madison disagreed. They believed in a strict interpretation of the Constitution. They claimed that unless the Constitution specifically mentioned government powers in a particular area the government had no authority to act.

In the presidential election of 1796, candidates sought office for the first time as members of a party rather than as individuals. The Federalists nominated Vice President John Adams and Charles Pinckney as their candidates. The Republicans put forth former secretary of state Thomas Jefferson and Aaron Burr. In the end Adams won. He took office on March 4, 1797.

President John Adams

Along with the stress of political party disagreement, the Adams administration faced growing tension with France. Between 1798 and 1800 the new American navy fought an undeclared war with the French navy.

The threat of war with France made Americans more suspicious of immigrants from other countries. Federalists in Congress responded with strict laws to protect the nation's security and punish those who spoke out against the government's actions. These measures were known as the **Alien and Sedition Acts.** Federalists used the laws to silence opposition.

For some Americans, fears of a strong central government abusing its power seemed to be coming true. The Democratic-Republicans looked to the states to protect the people's freedoms and fight what they regarded as Federalist tyranny.

Caught up in this political turmoil, President Adams refused to rush to war with France. He appointed a commission that sought peace with France. In 1800 the French agreed to stop attacks on American ships. Even though he had successfully avoided war, Adam's actions divided the Federalists and hurt his chances for re-election.

✓ **Reading Check** **Identifying** Which political party was led by Alexander Hamilton?

NATIONAL GEOGRAPHIC

The Louisiana Purchase and Western Exploration

Fort Clatsop · Lewis and Clark, 1805 · BRITISH · Lewis, 1806 · Fort Mandan · Lake Superior · ME. (Part of MASS.) · Pike, 1805–1806 · VT. · N.H. · MASS.

OREGON COUNTRY · Clark, 1806 · Lake Michigan · Lake Huron · Lake Ontario · N.Y. · R.I. 40°N · CONN.

ROCKY MTS. · Lewis and Clark, 1804 · MICHIGAN TERR. · Lake Erie · PA. · N.J. · DEL.

Great Salt Lake · Platte R. · Missouri R. · OHIO · Ohio · MD.

Pikes Peak · Mississippi R. · INDIANA TERR. · St. Louis · VA.

PACIFIC OCEAN · SPANISH · Colorado R. · LOUISIANA TERR. · Pike, 1806 · KY. · TENN. · N.C. · ATLANTIC OCEAN

Santa Fe · Arkansas R. · S.C. · 30°N

0 300 miles
0 300 kilometers
Azimuthal Equidistant projection

Boundary in Dispute, 1803–1819 · Red R. · MISSISSIPPI TERR. · GA.

Pike, 1807 · Rio Grande · New Orleans · SPANISH · 110°W · Disputed between U.S. and Spain, 1803–1819 · Gulf of Mexico · 90°W · TROPIC OF CANCER

Legend:
- ← Lewis and Clark
- ← Return trip
- ← Pike
- ■ Fort

The Jefferson Era

The Federalist and Democratic-Republican parties fought a bitter election campaign in 1800. Federalists supported President Adams and Charles Pinckney for a second term. The Democratic-Republicans again nominated Jefferson and Burr.

The Democratic-Republicans Take Power

When members of the Electoral College voted, Jefferson and Burr each received 73 votes. The House of Representatives had to decide the election. The Federalists worked for 35 ballots to prevent the election of Jefferson, but finally, at Hamilton's urging, Jefferson became president by a single vote.

When Jefferson entered office, he aimed to reduce the big federal government, protect individual liberties, and reduce the national debt of $83 million. The entire federal government in 1801 consisted of only a few hundred people, and some of those were part-time workers. This

Geography *Skills*

The purchase of the Louisiana Territory doubled the size of the United States. Americans quickly set out to explore the region and lands farther west.

1. **Place** What geographical barrier did Lewis and Clark have to cross in order to reach the Pacific Ocean?
2. **Region** What rivers flowed through the Louisiana Territory?

was exactly how Jefferson thought it should be. In his view the responsibilities of government should be limited to delivering the mail, collecting taxes on foreign imports, and conducting a census every 10 years.

Jefferson and the Courts

Jefferson hoped that some Federalists would support his policies. However, bitter feelings between the parties continued during his administration. Much of the ill will resulted from a disagreement between Jefferson and the Supreme Court.

Chief Justice **John Marshall,** a Federalist, made the Court an equal partner in government. He did this by declaring that the Supreme Court could review the actions of the executive and legislative branches. This power of judicial review has become a basic part of the system of checks and balances of our government today. Under Marshall the Court usually upheld the power of the national government over the rights of the states.

The Louisiana Purchase

In 1802 France needed money to continue financing its ongoing war with the British Empire. Consequently, French leader Napoleon Bonaparte agreed to sell the large **Louisiana Territory** that stretched west of the Mississippi River. Previously owned by Spain, France had acquired the territory just that year in a secret deal.

Jefferson's administration could not resist the opportunity to expand the country. The Louisiana Purchase would provide cheap and abundant land for farmers for generations to come. The Senate approved the sale in October 1803 and the size of the United States doubled.

Lewis and Clark

Even before the Louisiana Purchase was complete, Jefferson persuaded Congress to sponsor an expedition to explore the new territory and chart its geography.

In the spring of 1804 **Meriwether Lewis** and **William Clark** led an exploration crew of expert river men, gunsmiths, carpenters, scouts, and a cook. Interpreters also came along to help negotiate with Native Americans they met along the way. Lewis and Clark kept a journal of their voyage, making valuable notes on what they saw and did.

Jefferson instructed the explorers to find a route across the Rocky Mountains to the Pacific Ocean. They were also to learn as much as they could about the Native Americans who lived in the new territory and to treat them "in the most friendly and conciliatory manner." They were assisted in this effort by a young Shoshone woman named **Sacagawea** (SA•kuh•juh•WEE•uh). Married to one of the guides, she served as an interpreter and helped the explorers survive.

After 18 months and nearly 4,000 miles, Lewis and Clark reached the Pacific Ocean in November 1805. After spending the winter at the mouth of the Columbia River, they headed east on two separate routes. Both explorers arrived in St. Louis in September 1806. The expedition had collected valuable information on people, plants, animals, and the geography of the West. Perhaps most important, the journey gave hope to a nation of people eager to move westward.

✓ Reading Check **Evaluating** What was John Marshall's greatest contribution as Chief Justice?

SECTION 1 ASSESSMENT

Checking for Understanding

1. **Key Terms** Write a short paragraph in which you use the following key terms: precedent, cabinet, implied powers, judicial review
2. **Reviewing Facts** Who established the cabinet and what was its purpose?

Reviewing Themes

3. **Government and Democracy** How did the Supreme Court affect the balance of power between the state and federal government?

Critical Thinking

4. **Drawing Conclusions** Why might some Americans fear a strong central government in the newly formed United States?
5. **Organizing Information** Re-create the diagram below and describe the benefits of acquiring the Louisiana Territory in 1803.

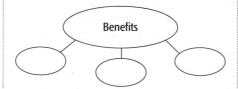

Benefits

Analyzing Visuals

6. **Geography Skills** Review the map on page 77. What was the farthest western point that the Lewis and Clark expedition reached? What is the straight-line distance between St. Louis and Pikes Peak?

Interdisciplinary Activity

Descriptive Writing Accurate descriptions and drawings in their journals made Lewis and Clark's observations valuable. Find an example of plants or animals that you can find in the area around where you live. Carefully draw and describe what you see.

SECTION 2

The Nation's New Challenges

Guide to Reading

Main Idea
The United States quickly expanded across the continent while its economy grew rapidly.

Key Terms
Industrial Revolution, cotton gin, sectionalism, favorite son, tariffs, secede, Manifest Destiny, annex

Reading Strategy
Identifying Central Issues As you read the section, re-create the diagram below and describe three ways in which the nation changed during this period.

Changes

Read to Learn
• how the Industrial Revolution affected the United States.
• how the idea of Manifest Destiny contributed to the growth of the United States.

Section Theme
Economic Factors Industrialization in the North and slave labor in the South led to rapid growth in the American economy.

Preview of Events

♦1800	♦1825	♦1850

1812
U.S. declares war on Britain

1820
Missouri Compromise passed

1823
Monroe Doctrine issued

1845
U.S. annexes Texas

AN American Story

In 1801 Washington, D.C., was slowly rising from a swampy site on the Potomac River. The nation's new capital had only two noteworthy buildings—the president's mansion (later called the White House) and the still-unfinished Capitol. Between them stretched a mile and a half of muddy streets on which pigs and chickens roamed freely.

Very few people liked being in Washington. It was hot and steamy in the summer, and the river and swamps were a breeding ground for mosquitoes. Abigail Adams called the new capital "the very dirtiest hole."

Conflict With Europe

From the swamps of Washington to the faraway lands of China, Americans were building a new nation. In 1785 the American ship Empress of China returned to New York from China with a highly prized cargo of tea and silk. The goods sold for a fabulous profit. Soon ships from New York, Philadelphia, and especially New England were sailing regularly to China and India carrying furs and other goods.

The young United States was beginning to assert its economic independence. The presence of American merchants on the seas, however, meant that the United States would be involved in the affairs of other nations as well.

A Disastrous Trade Ban

War broke out again between France and Great Britain in the mid-1790s. The United States continued to trade with both nations, claiming it was a neutral party. Trouble began when Britain and France began to stop and search American trade vessels on the Atlantic Ocean. Angry at this interference newly re-elected President Jefferson completely banned trade with both nations.

Federalist New England, the heart of the shipping industry, complained loudly about the ban. With ships stuck in their ports, unemployment began to rise. In the South tobacco meant for

Europe rotted on the docks and cotton went unpicked. In the West the price of wheat declined, and river traffic came to a halt.

In 1808, the new president, James Madison, faced even more problems. Madison struggled to resolve difficulties with Europe. He also tried to deal with angry Native Americans who objected to American settlers in the Ohio valley.

Convinced that the Native Americans in the Ohio valley were allied with the British, an angry group of western Democratic-Republicans in Congress known as **War Hawks** pressured the president to declare war on Britain. Eventually Madison asked Congress to declare war, although Americans in the Northeast remained strongly opposed to war.

The War of 1812

The United States began preparing for war too late. The regular army consisted of fewer than 7,000 troops. The state militias numbered nearly 70,000 but were poorly trained, and many states opposed "Mr. Madison's war."

Chart Skills

1. **Analyzing Information** When did U.S. exports reach their lowest level?
2. **Determining Cause and Effect** How did the Embargo Act affect imports and exports?

Imports and Exports, 1800–1820

Nonintercourse Act
Embargo Act
Panic of 1819
War of 1812

Millions of Dollars

180
160
140
120
100
80
60
40
20

1 **Exports:** goods sold
2 **Imports:** goods purchased
3 **Balance of trade:** difference between the value of a nation's exports and its imports

1800   1805   1810   1815   1820
Year

The war took place mostly in the Northeast, along the Great Lakes, and alongside the Atlantic Coast and the Gulf of Mexico. In August of 1814, the British sailed into Chesapeake Bay and directly attacked Washington, D.C. The Capitol and the president's mansion were burned. The same year, British leaders in London decided that the war was costly and unnecessary.

The Treaty of Ghent officially ended the war in December 1814. It did not change any existing borders. Before word of the treaty had reached the United States, one final battle occurred at New Orleans. Andrew Jackson's army defeated a British invasion of the city and killed about 700 British soldiers. Jackson became a hero, even though the battle did not affect the war's outcome.

cotton gin

✔ **Reading Check** **Explaining** Why did Federalists oppose the trade ban?

Growth and Expansion

Between 1790 and 1825 three developments changed the nation. First, manufacturing took on an important role in the American economy. Second, people moved westward across the continent in larger and larger numbers. Third, the United States slowly began to seek a role in world affairs.

Economic Growth

In the mid-1700s the way goods were made began to change in Great Britain. Instead of people using hand tools, machinery began to perform some of the work. This new system of producing goods brought about so many changes that this time in history is known as the Industrial Revolution.

The Industrial Revolution began to take root in the United States around 1800, appearing first in New England. The soil was poor, and farming was difficult, but it had many streams and rivers to power the waterpower machinery that ran in factories. Most important, merchants in New England had money to invest in machinery.

American inventors such as Oliver Evans improved the steam engine and developed a mechanical flour mill. In 1793 Eli Whitney invented the cotton gin, a simple machine that quickly separated the cotton seeds from the fiber.

Agriculture Expands

Although many New Englanders went to work in factories, most Americans still lived and worked on farms. In the 1820s more than 65 percent of Americans were farmers. In the South, cotton production increased dramatically. The demand for cotton had grown steadily with the development of industrial textile mills in New England and Europe.

Southern plantation owners used enslaved workers to plant, tend, and pick the cotton. The cotton gin made it possible to clean the cotton much faster and more cheaply than by hand. Between 1790 and 1820, cotton production soared from 3,000 to more than 300,000 bales a year.

Westward Bound

In 1790 the United States population was nearly 4 million. Most Americans lived east of the Appalachian Mountains and within a few hundred miles of the Atlantic coast. By 1820 the population of the country had reached about 10 million, with nearly 2 million living west of the Appalachians.

The nation needed good inland roads for travel and for the shipment of goods to and from seaports. Private companies built many roads and charged fees to help recover construction costs. When Ohio joined the Union in 1803, it asked the federal government to build a road to connect it with the East. In 1806 Congress approved funds for a **National Road** to the West.

Americans moved westward in waves. The first wave began before the 1790s and led to the admission of four new states between 1791 and 1803-Vermont, Kentucky, Tennessee, and Ohio. During the next 13 years, only one new state, Louisiana, entered the Union.

The westward movement slowed during the War of 1812. After the war, however, a second

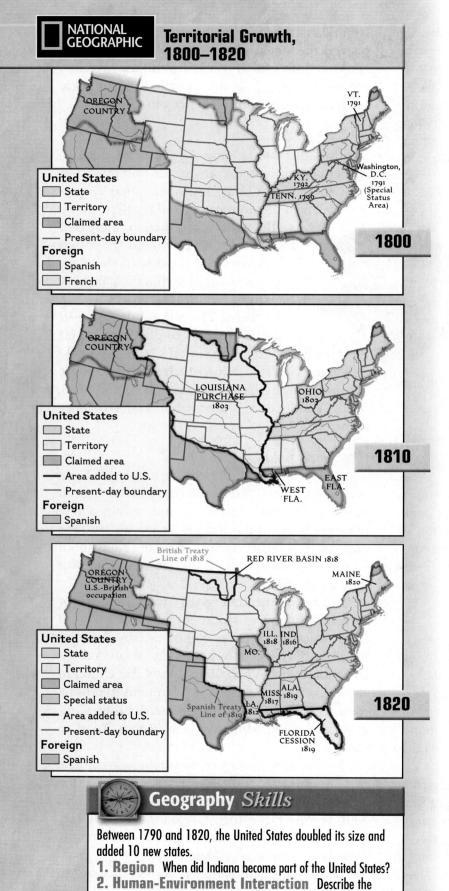

United States
- State
- Territory
- Claimed area
- — Present-day boundary

Foreign
- Spanish
- French

1800

OREGON COUNTRY

VT. 1791

KY. 1792

TENN. 1796

Washington, D.C. 1791 (Special Status Area)

United States
- State
- Territory
- Claimed area
- — Area added to U.S.
- — Present-day boundary

Foreign
- Spanish

1810

OREGON COUNTRY

LOUISIANA PURCHASE 1803

OHIO 1803

WEST FLA.

EAST FLA.

United States
- State
- Territory
- Claimed area
- Special status
- — Area added to U.S.
- — Present-day boundary

Foreign
- Spanish

1820

British Treaty Line of 1818

RED RIVER BASIN 1818

OREGON COUNTRY U.S.-British occupation

MAINE 1820

ILL. 1818

IND. 1816

MO.

ALA. 1819

MISS. 1817

LA. 1812

Spanish Treaty Line of 1819

FLORIDA CESSION 1819

Geography Skills

Between 1790 and 1820, the United States doubled its size and added 10 new states.

1. Region When did Indiana become part of the United States?

2. Human-Environment Interaction Describe the changes in French territory between 1800 and 1820.

wave of westward growth began. Between 1816 and 1821, five new western states were created—Indiana, Illinois, Mississippi, Alabama, and Missouri.

Unity and Sectionalism

The nation expanded economically and geographically during James Monroe's presidency, a period called the **Era of Good Feelings.** However, political cooperation began to decline as Americans began supporting the region where they lived. This regional loyalty, or sectionalism, became more intense as differences arose over national policies.

Sectional tension reached new heights in 1820 over the issue of slavery and how to admit new states to the Union. The South wanted Missouri, part of the Louisiana Purchase, admitted as a slave state. Northerners wanted Missouri to be free of slavery. The issue became the subject of debate throughout the country, exposing bitter regional disagreements.

Eventually Speaker of the House Henry Clay helped work out a compromise that preserved the balance between North and South. The **Missouri Compromise,** reached in March 1820, provided for the admission of Missouri as a slave state and Maine as a free state. The agreement banned slavery in the remainder of the Louisiana Territory north of the 36° 30′ N parallel. The question was settled, but only temporarily.

The Supreme Court

The Supreme Court also became involved in sectional and states' rights issues at this time. The state of Maryland imposed a tax on the Baltimore branch of the Second Bank of the United States—a federal institution. The Bank refused to pay the state tax, and the case reached the Court in 1819. In *McCulloch* v. *Maryland,* the Supreme Court ruled that since the Bank was a creation of the federal government, the state had no right to interfere with it.

Jackson campaign poster

Election of 1824			
Candidate	Electoral Vote	Popular Vote	House Vote
Jackson	99	153,544	7
Adams	84	108,740	13
Crawford	41	46,618	4
Clay	37	47,136	—

Chart Skills

The presidential election of 1824 was decided in the House of Representatives.

Analyzing Information Which candidate received the most electoral votes?

The Supreme Court's ruling strengthened the national government. It also contributed to the debate over sectional issues. People who supported states' rights believed the decision was a threat to individual liberties. Strong nationalists welcomed the decision's support for national power.

The Monroe Doctrine

In the 1820s Spain began having trouble with their colonies in the Western Hemisphere. All throughout Spain's colonial empire—which stretched from the southwestern United States, through Mexico, Central America, and most of South America—struggles for independence were breaking out.

In 1822 Spain turned to France, Austria, Russia, and Prussia for help in its fight against revolutionary forces in South America. The possibility of increased European involvement in North America led President Monroe to issue a statement, later known as the **Monroe Doctrine.**

In 1823 Monroe declared that while the United States would not interfere with any existing European colonies in the Americas, it would oppose any new ones. North and South America "are henceforth not be considered as subjects for future colonization by any European powers."

In 1823, the United States did not have the military power to enforce the Monroe Doctrine. Nevertheless, it became an important element in American foreign policy.

✓ **Reading Check** **Summarizing** What two factors allowed Southern plantations to be so productive?

The Jackson Era

A struggle for political rights took shape in the 1820s and 1830s, when many people questioned the limits of American democracy. From 1816 to 1824, the United States had only one political party—the Democratic-Republicans. However, within the party, differences had arisen among various groups with their own views and interests.

From Adams to Jackson

In 1824 James Monroe was finishing his second term as president. Following the example of earlier presidents, Monroe declined to run for a third term. Four candidates from the Democratic-Republican Party competed for the presidency.

The four candidates' opinions differed on the role of the federal government. They also spoke for different areas of the country. The party nominated William H. Crawford, from Georgia.

The other three Democratic-Republicans in the presidential race were favorite son candidates, meaning they received the backing of their home states rather than that of the national party. Henry Clay of Kentucky was Speaker of the House of Representatives. Clay fought for continued improvements of the country's transportation system, high taxes on imports, and a stronger national bank.

General Andrew Jackson of Tennessee was a hero of the War of 1812. Raised in poverty, Jackson claimed to speak for the Americans who had been left out of politics. His supporters included farmers in the South, settlers in the West, and laborers in the Eastern cities.

John Quincy Adams of Massachusetts, son of former president John Adams, received support from Northeastern merchants. Adams believed that the federal government should shift the nation's economy to manufacturing.

In the election no one received more than half of the electoral votes, so according to the **Twelfth Amendment,** the House of Representatives selected the president. With the help of Henry Clay, Adams received enough votes in the House to become president. Adams named Clay as his secretary of state. Jackson's followers accused the two men of making a "corrupt bargain" and stealing the election.

The Election of 1828

In 1828 Andrew Jackson tried again for the presidency, but by this time the party had divided into two separate parties: the Democratic-Republicans who supported Jackson and the National Republicans who supported Adams. Jackson's supporters, commonly called Democrats, favored states' rights and mistrusted strong central government.

After a bitter campaign, Jackson received most of the votes of the new frontier states while also receiving many votes from the South. Jackson defeated Adams in a landslide victory. He tallied 56 percent of the popular vote and 178 of 261 electoral votes.

Upon taking office, President Jackson promised "equal protection and equal benefits" for all Americans—at least for all white American men. During his first term, a spirit of equality and flourishing democracy spread through American politics.

Between 1824 and 1828, the percentage of white males voting in presidential elections increased from 36.9 to 57.6 percent. By 1828, 22 of the 24 states had also changed their constitutions to allow the people, rather than the state legislatures, to choose presidential electors.

Trail of Tears

The Tariff Debate

One of the most dividing issues in American politics was the use of tariffs, fees paid by merchants who imported goods. While northeastern manufacturers believed tariffs made American-made goods seem more affordable, Southerners hated tariffs. The South traded cotton to Europe for manufactured goods, and the new tariff made these items more expensive.

Southern politicians and plantation owners were so outraged by the rise of high tariffs during the 1820s and 1830s that some threatened to secede, or break away, from the United States and form their own government.

Jackson supported a congressional bill that lowered the tariff, while simultaneously persuading Congress to pass a bill that allowed him to use the military to enforce acts of Congress. The message was clear: If the South did not calm itself, it would face the army.

For a time, a crisis was avoided. Yet the South would remember this lesson—that the federal government would not allow a state to go its own way without a fight.

Conflicts Over Land

The United States had expanded westward by the 1830s, but large numbers of Native Americans still lived in the eastern part of the country. In Georgia, Alabama, Mississippi, and Florida, the Cherokee, Creek, Choctaw, Chickasaw, and Seminole held valuable lands.

In 1830 Congress passed the Indian Removal Act, which allowed the federal government to pay Native Americans to move west. Most agreed to move, and in 1834 Congress created the Indian Territory in present-day Oklahoma for Native Americans from the Southeast.

Sometimes, they did not agree to move. In 1838, Jackson ordered 7,000 federal troops to remove the Cherokee from their homes and lead them west. Brutal weather along the way claimed thousands of Cherokee lives. Their forced journey west became known to the Cherokee people as the Trail Where They Cried. Historians call it the **Trail of Tears.**

Jackson and the Bank

Another area of conflict during Jackson's time as president was the Second Bank of the United States. For years, Jackson had attacked the Bank as an organization of wealthy Easterners. The Bank held the federal government's money and controlled much of the country's money supply. Although Congress had chartered the Bank, it was run by private bankers.

In 1832 Jackson rejected a congressional bill to renew the Bank's charter for another twenty years. Most people supported this action, and Jackson was reelected in 1832 with 55 percent of the popular vote. Once re-elected, Jackson decided to "kill" the Bank by ordering the withdrawal of all government deposits from the Bank. The Bank was eventually forced to close.

✓**Reading Check** **Explaining** Why did Southern leaders oppose tariffs?

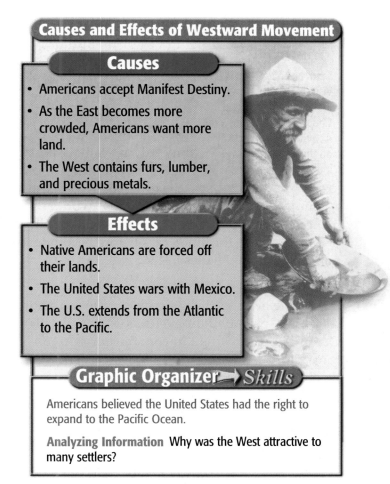

Causes and Effects of Westward Movement

Causes

- Americans accept Manifest Destiny.
- As the East becomes more crowded, Americans want more land.
- The West contains furs, lumber, and precious metals.

Effects

- Native Americans are forced off their lands.
- The United States wars with Mexico.
- The U.S. extends from the Atlantic to the Pacific.

Graphic Organizer *Skills*

Americans believed the United States had the right to expand to the Pacific Ocean.

Analyzing Information Why was the West attractive to many settlers?

Manifest Destiny

Since colonial times many Americans had believed their nation had a special role to fulfill. In the 1800s that mission seemed to be spreading freedom by occupying the entire continent. In the 1840s that mission was described as a "Manifest Destiny to overspread and to possess the whole of the continent which Providence has given us." This meant that the United States was clearly destined—set apart for a special purpose—to expand all the way to the Pacific.

The Oregon Country

A large northwestern part of the continent was called the Oregon country. For twenty years, Great Britain and the United States claimed and settled the area peacefully. However, Americans began to settle there in increasing numbers.

Democrat James Polk won the presidency in 1844, partly because he supported American claims to Oregon. Democrats campaigned using the slogan **"Fifty-four Forty or Fight,"** referring to the line of latitude that Democrats believed should be the nation's northern border in Oregon. In 1846, the two nations compromised and set the boundary between the United States and Canada at latitude 49°.

Independence for Texas

Manifest Destiny also demonstrated itself in the Southwest during the 1830s. Present-day Texas was once a possession of Spain. When Mexico won its independence from Spain in the 1820s, it assumed control of the Texas territory. Mexican leaders hoped to attract settlers to Texas by offering large tracts of land at low prices and postponing taxes for four years. In return, colonists agreed to obey Mexican law, convert to Catholicism, and learn Spanish. By 1830 Americans in Texas far outnumbered Mexicans. Further, these American settlers had not adopted Mexican ways.

Student Web Activity
Visit taj.glencoe.com
and click on **Prologue
Chapter 2—Student Web
Activities** for an activity
on the fight for Texas
independence.

When Mexico tried to assert its authority, American settlers called for independence. The American settlers fought the Mexican Army in several battles, most famously at a catholic mission named the Alamo. Despite losing at the Alamo, the Americans eventually won and gained their independence in 1836. The Republic of Texas existed for nine years before becoming part of the United States in 1845.

New Mexico and California

The Mexican territories of New Mexico and California extended from Texas to the Pacific Ocean and up to the Oregon Territory. Americans with the idea of Manifest Destiny viewed this land as valuable.

Shippers and manufacturers hoped to build ports on California's Pacific coast for trade with China and Japan. Polk twice offered to buy California and New Mexico from Mexico, but Mexico refused. Before long the United States would take over both regions by force.

War with Mexico

Relations between Mexico and the United States had been strained for some years. When the United States annexed, or took control of, Texas in 1845, the situation worsened. Mexico, which had never accepted the independence of Texas, charged that the annexation was illegal.

Words turned into blows on April 24, 1846, when Mexican soldiers attacked a small force of American soldiers. Polk's government decided that the attack was grounds for war with Mexico. Although Polk had clearly provoked the Mexicans, Americans felt justified by Manifest Destiny. Congress passed a declaration of war against Mexico. American forces quickly defeated the Mexican army and claimed New Mexico and California as part of the United States.

The United States lost over 12,000 men to war and disease, but Mexico losses were far greater. Mexico lost more than half its territory in the war.

In the peace treaty Mexico gave up all claims to Texas, surrendered New Mexico and California, and agreed to the Rio Grande River as the border between the two nations. In 1853 the United States paid Mexico an additional $10 million for a strip of land along the southern edge of present-day Arizona and New Mexico. With this, the United States mainland reached its present size. All that remained was to settle the newly acquired territories.

Reading Check **Identifying** What slogan was identified with the Oregon country?

SECTION 2 ASSESSMENT

Checking for Understanding

1. **Key Terms** Use each of these terms in a complete sentence that will help explain its meaning: Industrial Revolution, cotton gin, sectionalism, favorite son, tariffs, secede, Manifest Destiny, annex

2. **Reviewing Facts** Why did Southerners not like tariffs?

Reviewing Themes

3. **Economic Factors** How did the cotton gin affect production?

Critical Thinking

4. **Analyzing Information** How did the notion of Manifest Destiny help Americans justify their desire to extend the United States to the Pacific Ocean?

5. **Organizing Information** Re-create the diagram below and list three territories that once belonged to Mexico but later became American states. Explain how they became states.

Former Territories of Mexico		
Texas	New Mexico	California

Analyzing Visuals

6. **Geography Skills** Study the map on page 82. When did Tennessee gain statehood? Which of the maps shows the territory gained from the Louisiana Purchase? In what year was Florida ceded to the United States?

Interdisciplinary Activity

Art Write a campaign slogan for one of the presidential candidates in the election of 1824. Then design a campaign button that uses your slogan.

Study & Writing
SKILLBUILDER

Analyzing Primary Sources

Why Learn This Skill?

Historians determine what happened in the past by combing through bits of evidence to reconstruct events. This evidence—both written and illustrated—is called *primary sources.* Examining primary sources can help you understand history.

Choctaw forced from their land

Learning the Skill

Primary sources are records of events made by the people who witnessed them. They include letters, diaries, photographs and pictures, news articles, and legal documents. To analyze primary sources, follow these steps:

• Identify when and where the document was written.
• Read the document for its content and try to answer the five "W" questions: Who is it about? What is it about? When did it happen? Where did it happen? Why did it happen?
• Identify the author's opinions.

Practicing the Skill

The primary source that follows comes from Speckled Snake, an elder of the Creek Nation, in 1829. He was more than 100 years old at the time he said these words. Read the quote, then answer the questions that follow.

❝Brothers! I have listened to many talks from our Great Father. When he first came over the wide waters, he was but a little man. . . . But when the white man had warmed himself before the Indians' fire and filled himself with their hominy, he became very large. With a step he bestrode the mountains and his feet covered the plains and the valleys. His hand grasped the eastern and the western sea, and his head rested on the moon. Then he became our Great Father. Brothers, I have listened to a great many talks from our Great Father. But they always began and ended in this—'Get a little further; you are too near me.'❞

❶ What events are described?

❷ Who was affected by these events?

❸ What is the general feeling of the person who stated this opinion?

Applying the Skill

Analyzing Primary Sources Find a primary source from your past—a photograph, a report card, an old newspaper clipping, or your first baseball card. Bring this source to class and explain what it shows about that time in your life.

GO TO Glencoe's **Skillbuilder Interactive Workbook CD-ROM, Level 1,** provides instruction and practice in key social studies skills.

Sectionalism and Reform

Guide to Reading

Main Idea
Great change occurred as the nation began to divide into a distinct North and South.

Key Terms
canals, yeomen, tenant farmers, utopia, abolitionists, Underground Railroad

Reading Strategy
Categorizing Information As you read the section, re-create the diagram below and describe the goals of three different reform movements.

Reform movements and their goals		
1.	2.	3.

Read to Learn
• what differences arose between the North and the South.
• how reform brought about change in the mid-1800s.

Section Theme
Culture and Traditions Many reform movements throughout the country changed the cultural landscape of the United States.

Preview of Events

♦1825   ♦1850

1816
American Colonization Society is formed

1833
American Antislavery Society is formed

1848
First women's rights convention held in Seneca Falls, New York

1860
U.S. population climbs to over 30 million

AN American Story

In the 1840s, telegraph wires and railroads began to cross the nation. But traveling by rail had its discomforts, as writer Charles Dickens describes: "[T]here is a great deal of jolting, a great deal of noise, a great deal of wall, not much window, a locomotive engine, a shriek, and a bell. . . . In the center of the carriage there is usually a stove . . . which is for the most part red-hot. It is insufferably close; and you see the hot air fluttering between yourself and any other object you may happen to look at, like the ghost of smoke. . . ."

North and South

In the Northern states, technology changed the way Americans worked, traveled, and communicated. By the mid-1800s, power-driven machinery performed many tasks that were once done by hand. The South, on the other hand, did not change as radically as the North. It continued to be an agricultural region. In the 1800s, sharp economic and cultural differences existed between the Northern and the Southern states. The existence of slavery in the South was the sharpest difference between the regions. Political disagreements over the spread of slavery into newly acquired lands would divide the regions over time.

The North's Economy

The industrialization of the North developed in three phases. Initially, manufacturers made products by dividing the tasks involved among the workers. During the second phase, manufacturers built factories to bring specialized workers together. In the third phase, factory workers used machinery to perform some of their work. By 1860 the Northeast's factories produced about two-thirds of the country's manufactured goods.

Improved Transportation

Improvements in transportation contributed to the success of many of America's new industries. Between 1800 and 1850, construction crews built thousands of miles of roads and canals—artificial waterways. The canals opened new shipping routes by connecting many lakes and rivers. The growth of railroads in the 1840s and 1850s produced another means to speed the flow of goods.

The North's People

As the factory system developed in the North, working conditions worsened. As the workday got longer, on-the-job accidents increased.

Workers often labored under unpleasant conditions as well. Factory owners showed more concern for profit than for the comfort and safety of their employees. They knew that they could easily replace an unhappy worker with someone else eager for a job.

Slavery had largely disappeared from the North by 1820. African Americans, however, were not treated the same as others. Most communities would not allow free African Americans to attend public schools and barred them from public facilities as well. Often African Americans were forced into separate schools and hospitals. Although better off than the enslaved people of the South, Northern African Americans still suffered the cruel and lasting effects of discrimination.

Immigration

Immigration to the United States increased dramatically between 1840 and 1860. American manufacturers welcomed the tide of immigrants, many of whom were willing to work for long hours and for low pay.

Picturing History

A clipper ship, the *Flying Cloud,* set a new record by sailing from New York to California in less than 90 days. **How did clipper ships get their name?**

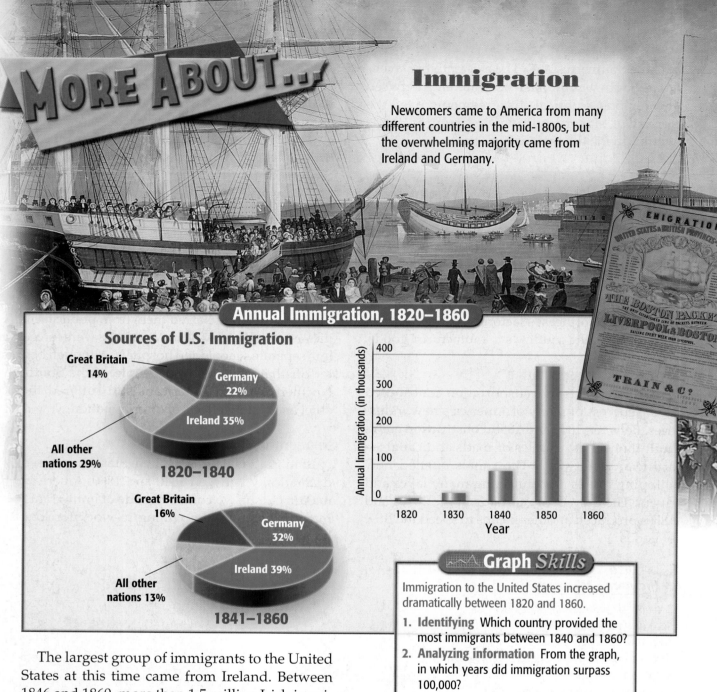

MORE ABOUT...

Immigration

Newcomers came to America from many different countries in the mid-1800s, but the overwhelming majority came from Ireland and Germany.

EMIGRATION
UNITED STATES & BRITISH PROVINCES OF N. AMERICA

THE BOSTON PACKETS,
THE ONLY ESTABLISHED LINE OF PACKETS BETWEEN
LIVERPOOL & BOSTON,
SAILING EVERY WEEK FROM LIVERPOOL.

TRAIN & C°

Annual Immigration, 1820–1860

Sources of U.S. Immigration

1820–1840
- Great Britain 14%
- Germany 22%
- Ireland 35%
- All other nations 29%

1841–1860
- Great Britain 16%
- Germany 32%
- Ireland 39%
- All other nations 13%

Annual Immigration (in thousands)

400
300
200
100
0

1820   1830   1840   1850   1860

Year

Graph Skills

Immigration to the United States increased dramatically between 1820 and 1860.

1. **Identifying** Which country provided the most immigrants between 1840 and 1860?
2. **Analyzing information** From the graph, in which years did immigration surpass 100,000?

The largest group of immigrants to the United States at this time came from Ireland. Between 1846 and 1860, more than 1.5 million Irish immigrants arrived in the country. Settling mostly in the Northeast, many Irish took low-paying factory jobs in Northern cities. The second largest group of immigrants in the United States between 1820 and 1860 came from Germany.

Southern Cotton Kingdom

The South did not receive as many immigrants as the North. This was because the southern region had developed along very different economic and social paths.

The growth of the British textile industry in the late 1700s had created a huge demand for cotton, and the cotton gin made it much easier to process the crop for shipping overseas. This made cotton very profitable.

Both the Upper South and the Deep South were agricultural, but their economies developed in different ways. The Upper South still produced tobacco, hemp, wheat, and vegetables. The Deep South was committed to cotton and, in some areas, to rice and sugarcane.

Industry never caught on in the South in the 1800s, in part because cotton growing was so profitable. Another disadvantage was the lack of money to invest in building industry. Most wealthy Southerners had their money tied up in land and slaves.

The South's People

Most white Southerners fit into one of four categories: yeomen, tenant farmers, the rural poor, or plantation owners. Yeomen—farmers who did not have slaves—made up the largest group of whites in the South. Most yeomen owned land. Although they lived throughout the nation, they were most numerous in the Upper South and in the hilly rural areas of the Deep South. Yeomen grew crops both for their own use and to sell.

Southern whites who did not own land rented it or worked as tenant farmers on landlords' estates. Others—the rural poor—lived in crude cabins in wooded areas where they could clear a few trees, plant some corn, and keep a hog or a cow. They also fished and hunted for food.

Plantations and Slavery

Plantation owners lived more comfortably than any of these other groups, though most did not live luxuriously. A small group of plantation owners—about 12 percent—held more than half of the slaves. About half of the planters held fewer than five enslaved workers.

Life for the enslaved worker on the plantation was one of hardship and misery. They worked hard, earned no money, and had little hope of freedom. In the face of these brutal conditions, enslaved African Americans maintained their family life as best they could and developed a culture all their own.

The Urban South

Although the South was primarily agricultural, it was the site of several large cities by the mid-1800s. Cities on the rise included Baltimore, Charleston, Richmond, and Memphis. The population of Southern cities included white city dwellers, some enslaved workers, and about 250,000 of the South's free African Americans.

Although some free African Americans prospered in the cities, their lives were far from secure. Between 1830 and 1860 Southern states passed laws that limited the rights of free African

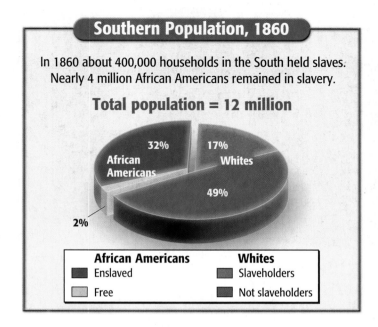

Southern Population, 1860

In 1860 about 400,000 households in the South held slaves. Nearly 4 million African Americans remained in slavery.

Total population = 12 million

32% African Americans
17% Whites
49%
2%

African Americans	Whites
■ Enslaved	■ Slaveholders
□ Free	■ Not slaveholders

Americans. Most states would not allow them to migrate from other states. Although spared the horrors of slavery, free African Americans were denied an equal share in economic and political life.

Reading Check Explaining Why was transportation important in the early 1800s?

The Age of Reform

A new reforming spirit arose in America in the early 1800s. The men and women who led the reform movement wanted to extend the nation's ideals of liberty and equality to all Americans. They believed the nation should live up to the noble goals stated in the Declaration of Independence and the Constitution.

The Reforming Spirit

The spirit of reform brought changes to American religion, politics, education, art, and literature. Some reformers sought to improve society by forming utopias, communities based on a vision of a perfect society.

In the early 1800s, a wave of religious fervor—known as the **Second Great Awakening**—stirred the nation. The Second Great Awakening increased church membership, especially among Methodists and Baptists. It also inspired people to become involved in missionary work and social reform movements.

TWO VIEWPOINTS

Is American Slavery Compassionate or Cruel?

More than any other factor, slavery isolated the South from the rest of the United States. While abolitionists cried out to bring the cruel practice to an end, Southern slaveholders defended the only way of life they knew.

Sojourner Truth, former slave, 1851

Look at me! Look at my arm! I have ploughed, and planted, and gathered into barns, and no man could head me! . . . I could work as much and eat as much as a man—when I could get it—and bear the lash as well! And ain't I a woman?

I have borne thirteen children, and seen them most all sold off to slavery, and when I cried out with my mother's grief, none but Jesus heard me! And ain't I a woman?

Sojourner Truth

Jeremiah Jeter, Southern slaveholder, c. 1820

I could not free them, for the laws of the State forbade it. Yet even if they had not forbidden it, the slaves in my possession were in no condition to support themselves. It was simple cruelty to free a mother with dependent children. Observation, too, had satisfied me that the free negroes were, in general, in a worse condition than the slaves. The manumission [setting free] of my slaves to remain in the State was not to be thought of. Should I send them to Liberia? Some of them were in a condition to go, but none of them desired to. If sent, they [would] be forced to leave wives and children belonging to other masters [on nearby plantations], to dwell in a strange land.

Learning From History

1. Why do you think Sojourner Truth was an effective speaker?
2. Why didn't Jeremiah Jeter just free his slaves?
3. Do the two excerpts contradict each other? In what way?

Reforming Education

Reformers also focused on education. They argued that the poor state of education threatened the nation's well-being. In the early 1800s, only New England states provided free elementary education.

By the 1850s, through the hard work of reformers, all states had accepted three basic principles of public education: that schools should be free and supported by taxes, that teachers should be trained, and that children should be required to attend school.

The Abolitionists

The spirit of reform in the early 1800s also included the efforts of abolitionists—members of the growing band of reformers who worked to abolish, or end, slavery.

The religious revival and the reform movements of the early and mid-1800s gave new life to the anti-slavery movement. Many Americans came to believe that slavery was wrong.

One effort to end slavery was the American Colonization Society, founded in 1816. The society planned to raise enough money to purchase land in Africa to resettle African Americans.

The American Colonization Society did not resettle African Americans as fast as the number of enslaved people increased in America. The Society could only resettle a small number at a time, and furthermore, most African Americans did not want to go. They simply wanted to be free in the country they had lived in for generations.

The Underground Railroad

Some abolitionists risked prison—even death—by secretly helping enslaved Africans escape. The network of escape routes out of the South became known as the Underground Railroad.

The Underground Railroad had no trains or tracks. Instead, passengers on this "railroad" traveled through the night, often on foot, and fled to the North. The railroad's "conductors" were whites and African Americans who helped guide the escaping slaves to freedom in the North.

Harriet Tubman escaped from slavery to become the most famous conductor on the Underground Railroad. She made many dangerous trips into the South and guided hundreds of enslaved people to freedom.

The antislavery movement led to an intense reaction against abolitionism. Southern slaveholders—and many Southerners who did not have slaves—opposed abolitionism because they believed it threatened the South's way of life.

Southerners claimed that slavery was essential to economic prosperity in the South. They also argued that they treated enslaved people well, and that for African Americans slavery was preferable to factory work in the North.

The conflict between the proslavery and antislavery groups continued to mount. At the same time, a new woman's rights movement was growing and many leading abolitionists were involved in that movement as well.

The Women's Movement

Women played a major role in all the American reform movements of the 1800s. In July 1848, Elizabeth Cady Stanton, Lucretia Mott, and a few other women organized the first women's rights convention in Seneca Falls, New York. The convention issued a Declaration of Sentiments and Resolutions modeled on the Declaration of Independence.

The women's declaration called for an end to all laws that discriminated against women. It demanded that women be allowed to enter the all-male world of trades, professions, and businesses. The most controversial issue at the Seneca Falls Convention was the demand to allow women the right to vote. The Seneca Falls Convention paved the way for the growth of the women's rights movement.

An Uncertain Future

The period of time from the 1820s to the 1860s was a time of conflict, compromise, and reform. The most pressing point of division remained the existence of slavery. Slavery would be the center of more and more arguments in the United States. This argument would eventually serve to split the nation in two.

Reading Check **Evaluating** Why was the Seneca Falls Convention important?

SECTION 3 ASSESSMENT

Checking for Understanding
1. **Key Terms** Use each of these terms in a complete sentence that will help explain its meaning: canals, yeomen, tenant farmers, utopia, abolitionists, Underground Railroad
2. **Reviewing Facts** List two differences between yeomen and plantation owners.

Reviewing Themes
3. **Culture and Traditions** Describe two goals of the women's movement.

Critical Thinking
4. **Comparing** Compare the arguments of Northerners and Southerners, for and against abolition.
5. **Comparing** Re-create the diagram below and describe how the life of a Northern industrial worker differed from a white Southern agricultural worker.

Northern worker	Southern worker

Analyzing Visuals
6. **Graph Skills** Study the graphs on page 90. What country provided about 1 of 4 immigrants to the U.S. between 1820 and 1840?

Interdisciplinary Activity

Art Design a poster to win support for the women's rights movement. Include viewpoints that will draw both men and women supporters.

SECTION 4 A Nation Divides and Reunites

AN American Story

Union sergeant Driscoll directed his troops at Malvern Hill on July 1, 1862. The enemy fought fiercely, especially one young Confederate soldier. Driscoll raised his rifle, took aim, and shot the boy. As he passed the spot where the boy had fallen, Driscoll turned the daring soldier over to see what he looked like. The boy opened his eyes and faintly murmured, "Father," then his eyes fluttered shut, never to open again. A Union captain later wrote, "I will forever recollect the frantic grief of Driscoll; it was harrowing to witness. He [had killed] his son, who had gone South before the war."

The Civil War

Like the Driscolls, many families were divided by the war. Neither side imagined, however, that the war would cost such a terrible price in human life. During the four years of fighting, hundreds of thousands of Americans were killed in battle. Division over slavery finally split the nation in 1860. During that year's

Seceding States, 1860–1861

WASHINGTON TERR.

OREGON

PACIFIC OCEAN

NEVADA TERR.

CALIF.

UTAH TERR.

DAKOTA TERR.

MINN.

WIS.

IOWA

NEBRASKA TERR.

COLORADO TERR.

KANSAS

NEW MEXICO TERR.

INDIAN TERR.

ARK.

TEXAS

LA.

MISS. ALA. GA.

MICH.

ILL. IND.

MO.

OHIO

KY.

TENN.

N.H.

VT. ME.

N.Y.

MASS.

R.I.

PA.

N.J. CONN.

W. VA. VA.

DEL.

MD.

N.C.

S.C.

FLA.

ATLANTIC OCEAN

0   500 miles
0   500 kilometers
Lambert Equal-Area projection

West Virginia seceded from Virginia in 1861 and was admitted to the Union in 1863.

On February 4, 1861, delegates met in Alabama to form a new nation.

South Carolina was the first state to secede from the Union.

Union Territories
Union free state
Union slave state
Slave state seceding before Fort Sumter, April 1861
Slave state seceding after Fort Sumter, April 1861
Boundary between Union and Confederacy

Geography *Skills*

After the attack on Fort Sumter, four more Southern states joined the seven that had already seceded from the Union.
1. **Region** Which slave states remained in the Union after the Fort Sumter attack?
2. **Analyzing Information** Which states did not secede until after the Fort Sumter attack?

presidential election, slavery divided the Democratic Party. This allowed the Republican candidate, Abraham Lincoln, to win the election.

The Republican platform tried to appeal to a wide range of Americans. It called for slavery to be left undisturbed where it existed, but for it to be excluded from the territories. This was not acceptable to most Southerners. Lincoln's name did not even appear on the ballot in most Southern states.

Secession and War

Many people in the South did not trust Lincoln and his Republican Party, fearing that the government would not protect Southern rights and slavery. On December 20, 1860, South Carolina became the first state to vote for secession—withdrawal from the union. By February 1861, Texas, Louisiana, Mississippi, Alabama, Florida, and Georgia joined South Carolina to form the Confederate States of America. They chose Jefferson Davis, a senator from Mississippi, as their president.

Fighting began when the South tried to hold federal forts. Confederate forces fired the first shots at **Fort Sumter,** a Union fort in South Carolina. When Confederate forces tried to claim Fort Sumter, a Union fort in South Carolina, they fired the first shots of the war. Thousands of cannonballs were fired at the fort, and the Civil War had begun. President Lincoln issued a call for 75,000 troops to fight to save the Union.

Choosing Sides

Virginia, North Carolina, Tennessee, and Arkansas joined the Confederacy. Border states—including Missouri, Kentucky, Maryland, and Delaware who allowed slavery—stayed with the Union. These states held many people sympathetic to the Confederacy. Likewise, some residents of Southern states opposed the secession. In 1861, 48 counties of Virginia organized themselves as a separate state called West Virginia. Congress admitted this new state to the Union in 1863.

Comparing North and South

The North enjoyed the advantages of a larger population, more industry, and more abundant resources than the South. It had a better banking system, which helped to raise money for the war. The North also possessed more ships, and almost all the members of the regular navy remained loyal to the Union. Finally, the North had a larger and more efficient railway network.

The North also faced disadvantages. Bringing the Southern states back into the Union would be difficult. The North would have to invade and hold the South—a large area filled with a hostile population. The South would also be fighting on familiar territory, defending their land, their homes, and their way of life. The South, also, had superior military leadership at the beginning of the war. Southern families had a strong tradition of military service and provided many experienced officers to the Confederate Army.

America's Bloodiest War

When the war began, each side expected an early victory. Each was very wrong. By the end of the war 850,000 men fought for the Confederacy. 2.1 million fought for the Union. The war lasted

Picturing **History**

Some paintings offered an idealized picture of the Civil War. Photographs provided a chilling account of life–and death–at the front lines. **In what ways might photographs have affected Americans' view of the war in a way that paintings did not?**

more than four years and was the most devastating conflict in American history.

Early Battles

Early battles were sobering for the nation. The first major battle of the war, the **First Battle of Bull Run** outside of Washington, D.C., resulted in a Southern victory. The North was shocked. Lincoln ordered one million more soldiers.

The war raged across the country, from the waters off of the East Coast to the western United States. Two ironclad warships—steam-powered, wooden ships covered in iron plates—fought each other for the first time off the coast of Virginia. The Union *Merrimack* and the Confederate *Monitor* fought each other to a stalemate because neither could sink the other.

The Battle of Shiloh raged in Tennessee, causing more than 20,000 casualties—people killed or wounded. The city of New Orleans fell to Union forces, giving the North control of most of the Mississippi River. The Battle of Antietam, occurring on 70 miles from Washington, was the single bloodiest day of the war.

Emancipation

Throughout the early part of the war, President Lincoln had no intention of ending slavery. His first priority was to save the Union. However, as the war went on, attitudes towards slavery began to change. More Northerners believed that slavery was helping the war effort in the South. They argued that enslaved people were raising crops to feed the armies and doing other heavy work in the trenches at army camps.

Lincoln was aware of the shift in public opinion. Lincoln signed the **Emancipation Proclamation,** which outlawed slavery in the Confederate states, on January 1, 1863. Since the policy only applied to the South, no enslaved people were actually freed. However, Lincoln knew that many of them would hear of the proclamation and might encourage them to run away from their slaveholders.

Only a year later, Congress prepared a constitutional amendment to end slavery in the United States. In 1865 Congress passed the **Thirteenth Amendment,** which was ratified, or approved, the same year by states loyal to the Union. It was this amendment that truly freed all of the enslaved Americans.

The Tide of War Turns

The winter of 1862–1863 saw gloom in the North and hope in the South. Confederate General Robert E. Lee won decisive victories at Fredericksburg and Chancellorsville, two Virginia towns.

However, in July 1863, the North won two victories that marked a turning point in the war. The **Battle of Gettysburg** occurred in Pennsylvania and involved over 100,000 troops. The North turned back a much larger force, although the day saw over 50,000 casualties. The battle at **Vicksburg,** Mississippi, ended when Confederate forces surrendered to Union general Ulysses S. Grant. The South would be on the defensive after the summer of 1863.

At the end of 1864, Union forces under General William Tecumseh Sherman led his army the historic "march to the sea" through the South, destroying everything in sight. Cities were burned, livestock was killed, and railroad lines were torn up. This method of waging war was known as total war.

Victory for the North

Confederate Army commander Lee finally surrendered on April 9, 1865, at a small village in Virginia called **Appomattox Court House.** Jefferson Davis, the president of the Confederacy, was captured in Georgia on May 10. The Civil War was over at last.

More than 600,000 soldiers died in the war. Billions of dollars of damage were suffered, most of it in the South. The war also created bitter feelings among defeated Southerners that lasted for generations.

The war had other consequences as well. The North's victory had saved the Union. The federal government was strengthened and was now clearly more powerful than the states. Finally, the war freed millions of African Americans. How the nation would treat those new citizens remained to be seen.

✓ **Reading Check** **Examining** What was the Emancipation Proclamation?

Reconstruction

Even before the war was over, Northerners disagreed about how to rebuild the South and allow the various states to rejoin the Union. This process was called Reconstruction, and it went through several different plans. President Lincoln had a plan, but it was short-lived. Lincoln was assassinated on April 14, 1865, at Ford's Theater in Washington, D.C.

Lincoln's vice president was Andrew Johnson, formerly a Southern Democrat from Tennessee. His plan was softer on the South than many in the Republican Congress wanted. The Congress, ruled by the "Radical Republicans," fought with the president over Reconstruction.

African American's Rights

In 1865, during the final weeks of the war, Congress established the **Freedmen's Bureau.** This government agency was meant to help former enslaved persons, or freedmen. The agency distributed food and clothing and established schools throughout the South.

Southern whites were making the lives of African Americans difficult. In 1865 and early 1866, the new Southern state legislatures passed a series of laws called black codes. These laws trampled the rights of African Americans. To freed men and women and many Northerners, the black codes looked like slavery in disguise.

In 1866, Congress passed a new amendment to the Constitution. The **Fourteenth Amendment** granted full citizenship to all individuals born in the United States. This was meant to protect the rights of newly freed African Americans.

Radical Reconstruction

The Republicans in Congress quickly took charge of Reconstruction. President Johnson could do little to stop them because Congress could easily override his vetoes. Thus began a period known as Radical Reconstruction.

Reconstruction Act of 1867

In 1867, Congress passed the First Reconstruction Act that called for the creation of new governments in the 10 Southern states that had not ratified the Fourteenth Amendment. The act divided these 10 states into five military districts, to be overseen by a military commander until new governments were formed.

Many white Southerners refused to take part in state government. Thousands of newly registered African American voters helped make the new state governments Republican-controlled.

Impeaching President Johnson

The Republican Congress was so opposed to President Johnson that it passed several laws limiting the president's power. One of these laws, the Tenure of Office Act, limited the president's control over his own government.

When Johnson broke this law, the House of Representatives voted to impeach—formally charge with wrongdoing—the president. The trial began in the Senate in March 1868 and lasted almost three months. Johnson survived by only one vote and served until the end of his term.

African Americans in Government

African Americans played an important role in Reconstruction politics both as voters and as elected officials. They did not control the government of any state, but held many important positions. At the national level, 16 African Americans served in the House of Representatives and 2 in the Senate between 1869 and 1880. One of the most famous of these men was **Hiram Revels,** a minister, a Civil War veteran, and educator. He served a year in the Senate, where he declared he received "fair treatment."

The Ku Klux Klan

Violence against African Americans and their white supporters became commonplace during Reconstruction. Much of this violence was committed by secret societies organized to prevent freed men and women from exercising their rights and to help whites regain power.

The most terrifying of these societies, the **Ku Klux Klan,** was formed in 1866. Members of the Klan dressed in white and intimidated African Americans, burning their homes, churches, and schools. The Klan killed as well. In Jackson County, Florida, the Klan murdered more than 150 people over a three-year period.

Life in the South

Despite the violence, Reconstruction brought important changes to the South. In the 1870s Reconstruction governments began creating public school systems for both races, which had not existed in the South before the war. Within a few years, more than 50 percent of the white children and about 40 percent of African American children in the South were enrolled in public schools.

Life was still difficult economically in the South, especially for African Americans. Most of them were not able to buy land after the war.

The End of Reconstruction

During the 1870s, the Republican Party began to decline in power and unity. Democrats gained power in some Southern states. The end of Reconstruction was near.

The presidential election of 1876 was a very close election and the results were disputed. Republicans and Democrats met in secret to work out an agreement.

The **Compromise of 1877** called for Republican Rutherford Hayes to take the presidency. The deal included various favors to the Democratic South, including the withdrawal of military troops. The message was clear. The federal government would no longer attempt to reshape Southern society. Reconstruction was over.

✓ **Reading Check** **Explaining** Why were the black codes passed in the South?

SECTION 4 ASSESSMENT

Checking for Understanding

1. **Key Terms** Use each of these terms in a complete sentence that will help explain its meaning: secession, border states, ironclad, casualties, ratified, Reconstruction, black codes, impeach
2. **Reviewing Facts** What advantages did the North have in the Civil War?

Reviewing Themes

3. **Individual Action** How were Southerners directly governed by the North after the war?

Critical Thinking

4. **Determining Cause and Effect** Why was controlling the Mississippi River vital to the North and the South?
5. **Organizing Information** Describe three consequences of the Civil War.

Effect of Civil War

Analyzing Visuals

6. **Geography Skills** Study the map on page 95. How many states made up the Confederacy? Which state seceded earlier-Mississippi or Arkansas?

Interdisciplinary Activity

Government Research to find out how many African Americans hold seats in Congress today. Make a list of the Congress members' name and the state he or she represents. Be sure to include members of both the House of Representatives and the Senate.

Chapter Summary

A Growing Nation

1789
- Washington becomes first president

1803
- Supreme Court establishes judicial review

1812
- U.S. declares war on Britain

1820
- Missouri Compromise passed

1823
- Monroe Doctrine issued

1825
- Erie Canal completed

1834
- Indian Territory created by Congress

1845
- U.S. annexes Texas

1849
- Thoreau writes "Civil Disobedience"

1860
- Abraham Lincoln elected

1861
- Civil War begins

1865
- Civil War ends

1877
- Reconstruction ends

Reviewing Key Terms

Explain why each of these terms is used in a chapter about early American History.

1. implied powers
2. judicial review
3. Industrial Revolution
4. Underground Railroad
5. Manifest Destiny
6. yeomen
7. abolitionists
8. secession
9. Reconstruction
10. impeach

Reviewing Key Facts

11. What was the main reason for the formation of political parties?
12. What Supreme Court justice was responsible for the policy of judicial review?
13. Explain the cause of the war with Mexico.
14. Why was there little industry in the South?
15. How did abolitionists support the antislavery movement from the 1830s to the 1850s?
16. During what years was the Civil War fought?
17. What did the Emancipation Proclamation state?
18. Describe the actions of the Freedmen's Bureau.

Critical Thinking

19. What do you think were Lewis and Clark's greatest contribution?
20. **Draw Conclusions** How did the notion of Manifest Destiny affect how many Americans viewed New Mexico and California?
21. **Analyzing Primary Sources** After being elected president in 1828, Andrew Jackson promised "equal protection and equal benefits" for all Americans. Do you think he included Native Americans in his promise? Why or why not?
22. **Organizing Information** Re-create the diagram below and describe two important consequences of the Compromise of 1877.

Consequences

Geography and History Activity

In 1819 Spain ceded Florida to the United States in the Adams-Onís Treaty. The Spanish had established colonies in Florida beginning in the 1500s. Study the map below and answer the questions that follow.

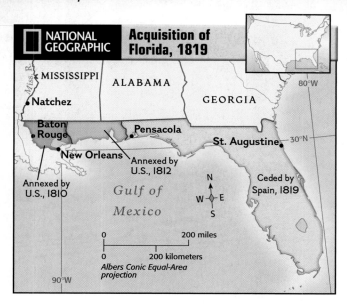

NATIONAL GEOGRAPHIC

Acquisition of Florida, 1819

MISSISSIPPI ALABAMA GEORGIA
80°W

Natchez

Baton Rouge
Pensacola

New Orleans
St. Augustine 30°N

Annexed by U.S., 1812

Annexed by U.S., 1810

Gulf of Mexico

N W-E S

Ceded by Spain, 1819

0   200 miles
0   200 kilometers
Albers Conic Equal-Area projection
90°W

23. **Region** When was the largest portion of Florida acquired from Spain?

24. **Movement** In what direction did the United States acquire the various parts of Florida?

25. **Location** What body of water blocked further expansion of Florida to the west?

Citizenship Cooperative Activity

26. **Analyzing Issues** With a partner, read the newspaper to find out what problems your state faces. Perhaps your state has a large budget deficit, or the crime rate has increased sharply. List the problems and describe what you would do if you were governor.

 ## Technology Activity

27. **Using the Internet** A patent gives an inventor the legal right to his or her invention for a period of time. Search the Internet for information about how to apply for a patent for an invention. Create a step-by-step list of directions describing the process.

Self-Check Quiz
Visit taj.glencoe.com and click on **Prologue Chapter 2—Self-Check Quizzes** to prepare for the chapter test.

Practicing Skills

28. **Analyzing Primary Sources** Imagine that historians in the distant future are analyzing primary sources to find out more about your life. What written or visual sources might they analyze? List as many specific examples as you can.

 ## Alternative Assessment

29. **Portfolio Writing Activity** If you were asked to make a film about one event described in this chapter, what would it be? In your journal describe the event and make a list of at least three people from history who would be in your movie.

Economic Activity

30. Economic differences had always existed between the North and South. From your reading of the chapter, would you say that the North or the South was better equipped economically for war? Explain your reasoning.

Standardized Test Practice

Directions: Choose the *best* answer to the following question.

The discovery of gold in California led to which of the following?

A Discovery of gold in the Black Hills of the Dakotas

B Increased western expansion and foreign immigration

C Annexation of California as a slave state

D War with Mexico over the independence of California

Test-Taking Tip:
This question is a good example of *cause and effect.* Think about other times in history when people have discovered something of value in an area. What effect did this discovery have on people's behavior?

UNIT 7

Reshaping the Nation

1858–1914

Traveler's trunk

Why It Matters

As you study Unit 7, you will learn that pioneers continued to spread across the continent, and immigrants flocked to industrial centers. The following resources offer more information about this period in American history.

Primary Sources Library

See pages 970–971 for primary source readings to accompany Unit 7.

 Use the **American History Primary Source Document Library CD-ROM** to find additional primary sources about the western frontier and the growth of industry.

Hudson River by
Gari Melchers

"*America! America! . . . From sea to shining sea!*"

—*Katherine Lee Bates, 1893*

The Western Frontier

1858–1896

Why It Matters

Many Native American nations lived on the Great Plains, along with the buffalo herds that were their primary source of food. Then, beginning in 1869, transcontinental railroad lines opened the West for white settlers, forever changing the Native American way of life.

The Impact Today

Settlement of the Great Plains came along with the development of machines for plowing, planting, and harvesting. This combination still makes the Midwest a leader in supplying meat and grain to the world.

 The American Journey Video The chapter 18 video, "Life on the Western Frontier," explores what life in the West was like for cowhands and Native Americans.

1862
- Homestead Act passed

1876
- Battle of Little Bighorn

 United States PRESIDENTS

Buchanan 1857–1861	Lincoln 1861–1865	A. Johnson 1865–1869	Grant 1869–1877	Hayes 1877–1881

1860   *1870*   *1880*

World

1861
- Italians establish a united kingdom

1869
- Suez Canal opens

1871
- Stanley and Livingstone meet in Africa

The Race by Mort Künstler The artist is well known for realistic portrayals of dramatic events in American history.

FOLDABLES™
Study Organizer

Evaluating Information Study Foldable
Make this foldable to organize information and ask yourself questions as you read about the western frontier of the United States.

Step 1 Fold a sheet of paper in half from side to side, leaving a ½ inch tab along the side.

Leave ½ inch tab here.

Step 2 Turn the paper and fold it into fourths.

Fold in half, then fold in half again.

Step 3 Unfold and cut up along the three fold lines.

Make four tabs.

Step 4 Label your foldable as shown.

| Miners | Ranchers | Farmers | Native Americans |

on the Western Frontier

Reading and Writing As you read the chapter, ask yourself and write down questions (under each appropriate tab) about the tragedies and triumphs these four groups of people experienced during the expansion of the western frontier.

1886
• Geronimo surrenders

1887
• Dawes Act passed

1890
• Wounded Knee massacre

1892
• Populist Party formed

| Garfield 1881 | Arthur 1881–1885 | Cleveland 1885–1889 | B. Harrison 1889–1893 | Cleveland 1893–1897 |

1890

1900

1885
• European powers partition Africa

1895
• X rays discovered by Wilhelm Roentgen

HISTORY
Online

Chapter Overview
Visit taj.glencoe.com and click on **Chapter 18— Chapter Overviews** to preview chapter information.

CHAPTER 18 The Western Frontier

527

The Mining Booms

Guide to Reading

Main Idea
Discoveries of gold and silver drew thousands of fortune seekers to the West.

Key Terms
lode, ore, vigilante, ghost town, subsidy, transcontinental

Reading Strategy
Analyzing Information As you read the section, re-create the diagram below and explain why these places were significant to the mining boom.

	Significance
Pikes Peak	
Comstock Lode	
Promontory Point	

Read to Learn
- how the rush to find gold and silver led to the growth of new communities in the West.
- how development of the railroads affected the nation.

Section Theme
Geography and History Rail lines and mining speeded the flow of settlers to the West.

Preview of Events

♦1855   ♦1865   ♦1875   ♦1885

1858
Gold is discovered at Pikes Peak

1869
Transcontinental railroad links East and West

1876
Colorado joins the Union

1883
Nation is divided into four time zones

AN American Story

"We'll cross the bold Missouri, and we'll steer for the West,
And we'll take the road we think is the shortest and the best,
We'll travel over plains where the wind is blowing bleak,
And the sandy wastes shall echo with—Hurrah for Pikes Peak."
                                        —"The Gold Seeker's Song"

Miners sang this hopeful song in 1859 as they headed for Pikes Peak, Colorado, where gold had been discovered.

Mining Is Big Business

By the mid-1850s the California Gold Rush had ended. Disappointed miners, still hoping to strike it rich, began prospecting in other parts of the West.

In 1858 a mining expedition found gold on the slopes of **Pikes Peak** in the Colorado Rockies. Newspapers claimed that miners were making $20 a day panning for gold—a large sum at a time when servants made less than a dollar a day. By the spring of 1859, about 50,000 prospectors had flocked to Colorado. Their slogan was "Pikes Peak or Bust."

Prospectors skimmed gold dust from streams or scratched particles of gold from the surface of the land. Most of the gold, however, was deep in underground lodes, rich streaks of ore sandwiched between layers of rock. Mining this rock, or ore, and then extracting the gold required expensive machinery, many workers, and an organized business. Companies made up of several investors had a better chance of getting rich in the goldfields than individual miners did. At most gold rush sites, mining companies soon replaced the lone miner.

Gold and silver mining attracted foreign as well as American investors. The British, for example, invested heavily in the American mining industry.

The Comstock Lode

In 1859 several prospectors found a rich lode of silver-bearing ore on the banks of the Carson River in Nevada. The discovery was called the **Comstock Lode** after Henry Comstock, who owned a share of the claim.

Thousands of mines opened near the site, but only a few were profitable. Mining companies reaped the largest share of the profits. When Comstock sold his share of the claim, he received $11,000 and two mules—a huge sum at the time. It was, however, just a tiny fraction of the hundreds of millions of dollars worth of gold and silver pulled from the Comstock Lode strike.

✓**Reading Check** **Describing** What was the Comstock Lode?

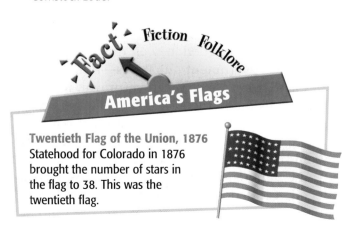

Fact · Fiction · Folklore

America's Flags

Twentieth Flag of the Union, 1876
Statehood for Colorado in 1876 brought the number of stars in the flag to 38. This was the twentieth flag.

The Mining Frontier

The gold strikes created **boomtowns**—towns that grew up almost overnight around mining sites. The Comstock boomtown was **Virginia City, Nevada.** In 1859 the town was a mining camp. Two years later it had a stock exchange, hotels, banks, an opera company, and five newspapers.

Boomtowns were lively, and often lawless, places filled with people from far-off regions. Gold and silver strikes attracted eager prospectors from Mexico, China, and other countries.

Money came quickly—and was often lost just as quickly through extravagant living and gambling. A fortunate miner could earn as much as $2,000 a year, about four times the annual salary of a teacher at that time. Still food, lodging, clothing, and other goods cost dearly in the boomtowns, draining the miners' earnings.

Violence was part of everyday life in boomtowns, where many people carried large amounts of cash and guns. Cheating and stealing were common. Few boomtowns had police or prisons, so citizens sometimes took the law into their own hands. These vigilantes dealt out their own brand of justice without benefit of judge or jury, often hanging the accused person from the nearest tree.

Women in the Boomtowns

Boomtowns were largely men's towns in the early days. Men outnumbered women by two to one in Virginia City, and children made up less than 10 percent of the population.

Eager to share in the riches of the boomtowns, some women opened businesses. Others worked as laundresses, cooks, or dance-hall entertainers. Women often added stability to the boomtowns, founding schools and churches and working to make the communities safer and more orderly.

Boom and Bust

Many mining "booms" were followed by "busts." When the mines no longer yielded ore, people left the towns. At its peak in the 1870s, Virginia City had about 30,000 inhabitants. By 1900 its population had dropped below 4,000.

The boomtown of Leadville, Colorado, surrounds a settler's cabin that sits in the middle of the main street.

Many boomtowns turned into ghost towns—deserted as prospectors moved on to more promising sites or returned home. Some ghost towns still exist in the West today, as reminders of the glory days of the mining frontier.

Mining Expands

Toward the end of the rush, gold and silver mining in some places gave way to the mining of other metals. Copper became the key metal found in Montana, New Mexico, and Arizona in the 1870s.

In the 1890s people began mining lead and zinc in some of the former silver-mining towns of Colorado. Finally, the mining frontier became part of American industry, providing raw materials for manufacturers.

New States Enter the Union

Many people who went west to seek their fortunes in gold or silver settled there permanently. Frontier areas around the boomtowns eventually became states. Colorado joined the United States in 1876. North Dakota, South Dakota, Washington, and Montana became states in 1889. Wyoming and Idaho were admitted to the Union in 1890.

Reading Check **Explaining** Why did many boomtowns turn into ghost towns?

Railroads Connect East and West

The western mines operated far from the industrial centers of the East and Midwest. For this reason transportation played a vital role in the survival of mining communities. Gold and silver had little value unless they could reach factories, ports, and markets. At the same time, the miners and others in the boomtowns needed shipments of food and other supplies.

Wagon trains and stagecoach lines could not move people and goods fast enough to meet these demands. Railroads could—and did. The nation's railroad network expanded rapidly between 1865 and 1890. During that period the miles of track in the United States soared from about 35,000 to more than 150,000.

Government and the Railroads

Railroad construction was often supported by large government subsidies—financial aid and land grants from the government. Railroad executives made the argument that their companies should receive free public land on which to lay track because a rail network would benefit the entire nation.

The national government and states agreed. In all, the federal government granted more than 130 million acres of land to the railroad companies. Much of the land was purchased or obtained by treaties from Native Americans. The government grants included the land for the tracks plus strips of land along the railway, 20 to 80 miles wide. Railroad companies sold those strips of land to raise additional money for construction costs.

States and local communities also helped the railroads. Towns offered cash subsidies to make sure that the railroads came to their communities. For example, Los Angeles gave the Southern Pacific Railroad money and paid for a passenger terminal to ensure that the railroad would come to the town.

Spanning the Continent

The search for a route for a transcontinental rail line—one that would span the continent and connect the Atlantic and Pacific coasts—began in the 1850s. Southerners wanted the route to run through the South, and Northerners through the North. During the Civil War, the Union government chose a northerly route. The government offered land grants to railroad companies willing to build the transcontinental line.

The challenge was enormous—laying track for more than 1,700 miles across hot plains and through rugged mountains. Two companies accepted the challenge. The Union Pacific Company began laying track westward from Omaha, Nebraska, while the Central Pacific Company worked eastward from Sacramento, California.

The two companies competed fiercely. Each wanted to cover a greater distance in order to receive more of the government subsidies.

The Central Pacific hired about 10,000 Chinese laborers to work on its tracks. The first Chinese were hired in 1865 at about $28 per month. The Union Pacific relied on Irish and African American workers. All workers toiled

TECHNOLOGY & History

Steam Locomotive

Since 1825, when the first steam locomotive was built in the United States, trains have crisscrossed the country. As America's transportation needs increased, so did the miles of railroad track linking its people. *Why do you think steam power was the first power source for locomotives?*

1 The **firebox** burns coal, wood, or sometimes oil.

2 Water in the **boiler**, heated by gases from the firebox, creates steam.

3 The **smokebox** draws hot gases from the firebox, and keeps an even fire burning.

4 In the **steam header tank**, the heated steam expands and creates great pressure.

5 Hot steam is piped to the **pistons**. The pistons power the **drive rods** which in turn push the **drive wheels**.

VIRGINIA & TRUCKEE.

for low wages in harsh conditions. In the choking heat of summer and the icy winds of winter, they cleared forests, blasted tunnels through mountains, and laid hundreds of miles of track. In the end the Union Pacific workers laid 1,038 miles of track, and the Central Pacific workers laid 742 miles. However, the Central Pacific covered a much harsher terrain.

The Transcontinental Railway

On May 10, 1869, construction was completed. A Chinese crew was chosen to lay the final ten miles of track, which was completed in only twelve hours. The two sets of track met at **Promontory Point** in Utah Territory. **Leland Stanford,** governor of California, drove a final golden spike into a tie to join the two railroads. Almost as the event occurred, telegraph lines flashed the news across the country:

      ❝The last rail is laid . . . the last spike driven.
. . . The Pacific Railroad is completed.❞

$ Economics

Effects of the Railroads

By 1883 two more transcontinental lines and dozens of shorter lines connected cities in the West with the rest of the nation. The economic consequences were enormous. The railroads brought thousands of workers to the West. Trains carried metals and produce east and manufactured goods west. As more tracks were laid, more steel was needed, and the demand boosted the nation's steel industry. Coal producers, railroad car manufacturers, and construction companies also flourished as the railroads spread across the West.

Towns sprang up along the rail lines that carried the settlers' agricultural goods to market. Some of these towns eventually grew into large cities such as Denver, Colorado. The railroads also brought the next wave of new settlers to the West—cattle ranchers and farmers.

Railroads even changed how people measured time. Before railroads, each community kept its own time. Clocks in Boston, for example, were 11 minutes ahead of clocks in New York. The demand for sensible train schedules, however, changed that. In 1883 the railroad companies divided the country into four **time zones.** All communities in each zone would share the same time, and each zone was exactly one hour apart from the zones on either side of it. Congress passed a law making this practice official in 1918.

✓ Reading Check **Identifying** To what California city did the transcontinental railroad extend?

SECTION 1 ASSESSMENT

Checking for Understanding

1. **Key Terms** Explain why each of these terms is used in a section about mining and the railroads: lode, ore, vigilante, ghost town, subsidy, transcontinental.
2. **Reviewing Facts** Describe life in a typical boomtown.

Reviewing Themes

3. **Geography and History** What physical features and climates made building the transcontinental railroad difficult?

Critical Thinking

4. **Drawing Conclusions** Some boomtowns thrived after the mining boom, while others became ghost towns. Why do you think some towns survived while others did not?
5. **Determining Cause and Effect** Re-create the diagram below and explain how railroads helped open the West to settlement.

Coming of the railroad
Effect   Effect

Analyzing Visuals

6. **Picturing History** Look at the diagram of the steam locomotive on page 531. What is the purpose of the firebox? How were the drive wheels set in operation?

Interdisciplinary Activity

Geography Draw a freehand outline map of the United States today. Shade in the area covered by the states that came into being during the period of the mining boom.

Social Studies SKILLBUILDER

Reading a Special-Purpose Map

Why Learn This Skill?

Maps that show information on specialized subjects, or themes, are called special-purpose maps. They differ from general-purpose maps in that they show more than basic physical features or political boundaries. Special-purpose maps can contain physical, economic, climatic, historic, or cultural information—almost anything that can be expressed geographically.

Learning the Skill

Begin by reading the map title and labels to determine the subject and purpose of the map. Then study the map key. Identify each symbol and color shown in the key and locate these on the map. Use this information to look for similarities and differences in the region shown on the map.

NATIONAL GEOGRAPHIC

Western Land Use, 1890

Key:
- Mining
- Farming
- Ranching
- Farming and ranching
- No activity

0 — 200 miles
0 — 200 kilometers
Lambert Equal-Area projection

Practicing the Skill

Look at the map of Western Land Use, 1890. Then answer the following questions.

1. What is the subject of the map?

2. What do the colors represent?

3. What are the most common uses of land in Texas?

4. What were the uses of land in Montana? In Nebraska?

Applying the Skill

Reading a Special-Purpose Map Look at the map on page 544. Where were Native American reservations placed in relation to productive ranching and farming land in 1890?

Glencoe's **Skillbuilder Interactive Workbook CD-ROM, Level 1,** provides instruction and practice in key social studies skills.

Ranchers and Farmers

Guide to Reading

Main Idea
Following the Civil War, settlers began to move west in great number.

Key Terms
open range, brand, vaquero, homestead, sodbuster, dry farming

Reading Strategy
Taking Notes As you read the section, re-create the diagram below and list the challenges settlers faced on the Great Plains.

Challenges

Read to Learn
• how the railroads helped create a "Cattle Kingdom" in the Southwest.
• how women contributed to the settling of the Great Plains.

Section Theme
Economic Factors Ranchers and farmers had to overcome many difficulties to make a profit.

Preview of Events

♦1860	♦1870	♦1880	♦1890
1862 Homestead Act gives free land to settlers	**1865** Missouri Pacific Railroad reaches Missouri	**1880** Railroad extends from Kansas to Santa Fe	**1889** Oklahoma land rush occurs

AN
American Story

An old Texas cowhand, E.C. Abbott, recalled the early days of riding the trail:
"Here [were] all these cheap long-horned steers overrunning Texas; here was the rest of the country crying for beef—and no railroads to get them out. So we trailed them out, across hundreds of miles of wild country that was thick with Indians. . . . In 1867 the town of Abilene was founded at the end of the Kansas Pacific Railroad and that was when the trail really started."

Cattle on the Plains

When the Spanish settled Mexico and Texas, they brought a tough breed of cattle with them. Called **longhorns** because of their prominent horns, these cattle gradually spread across Texas.

At this time much of Texas was open range—not fenced or divided into lots. Huge ranches covered other areas of the state. Ranchers added to their own herds by rounding up wild cattle. The ranchers burned a brand, or symbol, into the animals' hides to show who owned the cattle.

Railroads and Cow Towns

Although Texas ranchers had plenty of cattle, the markets for beef were in the North and the East. In 1866 the Missouri Pacific Railroad reached Missouri, and Texas cattle suddenly increased in value. The cattle could be loaded onto trains in Missouri for shipment north and east. Some Texans drove their combined herds—sometimes 260,000 head of cattle—north to **Sedalia, Missouri,** the nearest rail point. Longhorns that had formerly been worth $3 each quickly rose in value to $40.

Cattle drives to **cow towns**—towns located near railroads to market and ship cattle—turned into a yearly event. Over the next decade, cow towns such as **Abilene** and **Dodge City, Kansas,** and **Cheyenne, Wyoming,** became important rail stations.

★ Geography

The Long Drive

The sudden increase in the longhorns' value set off what became known as the **Long Drive**—the herding of cattle 1,000 miles or more to meet the railroads. The drives left Texas in the spring, when there was enough grass along the way to feed the cattle. The longhorns had to remain well fed because underweight cattle could not be sold.

Some of the largest Long Drives led from central Texas to Abilene, Kansas, on the **Chisholm Trail.** The **Goodnight-Loving Trail,** named for ranchers Charlie Goodnight and Oliver Loving, swung west through the New Mexico Territory and then turned north. During the heyday of the "Cattle Kingdom," from the late 1860s to the mid-1880s, the trails carried more than five million cattle north.

 Reading Check **Explaining** Why did the value of cattle increase in the mid-1860s?

Life on the Trail

The cattle drives and the cowhands who worked on them captured the imagination of the nation. Cattle driving, however, was hard work. Cowhands rode in the saddle up to 15 hours every day, in driving rain, dust storms, and blazing sun. Life on the trail was lonely too. Cowhands saw few outsiders.

History *Through Art*

Jerked Down **by Charles Russell** Celebrated for his detailed and dramatic scenes of Western life, Charles Russell depicts cowhands on their surefooted horses lassoing cattle. **Where did the traditions of cattle herding begin?**

Spanish Influence

Many cowhands were veterans of the Confederate army. Some were African Americans who moved west in search of a better life after the Civil War. Others were Hispanics. In fact, the traditions of cattle herding began with Hispanic ranch hands in the Spanish Southwest. These vaqueros developed many of the skills—riding, roping, and branding—that cowhands used on the drives. Much of the language of the rancher today is derived from Spanish words used by vaqueros for centuries. Even the word *ranch* comes from the Spanish word *rancho.*

The cowhand's equipment was based on the vaquero's equipment too. Cowhands wore wide-brimmed hats to protect themselves from the sun and leather leggings, called **chaps,** to shield their legs from brush and mishaps with cattle. They used ropes called **lariats** to lasso cattle that strayed from the herd.

Hazards on the Trail

During the months on the trail the cowhands faced violent storms, "rustlers" who tried to steal cattle, and many other dangers. They had to drive the herds across swift-flowing rivers, where cattle could be lost.

One of the greatest dangers on the trail was the **stampede,** when thousands of cattle ran in panic. Any sudden sound—a roar of thunder or the crack of a gunshot—could set off the cattle. The cowhands had to race on horseback with the stampeding cattle and bring them under control.

Nat Love was one of many African Americans who rode the cattle trails.

The "Wild West"

African American, Native American, Hispanic, and Anglo cowhands all met and worked together. Yet discrimination existed in the West just as it did elsewhere in the nation. Members of minorities rarely became trail bosses and often received less pay for their work. Some towns discriminated against Hispanics, segregated African Americans, and excluded Chinese cowhands altogether.

After many tiring weeks on the trail, the cowhands delivered their cattle and enjoyed some time off in cow towns. Cowhands drank and gambled, and got involved in fistfights and gunplay. Some towns, such as Dodge City and Abilene, were rowdy, lawless, and often violent. Eventually, though, they grew into settled, businesslike communities.

The Cattle Kingdom Ends

As profits from cattle increased, cattle ranching spread north from Texas. On the northern Plains, ranchers crossbred the longhorns with fatter Hereford and Angus cattle to produce hardy and plumper new breeds.

On the northern Plains, ranching began to replace the Long Drive. The sturdy crossbred cattle multiplied on open-range ranches. When cattle prices "boomed" in the early 1880s, ranchers became rich. The boom, however, was soon followed by a bust. Overgrazing depleted the grasslands. In addition, too many cattle glutted the beef market and prices fell. The bitterly cold winters of 1885 and 1886 killed large numbers of cattle.

The price collapse of the mid-1880s marked the end of the "Cattle Kingdom." Ranchers built fences and grew hay to feed their cattle during the harsh winters. Another type of life would rise on the Plains—farming.

✓ **Reading Check** **Describing**
Who were the vaqueros?

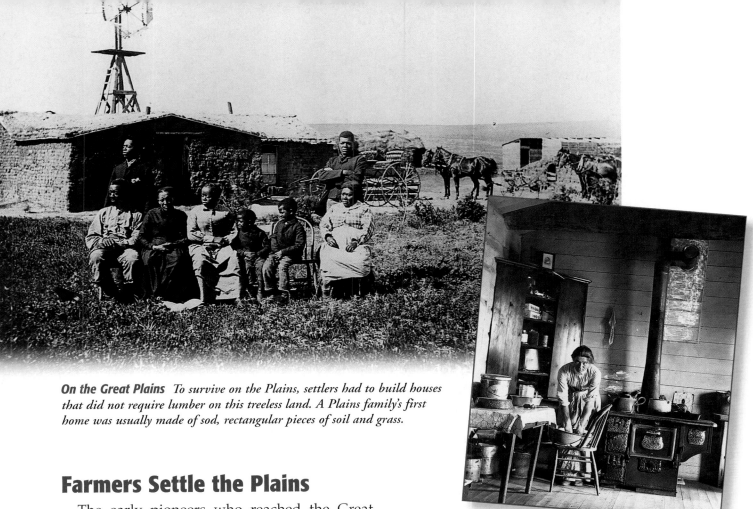

On the Great Plains *To survive on the Plains, settlers had to build houses that did not require lumber on this treeless land. A Plains family's first home was usually made of sod, rectangular pieces of soil and grass.*

Farmers Settle the Plains

The early pioneers who reached the Great Plains did not believe they could farm the dry, treeless area. In the late 1860s, however, farmers began settling there and planting crops. In a surprisingly short time, much of the Plains changed from "wilderness" to farmland. In 1872 a Nebraska settler wrote,

> 66One year ago this was a vast houseless, uninhabited prairie. . . . Today I can see more than thirty dwellings from my door.99

Several factors brought settlers to the Plains. The railroads made the journey west easier and cheaper. New laws offered free land. Finally, above-average rainfall in the late 1870s made the Plains better suited to farming.

The Homestead Act

In 1862 Congress passed the **Homestead Act,** which gave 160 free acres of land to a settler who paid a filing fee and lived on the land for five years. This federal land policy brought farmers to the Plains to homestead—earn ownership of land by settling on it.

Homesteading lured thousands of new settlers. Some were immigrants who had begun the process of becoming American citizens and were eligible to file for land. Others were women. Although married women could not claim land, single women and widows had the same rights as men—and they used the Homestead Act to acquire property. In Colorado and Wyoming, 12 percent of all those who filed homestead claims were women.

Promoting the Plains

Homesteaders came to the Plains to own land and be independent. They were also swayed by advertising paid for by railroads, steamship companies, land speculators, and western states and territories.

Railroad companies wanted to sell the strips of land alongside the rail lines to raise cash. Steamship companies went to great lengths to advertise the American Plains in Scandinavia. By 1880 more than 100,000 Swedes and Norwe-

European immigrants on a railroad flatcar view land open for settlement on the Great Plains.

gians had settled in the northern Plains—Minnesota and the Dakotas. The Scandinavian influence remains strong in this region today.

African American Settlers

Thousands of African Americans also migrated from the Southern states into Kansas in the late 1870s. They called themselves **"Exodusters,"** from the biblical book of Exodus, which describes the Jews' escape from slavery in Egypt.

The end of Reconstruction in 1877 had meant the end of federal protection for African Americans. Fearing for their safety in former slave regions, freed people sought land farther west. By 1881 more than 40,000 African Americans had migrated to Kansas. Some, however, had to return to the South because they lacked the money to start new farms or businesses.

★Geography
The Farmers' Frontier

The climate of the Plains presented farmers with their greatest challenge. Generally there was little rainfall, but in some years rain came down in torrents, destroying crops and flooding homesteads. The other extreme—drought—also threatened crops and lives. Fire was another enemy. In times of drought, brushfires swept rapidly through a region, destroying crops, livestock, and homes.

Summer might bring plagues of grasshoppers. Several times during the 1870s, swarms of the insects swept over the Plains. Thousands of grasshoppers would land on a field of corn. When they left, not a stalk would remain.

Winters presented even greater dangers. Winds howled across the open Plains, and deep snow could bury animals and trap families in their homes. Farm families had to plan ahead and store food for the winter.

Farm Families

Farming on the Great Plains was a family affair. Men labored hard in the fields. Women often did the same work, but they also cared for the children. A farm wife sewed clothing, made candles, and cooked and preserved food. In the absence of doctors and teachers, she also tended to the children's health and education. When her husband was away—taking the harvest to town or buying supplies—she bore all responsibility for keeping the farm running.

When children grew old enough, they too worked the farm. Children helped in the fields, tended animals, and did chores around the house. Farmwork often kept children from attending school.

Although separated by great distances, farm families socialized whenever they could. People took great pleasure in getting together for weddings, church services, picnics, and other occasions. As communities grew, schools and churches began to dot the rural landscape.

New Farming Methods

The Plains could not be farmed by the usual methods of the 1860s. Most parts of the region had little rainfall and too few streams for irrigation. The Plains farmers, known as sodbusters, needed new methods and tools.

One approach, called dry farming, was to plant seeds deep in the ground where there was some moisture. Wooden plows could not penetrate the tough layer of sod, but in the late 1870s farmers could use the newly invented lightweight steel plows to do the job.

The sodbusters had other tools to help them conquer the Plains—windmills to pump water from deep in the ground and a new fencing called **barbed wire.** With no wood to build fences, farmers used these wire fences to protect their land.

Dry farming, however, did not produce large crop yields, and the 160-acre grants were too small to make a living. Most farmers needed at least 300 acres, as well as advanced machinery, to make a Plains farm profitable. Many farmers went into debt. Others lost ownership of their farms and then had to rent the land.

The Oklahoma Land Rush

The last part of the Plains to be settled was the Oklahoma Territory, which Congress had designated as "Indian Territory" in the 1830s. In 1889, after years of pressure from land dealers and settlers' groups, the federal government opened Oklahoma to homesteaders.

On the morning of April 22, 1889—the official opening day—more than 10,000 people lined up on the edge of this land. At the sound of a bugle, the homesteaders charged across the border to stake their claims. The eager **boomers,** as the homesteaders were called, discovered to their dismay that some settlers had already slipped into Oklahoma. These so-called **sooners** had already claimed most of the best land. Within a few years, all of Oklahoma was opened to settlement.

Closing the Frontier

Not long after the Oklahoma land rush, the government announced in the 1890 census that the frontier no longer existed. Settlement had changed the Plains dramatically. No one felt these changes more keenly than the Native Americans who had lived on the Plains for centuries.

Reading Check **Explaining** Why was the Homestead Act important to settlers?

SECTION 2 ASSESSMENT

Checking for Understanding

1. **Key Terms** Use each of these terms in a sentence that will help explain its meaning: open range, brand, vaquero, homestead, sodbuster, dry farming.
2. **Reviewing Facts** Explain why cow towns developed.

Reviewing Themes

3. **Economic Factors** Discuss two developments that contributed to the collapse of the cattle industry during the mid-1880s.

Critical Thinking

4. **Analyzing Information** What opportunities did settlement on the Plains provide for women and African Americans?
5. **Determining Cause and Effect** Re-create the diagram below and explain how the Homestead Act encouraged settlement of the Great Plains.

Analyzing Visuals

6. **Picturing History** Study the photographs that appear on page 537. What image of life on the Plains do the photographs depict? How would you describe the mood of the people?

Interdisciplinary Activity

Art Create a poster that the United States government might have used to encourage farmers to move west. Think about what would tempt you to move west if you were a farmer. Display your posters in class.

What were people's lives like in the past?

What—and whom—were people talking about? What did they eat? What did they do for fun? These two pages will give you some clues to everyday life in the U.S. as you step back in time with TIME Notebook.

Profile

WYATT EARP *has been a buffalo hunter, a gambler, a con man, a bartender, and a legendary lawman. In Tombstone, Arizona, where his brother Virgil was sheriff, Wyatt served as a deputy U.S. marshal.*

IN OCTOBER 1881, A FEUD BETWEEN THE EARP FAMILY AND A GANG LED BY Ike Clanton led to one of the most famous gunfights of all time—the showdown at the O.K. Corral. The Earps and their friend Doc Holliday shot and killed three of Clanton's gang members (Billy Clanton, Frank McLaury and Tom McLaury). Wyatt claims they were simply trying to arrest the three. Others say the Earps used murder to settle the feud with the Clantons—and that Wyatt fired the first shot. Judge Spicer called a hearing to investigate the matter. Here's what Wyatt told him about the gunfight.

"Billy Clanton and Frank McLaury commenced to draw their pistols. The first two shots were fired by Billy Clanton and myself. . . . We fired almost together. I don't know which [gun] was fired first. . . ."

Wyatt Earp

BROWN BROTHERS

"We sat and looked as the lamp continued to burn, and the longer it burned, the more fascinated we were. None of us could go to bed. There was no sleep for any of us for 40 hours."

THOMAS EDISON
on inventing the light bulb, which he patented in 1883

TIME PIX

"'We the people' does not mean 'We the male citizens'."

SUSAN B. ANTHONY,
crusader for women's rights in 1872

"Every time you stop a school, you will have to build a jail. What you gain at one end you lose at the other. It's like feeding a dog on his own tail. It won't fatten the dog."

SAMUEL CLEMENS
(also known as Mark Twain)

"I asked a man in prison once how he happened to be there and he said he had stolen a pair of shoes. I told him if he had stolen a railroad, he would be a United States senator."

"MOTHER" MARY JONES,
labor activist

The Eighth Wonder of the World

Sixteen years after the project began, the **Brooklyn Bridge**—the largest suspension bridge in the world—opens in 1883. Schools and shops in Brooklyn are closed so everyone can celebrate. President Chester Arthur is the first to walk across.

Hung from great steel cables, with a span half again as long as that of any previous bridge, it was designed and built by John Roebling. During the project, John was killed on the job. His son, Washington, continued directing the work until he himself was injured. Then Washington's wife Emily completed the job, making her possibly the first woman field engineer.

NORTH WIND PICTURES

MILESTONES

PEOPLE AND EVENTS OF THE TIME

1870 LOUISA SWAIN, age 70, casts a ballot in Wyoming and thus becomes the first woman in the U.S. to vote in a public election.

BROWN BROTHERS

1871 Fire breaks out on October 8—by most accounts in Mrs. Patrick O'Leary's barn—on Chicago's West Side. Because of the city's 651 miles of wooden sidewalks and 60,000 mostly wooden buildings, Chicago's 200 firemen are unable to bring the blaze under control for 30 hours. In a city of about 300,000, some 100,000 are left homeless.

Alexander Graham Bell

NORTH WIND PICTURES

1876 In a building in Boston, **ALEXANDER GRAHAM BELL** makes the first phone call—to Mr. Watson, his assistant upstairs. Bell's message is simple: "Mr. Watson, come here. I want you!" Bell starts his own company because others dismiss the idea of the telephone as foolish. They see the telephone as just a toy.

1878 The first commercial telephone switchboard opens for business in New Haven, Connecticut. There are 21 subscribers.

NUMBERS

U.S. AT THE TIME

10,000 Number of people who watched the first Kentucky Derby in 1875

4 Number of time zones for the United States under 1883 system

5¢ Price for all the goods in F.W. Woolworth's "Great Five-Cent Store" in Utica, New York (1879)

11 Number of days the stock exchange closes as a result of a panic on Wall Street in 1873

14,000 Number of deaths in southern states because of a yellow fever epidemic that raged in 1878

Western Words

Settlers of the western United States are learning some "new" words that come from Spanish.

mesa: an elevated, flat-topped piece of land

stampede: a wild rush of frightened animals

mesquite: wood of a spiny, southwestern tree or shrub sometimes used in cooking

pinto: a horse or pony that's spotted with white and another color

lariat: lasso; a long rope with a noose used to catch livestock

corral: a pen or enclosure for holding livestock

The Well-Dressed Cowhand

These are prices from the Montgomery Ward catalogs of the 1880s.

Stetson hat	$10.00
Leather vest	$3.00
Cotton shirt *(no collar)*	$1.25
Chaps and pants	$8.00
Leather boots	$20.00
Spurs	$0.70
Raincoat	$2.75
Winchester rifle	$20.50
Colt pistol	$12.20
Holster, cartridge belt	$2.00
Horse *(usually provided by ranch)*	$35.00
Saddle	$40.00
Single-ear bridle	$2.30
Lariat	$7.75
Saddlebags	$5.00

SECTION 3 Native American Struggles

Guide to Reading

Main Idea
During the late 1800s, whites and Native Americans fought while Native Americans tried to preserve their civilizations.

Key Terms
nomadic, reservation

Reading Strategy
Determining Cause and Effect As you read the section, re-create the diagram below and describe how Western settlement affected Native Americans.

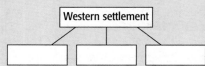

Read to Learn
- why the government forced Native Americans to move to reservations.
- how conflict between Native Americans and whites grew.

Section Theme
Culture and Traditions The settlement of white people in the West forced change on the Native Americans of the Plains.

Preview of Events

◆1860	◆1870	◆1880	◆1890
1864 Sand Creek massacre occurs	**1876** Sioux victorious at Little Bighorn	**1886** Geronimo surrenders to the army	**1890** Battle at Wounded Knee

AN American Story

In May 1876, George Crook led an army from the North Platte River to round up Native American bands. Sioux chief Crazy Horse urged on his warriors with the cry, "Come on Dakotas, it's a good day to die." The two sides fought until midafternoon. Then the Native Americans began to drift away. "They were tired and hungry, so they went home," one warrior later explained. The Native Americans retired to a large camp on the Little Bighorn River. Great leaders were there—Sitting Bull, Gall, Crazy Horse. A vast pony herd grazed nearby; the grass was green; there was dancing at night. . . .

Following the Buffalo

Starting in the mid-1850s, miners, railroads, cattle drives, and farmers came to the Plains. Each new group dealt another blow to Native Americans living there. The Sioux chief Red Cloud lamented,

❝The white children [settlers] have surrounded me and left me nothing but an island.❞

For centuries the Great Plains was home to many Native American nations. Some, like the Omaha and the Osage nations, lived in communities as farmers and hunters. Most of the Plains Indians, however, including the Sioux, the Comanche, and the Blackfeet, lived a nomadic life. They traveled vast distances following their main source of food—the great herds of buffalo that lived on the Great Plains.

Despite their differences, the people of the Plains were similar in many ways. Plains Indian nations, sometimes numbering several thousand people, were divided into bands consisting of up to 500 people each. A governing council headed each band, but most members participated in making decisions.

The women reared the children, cooked, and prepared hides. The men hunted, traded, and supervised the military life of the band. Most Plains Indians practiced a religion based on a belief in the spiritual power of the natural world.

Threats to the Buffalo

The Plains Indians had millions of buffalo to supply their needs. After the Civil War, though, American hunters hired by the railroads began slaughtering the animals to feed the crews building the railroad. The railroad companies also wanted to prevent huge herds of buffalo from blocking the trains. William Cody, hired by the Kansas Pacific Railroad, once claimed that he had killed more than 4,000 buffalo in less than 18 months. He became known as Buffalo Bill. Starting in 1872 hunters targeted buffalo to sell the hides to the East, where tanneries made them into leather goods.

✔ Reading Check **Describing** What is a nomadic way of life?

Conflict

As long as white people regarded the Plains as the "Great American Desert," they left the Native Americans who lived there more or less alone. When whites began settling the Plains, the situation changed. In the late 1860s, the government tried a new Indian policy.

Reservation Policy

In 1867 the federal government appointed the Indian Peace Commission to develop a policy toward Native Americans. The commission recommended moving the Native Americans to a few large reservations—tracts of land set aside for them. Moving Native Americans to reservations was not a new policy, and the government now increased its efforts in that direction.

Native Americans of the Great Plains settled in one place for only part of the year.

Native American Population

Population (in thousands)

500
400
300
200
100

1850 1860 1870 1880 1890 1900
Year

Source: Paul Stuart, *Nations within a Nation.*

📈 Graph *Skills*

Census figures show a declining Native American population before 1900.

Analyzing Information During what 10-year period did the Native American population decline the least?

NATIONAL GEOGRAPHIC

Western Native American Lands, 1860–1890

CANADA

WASH.
Spokane
Yakima
Nez Perce
Blackfoot
Walla Walla
OREGON
MONT.
Shoshone
ID. Shoshone
ROUTE OF NEZ PERCE 1877

Sitting Bull's and Crazy Horse's warriors defeated Custer and 200 U.S. troops at Little Bighorn.

Sioux
N.D.
Sioux
Chippewa
MINN.
Chippewa
WISC.
MICH.

Battle of Little Bighorn 1876
Fetterman Massacre 1866
S.D.

Arapaho
WYO.
Battle of Wounded Knee 1890

Sioux

Sioux warriors ambush U.S. troops on December 21, 1866.

The massacre of the buffalo changed the lives of the Plains Indians.

NEBR.
IOWA
IND. OHIO

Paiute
Ute
NEV.
UTAH TERR.
COLO.

About 200 Sioux and 25 soldiers were killed at Wounded Knee.

ILL.

CALIF.
Sand Creek Massacre 1864
KANSAS
MO.
KY.

PACIFIC OCEAN

Mojave
Navaho
Hopi
ARIZ. TERR.
Apache
Apache
Pueblo
N. MEX. TERR.
Apache

OKLA. TERR.
Cherokee
UNORG. TERR.
Arapaho
Comanche
Creek
Chickasaw
Choctaw
ARK.
TENN.
MISS. ALA. GA.

Geronimo surrenders 1886
TEXAS
LA.
FLA.

MEXICO

0 — 400 miles
0 — 400 kilometers
Lambert Equal-Area projection

Indian reservations in 1890
✦ Battle

Geography Skills

During the late 1800s, Native Americans and the United States Army fought many battles over land.

1. **Location** In what state did the Battle of Little Bighorn take place?
2. **Analyzing Information** Which Native American nations resettled in present-day Oklahoma?

One large reservation was in **Oklahoma,** the "Indian Territory" that Congress had created in the 1830s for Native Americans relocated from the Southeast. Another one, meant for the Sioux people, was in the **Dakota Territory.** Managing the reservations would be the job of the federal Bureau of Indian Affairs.

Government agents often used trickery to persuade Native American nations to move to the reservations. Many reservations were located on poor land. In addition the government often failed to deliver promised food and

supplies, and the goods that were delivered were of poor quality.

A great many Native Americans accepted the reservation policy at first. Many southern Kiowa, Comanche, Cheyenne, and Arapaho agreed to stay on the Oklahoma reservation. Thousands of Sioux agreed to move onto the Dakota reservation in the North.

Pockets of resistance remained, however. Some Native Americans refused to make the move, and some who tried reservation life abandoned it. The stage was set for conflict.

Conflict on the Plains

During the 1860s, many armed clashes between Native Americans and whites took place. Minnesota was the site of one especially bloody confrontation. Resentful of the settlers,

Sioux warriors, led by **Little Crow,** burned and looted white settlers' homes in the summer of 1862. Hundreds died before troops arrived from St. Paul and put down the uprising.

Following the Minnesota uprising, the army sent patrols far out onto the northern Great Plains. This action brought troops into contact with another branch of the Sioux—the nomadic **Lakota.** The Lakota fought hard to keep control of their hunting grounds, which extended from the Black Hills and the surrounding Badlands—rocky and barren terrain in the western parts of the Dakotas and northwestern Nebraska—westward to the Bighorn Mountains.

The Sioux, along with Cheyenne and Arapaho warriors, staged a series of attacks from 1865 to 1867. The bloodiest incident occurred on December 21, 1866. Army troops were manning a fort on the Bozeman Trail, used by prospectors to reach gold mines in Montana. A Sioux military leader, **Crazy Horse,** acted as a decoy and lured the troops into a deadly trap. He tricked the fort's commander into sending a detachment of about 80 soldiers in pursuit. Hundreds of warriors were waiting in ambush and wiped out the entire detachment. This incident was known as the **Fetterman Massacre.**

Colorado was another site of conflict. The number of miners who had flocked to Colorado in search of gold and silver grew. Bands of Cheyenne and Arapaho began raiding wagon trains and stealing cattle and horses from ranches. By the summer of 1864, travelers heading to Denver or the mining camps were no longer safe. Dozens of ranches had been burned and an estimated 200 settlers had been killed. The territorial governor of Colorado ordered the Native Americans to surrender at Fort Lyon, where he said they would be given food and protection.

Although several hundred Native Americans surrendered at the fort, many others did not. In November 1864, Chief **Black Kettle** brought several hundred Cheyenne to negotiate a peace deal. They camped at Sand Creek. Shortly after, Colonel John Chivington led the Colorado Volunteers on an attack on the unsuspecting Cheyenne. Fourteen volunteers and hundreds of Cheyenne died. Retaliation by the Cheyenne was swift, provoking widespread uprisings before some of the Cheyenne and Arapaho leaders agreed to stop the fighting in October 1865.

Little Bighorn

An 1868 treaty was supposed to bring peace, but tensions remained and erupted in more fighting a few years later.

This time the conflict arose over the **Black Hills** of the Dakotas. The government had promised that "No white person or persons shall be permitted to settle upon or occupy" or even "to pass through" these hills. However, the hills were rumored to contain gold. In 1874 Custer led an army expedition to check on the rumors and confirmed that there was gold, "from the grass roots down." Prospectors swarmed into the area.

The Sioux protested against the trespassers. Instead of protecting the Sioux's rights, the government tried to buy the hills. **Sitting Bull,** an important leader of the Lakota Sioux, refused. "I do not want to sell any land. Not even this much," he said, holding a pinch of dust.

Sitting Bull gathered Sioux and Cheyenne warriors along the **Little Bighorn River** in present-day Montana. They were joined by **Crazy Horse,** another Sioux chief, and his

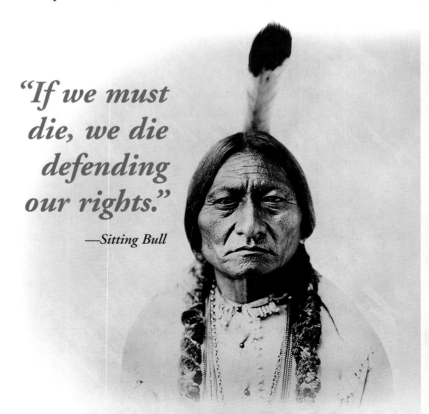

"If we must die, we die defending our rights."

—*Sitting Bull*

Chief Joseph 1840—1904

In 1877 the United States government demanded the Nez Perce give up their lands and move onto a reservation in Idaho. Chief Joseph was preparing his people for the move when he learned that several young braves had attacked a group of white settlers. Fearing revenge, Chief Joseph led his followers over 1,000 miles across Oregon, Washington, Idaho, and Montana.

For more than three months he managed to evade a U.S. force ten times larger than his group. Along the way, he won the admiration of many whites for his humane treatment of prisoners, and for his concern for women, children, and the elderly.

Just 40 miles from the Canadian border the Nez Perce were surrounded. Chief Joseph's words of surrender reflect the tragedy of his people:

"The little children are freezing to death. My people . . . have no blankets, no food . . . . I am tired; my heart is sick and sad. From where the sun now stands I will fight no more forever. "

forces. The United States Army was ordered to round up the warriors and move them to reservations. The Seventh Cavalry, led by Lieutenant Colonel **George Custer,** was ordered to scout the Native American encampment.

Custer wanted the glory of leading a major victory. He divided his regiment and attacked the Native Americans on June 25, 1876. He had seriously underestimated their strength, however. With about 250 soldiers, Custer faced a Sioux and Cheyenne force of thousands. Custer and his entire command lost their lives. News of the army's defeat shocked the nation.

The Native American triumph at Little Bighorn was short-lived. The army soon crushed the uprising, sending most of the Native Americans to reservations. Sitting Bull and his followers fled north to Canada. By 1881, exhausted and starving, the Lakota and Cheyenne agreed to live on a reservation.

The Apache Wars

Trouble also broke out in the Southwest. The Chiracahua Apache had been moved from their homeland to the San Carlos reservation in Arizona in the mid-1870s. Many Apache resented confinement to this reservation. The Apache leader, **Geronimo,** escaped from San Carlos and fled to Mexico with a small band of followers. During the 1880s he led raids against settlers and the army in Arizona.

Thousands of troops pursued Geronimo and his warriors. Several times he went back to the reservation. Geronimo said,

❝Once I moved about like the wind. Now I surrender to you.❞

But again he left the reservation. In 1886 Geronimo finally gave up—the last Native American to surrender formally to the United States.

A Changing Culture

Many things contributed to changing the traditional way of life of Native Americans—the movement of whites onto their lands, the slaughter of the buffalo, United States Army attacks, and the reservation policy. More change came from well-meaning reformers who wanted to abolish reservations and absorb the Native Americans into white American culture.

American reformers such as **Helen Hunt Jackson** were horrified by the massacres of Native Americans and by the cruelty of the reservation system. Describing the whites' treatment of Native Americans in her 1881 book, *A Century of Dishonor,* Jackson wrote:

❝It makes little difference . . . where one opens the record of the history of the Indians; every page and every year has its dark stain.❞

Congress changed government policy with the **Dawes Act** in 1887. The law aimed to eliminate what Americans regarded as the two weaknesses of Native American life: the lack of private property and the nomadic tradition.

The Dawes Act proposed to break up the reservations and to end identification with a tribal group. Each Native American would receive a plot of reservation land. The goal was to encourage native peoples to become farmers and, eventually, American citizens. Native American children would be sent to white-run boarding schools. Some of the reservation lands would be sold to support this schooling.

Over the next 50 years, the government divided up the reservations. Speculators acquired most of the valuable land. Native Americans often received dry, gravelly plots that were not suited to farming.

Wounded Knee

The Dawes Act changed forever the Native American way of life and weakened their cultural traditions. In their despair the Sioux turned in 1890 to Wovoka, a prophet. Wovoka claimed that the Sioux could regain their former greatness if they performed a ritual known as the **Ghost Dance.**

The Ghost Dance was a way for the Sioux to express their culture that was being destroyed. As the ritual spread, reservation officials became alarmed and decided to ban the dance. Believing that their chief, Sitting Bull, was the leader of the movement, police went to his camp to arrest him. During a scuffle, they shot Sitting Bull.

Several hundred Lakota Sioux fled in fear after Sitting Bull's death. They gathered at a creek called **Wounded Knee** in southwestern South Dakota. On December 29, 1890, the army went there to collect the Sioux's weapons. No one knows how the fighting started, but when a pistol shot rang out, the army responded with fire. More than 200 Sioux and 25 soldiers were killed.

Wounded Knee marked the end of armed conflict between whites and Native Americans. The Native Americans had lost their long struggle.

✓ **Reading Check** **Describing** What was the purpose of the Dawes Act?

SECTION 3 ASSESSMENT

Checking for Understanding

1. **Key Terms** Use each of these terms in a sentence that will help explain its meaning: nomadic, reservation.
2. **Reviewing Facts** Who were Geronimo and Chief Joseph?

Reviewing Themes

3. **Culture and Traditions** What two aspects of Native American life was the Dawes Act supposed to eliminate?

Critical Thinking

4. **Identifying Central Issues** Re-create the diagram below and identify ways the government reservation policy ignored the needs of Native Americans.

5. **Drawing Conclusions** Did the Dawes Act reflect an effort by the United States government to change Native American life? If so, how?

Analyzing Visuals

6. **Geography Skills** Study the map on page 544. When did the Battle of Wounded Knee occur? Where were the Shoshone reservations located?

Interdisciplinary Activity

Science Research to find out more about the buffalo. With the buffalo at the center, create a diagram that shows the importance of this animal in the everyday life and culture of Plains Native Americans.

Guide to Reading

Main Idea
In the late 1800s, farmers began to band together in groups and associations to fight their problems.

Key Terms
National Grange, cooperative, Populist Party, free silver

Reading Strategy
Identifying Central Issues As you read the section, re-create the diagram below and identify the problems farmers faced in the late 1800s.

Farmers' problems

Read to Learn
• why farmers faced hard times in the late 1800s.
• how farmers tried to solve their problems.

Section Theme
Groups and Institutions During the late 1800s, farmers worked together to try to improve their lives.

Preview of Events

◆1870	◆1880	◆1890	◆1900
1870s The Grange works to reduce shipping costs	**1880s** Farmers' Alliances seek federal support	**1890** Alliance members form the Populist Party	**1896** William McKinley is elected president

AN American Story

In the last decades of the 1800s, farmers suffered from falling prices and rising costs. They expressed their frustration in a popular song:

"When the banker says he's broke
And the merchant's up in smoke
They forget that it's the farmer feeds them all. . . .
The farmer is the man,
Lives on credit till the fall;
With the interest rates so high,
It's a wonder he don't die,
For the mortgage man's the one who gets it all."

The Farmers Organize

After the Civil War, farming expanded in the West and the South, and more land came under cultivation. The supply of crops grew faster than the demand for them, however, and prices fell steadily. In 1866 a bushel of wheat sold for $1.45. By the mid-1880s the price had dropped to 80 cents and by the mid-1890s to 49 cents. At the same time, farmers' expenses—for transporting their goods to market, for seed, and for equipment and other manufactured goods—remained high. The farmers' plight gave rise to bitter feelings.

Farmers blamed their troubles on three groups in particular. They resented the railroad companies, which charged farmers more to ship crops than they charged manufacturers to ship goods. They were angry at the Eastern manufacturers, who charged high prices for their products. They also had problems with bankers.

Farmers needed to borrow money to buy seed, equipment, and other goods. After they sold their crops, they had to pay the high interest rates set by bankers. If crops failed and farmers could not repay the loans, they were in danger of losing their farms.

Farmers with small and middle-sized holdings struggled to survive. Senator William A. Peffer of Kansas summed up the farmers' plight when he noted that the railroad companies "took possession of the land" and the bankers "took possession of the farmer."

The Grange

Farmers began to organize in an effort to solve their problems. Within a short time, they had created a mass political movement.

The first farmers' organization of this period was a network of local self-help organizations that eventually came to be called the National Grange. The Grange offered farmers education, fellowship, and support. For inexperienced farmers, the Grange provided a library with books on planting and livestock raising. For lonely farm families, it organized social gatherings. In an 1874 declaration of purposes, the Grange said,

❝We propose meeting together, talking together, working together, buying together, selling together....❞

Above all, the Grange tried to encourage economic self-sufficiency. It set up "cash-only" cooperatives, stores where farmers bought products from each other. The cooperatives charged lower prices than regular stores and provided an outlet for farmers' crops. The purpose of the "cash-only" policy was to remove the burden of credit buying that threatened farmers.

In the 1870s the Grange tried to cut farmers' costs by getting state legislatures to limit railroad shipping rates. Many Midwestern states did pass such laws. By 1878, however, the railroads had put so much pressure on state legislatures that these states repealed the rate regulations.

HISTORY Online

Student Web Activity
Visit taj.glencoe.com and click on Chapter 18— Student Web Activities for an activity on the life of a farmer in the late 1800s.

The Grange cooperatives also failed. Farmers were always short of cash and had to borrow money until their next crop was sold. The cash-only cooperative could not work if borrowing was necessary. By the late 1870s, the Grange had declined. Rural reformers then tried to help farmers through the Farmers' Alliances.

The Farmers' Alliances

The **Farmers' Alliances** were networks of organizations that sprang up in the West and the South in the 1880s. The Southern Alliance was founded in Texas when farmers rallied against the railroads and against "money power."

Alliance leaders extended the movement to other states. By 1890 the Southern Alliance had more than three million members, and the Colored Farmers' National Alliance, a separate organization of African American farmers, had one million members. An Alliance movement developed in the Plains states as well.

Like the Grange, the Farmers' Alliances sponsored education and cooperative buying and selling. The Alliances also proposed a plan in which the federal government would store farmers' crops in warehouses and lend money to the farmers. When the stored crops were sold, the farmers would pay back the government loans. Such a plan would reduce the power that railroads, banks, and merchants had over farmers and would offer farmers some federal protection.

If the Alliances had remained united, they would have been a powerful political force. Regional differences and personality clashes kept the groups apart, however.

✔ **Reading Check** **Describing** What is the purpose of a cooperative?

A PARTY OF PATCHES.
Grand Balloon Ascension—Cincinnati, May 20th, 1891.

Analyzing *Political Cartoons*

Party of Patches The cartoonist shows the Populist Party as a collection of special interest groups and minor political parties. **Does the cartoon support or ridicule the Populist Party? Explain.**

A Party of the People

In the 1890 election, the Alliances became active in political campaigns. Candidates they supported won 6 governorships, 3 seats in the United States Senate, and 50 seats in the House of Representatives.

The Populist Party

Pleased with such successes, Alliance leaders worked to turn the movement into a national political party. In February 1890, Alliance members had formed the People's Party of the U.S.A., also known as the Populist Party. The goals of this new party were rooted in **populism,** or appeal to the common people.

The new party claimed that the government, not private companies, should own the railroads and telegraph lines. The Populists also wanted to replace the country's gold-based currency system with a flexible currency system that was based on free silver—the unlimited production of silver coins. They believed that putting more silver coins into the economy would give farmers more money to pay their debts.

The Populist Party supported a number of political and labor reforms. They wanted election reforms such as limiting the president and vice president to a single term, electing senators directly, and introducing the use of secret ballots. They also called for shorter hours for workers and the creation of a national income tax.

Populist Gains and Problems

At a convention in **Omaha, Nebraska,** in July 1892, the Populist Party nominated **James B. Weaver** of Iowa to run for president. In the election Weaver received more than 1 million votes—8.5 percent of the total—and 22 electoral votes. **Grover Cleveland,** the Democratic candidate, won the election, but the Populists had done well for a third party.

The Populists made a strong showing in the state and local elections of 1894 and had high hopes for the presidential election of 1896. The party nominated a number of energetic candidates, but it lacked money and organization.

$ Economics
Free Silver

To make matters worse, antagonism between the North and the South plagued the Populist Party. In addition many white Southerners could not bring themselves to join forces with African American Populists.

Another blow against populism was struck by the Democratic Party in the South. In the 1890s Democrat-controlled Southern state legislatures placed strict limits on the rights of African Americans to vote. Many freedmen—who might have supported the Populists—were unable to vote.

The Populist crusade for free silver and against the "money power" continued, however. Banking and business interests warned that coining unlimited amounts of new currency would lead to inflation and ruin the economy.

Farmers were joined by debtors in supporting free silver, hoping that loans could be repaid more cheaply. Silver-mining companies in the West also supported the cause. If the government coined large quantities of silver, they had a place to sell their metal.

In the mid-1890s Democrats from farm and silver-producing states took up the free silver issue. This created a problem for Populists. Should they ally themselves with these Democrats? Or should they remain a separate party and risk dividing the free-silver vote?

The Election of 1896

President Grover Cleveland, a Democrat, opposed free silver. At their 1896 convention, however, the Democrats chose a candidate for president who supported free silver and other Populist goals. He was 36-year-old **William Jennings Bryan,** known as the Great Commoner because of his appeal to average Americans. Bryan passionately believed in the farmers' causes.

The Populists decided to endorse Bryan as their candidate for president and to nominate their own candidate, Tom Watson of Georgia, for vice president. The Republicans nominated **William McKinley** of Ohio for president. A former representative and governor of Ohio, McKinley was a shrewd politician who opposed free silver.

A fiery speaker, Bryan proved to be an outstanding campaigner. He crossed the nation giving one dynamic speech after another, attacking bankers and other money interests.

Bryan's strenuous campaigning was in vain. By the time of the election, an economic depression that had slowed business in the early 1890s was nearly over. Voters believed that good times were returning, and they put their trust in the Republican candidate McKinley, who represented stability. Even the economic situation of the farmers was improving. The Populists' message no longer seemed urgent. McKinley won 271 electoral votes to Bryan's 176. McKinley received 7.1 million popular votes to 6.5 million for Bryan. The Populist ticket received only 222,600 popular votes and won no electoral votes.

The Populist Legacy

In one sense, however, the Populists were victorious. Reformers adopted many Populist ideas and succeeded in getting many new laws passed. In the 1900s, the United States abandoned the gold standard, adopted an eight-hour workday, and introduced an income tax. Election reforms brought in the secret ballot and direct election of senators. These were Populist goals.

✓ **Reading Check** **Examining** Which of the Populists' political reforms are a part of our political system today?

SECTION 4 ASSESSMENT

Checking for Understanding

1. **Key Terms** Write a one-page newsletter for the Populist Party that uses these terms: National Grange, cooperative, Populist Party, free silver.

2. **Reviewing Facts** Who were the presidential candidates in the election of 1896?

Reviewing Themes

3. **Groups and Institutions** Why were granges and alliances formed?

Critical Thinking

4. **Making Inferences** Why do you think the Populists considered themselves to be a party of the people?

5. **Analyzing Information** Re-create the diagram below and explain what actions farmers took to address their problems.

```
       Farmers' problems
      /       |        \
Action:   Action:    Action:
```

Analyzing Visuals

6. **Analyzing Political Cartoons** Look at the cartoon on page 550. Why are the names of many groups shown on the balloon?

Interdisciplinary Activity

Citizenship Write a campaign slogan for a Populist candidate who is running for office, and make a bumper sticker displaying your slogan.

Chapter Summary
The Western Frontier

Mining
- Gold is discovered on Pikes Peak
- Comstock Lode discovered
- Mining companies form
- Boomtowns appear
- Many boomtowns turn into ghost towns

Railroads
- Railroads expand to meet needs of Western mines
- Railroads receive government grants
- Transcontinental rail line completed
- More settlers move west
- Raw materials shipped east; manufactured goods shipped west

Western Frontier

Ranchers and Farmers
- Long drives move cattle to railroad towns
- Cow towns become important stations
- Homestead Act increases settlement of Great Plains
- Oklahoma opened to homesteaders

Native Americans
- Plains Native Americans depend on the buffalo
- Whites massacre the buffalo
- Government moves Native Americans to reservations
- Native American resistance leads to war
- Conflict with Native Americans ends with massacre at Wounded Knee

Reviewing Key Terms

On a sheet of paper, create a crossword puzzle using the following terms. Use the terms' definitions as your crossword clues.

1. lode
2. ore
3. vigilante
4. cooperative
5. nomadic
6. reservation

Reviewing Key Facts

7. In what ways did the transcontinental railroad help to boost the American economy?
8. Where did the Chisholm Trail begin?
9. What attracted farmers to the Great Plains?
10. Who were the Exodusters?
11. What problem did dry farming address?
12. What actions by whites destroyed the buffalo population?
13. In what present-day state was the Indian Territory located?
14. Who was Geronimo?
15. How did the Grange help farmers?
16. What political reforms did the Populists support?

Critical Thinking

17. **Geography and History** How did the rush to find gold and silver spark the creation of new communities in the West?
18. **Analyzing Themes: Economic Factors** Why was the Cattle Kingdom dependent on the railroads?
19. **Analyzing Themes: Groups and Institutions** Describe the problems that led farmers to organize granges and alliances.
20. **Analyzing Themes: Culture and Traditions** Re-create the diagram below and describe what actions by the United States government and white settlers brought an end to the traditional Native American way of life.

Actions

Geography and History Activity

Study the map on page 544 and answer these questions.

21. **Location** In what state did the Battle of Little Bighorn take place?

22. **Movement** In which direction from Wyoming did the Nez Perce people travel?

23. **Region** In what area did the Hopi people live?

Practicing Skills

Reading a Special-Purpose Map

Study the special-purpose map below; then answer the questions that follow.

24. What geographic region is shown?

25. In what part of Texas were most of the large cattle ranches located?

26. Where did the Western Trail end?

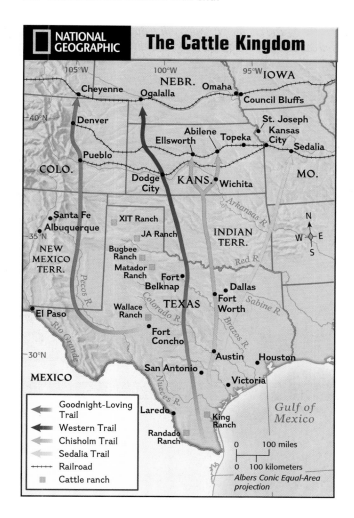

The Cattle Kingdom

Legend:
- → Goodnight-Loving Trail
- → Western Trail
- → Chisholm Trail
- → Sedalia Trail
- +++++ Railroad
- ▪ Cattle ranch

0 100 miles
0 100 kilometers
Albers Conic Equal-Area projection

Self-Check Quiz
Visit taj.glencoe.com and click on **Chapter 18—Self-Check Quizzes** to prepare for the chapter test.

Citizenship Cooperative Activity

27. **Constitutional Interpretations** With a partner, find information about the Civil Rights Act of 1964, the Voting Rights Act of 1975, and Americans with Disabilities Act of 1990. Prepare an informational brochure that describes these acts.

Economics Activity

28. **History and Economics** Today many Native Americans still live on reservations. Some reservations have developed their own businesses and industries to help make them more self-sufficient. With a partner, research to find information about a reservation in the United States today. Write a report describing one of the major businesses on that reservation.

Alternative Assessment

29. **Portfolio Writing Activity** Reread and take notes on the section of the chapter that discusses the chores of a farm woman. Use your notes to create an hour-by-hour schedule to show one day's typical activities for a farm wife living on the Great Plains.

Standardized Test Practice

Directions: Choose the *best* answer to the following question.

People in the late 1800s took advantage of the open grasslands of the West to develop which of these industries?

A Banking

B Manufacturing

C Ranching

D Mining

Test-Taking Tip

The important words in this question are *open grasslands.* Banking and manufacturing do not need open grasslands, so you can easily eliminate answers **A** and **B**.

CHAPTER 19

The Growth of Industry

1865–1914

Why It Matters

Innovations in technology and new business combinations helped the United States develop into a great industrial power. By the year 1900, United States industrial production was the greatest in the world.

The Impact Today

Innovations in technology and economics have transformed national and regional economies into a global economy. Developments in transportation and communications have made international trade an economic driving force in today's world.

The American Journey Video *The chapter 19 video, "The Builders of Our Railroads," examines the life and hardships that immigrants faced as workers on the railroads.*

1869
• First transcontinental railroad completed

1870
• Rockefeller organizes Standard Oil Company

1876
• Bell patents the telephone

1879
• Edison invents electric light

1886
• Trade unions form AFL

United States PRESIDENTS

A. Johnson 1865–1869

Grant 1869–1877

Hayes 1877–1881

Garfield 1881

Arthur 1881–1885

1860

1870

1880

World

1867
• Canada becomes self-governing dominion

Identifying Main Ideas Study Foldable Make this foldable to describe the growth of industry in the United States in the late 1800s.

Step 1 Fold two sheets of paper in half from top to bottom. Cut the papers in half along the folds.

Cut along the fold lines.

Step 2 Fold each of the four papers in half from top to bottom.

Step 3 On each folded paper, make a cut 1 inch from the side on the top flap.

1"

Cut 1 inch from the edge through the top flap only.

Step 4 Place the folded papers one on top of the other. Staple the four sections together and label each of the tabs **Railroads, Inventions, Big Business,** and **Industrial Workers.**

Staple here.

Railroads

Reading and Writing As you read, write what you learn about the developments of industry under each appropriate tab.

The Ironworkers' Noontime by Thomas Pollock Anshutz Factory workers in Wheeling, West Virginia, take their noontime break.

1890
• Sherman Antitrust Act passed

1896
• Ford's first auto built

1903
• Wright brothers fly first motorized airplane

1908
• Ford introduces Model T

Cleveland 1885–1889

B. Harrison 1889–1893

Cleveland 1893–1897

McKinley 1897–1901

Roosevelt 1901–1909

1890

1900

1895
• Marconi sends first radio signals
• Lumière brothers introduce motion pictures

1901
• Australia becomes self-governing dominion

1907
• New Zealand becomes self-governing dominion

HISTORY
Online

Chapter Overview
Visit taj.glencoe.com and click on **Chapter 19— Chapter Overviews** to preview chapter information.

Railroads Lead the Way

Guide to Reading

Main Idea
A growing transportation network spread people, products, and information across the nation.

Key Terms
consolidation, standard gauge, rebate, pool

Reading Strategy
Analyzing Information As you read the section, complete a diagram like the one shown by describing the contributions of the railroad to the growth of industry.

The role of the railroad

Read to Learn
• how the railroad barons made huge fortunes.
• how the national railroad system changed the American economy.

Section Theme
Geography and History As the railroads expanded, the centers of some industries shifted.

Preview of Events

◆1860	◆1870	◆1880	◆1890

1869
First transcontinental railroad completed

1880s
Standard width for railroad tracks adopted

1883
Northern Pacific Railroad opens

1890s
Five railway lines cross the country

AN American Story

Rugged construction gangs labored on the Union Pacific and other railways during the transportation boom of the late 1800s. The chorus of a favorite song told of the hard work of the tarriers, or drillers:

And drill, ye tarriers, drill!
Drill, ye tarriers, drill!
For it's work all day for sugar in
*   your tay,*

Down behind of the railway and,
Drill, ye tarriers, drill!
And blast!
And fire!

Railroad Expansion

During the Civil War, trains carried troops, weapons, and supplies to the front. The superior railroad system of the North played an important role in its victory over the South. In the decades after the war, railroads became a driving force behind America's economic growth. The first transcontinental railroad, completed in 1869, was soon followed by others. By the 1890s five railway lines crossed the country, and hundreds of smaller lines branched off from them. The railroad system grew rapidly. In 1860 the United States had about 30,000 miles (48,270 km) of railroad track. By 1900, the nation had nearly 250,000 miles (402,250 km) of track.

Work songs such as "John Henry" and "I've Been Working on the Railroad" were popular among those who labored to build these miles of track. They sang:

> ❝I've been working on the railroad,
> All the live-long day,
> I've been working on the railroad,
> Just to pass the time away.❞

The expansion of the railroad system was accompanied by consolidation—the practice of combining separate companies—in the industry. Large railroad companies expanded by buying smaller companies or by driving them out of business. Consolidation made the large companies more efficient. After consolidation, a few powerful individuals known as **railroad barons** controlled the nation's rail traffic.

Railroad Barons

New Yorker Cornelius Vanderbilt, one of the first railroad barons, gained control of the New York Central line and then made a fortune by consolidating several companies. His railroad empire stretched from New York City to the Great Lakes.

Another railroad baron, James J. Hill, built the Great Northern line between Minnesota and Washington State. Until his death in 1916, Hill continued building and directing his ever-growing business empire. Collis P. Huntington, Leland Stanford, and two other partners founded the Central Pacific, which connected California and Utah.

The railroad barons were aggressive and competitive. They lived in an age when few laws had been passed to regulate business, and some of their methods were highly questionable. Nevertheless, the railroad barons played an important part in building the nation's transportation system.

✓ **Reading Check** **Analyzing** What did consolidation mean for many small companies?

$ Economics

Railroads Stimulate the Economy

The fast-growing national rail system created new economic links in the country. The railroads carried raw materials such as iron ore, coal, and timber to factories. They also carried manufactured goods from factories to markets and transported produce from farming areas to the cities.

The national railroad system encouraged the expanding economy in many other ways. At first the demand for iron tracks and locomotives helped the iron mining and processing industries grow. Around 1880 railroad companies began using tracks of steel—a metal made stronger by adding carbon and other elements to refined iron. The use of steel in railroad tracks stimulated America's steel industry.

The railroads also helped other industries to thrive. The lumber industry, which supplied wood for railway ties, and the coal industry, which provided fuel for locomotives, saw extraordinary growth. In addition railroad companies provided work for thousands of people who laid tracks and built stations and for those who manufactured railway cars and equipment.

Improving the Railroads

Increased use made it necessary for railroads to expand and unify their systems. While railroads were being built across the country, different lines used rails of different gauges, or widths. As a result trains of one line could not use another line's tracks. Many early local lines carried goods for short distances and did not even

Labor

Railroads employed more workers in the late 1800s than any other industry. In the late 1800s, railroads became the nation's largest industry. It surpassed all others as a buyer of iron, steel, and coal, and became the nation's largest employer.

NATIONAL GEOGRAPHIC
Major Western Railroads before 1900

By 1883 several railroads crossed the West. The transcontinentals shipped settlers and goods there and hauled out raw resources.

Trains could carry passengers from New York City to San Francisco in less than 10 days.

The refrigerated railroad car in the 1870s allowed fresh meat and produce to be transported all over the nation.

0   300 miles
0   300 kilometers
Lambert Equal-Area projection

Railroads
Mining centers

Geography *Skills*

By the 1890s more than 150,000 miles (241,350 km) of tracks had been laid.

1. **Identifying** Which railroad connected Los Angeles to New Orleans?
2. **Analyzing Information** Which railroads would a traveler use from St. Louis to Virginia City?

connect with other lines. The gaps in service between the various lines made long-distance railroad travel slow and inefficient.

As the railroad companies consolidated, railroad barons saw the advantages of being part of a national railroad network. During the late 1880s, almost all companies adopted a standard gauge of 4 feet, 8.5 inches as the width of the railroad track. A standard gauge allowed faster shipment of goods at a reduced cost. It was no

longer necessary to load and unload goods from one train to another. One train could make the entire journey.

Railroad Technology

Railway transportation also improved with the introduction of new technology. Four developments were particularly important. Inventor **George Westinghouse** devised air brakes that improved the system for stopping trains, making train travel safer. Janney car couplers, named after inventor **Eli H. Janney,** made it easier for railroad workers to link cars. Refrigerated cars, developed by **Gustavus Swift,** enabled the railroads to ship meat and other perishable goods over long distances. Finally, **George M. Pullman** developed the Pullman sleeping car—

a luxury railway car with seats that converted into beds for overnight journeys. Pullman also introduced improved dining cars, raising train travel to a new level of comfort.

Competing for Customers

As the railroad network expanded, the railroad companies competed fiercely with one another to keep old customers and to win new ones. Large railroads offered secret discounts called rebates to their biggest customers. Smaller railroads that could not match these rebates were often forced out of business. Giving discounts to big customers raised freight rates for farmers and other customers who shipped small amounts of goods.

The railroad barons also made secret agreements among themselves, known as pools. They divided the railway business among their companies and set rates for a region. With no other competition in its region, a railroad could charge higher rates and earn greater profits. Although Congress and some states passed laws to regulate the railroads, these laws did little to curb the railroad barons.

Railroads Change America

The growing railroad network paved the way for American industry to expand into the West. The center of the flour milling industry, for example, shifted westward in the 1800s, moving from the East Coast to Ohio, to Minneapolis, and finally to Kansas City. Other industries followed the same pattern. As farmers settled the Great Plains, the manufacturing center for agricultural equipment moved from central New York State to Illinois and Wisconsin.

Railroads also touched the lives of thousands of Americans. Trains redistributed the population. They carried homesteaders into the Great Plains and the West. Trains also made it easy for people to move from rural areas to the cities.

Time Zones

Railroads affected the way Americans thought about time as well. As train travel became more common, people began measuring distances by how many hours the trip would take rather than by the number of miles traveled. The spread of the railroad system led to a national system of time with four time zones.

The railroads opened the entire United States to settlement and economic growth and united the different regions of the country into a single network. At the same time, inventions that revolutionized transportation and communication brought Americans together in new ways.

Reading Check **Explaining** Why was adopting standard-gauge tracks important for the railroad industry?

SECTION 1 ASSESSMENT

Checking for Understanding

1. **Key Terms** Use each of these terms in a sentence that will help explain its meaning: **consolidation, standard gauge, rebate, pool.**
2. **Reviewing Facts** Describe the methods used by railroad barons to drive smaller companies out of business.

Reviewing Themes

3. **Geography and History** How did the railroads pave the way for the expansion of industry in the West?

Critical Thinking

4. **Making Inferences** Do you think the federal government should have intervened to regulate the unfair practices of the railroad barons? Why or why not?
5. **Organizing Information** Re-create the diagram below and identify the developments in technology that improved railroad transportation.

Railroad technology

Analyzing Visuals

6. **Geography Skills** Study the map of the major western railroads that appears on page 558. Through what states did the Great Northern Railroad pass? Through what cities in Montana did railroads pass?

Interdisciplinary Activity

Art Create an ad with words and pictures to announce the development of the new Pullman sleeping car.

Social Studies SKILLBUILDER

Reading a Time Zone Map

NATIONAL GEOGRAPHIC

United States Time Zones

ARCTIC CIRCLE

International Date Line

2:00 P.M. — Alaska Time
3:00 P.M. — Pacific Time
4:00 P.M. — Mountain Time
5:00 P.M. — Central Time
6:00 P.M. — Eastern Time
7:00 P.M. — Atlantic Time

60°N

12:00 P.M.

1:00 P.M. — Hawaii-Aleutian Time

7:30 P.M. — New-foundland Time

30°N

TROPIC OF CANCER

0   1,000 miles
0   1,000 kilometers
Mercator projection   120°W

150°W   90°W   60°W

Earth's surface is divided into 24 time zones. Each zone represents 15° longitude, or the distance the earth rotates in one hour. The 0° line of longitude—the Prime Meridian—is the starting point for figuring time around the world. Traveling west from the Prime Meridian, it becomes one hour earlier; traveling east, it becomes one hour later. To read a time zone map, follow these steps:

- Locate a place where you know what time it is and select another place where you wish to know the time.
- Notice the time zones you cross between these two places.
- If the second place lies east of the first, add an hour for each time zone. If it lies west, subtract an hour for each zone.

Practicing the Skill

1. Describe how U.S. time changes as you move from east to west.

2. What U.S. time zone lies farthest west?

3. If it is 6:00 P.M. in Washington, D.C., what time is it in San Diego, California?

Applying the Skill

Reading a Time Zone Map It takes two hours to fly from Denver, Colorado, to Chicago, Illinois. If you leave Denver at 2:00 A.M., what time will it be in Chicago when you arrive?

GO TO

Glencoe's **Skillbuilder Interactive Workbook CD-ROM, Level 1,** provides instruction and practice in key social studies skills.

Inventions

Guide to Reading

Main Idea
Inventions improved the transportation and communication networks that were vital to the nation's industrial growth.

Key Terms
assembly line, mass production

Reading Strategy
Organizing Information As you read the section, re-create the diagram below to list each person's invention and to explain the significance of each invention to industrial growth.

	Invention	Significance
Samuel Morse		
Alexander Bell		
Thomas Edison		

Read to Learn
- what changes in transportation and communication transformed America.
- how labor-saving inventions affected life.

Section Theme
Science and Technology New inventions promoted economic growth.

Preview of Events

♦1870   ♦1890   ♦1910

1868
Christopher Sholes invents the typewriter

1876
Alexander Bell develops the telephone

1879
Edison develops first practical lightbulb

1903
The Wright brothers fly at Kitty Hawk

1908
Henry Ford introduces the Model T

AN American Story

In the early 1900s, American songwriters were caught up in the public fascination with new inventions. One of the most popular songs of 1905, "In My Merry Oldsmobile," celebrated the automobile:

"Come away with me Lucile,
In my merry Oldsmobile.
Down the road of life we'll fly,
Automobubbling you and I.

To the church we'll swiftly steal,
Then our wedding bells will peal;
You can go as far as you like, . . .
In my merry Oldsmobile."

Communication Changes

By 1910 Americans in cities drove cars through streets lit with electric lights. They went to department stores where they bought everything from kitchen sinks to shoes. Americans could also do their shopping by mail—or pick up the telephone and order groceries from the local store. The automobile, the electric light, and the telephone were all invented after 1870. Within a generation they had become part of everyday life for millions of people. New inventions helped people communicate more quickly over long distances. Improvements in communication helped unify the regions of the country and promoted economic growth.

Why It Matters

The First Flight at Kitty Hawk

A small crowd of people assembled on the sand dunes at Kitty Hawk, North Carolina, to test the Wrights' Flyer. Covering a few hundred feet in 12 seconds, the flight came to a halt when the Flyer's wing caught on one of the dunes. It was enough to encourage the Wrights to try further flights. They would soon have a practical aircraft and the world would have a new form of transportation.

Space shuttle Discovery, 1990

The Beginning of Controlled, Powered Flight

Inventors experimented with engine-powered aircraft in the 1800s, but the age of air travel did not begin until 1903 at Kitty Hawk, North Carolina. Orville and Wilbur Wright, brothers and bicycle mechanics, built a wood-and-canvas plane with a 12-horsepower engine. On the morning of December 17, Orville Wright took off in their plane and flew a distance of 120 feet.

Firsts in Aviation History

In less than 100 years, aviators advanced from making the first flight in a glider to breaking the speed of sound.

1853 → Human-carrying flight in a glider built by Sir George Cayley takes place	**1874** → Steam-powered monoplane is briefly airborne	**1903** → Wright brothers take flight at Kitty Hawk	**1909** → Louis Blériot flies across the English Channel	**1914** → Scheduled airline service opens between St. Petersburg and Tampa, Florida

The Telegraph

Samuel Morse had introduced the telegraph in 1844. By 1860 the United States had thousands of miles of telegraph lines, which were controlled for the most part by the Western Union Telegraph Company. At telegraph offices, trained operators transmitted messages in Morse code. Telegrams offered almost instant communication and had many uses. Shopkeepers relied on telegrams to order goods, and reporters used them to transmit stories to their newspapers. Americans also began sending personal messages by telegram.

The telegraph soon linked the United States and Europe. In the 1860s news from Europe traveled to this country by ship and took several weeks. **Cyrus Field** wanted to speed up the process. After several unsuccessful attempts, in 1866 Field managed to lay a telegraph cable across the Atlantic Ocean. The new transatlantic telegraph carried messages in a matter of seconds, bringing the United States and Europe closer together.

The Telephone Rings In

Alexander Graham Bell invented a device that revolutionized communications even more than Morse's telegraph. Born and educated in Scotland, Bell moved to the United States, where he studied ways of teaching hearing-impaired people to speak. At the same time, he experimented with sending voices through electrical wires.

Bi-wing plane, early 1900s

Taking to the Air

- The Flyer was a biplane with a light and powerful gas engine.

- The Wrights used adjustable rudders to control the aircraft as it turned.

- The two propellers were each $8\frac{1}{2}$ feet in diameter.

- The wingspan reached 40 feet, 4 inches.

- The distance from the nose to the tail was 21 feet, 1 inch.

- The weight of the craft was 605 pounds.

Chuck Yeager and the Bell X-1

1914 → Aerial combat between German and French World War I pilots

1919 → First nonstop flight across the Atlantic Ocean

1927 → Lindbergh completes first nonstop solo transatlantic flight

1939 → German Heinkel is first jet-powered aircraft to fly

1947 → Chuck Yeager is first to fly faster than the speed of sound

By 1876 Bell developed a device that transmitted speech—the telephone. While Bell was preparing to test the device, he accidentally spilled some battery acid on his clothes. In panic Bell called out to his assistant in another room: "Mr. Watson, come here. I want you!" Watson heard Bell's voice coming through the telephone. The invention was a success.

Bell formed the Bell Telephone Company in 1877. By the 1890s he had sold hundreds of thousands of phones. Most early telephone customers were businesses. Before long, though, telephones became common in homes.

✓ **Reading Check** **Explaining** How did the telegraph affect communication?

The Genius of Invention

The late 1800s saw a burst of inventiveness in the United States. Between 1860 and 1890, the United States government granted more than 400,000 patents for new inventions.

Many of the inventions helped businesses operate more efficiently. Among these were Christopher Sholes's typewriter (1868) and William Burroughs's adding machine (1888).

Other inventions affected everyday life. In 1888 **George Eastman** invented a small box camera—the Kodak—that made it easier and less costly to take photographs. **John Thurman** developed a vacuum cleaner in 1899 that simplified housework.

Thomas Edison

The Wizard of Menlo Park

Thomas Edison was called "dull" by his teachers. Because of poor hearing he had trouble in school and often didn't attend. His mother finally removed him from school and taught him at home. He loved anything related to science, and she allowed him to set up a chemistry lab in the family's basement. When he was 12, he got a job working for the railroad, where he set up a new lab in an empty freight car. One day, Edison saved the life of a child who had fallen onto the tracks of an oncoming train. The child's father took an interest in Edison and taught him to use the telegraph. Edison's first invention was a gadget that sent automatic telegraph signals—which he invented so he could sleep on the job.

While still in his 20s, Edison decided to go into the "invention business." In 1876 Edison set up a workshop in Menlo Park, New Jersey. Out of this famous laboratory came the phonograph, the motion picture projector, the telephone transmitter, and the storage battery. But Edison's most important invention was the electric lightbulb.

Edison developed the first workable lightbulb in 1879. He then designed power plants that could produce electric power and distribute it to lightbulbs. For Christmas in 1880, Edison used 40 bulbs to light up Menlo Park. Visitors flocked to see the "light of the future." He built the first central electric power plant in 1882 in New York City—illuminating 85 buildings!

Inventor **George Westinghouse** took Thomas Edison's work with electricity even further. In 1885 Westinghouse developed and built transformers that could send electric power more cheaply over longer distances. Soon electricity powered factories, trolleys, streetlights, and lamps all over America. Westinghouse also developed a system for transporting natural gas and invented many safety devices.

African American Inventors

A number of African Americans contributed to the era of invention. **Lewis Howard Latimer,** an engineer, developed an improved filament for the lightbulb and joined Thomas Edison's company. **Granville Woods,** an electrical and mechanical engineer from Ohio, patented dozens of inventions. Among them were an electric incubator and railroad improvements such as an electromagnetic brake and an automatic circuit breaker. **Elijah McCoy** invented a mechanism for oiling machinery.

Jan E. Matzeliger, another African American inventor, developed a shoe-making machine that performed many steps previously done by hand. His device, which revolutionized the shoe industry, was adopted in shoe factories in the United States and overseas.

✓ **Reading Check** **Evaluating** Which of Edison's inventions do you think is the most valuable to our world? Explain your reasoning.

A Changing Society

In the 1900s improvements ushered in a new era of transportation. After a period of experimentation, the automobile became a practical method of getting from place to place.

Henry Ford's Automobiles

Henry Ford wanted to build an inexpensive car that would last a lifetime. While working as an engineer in **Detroit, Michigan,** in the 1890s, Ford had experimented with an automobile engine powered by gasoline. In 1903 he established an automaking company and began designing cars.

In 1906 Ford had an idea for a new type of car. He told Charles Sorenson, later Ford's general superintendent, "We're going to get a car now that we can make in great volume and get the prices way down." For the next year, Ford and Sorenson worked on the **Model T,** building the car and testing it on rough roads. In 1908 Ford introduced the Model T to the public. Sorenson described the sturdy black vehicle as

66 . . . a car which anyone could afford to buy, which anyone could drive anywhere, and which almost anyone could keep in repair. **99**

These qualities made the Model T immensely popular. During the next 18 years, Ford's company sold 15 million Model T's. Henry Ford also pioneered a new, less expensive way to manufacture cars—the assembly line. On the assembly line, each worker performed an assigned task again and again at a certain stage in the production of the automobile. The assembly line

MORE ABOUT...

Changing the Way We Live

Inventions American ingenuity, innovation, and imagination led to the inventions that changed the way we live and how we communicate.

The Telephone Alexander Graham Bell demonstrated the telephone in 1876. The telephone soon became a necessity. By 1900 there were 2 million in use.

Phonograph The first practical phonograph was built by Thomas Edison in 1877.

Lighting the World Lewis Latimer improved on Edison's version, creating a bulb that lasted much longer, and developed the threaded socket. Latimer directed the installation of electric street lights in New York City, Philadelphia, Montreal, and London.

Kodak Camera In 1888 George Eastman invented a small camera that made it easier and less costly to take photographs.

1912 Model T Ford

revolutionized industry, enabling manufacturers to produce large quantities of goods more quickly. This mass production of goods decreased manufacturing costs, so products could be sold more cheaply.

Selling Goods

With factories churning out more and more products, merchants looked for better ways to sell their goods. One way was through the mail. In 1863 mail delivery to homes began—up to then, service was only to post offices. By the 1890s, the U.S. Post Office had expanded its delivery service in rural areas.

Merchants could now send goods across the country nearly as easily as across town. Some firms developed mail order businesses, receiving and shipping orders by mail. Companies such as Montgomery Ward and Sears Roebuck published catalogs that offered a wide range of goods from shoes to farm equipment. Catalogs introduced rural families to a wide assortment of goods not found in country stores.

Chain stores—stores with identical branches in many places—grew rapidly. F.W. Woolworth's chain of "five-and-ten-cent stores" specialized in the sale of everyday household and personal items at bargain prices. By 1911 more than a thousand Woolworth's were in operation. The Woolworth Building, erected in New York City in 1913, stood 792 feet (241 meters) tall—the tallest building in the world at that time.

✓ **Reading Check** **Describing** What qualities made the Model T popular?

HISTORY Online

Student Web Activity
Visit taj.glencoe.com and click on **Chapter 19— Student Web Activities** for an activity on inventions.

SECTION 2 ASSESSMENT

Checking for Understanding

1. **Key Terms** Use the terms assembly line and mass production in a complete sentence that explains their meaning.
2. **Reviewing Facts** Name and describe two inventions that changed the way Americans communicated in the 1800s.

Reviewing Themes

3. **Science and Technology** How was transportation improved during the early 1900s?

Critical Thinking

4. **Drawing Conclusions** Which invention do you think brought about the most dramatic change in people's lives? Explain.
5. **Organizing Information** Re-create the diagram below. From the description of inventions in this section, classify each invention in one of the categories.

Mostly rural use	Mostly urban use	Both urban and rural	Mostly used by business and industry

Analyzing Visuals

6. **Artifacts** Study the photographs of the inventions and products that appear in Section 2. Which have undergone the greatest change? Why do you think this is so?

Interdisciplinary Activity

Science Write a one-page paper describing how the inventions mentioned in this section changed the way Americans viewed the world. Discuss how these inventions led to further advances in scientific theory.

An Age of Big Business

Guide to Reading

Main Idea
Business growth was driven by the formation of corporations and the ambition of their owners.

Key Terms
corporation, stock, shareholder, dividend, horizontal integration, trust, monopoly, vertical integration, philanthropy, merger

Reading Strategy
Analyzing Information As you read the section, re-create the diagram below and explain the significance of each term to business in the late 1800s.

	Significance
Shareholders	
Stock exchanges	
Mergers	

Read to Learn
- how new discoveries and inventions helped industries grow.
- why the development of large corporations brought both benefits and problems.

Section Theme
Economic Factors Corporations changed the American economy of the late 1800s.

Preview of Events

♦1850	♦1875		♦1900
1859 Oil discovered in Titusville, Pennsylvania	**1870** Rockefeller organizes the Standard Oil Company	**1890** Sherman Antitrust Act prohibits monopolies	**1900** Andrew Carnegie rules the steel industry

AN American Story

John D. Rockefeller, a young oil man, never tired until he got what he wanted. One person commented: "The only time I ever saw John Rockefeller enthusiastic was when a report came in . . . that his buyer had secured a cargo of oil at a figure much below the market price. He bounded from his chair with a shout of joy, danced up and down, hugged me, threw up his hat, acted so like a madman that I have never forgotten it. . . ."

Foundations for Growth

In the hills of western Pennsylvania, a sticky black substance—petroleum—seeped from the ground. For a while promoters sold the oil as medicine. Then in the 1850s researchers found they could burn petroleum to produce heat and smoke-free light. It could also be used to lubricate machinery. Suddenly oil became valuable. A former railroad conductor named Edwin L. Drake believed that he could find petroleum by digging a well. People thought Drake was wrong. Few people knew that pools of oil did indeed exist underground.

In 1859 Drake decided to test his belief. He drilled a well in **Titusville, Pennsylvania,** and struck oil. This led to the creation of a multimillion-dollar petroleum industry.

Factors of Production

The period from the end of the Civil War to 1900 was an era of unmatched economic growth in the United States. New methods in technology and business allowed the country to tap its rich supply of natural resources, increase its production, and raise the money needed for growth. The growing transportation system made it easier for merchants to reach distant markets.

The change from an agricultural economy to an industrial one was possible because the United States had the resources needed for a growing economy. Among these resources were what economists call the **factors of production**: land, labor, and capital.

The first factor of production, **land,** means not just the land itself but all natural resources. The United States held a variety of natural resources that were useful for industrial production.

The second production factor is **labor.** Large numbers of workers were needed to turn raw materials into goods. This need was met by the rapid growth of population. Between 1860 and 1900, the population of the country more than doubled.

The third production factor, **capital,** is the equipment—buildings, machinery, and tools—used in production. Land and labor are needed to produce capital goods. These goods, in turn, are essential for the production of consumer goods.

The term "capital" is also used to mean money for investment. Huge amounts of money were needed to finance industrial growth. One source of money was the selling of stock by corporations. Another was corporate savings, or businesses investing a portion of their earnings in better equipment.

Raising Capital

With the economy growing after the Civil War, many railroads and other businesses looked for ways to expand. To do so they had to raise capital. They needed capital to buy raw materials and equipment, to pay workers, and to cover shipping and advertising costs.

One way a company could raise capital was by becoming a corporation. A corporation is a company that sells shares, or stock, of its business to the public. The people who invest in the corporation by buying stock are its shareholders, or partial owners.

In good times shareholders earn dividends—cash payments from the corporation's profits—on the stock they own. If the company prospers, its stock rises in value, and the shareholders can sell it for a profit. If the company fails, however, the shareholders lose their investment. In the late 1800s hundreds of thousands of people shared in corporate profits by buying and selling stocks in special markets known as **stock exchanges.**

Growth of Corporations

Railroads were the first businesses to form corporations, or "incorporate." Soon manufacturing firms and other businesses were incorporating as well. The growth of corporations helped fuel America's industrial expansion in the years following the Civil War.

Banks played a major role in this period of economic growth. Businesses borrowed money from banks to start or expand their operations. The banks, in turn, made profits on the loans.

✓ **Reading Check**
Explaining What are dividends?

Sign advertising oil

| (A) Standard Oil | (B) Government | (C) Suppliers |

The Oil Business

The oil industry grew rapidly in the late 1800s. Edwin Drake's Titusville well produced 15 barrels of petroleum a day. As word of his success spread, prospectors and investors hurried to western Pennsylvania. "Oil rush" towns with names such as Oil City and Petroleum Center sprang up overnight. The oil boom expanded as prospectors struck oil in Ohio and West Virginia.

John D. Rockefeller

Born in Richford, New York, in 1839, **John D. Rockefeller** made his fortune from oil. When Rockefeller was 26 years old, he and four partners set up an oil refinery—a plant to process oil—in **Cleveland, Ohio.**

In 1870 Rockefeller organized the Standard Oil Company of Ohio and set out to dominate the oil industry. He acquired most of the oil refineries in Cleveland and other cities.

One method Rockefeller used to build his empire was horizontal integration—combining competing firms into one corporation. The corporation produced and used its own tank cars, pipelines, and even its own wooden barrels—made from forests owned by Standard Oil. Standard Oil grew in wealth and power, becoming the most famous corporate empire of the day.

The Standard Oil Trust

To strengthen Standard Oil's position in the oil industry, Rockefeller lowered his prices to drive his competitors out of business. In addition he pressured customers not to deal with rival oil companies, and he persuaded the railroads to grant him rebates in exchange for his business.

Rockefeller increased his control of the oil industry in 1882 by forming a trust, a group of companies managed by the same board of directors. First he acquired stock in many different oil companies. Then the shareholders of these companies traded their stock for Standard Oil stock, which paid higher dividends. This gave Standard Oil's board of directors ownership of the

"Success can be attained in any branch of human labor. There is always room at the top in every pursuit."

—Andrew Carnegie, 1903

other companies' stock and the right to manage those companies. Rockefeller had created a monopoly—almost total control by a single producer—of the oil industry.

✓ **Reading Check** **Explaining** What method did Rockefeller use to build his oil empire?

The Steel Business

Steel also became a huge business in the late 1800s. Steel is a strong and long-lasting form of iron treated with carbon—the ideal material for railroad tracks, bridges, and many other products. Before the 1860s, however, steel was not widely used because it was expensive to manufacture. The development of new manufacturing techniques helped to overcome this problem.

Steel Industry Growth

Two new methods of making steel—the Bessemer process, developed by Henry Bessemer of England, and the open-hearth process—changed the industry. With the new methods, mills could produce steel at affordable prices and in large quantities. In the 1870s large steel mills emerged close to sources of iron ore in western Pennsylvania and eastern Ohio.

Pittsburgh, Pennsylvania, became the steel capital of the United States. Cities located near the mines and close to waterways like Cleveland, Chicago, Detroit, and Birmingham, Alabama, also became centers of steel production.

Andrew Carnegie

The leading figure in the early years of the American steel industry was **Andrew Carnegie,** son of a Scottish immigrant. Starting as a telegraph operator, Carnegie worked his way up to become manager of the Pennsylvania Railroad. In 1865 he left that job to invest in the growing iron industry.

Carnegie soon realized that steel would have an enormous market. After learning about the Bessemer process, he built a steel plant near Pittsburgh that used the new process. Carnegie named the plant the J. Edgar Thompson Steel Works, after the president of the Pennsylvania Railroad—his biggest customer.

Vertical Integration

By 1890 Andrew Carnegie dominated the steel industry. His company became powerful through vertical integration, acquiring companies that provided the equipment and services he needed. Carnegie bought iron and coal mines, warehouses, ore ships, and railroads to gain control of all parts of the business of making and selling steel. When Carnegie combined all his holdings into the Carnegie Steel Company in 1900, he was producing one-third of the nation's steel.

In 1901 Carnegie sold his steel company to banker **J. Pierpont Morgan.** Morgan combined the Carnegie company with other businesses to form the United States Steel Corporation, the world's first billion-dollar corporation.

Philanthropists

Andrew Carnegie, John D. Rockefeller, and other industrial millionaires of the time grew interested in philanthropy—the use of money to benefit the community. The philanthropists founded schools, universities, and other civic institutions across the United States.

Carnegie donated $350 million to various organizations. He built Carnegie Hall in New York City, one of the world's most famous concert halls; the Carnegie Foundation for the Advancement of Teaching; and more than 2,000 libraries worldwide. Rockefeller used his fortune to establish the University of Chicago in 1890 and New York's Rockefeller Institute for Medical Research.

Corporations Grow Larger

In 1889 New Jersey encouraged the trend toward business monopolies by allowing holding companies to obtain charters, a practice that some states prohibited. A holding company would buy controlling interests in the stock of other companies instead of purchasing the companies outright. Rockefeller formed Standard Oil of New Jersey so that the corporation could expand its holdings. Other states also passed laws that made corporate mergers—the combining of companies—easier.

Mergers concentrated economic power in a few giant corporations and a few powerful individuals, such as Rockefeller and banker J. Pierpont Morgan. By 1900 one-third of all American manufacturing was controlled by just 1 percent of the country's corporations. These giant corporations were the driving force behind the great economic growth of the period, but they also posed problems. On the one hand, many Americans admired the efficiencies that large businesses provided. On the other hand, some argued that a lack of competition hurt consumers. Without competition, corporations had no reason to keep their prices low or to improve their goods and services.

Government Regulation

State governments responded to the growing opposition to trusts and monopolies. During the 1880s, several states passed laws restricting business combinations. Corporations, however, avoided these laws by doing business in states that had no such laws.

Public pressure for a federal law to prohibit trusts and monopolies led Congress to pass the **Sherman Antitrust Act** in 1890. The law sought "to protect trade and commerce against unlawful restraint and monopoly." The act did not clearly define either "trusts" or "monopolies," however.

In its early years, the Sherman Antitrust Act did little to curb the power of big business. By contrast, in the 1890s the government did use the act to stop a strike by railroad workers that threatened to "restrain" the nation's mail delivery.

Reading Check **Comparing** How does vertical integration differ from horizontal integration?

SECTION 3 ASSESSMENT

Checking for Understanding

1. **Key Terms** Use the key terms that follow to write a newspaper article about Andrew Carnegie: corporation, monopoly, vertical integration, philanthropy.
2. **Reviewing Facts** What cities became centers of steel production in the late 1800s?

Reviewing Themes

3. **Economic Factors** Summarize the steps that John D. Rockefeller took to gain control of the oil industry.

Critical Thinking

4. **Determining Cause and Effect** Recreate the diagram below and list the benefits of competition to consumers.

Competition

5. **Comparing** Compare the methods used by Rockefeller and Carnegie to build their industrial empires. Describe any differences between the two.

Analyzing Visuals

6. **Analyzing Political Cartoons** Study the cartoon on page 569. Whom do the figures represent? What is the cartoon saying about the Standard Oil Company?

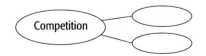

Citizenship Research to find a philanthropist who has provided benefits to the community in which you live—in the past or present. Share your findings with the class.

SECTION 4 Industrial Workers

Guide to Reading

Main Idea
Workers organized to demand better pay and working conditions.

Key Terms
sweatshop, trade union, collective bargaining, strikebreaker, injunction

Reading Strategy
Organizing Information As you read the section, re-create the diagram below and list actions labor unions took to improve working conditions.

Labor Unions

Read to Learn
• why workers demanded changes in their working conditions and wages.
• how labor unions helped workers gain economic and political power.

Section Theme
Groups and Institutions Industrial workers labored long hours for low pay.

Preview of Events

♦1870	♦1880	♦1890
1869 Knights of Labor organized	**1877** Railroad workers on strike	**1886** Riots erupt in Haymarket Square

AN American Story

On a spring day in 1886, about 12,000 workers in Chicago's Haymarket Square manufacturing district were on strike. Nearly all were immigrants, and many wore small red ribbons on their jackets. At 2 o'clock a man climbed up on an empty freight car near the crowd. He moved to the edge of the roof and waved frantically at the crowd below. "Stand firm," he yelled. "Let every man stand shoulder to shoulder and we will win this fight. We must have our rights. Strike while the iron is hot. . . ."

Working Conditions

The industrial growth of the late 1800s created new jobs. Growth also raised the standard of living for many American workers. That is, necessities and luxuries were more available and affordable. Yet workers paid a price for economic progress. Factories had once been small workplaces where employers and employees knew one another and often worked side by side. As mass production spread, however, factories became larger and less personal.

Industrial laborers worked for 10 or 12 hours a day, six days a week. They could be fired at any time for any reason. Many lost their jobs during business downturns or were replaced by immigrants who were willing to work for lower pay.

Factories and mines were noisy, unhealthy, and unsafe. Accidents were common. Steel workers suffered burns from spills of hot steel. Coal miners died in cave-ins and from the effects of gas and coal dust. Textile workers' lungs were damaged by airborne lint. Garment workers toiled in crowded urban factories called sweatshops, where their eyesight was ruined by sewing for hours in poor light. Filled with flammable materials, the sweatshops were also terrible firetraps.

📖 (See page 971 for a first-person account of sweatshop conditions.)

Women Workers

Although the majority of working women in the late 1800s had jobs as domestic servants, women also joined the industrial workforce, especially the textile industry. By 1900 more than one million women worked in industry. However, because no laws regulated workers' salaries, women generally received about half of what men earned for the same work.

Child Labor

Industries also hired children. In 1900, hundreds of thousands of children under 16 years of age worked in factories. Concerned groups brought child labor to the attention of their state legislatures. As a result many states passed child-labor laws. These laws stated that children working in factories had to be at least 12 years old and should not work more than 10 hours a day. Employers widely ignored child-labor laws, however. Also, the laws did not apply to agriculture, which employed about one million children.

✔ **Reading Check** **Examining** How did mass production change the size of factories?

Labor Unions Form

Dissatisfied workers organized into groups—labor unions—to demand better pay and working conditions from their employers. Earlier in the 1800s, skilled workers had formed unions to represent workers in certain crafts or trades, such as carpentry. These trade unions had little influence because each represented only one trade. By the mid-1800s labor leaders looked to expand their unions.

In 1869 garment cutters in Philadelphia founded the Noble and Holy Order of the **Knights of Labor.** Employers fired workers who joined labor organizations, so the Knights met secretly and used special handshakes to identify each other. Under the leadership of **Terence V. Powderly,** the Knights of Labor became a national labor organization in the 1880s. Unlike most unions, the Knights recruited people who had been kept out of trade unions, including women, African Americans, immigrants, and unskilled laborers.

The Knights of Labor grew rapidly to more than 700,000 members by 1886. However, a wave of strikes turned public opinion against the union, and it lost members and power in the 1890s.

In 1881 a group of national trade unions formed a federation that five years later became known as the **American Federation of Labor (AFL).** The AFL represented skilled workers in various crafts.

Young coal miners in Kingston, Pennsylvania, c. 1900

NATIONAL GEOGRAPHIC

Labor's Struggle for Justice, 1877–1914

Labor Unrest

1. **1877 Great Railway Strike**
   Workers protest pay cuts
2. **1886 Haymarket Affair**
   Labor rally ends in violence
3. **1892 New Orleans**
   Workers from 42 unions demand shorter
   hours and better pay
4. **1892 Homestead Strike**
   Steelworkers protest wage cut
5. **1892 Silver Mines Unrest**
   State jails hundreds of striking workers
6. **1894 Pullman Strike**
   Federal troops quell riots
7. **1902 Anthracite Coal Strike**
   Miners strike to win union recognition
8. **1914 Ludlow Massacre**
   State militia burns striking miners' tent colony

Geography *Skills*

The strike was the major weapon for workers against the management for whom they worked.
1. **Location** Which strikes involved miners?
2. **Analyzing Information** Which strike occurred in Martinsburg?

The AFL was led by **Samuel Gompers,** the tough, practical-minded president of the Cigar Makers' Union. The organization pressed for higher wages, shorter hours, better working conditions, and the right to bargain collectively with employers. In collective bargaining, unions represent workers in bargaining with management.

Although violent strikes turned public feeling against workers and unions in the late 1880s, the AFL survived and grew. By 1904 the AFL claimed more than 1.6 million members.

Women and the Unions

Many unions would not admit women workers, so some women formed their own unions. **Mary Harris Jones,** better known as Mother Jones, spent 50 years fighting for workers' rights.

In 1911 a fire broke out at the **Triangle Shirtwaist Company** factory, a crowded sweatshop in New York City. The workers, mostly young immigrant women, could not escape from the building because the company had locked the doors to prevent employees from leaving early. Nearly 150 workers died in the fire. The disaster led the **International Ladies' Garment Workers Union** (ILGWU) to push for a safer working environment.

✓ **Reading Check** **Comparing** Who was eligible for membership in the AFL? In the Knights of Labor?

The Unions Act

Economic depressions in the 1870s and the 1890s led companies to fire workers and lower wages. Unions responded with large strikes that sometimes sparked violence.

Economic depression hit the nation following a financial panic in 1873. To cut costs, companies forced their workers to take pay cuts. In July 1877 angry strikers burned rail yards, ripped up track, and destroyed railroad property. The companies hired strikebreakers to replace the striking workers, and federal troops restored order.

Antilabor feeling grew stronger after a bloody clash between police and strikers in Chicago's Haymarket Square in May 1886. Striking workers from the McCormick Harvester Company gathered to protest the killings of four strikers the previous day. When police ordered the crowd to break up, an unidentified person threw a bomb that killed a police officer. Several more were killed in a riot that followed. Following the **Haymarket Riot,** many Americans associated the labor movement with terrorism and disorder.

In 1892 workers went on strike at Andrew Carnegie's steel plant in Homestead, Pennsylvania. Plant managers had cut workers' wages, hoping to weaken the steelworkers' union. When the union called a strike, Homestead managers hired nonunion workers and brought in 300 armed guards to protect them. A fierce battle left at least 10 people dead. Pennsylvania's governor sent the state's militia to Homestead to restore order. The plant reopened with nonunion workers, protected by the troops. After the failure of the **Homestead Strike,** the steelworkers' union dwindled.

The employees of George Pullman's railway-car plant near Chicago went on strike in May 1894, when the company cut wages. Pullman responded by closing the plant. One month later, workers in the American Railway Union supported the strikers by refusing to handle Pullman cars, paralyzing rail traffic.

Pullman and the railroad owners fought back. They persuaded U.S. Attorney General Richard Olney to obtain an injunction, or court order, to stop the union from "obstructing the railways and holding up the mails." The workers and their leader, **Eugene V. Debs,** refused to end the strike. Debs was sent to jail.

President **Grover Cleveland** sent federal troops to Chicago, and soon the strike was over. The failure of the **Pullman Strike** dealt another blow to the union movement. Despite these setbacks, workers continued to organize to work for better wages and working conditions.

✓ **Reading Check** **Describing** Why did the Pullman workers go on strike?

SECTION 4 ASSESSMENT

Checking for Understanding

1. **Key Terms** Write a paragraph about the American Federation of Labor. Use the following terms: sweatshop, trade union, collective bargaining, strikebreaker, injunction.
2. **Reviewing Facts** What role did Samuel Gompers play in union growth?

Reviewing Themes

3. **Groups and Institutions** What were the goals of the American Federation of Labor when it was founded?

Critical Thinking

4. **Drawing Conclusions** Why do you think many Americans did not immediately support the labor unions?
5. **Organizing Information** Re-create the diagram below and describe the roles each played in labor-management issues.

Individual	Role
Terence Powderly	
Mary Harris Jones	
George Pullman	
Grover Cleveland	

Analyzing Visuals

6. **Geography Skills** Study the map on page 574. Which of the incidents shown on the map occurred in the 1890s? What events took place in Illinois? When did they occur?

Interdisciplinary Activity

Art Design a board game in which players can experience the ups and downs of factory work in the late 1800s. Include spaces such as "Workday extended to 12 hours. Miss a turn." and "Your union wins a pay hike. Collect $5."

Chapter Summary

The Growth of Industry

Railroads

- Settlers are transported west.
- Railroads deliver raw materials and finished goods.
- Thousands of jobs are provided.
- Large railroads offer secret rebates to customers and make secret agreements that raise rates.

Inventions

- The telegraph links the United States and Europe.
- Alexander Graham Bell invents the telephone.
- Thomas Alva Edison invents the electric lightbulb.
- Henry Ford uses assembly lines to mass-produce the automobile.
- Wright brothers fly airplane at Kitty Hawk.
- New processes improve steel production.

Companies

- Railroads are the first businesses to incorporate.
- John D. Rockefeller organizes Standard Oil, forms a trust, and creates a monopoly.
- Andrew Carnegie forms Carnegie Steel Company.
- Congress passes the Sherman Antitrust Act.

Labor Movement

- Working conditions in factories and mines are unhealthy.
- Women workers paid half of men's wages for same work.
- Child workers are exploited.
- Labor unions form to improve wages and working conditions.
- Labor union strikes sometimes result in violence.

Reviewing Key Terms

Use each of the following terms in a statement that might have been made by the person indicated.

1. **Railroad owner:** rebate, pool, standard gauge
2. **Union member:** trade union, collective bargaining
3. **Factory owner:** mass production, assembly line
4. **Shareholder:** stock, dividend

Reviewing Key Facts

5. What improvements in railway transportation were brought about by new technology?
6. What were four of Thomas Edison's inventions?
7. What inventions improved communications in the late 1800s?
8. What manufacturing methods did Henry Ford use to make his new automobile affordable?
9. What is vertical integration?
10. What action did Congress take to control trusts and monopolies in response to pressure from the American people?
11. What is collective bargaining?
12. How did the Haymarket Riot of 1886 affect public opinion about the labor movement?

Critical Thinking

13. **Analyzing Information** Describe the contributions of African American inventors in the late 1800s.
14. **Analyzing Themes: Economic Factors** How did horizontal integration differ from vertical integration?
15. **Drawing Conclusions** Why did workers think that forming organized labor unions would help them get what they wanted from employers?
16. **Analyzing Themes: Geography and History** Re-create the diagram below and describe two ways in which the growing railroad network helped American industry.

Railroad network

Geography and History Activity

Study the map below and answer the questions that follow.

Economics Activity

24. Using a product that is familiar to you, explain how each of the factors of production was used in its creation.

 ### Technology Activity

25. **Using a Spreadsheet** Become an imaginary shareholder in a corporation. Search for stock market data in a daily newspaper. Choose one stock to follow for a two-week period. Track the performance of the stock on a spreadsheet by marking its daily increases and decreases. Compare your spreadsheet with classmates' results and decide if you made a good investment.

 ### Alternative Assessment

26. **Portfolio Writing Activity** Review the chapter for information about the four major union strikes between 1877 and 1894. Write a headline for each that might have appeared in newspapers following the strike.

17. **Movement** What forms of transportation moved goods into and out of this region?

18. **Human/Environment Interaction** What industry grew in the timbered regions of Wisconsin and Michigan?

19. **Location** Identify the major iron/steel manufacturing centers shown on the map.

Practicing Skills

Reading a Time Zone Map *Study the time zone map on page 560. Use the map to answer the following questions.*

20. If you traveled from Florida to California, what time zones would you cross?

21. If it is 6:00 a.m. in Maine, what time is it in Hawaii?

22. If it is 3:00 p.m. in Texas, what time is it in Alaska?

Citizenship Cooperative Activity

23. **Labor Unions** With another student, write a short essay in which you support or criticize labor unions from the point of view of a young person who has just entered the workforce. Note how you think a union could or could not improve your life. Share your essay with the class.

Standardized Test Practice

Directions: Choose the *best* answer to the following question.

The development of the transformers that Westinghouse built led to an increase in

F the price of electricity.

G the use of gas to heat homes.

H the use of electricity to power factories.

J imported goods.

Test-Taking Tip

The phrase *led to* indicates that this question is looking for a *cause-and-effect* relationship. Remember that a *cause* is any person, event, or condition that makes something happen. What happens as a result is known as an *effect*.

Building a Conductivity Tester

What role does electricity play in your life? Can you imagine your life without electricity? Electricity powers lights, TVs, radios, ovens, microwaves, and computers, along with countless other objects you use every day.

The Way It Was

The Civil War had ended. No longer divided by war, Americans set about improving their lives. Inventors led the way. Inventors such as George Westinghouse, Lewis Howard Latimer, and Thomas Edison learned from one another, and together pushed the United States to become an industrial nation. To create the lightbulb, Edison first had to understand how electricity works. Now, conduct your own investigation of electrical currents, much as Edison did, and experience the life of an inventor. Find out which common objects are conductors and which are insulators by building and testing a battery-powered conductivity tester.

Believe It or Not

Thomas Edison suffered from hearing problems throughout his life. Although an operation could have saved his hearing, Edison refused it. He claimed he preferred deafness because it helped him concentrate.

Materials

- ✓ flashlight with one fresh D cell (battery)
- ✓ 3 pieces of insulated wire (each about 6 inches (15 cm) long, with the ends stripped)
- ✓ roll of masking or duct tape
- ✓ a penny
- ✓ a plastic comb
- ✓ several pieces of fabric
- ✓ a metal fork or spoon
- ✓ several different rocks
- ✓ various other objects to test

What To Do

Build your conductivity tester by unscrewing the top of the flashlight. You will find that the flashlight contains a bulb assembly.

1 Take one wire and tape it to the metal tip of the flashlight lightbulb. Tape a second wire to the metal ring that touches the side of the bulb.

2 Tape the other end of the wire that is connected to the tip of the lightbulb to the positive (+) end of a D cell (battery) and touch the free end of the second wire to the negative (–) end of the cell. The light should go on because you have made an electrical current. (If the light does not go on, make sure all the connections are taped tightly and make good contact.)

3 Tape one end of a third wire to the negative (–) end of the cell and touch the free end of that wire to the wire coming from the bulb holder. Again, the light should go on. Try touching the two free ends of the wires to the penny at the same time. The bulb should light because the penny is a good conductor.

Test your other objects in the same way that you tested the penny. Record whether they are conductors or insulators.

Project Report

1. In general, what types of materials make the best conductors?

2. From your experiment, how would you define an electrical current?

3. **Drawing Conclusions** What are some of the risks inventors take when experimenting with unfamiliar materials?

Go a Step Further

How was Edison able to invent such useful things? How would you go about inventing something? Research and learn about some of the inventors from the late 1800s and early 1900s. Note how these inventors got started. Then create a diagram that explains how you would go about creating a new invention.

CHAPTER 20

Toward an Urban America

1865–1914

Why It Matters

By 1914 as many Americans lived in cities as in rural areas. Between 1860 and 1910, the urban population of the nation grew from a little over 6 million people to more than 40 million.

The Impact Today

During these years of urban growth, many aspects of modern city life emerged. Problems arose, such as poverty, crime, and inadequate housing, but benefits such as daily newspapers, libraries, and public parks appeared as well.

 The American Journey Video *The chapter 20 video, "Ellis Island: In the Shadow of Lady Liberty," details the hardships immigrants faced when arriving in America.*

1882
- Chinese Exclusion Act passed

1884
- First skyscraper built in Chicago

1871
- Great Chicago fire

1886
- Statue of Liberty dedicated

United States PRESIDENTS

| A. Johnson 1865–1869 | Grant 1869–1877 | Hayes 1877–1881 | Garfield 1881 | Arthur 1881–1885 | Cleveland 1885–1889 | B. Harrison 1889–1893 |

1865   1875   1885

World

1866
- Transatlantic telegraph line successfully completed

1889
- Eiffel Tower erected

1900
- Freud's *Interpretation of Dreams* published

New York City, East Side, 1900 New arrivals crowded into America's cities and brought with them the cultural heritage of their homelands.

1892
- Ellis Island admits immigrants

1900
- Nation's population passes 75 million

1906
- San Francisco rocked by earthquake

1913
- Ford develops first moving assembly line

Cleveland 1893–1897

McKinley 1897–1901

T. Roosevelt 1901–1909

Taft 1909–1913

1895

1905

1915

c. 1907
- Cubism arises in art

1911
- Italy seizes Libya

HISTORY Online

Chapter Overview
Visit taj.glencoe.com and click on **Chapter 20— Chapter Overviews** to preview chapter information.

The New Immigrants

Guide to Reading

Main Idea
In the late 1800s and early 1900s, the pattern of immigration was changing.

Key Terms
emigrate, ethnic group, steerage, sweatshop, assimilate

Reading Strategy
Analyzing Information As you study Section 1, re-create the diagram below and write the reasons immigrants came to America.

Reasons for immigrating

Read to Learn
• what opportunities and difficulties immigrants found in the United States.
• how the arrival of new immigrants changed American society.

Section Theme
Culture and Traditions The number of immigrants from southern and eastern Europe increased dramatically.

Preview of Events

♦1880	♦1900	♦1920

1882
Chinese Exclusion Act is passed

1886
Statue of Liberty is erected

1892
Ellis Island starts processing immigrants

1917
Immigration Act of 1917 requires literacy

AN American Story

In the 1870s two young brothers left Italy for America. "We were so long on the water that we began to think we should never get to America. . . . We were all landed on an island and the bosses there said that Francisco and I must go back because we had not enough money, but a man named Bartolo came up and told them that . . . he was our uncle and would take care of us. . . . We came to Brooklyn to a wooden house on Adams Street that was full of Italians from Naples. Bartolo had a room on the third floor and there were fifteen men in the room, all boarding with Bartolo. . . . It was very hot in the room, but we were soon asleep, for we were very tired."

A Flood of Immigrants

Before 1865 most immigrants to the United States—except for the enslaved —came from northern and western Europe. The greater part of these "old" immigrants were Protestant, spoke English, and blended easily into American society. After the Civil War, even greater numbers of immigrants made the journey to the United States. The tide of new-comers reached a peak in 1907 when nearly 1.3 million people came to America.

★Geography

New Immigration

In the mid-1880s the pattern of immigration started to change. Large groups of "new" immigrants arrived from eastern and southern Europe. Greeks, Russians, Hungarians, Italians, Turks, and Poles were among the newcomers. At the same time, the number of "old" immigrants started to decrease. By 1907 only about 20 percent of the immigrants came from northern and western Europe, while 80 percent came from southern and eastern Europe.

Many of the newcomers from eastern and southern Europe were Catholics or Jews. Few spoke English. Because of this, they did not blend into American society as easily as the "old" immigrants had. Many felt like outsiders, and they clustered together in urban neighborhoods made up of people of the same nationality.

After 1900 immigration from Mexico also increased. In addition many people came to the United States from China and Japan. They, too, brought unfamiliar languages and religious beliefs and had difficulty blending into American society.

Leaving Troubles Behind

Why did so many people leave their homelands for the United States in the late 1800s and early 1900s? They were "pushed" away by difficult conditions at home and "pulled" to the United States by new opportunities.

Many people **emigrated,** or left their homelands, because of economic troubles. In Italy and Hungary, overcrowding and poverty made jobs scarce. Farmers in Croatia and Serbia could not own enough land to support their families. Sweden suffered major crop failures. New machines such as looms put many craft workers out of work.

Persecution also drove people from their homelands. In some countries the government passed laws or followed policies against certain **ethnic groups**—minorities that spoke different languages or followed different customs from those of most people in a country. Members of these ethnic groups often emigrated to escape discrimination or unfair laws. Many Jews fled persecution in Russia in the 1880s and came to the United States.

Seeking Opportunity

Immigrants saw the United States as a land of jobs, plentiful and affordable land, and opportunities for a better life. Although some immigrants returned to their homelands after a few years, most came to America to stay.

✓ Reading Check **Describing** Who were the "new" immigrants?

Picturing **History**

Immigrants arrive in New York Harbor from Hamburg, Germany, in 1906. **Where did most immigrants to America come from after 1880?**

Fact · Fiction · Folklore

Ellis Island

The first stop for millions of immigrants was Ellis Island. About 12 million people passed through the Ellis Island immigration center between 1892 and 1954. The main building was reopened in 1990 as the Ellis Island Museum of Immigration. Located a short distance north of the Statue of Liberty in New York Harbor, Ellis Island stands as a memorial to the traditions of freedom and opportunity in America.

The Journey to America

Immigrants often had a difficult journey to America. Many had to first travel to a seaport to board a ship. Often they traveled for hundreds of miles on foot or on horseback and through foreign countries to get to the port cities.

Then came the long ocean voyage to America—12 days across the Atlantic or several weeks across the Pacific. Immigrants usually could afford only the cheapest tickets, and they traveled in steerage—cramped, noisy quarters on the lower decks.

The Statue of Liberty

Most European immigrants landed at New York City. After 1886 the magnificent sight of the **Statue of Liberty** greeted the immigrants as they sailed into **New York Harbor.** The statue, a gift from France, seemed to promise hope for a better life in the new country. On the base of the statue, the stirring words of **Emma Lazarus,** an American poet, welcomed immigrants from Europe:

    ❝Give me your tired, your poor,
    Your huddled masses yearning to breathe free,
    The wretched refuse of your teeming shore.
    Send these, the homeless, tempest-tossed to me,
    I lift my lamp beside the golden door!❞

Entering America

Bianca De Carli arrived from Italy in 1913 as a young girl. Many years later she remembered how she felt as her ship reached New York City:

❝We all trembled because of the strangeness and the confusion. . . . Some were weak from no movement and exercise, and some were sick because of the smells and the unfresh air. But somehow this did not matter because we now knew it was almost over.❞

Before the new arrivals could actually pass through the "golden door" to America, they had to register at government reception centers. In the East immigrants were processed at Castle Garden, a former fort on Manhattan Island, and after 1892 at **Ellis Island** in New York Harbor. Most Asian immigrants arrived in America on the West Coast and went through the processing center on **Angel Island** in **San Francisco Bay.**

Examiners at the centers recorded the immigrants' names—sometimes shortening or simplifying a name they found too difficult to write. The examiners asked the immigrants where they came from, their occupation, and whether they had relatives in the United States. The examiners also gave health examinations. Immigrants with contagious illnesses could be refused permission to enter the United States.

✓ **Reading Check** **Describing** How long did the ocean voyage across the Atlantic take?

The Immigrant Experience

After passing through the reception centers, most immigrants entered the United States. Where would they go? How would they live? Some had relatives or friends to stay with and to help them find jobs. Others knew no one and would have to strike out on their own.

Finding Work

An immigrant's greatest challenge was finding work. Sometimes organizations in his or her homeland recruited workers for jobs in the United States. The organization supplied American employers with unskilled workers who worked unloading cargo or digging ditches.

Some of America's fastest-growing industries hired immigrant workers. In the steel mills of Pittsburgh, for example, most of the common laborers in the early 1900s were immigrant men. They might work 12 hours a day, seven days a week.

Many immigrants, including women and children, worked in sweatshops in the garment industry. These were dark, crowded workshops where workers made clothing. The work was repetitious and hazardous, the pay low, and the hours long.

Pauline Newman, who later became an official in the International Ladies' Garment Workers Union, worked in a New York sweatshop as a child. She recalled:

66 We started work at seven-thirty in the morning, and during the busy season we worked until nine in the evening. They didn't pay you any overtime and they didn't give you anything for supper money. Sometimes they'd give you a little apple pie if you had to work very late. 99

Adjusting to America

In their new homes, immigrants tried to preserve some aspects of their own cultures. At the same time, most wanted to assimilate, or become part of the American culture. These two desires sometimes came into conflict.

Language highlighted the differences between generations. Many immigrant parents continued to speak their native languages. Their children spoke English at school and with friends, but they also spoke their native language at home. On the other hand, the grandchildren of many immigrants spoke only English.

HISTORY Online
Student Web Activity
Visit taj.glencoe.com and click on Chapter 20—Student Web Activities for an activity on immigration.

The role of immigrant women also changed in the United States, where women generally had more freedom than women in European and Asian countries. New lifestyles conflicted with traditional ways and sometimes caused family friction. (See page 971 of the Primary Sources Library for one woman's account of leaving her native country.)

Building Communities

Most of the new immigrants were from rural areas. Because they lacked the money to buy farmland in America, however, they often settled in industrial cities. With little or no education, they usually worked as unskilled laborers.

Relatives who had immigrated earlier helped new arrivals get settled, and people of the same ethnic group naturally tended to form

Immigrant children learn American ways in the classroom.

TWO VIEWPOINTS

Should We Welcome or Prevent Immigration to Our Country?

Immigrants struggled to find their place in American society. They changed American society with customs from their cultures. Many Americans resisted these changes and warned against further immigration.

San Francisco Real Estate Circular, September 1874

The Chinese come for a season only; and, while they give their labor, they do not [spend the money they earn] in the country. They do not come to settle or make homes . . . To compare the Chinese with even the lowest white laborers is, therefore, absurd.

Our best interests are suffering of these Asiatic slaves; we are trying to make them live decently while here, and to discourage their arrival in such numbers as to drive white laborers out of the country. . . .

Chinese immigrants

Attorney Louis Marshall Speaks Out Against Limiting Immigration, 1924

In common with all other immigrants, those who have come from the countries sought to be tabooed [forbidden] have been industrious, and law-abiding and have made valuable contributions to our industrial, commercial and social development. . . .

To say that they are not assimilable argues ignorance. The facts show that they adopt American standards of living and that they are permeated [filled] with the spirit of our institutions. It is said that they speak foreign languages, but in those foreign languages they are taught to love our Government. . . .

Louis Marshall

Learning From History

1. What did the writer from San Francisco seem to fear?
2. What did Louis Marshall claim about the immigrants' contributions?
3. What facts does Marshall use to support his view that the newcomers are "assimilable"?

communities. As a result neighborhoods of Jewish, Italian, Polish, Chinese, and other groups quickly developed in New York, Chicago, San Francisco, and other large cities.

The immigrants sought to re-create some of the life they had left behind. The communities they established revolved around a number of traditional institutions. Most important were the houses of worship—the churches and synagogues—where worship was conducted and holidays were celebrated as they had been in their homelands. Priests and rabbis often acted as community leaders.

The immigrants published newspapers in their native languages, opened stores and theaters, and organized social clubs. Ethnic communities and institutions helped the immigrants preserve their cultural heritage.

✓ **Reading Check** **Describing** What is assimilation?

Nativist Movement

Assimilation was also slowed by the attitudes of many native-born Americans. Although employers were happy to hire immigrant workers at low wages, some American-born workers resented the immigrants. These Americans feared that the immigrants would take away their jobs or drive down everyone's wages by accepting lower pay.

Ethnic, religious, and racial differences contributed to tensions between Americans and the new immigrants. Some Americans argued that the new immigrants—with their foreign languages, unfamiliar religions, and distinctive customs—did not fit into American society.

People found it easy to blame immigrants for increasing crime, unemployment, and other problems. The nativist movement, for example, had opposed immigration since the 1830s. Nativism gained strength in the late 1800s. Calls for restrictions on immigration mounted.

New Immigration Laws

Lawmakers responded quickly to the tide of anti-immigrant feeling. In 1882 Congress passed the first law to limit immigration—the **Chinese Exclusion Act.** This law prohibited Chinese workers from entering the United States for 10 years. Congress extended the law in 1892 and again in 1902.

In 1907 the federal government and Japan came to a "gentleman's agreement." The Japanese agreed to limit the number of immigrants to the United States, while the Americans pledged fair treatment for Japanese Americans already in the United States.

Other legislation affected immigrants from all nations. An 1882 law made each immigrant pay a tax and also barred criminals from entering the country. In 1897 Congress passed a bill requiring immigrants to be able to read and write in some language. Although President Cleveland vetoed the bill as unfair, Congress later passed the **Immigration Act of 1917,** which included a similar literacy requirement.

Support for Immigrants

Despite some anti-immigrant sentiment, many Americans—including **Grace Abbott** and **Julia Clifford Lathrop,** who helped found the Immigrants' Protective League—spoke out in support of immigration. These Americans recognized that the United States was a nation of immigrants and that the newcomers made lasting contributions to their new society.

Immigrants' Contributions

The new immigrants supplied the country's growing industries with the workers that were necessary for economic growth. At the same time, the new immigrants and their children—like the old immigrants before them—helped shape American life. They gave the nation its major religious groups—Protestants, Catholics, and Jews. As they became part of the society around them, they enriched that society with the customs and cultures and the language and literature of their homelands.

The effects of immigration were most visible in the cities, with their fast-growing ethnic neighborhoods. The flow of immigrants was one of the factors that transformed America's cities in the late 1800s and the early 1900s.

✓ **Reading Check** **Explaining** What was the nativist movement?

SECTION 1 ASSESSMENT

Checking for Understanding

1. **Key Terms** Use each of these terms in a sentence that will help explain its meaning: emigrate, ethnic group, steerage, sweatshop, assimilate.

2. **Reviewing Facts** Explain the difference between "old immigration" and "new immigration."

Reviewing Themes

3. **Culture and Traditions** What were some of the cultural differences that immigrants had to adjust to in the United States?

Critical Thinking

4. **Drawing Conclusions** Why do you think some Americans blamed the "new" immigrants for many of society's problems?

5. **Organizing Information** Re-create the diagram below and give three reasons why some Americans did not accept the new immigrants.

Anti-immigrant feelings

Analyzing Visuals

6. **Picturing History** Select one of the photographs that appear in Section 1 and write a paragraph in which you describe the scene. Include a title for the photograph.

Interdisciplinary Activity

Art Create a collage illustrating the origins of immigrants who came to the United States after 1880. Clip photographs from advertisements and newsmagazines to make your collage.

NEW AMERICANS

BETWEEN 1890 AND 1930 people viewed the United States as a land of opportunity because growing American industries were searching for workers. More than 20 million immigrants poured into the country. The largest groups came from southern, central, and eastern Europe. Immigrants came seeking jobs and freedom. They fled from crop failures, political repression, and military service.

LIFE IN AMERICA

Most newcomers settled near other immigrants from their own country. The largest group, Italians, settled primarily in the Midwest and Northeast. They were escaping from a disastrous cholera epidemic and repeated crop failures. Although they had been farm workers in southern Italy, they settled in cities and found jobs building railroads, streets, and buildings, or selling produce. Many of the women went to work for the garment industry.

Poles, Czechs, Serbs, Croats, and Russians came seeking more freedom. Poles tended to form close-knit communities in the industrial cities of the Midwest and Northeast. For many of them life centered on the Catholic Church, and they sent their children to parochial schools. Women tended to establish boardinghouses or laundries. The men worked in steel mills and slaughterhouses.

Japanese immigrants settled in Hawaii, California, and the Pacific Northwest. They found work in agriculture, forestry, and fisheries. Soon Japanese immigrants were growing 10 percent of California's produce.

The tide of immigration slowed in the early 1920s, when the government imposed new restrictions. Nevertheless, immigrants still continued to play an important role shaping American culture.

LEARNING from GEOGRAPHY

1. **Why do you think Italian, Polish, and Japanese immigrants settled where they did?**

2. **In what regions of the world did the number of emigrants change the most from 1890 to 1930?**

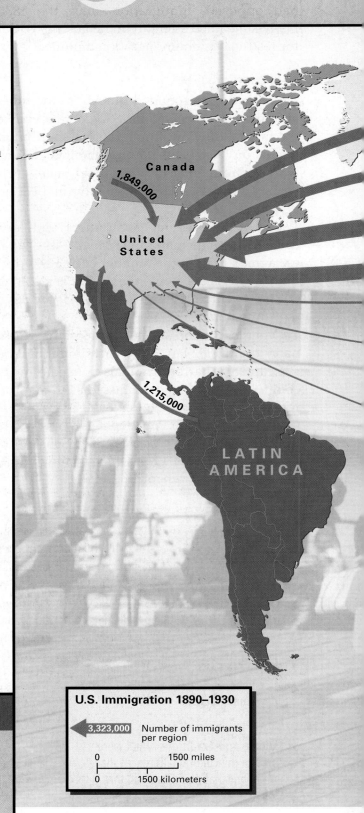

U.S. Immigration 1890–1930

3,323,000 — Number of immigrants per region

0   1500 miles

0   1500 kilometers

3,761,000

NORTHERN
EUROPE
3,323,000

Poland
CENTRAL
EUROPE
5,617,000

Italy
SOUTHERN
EUROPE
5,108,000

617,000

22,000

40,000

EASTERN EUROPE and Russia

A S I A

Japan

China

India

Turkey

AFRICA

OCEANIA

1890
Other 2%
(Canada, Africa, Asia,
Latin America, Oceania)

Southern Europe
12%

Eastern Europe
and Russia 8%

Northern Europe
43%

Central Europe
35%

1930
Other 1%
(Africa, Latin America, Oceania)

Latin America
9%

Northern Europe
29%

Canada
27%

Central Europe
19%

2% Asia

Southern Europe
11%

Eastern Europe
and Russia
2%

Italian

Polish

Japanese

**Where Immigrants Settled
1900–1930**

More than 100,000

50,000–100,000

10,000–49,999

5,000–9,999

Less than 5,000

SECTION 2 Moving to the City

Guide to Reading

Main Idea
Cities in the United States expanded rapidly in the late 1800s.

Key Terms
tenement, slum, suburb, The Gilded Age, settlement house

Reading Strategy
Analyzing Information As you study Section 2, re-create the diagram below and list three serious problems facing American cities in the late 1800s.

Urban problems

Read to Learn
• how American cities grew and changed.
• what problems cities faced and how people tried to solve them.

Section Theme
Science and Technology Many Americans left the nation's farms, hoping to make their fortunes in the cities.

Preview of Events

1870	1880	1890

1873
The Gilded Age is published

1883
The Brooklyn Bridge opens

1884
First skyscraper constructed in Chicago

1889
Jane Addams founds Hull House

AN American Story

A train pulling into Chicago in 1884 carried a young passenger named Hamlin Garland. For Garland, who had grown up on a farm, the big city was a bewildering sight. Garland later became famous for his stories about the Midwest. In one novel he described his feeling of dismay when he first saw Chicago. "The mere thought of a million people stunned my imagination." Garland wondered, "How can so many people find a living in one place?"

Growth of Cities

American cities grew rapidly after the Civil War. In 1870, one American in four lived in cities with 2,500 or more people. By 1910 nearly half of the American population were city dwellers. The United States was changing from a rural to an urban nation.

Immigrants played an enormous part in the growth of cities. In major urban centers such as New York, Detroit, and Chicago, immigrants and their children made up 80 percent or more of the population in 1890.

Native-born Americans also contributed to urban growth. Americans moved in huge numbers from farming areas to cities, looking for jobs.

The industrialization of America had changed work on farms. New farm machinery made it possible to produce crops, using fewer farmworkers. In addition women in rural areas no longer had to make clothing and household goods. These items, made by machine, could now be bought in stores or from catalogs. Freed from such chores, many women left farms to look for jobs in the cities.

African Americans also migrated to cities in large numbers. The vast majority of the country's African American population lived in the rural South in great poverty. Many African Americans began moving to Southern cities in search of jobs and to escape debt, injustice, or discrimination. After 1914 a large number of African Americans moved to Northern cities, which offered more jobs in industry and manufacturing than Southern cities did. Many African Americans also hoped to find less discrimination and violence in the North.

Transportation and Resources

America's expanding railroad network fed the growth of the cities. Railroads helped people move to the cities, and they transported the raw materials for industry. Trains carried cattle to Chicago and **Kansas City,** making these cities great meatpacking centers.

Some cities flourished because of nearby resources. **Pittsburgh** developed rapidly as a center for iron and steel manufacturing because both iron ore and coal—to fuel the industry's huge furnaces—were found in the area.

Seaports such as **New York** and **San Francisco** developed as American trade with the rest of the world increased. In addition the immigrant population of these cities provided a large pool of workers who were available for low wages.

Tenement Living

Cities were exciting places that offered jobs, stores, and entertainment. But there was also substandard housing and desperate poverty. People poured into the cities faster than housing could be built to accommodate them. In the biggest, most crowded cities, the poorest residents—including most immigrants—lived in tenements. Originally a tenement was simply a building in which several families rented rooms. By the late 1800s, however, a tenement had come to mean an apartment building in the slums— poor, run-down urban neighborhoods.

Tenements had many small, dark rooms. One young immigrant from Poland spoke of living in the dimly lit rooms in the back of a New York City tenement:

> 66We would so like to live in the front, but we can't pay the rent. . . . Why, they have the sun in there. When the door is opened the light comes right in your face.99

Three, four, or more people lived in each room. Usually several families had to share a cold-water tap and a toilet. Few tenement houses had hot water or bathtubs. A government inspector wrote of the "filthy and rotten tenements" of the Chicago slums in 1896, where children filled "every nook, eating and sleeping in every windowsill, pouring in and out of every door."

Urban and Rural Population Growth, 1860–1900

Population (in millions)

Urban Rural

Year

Source: *Historical Statistics of the United States.*

Graph *Skills*

The gap between the urban and rural populations narrowed in the late 1800s.

Comparing About how many more people lived in urban areas in 1900 than in 1860?

People In History

Jacob Riis 1849–1914

Jacob Riis came to the United States from Denmark when he was 21. Riis worked as a reporter and photographer for New York City newspapers for 20 years. Many of his stories and pictures called attention to the living conditions in the poorer sections of the city. In 1890 Riis wrote *How the Other Half Lives.*

By taking pictures of the tenements, Riis was able to bring the terrible conditions of the slums to the attention of readers. His book helped establish housing codes to prevent the worst abuses.

When Theodore Roosevelt became the city's police commissioner, he asked Riis to present a reform program. Through Riis's efforts, many playgrounds and parks were established in the city. Riis helped make others aware of the problems many urban Americans faced in their daily lives. In addition, he served as an example of what individuals could do to lessen these problems.

Middle-Class Comfort

The cities also had a growing middle class. The middle class included the families of professional people such as doctors, lawyers, and ministers. An increasing number of managers and salaried office clerks also became part of the middle class.

The middle class enjoyed a comfortable life. Many families moved from cities to the suburbs, residential areas that sprang up outside of city centers as a result of improvements in transportation. There they lived in houses with hot water, indoor toilets, and—by 1900—electricity. Middle-class families might have one or two servants and the leisure time to enjoy music, art, and literature.

The Gilded Age

At the top of the economic and social ladder stood the very rich. The wealthy lived very different lives from most Americans. They built enormous mansions in the cities and huge estates in the country. Some homes, such as those of J.P. Morgan and Henry Clay Frick in New York City, are now museums.

In these mansions, the rich lived lives of extreme luxury, throwing enormous parties and dinners. In 1883 Alva and William Kissam Vanderbilt gave a party for more than 1,000 guests at their New York mansion. The party was estimated to have cost $75,000 for food and entertainment, which is equal to about $1.3 million today.

Mark Twain and Charles Dudley Warner published a novel in 1873 called *The Gilded Age.* The name—which refers to something covered with a thin layer of gold—became associated with America of the late 1800s. The Gilded Age suggested both the extravagant wealth of the time and the terrible poverty that lay underneath.

✓ **Reading Check** **Describing** Why was tenement living difficult?

Cities in Crisis

The rapid growth of the cities produced serious problems. The terrible overcrowding in tenement districts created sanitation and health problems. Garbage and horse manure accumulated in city streets, and the sewers could not handle the flow of human waste. Filth created a breeding ground for diseases, which spread rapidly through the crowded districts.

Fires were an ever-present threat. About 18,000 buildings were destroyed and 100,000 Chicagoans lost their homes in the Chicago fire of 1871. Two years later, Boston experienced a devastating fire.

Health and Crime Problems

In a poor Chicago neighborhood in 1900, babies often died of whooping cough, diphtheria, or measles before their first birthday. A section of New York was called the "lung block" because so many residents had tuberculosis.

In an effort to control disease, New York City began to screen schoolchildren for contagious diseases and to provide visiting nurses to mothers with young children. The city also established public health clinics for those who could not pay for medical care.

The poverty in the cities inevitably led to crime. Orphaned and homeless children sometimes resorted to picking pockets and other minor crimes to survive. Gangs roaming the poor neighborhoods committed more serious crimes. **Jacob Riis** reported:

> 66The gang is an institution in New York. The police deny its existence while nursing the bruises received in nightly battles with it. . . . The gang is the ripe fruit of tenement-house growth. It was born there.99

Seeking Solutions

The problems of the cities did not go unnoticed. Many dedicated people worked to improve urban life and help the poor.

Religious groups aided the poor. Some religious orders helped the poor in orphanages, prisons, and hospitals. Organizations such as the **YMCA** (Young Men's Christian Association) and **YWCA** (Young Women's Christian Association) offered recreation centers where city youngsters could meet and play.

The poor also received assistance from establishments called settlement houses. The settlement house movement had spread to the United States from Britain. Located in poor neighborhoods, settlement houses provided medical care, playgrounds, nurseries, and libraries as well as classes in English, music, and arts and crafts. Settlement workers—mostly women—also tried to get better police protection, garbage removal, and public parks for poor districts.

One of the most famous settlement houses was Chicago's **Hull House,** founded by **Jane Addams** in 1889. Addams explained:

> 66We were ready to perform the humblest neighborhood services. We were asked to wash the new-born babies, and to prepare the dead for burial, to nurse the sick, and to 'mind the children.'99

Jane Addams

✓ **Reading Check** **Explaining** What purpose did settlement houses serve?

The Changing City

Urban growth led to important new developments. In the late 1800s, cities saw the introduction of a new type of building, new kinds of public transportation, and public parks.

Building Up—Not Out

Because of the limited space in cities, imaginative architects began building upward rather than outward. In the 1860s architects started to use iron frames to strengthen the walls of buildings. Iron supports—together with the safety elevator that **Elisha Otis** invented in 1852—made taller buildings possible.

In 1884 **William LeBaron Jenney** constructed a 10-story office building in Chicago. Supported by an iron-and-steel frame, it was the world's first **skyscraper.** Architect **Louis Sullivan** gave style to the skyscraper. "It must be every inch a proud and soaring thing, rising

The Woolworth building was designed and built to be the tallest building in the world.

in sheer exultation," he said. Sullivan and his colleagues changed the face of America's cities. Soon people built even higher structures. New York's **Woolworth Building,** completed in 1913, soared an incredible 55 stories—792 feet (241 m) high. People called the building the Cathedral of Commerce.

New Designs

Some people looked to reshape the urban landscape. A group known as the "City Beautiful" movement believed city dwellers should be able to enjoy the beauties of nature. **Frederick Law Olmsted,** a leader in this movement, designed New York's Central Park as well as several parks in Boston.

In 1892 and 1893, Chicago hosted a World's Fair on fairgrounds designed by Olmsted. The Fair revealed that American architecture was dynamic and original. The best architects thoroughly understood European styles and adapted them for modern use. The firm of

McKim, Mead, and White used the Italian Renaissance style in its design for the Boston Public Library. Henry Richardson adapted styles from ancient Rome in his design for churches, libraries, and even department stores.

New Forms of Transportation

As cities grew, people needed new means of transportation. Mark Twain complained in 1867 that

66New York is too large. You cannot accomplish anything . . . without devoting a whole day to it. . . . The distances are too great.99

Streetcars, which horses pulled on tracks, provided public transportation at the time. Horses were slow, however, and left piles of manure. In 1873 San Francisco began construction of cable-car lines. A large underground cable powered by a motor at one end of the rail line moved passengers along. In 1888 Richmond,

Virginia, pioneered the use of the trolley car, a motorized train that was powered by electricity supplied through overhead cables. By the turn of the century, the trolley was everywhere. In 1897, Boston opened the nation's first subway, or underground railway. In 1904, New York City opened the first section of what was to become the largest subway system in the world.

Another improvement that helped transportation was the paving of streets. During most of the 1800s, city streets remained poorly paved. For example, although the rapid growth of Cleveland, Ohio, made that city an important urban center, most of its streets were nothing more than sand and gravel. Other cities used wood blocks, brick, or cobblestone, all of which were bumpy, noisy, and hard to repair. The growing use of asphalt—a by-product of petroleum refining—beginning in the 1890s made city streets smoother and quieter.

Building Bridges

Bridge construction provided another improvement in urban transportation. Many American cities were divided or bounded by rivers. Using new construction technology, architects and engineers designed huge steel bridges to link sections of cities. The 520-foot (156-m) **Eads Bridge** across the Mississippi River in St. Louis opened in 1874. Ten years later

Skyscrapers

The Empire State Building is the world's tallest building. That was once true, but no longer. By 1931 the Empire State Building dwarfed all other buildings in the world at 102 stories. Today the nation's tallest building is the Sears Tower in Chicago. It is 1,450 feet (442 m) high and has 110 stories.

New York's majestic **Brooklyn Bridge,** 1,600 feet (488 m) long, connected Manhattan and Brooklyn. Both bridges remain in use today.

The new forms of transportation not only helped people travel within the cities, but they also helped the cities grow. Middle-class suburbs developed along train or trolley lines stretching away from city centers. People who moved out of the city centers could easily travel downtown to work or shop.

The increase in immigration and the growth of the cities went hand in hand with other changes in American life. Education, culture, and recreation were changing too.

✓ **Reading Check** **Summarizing** What new forms of urban transportation were developed?

SECTION 2 ASSESSMENT

Checking for Understanding

1. **Key Terms** Use the vocabulary terms that follow to write a paragraph about life in the cities: tenement, slum, suburb, settlement house.
2. **Reviewing Facts** Who founded Hull House?

Reviewing Themes

3. **Science and Technology** What improvements in transportation helped cities and suburbs grow?

Critical Thinking

4. **Analyzing Information** How did the efforts of religious groups help those living in poverty?
5. **Summarizing Information** Re-create the diagram below and describe three efforts made to improve living conditions in the cities.

Analyzing Visuals

6. **Graph Skills** According to the graph on page 591, what was the range of urban population between 1890 and 1900? About how many more people lived in rural than in urban areas in 1860?

Interdisciplinary Activity

Art Draw the front of a postcard that shows a scene of an American city in 1900. On the reverse side, write a note that an immigrant may have sent home to relatives.

Reading a Line Graph

Why Learn This Skill?

Graphs are a way of showing numbers visually, making them easier to read and understand. Graphs are often used to compare changes over time or differences between places, groups of people, or related events.

Learning the Skill

On a line graph, numbers usually appear along the left side of the graph, or the vertical axis. Time is usually shown along the bottom of the graph, or the horizontal axis. A line on the graph shows whether the numbers go up or down over time. Sometimes a graph contains more than one line to record two or more related quantities.

To read a line graph, follow these steps:

• Read the title of the graph.
• Read the information on the horizontal axis and the vertical axis.
• Study the points where the line intersects the grid on the line graph. This step tells you what amount existed at a given time.
• Study the changes over time that the line on the graph illustrates. Look for increases, decreases, and sudden shifts.
• Draw conclusions from the statistics presented. What trends or patterns appear?

Practicing the Skill

Study the line graph on this page and answer the following questions.

❶ What is the subject of this line graph?

❷ What information is presented on the horizontal axis? On the vertical axis?

❸ In about what year did immigration from northern and western Europe peak?

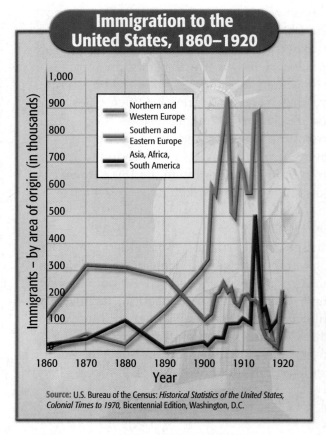

Immigration to the United States, 1860–1920

Immigrants – by area of origin (in thousands)

Legend:
— Northern and Western Europe
— Southern and Eastern Europe
— Asia, Africa, South America

Source: U.S. Bureau of the Census: *Historical Statistics of the United States, Colonial Times to 1970,* Bicentennial Edition, Washington, D.C.

❹ In about what year was immigration from Asia, Africa, and South America the lowest?

❺ During what two decades did immigration from southern and eastern Europe peak?

Applying the Skill

Making a Line Graph Keep track of the number of hours you spend on homework each day for a one-week period. Chart the information on a line graph.

 Glencoe's **Skillbuilder Interactive Workbook CD-ROM, Level 1,** provides instruction and practice in key social studies skills.

SECTION 3 A Changing Culture

Guide to Reading

Main Idea
The states worked to expand and improve the system of education.

Key Terms
land-grant college, yellow journalism, realism, regionalism, ragtime, vaudeville

Reading Strategy
Classifying Information As you study Section 3, re-create the diagram below and describe the achievements of the persons listed.

	Achievements
John Dewey	
George Washington Carver	
Mary Cassatt	
Scott Joplin	

Read to Learn
• how education became more widely available.
• how Americans spent their leisure time.

Section Theme
Continuity and Change A distinctive American culture was developing that affected many parts of American life.

Preview of Events

♦1860 ♦1870 ♦1880 ♦1890

1862
Morrill Act is passed

1879
Carlisle Indian Industrial School is founded

1881
Booker T. Washington opens the Tuskegee Institute

1883
Joseph Pulitzer purchases the New York *World*

AN American Story

Mary Antin, a young girl who came to the United States from Russia in 1894, never forgot her first day of school. "Father himself conducted us to school. He would not have delegated that mission to the president of the United States." For her father, Mary explained, education was "the essence of American opportunity, the treasure no thief could touch, not even misfortune or poverty. . . . The door stood open for every one of us."

Expanding Education

Most Americans in 1865 had attended school for an average of only four years. Government and business leaders and reformers believed that for the nation to progress, the people needed more schooling. Toward the end of the 1800s, the "treasure" of education became more widely available to Americans.

By 1914 most states required children to have at least some schooling. More than 80 percent of all children between the ages of 5 and 17 were enrolled in elementary and secondary schools.

Public Schools

The expansion of public education was particularly notable in high schools. The number of public high schools increased from 100 in 1860 to 6,000 in 1900, and increased to 12,000 in 1914. Despite this huge increase, however, many teenagers did not attend high school. Boys often went to work to help their families instead of attending school. The majority of high school students were girls.

The benefits of a public school education were not shared equally by everyone. In the South many African Americans received little or no education. In many parts of the country, African American children had no choice but to attend segregated elementary and secondary schools.

Progressive Education

Around 1900 a new philosophy of education emerged in the United States. Supporters of this "progressive education" wanted to shape students' characters and teach them good citizenship as well as facts. They also believed children should learn through the use of "hands-on" activities. These ideas had the greatest effect in elementary schools.

John Dewey, the leading spokesperson for progressive education, criticized schools for overemphasizing memorization of information. Instead, Dewey argued, schools should relate learning to the interests, problems, and concerns of students.

Higher Education

Colleges and universities also changed and expanded. An 1862 law called the **Morrill Act** gave the states large amounts of federal land that could be sold to raise money for education. The states used these funds to start dozens of schools called land-grant colleges. Wealthy individuals also established and supported colleges and universities. Some schools were named for the donors—for example, Cornell University for Ezra Cornell and Stanford University for Leland Stanford.

What Life Was Like...

School Days

◀ ### On the Bus
Students line up for a ride to school in Fresno, California. Few schools were lucky enough to have their own buses in the early 1900s. Not until 1939 were national standards for school buses adopted, including the color "school-bus yellow" to promote visibility and safety.

Women and Higher Education

In 1865 only a handful of American colleges admitted women. The new land-grant schools admitted women students, as did new women's colleges—Vassar, Smith, Wellesley, and Bryn Mawr—founded in the late 1800s. By 1890 women could attend a wide range of schools, and by 1910 almost 40 percent of all American college students were women.

Writing

By 1900, the Palmer method of penmanship was taught everywhere. In the Palmer method, some capital letters were no longer written separately, and entire words could be completed before the pen was lifted to cross a "t" or dot an "i." Writing sets included ink bottles like this one. Its double covers prevented evaporation and protected against leakage.

Crossing Guard

A New York City police officer guides students on their way to school in 1899. By the early 1900s, the police provided this service in many communities.

Bookmobile

Librarians attempted to provide reading material to rural communities. Here, a traveling library makes book deliveries in Washington County, Maryland.

The Classroom

Students observe an experiment and take notes during science class in 1900.

Elementary Students

The classroom was the major place where immigrant children learned American ways.

Minorities and Higher Education

Some new colleges, such as Hampton Institute in Virginia, provided higher education for African Americans and Native Americans. Howard University in Washington, D.C., founded shortly after the Civil War, had a largely African American student body. By the early 1870s, Howard offered degrees in theology, medicine, law, and agriculture. Prominent graduates of Howard include Thurgood Marshall, who later became a justice of the Supreme Court, writer Toni Morrison, and political scientist Ralph Bunche, the first African American to win the Nobel Peace Prize.

One Hampton Institute student, **Booker T. Washington,** became an educator. In 1881 Washington founded the **Tuskegee Institute** in Alabama to train teachers and to provide practical education for African Americans. As a result of his work as an educator and public speaker, Washington became influential in business and politics.

In 1896, scientist **George Washington Carver** joined the Tuskegee faculty. His research transformed agricultural development in the South. From the peanut, which was formerly of little use, Carver developed hundreds of products, including plastics, synthetic rubber, shaving cream, and paper.

These two photographs of a young Navajo, Tom Torlino, show how his appearance changed a short time after he entered the Carlisle Indian School.

Schools for Native Americans

Reservation schools and boarding schools also opened to train Native Americans for jobs. The Carlisle Indian Industrial School in Pennsylvania was founded in 1879, and similar schools opened in the West. Although these schools provided Native Americans with training for jobs in industry, they also isolated Native Americans from their tribal traditions. Sometimes, boarding schools were located hundreds of miles away from a student's family.

✓ **Reading Check** **Comparing** What did the colleges Bryn Mawr, Vassar, and Smith have in common?

A Nation of Readers

As opportunities for education grew, a growing number of Americans became interested in reading. Public libraries opened across the nation, and new magazines and newspapers were created for the reading public.

Public Libraries

In 1881 **Andrew Carnegie,** the wealthy steel industrialist, made an extraordinary announcement. He pledged to build a public library in any city that would agree to pay its operating costs. In the next 30 years, Carnegie donated more than $30 million to found more than 2,000 libraries throughout the world. With gifts from Carnegie and others, and the efforts of state and local governments, every state in the Union established free public libraries.

Spreading the News

Technological advances in printing, paper making, and communications made it possible to publish a daily paper for a large number of readers. The growing cities provided readers for the newspapers.

In 1883 **Joseph Pulitzer** purchased the New York *World* and created a new kind of newspaper. The paper grabbed the reader's attention with illustrations, cartoons, and sensational stories with huge, scary headlines—such as "ANOTHER MURDERER TO HANG." Under Pulitzer's management, the *World* built up its circulation to more than one million readers every day.

Other newspapers soon imitated Pulitzer's style. **William Randolph Hearst's** New York *Morning Journal* became even more successful than the *World,* attracting readers by exaggerating the dramatic or gruesome aspects of stories. This style of sensational writing became known as yellow journalism—a name that came from the paper's popular comic strip, "The Yellow Kid."

Ethnic and minority newspapers thrived as well. By 1900 there were six daily Jewish-language newspapers operating in New York City. African Americans started more than 1,000 newspapers between 1865 and 1900.

More magazines took advantage of printing improvements and mass circulation techniques to reach a national market. Between 1865 and 1900, the number of magazines in the United States rose from about 700 to 5,000. Some magazines of that era—the *Atlantic Monthly, Harper's Magazine,* and *Ladies' Home Journal*—are still published today.

Changes in Literature

Many writers of the era explored new themes and subjects. Their approach to literature was called realism because they sought to describe the lives of people. Related to realism was regionalism, writing that focused on a particular region of the country.

Mark Twain was a realist and a regionalist. Many of his books, including *Adventures of Huckleberry Finn* and *The Adventures of Tom Sawyer,* are set along the Mississippi River, where Twain grew up.

Stephen Crane wrote about city slums in *Maggie* and about the Civil War in *The Red Badge of Courage.* In books such as *The Call of the Wild* and *The Sea Wolf,* **Jack London** portrayed the lives of miners and hunters in the far Northwest. **Edith Wharton** described the joys and sorrows of the upper-class Easterners in *The House of Mirth* and *The Age of Innocence.*

Paul Laurence Dunbar, the son of former slaves, wrote poetry and novels that used the dialects and folktales of Southern African Americans. Dunbar was one of the first African American writers to gain fame worldwide.

Paperback books appeared for the first time in the late 1800s, and these inexpensive books helped expand the reading public. Many paperbacks featured lively adventure tales or stories of athletic boys and girls.

Horatio Alger wrote a successful series of young adult books with such titles as *Work and Win* and *Luck and Pluck.* Based on the idea that hard work and honesty brought success, Alger's books sold millions of copies.

✓ **Reading Check** **Explaining** What is regionalism?

Art, Music, and Leisure

For most of the 1800s, the work of American artists and musicians reflected a European influence. After the Civil War, Americans began to develop a distinctively American style.

American Artists

Some American painters pursued realist themes. **Thomas Eakins** painted the human anatomy and surgical operations. One of Eakins's students, **Henry Tanner,** depicted warm family scenes of African Americans in the South. **Frederic Remington** portrayed the American West, focusing on subjects such as cowhands and Native Americans. **Winslow Homer** painted Southern farmers, Adirondack campers, and stormy sea scenes. **James Whistler's** *Arrangement in Grey and Black,* commonly known as "Whistler's Mother," is one of the best-known American paintings. **Mary Cassatt** was influential in the French Impressionist school of

painting. Impressionists tried to capture the play of light, color, and patterns as they made immediate impressions on the senses.

Music in America

More distinctively American kinds of music were also becoming popular. Bandleader **John Philip Sousa** composed many rousing marches, including "The Stars and Stripes Forever." African American musicians in New Orleans in the late 1800s developed an entirely new kind of music—jazz. **Jazz** combined elements of work songs, gospel music, spirituals, and African rhythms. Related to jazz was ragtime music. For about 20 years, beginning around the turn of the century, ragtime—with its complex rhythms—was the dominant force in popular music. One of the best-known ragtime composers is **Scott Joplin.** He wrote "Maple Leaf Rag" and many other well-known works.

The symphony orchestras of New York, Boston, and Philadelphia—all founded before 1900—were among the world's finest. Great singers and conductors came from all over the world to perform at New York's Metropolitan Opera House.

Leisure Time

Although sweatshop workers labored long hours for six or even seven days a week, middle-class people and even some factory workers enjoyed increasing amounts of leisure time.

History *Through Art*

Girls with Lobster by Winslow Homer Homer painted scenes of people enjoying the New Jersey and New England seashores. **What themes did many American painters represent in their works?**

Unlike round-the-clock farmwork, professional and industrial jobs gave people hours and even days of free time. Americans developed new forms of recreation.

A favorite leisure-time activity for many people was watching and following sports. Baseball became the most popular **spectator sport** in America. By the turn of the century, both the National and American Leagues had been founded—each made up of teams from major cities. Their games drew large crowds of enthusiastic fans, and in 1903 the first World Series was held.

Another popular spectator sport was football, which developed from the English game of rugby. By the 1890s college games were drawing huge crowds.

Basketball, invented by Dr. James Naismith of Springfield, Massachusetts, also became popular. Naismith developed the game in the 1890s as an indoor winter sport for the boys in his YMCA physical education classes. Considered the only major sport that is completely American in origin, basketball soon spread to other countries.

Americans not only watched but also participated in sports. Tennis and golf were enjoyed by the wealthy, usually in exclusive private clubs. Bicycling grew in popularity after the "safety" bicycle was developed. Older bicycles had metal-rimmed wheels—a large one in front and a small one in back—while the new ones had two air-filled rubber tires of the same size.

These improvements helped bicycle riding take the country by storm. One romantic song celebrated the bicycle:

> **66**It won't be a stylish marriage,
> I can't afford a carriage,
> But you'll look sweet on the seat of a
> bicycle built for two.**99**

Large cities had many theaters. Plays performed ranged from serious dramas by Shakespeare to vaudeville shows, which were variety shows with dancing, singing, comedy, and magic acts. Many people could afford the price of a ticket, and in the early 1900s, vaudeville offered the most popular shows in town. The circus also attracted large crowds. In 1910 the United States had about 80 traveling circuses.

Thomas Edison invented "moving pictures" in the 1880s. The "movies" soon became enormously popular. Some theaters, called nickelodeons, charged five cents to see short films. The nickelodeons were the beginning of today's film industry.

✓ **Reading Check** **Describing** What elements made up jazz music?

SECTION 3 ASSESSMENT

Checking for Understanding

1. **Key Terms** Use each of these terms in a complete sentence that will help explain its meaning: land-grant college, yellow journalism, realism, regionalism, ragtime, vaudeville.
2. **Reviewing Facts** Summarize the new philosophy of education that emerged around 1900.

Reviewing Themes

3. **Continuity and Change** What sparked an increase in the number of newspapers, magazines, and books in the late 1800s?

Critical Thinking

4. **Determining Cause and Effect** Explain the connection between leisure time and the development of the arts.
5. **Analyzing Information** Re-create the diagram below and describe the work of each of these writers.

Writer	Description of work
Horatio Alger	
Stephen Crane	
Edith Wharton	

Analyzing Visuals

6. **Picturing History** Look at the pictures of classrooms that appear in the section. In what ways are they similar to and in what ways are they different from classrooms today?

Interdisciplinary Activity

Art Create your own moving pictures by making a series of drawings (that build on one another) on 2-inch by 4-inch slips of paper. Staple the slips of paper together on one side, then flip through them slowly to view your motion picture.

America's LITERATURE

Life on the Mississippi

When I was a boy, there was but one permanent ambition among my comrades in our village on the west bank of the Mississippi River. That was, to be a steamboatman. . . .

Once a day a cheap, gaudy **packet** arrived upward from St. Louis, and another downward from **Keokuk.** Before these events, the day was glorious with expectancy; after them, the day was a dead and empty thing. Not only the boys, but the whole village, felt this. After all these years I can picture that old time to myself now, just as it was then: the white town drowsing in the sunshine of a summer's morning; the streets empty, . . . the magnificent Mississippi, rolling its mile-wide tide along, shining in the sun; . . . Presently a film of dark smoke appears . . . ; instantly a . . . **drayman,** famous for his quick eye and prodigious voice, lifts up the cry, "S-t-e-a-m-boat a-comin'!" and the scene changes! . . . [A]ll in a twinkling the dead town is alive and moving. Drays, carts, men, boys, all go hurrying from many quarters to a common center, the wharf. Assembled there, the people fasten their eyes upon the coming boat as upon a wonder they are seeing for the first time. And the boat *is* rather a handsome sight, too. . . . [T]he captain stands by the big bell,

calm, imposing, the envy of all; great volumes of the blackest smoke are rolling and tumbling out of the chimneys; . . . the captain lifts his hand, a bell rings, the wheels stop; then they turn back, churning the water to foam, and the steamer is at rest. Then such a scramble as there is to get aboard, and to get ashore, and to take in freight and to discharge freight, all at one and the same time; . . . Ten minutes later the steamer is under way again, with no flag on the jack-staff and no black smoke issuing from the chimneys. After ten more minutes the town is dead again. . . .

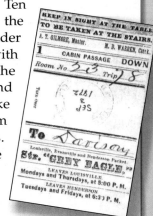

ANALYZING LITERATURE

1. **Recall and Interpret** What major event takes place once a day?
2. **Evaluate and Connect** Why is the event so important?

Interdisciplinary Activity

Art Read again Twain's descriptions. Then draw a picture of one of these scenes. Be sure to add details that reflect Twain's words.

Chapter Summary
Toward an Urban America

Cities grow as immigrants and people from rural areas move to them.

An Urban America was replacing a rural one.

Cities grew upward as space became limited.

Transportation improvements allowed families to live in suburbs.

Urban America

Limited housing in crowded cities meant many lived in tenements.

Problems in cities included overcrowding, crime, and public health dangers.

Reviewing Key Terms

On a sheet of paper, define the following terms.

1. ethnic group
2. tenement
3. settlement house
4. yellow journalism
5. ragtime
6. assimilate

Reviewing Key Facts

7. What did nativist groups try to do?
8. What was the purpose of the Morrill Act?
9. What project did Andrew Carnegie fund?

Critical Thinking

10. **Analyzing Information** What new styles of writing did American authors adopt during this period?
11. **Drawing Conclusions** Re-create the diagram below and describe three ways newcomers to America tried to preserve their culture.

Preserving cultural heritage

Practicing Skills

Reading a Line Graph *Study the line graph below and answer the questions that follow.*

12. What was the average number of school days in 1920?
13. What trend is shown in this line graph?

Length of School Year, 1880–1920

Average number of days attended per year

130
120
110
100
90
80

1880 1890 1900 1910 1920

Year

Source: Department of Education.

Geography and History Activity

Study this map and answer the questions below.

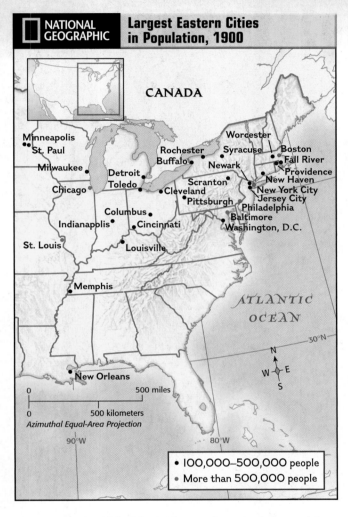

NATIONAL GEOGRAPHIC

Largest Eastern Cities in Population, 1900

CANADA

Minneapolis
St. Paul
Milwaukee
Chicago
Detroit
Toledo
Cleveland
Rochester
Buffalo
Worcester
Syracuse
Boston
Fall River
Newark
Providence
New Haven
Scranton
New York City
Jersey City
Pittsburgh
Philadelphia
Columbus
Baltimore
Indianapolis
Cincinnati
Washington, D.C.
St. Louis
Louisville
Memphis

ATLANTIC OCEAN

30°N

New Orleans

0   500 miles
0   500 kilometers
Azimuthal Equal-Area Projection

90°W   80°W

N
W   E
S

• 100,000–500,000 people
• More than 500,000 people

14. Location Which cities had more than 500,000 people?

15. Place About how many people lived in Louisville?

16. Location What do the cities with more than 500,000 people have in common?

Citizenship Cooperative Activity

17. Citizenship Test Immigrants who want to become United States citizens today must pass a written test to qualify. Many of the questions on the test deal with United States history and customs. Work with members of your group to design a 15-question test that you think prospective citizens should be required to pass.

HISTORY Online

Self-Check Quiz
Visit taj.glencoe.com and click on **Chapter 20—Self-Check Quizzes** to prepare for the chapter test.

Economics Activity

18. Research for information, and then summarize your findings in a short report that answers these questions. What field or career area interests you? What education and skills are required to enter it? What attitudes, work habits, and other qualities does it take to succeed on the job?

Alternative Assessment

19. Portfolio Writing Activity Choose a problem of the early 1900s that interests you and describe what you would do to help correct it.

Standardized Test Practice

Read the passage about American life and choose the *best* answer to the question that follows.

"Between 1860 and 1900 American urban areas grew twice as fast as the total population. Chicago, which in the 1830s had been a frontier town with a few hundred residents, became a vast metropolis. New York became the second-largest city in the world. During the same span of years, the populations of Boston, Baltimore, and Philadelphia also grew rapidly."

The main idea of the passage is best expressed by

A New York City grew rapidly.

B Only cities in the northeastern United States grew rapidly.

C Population of urban America grew at a very fast rate during this era.

D Rural growth continued, but not as quickly as urban growth.

Test-Taking Tip

Make sure that your answer is supported by information in the quotation. Do not rely only on your memory. Keep in mind that a *metropolis* is a "large city."

UNIT

8

Reform, Expansion, and War

1865–1920

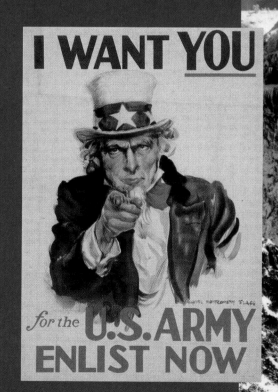

World War I enlistment poster

Why It Matters

As you study Unit 8, you will learn that progressive reforms affected many areas of American life during this era. You will also learn why the United States took a more active role in international affairs. The following resources offer more information about this period in American history.

Primary Sources Library

See pages 972–973 for primary source readings to accompany Unit 8.

 Use the American history
Primary Source Document Library CD-ROM *to find additional primary sources about reform, expansion, and World War I.*

Yosemite Valley
by Ansel Adams

"Suffrage is the pivotal right."

—Susan B. Anthony, 1897

CHAPTER 21

Progressive Reforms

1877–1920

Why It Matters

The spirit of reform gained strength in the late 1800s and thrived during the early 1900s. The reformers, called progressives, were confident in their ability to improve government and the quality of life.

The Impact Today

Progressive reforms affected many areas of American life. Among these are government, consumers' rights, and education.

 The American Journey Video *The chapter 21 video "The Progressive Movement," studies the movement and how it gained strength over time.*

1887
• Interstate Commerce Commission formed

1901
• President McKinley assassinated

United States PRESIDENTS

| Hayes 1877–1881 | Garfield 1881 | Arthur 1881–1885 | Cleveland 1885–1889 | B. Harrison 1889–1893 | Cleveland 1893–1897 | McKinley 1897–1901 |

1880   *1890*   *1900*

World

1879
• British win Zulu War

1889
• Brazil becomes a republic

1893
• New Zealand grants women suffrage

1897
• First World Zionist Congress convenes

The Lone Tenement by George Bellows, 1909 Bellows's favorite themes, which include city scenes and athletic events, mark him as a uniquely American painter.

FOLDABLES™
Study Organizer

Analyzing Information Study Foldable
Make this foldable to help you analyze information about the Progressive movement.

Step 1 Fold a sheet of paper in half from side to side, leaving a ½ inch tab along the side.

> Leave ½ inch tab here.

Step 2 Turn the paper and fold into fourths.

> Fold in half, then fold in half again.

Step 3 Unfold and cut up along the three fold lines.

> Make four tabs.

Step 4 Label your foldable as shown.

WHAT was the Progressive movement? | HOW did it change the roles of women? | WHO were the Progressive presidents? | WHY were some groups excluded from reform?

Reading and Writing As you read, find and write answers to the four questions under the appropriate tab of your foldable.

1906
• Sinclair's *The Jungle* published

1909
• The NAACP is formed

1919
• Eighteenth Amendment prohibits alcohol

1920
• Nineteenth Amendment grants woman suffrage

Roosevelt 1901–1909

Taft 1909–1913

Wilson 1913–1921

1910

1920

1905
• Einstein announces theory of relativity

1911
• Rutherford discovers structure of atom

HISTORY
Online

Chapter Overview
Visit <u>taj.glencoe.com</u> and click on **Chapter 21— Chapter Overviews** to preview chapter information.

The Progressive Movement

Guide to Reading

Main Idea
Many men and women became part of a widespread movement to bring about reform.

Key Terms
political machine, patronage, civil service, trust, muckraker, primary, initiative, referendum, recall

Reading Strategy
Organizing Information As you read Section 1, re-create the diagram below and list two or more reforms for each category.

Reforms		
Government	Business	Voting

Read to Learn
- how journalists helped shape the reform movement.
- how cities, states, and Congress answered the call for reform of the government.

Section Theme
Government and Democracy Americans took action against corruption in business and government.

Preview of Events

| 1885 | 1895 | 1905 | 1915 |

1887
Interstate Commerce Commission is established

1890
Congress passes Sherman Antitrust Act

1906
Upton Sinclair writes *The Jungle*

1912
Congress passes the Seventeenth Amendment

AN American Story

Newspaper reporter Jacob Riis shocked Americans in 1890 with his book *How the Other Half Lives.* With words and powerful photographs, Riis vividly portrayed immigrant life in New York City's crowded tenements. Said Riis: "We used to go in the small hours of the morning into the worst tenements to count noses and see if the law against overcrowding was violated and the sights I saw there gripped my heart until I felt that I must tell of them, or burst."

Fighting Corruption

Many Americans called for reform in the late 1800s. The reformers had many different goals. Progressive reformers focused on urban problems, government, and business. They claimed that government and big business were taking advantage of the American people rather than serving them.

Political machines—powerful organizations linked to political parties—controlled local government in many cities. In each ward, or political district within a city, a machine representative controlled jobs and services. This representative was the **political boss.** The bosses gained votes for their parties by doing favors for people, such as offering turkey dinners and summer boat rides, providing jobs for immigrants, and helping needy families. A political boss was often a citizen's closest link to local government. Although they did help people, many bosses were dishonest.

Corrupt politicians found numerous ways to make money. They accepted bribes from tenement landlords in return for overlooking violations of city housing codes. They received campaign contributions from contractors hoping to do business with the city. They also accepted kickbacks. A **kickback** is an arrangement in which contractors padded the amount of their bill for city work and paid, or "kicked back," a percentage of that amount to the bosses.

Some politicians used their knowledge of city business for personal profit. A person who knew where the city planned to build a road could buy land there before the route became public knowledge. Later the land could be sold for a huge profit.

One of the most corrupt city bosses, William M. Tweed, known as **Boss Tweed,** headed New York City's Democratic political machine in the 1860s and 1870s. Tweed and a network of city officials—the Tweed ring—controlled the police, the courts, and some newspapers. They collected millions of dollars in illegal payments from companies doing business with the city. Political cartoonist Thomas Nast exposed the Tweed ring's operations in his cartoons for *Harper's Weekly.* Tweed was convicted and sentenced to prison.

Citizenship
New Ways to Govern Cities

To break the power of political bosses, reformers founded organizations such as the National Municipal League in Philadelphia. These groups worked to make city governments more honest and efficient.

Cities troubled by poor management or corruption tried new forms of government. After a tidal wave devastated **Galveston, Texas,** in 1900, the task of rebuilding the city overwhelmed the mayor and city council. Galveston's citizens persuaded the Texas state legislature to approve a new charter that placed the city government in the hands of five commissioners. The new commission efficiently rebuilt the city. By 1917

Analyzing *Political Cartoons*

The Tweed Ring Boss Tweed and New York City officials are shown pointing to one another in response to the question "Who stole the people's money?" On Tweed's right a man holds a hat labeled "Chairs," a reference to the $179,000 New York City paid for 40 chairs and three tables. Other contractors and cheats—their names on their coats—complete the "ring." **How did political bosses gain votes for their parties?**

"WHO STOLE THE PEOPLE'S MONEY?" — DO TELL . N.Y.TIMES   'TWAS HIM.

A Boss Tweed   **B** Peter Sweeny   **C** Richard Connelly   **D** Mayor A. Oakey Hall

HISTORY Online

Student Web Activity
Visit taj.glencoe.com and click on **Chapter 21— Student Web Activities** for an activity on the Progressive movement.

commissions governed nearly 400 cities. Many other cities, mostly small ones, hired professional city managers.

One successful civic reformer was **Tom Johnson,** mayor of Cleveland, Ohio, from 1901 to 1909. He battled corporations and party bosses to lower streetcar fares, improve food inspections, and build parks. Because of Johnson's reforms, Cleveland became known as the best-governed city in the United States.

Fighting the Spoils System

The spoils system—rewarding political supporters with jobs and favors—had been common practice since the time of Andrew Jackson. Whenever a new president came to power, job seekers flooded the nation's capital.

The spoils system—also called patronage—existed at all levels of government and led to numerous abuses. Many who received government jobs were not qualified. Some were dishonest.

Presidents **Rutherford B. Hayes** (1877–1881) and **James Garfield** (1881) wanted to change the spoils system. Hayes tried to do this by reforming the civil service—the body of nonelected government workers—but neither the Democratic nor the Republican Party supported his efforts.

Garfield also hoped to reform the civil service. He believed that people should be appointed to government jobs not as a reward for political support but because of their qualifications. Garfield took office in 1881 but was assassinated by an unsuccessful office seeker before he could launch his reforms.

When Vice President **Chester A. Arthur** succeeded Garfield, he tried to end the spoils system. In 1883 Congress passed the **Pendleton Act,** which established the **Civil Service Commission** to set up competitive examinations for federal jobs. Applicants had to demonstrate their abilities in this examination. By 1900 the commission controlled the hiring of many federal employees.

✓ **Reading Check** **Explaining** Whom did the spoils system reward?

⑤ Economics

Controlling Business

During the late 1800s, many Americans came to believe that trusts, or combinations of companies, were becoming too large. They believed these trusts had too much control over the economy and the government. This public concern led to new laws regulating big business.

In 1890 Congress passed the **Sherman Antitrust Act,** the first federal law to control trusts and monopolies. Supporters of the law hoped it would keep trusts from limiting competition. During the 1890s, however, the government rarely used the Sherman Act to curb business. Instead, it applied the act against labor unions, claiming that union strikes interfered with trade. Not until the early 1900s did the government win cases against trusts by using the Sherman Act.

Reining in the Railroads

The railroads functioned as an **oligopoly**—a market structure in which a few large companies control the prices of the industry. Reformers called for regulations on railroad rates, but the Supreme Court ruled that only Congress could enact legislation to regulate commerce that crossed state lines.

So in 1887 Congress passed the **Interstate Commerce Act,** which required railroads to charge "reasonable and just" rates and to publish those rates. The act also created the **Interstate Commerce Commission** (ICC) to supervise the railroad industry and, later, the trucking industry.

Lowering Tariffs

Reformers also wanted to lower tariffs. Many people believed that high tariffs led to higher prices for goods. In 1890 the Republicans raised tariffs sharply to protect American businesses from international competition. Voters showed their opposition to high tariffs by sending many Democrats to Congress. **Grover Cleveland,** who became president in 1893, also supported lower tariffs.

✓ **Reading Check** **Explaining** Why did many people want lower tariffs?

The New Reformers

In the early 1900s, new ideas for correcting injustice and solving social problems emerged among American reformers. Socialism and progressivism were two such ideas.

Socialists believed a nation's resources and major industries should be owned and operated by the government on behalf of all the people—not by individuals and private companies for their own profit. **Eugene V. Debs** helped found the American Socialist Party in 1898. Under Debs's leadership the party won some support in the early 1900s. Debs ran for president five times but never received more than 6 percent of the popular vote.

During the same period, progressives brought new energy to the reform movement. Like the socialists, many progressives were alarmed by the concentration of wealth and power in the hands of a few. Progressives rejected the socialist idea of government ownership of industries. Instead, they supported government efforts to regulate industry.

They also sought to reform government, to make it more efficient and better able to resist the influence of powerful business interests. Progressives also believed that society had an obligation to protect and help all its members. Many progressive reforms aimed to help those who lacked wealth and influence.

Muckrakers Expose Problems

Journalists aided the reformers by exposing injustices and corruption. Investigative reporters wrote newspaper and magazine stories that brought problems to the attention of the public—and gained readers. These journalists were called muckrakers because they "raked" (brought to light) the "muck" (dirt and corruption) underlying society.

One of the most effective muckrakers, **Lincoln Steffens,** reported for *McClure's Magazine.* Steffens exposed corrupt machine politics in New York, Chicago, and other cities. His articles, collected in a book called *The Shame of the Cities* (1904), strengthened the demand for urban reform.

"It is the duty of the public to know."

—*Ida Tarbell, 1905*

Ida Tarbell, also writing for *McClure's,* described the unfair practices of the oil trust. Her articles led to public pressure for more government control over big business. In her 1904 book, *The History of the Standard Oil Company,* she warned of the giant corporation's power.

In his novel *The Jungle* (1906), **Upton Sinclair** described the horrors of the meatpacking industry in Chicago. Although Sinclair's aim was to arouse sympathy for the workers, his vivid descriptions shocked Americans. The uproar caused by Sinclair's book helped persuade Congress to pass the **Meat Inspection Act** in 1906. That same year Congress also passed the **Pure Food and Drug Act,** requiring accurate labeling of food and medicine and banning the sale of harmful food.

Reading Check **Identifying** Who wrote about unfair practices in the oil industry?

🎙Citizenship

Expanding Democracy

In the early 1900s, progressives backed a number of reforms designed to increase the people's direct control of the government. **Robert La Follette** led Wisconsin's reform-minded Republicans. "Fighting Bob," as he was called, won the support of farmers and workers with his fiery attacks on big business and the railroads. While governor, La Follette brought

Fact · Fiction · Folklore

Presidential Elections

Debs ran for president while in prison. Eugene Debs was the candidate of the Socialist Party for president in 1904, 1908, and 1912. For his opposition to the entry of the United States into World War I, Debs was convicted in 1918 and sentenced to 10 years in prison. While in prison in 1920 he ran again for president on the Socialist ticket and received almost 1 million votes—about 3.5 percent of the total. His sentence was commuted in 1921.

about reforms such as improving the civil service. His greatest achievement, however, was reforming the state electoral system. Candidates for general elections in Wisconsin had been chosen at state conventions run by party bosses. La Follette introduced a direct primary election, allowing the state's voters to choose their party's candidates. Reformers in other states copied this "Wisconsin idea."

The Oregon System

The state of Oregon also made important changes in the political process to give voters more power and to limit the influence of political parties. The reforms in Oregon included a direct primary election and the initiative, the referendum, and the recall.

The initiative allowed citizens to place a measure or issue on the ballot in a state election. The referendum gave voters the opportunity to accept or reject measures that the state legislature enacted. The recall enabled voters to remove unsatisfactory elected officials from their jobs. These reforms were called the **Oregon System.** Other western states soon adopted the reforms.

The Seventeenth Amendment

Progressives also changed the way United States senators are elected. The Constitution had given state legislatures the responsibility for choosing senators, but party bosses and business interests often controlled the selection process. Progressives wanted to give the people an opportunity to vote for their senators directly. Support for this idea grew. In 1912 Congress passed the **Seventeenth Amendment** to the Constitution to provide for the direct election of senators. Ratified in 1913, the amendment gave the people a voice in selecting their representatives. 📖 *(See page 248 for the text of the Seventeenth Amendment.)*

✔ **Reading Check** **Identifying** What reform allowed voters to place a measure on the ballot?

SECTION 1 ASSESSMENT

Checking for Understanding

1. **Key Terms** Use each of these terms in a complete sentence that will help explain its meaning: political machine, patronage, civil service, trust, muckraker, primary, initiative, referendum, recall.
2. **Reviewing Facts** Explain how the Civil Service Commission helped to eliminate the spoils system.

Reviewing Themes

3. **Government and Democracy** Identify and describe three reforms that gave the American people more direct control of the government.

Critical Thinking

4. **Comparing** Compare socialist and progressive views on industry.
5. **Organizing Information** Re-create the diagram below and show how the Seventeenth Amendment reformed the political process.

Seventh Amendment	
Policy before	Policy after

Analyzing Visuals

6. **Analyzing Political Cartoons** Examine the political cartoon on page 611. Why are the individuals pointing to someone else? What statement is cartoonist Thomas Nast making about the extent of political corruption in New York City?

Interdisciplinary Activity

Civics Citizens must prepare to vote. Create a pamphlet describing the kinds of things voters should know in order to make their ballots meaningful.

SECTION 2 Women and Progressives

Guide to Reading

Main Idea
Women worked for the right to vote, for improved working conditions, and for temperance.

Key Terms
suffragist, prohibition

Reading Strategy
Organizing Information As you read the section, re-create the diagram below and describe the role of each individual.

Individual	Role in Progressive movement
Mary Church Terrell	
Susan B. Anthony	
Frances Willard	

Read to Learn
• how the role of American women changed during the Progressive Era.
• how women fought for the right to vote.

Section Theme
Groups and Institutions Many women worked for a constitutional amendment to gain suffrage.

Preview of Events

◆1890   ◆1900   ◆1910   ◆1920

1890
National American Woman Suffrage Association emerges

1896
National Association of Colored Women is formed

1919
The Eighteenth Amendment is ratified

1920
The Nineteenth Amendment is ratified

AN American Story

Nurse Lillian Wald followed a young girl up a rickety staircase in a filthy tenement house on New York City's Lower East Side. The girl had begged Wald to help her mother who had just given birth to a baby. A doctor had refused to treat the girl's mother because she could not pay his fee. The sight of the desperate mother and her baby was a turning point in Wald's life. Wald dedicated herself to helping poor people and educating them about health care. Eventually Wald became a national reform leader who was known to say, "The whole world is my neighborhood."

Women's Roles Change

Many leaders of the urban reform movement, including Lillian Wald, were middle-class women. The situation of middle-class women changed during the late 1800s. Their responsibilities at home lessened as families became smaller, more children spent the day at school, and men worked away from home. Women also gained more free time as technology made housework easier.

CHAPTER 21 Progressive Reforms   **615**

Many more middle-class women were gaining higher education. About 40 percent of all college students in 1910 were women. Women were also starting professional careers—mostly in teaching but also in nursing, medicine, and other fields. Between 1890 and 1910, the number of women working outside the home increased from 4 million to nearly 7.5 million.

These changes created the "new woman"—a popular term for educated, up-to-date women who pursued interests outside their homes. Many such women became role models.

As you read in Chapter 20, **Jane Addams** established Hull House, a settlement house, in **Chicago.** Working there gave Addams an outlet for her energy and intelligence, as well as a sense of satisfaction with helping poor people. *(See page 972 for an account of settlement houses.)*

Settlement workers such as Addams gained notice as writers, public speakers, fund-raisers, and reformers. Many young women followed the example of these talented public figures. Others found inspiration in the life of **Mother Cabrini,** an Italian nun who came to the United States to work with the poor.

Women's Clubs

Women found another outlet for their talent and energy in women's clubs, which rapidly increased in number. At first the clubs focused on such cultural activities as music and painting. Many clubs gradually became more concerned with social problems.

When some clubs refused to admit African Americans, African American women established their own network of clubs. Clubs such as the Phyllis Wheatley Club of New Orleans organized classes, recreational activities, and social services. In 1896 women from these clubs formed the **National Association of Colored Women.** Its first president, **Mary Church Terrell,** was an active

Mary Church Terrell

leader for women's rights. The association established homes for orphans, founded hospitals, and worked for woman suffrage, fulfilling its motto "Lifting As We Climb."

✔**Reading Check** **Identifying** Who was Mary Church Terrell?

The Fight for Suffrage

At the Seneca Falls Convention in 1848, women had called for the right to vote. After the Civil War, Congress passed the Fifteenth Amendment, giving voting rights to freed men—but not to women. Some leading abolitionists became suffragists, men and women who fought for woman suffrage, or women's right to vote.

Like other reformers, the suffragists formed organizations to promote their cause. **Elizabeth Cady Stanton** and **Susan B. Anthony** founded the **National Woman Suffrage Association,** which called for a constitutional amendment allowing women to vote in national elections. A second organization, the American Woman Suffrage Association, focused on winning woman suffrage in state elections.

In 1890 the two groups merged to form the National American Woman Suffrage Association. Led by **Anna Howard Shaw,** a minister and doctor, and **Carrie Chapman Catt,** an educator and newspaper editor, this organization grew to more than two million members by 1917. In a speech to the association in 1902, Catt declared:

> ❝The whole aim of the [women's] movement has been to destroy the idea that obedience is necessary to women; to train women to such self-respect that they would not grant obedience and to train men to such comprehension of equity [fairness] they would not exact [demand] it.❞

Opposition to Woman Suffrage

Groups formed to protest the idea of giving women the vote. These organizations—supported by some women as well as by men—claimed that woman suffrage would upset society's "natural" balance and lead to divorce and neglected children.

CANADA

WASH.
1910

OREGON
1912

MONTANA
1914

N. DAK.

MINN.

IDAHO
1896

WYOMING
1869

S. DAK.
1918

WIS.

NEVADA
1914

UTAH
1870

NEBRASKA

IOWA

MICH.
1918

N.H.
VT.   MAINE

N.Y.
1917

MASS.

R.I.
CONN.

CALIF.
1911

COLORADO
1893

KANSAS
1912

ILL.   IND.

OHIO

PA.

N.J.

DEL.

ARIZONA
1912

NEW
MEXICO

OKLA.
1918

MO.

W.
VA.   VA.

MD.

KY.

ARK.

TENN.

N.C.

S.C.

ATLANTIC
OCEAN

PACIFIC
OCEAN

TEXAS

LA.

MISS.   ALA.   GA.

FLA.

Gulf of Mexico

0   500 miles

0   500 kilometers
Azimuthal Equal-Area projection

40iN

30iN

90iW   80iW

N
W   E
S

MEXICO

Equal suffrage, date effective

Partial suffrage

No statewide suffrage

Geography Skills

By 1919 a total of 15 states allowed women to vote in all elections.
1. Place Where were women first granted equal suffrage?
2. Comparing What was the status of woman suffrage in your state by 1919?

The suffrage movement gained strength, however, when respected public figures such as Jane Addams spoke out in support of the vote for women. Alice Duer Miller brought humor to the struggle for the right to vote:

"Said Mr. Jones in 1910:
'Women, subject yourselves to men.'
Nineteen-Eleven heard him quote:
'They rule the world without the vote.'

. . . .

By Nineteen-Thirteen, looking glum,
He said that it was bound to come.

. . . .

By Nineteen-Fifteen, he'll insist
He's always been a suffragist."

The suffragists won their early victories in the West. First as a territory in 1869 and then as a state in 1890, **Wyoming** led the nation in giving women the vote. Between 1910 and 1913, five other states adopted woman suffrage. By 1919 women could vote in at least some elections in most of the 48 states.

Continuing the Fight

In the meantime suffragists continued their struggle to win the vote everywhere. **Alice Paul,** a Quaker who founded the National Woman's Party in 1916, was a forceful leader of the suffragist movement. She sought greater economic and legal equality as well as suffrage for women.

During a visit to Great Britain, Paul saw suffragists use protest marches and hunger strikes to call attention to their cause. When she returned to the United States, she, too, used these methods in the fight for suffrage.

In 1917 Alice Paul met with President **Woodrow Wilson** but failed to win his support for woman suffrage. Paul responded by leading women protestors in front of the White House. Day after day they marched carrying banners demanding votes for women. When Paul and other protestors were arrested for blocking the sidewalk, they started a much-publicized hunger strike. Alva Belmont, one of the protestors, proudly declared that all the women had done was to stand there "quietly, peacefully, lawfully, and gloriously."

Women Vote Nationally

By 1917 the national tide was turning in favor of woman suffrage. New York and, a year later, South Dakota and Oklahoma granted equal suffrage. Meanwhile Congress began debating the issue, and President Wilson agreed to support an amendment to the Constitution.

In 1919 the Senate voted in favor of the **Nineteenth Amendment,** which allowed woman suffrage. The amendment was ratified in 1920, in time for women to vote in that year's presidential election. For the first time, American women were able to participate in the election of their national leaders.

✓ Reading Check **Identifying** What state was the first to give women the right to vote?

Women and Social Reform

During the Progressive Era, women involved themselves in many reform movements besides woman suffrage. In 1912, for example, pressure from women's clubs helped persuade Congress to create the Children's Bureau in the Labor Department. The bureau's task was to develop federal policies that would protect children.

Working for a Better Life

While they struggled to gain rights for themselves, many middle-class women also worked to improve the lives of working-class people, immigrants, and society as a whole. They supported and staffed libraries, schools, and settlement houses and raised money for charities.

Some women promoted other causes. They challenged business interests by sponsoring laws to regulate the labor of women and children and to require government inspection of workplaces. Women also played an important role in the movement to reform and regulate the food and medicine industries.

In many states across the country, women pressured state legislatures to provide pensions for widows and abandoned mothers with children. These pensions later became part of the Social Security system.

Labor Movement

Reform efforts brought upper-class women reformers into alliance with working women. In 1903 women's groups joined with working-class union women to form the **Women's Trade Union League** (WTUL).

The WTUL encouraged working women to form women's labor unions. It also supported laws to protect the rights of women factory workers. WTUL members raised money to help striking workers and to pay bail for women who were arrested for participating in strikes.

The Temperance Crusade

A crusade against the use of alcohol had begun in New England and the Midwest in the early 1800s. The movement continued throughout the late 1800s. Protestant churches strongly supported the anti-alcohol movement.

Two driving forces in the crusade were the **Woman's Christian Temperance Union** (WCTU), established in 1874, and the **Anti-Saloon League,** founded 20 years later. They called for temperance, urging individuals to stop drinking, and prohibition, the passing of laws to prohibit the making or selling of alcohol.

In 1879 **Frances Willard** became head of the WCTU. Willard led a campaign to educate the public about the links between alcohol abuse and violence, poverty, and unemployment. She turned the WCTU into a powerful organization with chapters in every state.

The WCTU's main goal was prohibition. However, the WCTU also supported other causes, including prison reform, woman suffrage, improved working conditions, and world peace. Through WCTU chapters, thousands of women combined their traditional role as guardians of the family and home with social activism.

Carry Nation was an especially colorful crusader for temperance. Her most dramatic protests occurred when she pushed her way into saloons and broke bottles and kegs with an ax.

Carry Nation went from praying outside taverns to destroying them with a hatchet.

Temperance poster

The Prohibition Amendment

The anti-alcohol movement grew during the early 1900s. Progressive reformers who wanted to ban alcohol for social reasons were joined by Americans who opposed alcohol for religious or moral reasons. In 1917 they persuaded Congress to pass a constitutional amendment making it illegal to make, transport, or sell alcohol in the United States. The **Eighteenth Amendment,** known as the Prohibition Law, was ratified in 1919. 📖 *(See page 249 for the text of the Eighteenth Amendment.)*

✓ **Reading Check** **Describing** What was the goal of the temperance movement?

SECTION 2 ASSESSMENT

Checking for Understanding

1. **Key Terms** Use each of these terms in a complete sentence that will help explain its meaning: suffragist, prohibition.

2. **Reviewing Facts** What did the Nineteenth Amendment provide?

Reviewing Themes

3. **Groups and Institutions** How did women's clubs help to change the role of women?

Critical Thinking

4. **Drawing Conclusions** Why do you think the right to vote was important to women?

5. **Sequencing Information** Re-create the time line below and identify the events regarding woman suffrage that happened in these years.

1848	1869	1896	1920

Analyzing Visuals

6. **Geography Skills** Examine the map on page 617. Which regions of the country provided no statewide suffrage?

Interdisciplinary Activity

Expository Writing Find a newspaper article about the role of women today. Rewrite the article to reflect how this information might have been presented in the early 1900s.

Progressive Presidents

Guide to Reading

Main Idea
Presidents during the Progressive Era worked to control big business and to deal with labor problems.

Key Terms
trustbuster, arbitration, square deal, laissez-faire, conservation

Reading Strategy
Taking Notes As you read Section 3, re-create the diagram below and explain why each of these acts of legislation is important.

Legislation	Importance
Sixteenth Amendment	
Pure Food and Drug Act	
Federal Reserve Act	

Read to Learn
- how President Theodore Roosevelt took on big business.
- why the progressives formed their own political party.

Section Theme
Economic Factors Government tried various means to regulate big business.

Preview of Events

1900	1910	1920

1901
President McKinley is assassinated

1905
Roosevelt proposes the U.S. Forest Service

1913
Federal Reserve Act creates 12 regional banks

1914
Congress establishes the Federal Trade Commission

AN American Story

"We were still under a heavy fire and I got together a mixed lot of men and pushed on from the trenches and ranch houses which we had just taken, driving the Spaniards through a line of palm-trees, and over the crest of a chain of hills. . . ." With these words, a young lieutenant colonel named Theodore Roosevelt described his military adventures in Cuba during the Spanish-American War. Known for his vigor, enthusiasm, and a colorful personality, Roosevelt became president in 1901 upon the assassination of President William McKinley.

Theodore Roosevelt

When **Theodore Roosevelt** received the Republican vice-presidential nomination in 1900, the powerful Republican leader Mark Hanna warned that there would be only one life between "that cowboy" and the White House. When the election resulted in a Republican victory, Hanna turned to McKinley and said, "Now it is up to you to live." Less than a year later, President McKinley was assassinated. Suddenly, 42-year-old Theodore Roosevelt became president—the youngest president in the nation's history. When Roosevelt moved into the White House in 1901, he brought progressivism with him.

The "Trustbuster"

President McKinley had favored big business, but President Roosevelt was known to support business regulation and other progressive reforms. In 1902 Roosevelt ordered the Justice Department to take legal action against certain trusts that had violated the Sherman Antitrust Act. His first target was the **Northern Securities Company,** a railroad monopoly formed by financiers J.P. Morgan and James J. Hill to control transportation in the Northwest. Northern Securities fought the government's accusations of illegal activity all the way to the Supreme Court. Finally, in 1904 the Justice Department won its case. The Supreme Court decided that Northern Securities had illegally limited trade and ordered the trust to be taken apart.

During the rest of Roosevelt's term as president, he obtained a total of 25 indictments (legal charges) against trusts in the beef, oil, and tobacco industries. Although hailed as a trustbuster, Roosevelt did not want to break up all trusts. As he saw it, trusts should be regulated, not destroyed. He distinguished between "good trusts," which were concerned with public welfare, and "bad trusts," which were not.

Labor Crisis

In 1902 Roosevelt faced a major labor crisis. More than 100,000 Pennsylvania coal miners, members of the **United Mine Workers,** went on strike. They demanded better pay, an eight-hour workday, and recognition of the union's right to represent its members in discussions with mine owners.

The mine owners refused to negotiate with the workers. The **coal strike** dragged on for months. As winter approached, coal supplies dwindled. Public opinion began to turn against the owners. As public pressure mounted, Roosevelt invited representatives of the owners and miners to a meeting at the White House. Roosevelt was outraged when the owners refused to negotiate. He threatened to send federal troops to work in the mines and produce the coal. The owners finally agreed to arbitration—settling the dispute by agreeing to accept the decision of an impartial outsider. Mine workers won a pay increase and a reduction in hours, but they did not gain recognition for the union.

Roosevelt's action marked a departure from normal patterns of labor relations at the time. Earlier presidents had used troops against strikers, but Roosevelt had used the power of the federal government to force the company owners to negotiate. In other labor actions, however, Roosevelt supported employers in disputes with workers.

Square Deal

Roosevelt ran for the presidency in 1904, promising the people a square deal—fair and equal treatment for all. He was elected with more than 57 percent of the popular vote.

Roosevelt's "square deal" called for a considerable amount of government regulation of business. This contrasted with an attitude toward business that dated back to the presidency of Thomas Jefferson, which was summed up in the phrase laissez-faire (LEH•say FEHR). This French term generally means, "let people do as they choose."

McKinley/Roosevelt glass canteen, 1900

Roosevelt introduced a new era of government regulation. He supported the **Meat Inspection** and **Pure Food and Drug Acts;** these acts gave the Department of Agriculture and the Food and Drug Administration the power to visit businesses and inspect their products.

Conserving the Wilderness

Roosevelt held a lifelong enthusiasm for the great outdoors and the wilderness. He believed in the need for conservation, the protection and preservation of natural resources.

As president, Roosevelt took steps to conserve the country's forests, mineral deposits, and water resources. In 1905 he proposed the **U.S. Forest Service.** He pressured Congress to set aside millions of acres of national forests and created the nation's first wildlife sanctuaries. Roosevelt also formed the National Conservation Commission, which produced the first survey of the country's natural resources.

Roosevelt has been called America's first environmental president. While he made conservation an important public issue, Roosevelt also recognized the need for economic growth and development. He tried to strike a balance between business interests and conservation.

✓ Reading Check **Describing** What is conservation?

William Howard Taft

No president before had ever served more than two terms. In keeping with that tradition, Roosevelt decided not to run for reelection in 1908. Instead Roosevelt chose William Howard Taft, an experienced diplomat, to run for president. In the election of 1908, Taft easily defeated Democrat William Jennings Bryan.

Although he had none of Roosevelt's flair, Taft carried out—and went beyond—many of Roosevelt's policies. The Taft administration won more antitrust cases in four years than Roosevelt had won in seven. Taft also favored the introduction of safety standards for mines and railroads.

Taft supported the **Sixteenth Amendment,** which gave Congress the power to tax people's incomes to generate revenue for the federal

Why It Matters

The Influence of
Minor Political Parties

Minor Political Parties The Republican and Democratic parties dominate the nation's two-party system. Yet the United States has a long history of other political parties that have risen to challenge the major parties. Minor parties pushed for an end to slavery, and supported voting rights for women, and child and labor regulation long before the major parties did.

Populist proposals that are in effect today include the federal income tax, the secret ballot, and the initiative and referendum.

government. Progressives hoped the income tax would enable the government to lower tariffs. In their view high tariffs led to higher prices for goods, which caused hardship for the poor. Progressives believed that taxes based on income were fairer. The Sixteenth Amendment, added to the Constitution in 1913, did not specify how income would be taxed. Congress passed additional laws so that higher incomes were taxed at a higher rate than lower incomes.

Despite his progressive reforms, President Taft disappointed progressives in two important areas—tariffs and conservation. He failed to fight for a lower tariff, and he modified some conservation policies so that they favored businesses.

Some third parties have presented a strong challenge to the major parties. The Republican Party was itself a third party in 1856. Four years later it captured the White House.

For the People
PEROT ★
By the People

Third-Party Results

Presidential Election Year	Candidate/party	Results: % of popular vote	Electoral votes
1848	Martin Van Buren, Free Soil	10.1	0
1856	John C. Fremont, Republican	33.1	114
1892	James Weaver, Populist	8.5	22
1912	Theodore Roosevelt, Progressive	27.4	88
1924	Robert La Follette, Progressive	16.6	13
1948	Strom Thurmond, States Rights	2.4	39
1968	George Wallace, Am. Independent	13.5	46
1992	Ross Perot, Reform	19.0	0
2000	Ralph Nader, Green	2.7	0

"Look up, not down—
Look out, not in—
Look forward, not backward—
And lend a hand."

Founders' Day
October 27, 1912
THE
Progressive
Party

A SQUARE DEAL
NATIONAL PRESIDENTIAL CLUB 1912

Former President Theodore Roosevelt left the Republican Party to form the Progressive, or "Bull Moose," Party.

Roosevelt Challenges Taft

By 1912 Roosevelt had become completely disappointed in Taft. With a new presidential election on the horizon, Roosevelt decided to challenge Taft for the Republican presidential nomination. Roosevelt claimed that Taft had "completely twisted around" his own policies.

The showdown between Roosevelt and Taft came at the Republican national convention in Chicago in June. Although Roosevelt won every primary and had many supporters, Taft had the backing of Republican Party leaders and influential business interests who controlled the party machinery. When Taft received the nomination on the first ballot, Roosevelt charged the Republican party leaders with stealing the presidential nomination from him.

A fiery Roosevelt led his supporters out of the convention hall. He and his followers formed a new party, the **Progressive Party.** In August the Progressives held their own convention in Chicago and nominated Roosevelt for president.

When a reporter asked Roosevelt about his health, the candidate thumped himself on the chest and declared, "I feel as strong as a bull moose!" From then on, the Progressive Party was known as the **Bull Moose Party.**

The Election of 1912

The split in the Republican Party hurt both Taft and Roosevelt. While Republicans and Progressives battled each other at the polls, Democrat **Woodrow Wilson** gathered enough support to defeat them in the election. Wilson had

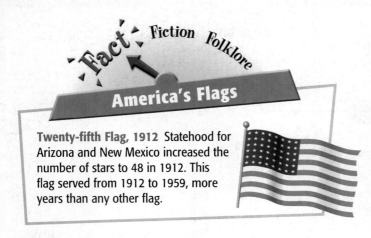

America's Flags

Twenty-fifth Flag, 1912 Statehood for Arizona and New Mexico increased the number of stars to 48 in 1912. This flag served from 1912 to 1959, more years than any other flag.

acquired a reputation as a progressive reformer while serving as president of Princeton University and governor of New Jersey.

Wilson gained only 42 percent of the popular vote, with Roosevelt receiving 27 percent and Taft 23 percent. However, Wilson won the presidency by the largest electoral majority up to that time, sweeping 435 of the 531 electoral votes.

Wilson in the White House

During his campaign Woodrow Wilson had criticized big government as well as big business. Wilson called his program the "New Freedom."

In 1913 Wilson achieved a long-awaited progressive goal—tariff reform. He persuaded the Democrat-controlled Congress to adopt a lower tariff on imported goods such as sugar, wool, steel, and farm equipment. Wilson believed that the pressure of foreign competition would lead American manufacturers to improve their products and lower their prices. The government income lost by lowering tariffs would be replaced by the new income tax.

That same year Congress also passed the **Federal Reserve Act** to regulate banking. By creating 12 regional banks supervised by a central board in Washington, D.C., the act gave the government more control over banking activities. Banks that operated nationally were required to join the Federal Reserve System and abide by its regulations.

Wilson also worked to strengthen government control over business. In 1914 Congress established the **Federal Trade Commission** (FTC) to investigate corporations for unfair trade practices. Wilson also supported the **Clayton Antitrust Act** of 1914, which joined the Sherman Antitrust Act as one of the government's chief weapons against trusts. The government also tried to regulate child labor. The Keating-Owen Act of 1916 banned goods produced by child labor from being sold in interstate commerce. The act was struck down as unconstitutional just two years later.

By the end of Wilson's first term, progressives had won many victories. The Progressive movement lost some of its momentum as Americans turned their attention to world affairs—especially the war that had broken out in Europe in 1914.

Reading Check **Analyzing** How did Roosevelt's run for the presidency affect the election of 1912?

SECTION 3 ASSESSMENT

Checking for Understanding

1. **Key Terms** Write a paragraph in which you use all of the following key terms: trustbuster, arbitration, laissez-faire.
2. **Reviewing Facts** What candidate won the presidential election of 1912?

Reviewing Themes

3. **Economic Factors** Why did progressives support an income tax?

Critical Thinking

4. **Analyzing Information** Explain why Roosevelt preferred regulation to trustbusting.
5. **Determining Cause and Effect** Re-create the diagram below and explain the reasons for, and the outcome of, the 1902 coal strike.

Analyzing Visuals

6. **Chart Skills** Study the chart on page 623. What party did James Weaver represent? What third party received the largest percentage of the popular vote? The largest number of electoral votes?

Interdisciplinary Activity

Art Draw a political cartoon that supports Theodore Roosevelt's actions as a "trustbuster."

Social Studies SKILLBUILDER

Interpreting a Political Cartoon

Why Learn This Skill?

You've probably heard the saying, "A picture is worth a thousand words." For more than 200 years, political cartoonists have drawn pictures to present their opinions about a person or event. Learning to interpret political cartoons can help you understand issues of both the past and present.

Learning the Skill

Political cartoons state opinions about particular subjects. To illustrate those opinions, cartoonists provide clues, using several different techniques. They often exaggerate a person's physical features or appearance in a special effect called "caricature." A caricature can be positive or negative, depending on the artist's point of view.

Cartoonists also use symbols to represent something else. The bald eagle is often shown in political cartoons as a symbol of the United States. Sometimes cartoonists help readers interpret their message by adding labels or captions.

To interpret a political cartoon, follow these steps:

* Read the caption and any other words printed in the cartoon.
* Analyze each element in the cartoon.
* Identify the clues: What is happening in the cartoon? Who or what is represented by each part of the drawing? What or whom do the figures represent? To what do the symbols refer?
* Study all these elements to decide the point the cartoonist is making.

Practicing the Skill

The cartoon on this page shows Theodore Roosevelt looking in a window at President Taft. Analyze the cartoon, and then answer the following questions.

1 What is going on in this picture?

2 What caricatures are included in this cartoon?

3 What symbols are shown in the cartoon? What do these symbols represent?

4 What point is the cartoonist making?

Applying the Skill

Interpreting a Political Cartoon Bring to class a copy of a political cartoon from a recent newspaper or magazine. Explain the cartoonist's point of view and the tools used to express it.

 Glencoe's **Skillbuilder Interactive Workbook CD-ROM, Level 1,** provides instruction and practice in key social studies skills.

WILD WONDERS

GRIZZLY BEARS, WOLVES, MOOSE, CARIBOU, DALL'S SHEEP and many other animals roam Alaska's Denali National Park and Preserve. Larger than Massachusetts, the six-million-acre park includes the highest mountain in North America.

The Alaskan wilderness area set aside as Mount McKinley National Park in 1917 was renamed Denali in 1980 when Congress tripled the size of the park. Denali was the peak's Native American name, meaning "the High One."

The idea of setting aside areas of natural beauty and historic importance for the benefit of the people dates back to the mid-1800s. Before then Americans had viewed wild places either as obstacles or as a source of natural resources for people to use.

The conservation movement gained popularity in the early 1900s when President Theodore Roosevelt and other conservationists urged Americans to protect natural resources.

Today conservation continues to be an important issue. Although many of us enjoy visiting national parks such as Denali, the parks also serve as refuges for wildlife. Scientists study the plants and animals so that they can protect them. With 430 species of flowering plants, 37 species of mammals, and 156 species of birds, Denali stands as one of America's great areas of unspoiled wilderness.

Mt. Foraker
17,400 ft. (5,303 m)

Avalanche Spire
10,105 ft. (3,080 m)

Kahiltna Glacier

ALASKA

Yukon River

CANADA
U.S.

Denali National Park
and Preserve

N
W E
S

| 0 | | 500 miles |
| 0 | | 500 kilometers |

LEARNING *from* GEOGRAPHY

1. Which peaks are higher than 15,000 feet?

2. Do you think it is necessary for the government to aid environmental programs? Explain.

Mt. McKinley (Denali)
20,320 ft. (6,194 m)

The Mooses Tooth
10,335 ft. (3,150 m)

Sheldon
Amphitheater

Tokositna Glacier

Ruth Glacier

Buckskin Glacier

AREA CLOSED

CLOSED TO ALL ENTRY
CRITICAL WILDLIFE HABITAT

Growth of the National Park System

■ National Parks
□ Other sites managed by
   National Park Service

Denali National Park 1980

Wild and Scenic Rivers Act 1968
National Trails Systems Act 1968

Historic Sites Act 1934

Mt. McKinley National Park 1917

National Park Service Act 1916

National Forest Service 1905

Yellowstone NP 1872

Number of sites / parks

350
300
250
200
150
100
50

1872 1880   1900   1920   1940   1960   1980   2000

SECTION 4 Excluded from Reform

Guide to Reading

Main Idea
Progressive reform did little to expand the rights and opportunities for minorities.

Key Terms
discrimination, barrio

Reading Strategy
Taking Notes As you read Section 4, re-create the diagram below and describe each person's accomplishments.

Individual	Accomplishments
Booker T. Washington	
Ida Wells	
W.E.B. Du Bois	
Carlos Montezuma	

Read to Learn
- why progressive reforms did not include all Americans.
- how minorities worked to move toward greater equality.

Section Theme
Civic Rights and Responsibilities Minorities discovered that progressive reforms often did not advance their own rights and responsibilities.

Preview of Events

♦ 1880   ♦ 1900   ♦ 1920

1887 American Protective Association targets Catholics

1907 Gentlemen's Agreement restricts Japanese immigration

1909 W.E.B. Du Bois helps form the NAACP

1915 Ku Klux Klan reappears

AN American Story

Like many seeking their fortunes, 16-year-old Lee Chew left his farm in China and booked passage on a steamer. When he and other Chinese immigrants arrived in San Francisco, they confronted a great wave of anti-Asian feeling. In the city's Chinese quarter, immigrants ran markets, laundries, and other small shops. Chew worked for an American family. "Chinese laundrymen [like me] were taught by American women," he said. "There are no laundries in China."

Prejudice and Discrimination

During the 1800s the overwhelming majority of Americans were white and Protestant and had been born in the United States. Many Americans believed that the United States should remain a white, Protestant nation. Nonwhite, non-Protestant, and non-native residents often faced discrimination—unequal treatment because of their race, religion, ethnic background, or place of birth. The government rarely interfered with this discrimination.

In 1908 violence erupted in **Springfield, Illinois,** when a white woman claimed to have been attacked by an African American man. Authorities jailed the man, but by that time, white townspeople had formed an angry mob.

Armed with axes and guns, the mob stormed through African American neighborhoods, destroying businesses and driving people from their homes. Rioters lynched two African American men and injured dozens more. Yet no one was ever punished for these violent crimes. Later, the woman who claimed she was attacked admitted that her accusation was untrue.

The Springfield riot shocked the nation and highlighted the deep racial divisions in American life. The riot took place in the hometown of Abraham Lincoln, the president who signed the Emancipation Proclamation. African Americans were no longer enslaved—but they were still pursued by prejudice and racial hatred.

Anti-Catholicism

Some Americans faced discrimination because of their religion. America's largely Protestant population feared that Catholic immigrants threatened the "American" way of life. Anti-Catholic Iowans formed the American Protective Association (APA) in 1887. By the mid-1890s, the APA claimed a membership of two million across the nation. Among other activities, the APA spread rumors that Catholics were preparing to take over the country.

Anti-Semitism

Many Jewish immigrants came to the United States to escape prejudice in their homelands. Some of them found the same anti-Semitic attitudes in America. Landlords, employers, and schools discriminated against Jews. Eastern European Jews faced prejudice both as Jews and as eastern Europeans, whom many Americans regarded as more "foreign" than western Europeans.

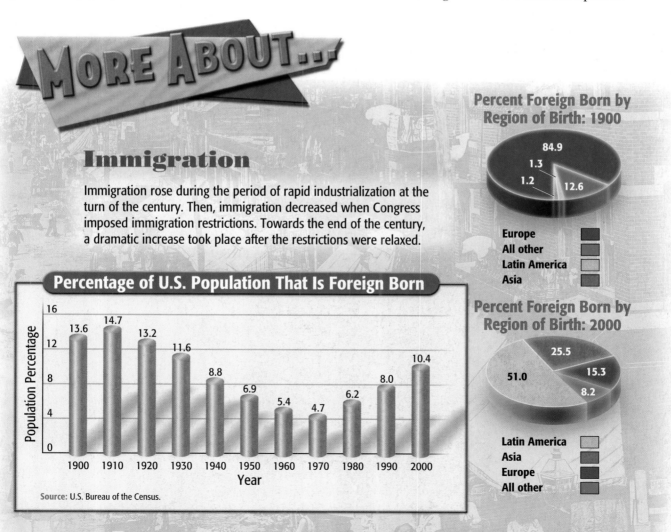

MORE ABOUT...

Immigration

Immigration rose during the period of rapid industrialization at the turn of the century. Then, immigration decreased when Congress imposed immigration restrictions. Towards the end of the century, a dramatic increase took place after the restrictions were relaxed.

Percentage of U.S. Population That Is Foreign Born

Population Percentage by Year:
- 1900: 13.6
- 1910: 14.7
- 1920: 13.2
- 1930: 11.6
- 1940: 8.8
- 1950: 6.9
- 1960: 5.4
- 1970: 4.7
- 1980: 6.2
- 1990: 8.0
- 2000: 10.4

Source: U.S. Bureau of the Census.

Percent Foreign Born by Region of Birth: 1900
- 84.9
- 1.3
- 1.2
- 12.6

Europe
All other
Latin America
Asia

Percent Foreign Born by Region of Birth: 2000
- 51.0
- 25.5
- 15.3
- 8.2

Latin America
Asia
Europe
All other

Anti-Asian Policies

Discrimination was also based on race. In California and other western states, Asians struggled against prejudice and resentment. White Americans claimed that Chinese immigrants, who worked for lower wages, took away jobs. Congress passed the Chinese Exclusion Act in 1882 to prevent Chinese immigrants from entering the United States.

America's westward expansion created opportunities for thousands of Japanese immigrants who came to the United States to work as railroad or farm laborers. Like the Chinese before them, Japanese immigrants encountered prejudice. California would not allow them to become citizens. In 1906 in San Francisco, the school board tried to make Japanese children attend a separate school for Asians until President Roosevelt stepped in to prevent such segregation.

Roosevelt yielded to a rising tide of anti-Japanese feeling, however, and authorized the **Gentlemen's Agreement** with Japan in 1907. This accord restricted Japanese immigration to the United States, but it did not bring an end to anti-Japanese feeling. In 1913 California made it illegal for Japanese immigrants to buy land. Other Western states passed similar laws.

Discrimination Against African Americans

African Americans faced discrimination in both the North and the South. Although officially free, African Americans were systematically denied basic rights and restricted to second-class citizenship.

Four-fifths of the nation's African Americans lived in the South. Most worked as rural sharecroppers or in low-paying jobs in the cities. They were separated from white society in their own neighborhoods, schools, parks, restaurants, theaters, and even cemeteries. In 1896 the Supreme Court legalized segregation in the case of *Plessy* v. *Ferguson*, which recognized "separate but equal" facilities.

The **Ku Klux Klan,** which had terrorized African Americans during Reconstruction, was reborn in Georgia in 1915. The new Klan wanted to restore white, Protestant America. The Klan lashed out against minorities—Catholics, Jews, and immigrants, as well as African Americans. Calling for "100 percent Americanism," the Klan kept growing and claimed more than two million members by 1924, many of them in Northern cities and towns.

Picturing **History**

A Ku Klux Klan pamphlet (right) promotes the Klan's hate campaign. Meanwhile, opponents of lynching called for an end to racial murders. **What two groups experienced the terror of lynching?**

Booker T. Washington (seated, second from left) founded the National Negro Business League. **Why did Washington stress economic power among African Americans?**

Racial Violence

People who lost their jobs during the economic depressions of 1893 and 1907 sometimes unleashed their anger against African Americans and other minorities. More than 2,600 African Americans were lynched between 1886 and 1916, mostly in the South. Lynchings were also used to terrorize Chinese immigrants in the West.

Progressivism and Prejudice

In the late 1800s and the early 1900s, many Americans held biased views. They believed that white, male, native-born Americans had the right to make decisions for all of society.

Most of the progressive reformers came from the middle and upper classes. They saw themselves as moral leaders working to improve the lives of people less fortunate than themselves. Nevertheless, the reforms they supported often discriminated against one group as they tried to help another group.

Trade unions often prohibited African Americans, women, and immigrants from joining. Skilled laborers, these unions argued, could obtain better working conditions for themselves if they did not demand improved conditions for all workers.

Sometimes reforms instituted by the progressives were efforts to control a particular group. The temperance movement, for example, was partly an attempt to control the behavior of Irish Catholic immigrants. Civil service reforms required job applicants to be educated—this reduced the political influence that immigrants had begun to have in some cities. In spite of their contradictions, progressive reforms did succeed in improving conditions for many Americans.

Reading Check **Identifying** What Supreme Court decision legalized segregation?

Struggle for Equal Opportunity

Often excluded from progressive organizations because of prejudice, minorities battled for justice and opportunity on their own. African Americans, Hispanics, and Native Americans took steps to improve their lives.

African Americans rose to the challenge of achieving equality. **Booker T. Washington,** who had been born enslaved and taught himself to read, founded the Tuskegee Institute in 1881. The institute taught African Americans farming and industrial skills.

People In History

W.E.B. Du Bois 1868–1963

W.E.B. Du Bois was the first African American to receive a doctorate degree from Harvard. As an educator he refused to accept racial inequality. Du Bois helped start the Niagara Movement in 1905 to fight against racial discrimination and demand full political rights and responsibilities for African Americans. Later, Du Bois joined others to form the National Association for the Advancement of Colored People (NAACP). This group today remains a force in the efforts to gain legal and economic equality for African Americans.

Du Bois rejected Booker T. Washington's emphasis on job skills and argued that the right to vote was the way to end racial inequality, stop lynching, and gain better schools. "The power of the ballot we need in sheer self-defense," he said, "else what shall save us from a second slavery?"

Washington believed that if African Americans had more economic power they would be in a better position to demand social equality and civil rights. Washington founded the **National Negro Business League** to promote business development among African Americans. In Washington's autobiography, *Up from Slavery*, he counseled African Americans to work patiently toward equality. Washington argued that equality would be achieved when African Americans gained the education and skills to become valuable members of their community.

Some African Americans thought that they would be better off in separate societies, either in the United States or in Africa. They founded organizations to establish African American towns and promoted a back-to-Africa movement. These movements were not popular, however, and their goals gained few supporters.

African American Women Take Action

African American women worked together through groups such as the National Association of Colored Women to fight the practice of lynching and other forms of racial violence. **Ida B. Wells,** the editor of an African American newspaper in Memphis, Tennessee, was forced to leave town after publishing the names of people involved in a lynching. The incident started Wells on a national crusade against the terrible practice of lynching.

In her 1895 book, *A Red Record,* Wells showed that lynching was used primarily against African Americans who had become prosperous or who competed with white businesses. "Can you remain silent and inactive when such things are done in your own community and country?" she asked.

Other Successes

During the early 1900s African Americans achieved success in a variety of professions. Chemist **George Washington Carver,** director of agricultural research at Tuskegee Institute, helped improve the economy of the South through his discoveries of plant products. **Maggie Lena** founded the St. Luke Penny Savings Bank in Richmond, Virginia. She was the first American woman to serve as a bank president.

Native Americans Seek Justice

The federal government's efforts to assimilate Native Americans into white society threatened to break down traditional native cultures. In 1911 Native American leaders from around the country formed the **Society of American Indians** to seek justice for Native Americans, to improve their living conditions, and to educate white Americans about different Native American cultures.

One of the society's founding members was **Dr. Carlos Montezuma,** an Apache who had been raised by whites. Convinced that federal policies were hurting Native Americans, Montezuma became an activist, exposing government abuse of Native American rights. Montezuma believed that Native Americans should leave the reservations and make their own way in white society.

Mexican Americans Work Together

Immigrants from Mexico had long come to the United States as laborers, especially in the West and Southwest. Between 1900 and 1914, the Mexican American population grew dramatically as people crossed the border to escape revolution and economic troubles in Mexico.

Like the Japanese and other immigrant groups, Mexican Americans encountered discrimination and violence. Relying on themselves to solve their problems, they formed *mutualistas*—self-defense associations—to raise money for insurance and legal help. One of the first *mutualistas* was the *Alianza Hispano Americo* (Hispanic American Alliance), formed in Tucson, Arizona, in 1894. Another *mutualista,* the

"Is there no redress, no peace, no justice in this land for us? Tell the world the facts."

—*Ida B. Wells*

Orden Hijos de America (Order of Sons of America), formed in San Antonio, Texas, in 1921 to work for equality and raise awareness of Mexican Americans' rights as U.S. citizens. In labor camps and Mexican neighborhoods called barrios, *mutualistas* organized self-help groups to deal with overcrowding, poor sanitation, and inadequate public services.

Widespread prejudice excluded Mexican Americans from many reform groups. Yet Mexican Americans produced dynamic leaders and created organizations to improve their circumstances and fight for justice.

✓ **Reading Check** **Describing** Against what type of violence did Ida B. Wells speak out?

SECTION 4 ASSESSMENT

Checking for Understanding

1. **Key Terms** Define discrimination and barrio.
2. **Reviewing Facts** What were the results of the Gentlemen's Agreement with Japan, authorized by Theodore Roosevelt?

Reviewing Themes

3. **Civic Rights and Responsibilities** Give an example of a progressive reform that resulted in discrimination.

Critical Thinking

4. **Comparing** How did the views of Booker T. Washington differ from those of W.E.B. Du Bois?
5. **Analyzing Information** Re-create the diagram below and list the actions these groups took to battle prejudice and discrimination.

Groups	Actions taken
Native Americans	
Mexican Americans	
African Americans	

Analyzing Visuals

6. **Graph Skills** Study the graphs on page 629. What was the percentage of foreign-born people in 1900? In 2000? Did Latin American people make up a larger percentage of the foreign-born population in 2000 or in 1900? Explain.

Interdisciplinary Activity

Art Create a title and cover design for a book about discrimination that might have been written during this time.

Chapter Summary
Progressive Reforms

Civic Reform

- City Commissions / City Managers
- Civic Service Commission

Business Reform

- Sherman Antitrust Act
- Regulation/ Trustbusting
- Clayton Antitrust Act
- Interstate Commerce Act
- Federal Trade Commission

Political Reform

- Direct Primary
- Initiative
- Referendum
- The Seventeenth Amendment

Women's Rights

- Suffragist movement
- Labor movement
- The Nineteenth Amendment

Reviewing Key Terms

You are a journalist writing about the impact of progressive reforms. Write an article in which you use at least three of the following key terms.

1. political machine
2. civil service
3. primary
4. referendum
5. initiative
6. recall

Reviewing Key Facts

7. How did corrupt political bosses get voters for their parties?
8. Why were journalists important to the reform movement?
9. What amendment provided for the direct election of senators?
10. What amendment provided for woman suffrage?
11. What is arbitration?
12. Why did progressives form their own political party?
13. What was the purpose of the Federal Reserve Act?
14. What is discrimination?
15. What did Dr. Carlos Montezuma think about Native American reservations?
16. Why did Mexican Americans organize *mutualistas*?

Critical Thinking

17. **Analyzing Themes: Government and Democracy** How did the Seventeenth Amendment give people a greater voice in government?
18. **Determining Cause and Effect** Why was the railroad industry subject to so many government regulations?
19. **Analyzing Themes: Civic Rights and Responsibilities** Re-create the diagram below and identify how these laws promote justice and insure citizens' rights.

- 19th Amendment
- Recall
- Rights of Citizens
- Initiative
- Referendum

Practicing Skills

Interpreting a Political Cartoon *Study the cartoon on this page; then answer the following questions.*

20. Who are the people grouped on the left of the cartoon?
21. What is the meaning of the comment made by the person on the right?
22. How does the cartoonist define "illegal immigrants?"

 ## Geography and History Activity

Examine the map on voting rights for women on page 617 and answer the questions that follow.

23. Which state was the first to provide equal suffrage?
24. By 1919 how many states allowed equal suffrage?
25. **Making Generalizations** Why do you think the percentage of states allowing woman suffrage was much higher in the West than in the East?

 ## Technology Activity

26. **Using E-Mail** Research the names of five modern organizations that have some of the same goals as the progressive reformers of the late 1800s and early 1900s. Choose one organization that interests you and make contact through E-mail to get more information about the group.

Self-Check Quiz
Visit **taj.glencoe.com** and click on **Chapter 21—Self-Check Quizzes** to prepare for the chapter test.

Citizenship Cooperative Activity

27. **Consumer Rights** Working with a partner, contact a local consumer league to learn about consumer rights. Then prepare a pamphlet on consumer rights. List the various rights consumers have and provide the names, addresses, and phone numbers of consumer groups to contact with problems. Distribute this pamphlet to people in your neighborhood.

Alternative Assessment

28. **Portfolio Activity** Scan the chapter and make a list of the constitutional amendments that were passed during the Progressive Era. Make a cause-and-effect chart to show what needs, actions, or abuses led to the passage of each. Save your work for your portfolio.

Standardized Test Practice

Directions: Choose the *best* answer to the following question.

The main goal of the Woman's Christian Temperance Union was to pass laws to ban the making or selling of alcohol. Which of the following was a secondary goal?

A prison reform

B limit immigration

C promote the Square Deal

D pass the Gentlemen's Agreement

Test-Taking Tip

This question requires you to remember a *fact* about the WCTU. By reading the question carefully, you can find clues about the organization. It worked for *reform*. Which answer fits best with this information?

CHAPTER 22

Overseas Expansion

1865–1917

Why It Matters

International power came to the United States with political strength and industrial growth. As its power increased, the United States moved beyond its territorial limits in search of new markets and colonies.

The Impact Today

The United States began to compete with other nations for more trade and more land. From this rivalry, the United States rose to take a major role in shaping world affairs.

 The American Journey Video The chapter 22 video, "Bring Me the Pictures and I'll Bring You the War," discusses the rise of yellow journalism and its role in the Spanish-American War.

1889
• Pan-American Union established

1887
• U.S. establishes naval base at Pearl Harbor

1867
• Alaska purchased from Russia

 United States PRESIDENTS

| Johnson 1865–1869 | Grant 1869–1877 | | Hayes 1877–1881 | Garfield 1881 | Arthur 1881–1885 | Cleveland 1885–1889 | B. Harrison 1889–1893 |

1865   *1875*   *1885*

World

1865

1867
• Japan ends 675-year shogun rule

1875
• Suez Canal comes under British control

1883
• Vietnam becomes French protectorate

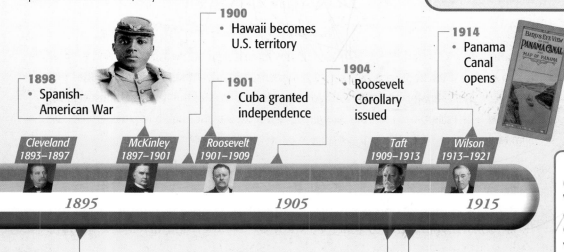

San Juan Hill Theodore Roosevelt, who later became the twenty-sixth president of the United States, leads the Rough Riders cavalry regiment during the Spanish-American War, July 1898.

FOLDABLES™
Study Organizer

Drawing Conclusions Study Foldable
Investigate the pros, or positive outcomes, and the cons, or negative outcomes, of overseas expansion by making this foldable.

Step 1 Fold one sheet of paper in half from top to bottom.

Step 2 Fold it in half again, from side to side.

Step 3 Unfold the paper once. Cut up the fold of the top flap only.

This cut will make two tabs.

Step 4 Label the foldable as shown.

PROS of Overseas Expansion | CONS of Overseas Expansion

Reading and Writing As you read, write what you learn about the positive and negative effects of United States overseas expansion under the appropriate tabs of your foldable.

1900
• Hawaii becomes U.S. territory

1898
• Spanish-American War

1901
• Cuba granted independence

1904
• Roosevelt Corollary issued

1914
• Panama Canal opens

Cleveland 1893–1897

McKinley 1897–1901

Roosevelt 1901–1909

Taft 1909–1913

Wilson 1913–1921

1895   *1905*   *1915*

1895
• José Martí leads revolt in Cuba

1910
• British form Union of South Africa

1911
• Qing dynasty overthrown in China

HISTORY
Online
Chapter Overview
Visit taj.glencoe.com and click on **Chapter 22—Chapter Overviews** to preview chapter information.

Expanding Horizons

Guide to Reading

Main Idea
In the late 1800s the United States acquired lands overseas.

Key Terms
isolationism, expansionism, imperialism

Reading Strategy
Analyzing Information As you read the section, re-create the diagram below and explain how the United States made its presence felt in each country or region.

	U.S. role
Japan	
Latin America	
Russia	

Read to Learn
- what factors contributed to the growth of American imperialism.
- how the United States expanded its economic and political influence in the late 1800s.

Section Theme
Economic Factors Americans expanded trade with other countries and competed for political influence.

Preview of Events

♦1850	♦1870	♦1890

1853
Matthew Perry sails into Tokyo Bay

1854
Japan signs Treaty of Kanagawa

1867
William Seward signs treaty to buy Alaska

1889
Pan-American Union established

AN American Story

In the late 1800s and early 1900s, Americans looked beyond their borders and yearned for an empire. Merchants desired overseas markets, and adventurers wanted another frontier to conquer. Senator Albert Beveridge voiced the feelings of many when he proclaimed in 1900: "The Philippines are ours forever.... And just beyond the Philippines are China's illimitable markets. We will not retreat from either.... The Pacific is our ocean."

American Foreign Policy

When President George Washington published his Farewell Address in 1796, he advised Americans to increase trade with other countries but to have "as little political connection as possible." Above all else, he warned Americans to "steer clear of permanent alliances with any portion of the foreign world." These principles guided American foreign policy for about 100 years. However, various people interpreted Washington's words in different ways. Some believed he meant that the United States should follow a policy of isolationism, or noninvolvement, in world affairs. Others pointed out that Washington supported trade with other countries and was not calling for complete isolation from the world.

American Expansionism

For many years some Americans dreamed of expanding their territory from ocean to ocean. Seeking land and better opportunities, many Americans moved to territories in the West and the South. This expansionism was a driving force in American history. During the Civil War, while the nation was torn apart, expansion came to a halt. After the war the United States began rebuilding and expanding again.

Americans settled the vast Great Plains, built railroads, and created large cities booming with people and busy factories. In 1890, when the nation spanned the North American continent from the Atlantic Ocean to the Pacific Ocean, the government issued a report announcing the end of the "frontier." Although areas of unsettled land remained, settlements could now be found from coast to coast.

To many Americans the frontier meant growth and opportunity. The idea that the frontier no longer existed was alarming. Americans began to look beyond the nation's borders to frontiers overseas where they could expand trade and compete for political influence.

Foreign Trade

In the mid-1800s, American merchants carried on a profitable trade with China and hoped to expand trade in other areas of the world. Many wanted to open trading relations with Japan, which had long been isolated from the West.

In 1853 President Millard Fillmore sent Commodore **Matthew Perry** on a mission to Japan. After steaming into Tokyo Bay with four warships, Perry asked the Japanese to open up their ports to U.S. ships. He told them he would return in several months for their answer.

The American show of force alarmed the Japanese. When Perry returned in 1854, the Japanese signed the **Treaty of Kanagawa** and opened two ports to American ships. Perry's successful mission began a period of trade between Japan and the United States. It also marked the start of greater American involvement in Asia.

Reading Check **Explaining** What did Washington say about alliances in his Farewell Address?

An Age of Imperialism

The United States was not the only Western nation expanding its trade and influence in Asia and other parts of the world. The late 1800s and

History *Through Art*

Perry's First Landing in Japan at Kurihama by Gessan Ogata A Japanese artist depicts Commodore Matthew Perry's 1853 arrival in Japan. **Why was Perry sent on a mission to Japan?**

the early 1900s were called an age of imperialism, a time when powerful European nations created large empires by exercising economic and political control over weaker regions.

The search for materials and markets drove imperialism. The industrial nations of Europe needed raw materials from Asia and Africa. The Europeans also sought new markets for the goods they manufactured. In their drive for raw materials and new markets, European powers competed with one another for power and influence in Asia and Africa.

Toward an Empire

American interest in political as well as economic expansion developed after the Civil War. Some Americans wanted the nation to build an empire. By annexing new lands, they argued, the United States would join the ranks of the world's great powers and take its rightful place at the center of power.

Secretary of State **William H. Seward,** appointed by Abraham Lincoln, supported this view. Seward pictured an American empire that dominated the Caribbean, Central America, and the Pacific. Holding this empire together would be a canal across Central America linking the Atlantic and Pacific Oceans, a thriving transcontinental railroad system, and rapid communication by means of the telegraph.

The Purchase of Alaska

Seward took a major step toward making his vision a reality with the purchase of **Alaska.** In 1867 Seward signed a treaty with Russia to buy the Russian colony for $7.2 million—an extraordinary bargain for a territory that was twice the size of Texas.

At the time many people ridiculed Seward's purchase. They regarded Alaska as a barren, icebound land. Newspapers mocked the purchase as "Seward's Ice Box" and a "polar bear garden." After gold was discovered in Alaska in the 1890s, however, Seward's "folly" began to seem more like a wise purchase. In 1912 Alaska became a territory of the United States.

A Sense of Mission

Some Americans had another reason for imperialist expansion. They had a sense of mission—a belief that they could "lift up" people they considered "uncivilized" by sharing Christianity and Western civilization with the rest of the world. **Josiah Strong,** a Congregational minister, proposed an "imperialism of righteousness," with Americans bringing their religion and their culture to the peoples of Africa, Asia, and the United States's closest neighbor, Latin America.

American Interest in Latin America

Since colonial times, the United States had carried on a flourishing trade with Latin America, including the Caribbean region. Fear of European influence in the region was a factor that led to the Monroe Doctrine in 1823, when President James Monroe warned European nations not to attempt to establish new colonies in North or South America.

United States merchants used the Monroe Doctrine to their advantage. In 1884 **James G. Blaine,** then the Republican nominee for president, declared:

> ❝While the great powers of Europe are steadily enlarging their colonial domination in Asia and Africa, it is the [particular] province of this country to improve and expand its trade with the nations of America.❞

Meanwhile, the United States signed treaties with a number of Latin American countries, allowing American businesses to influence those nations' economies.

As secretary of state in 1889, Blaine invited Latin American countries to attend a Pan-American Conference held in Washington, D.C. Blaine hoped to develop economic and political ties among the nations of the region. Although many Latin American countries worried about American domination, they decided to attend the meeting. The conference established the **Pan-American Union** to share information among member nations.

Building Sea Power

As the United States looked to expand its horizons, Captain **Alfred Thayer Mahan,** president of the Naval War College, called for improving and enlarging the navy. Mahan argued that sea power would protect shipping and provide access to world markets:

> ❝Sea power is essential to the greatness of every splendid people.❞

To maintain a powerful navy, the United States would need overseas colonies where ships could be refueled.

Transforming and expanding the navy began in 1883, when Congress authorized construction of the first steel-hulled warships. In the following years, the navy gradually shifted from sails to steam power and from wood to steel hulls. By the early 1900s, the United States had the naval power it needed to back up an expanded role in foreign affairs.

✓ Reading Check **Explaining** Why did many people criticize the purchase of Alaska?

SECTION 1 ASSESSMENT

Checking for Understanding

1. **Key Terms** Use the following terms to create a newspaper article about United States expansion during the late 1800s: isolationism, expansionism, imperialism.
2. **Reviewing Facts** Discuss the main points of the Monroe Doctrine.

Reviewing Themes

3. **Economic Factors** What price did the United States pay for Alaska? Why was the purchase of this territory ridiculed?

Critical Thinking

4. **Determining Cause and Effect** What did Alfred Thayer Mahan say would result from American sea power?
5. **Organizing Information** Re-create the diagram below and list two economic reasons for United States expansion.

(diagram: Reasons for expansion — with two empty ovals)

Analyzing Visuals

6. **Picturing History** Study the painting on the chapter opening page on page 637. What does it show? What idea do you think the artist is expressing?

Interdisciplinary Activity

Geography Research the natural resources of Alaska. Draw a map of the state and use symbols to represent each resource and show its location in the state.

STEP BACK IN TIME

What—and who—were people talking about? What did they eat? What did they do for fun? These two pages will give you some clues to everyday life in the U.S. as you step back in time with TIME Notebook.

Profile

BOOKER T. WASHINGTON *Teaching industrial training as a means to success, in 1881 Washington founded the Tuskegee Institute in Alabama. Here is an excerpt from his autobiography,* Up From Slavery.

FROM THE VERY BEGINNING, AT TUSKEGEE, I was determined to have the students do not only the agricultural and domestic work, but to have them erect their own buildings. My plan was to have them, while performing this service, taught the latest and best methods of labour, so that the school would not only get the benefit of their efforts, but the students themselves would be taught to see not only utility in labour, but beauty and dignity. ... My plan was not to teach them to work in the old way, but to show them how to make the forces of nature—air, water, steam, electricity, horse-power— assist them in their labour.

Booker T. Washington

VERBATIM

WHAT PEOPLE ARE SAYING

❝ If you pick up a starving dog and make him prosperous, he will not bite you. This is the principal difference between a dog and a man. ❞

MARK TWAIN,
author of
The Adventures of Tom Sawyer

❝ Speak softly and carry a big stick; you will go far. ❞
PRESIDENT TEDDY ROOSEVELT,
proposing action when asked how the United States will deal with its new far-flung colonies in 1901

❝ Give me your tired, your poor, your huddled masses yearning to breathe free. ❞
WORDS BY EMMA LAZARUS,
engraved on the Statue of Liberty in 1903

❝ Mountains! Look at them! ❞
EDWARD CORSI,
10-year-old Italian immigrant on spotting the high-rise buildings in New York City for the first time in 1907

It's The Law

Two laws were passed in 1902 to deal with the automobile.

1 Tennessee demands all drivers give the public a week's notice before they start any trip.

2 Vermont states an adult waving a red flag has to walk in front of any moving automobile.

MILESTONES
EVENTS AND PEOPLE OF THE TIME

SIGNED UP. Sharpshooter **ANNIE OAKLEY** to Buffalo Bill's Wild West Show in 1885.

FLEW. 19-year-old Cromwell Dixon over the Continental Divide in 1911 in a biplane. At age 14, Dixon was building **DIRIGIBLES** (sausage-shaped balloons), including a model that could be pedaled through the air like a bicycle. Dixon later traveled around the country, flying at state fairs.

Annie Oakley

BETTMANN/CORBIS

AMERICAN SCENE
Average Lifespans in 1900

Average life expectancy: **47.3 years**

Male life expectancy: **46.3 years**

Female life expectancy: **48.3 years**

White life expectancy: **47.6 years**

Nonwhite life expectancy: **33.0 years**

| 0 | 10 | 20 | 30 | 40 | 50 years |

TRANSPORTATION
Take a Ride in My Car!

Here's what one magazine from the early 1900s recommends you carry in your car at all times:

1 Efficient tire pump

1 Strong two-gallon can extra gasoline

1 Sheet fine sandpaper

1 Small, short-handled axe

1 Ball asbestos cord

4 Half-pound cans of meat or fish

2 Pounds sweet chocolate

BETTMANN/CORBIS

NUMBERS
U.S. AT THE TIME

12¢ Price of a dozen eggs in 1910

$12 Price of a sewing machine in 1900

SCHENECTADY MUSEUM/HALL OF ELECTRICAL HISTORY FOUNDATION/CORBIS

$12 Lowest price for a steamship ticket from Italy to America in 1905

$12 Average weekly salary (seven-day weeks/12-hour days) for arriving immigrants in 1907

Wright brothers

BETTMANN/CORBIS

12 seconds Air time of Wright brothers' first flight in 1903

1.2 million Approximate number of immigrants who entered the U.S. in 1907

395,000 Approximate number of immigrants in 1908 who gave up on America and returned home

50¢ Price of cheapest seat at baseball's first World Series in 1903

Imperialism in the Pacific

Guide to Reading

Main Idea
The United States expanded into the Pacific Ocean region to set up trading bases.

Key Terms
annexation, spheres of influence, Open Door policy

Reading Strategy
Sequencing Information As you read the section, complete a time line like the one shown with important events in Hawaii's history.

1820 1842 1875 1887 1891 1898 1900

Read to Learn
• how the United States gained control of Hawaii and Samoa.
• how competition for influence in China and the Pacific region led to new foreign policies.

Section Theme
Geography and History The United States exercised its influence in China and the Pacific region.

Preview of Events

♦1890   ♦1900   ♦1910

1893
American planters overthrow Queen Liliuokalani

1899
U.S., Britain, and Germany divide Samoa

1900
Hawaii becomes a U.S. territory

1907
The Great White Fleet begins its voyage

AN
American Story

As more Americans arrived in Honolulu, many Hawaiians feared that time was running out for their people. Kaona, a local judge in Honolulu, had visions that the end of the world was near. When volcanoes erupted and earth tremors plagued the island, his visions seemed to be coming true. Kaona and his followers prepared for the end. They dressed in flowing white robes and prayed loudly. Kaona had indeed been correct. The world that he and native Hawaiians had known would soon end.

✦Geography

Hawaii

Secretary of State William H. Seward believed the United States could build its empire in Hawaii and other regions through trade. The Pacific region played a key part in Seward's plan. In 1867 Seward acquired the two small Pacific islands of **Midway**. He thought that these islands, more than 3,000 miles (4,800 km) west of California, would serve as an important stopping place for American ships en route to China. American merchants and the United States Navy would need more than two small islands, however, to establish a secure foothold in the vast stretches of the Pacific.

The lush Hawaiian Islands, a chain of 8 large and 100 or so smaller islands, lay about 2,000 miles (3,200 km) west of California. The Hawaiian people dwelled in independent communities, each with its own chieftain, and lived by farming and fishing. American trading ships and whalers often stopped at the islands to take on supplies and fresh water.

In the 1790s Americans began trading with the Hawaiians for local resources. About that same time, King Kamehameha I unified the islands. Villages with good ports such as **Honolulu** and **Lahaina** (luh•HY•nuh) began to grow in importance, and trade increased. However, American and European ships also brought infectious diseases to the islands. These diseases devastated the island population just as they had once devastated the Native Americans.

Missionaries and Sugar Growers

In 1820 Christian missionaries from the United States began arriving in Hawaii. They established schools, created a written Hawaiian alphabet, and translated the Bible into Hawaiian. Increasing numbers of American merchants in the whaling trade came to settle there, too.

An American firm introduced sugarcane in Hawaii in the 1830s, and the missionaries and traders began buying land and establishing sugar plantations. The sugar industry grew quickly, and plantation owners brought in thousands of immigrants from Japan, China, and other Pacific lands to work in the fields. Gradually the Americans took control of most of the land and businesses. They also influenced Hawaiian politics, serving as advisers to the Hawaiian ruling family. Although the United States recognized Hawaiian independence in 1842, the islands came increasingly under American influence.

In 1875 the United States agreed to allow Hawaiian sugar to enter the country without tariffs. As sugar exports to the United States soared, American planters in Hawaii reaped enormous profits. In 1887, in return for renewal of the trade agreement, the United States pressured King Kalakaua (kah•LAH•KAH•u•ah) to allow it to establish a naval base at **Pearl Harbor,** the best seaport in the islands.

In the early 1890s, under pressure from American sugar producers, Congress revised the tariff laws and eliminated the exemption for Hawaiian sugar. As a result, Hawaiian sugar planters had to drop their prices drastically in order to sell any sugar. Sugar exports to the United States dropped sharply. Facing ruin, the planters plotted a way to avoid the new tariff. They decided to make Hawaii a territory of the United States.

American Planters' Revolt

The Hawaiians, meanwhile, had begun to resist the growing influence of Americans. In 1891 Queen **Liliuokalani** (lih•LEE•uh•woh•kuh•LAH•nee) came to the throne. The new ruler wanted Hawaiians to regain economic control of their islands, and she took away powers that the American sugar planters had held. In response, the white planters overthrew Liliuokalani and set up their own **provisional,** or temporary, government in 1893. The queen left under protest:

❝Now, to avoid any collision of armed forces and perhaps the loss of life, I . . . yield my authority.❞

Queen Liliuokalani

Annexation

The success of the planters' revolt stemmed in part from the support of the chief American diplomat in Hawaii, **John Stevens,** who arranged for marines from the warship *Boston* to assist in the uprising. Stevens immediately recognized the new government, which sent a delegation to Washington to seek a treaty of annexation that would add Hawaii to the United States. President Benjamin Harrison signed the treaty during the final days of his administration and forwarded it to the Senate for approval.

United States Overseas Possessions, 1900

0   2,500 miles
0   2,500 kilometers
Mercator projection

U.S. possessions with date acquired
• Ports open to U.S. trade

RUSSIA

Alaska (1867)

ASIA

NORTH AMERICA

CHINA
Shanghai
Canton
JAPAN
Nagasaki

PACIFIC OCEAN

UNITED STATES

ATLANTIC OCEAN

EUROPE

AFRICA

Midway Islands (1867)

TROPIC OF CANCER

Philippines (1898)
Guam (1898)
Wake I. (1899)
Howland I. (1857)
Johnston I. (1858)
Hawaiian Islands (1898)
Kingman Reef (1858)
Palmyra Atoll (1898)
Puerto Rico (1898)

EQUATOR

Baker I. (1857)
Jarvis I. (1857)
American Samoa (1899)

SOUTH AMERICA

TROPIC OF CAPRICORN

AUSTRALIA

Geography Skills

1. **Location** Locate Puerto Rico, Guam, and the Philippines. Which of these is the farthest from the continental United States?
2. **Analyzing Information** When were the Hawaiian Islands acquired?

However, the Senate did not act quickly enough. It failed to ratify the treaty before Harrison left office. The new president, **Grover Cleveland,** opposed annexation and withdrew the treaty from the Senate after discovering that Hawaiians did not support the revolt. Cleveland called American interference in the Hawaiian revolution "disgraceful."

Although most of the Hawaiians and the Asian immigrants in Hawaii opposed annexation, their opposition made no difference. A small, powerful group of American sugar growers, traders, and missionaries—and their Hawaiian allies, along with influential people in the United States—had the final word. Congress approved the annexation of Hawaii in 1898, after William McKinley became president. In 1900 Hawaii became a territory of the United States.

The Islands of Samoa

About 3,000 miles (4,800 km) south of Hawaii lay the **Samoa Islands,** directly on the trade route linking Australia and the United States. As early as the 1830s, missionaries from the United States landed in Samoa and began converting the people to Christianity.

In 1878 Samoa agreed to give Americans special trading rights and permission to build a naval station at the port of Pago Pago. Great Britain and Germany also secured trading rights. During the 1880s, tensions mounted as the three rivals competed for power in Samoa.

In 1899 the United States, Great Britain, and Germany met in Berlin and—without consulting the Samoans—decided to divide up the islands. The United States and Germany split Samoa between them, while Great Britain agreed to withdraw from the area in return for rights on other Pacific islands. The Americans annexed their portion of Samoa the same year.

✓ **Reading Check** **Explaining** Why did some American planters want to make Hawaii a territory of the United States?

China and the Open Door

For Americans the island territories in the Pacific, while important in themselves, represented stepping-stones to a larger prize—China. Torn apart by warring factions and lacking industry, China was too weak to resist the efforts of foreign powers that wanted to exploit its vast resources and markets.

Rivalries in China

By the late 1890s, Japan and the leading European powers had carved out spheres of influence in China—sections of the country where each of the foreign nations enjoyed special rights and powers. Japan held the island of Formosa and parts of the Chinese mainland. Germany controlled the Shandong area in east-central China. Great Britain and France held a number of Chinese provinces, and Russia moved into Manchuria and other areas in northern China.

An Open Door to China

In the United States, some government and business leaders worried about being squeezed out of the profitable China trade. Although the United States could not force the other foreign powers out of China, Secretary of State **John Hay** wanted to protect and expand American trading interests in the country. Hay proposed an Open Door policy under which each foreign nation in China could trade freely in the other nations' spheres of influence.

The Boxer Rebellion

The other major powers were reluctant to accept a policy that would benefit the United States most of all. The situation soon changed, however. Beginning in late 1899 a secret Chinese martial arts society, known as the Boxers, led a violent uprising against the "foreign devils" in China. Many died and for nearly two months, hundreds more were trapped in the besieged capital city of **Beijing.** Finally, in August 1900, foreign troops broke the siege and defeated the Boxers.

Out of the Boxer Rebellion came a second Open Door proposal, which stressed the importance of maintaining China's independence and respecting its borders. Alarmed by the rebellion, the other foreign powers accepted Hay's policy.

Reading Check **Analyzing** What was the purpose of the Open Door policy?

History *Through Art*

View of Peking After the Boxer Rebellion by Yoshikazu Ichikawa American soldiers march through the Chinese capital after the Boxer Rebellion. **What policy did the United States want for China?**

Japan

Eager to expand its power in Asia, Japan began to ignore the Open Door policy. Japan's actions led to war with Russia and conflict with the United States.

In the early 1900s, Japan and Russia clashed over Manchuria, a Chinese province rich in natural resources. On February 8, 1904, Japan launched an attack on the Russian fleet at Port Arthur in southern Manchuria, starting the **Russo-Japanese War.** By the spring of 1905, both Japan's and Russia's resources were nearly exhausted, and both countries were eager to make peace.

Treaty of Portsmouth

President Theodore Roosevelt offered to meet with their leaders in Portsmouth, New Hampshire, to help settle the conflict. In September 1905, Japan and Russia signed the **Treaty of Portsmouth,** which recognized Japan's control of Korea in return for a pledge by Japan to halt its expansion.

Roosevelt hoped the treaty would preserve a balance of power in Asia, but it failed to do so. Japan emerged as the strongest naval power in the Pacific, and it challenged the United States for influence in the region. Relations between the two nations deteriorated steadily.

Strained Relations

During the Russo-Japanese War, Japanese immigration to the United States—especially to California—increased. Many Americans resented the Japanese newcomers, claiming that they took jobs from Americans.

As you read in Chapter 21, in 1906 the San Francisco Board of Education ordered that all Asian students attend separate schools. The Japanese government protested. An 1894 treaty had guaranteed that Japanese living in the United States would be treated well. The Japanese felt that the treaty had been broken.

President Roosevelt forced the San Francisco school board to change its policies. In return, he persuaded Japan to consent to an agreement, promising to restrict emigration. The Japanese resented the agreement and relations between the two nations worsened. Some Americans called for war.

Although President Roosevelt had no plan for war, in 1907 he sent 16 gleaming white battleships on a cruise around the world to display the nation's naval power. The **"Great White Fleet"** greatly impressed the Japanese. By 1909 the United States and Japan had resolved many of their differences.

✓ **Reading Check** **Identifying** Who offered to help settle the Russo-Japanese War?

SECTION 2 ASSESSMENT

Checking for Understanding

1. **Key Terms** Use each of these terms in a complete sentence that will help explain its meaning: annexation, spheres of influence, Open Door policy.
2. **Reviewing Facts** Name three Pacific Islands that the United States acquired in the late 1800s and early 1900s.

Reviewing Themes

3. **Geography and History** Why were American political leaders interested in the Pacific islands in the 1800s?

Critical Thinking

4. **Making Inferences** Why do you think Roosevelt considered the cruise of the Great White Fleet to be "the most important service [he] rendered for peace"?
5. **Determining Cause and Effect** Re-create the diagram below and list the cause and effects of the Boxer Rebellion.

Analyzing Visuals

6. **Geography Skills** Study the map on page 646. What particular geographic region of the world is the focus of the map? Which location is farthest west—Hawaii, Baker Island, or Wake Island?

Interdisciplinary Activity

Science Research the process of turning sugarcane into the refined sugar available in supermarkets. Draw a diagram showing the steps involved.

Spanish-American War

Guide to Reading

Main Idea
The Spanish-American War emerged out of events in Cuba, where the Cuban people were resisting Spanish rule.

Key Terms
yellow journalism, armistice, protectorate

Reading Strategy
Analyzing Information As you read the section, complete a diagram like the one shown by listing two reasons the United States went to war over Cuba.

War

Read to Learn
• why the Spanish-American War began.
• how the United States's role in global affairs grew after the war.

Section Theme
Continuity and Change Through the Spanish-American War, the United States took control of new territory.

Preview of Events

♦1894　　　　　♦1896　　　　　♦1898　　　　　♦1900

1895
José Martí leads revolt in Cuba

1897
William McKinley becomes president

1898
The *Maine* explodes; the Spanish-American War takes place

1900
Foraker Act sets up new government in Puerto Rico

AN
American Story

African Americans had fought in military conflicts since colonial times. The Buffalo Soldiers—named for their bravery and fighting ability by their Apache and Cheyenne foes—also answered the nation's call to arms during the Spanish-American War. On the front lines of the Spanish-American War, the 9th and 10th Cavalry, with valiant soldiers like Charles Young, led the charge up San Juan Hill with Colonel Teddy Roosevelt and his Rough Riders.

The Cuban Rebellion

The people of Cuba had lived under Spanish rule for centuries. The Cubans rebelled several times in the late 1800s, but each time the Spanish overpowered them and smashed their dreams of independence. **José Martí,** one of the heroes of the Cuban independence movement, fled to the United States to gather money, arms, and troops. In 1895, as economic conditions in Cuba worsened, Martí returned to Cuba to lead his people in a new revolt.

Martí's revolution led to terrible losses in human life and property. The rebels burned sugarcane fields and destroyed buildings in hopes of forcing the Spaniards to leave. In retaliation Spanish troops herded Cuban people into camps to separate them from the rebels and to break their morale. Thousands of Cubans died of starvation and disease.

War Fever

The Cuban people's struggle against Spain attracted much sympathy in the United States. Businesspeople worried about the destruction of trade and their loss of investments in Cuba. Government leaders were concerned about a rebellion so close to the United States. Many Americans were horrified by the atrocities against Cuban citizens and called for the government to do something about it.

President Grover Cleveland opposed any American involvement in Cuba. In March 1897, **William McKinley** became president. He, too, hoped the conflict could be settled peacefully.

The American press reported the unfolding tragedy in Cuba in graphic detail, and its coverage intensified the debate over America's role in the crisis. Newspapers, including **Joseph Pulitzer's** *World* and **William Randolph Hearst's** *Journal,* tried to outdo each other with shocking reports on the revolution. Hearst supposedly told an artist who was illustrating a story on Cuba, "You furnish the pictures, and I'll furnish the war." This type of sensational, biased, and often false reporting—known as yellow journalism—played a major role in fanning the flames of prowar sentiment in the United States. *(See page 973 for one newspaper's account of Cuba's struggle.)*

"Remember the *Maine*"

The pressure on President McKinley to take action seemed to grow by the hour. After rioting broke out in the Cuban capital of Havana in January 1898, McKinley sent the battleship *Maine* to protect American citizens and property.

The ship remained quietly at anchor in Havana Harbor for three weeks. Then, on the night of February 15, 1898, an enormous explosion shattered the *Maine,* killing 260 officers and crew members. American newspapers immediately blamed the Spanish, and the slogan **"Remember the *Maine*"** became a rallying cry for revenge. Spain denied responsibility for the explosion. Much later, evidence indicated that the explosion may have been accidental, but at the time, Americans clamored for war with Spain.

After the *Maine* incident, President McKinley sent the Spanish a strong note demanding a truce and an end to brutality against the Cubans. The Spanish agreed to some American demands, but not enough to satisfy McKinley or Congress. On April 19 Congress recognized Cuban independence. It also demanded the withdrawal of Spanish forces and authorized the president to use the army and navy to enforce American aims. On April 25, 1898, Congress declared war on Spain.

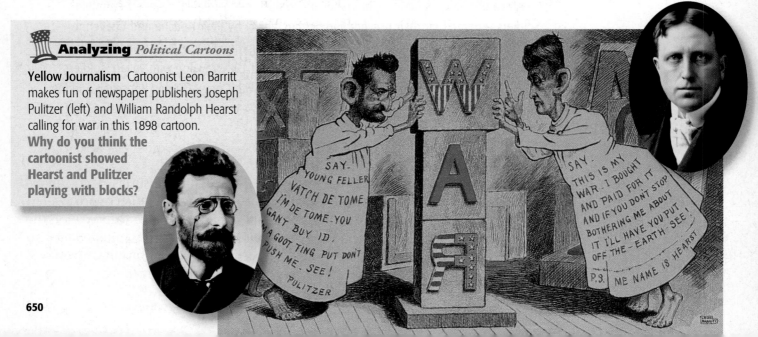

Analyzing *Political Cartoons*

Yellow Journalism Cartoonist Leon Barritt makes fun of newspaper publishers Joseph Pulitzer (left) and William Randolph Hearst calling for war in this 1898 cartoon. **Why do you think the cartoonist showed Hearst and Pulitzer playing with blocks?**

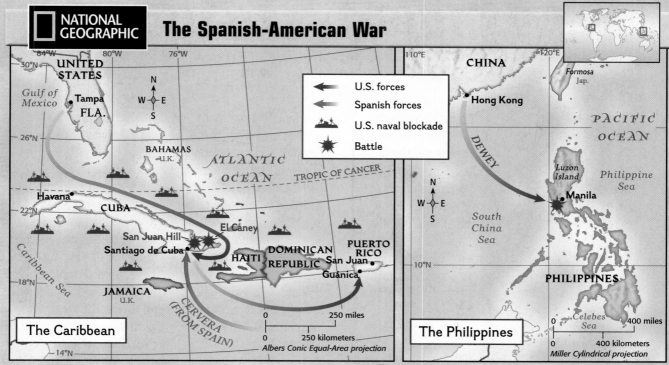

NATIONAL GEOGRAPHIC
The Spanish-American War

Map Legend:
- ← U.S. forces
- ← Spanish forces
- U.S. naval blockade
- Battle

The Caribbean

The Philippines

Albers Conic Equal-Area projection

Miller Cylindrical projection

Geography *Skills*

American troops sailed from Tampa, Florida, to the south coast of Cuba in June 1898. Admiral Dewey had already sailed from Hong Kong to Manila.

1. **Movement** According to the two maps, in which area did more of the fighting take place?
2. **Analyzing Information** On what two Caribbean islands did United States forces land?

War in the Philippines

Although events in Cuba triggered the Spanish-American War, the war's first military actions happened thousands of miles away in the Spanish colony of the **Philippines.** These islands served as a base for part of the Spanish fleet. In late February 1898, Assistant Secretary of the Navy **Theodore Roosevelt** had wired Commodore **George Dewey** and his squadron of navy vessels to prepare for action in the Philippines "in the event of declaration of war." In the early morning hours of May 1, Dewey launched a surprise attack on the Spanish fleet in Manila Bay, destroying most of the ships.

American troops arrived in July. With the help of Filipino rebels led by **Emilio Aguinaldo** (AH•gee•NAHL•doh), the Americans captured the city of Manila. As in Cuba, the Filipino rebels had struggled for years to win independence from Spain. Using American-supplied arms, they seized the main island of **Luzon,** declared independence, and created a democratic republic. The rebels expected the United States to support their independence. However, the United States debated what to do with the islands.

Fighting in Cuba

Meanwhile in the Caribbean, a Spanish fleet entered the harbor of **Santiago** on the southeastern shore of Cuba on May 19. Several days later, an American naval force blockaded the coast, trapping the Spanish in the harbor.

An American land force of about 17,000—nearly a quarter of them African American—landed near the city of Santiago. The inexperienced, ill-equipped Americans disembarked while forces under Cuban general Calixto García drove off the Spanish soldiers. When the Cuban and American forces advanced, Sergeant Major Frank W. Pullen, Jr., wrote that they faced "a perfect hailstorm of bullets, which, thanks to the poor marksmanship of the Spaniards, 'went high.'" Heavy fighting followed.

People In History

Theodore Roosevelt 1858–1919

Theodore Roosevelt was not only the twenty-sixth president of the United States—he was also a writer, historian, explorer, soldier, conservationist, and rancher. His life was one of constant activity, great energy, and many accomplishments.

Struggling with poor health as a child, Theodore Roosevelt began to exercise vigorously, gaining strength and a love of the outdoors that lasted throughout his life. After serving in the New York State Assembly, Roosevelt headed west in 1883, where he hunted and also operated a cattle ranch. He drew on these experiences to write several books about life in the West.

Roosevelt gained political experience working for reform at the local and national levels. In 1897 he was appointed assistant secretary of the navy and helped prepare the navy for war with Spain. When the war broke out in 1898, he resigned from his post and helped organize the "Rough Riders." Roosevelt came home a war hero and was elected governor of New York in 1898. Two years later he was elected vice president on the McKinley ticket. With the assassination of President McKinley in 1901, Roosevelt became president.

The Rough Riders

Theodore Roosevelt resigned his position as assistant secretary of the navy to join the fighting in Cuba. He led the First Regiment of U.S. Cavalry Volunteers, an assorted group of former cowhands and college students, popularly known as the **Rough Riders.** On July 1 the Rough Riders, with African American soldiers of the Ninth and Tenth Cavalries, joined the **Battle of San Juan Hill.** "I waved my hat and we went up the hill with a rush," Roosevelt wrote later.

The Americans captured San Juan Hill after intense fighting. Two days later the Spanish fleet attempted to break out of Santiago. In a battle that lasted about four hours, the Spanish fleet was completely destroyed. This defeat ended Spanish resistance in Cuba.

The United States then turned its attention to the Spanish colony of **Puerto Rico,** east of Cuba. American troops landed on Puerto Rico in late July and quickly took control of the island. On August 12 the Spanish signed an armistice—a peace agreement—ending the war.

"A Splendid Little War"

Secretary of State John Hay called the Spanish-American War "a splendid little war." The war lasted fewer than four months, and about 400 Americans were killed in battle or died from wounds received in the fighting.

Yet the war had other aspects that were not at all "splendid." More than 2,000 Americans died of diseases such as yellow fever, malaria, and other diseases contracted in the tropical climate. The African Americans who served faced the additional burden of discrimination. Serving in segregated units, African Americans battled alongside the Cuban rebel army, in which black and white troops fought as equals.

Reading Check **Explaining** Why did Filipino rebels help the United States fight against Spain?

Acquisitions

The United States and Spain signed the Treaty of Paris on December 10, 1898, marking the official end of the war. The treaty dissolved most of the Spanish empire. Cuba became an American protectorate, a country that is technically independent but actually under the control of another country. Puerto Rico and the Pacific island of **Guam** became territories of the United States. Spain also surrendered the Philippines to the United States in exchange for $20 million. The American empire had become a reality, and with the empire came new responsibilities.

Cuban Protectorate

Americans debated what to do about Cuba. Many congressional leaders believed that the Cubans were not ready for complete self-government. American business leaders feared that leaving Cuba might weaken the political stability of Cuba and jeopardize American interests there.

While Congress considered the matter, American troops remained in Cuba. Finally, in 1901, the United States agreed to grant Cubans full independence, but only if their new constitution included clauses giving the United States certain rights. Known as the **Platt Amendment,** these clauses prohibited Cuba from making treaties with other nations and gave America control of a naval base at Guantanamo Bay. The Platt Amendment also gave the United States the right to intervene in Cuban affairs if the country's independence was threatened.

New Government for Puerto Rico

After the war, Puerto Rico remained under direct military rule. In 1900 the United States set up a new Puerto Rican government under the **Foraker Act.** The American government controlled the new administration. In 1917 the Jones Act made Puerto Rico a territory of the United

TWO VIEWPOINTS

Should the United States Take the Philippines?

In the late 1800s, the United States stretched its power by acquiring Puerto Rico, Hawaii, and many Pacific islands, including the Philippines. While some Americans applauded the additions to their nation, others condemned its ideals.

President William McKinley Relates His Decision to Annex the Philippines, 1899

I walked the floor of the White House night after night until midnight; and I am not ashamed to tell you, gentlemen, that I went down on my knees and prayed Almighty God for light and guidance more than one night. And one night late it came to me this way—I don't know how it was, but it came. . . . [T]hat there was nothing left for us to do but to take them all, and to educate the Filipinos, and uplift and civilize and Christianize them, and by God's grace do the very best we could by them, as our fellow-men for whom Christ also died. And then I went to bed, and went to sleep, and slept soundly, and the next morning I sent for the chief engineer of the War Department (our map-maker), and I told him to put the Philippines on the map of the United States [pointing to a large map on the wall of his office], and there they are, and there they will stay while I am President!

President McKinley

The Platform of the Anti-Imperialist League, 1900

We hold that the policy known as imperialism is hostile to liberty and tends toward militarism, an evil from which it has been our glory to be free. We regret that it has become necessary in the land of Washington and Lincoln to reaffirm that all men, of whatever race and color, are entitled to life, liberty and the pursuit of happiness. We maintain that governments derive their just powers from the consent of the governed. We insist that the subjugation [conquer and control] of any people is "criminal aggression." . . .

Learning From History

1. Why did President McKinley decide to take over the Philippines?
2. Why did members of the Anti-Imperialist League condemn McKinley's action?
3. What do you think each side believed the mission of the United States was at this time?

States and granted American citizenship to all Puerto Ricans. However, many Puerto Ricans still wanted independence.

Acquiring the Philippines

The United States had gained possession of the Philippines in the treaty that ended the Spanish-American War. But acquisition of the Philippines aroused fierce debate.

During the 1890s some people—**anti-imperialists**—opposed the American enthusiasm for foreign expansion and the Spanish-American War. After the war the anti-imperialists fought approval of the treaty. Some argued that American rule of the Philippines contradicted the principles on which the United States was founded. Others opposed the large standing army that would be necessary to control the Philippines. Still others feared competition from Filipino laborers.

Many Americans—including Carl Schurz, Andrew Carnegie, and Mark Twain—joined the anti-imperialist campaign. The imperialists, however, led by Senators Henry Cabot Lodge and Albert Beveridge, eventually won out. The Senate ratified the Treaty of Paris on February 6, 1899.

In February 1899, Emilio Aguinaldo's forces began a fight for independence. This conflict became a mammoth undertaking for the United

Fact · Fiction · Folklore

Puerto Rico

Puerto Rico has its own constitution. Puerto Rico was granted status as a commonwealth in 1952. This means that it is a territory of the United States but governs itself under its own constitution. Even though they are citizens, Puerto Ricans pay no federal income tax and they cannot vote for president. Many Puerto Ricans have immigrated to the United States mainland, which as citizens they can do freely.

States. More than 4,000 Americans died. Filipinos suffered far greater casualties—at least 200,000 soldiers and civilians died.

When Aguinaldo was captured in March 1901, many Filipino military officers and soldiers surrendered. Others refused to give up even after Aguinaldo urged them to stop fighting.

In the summer of 1901, the United States transferred authority in the Philippines from the military to a civilian government headed by **William Howard Taft.** Taft set out to prepare the islands for eventual self-rule. However, the Philippines did not gain full independence until 1946.

✓ **Reading Check** **Describing** What is a protectorate?

SECTION 3 ASSESSMENT

Checking for Understanding

1. **Key Terms** Write a one-page newspaper article about events during the Spanish-American War. Use these terms in your article: yellow journalism, armistice, protectorate.
2. **Reviewing Facts** Summarize how yellow journalism influenced Americans' views of going to war with Spain.

Reviewing Themes

3. **Continuity and Change** How did the United States govern Puerto Rico and the Philippines?

Critical Thinking

4. **Drawing Conclusions** Do you think the United States should have taken permanent control of Cuba and made it part of its empire? Why or why not?
5. **Analyzing Information** Re-create the diagram below and list the reasons some Americans opposed making the Philippines a United States possession.

Opposition

Analyzing Visuals

6. **Geography Skills** Study the maps of the war on page 651. Near what Cuban city was the Battle of San Juan Hill fought?

Interdisciplinary Activity

Expository Writing Write a 45-second news report to convince viewers that they should pressure the United States to get involved in a war with Spain over Cuba. Be as persuasive as possible. Present your report to the class.

Technology
SKILLBUILDER

Developing Multimedia Presentations

Why Learn This Skill?

You want to present a research report to the rest of your class, and you want to really hold their attention. How do you do it? Your presentation can be exciting if you use various media.

Learning the Skill

At its most basic, a multimedia presentation involves using several types of media. To discuss life in the Philippines, for example, you might show photographs of the country. You could also play a recording of the country's language and music, or present a video showing the Filipino people at work and at play.

You can also develop a multimedia presentation on a computer. Multimedia, as it relates to computer technology, is the combination of text, video, audio, and animation in a computer program.

In order to create multimedia productions or presentations on a computer, you need to have certain tools. These may include traditional computer graphic tools and drawing programs, animation programs that make still images move, and authoring systems that tie everything together. Your computer manual will tell you which tools your computer can use.

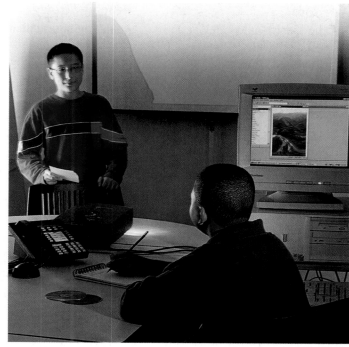

Practicing the Skill

This chapter focuses on the overseas expansion of the United States in the late 1800s and early 1900s. Ask yourself questions like the following to develop a multimedia presentation on the people, politics, and industries of that era:

- Which forms of media do I want to include? Video? Sound? Animation? Photographs? Graphics? Other?

- Which of these media forms does my computer support?
- What kind of software programs or systems do I need? A paint program? A drawing program? An animation program? A program to create interactive, or two-way, communication? An authoring system that will allow me to change images, sound, and motion?
- Is there a "do-it-all" program I can use to develop the kind of presentation I want?

Developing Multimedia Presentations
Keeping in mind the four guidelines given above, write a plan describing a multimedia presentation you would like to develop. Indicate what tools you will need and what steps you must take to make the presentation a reality.

SECTION 4 Latin American Policies

Guide to Reading

Main Idea
After the Spanish-American War, the United States attempted to extend its political and economic influence in Latin America.

Key Terms
isthmus, anarchy, dollar diplomacy

Reading Strategy
Analyzing Information As you read the section, re-create the diagram below and describe these policies.

	Description
Roosevelt Corollary	
Dollar Diplomacy	
Moral Diplomacy	

Read to Learn
• what shaped the policies the United States followed in Latin America.
• where and how the United States intervened in Latin America.

Section Theme
Global Connections American investments in Latin America grew in the early 1900s.

Preview of Events

♦1900 ———————————————— ♦1910 ———————————————— ♦1920

1904
Roosevelt Corollary is issued

1911
Revolution occurs in Mexico

1914
Panama Canal opens

1916
Francisco "Pancho" Villa launches uprising in Mexico

AN
American Story

On August 15, 1914, something described as the "greatest liberty that Man has taken with Nature" occurred. On that day, the first ship, the *Ancon,* traveled through the newly built Panama Canal. The world barely noticed, however. Most eyes were watching Europe, where World War I was beginning. As the ship passed the words on the great seal of the Panama Canal Zone—THE LAND DIVIDED, THE WORLD UNITED—the world was setting out to tear itself to pieces.

Panama

Americans and Europeans had dreamed of building a canal across Central America to connect the Atlantic and Pacific Oceans and to eliminate the long and dangerous sea voyage around South America. Now that the United States controlled territory in both oceans, a canal that would allow easier access to American overseas territory became increasingly important.

In 1879 a French company had acquired a lease from the government of Colombia to construct a canal across its province of **Panama.** Panama was an isthmus—a narrow strip of land connecting two larger bodies of land—about 50 miles (80 km) wide. Wedged between the Caribbean Sea and the Pacific Ocean, Panama seemed like the perfect site for the canal.

French efforts to build a canal failed, and in 1901 the United States bought the lease from the French for $40 million. In 1903 Secretary of State John Hay negotiated a treaty with Colombia that granted the United States a 99-year lease on a strip of land across Panama in return for a payment of $10 million and an annual rent of $250,000.

In Colombia, opposition to the low price offered by the Americans led the Colombian senate to reject the treaty. In a fit of anger, President Roosevelt referred to the Colombians who rejected the treaty as "bandits." He believed the canal was vital to America's national defense.

Revolution in Panama

Roosevelt began looking for other ways to get land for the canal, and he wrote that he would "be delighted if Panama were an independent state." The Panamanians had staged revolts against Colombia in the past, but never with success. This time, however, the Panamanians had reason to believe that the Americans would support them in a revolt against Colombia.

On November 2, 1903, the American warship *Nashville* steamed into the port of Colón on the Caribbean coast of Panama. Encouraged by this show of support, the Panamanians revolted the next day and declared their independence. When Colombia sent forces to stop the revolt, the United States intervened and turned them back.

The Panama Canal

On November 6, the United States recognized Panama's independence. Less than two weeks later, Hay signed a treaty with the new nation of Panama. It gave the United States a 10-mile (16-km) strip of land across the country for the same amount offered earlier to Colombia. The United States now had land to build a canal. Roosevelt's actions in Panama angered many Latin Americans and some members of Congress and other Americans. The president, however, took great pride in his accomplishment. "I took the canal zone and let Congress debate," he said later, "and while the debate goes on, the canal does also."

The United States could now start work on the canal—not an easy undertaking. Disease struck the workers. An English writer described Panama as "a damp, tropical jungle, intensely hot, swarming with mosquitoes." These mosquitoes carried two deadly diseases—yellow fever and malaria.

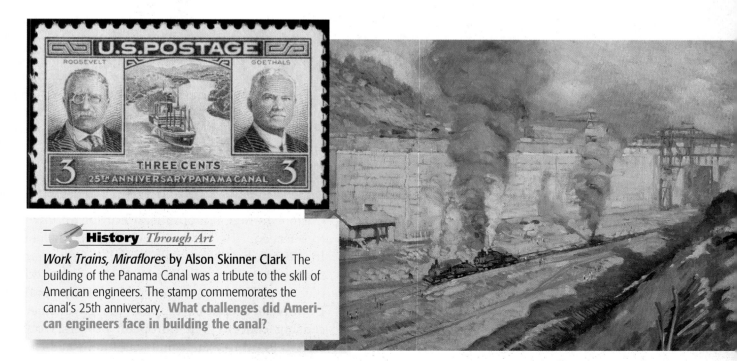

History *Through Art*

Work Trains, Miraflores by Alson Skinner Clark The building of the Panama Canal was a tribute to the skill of American engineers. The stamp commemorates the canal's 25th anniversary. **What challenges did American engineers face in building the canal?**

Colonel **William Gorgas,** an army doctor who had helped eliminate yellow fever in Cuba, went to Panama to fight the diseases. Gorgas instructed workers to drain swamps, spray insecticides, spread oil on stagnant pools of water, and cut grassy marshes in order to destroy mosquito breeding places. By 1906 these measures had eliminated yellow fever and greatly reduced the number of malaria cases. Without controlling disease, the United States could not have built the canal.

The Panama Canal was regarded as one of the great engineering feats of the time. Thousands of workers struggled to carve a path through the dense jungle and over mountains. They dug out huge amounts of earth and rock and used them to build a dam. They created a large lake and constructed giant locks to raise and lower ships from sea level over the mountains and then back to sea level again on the other side of the isthmus.

The Grand Opening

The Panama Canal opened on August 15, 1914, and a cargo ship, the *Ancon,* made the first trip through the canal. A great success from the start, the canal reduced shipping costs by cutting more than 7,000 miles off the voyage from New York City to San Francisco. The canal also helped extend American naval power by allowing the United States fleet to move freely between the Atlantic and Pacific Oceans.

In the long run, the canal guaranteed a strong American presence in Latin America, where the United States now had a valuable

property it intended to protect. Yet many Latin Americans remained bitter over how the Canal Zone was acquired. This resentment soured relations between the United States and Latin America for years.

Reading Check **Analyzing** Why was Panama chosen as the site for a canal connecting the Atlantic and Pacific Oceans?

Policing the Western Hemisphere

President Roosevelt often quoted an African proverb, "Speak softly and carry a big stick." He believed the United States should respond to foreign crises not by threats but by military action. Roosevelt became known for his "big stick" approach to foreign affairs. America must exercise "an international police power," he maintained, to preserve order and prevent the world from falling into anarchy—disorder and lawlessness.

Roosevelt Corollary

Roosevelt worried that instability in the Caribbean region would lead European powers to intervene. Two incidents confirmed his fears. In 1902, when Venezuela failed to meet payments on its loans, European nations imposed a blockade. The following year a revolution in the Dominican Republic toppled the government, causing concern that European powers would step in to protect their financial interests there.

The president responded to these incidents in 1904 by asserting America's right to act as a "policeman" in Latin America, intervening "however reluctantly . . . in cases of wrongdoing." This policy, known as the **Roosevelt Corollary,** was an addition to the Monroe Doctrine. Up to that time, the United States had used the Monroe Doctrine only to prevent European intervention in Latin America. Under the Roosevelt Corollary, the United States now claimed the right to intervene in the affairs of Latin American nations whenever those nations seemed unstable.

The United States first applied the Roosevelt Corollary in 1905, when it took control of the Dominican Republic's finances. This arrangement continued for more than 30 years. The United States used the policy again in 1906, when troops were sent to Cuba to stop a revolution there.

Dollar Diplomacy

Theodore Roosevelt thought of American power mostly in military terms. His successor in the White House, William Howard Taft, took a different view. Taft hoped to modify American foreign policy by "substituting dollars for bullets."

President Taft was willing to intervene in other nations whenever American business interests were threatened. He believed that American investments would bring stability to troubled areas of the world, as well as profit and power to the United States, without the need for force. Taft's policy of linking American business interests to diplomatic interests abroad was known as dollar diplomacy. This policy set in motion some positive effects.

Encouraged by dollar diplomacy, American investments in Latin America grew in the early 1900s. American investments helped build roads, railroads, and harbors, which stimulated trade and brought benefits to both Latin American countries and the United States.

Analyzing *Political Cartoons*

Uncle Sam is the nickname of the character often used to represent the United States in political cartoons. In this cartoon, Uncle Sam uses the Monroe Doctrine to warn the leaders of Europe not to interfere in the affairs of Latin America. **How are the European leaders reacting to Uncle Sam?**

Ⓐ European Leaders   Ⓑ Uncle Sam   Ⓒ Latin America

People In History

Jovita Idar 1885-1946

Through her work as a teacher and newspaper writer, Jovita Idar championed the cause of equal rights for Mexican Americans. Born in Laredo, Texas, Jovita Idar grew up in a family that devoted its skills to the cause. Her father, Clemente Idar, formed unions and spoke out against injustice in his newspaper, *La Crónica*.

In 1910 and 1911, Jovita, along with her father, wrote a series of articles about the discrimination and violence against Mexican Americans in South Texas. Calling on both the U.S. and Mexican governments for help, the Idar newspaper demanded equal treatment for Mexican American students and for Mexican Americans in the justice system.

During the Mexican Revolution of 1910, Jovita helped organize the White Cross to care for the wounded on both sides of the battle.

She was also instrumental in forming the League of Mexican Women. Jovita became its first president and worked hard to provide education for Mexican American students. The organization also provided free food and clothing for the needy in the community.

Dollar diplomacy also resulted in a stronger role for the United States overseas. Large American companies gained great power in Latin America and controlled the politics of some nations in the region. Furthermore, when American business interests were endangered, military intervention often followed. In 1912, when a revolution in Nicaragua threatened American business interests, the United States quickly sent marines to restore peace. Such interference led to increased anti-U.S. feelings throughout Latin America.

Relations with Mexico

In the early 1900s, Mexico was a poor country controlled by a tiny group of rich landholders. Investors in the United States poured millions of dollars into Mexican oil wells and other businesses. Then, in 1910, Mexico entered a turbulent period in its history—one that threatened American investments, revealed the weaknesses of dollar diplomacy, and led to military intervention by the United States.

In 1911 a popular Mexican reformer named **Francisco Madero** (muh•DEHR•oh) led a revolution to overthrow Mexico's brutal dictator **Porfirio Díaz** (DEE•ahs). Although foreign business and some Mexican politicians and landowners had prospered under the rule of Díaz, the lives of most Mexicans had grown worse.

Two years after taking power, Madero was overthrown and killed by General **Victoriano Huerta** (WEHR•tuh), who—like Díaz—favored the wealthy and foreign interests. President **Woodrow Wilson,** who had just taken office, refused to recognize Huerta's "government of butchers."

Wilson's "Moral Diplomacy"

A sincere believer in the ideals of democracy, Wilson thought the United States had a duty "to teach the South American republics to elect good men." Like Roosevelt and Taft, Wilson recognized the importance of military power and economic interests. Yet Wilson also attempted to follow a foreign policy based on moral principles.

Wilson's "moral diplomacy" faced a serious challenge in Mexico. After Huerta took power, a civil war broke out in Mexico. Wilson hoped that the Huerta government, without American support, would fall. When that did not happen, Wilson authorized arms sales to Huerta's rival, **Venustiano Carranza** (kuh•RAN•ZUH).

In April 1914, after Huerta's troops arrested some American sailors, Wilson ordered United States troops to seize the port of **Veracruz.** This show of force strengthened Carranza's position and forced Huerta to flee in August. Carranza took power, and American troops withdrew.

Francisco "Pancho" Villa

Huerta's resignation did not end civil war in Mexico. Rebel leader **Francisco "Pancho" Villa** launched an uprising against Carranza. In January 1916, Villa seized and shot 16 Americans because of United States support for the Carranza government. Villa hoped his action would damage relations between the United States and the Carranza government, but the United States did not take steps

against Mexico. Then Villa and his rebels crossed the border into New Mexico and burned the town of Columbus, killing 18 Americans there.

Villa's actions outraged the American public. The president sent General **John J. Pershing** with a large force of troops across the border into Mexico to capture Pancho Villa. For almost a year, Pershing's troops pursued Villa across Mexico, but the Mexican people protected Villa.

In 1917, when America's attention turned to the war raging in Europe, President Wilson withdrew the troops from Mexico. Mexico and the United States had come close to war, and American actions had caused great resentment in Mexico. America's experience in Mexico, like its policies in the Caribbean, showed that it would willingly use its power when it believed its interests or honor was threatened.

Pancho Villa

Reading Check

Explaining On what principles did Wilson base his foreign policy?

SECTION 4 ASSESSMENT

Checking for Understanding

1. **Key Terms** Use each of these terms in a sentence that helps explain its meaning: *isthmus, anarchy, dollar diplomacy.*
2. **Reviewing Facts** Describe how the United States used Panama's desire for independence to its advantage.

Reviewing Themes

3. **Global Connections** Compare the different diplomacy styles of Presidents Roosevelt, Taft, and Wilson.

Critical Thinking

4. **Making Generalizations** Do you think our government today follows Roosevelt's, Taft's, or Wilson's diplomatic ideas in setting foreign policy? Explain.
5. **Compare and Contrast** Re-create the diagram below and list the differences between the Roosevelt Corollary and the Monroe Doctrine.

Monroe Doctrine	Roosevelt Corollary

Analyzing Visuals

6. **Analyzing Political Cartoons** Examine the cartoon on page 659. Whom do the figures on the left represent? Who is stopping them from crossing to the other side?

Interdisciplinary Activity

Economics Use a reference such as *Historical Abstract of the United States* to find the value of the U.S. imports and exports to a Latin American country from 1890 to 1910. Create a graph showing this information.

Chapter Summary
Overseas Expansion

Expansion
- Acquisition of Alaska, new trading ties with Hawaii and Latin America, and a strong stand against European intervention in the Americas raise the stature of the United States.

Spanish-American War
- In fighting the Spanish-American War, the United States establishes its willingness to become involved in conflict to help oppressed people and to protect its own interests.

Building an Empire
- As a result of the war, the United States gains a colonial empire and with it the challenge of governing overseas possessions.

BIRD'S EYE VIEW OF THE PANAMA CANAL AND MAP OF PANAMA

Diplomacy
- United States intervention in foreign countries is accomplished with the use or show of force—sanctioned by Roosevelt's Big Stick diplomacy. Later, in the Pacific and East Asia, a combination of diplomacy and dollars helps the United States engage in trade and spread its influence.

Reviewing Key Terms
For each of the pairs of terms below, write a sentence or short paragraph showing how the two are related.
1. expansionism, imperialism
2. spheres of influence, dollar diplomacy
3. annexation, protectorate

Reviewing Key Facts
4. Why did many Americans oppose the purchase of Alaska?
5. How did the United States gain access to trade in China?
6. Who were the Rough Riders?
7. Why did the United States encounter difficult problems in trying to govern the Philippines?
8. What was the purpose of the Roosevelt Corollary?

Critical Thinking
9. **Analyzing Themes: Economic Factors** What economic reasons did the United States have for expanding its foreign interests?
10. **Drawing Conclusions** Re-create the diagram below and list the three types of diplomacy. Underline which type was the most effective during this period. Explain why you think so.

Type of Diplomacy

Practicing Skills
11. **Developing Multimedia Presentations** Study the list of topics below. Choose one of the topics and explain how you would use at least three types of media in a presentation to best teach the topic to your class.
    - Matthew Perry's mission to Japan
    - The development of the American navy
    - How the United States changed Hawaii forever
    - The Battle of San Juan Hill
    - Building the Panama Canal

Geography and History Activity

The building of the Panama Canal was regarded as a great engineering feat. Study the map of the canal below; then answer the questions that follow.

NATIONAL GEOGRAPHIC

The Panama Canal

Caribbean Sea
80°W
Colón
Cristobal
GATUN LOCKS
Madden Lake
Gatun Lake
GAILLARD CUT
PEDRO MIGUEL LOCKS
PANAMA
MIRAFLORES LOCKS
Balboa
Panama
9°N
N W E S
Bay of Panama

Canal Zone
Canal route
Railroad
Locks

0   10 miles
0   10 kilometers
Lambert Azimuthal
Equal-Area projection

12. **Location** What bodies of water are shown on the map of the Panama Canal?

13. **Human-Environment Interaction** What is the approximate length of the Panama Canal? How did you determine your answer?

14. **Location** What cities are located near the path of the canal?

15. **Movement** In which direction would a ship en route to Cristobal from Balboa travel?

16. **Human-Environment Interaction** What does the location of Panama tell you about the climatic conditions the canal workers faced?

Citizenship Cooperative Activity

17. **Community Service** Working in groups of three, interview one of your community's officials to learn how you can begin taking an active role in the community. Members of your group may wish to volunteer for some sort of community service, then perform the service and report your experiences to your classmates.

Self-Check Quiz
Visit taj.glencoe.com and click on **Chapter 22—Self-Check Quizzes** to prepare for the chapter test.

Economics Activity

18. Work with a partner to create a map showing all of the areas acquired by the United States during the late 1800s and early 1900s. Research to find out about the natural resources that existed in each area and the importance of the area's location in world trade. Then, starting with these two factors, rank each of the areas on your map as to its economic value to the United States. The area ranked number "1" should be the most valuable. Compare your maps and rankings with other members of the class and create a chart of the overall ratings.

 ## Alternative Assessment

19. **Portfolio Writing Activity** Review the chapter for information about treaties and agreements between various nations during this period. Make a list of the agreements and draw a picture or symbol next to each that will help you recall its terms.

Standardized Test Practice

Directions: Choose the *best* answer to the following question.

The manner in which President Roosevelt acquired the Panama Canal Zone

A angered some members of Congress.

B led to better relations with Latin America.

C ended the Spanish-American War.

D led to McKinley's election.

Test-Taking Tip.

Be aware of the order of events asked about in a question. This question specifically asks about the takeover of the Panama Canal Zone. Both choices **C** and **D** are events that occurred before the events in Panama. Therefore, answers **C** and **D** are incorrect.

World War I

1914–1919

Why It Matters

World War I changed the world. The people of the time called the conflict the Great War, and they believed that there could never again be another like it. Although the United States tried to remain neutral, it was drawn into the conflict.

The Impact Today

The war touched all aspects of life. When the fighting was over, the United States emerged as one of the great powers in the world.

 The American Journey Video The chapter 23 video, "Over There," examines the impact of technology in World War I.

1917
- Zimmermann telegram angers U.S.
- United States enters WW I
- Selective Service Act passed

1914
- Beginning of Great Migration

1915
- Germany torpedoes the *Lusitania*

United States PRESIDENTS

Wilson 1913–1921

1914

1916

World

1914
- Franz Ferdinand assassinated
- World War I begins

1917
- Lenin leads Bolshevik Revolution

To the Front World War I combined traditional means of warfare, such as the cavalry, with modern means, such as the tank and the airplane.

1918
- National War Labor Board is set up

1920
- Senate rejects League of Nations

1918 *1920*

1918
- World War I ends
- Flu epidemic kills more than 20 million worldwide

1919
- Treaty of Versailles signed

HISTORY Online

Chapter Overview
Visit taj.glencoe.com and click on **Chapter 23— Chapter Overviews** to preview chapter information.

War in Europe

Main Idea
When Europe went to war in 1914, the United States tried to stay out of the conflict.

Key Terms
nationalism, ethnic groups, militarism, alliance system, entente, balance of power

Reading Strategy
Organizing Information As you read the section, re-create the diagram below, and identify four causes of World War I.

Causes of WWI

Read to Learn
• what factors led to World War I.
• how the early fighting progressed in Europe.

Section Theme
Science and Technology New weapons and other technology were used in fighting the war.

Preview of Events

♦1914	♦1915	♦1916

June 1914
Franz Ferdinand is assassinated

July 1914
Austria-Hungary declares war on Serbia

August 1914
Germany declares war on Russia and France

1916
France and Germany fight the Battle of Verdun

AN
American Story

The swift chain of events that led to war in Europe in 1914 stunned Americans. Most agreed with Jeannette Rankin—the first woman to serve in the U.S. Congress at a time when women could not even vote in most states—that "You can no more win a war than you can win an earthquake." Most Americans wanted the country to stay out of other countries' affairs. They saw no good reason to get involved in a conflict that they believed grew out of national pride and greed. As time went on, the United States found it more and more difficult to remain neutral.

Troubles in Europe

The people of Sarajevo crowded the streets of their city on the morning of June 28, 1914. They wanted to see **Archduke Franz Ferdinand,** the heir to the throne of the Austro-Hungarian Empire. The royal couple had come on a state visit to **Bosnia,** an Austrian province. Suddenly shots rang out. The archduke and his wife were hit and died soon after. The assassination destroyed the delicate balance of European stability. Within weeks Europe was at war. The tensions that led to World War I had roots that went back many years. The conflicts grew as European nations pursued dreams of empires, built up their armies, and formed alliances.

Nationalism

Nationalism, a feeling of intense loyalty to one's country or group, caused much of the tension in Europe. On the one hand, nationalism encouraged new nations, such as Italy and Germany, to unify and to establish their power in the world. Italy had become a kingdom in the 1860s, and the German states had united in the 1870s. Their actions challenged the position of older nations such as Great Britain and France.

On the other hand, nationalism inspired certain groups of people to break away from existing nations. Some of these ethnic groups—people who share a common language and traditions—demanded independent nations of their own.

Imperial Expansion

Tension in Europe also grew out of the desire of nations to expand their empires. Nations competed for colonies in Africa, Asia, and other parts of the world. These colonies not only brought new markets and raw materials, they also added to a nation's prestige.

Great Britain and France already possessed large overseas empires, but they wanted to expand them even more. Germany, Italy, and Russia wanted to increase their colonial holdings as well. Because few areas were left to colonize, however, expansion by one European nation often brought it into conflict with another power.

Military Buildup

As European nations competed for colonies, they strengthened their armies and navies to protect their interests. If one nation increased its military strength, its rivals felt threatened and built up their own military in response. In this atmosphere of militarism, Germany, France, and Russia developed huge armies in the early 1900s.

Great Britain, an island nation, had the world's largest and strongest navy. When Germany began to challenge Britain's naval power in the early 1900s, a bitter rivalry grew between the two nations. The rivalry led to an arms race that threatened peace in Europe.

Forming Alliances

Along with militarism came a strengthening of the alliance system, or the defense agreements among nations. By 1914 two major alliances had been established. Germany, Austria-Hungary, and Italy banded together in the **Triple Alliance,** while Great Britain, France, and Russia joined in the **Triple Entente.** An entente is an understanding among nations.

The alliances aimed to keep peace by creating a balance of power—a system that prevents any one country from dominating the others. Yet the alliance system actually posed a great danger. An attack on one nation was all that was needed to trigger a war involving many countries.

Europe was like a powder keg. One American diplomat noted that it would take "only a spark to set the whole thing off." That spark was ignited in the **Balkans.**

✓ **Reading Check** **Describing** What was the purpose of the alliance system?

Crisis in the Balkans

The Balkan Peninsula in southeastern Europe was a hotbed of nationalist and ethnic rivalries in the early 1900s. The nations of Greece, Albania, Romania, and Bulgaria argued over territory, while Slavic nationalists hoped to unite all the Slavic peoples in the region. Especially bitter was the dispute between Austria-Hungary, whose Slavic people desired independence, and the neighboring nation of Serbia, which supported the Slavs and opposed the empire.

An Assassination Leads to War

Franz Ferdinand's assassin, Gavrilo Princip, was a member of a Serbian nationalist group. Princip and other terrorists had plotted the murder to advance the cause of the unification of Slavic peoples.

Archduke Franz Ferdinand

NATIONAL GEOGRAPHIC   Europe in World War I, 1914

| Allies |
| Central Powers |
| Neutral nations |

1 June 28   Franz Ferdinand assassinated
2 July 28   Austria-Hungary declares war on Serbia
3 July 30   Russia mobilizes armed forces
4 Aug. 1   Germany declares war on Russia
5 Aug. 3   Germany declares war on France
6 Aug. 4   Germany invades Belgium
7 Aug. 4   Britain declares war on Germany
8 Aug. 6   Austria-Hungary declares war on Russia
9 Aug. 12   France and Britain declare war on Austria-Hungary

0   500 miles
0   500 kilometers
Azimuthal Equidistant projection

Geography Skills

1. **Region** What nations made up the the Central Powers?
2. **Drawing Conclusions** What incident sparked the beginning of World War I?

The rulers of Austria-Hungary blamed the Serbian government for the assassination and moved to crush the Serbian nationalist movement. After making sure its ally, Germany, supported its decision, Austria-Hungary sent a letter to Serbia listing harsh demands. When Serbia refused the conditions, Austria-Hungary declared war on Serbia on July 28, 1914.

Europe's system of alliances caused the war to spread. Russia, which had agreed to protect Serbia, prepared for war. This brought Germany to the side of its ally, Austria-Hungary. Germany declared war on Russia on August 1, 1914. Knowing France was an ally of Russia, Germany declared war on France on August 3.

A day later, Germany invaded Belgium as part of a plan to sweep across eastern and northern France. In doing so, Germany violated a treaty signed in 1839 guaranteeing Belgium's neutrality. The invasion of Belgium prompted Great Britain to honor its pledge to protect Belgium, and Britain declared war on Germany.

Reading Check **Describing** What actions did Austria-Hungary take after the assassination of Franz Ferdinand?

A World War Begins

The "Great War" had begun. On one side were the **Allied Powers,** or the Allies—Great Britain, France, and Russia. On the other were the **Central**

Powers—Germany, Austria-Hungary, and the Ottoman (Turkish) Empire, which joined the war in October 1914. **Japan,** a rival of Germany in Asia, joined the Allies in late August 1914. Italy refused to honor its alliance with Germany and Austria-Hungary. Instead, it joined the Allies in 1915 after being promised territory in Austria after the war.

Fighting on the Western Front

In launching an offensive through Belgium, Germany hoped to defeat France quickly and destroy the French armies. This would allow Germany to move troops east against Russia.

The plan almost succeeded. The Belgians, however, held out heroically for nearly three weeks against the powerful German army. This delay gave the French and British time to mobilize their forces.

After defeating the Belgians, the Germans marched into France and advanced to within 15 miles of Paris. The British and French finally managed to stop the German advance at the Marne River just a few miles east of the city. The **Battle of the Marne,** fought between September 5 and 12, 1914, saved Paris from invasion by the Germans and boosted French morale. It also made it clear that neither side was capable of winning the war quickly or easily.

After the Battle of the Marne, the fighting in western Europe reached a stalemate. For the next three years, the opposing armies faced each other across an elaborate network of deep **trenches.** Trenches along the front lines provided some protection from flying bullets and artillery shells. Support trenches behind the lines served as headquarters, first-aid stations, and storage areas.

In 1916 both sides attempted to break the deadlock of trench warfare by launching major offensives. The German offensive, the **Battle of Verdun** in northeastern France, began in February and continued on and off until December. At first the Germans made small gains, but these were lost after the French counterattacked. Verdun was one of the longest and bloodiest battles of the war. When it was over, more than 750,000 French and German soldiers had lost their lives.

While the Battle of Verdun raged, the British and French launched their own offensive in northern France in July—the **Battle of the Somme.** Again the number of casualties was extremely high. The Allies gained only about 7 miles (11.2 km) in the offensive.

Deadly Technology

New and more deadly weapons accounted for the terrible slaughter during these battles. Improved cannons and other artillery fired larger shells greater distances than ever before. Better rifles enabled soldiers to hit targets with greater accuracy.

Poison gas, another new and devastating weapon, was first used by the Germans over Allied lines in April 1915. The gas could kill or seriously injure anyone who breathed it. A British officer said,

❝They fought with terror, running blindly in the gas cloud, and dropping . . . in agony.❞

Airplanes were first used in combat during World War I.

United States neutrality was put to a test when German U-boats (shown here) attacked American ships.

The Allies began to use poison gas also, and gas masks became necessary equipment for soldiers in the trenches.

The armored tank, first used in World War I in January 1916, proved effective for crossing battle lines to fire on the enemy at close range. Tanks also could crush barbed wire, providing an easier route for advancing troops. After the Germans saw the effectiveness of tanks, they produced them too.

The most dramatic new weapon—the airplane—added a new dimension to fighting in World War I. Both sides used airplanes for watching troop movements and bombing enemy targets. Daring pilots waged duels in the skies called "dogfights." The first fighter planes were only equipped with machine guns, which were fastened to the top wing. The most famous pilots included Germany's "Red Baron," **Baron von Richthofen,** and America's **Eddie Rickenbacker,** who served in the French air force. The Germans used the zeppelin, or blimp, to bomb Allied cities.

On the Seas

With their land armies deadlocked in western Europe, both sides looked to the sea to gain an advantage in the war. Great Britain blockaded all ports under German control, eventually causing serious shortages. Many Germans suffered from malnutrition and illness because of lack of food and other supplies.

Germany had an effective naval weapon of its own: the submarine. Known as **U-boats**—from the German word for submarine, *Unterseeboot*—submarines prevented supplies, including food, from reaching Great Britain. U-boat attacks on ships at sea eventually affected the United States and changed the course of the war.

Reading Check **Explaining** What did both sides realize after the Battle of the Marne?

SECTION 1 ASSESSMENT

Checking for Understanding

1. **Key Terms** Write headlines for events during the World War I era; use each of the following terms: nationalism, militarism, alliance system, entente.

2. **Reviewing Facts** What nations made up the Triple Alliance? The Triple Entente?

Reviewing Themes

3. **Science and Technology** Why were casualties so high in World War I?

Critical Thinking

4. **Determining Cause and Effect** How did forming alliances increase the likelihood of war in Europe?

5. **Determining Cause and Effect** Re-create the diagram below and describe two effects that militarism had on rival nations.

Analyzing Visuals

6. **Geography Skills** Examine the map on page 668. When did Germany declare war on France? On what side did Belgium fight?

Interdisciplinary Activity

Science Research the inventions that were developed in World War I. Make a chart in which you describe each invention and a possible peacetime use of the invention.

SECTION 2 America's Road to War

Guide to Reading

Main Idea
The United States entered the conflict on the side of the Allies.

Key Terms
propaganda, autocracy

Reading Strategy
Analyzing Information As you read the section, re-create the diagram below and list two reasons the United States found it difficult to maintain neutrality.

Maintaining neutrality

Read to Learn
• how Americans responded to the war in Europe.
• what led to American involvement in the war.

Section Theme
Government and Democracy The United States, officially neutral at first, entered the conflict.

Preview of Events

♦1914	♦1916	♦1918

August 1914
Europe goes to war

May 1915
Germany torpedoes the *Lusitania*

March 1917
Zimmermann telegram angers U.S.

April 1917
U.S. declares war on Germany

AN
American Story

President Wilson struggled to remain neutral, even after Americans had been killed at the outbreak of World War I. Others felt differently. An American businessman cabled the president after the *Laconia* was sunk by Germans: "My beloved mother and sister . . . have been foully murdered on the high seas. . . . I call upon my government to preserve its citizens' self-respect and save others of my countrymen from such deep grief as I now feel. I am of military age, able to fight. If my country can use me against these brutal assassins, I am at its call." Remaining neutral grew more and more difficult.

American Neutrality

President Wilson had to make some difficult decisions. He declared that the United States would be neutral in the war and called on Americans to be "neutral in fact as well as in name, impartial in thought as well as in action." Other influential political leaders also argued strongly in favor of neutrality.

NOTICE!

TRAVELLERS intending to embark on the Atlantic voyage are reminded that a state of war exists between Germany and her allies and Great Britian and her allies; that the zone of war includes the waters adjacent to the British Isles; that, in accordance with formal notice given by the Imperial German Government, vessels flying the flag of Great Britian, or of any of her allies, are liable to destruction in those waters and that travellers sailing in the war zone on ships of Great Britian or her allies do so at their own risk.

IMPERIAL GERMAN EMBASSY,
WASHINGTON, D. C., APRIL 22, 1915.

Picturing History

The *Lusitania* left New York for England on May 1, 1915. Germany had placed a warning notice in American newspapers, but few people took it seriously. **How did the United States respond to German U-boat attacks?**

When Europe went to war in August 1914, most Americans believed that the war did not concern them. Many shared the view expressed in an editorial in the *New York Sun:*

66There is nothing reasonable in such a war, and it would be [foolish] for the country to sacrifice itself to the . . . policies and the clash of ancient hatreds which is urging the Old World to destruction.99

Despite Wilson's plea to remain neutral, Americans soon began to take sides. More than one-third of the nation's 92 million people were either foreign-born or the children of immigrants. Many of these people naturally sympathized with their countries of origin. Some of the 8 million Americans of German or Austrian descent and the 4.5 million Irish Americans— who hated the British because they ruled Ireland—favored the Central Powers.

Even more Americans, however, including President Wilson, felt sympathetic to the Allies. Ties of language, customs, and traditions linked the United States to Great Britain, and many Americans were of British descent. President Wilson told the British ambassador: "Everything I love most in the world is at stake." A German victory "would be fatal to our form of government and American ideals."

Using Propaganda

To gain the support of Americans, both sides in the war used propaganda—information designed to influence opinion. Allied propaganda emphasized the German invasion of neutral Belgium and included horror stories of German atrocities. It called the Germans "Huns" and pictured them as savage barbarians.

The propaganda from the Central Powers was equally horrible, but because of British sympathies, the Allied propaganda was more effective in influencing Americans.

America's Early Involvement

Trade between the United States and the Allies helped build support for the Allied cause. As a neutral nation, America sought to trade with both sides, but Britain's blockade of Germany made this difficult.

The British navy stopped and searched American ships headed for German ports, often seizing the ships' goods. The United States protested that its ships should be able to pass without interference. The British responded with the defense that they were fighting for their survival. "If the American shipper grumbles," wrote a London paper, "our reply is that this war is not being conducted for his pleasure or profit." The United States government could do nothing about the blockade. Barred from trading with Germany, it continued trading with Britain.

Indeed, American trade with the Allies soared. In addition, Great Britain and France borrowed billions of dollars from American banks to help pay for their war efforts. All this business caused an economic boom in the United States. It also upset the Germans, who watched the United States—supposedly a neutral nation—helping the Allies.

Submarine Warfare

To stop American aid to Britain, Germany announced in February 1915 that it would use its U-boats to sink any vessels that entered or left British ports. President Wilson warned that America would hold Germany responsible for any American lives lost in submarine attacks. Determined to cut off supplies to Great Britain, the Germans ignored this threat.

On May 7, 1915, a German U-boat torpedoed the British passenger liner *Lusitania* off the coast of Ireland. W.T. Turner, the captain, reported:

> ❝I saw the torpedo speeding towards us. Immediately I tried to change our course, but was unable to maneuver out of its way. There was a terrible impact as the torpedo struck the starboard side of the vessel. . . . It was cold-blooded murder.❞

The *Lusitania* sank in about 15 minutes. More than 1,000 people died, including 128 United States citizens. Americans were outraged, and President Wilson denounced the attack. Later it was learned that the ship carried war materials.

📖 *(See page 973 for a passenger's account of the sinking.)*

TECHNOLOGY & History

Submarine

During World War I, German U-boats, or submarines, became the terror of the seas. *What part of the craft guided the submarine up and down?*

1 The **conning tower** is the attack center.

Periscope

2 The **diving rudders** guide the submarine to different depths.

Deck gun

Engine room

Crew's quarters

Control room

3 The **rudder** steers the vessel.

4 **Torpedo tubes** were always loaded. About 12 torpedoes could be carried at a time.

The United States began building its own submarine fleet during the war. The fastest American submarines reached a top surface speed of 14 knots (a little more than 16 miles per hour).

Several months later a German U-boat torpedoed the unarmed French passenger ship *Sussex*, injuring several Americans. Fearing that the Americans might enter the war, Germany offered to compensate Americans injured on the *Sussex* and promised to warn neutral ships and passenger vessels before attacking. The Sussex Pledge, as it was called, seemed to resolve the issue.

✔ **Reading Check** **Describing** What is the aim of propaganda?

The End of Neutrality

The crisis over submarine warfare led the United States to take steps to strengthen its military. In the summer of 1916, Congress passed legislation that doubled the size of the army and provided funds to build new warships. President Wilson still hoped, however, to stay out of the war.

Antiwar sentiment remained very strong. Some Americans criticized the nation's military buildup, seeing it as a step toward entering the war. A popular song in 1915 expressed this opposition:

❝I didn't raise my boy to be a soldier,
I brought him up to be my pride and joy.
Who dares place a musket on his shoulder,
To shoot some other mother's darling boy?❞

Antiwar sentiment was strong at the 1916 Democratic national convention, where all references to the president's efforts to keep the country out of war brought wild applause. After Wilson was nominated for a second term, the phrase "He Kept Us Out of War" became the Democrats' slogan. The question of neutrality divided the Republicans, and Republican presidential candidate Charles Evans Hughes avoided discussing the issue. Wilson narrowly defeated Hughes.

What If...

The British Had Not Intercepted the Zimmermann Note?

In January 1917 German foreign minister Arthur Zimmermann cabled the German ambassador in Mexico instructing him to make an offer to the Mexican government. Zimmermann proposed that Mexico help Germany in the event that the United States entered the war. To encourage Mexico's cooperation, Germany promised that Mexico would regain some of the region that it lost to the United States in 1848. A British official intercepted Zimmermann's telegram. The telegram read:

❝On the first of February we intend to begin submarine warfare unrestricted. In spite of this, it is our intention to endeavor to keep neutral the United States of America.

If this attempt is not successful, we propose an alliance on the following basis with Mexico: That we shall make war together and together make peace. We shall give generous financial support, and it is understood that Mexico is to reconquer the lost territory in New Mexico, Texas, and Arizona. The details are left to you for settlement....

You are instructed to inform the President of Mexico of the above in the greatest confidence as soon as it is certain that there will be an outbreak of war with the United States and suggest that the President of Mexico, on his own initiative, should communicate with Japan suggesting adherence at once to this plan; at the

same time, offer to mediate between Germany and Japan.

Please call to the attention of the President of Mexico that the employment of ruthless submarine warfare now promises to compel England to make peace in a few months.❞

Widely publicized by British and in the American press, the Zimmermann telegram angered Americans and helped build popular sentiment for the war. Then, between March 12 and March 19, four American merchant ships were sunk without warning. On April 2, 1917, President Wilson asked the members of Congress to declare war on Germany.

—adapted from *Almost History*, Roger Bruns ©2000

On the Brink of War

In January 1917, Germany reversed its policy on submarine warfare. It announced that it would sink on sight all merchant vessels, armed or unarmed, sailing to Allied ports. While realizing that their policy might bring the Americans into the war, the Germans believed they could defeat the Allies before the United States became heavily involved. An angry President Wilson broke off diplomatic relations with Germany.

A few weeks later, a secret telegram—intercepted by the British government—set off a new wave of anti-German feeling. In late February the German foreign minister, Arthur Zimmermann, sent a telegram to Mexico with an offer to the Mexican government:

> 66[W]e shall make war together and together make peace. . . . [A]nd it is understood that Mexico is to reconquer the lost territory in New Mexico, Texas, and Arizona.99

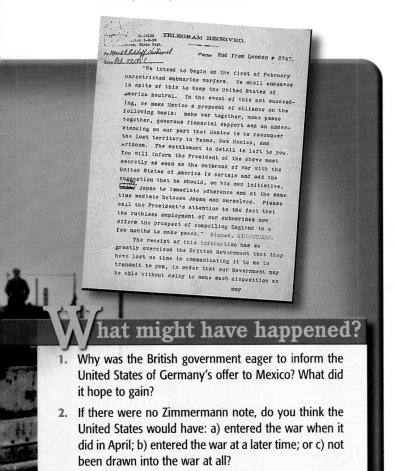

What might have happened?

1. Why was the British government eager to inform the United States of Germany's offer to Mexico? What did it hope to gain?

2. If there were no Zimmermann note, do you think the United States would have: a) entered the war when it did in April; b) entered the war at a later time; or c) not been drawn into the war at all?

Newspapers published the secret **Zimmermann telegram** on March 1, and Americans reacted angrily to the German action.

Revolution in Russia

In the weeks following publication of the Zimmermann telegram, dramatic events pushed the United States to the brink of war. First, a revolution took place in Russia. Following a period of rioting and strikes, the Russian people overthrew the monarchy. In its place they established a temporary government that promised free elections.

Many Americans believed that the new Russian government, which vowed to defeat Germany, would help the Allies. With Russia's change to a democratic form of government, Wilson could now claim that the Allies were fighting a war of democracy against autocracy—rule by one person with unlimited power.

Other critical events took place at sea. In March 1917, within a few days time, the Germans attacked and sank four American ships—the *Algonquin*, the *City of Memphis*, the *Illinois*, and the *Vigilancia*. Thirty-six lives were lost.

President Wilson continued to struggle with his conscience. He was convinced that war would destroy much of the optimism and sympathy to human needs that had allowed America to make the social progress it had. His cabinet, on the other hand, strongly favored war. One government official later explained:

> 66If we had stayed out of the war, and Germany had won, there would no longer have been a balance of power in Europe, or a British fleet to support the Monroe Doctrine and to protect America.99

President Wilson decided that the United States could no longer remain neutral.

America Enters the War

On the cold, rainy evening of April 2, 1917, President Wilson stood before a special session of Congress to ask for a declaration of war against Germany.

66The world must be made safe for democracy. . . . It is a fearful thing to lead this great peaceful people into war, into the most terrible and disastrous of all wars. . . . But the right is more precious than peace. . . .99

Congress did not agree at once to a formal resolution of war. Some members of Congress agreed with Senator George Norris of Nebraska. He held that America's involvement in the war was the fault of American financiers and arms manufacturers who were determined to profit from the war no matter what it cost the rest of the country.

In the end, however, most members of Congress agreed that if the United States wished to remain a great world power it must defend its rights. As a result, Congress passed a declaration of war, and Wilson signed it on April 6. Fifty-six members of the House and Senate voted against war, including Representative Jeannette Rankin of Montana—the first woman to serve in Congress.

The United States had to raise an army quickly. On May 18, Congress passed the **Selective Service Act,** establishing a military draft. Unlike the draft during the Civil War that led to riots, this draft had the support of most of the American public.

Men aged 21 to 30 (later the draft age was extended from 18 to 45) registered by the millions. By the end of the war, some 24 million men had registered. Of those, about 3 million were called to serve; another 2 million joined the armed forces voluntarily.

In addition thousands of women enlisted in the armed forces—the first time they were allowed to do so. Women did noncombat work, serving as radio operators, clerks, and nurses.

Many African Americans also wanted to serve their country. More than 300,000 joined the army and navy—the marines would not accept them. African Americans faced discrimination and racism in the armed forces just as they did in civilian life. Most held low-level jobs on military bases in the United States. Among the 140,000 African American soldiers sent to Europe, 40,000 saw actual combat. Many served with distinction. An African American regiment received medals for bravery from the French government. One of its members, Henry Johnson, was the first American to receive the French Croix de Guerre [Cross of War] for bravery.

✓ **Reading Check** **Describing** What was the purpose of the Selective Service Act?

HISTORY Online
Student Web Activity
Visit taj.glencoe.com and click on **Chapter 23— Student Web Activities** for an activity on World War I.

SECTION 2 ASSESSMENT

1. **Key Terms** Define propaganda and autocracy.
2. **Reviewing Facts** What did the Zimmermann telegram promise to Mexico?

Reviewing Themes

3. **Government and Democracy** What steps did President Wilson have to take to make an official declaration of war?

Critical Thinking

4. **Determining Cause and Effect** Explain how the war in Europe brought about an economic boom in the United States.
5. **Sequencing Information** Re-create the diagram below and explain how these events led the United States into the war.

Event	
Sinking of *Lusitania*	
Zimmermann note	

Analyzing Visuals

6. **Picturing History** Examine the submarine on page 673. What was the top speed of American submarines? What was the purpose of the diving rudders?

Interdisciplinary Activity

Expository Writing Create headlines announcing major events described in Section 2. Keep in mind that headlines condense much information into a few words.

SECTION 3 Americans Join the Allies

Guide to Reading

Main Idea
With the help of American troops and supplies, the Allies turned the tide against Germany.

Key Terms
convoy, front, armistice

Reading Strategy
Sequencing Information As you read the section, re-create the time line below and identify the events that took place.

Nov. 1917	June 1918	Oct. 4, 1918	Nov. 11, 1918

Read to Learn
• what was happening in Europe when the United States entered the war.
• what role American troops played in the fighting.

Section Theme
Global Connections The entry of the United States into the war made an immediate difference, eventually leading to Germany's surrender.

Preview of Events

♦1917 ————————————————— ♦1918 ————————————————— ♦1919

June 1917
American troops land in France

March 1918
Russia withdraws from the war

June 1918
American Expeditionary Force begins to fight

November 1918
Armistice ends World War I

AN American Story

Drafted into the United States Army in 1917, Alvin York was reluctant to serve. "I was worried clean through," he said. "I didn't want to go and kill." York had grown up in the mountains of Tennessee, where he learned to shoot while hunting wild turkeys. Applying his sharpshooting skills in World War I, York killed 17 German soldiers with 17 shots. He also took 132 Germans prisoner and captured 35 enemy machine guns. For his actions and bravery in combat, Sergeant York received the Medal of Honor.

Supplying the Allies

In 1917 the Allies desperately needed the help of American soldiers. Years of trench warfare had exhausted the Allied armies, and some French troops refused to continue fighting after a failed offensive in 1917. The British had started to run out of war supplies and food; their people were starving. Furthermore, German submarines were taking a deadly toll on Allied shipping—sinking one of every four ships that left British ports.

The American entry into the war made an immediate difference. To ensure that needed supplies reached Great Britain, the United States Navy took two steps. First, it helped the British find and destroy German submarines. Then convoys—teams—of navy destroyers escorted groups of merchant ships across the Atlantic. The convoy system worked well. In one year it reduced Allied shipping losses from 900,000 to 300,000 tons a month. With the convoy system, not one American soldier bound for Europe was lost to submarine attack.

Russian Withdrawal

The Allies needed more troops because of a second revolution in Russia. In November 1917, the **Bolsheviks,** a group of communists, overthrew the democratic Russian government established in March 1917.

Led by **Vladimir Lenin,** the Bolsheviks wanted to end Russia's participation in the war so they could focus their energies and resources on setting up a new Communist state. Lenin took Russia out of the war in December. In March 1918, he signed the **Treaty of Brest-Litovsk** with

NATIONAL GEOGRAPHIC
Europe During World War I, 1914–1918

Allies
Central Powers
Neutral nations

0   250 miles
0   250 kilometers
Lambert Azimuthal
Equal-Area projection

May, 1915 Germany sinks *Lusitania*

NORWAY
SWEDEN
North Sea
DENMARK
Baltic Sea
UNITED KINGDOM
Western Front
GERMANY
BELGIUM
LUX.
ATLANTIC OCEAN
RUSSIA
Eastern Front
FRANCE
AUSTRIA-HUNGARY
Western Front
ROMANIA
Black Sea
PORTUGAL
ITALY
SERBIA
BULGARIA
SPAIN
Mediterranean Sea
GREECE
OTTOMAN EMPIRE

Major Battles
1 Tannenberg, Aug. 1914   4 Verdun, Feb.–Dec. 1916   7 2nd Marne, July 1918
2 1st Marne, Sept. 1914   5 Somme, July–Nov. 1916   8 St. Mihiel, Sept. 1918
3 Gallipoli, Apr. 1915 –   6 Château-Thierry and   9 Meuse-Argonne, Sept.–Nov. 1918
  Jan. 1916   Belleau Wood, June 1918

Geography *Skills*

1. Location What country was the site of most Western Front battles?

2. Location Nearest to what front was the battle of Tannenberg fought?

Life in the trenches was miserable. Soldiers lived in dirt and mud for months at a time. Between the enemy lines lay a "no-man's land" of barbed wire and land mines. Endless days of shelling the enemy might sometimes be interrupted by an attempt to "break out" of the trenches and advance into enemy territory.

Germany, surrendering Poland, the Ukraine, and other territory to the Germans. Russia's withdrawal from the war allowed the Germans to move hundreds of thousands of troops from the Eastern Front—line of battle—to the Western Front in France.

New German Offensive

Reinforced by the transfer of troops, the Germans now launched a powerful offensive against the Allies. German military leaders hoped to drive a wedge in the Allied lines and to capture the city of Amiens before proceeding to Paris. Between March and June 1918, they hammered at Allied lines, pushing them back to within 40 miles (64 km) of Paris. After years of stalemate along the Western Front—the area along the French-German border—it suddenly looked as if Germany might win the war.

American Troops in the War

Although the first American soldiers had reached France in June 1917, many months passed before they were ready for battle. When they finally began to fight, the Americans helped turn the war around.

General **John J. Pershing** led the **American Expeditionary Force** (AEF), the American troops in Europe. American correspondent Floyd Gibbons described the tremendous welcome the French gave Pershing and his troops in Paris:

> 66The sooty girders of the Gare du Nord [railroad station] shook with cheers when the special train pulled in. . . . A minute later, there was a terrific roar from beyond the walls of the station. The crowds outside had heard the cheering within. . . . Pershing took Paris by storm.99

The AEF reached full strength in Europe in the spring of 1918. The French and British wanted to use the American soldiers to build up their own troops, but General Pershing refused. He preferred to keep the AEF a separate force.

The American Expeditionary Force saw its first serious fighting in early June 1918. It helped turn back a German offensive at **Château-Thierry** on the **Marne River** east of Paris. The American troops then advanced to nearby **Belleau Wood.** For 24 hours a day for the next three weeks, American forces fought their way through the forest against a solid wall of German machine-gun fire. In July the Americans and the French fought back German attacks on Allied forces along the Marne and the Somme Rivers.

By the middle of July, the Allies had stopped the German offensive. General Pershing wrote that the battles had "turned the tide of war." The Allies now began an offensive of their own. In mid-September about 500,000 "doughboys"—the nickname given to American soldiers—fighting alone, defeated the Germans at Saint Mihiel, east of **Verdun.** Later in the month, more than one million American troops joined the Allies in the **Battle of the Argonne Forest,** west of Verdun.

The Battle of the Argonne Forest raged for nearly seven weeks, with soldiers struggling over the rugged, heavily forested ground. Rain, mud, barbed wire, and withering fire from German machine guns hindered the Allies' advance, and many lives were lost.

American lieutenant Elden Betts wondered if he would survive the battle and wrote home—in case "I get mine tomorrow." He said he hoped his family would be proud of him, ending with "Now good-bye, and thank you Pop, Edie and Margie." Four days later Betts was killed.

The Battle of the Argonne Forest ended in early November, when the Allies finally pushed back the Germans and broke through the enemy lines. The Germans now were faced with an invasion of their own country.

✓ **Reading Check** **Identifying** What was the first major battle to involve Americans?

The End of the War

With their troops in retreat, German military leaders realized they had little chance of winning the war. The Allied forces were now fortified by the Americans. In addition, the Germans suffered from severe shortages of food and other essential supplies.

Request for an Armistice

On October 4, 1918, the German government appealed to President Wilson for an armistice. An armistice is an agreement to end the fighting. Wilson consented under certain conditions. Germany must accept his plan for peace and

In 1915 the Germans introduced a new weapon—poison gas. In time, all of the combatants would use gas warfare. Artillery shells containing gas were fired at the enemy, and wind carried the gas into trenches, causing blindness, choking, damaged lungs, and death.

promise not to renew hostilities. All German troops must leave Belgium and France. Finally, Wilson would deal only with civilian leaders, not with the military.

While German leaders considered Wilson's demands, political unrest erupted in Germany. On November 9, the German **kaiser,** or emperor, **Wilhelm II,** was forced to give up his throne. Germany became a republic, and its new leaders quickly agreed to Wilson's terms for the armistice.

Peace Begins

The armistice began on November 11, 1918. Germany agreed to withdraw all land forces west of the **Rhine River,** withdraw its fleet to the Baltic Sea, and surrender huge amounts of equipment.

With the signing of the armistice, the Great War ended. President Wilson announced:

❝Everything for which America fought has been accomplished. It will now be our duty to assist by example, by sober, friendly counsel, and by material aid in the establishment of just democracy throughout the world.❞

✓**Reading Check** **Describing** What conditions did Germany accept to end the fighting?

Linking Past & Present

Honoring the Veterans

Armistice Day, first observed on November 11, 1919, honored the Allied soldiers who died in World War I. In 1954 Armistice Day was renamed Veterans' Day in honor of all those, living and dead, who had served with U.S. armed forces in wartime. Similar commemorations take place in Canada on Remembrance Day and the United Kingdom on Remembrance Sunday.

Soldiers receive the Distinguished Service Cross.

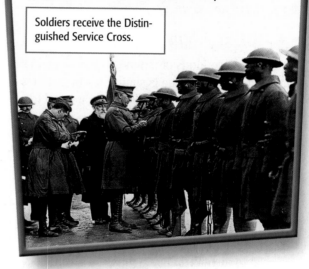

SECTION 3 ASSESSMENT

Checking for Understanding

1. **Key Terms** Write headlines for three news stories about World War I; use each of the following terms: convoy, front, armistice.

2. **Reviewing Facts** Who led the American forces in Europe?

Reviewing Themes

3. **Global Connections** According to the armistice, from where did Germany agree to withdraw its land forces?

Critical Thinking

4. **Predicting Consequences** Do you think the Allies would have won the war if the United States had not intervened? Why or why not?

5. **Determining Cause and Effect** Re-create the diagram below and list three reasons the Allies needed the help of American forces.

Allied needs

Analyzing Visuals

6. **Geography Skills** Examine the map on page 678. When was the battle at St. Mihiel fought? When was the Battle of Gallipoli fought? Do you think it was easier for Norway, Spain, and Sweden to remain neutral than it was for Switzerland? Why?

Interdisciplinary Activity

Descriptive Writing Write the text for a radio broadcast announcing the arrival of American soldiers in Paris in 1917.

Study & Writing SKILLBUILDER

Outlining

Why Learn This Skill?

To sketch a scene, you first draw the rough shape, or outline, of the picture. Then you fill in this rough shape with details. Outlining written material is a similar process. You begin with the rough shape of the material and gradually fill in the details.

Learning the Skill

There are two kinds of outlines—formal and informal. An informal outline is similar to taking notes. You write only the words and phrases needed to remember main ideas.

A formal outline has a standard format. In a formal outline, label main heads with Roman numbers, subheads with capital letters, and details with Arabic numerals and lowercase letters. Each level should have at least two entries and should be indented from the level above.

When outlining written material, first read the material to identify the main ideas. In textbooks, section heads provide clues to main topics. Then identify the subheads. Place supporting details under the appropriate head.

Practicing the Skill

Study the partial outline of Section 3 on this page. Then answer the following questions.

❶ Is this a formal or an informal outline?

❷ What are the three main topics?

❸ If you wanted to add two facts about the AEF, where would you put them in the outline? Would you use numbers or letters to label the facts?

Outline of Chapter 23, Section 3

I. European Allies need help.
   A. Allied armies are exhausted.
      1. Trench warfare depletes supplies.
      2. Russia leaves war.
   B. Civilians are in trouble.
      1. People are starving.
      2. Supply ships are sunk by Germans.
II. Americans enter the war.
   A. United States Navy patrols seas.
      1. German U-boats are destroyed.
      2. Convoys protect Allied ships.
         a. Losses are reduced by two-thirds.
         b. No American soldiers are killed.
   B. American Expeditionary Force (AEF) lands in Europe.
      1. Germans lose at Château-Thierry.
      2. Germans are defeated at Belleau Wood.
III. Allies take the offensive.
   A. Battle of Argonne Forest is fought.
   B. President Wilson lists conditions for armistice.

Applying the Skill

Outlining Following the guidelines above, prepare an outline for Section 2 of Chapter 23.

 Glencoe's **Skillbuilder Interactive Workbook CD-ROM, Level 1,** provides instruction and practice in key social studies skills.

SECTION 4 The War at Home

Guide to Reading

Main Idea

World War I drastically changed life in the United States.

Key Terms

mobilization, dissent, socialist, pacifist, espionage, sabotage

Reading Strategy

Analyzing Information As you read the section, re-create the diagram below and describe the goals of these agencies.

Agency	Goals
Food Administration	
War Industries Board	
Committee on Public Information	

Read to Learn

- what steps the United States took to organize and prepare for World War I.
- how the war affected Americans.

Section Theme

Economic Factors America's involvement in the war in Europe led to economic challenges and opportunities at home.

Preview of Events

♦1917   ♦1918   ♦1919

July 1917
Race riots occur in East St. Louis

April 1918
National War Labor Board is set up

June 1918
Congress passes Sabotage and Sedition acts

AN American Story

"Over there, over there,
Send the word, send the word
over there
That the Yanks are coming, the Yanks
are coming,
The drums rum-tumming ev'rywhere

So prepare, say a pray'r,
Send the word, send the word to
beware,
We'll be over, we're coming over,
And we won't come back till it's over
over there."

George M. Cohan wrote this rousing song to help create enthusiasm for America's participation in World War I. "Over There" was performed at rallies to raise money for the war.

Mobilizing the Nation

After declaring war on Germany in 1917, Americans immediately focused their energies on getting ready to fight a war. Mobilization—the gathering of resources and the preparation for war—affected almost every part of American life.

To ensure production of vital war materials, the government created the **National War Labor Board** in April 1918. The board pressured businesses to grant some of the workers' pressing demands. As a result workers won an eight-hour working day, extra pay for overtime, equal pay for women, and the right to form unions. In return workers agreed not to go on strike.

Workers During the War

To meet the need for supplies and weapons, the nation's industries had to expand. At the same time, however, millions of men left their jobs in industry to serve in the armed forces, and few European immigrants—who might have taken these jobs—came to the United States during the war.

The labor shortage provided new job opportunities for women and minorities. Many women joined the workforce for the first time. Women were hired for jobs previously held by men.

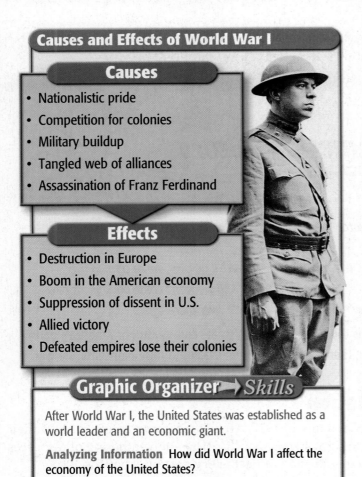

Causes and Effects of World War I

Causes
- Nationalistic pride
- Competition for colonies
- Military buildup
- Tangled web of alliances
- Assassination of Franz Ferdinand

Effects
- Destruction in Europe
- Boom in the American economy
- Suppression of dissent in U.S.
- Allied victory
- Defeated empires lose their colonies

Graphic Organizer → Skills

After World War I, the United States was established as a world leader and an economic giant.

Analyzing Information How did World War I affect the economy of the United States?

The prospect of finding good jobs also brought hundreds of thousands of African Americans to Northern cities from the rural South. In addition, thousands of Mexicans migrated to the United States in search of jobs.

Paying for the War

War is costly. World War I cost the United States an enormous amount of money—about $32 billion. Two-thirds of this money was raised by selling the American people war bonds, or **Liberty Bonds.**

The federal government also raised money for the war by increasing taxes and requiring a greater number of Americans to pay income taxes. It taxed wealthy Americans at rates as high as 70 percent of their income. The government also imposed steep taxes on business profits.

Ⓢ Economics

Producing Supplies

The United States had to produce food not only for its own needs but also for the Allies. President Wilson appointed **Herbert Hoover,** who had helped organize food for war refugees in Europe, to head a new **Food Administration.** This agency launched a campaign to encourage American farmers to produce more and to persuade the public to eat less. The agency urged people to observe "Wheatless Mondays," "Meatless Tuesdays," and "Porkless Thursdays," and to add to their own store of food by planting "victory gardens." Slogans such as "Serve Just Enough" and "Use All Leftovers" reminded Americans to conserve food.

The Food Administration also imposed price controls on various agricultural products to encourage voluntary **rationing**—limitation of use. As a result of such efforts, Americans consumed less food, expanded food production, and increased food exports.

Another government agency, the **War Industries Board,** supervised the nation's industrial production. The board's responsibilities included converting factories to the production of war-related goods and setting prices for key consumer products.

People In History

Edward Rickenbacker 1890–1973

The son of Swiss immigrants who settled in Ohio, Edward Rickenbacker was the leading American combat pilot of World War I. "Captain Eddie" recorded 26 official victories against German aircraft during World War I and was awarded the Medal of Honor.

From his youngest days, Rickenbacker was fascinated by technology and speed. He worked on automobile engines, then struck out on his own as a race car driver; he won many championships and set a world record for speed driving.

When the United States entered the war, Rickenbacker volunteered. After less than three weeks of training he was assigned to the 94th Aero Squadron. The 94th was the first patrol flown in France by an all-American squadron and won more victories than any other squadron.

After the war, Rickenbacker was associated with several automotive and aviation companies. He purchased and managed the Indianapolis Motor Speedway. He also built Eastern Airlines into one of the nation's largest airlines.

Mobilizing Support

The federal government also needed to mobilize public support for the war because antiwar sentiment remained strong even after the United States entered the war. President Wilson appointed journalist George Creel to head the **Committee on Public Information.** The mission of the committee was to persuade Americans that the war represented a battle for democracy and freedom.

The Committee on Public Information distributed millions of pro-war pamphlets, posters, articles, and books. It provided newspapers with government accounts of the war and advertisements. It arranged for short patriotic talks, called Four-Minute Speeches, to be presented before plays and movies. The committee hired speakers, writers, artists, and actors to build support for the war. It was the greatest propaganda campaign the nation had ever seen.

✓ **Reading Check** **Explaining** Why did the United States face a labor shortage during the early days of World War I?

Americans and the War

World War I provided a boost for the American economy. Yet the war had harmful effects on American society as well. In the interest of national unity, the government stifled voices of dissent, or opposition. Racial and other tensions remained, and many Americans became intolerant of those who were "different."

African American Migration

From 1914 to 1920, between 300,000 and 500,000 African Americans left their homes in the rural South to seek jobs and settle in Northern cities. Known as the **Great Migration,** this tremendous population movement continued the northward migration that had begun in the late 1800s.

Many African American workers who traveled north did find jobs. But their new lives were not easy. Often they lived in tiny, crowded apartments in segregated neighborhoods, and they found that racial prejudice continued to haunt their lives in the North.

Terrible race riots took place in several Northern cities during the war years. One of the worst occurred in **East St. Louis, Illinois.** In July 1917, a white mob attacked an African American neighborhood, burning houses and firing on residents as they tried to escape. During the riot, as many as 40 African Americans died and thousands lost their homes.

Controlling Public Opinion

Even after America entered the war, opposition to it remained strong. Some German Americans and Irish Americans sympathized with the Central Powers. Many socialists—people who believe industries should be publicly owned—opposed the war because they thought it would only help rich business owners and hurt working people. Also against the war were pacifists—people opposed to the use of violence.

During the war, the Committee on Public Information began trying to silence dissent and portrayed people who were against the war as unpatriotic. **The Espionage Act** that Congress passed in 1917 gave the government a new weapon to combat dissent to the war. The law provided stiff penalties for espionage, or spying, as well as for aiding the enemy or interfering with army recruiting. Congress passed even harsher measures in 1918—the **Sabotage Act** and

the **Sedition Act.** These laws made it a crime to say, print, or write almost anything perceived as negative about the government. Such acts would be considered sabotage—secret action to damage the war effort. Thousands of people—especially immigrants, socialists, pacifists, and labor activists—were convicted under the laws.

People became suspicious of German Americans. A few communities prohibited such activities as performing German music and teaching the German language in schools. As a result some German Americans concealed their ancestry. They even gave patriotic names—such as "liberty cabbage" and "liberty sausage"—to German-sounding words such as *sauerkraut* and *frankfurter.*

Some people spoke out against these laws and the intolerance they produced. Most Americans, however, believed that in wartime no measure could be "too drastic" toward traitors and disloyal Americans.

✓ **Reading Check** **Identifying** What act provided stiff penalties for spies?

SECTION 4 ASSESSMENT

Checking for Understanding

1. **Key Terms** Use each of these terms in a sentence that will help explain its meaning: mobilization, dissent, socialist, pacifist, espionage, sabotage.
2. **Reviewing Facts** Describe the role of the Committee on Public Information.

Reviewing Themes

3. **Economic Factors** Where did the United States get most of the money to finance the war?

Critical Thinking

4. **Predicting Consequences** Do you think it was necessary for the government to take strong measures against people who opposed the war? Explain.
5. **Organizing Information** Re-create the diagram below and describe three ways that Americans supported the war effort at home.

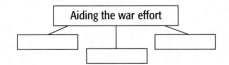

Aiding the war effort

Analyzing Visuals

6. **Graphic Organizer Skills** Examine the cause-and-effect chart on page 684. What happened to the colonies of the defeated nations after World War I ended in 1918?

Interdisciplinary Activity

Citizenship Suppose that the United States was at war today. Write a law that states who is eligible to be drafted and what to do about people who refuse to serve.

America's LITERATURE

George M. Cohan (1878–1942)

As the United States entered World War I, rousing songs helped bolster the spirits of soldiers and civilians alike. Composer George M. Cohan was awarded the Medal of Honor for writing "Over There," the most popular patriotic song of the war, and for writing "You're a Grand Old Flag."

READ TO DISCOVER

As you read the lyrics for the following song, think about its purpose. How might it have helped the country's war effort? What words used by the composer are especially patriotic?

READER'S DICTIONARY

Jubilee: celebration
emblem: symbol
auld: old

You're a Grand Old Flag

There's a feeling comes a-stealing,
 And it sets my brain a-reeling,
When I'm listening to the music
 of a military band.

Any tune like "Yankee Doodle"
 Simply sets me off my noodle,
It's that patriotic something that
 no one can understand.

"Way down South, in the
 land of cotton,"
 Melody untiring,
 Ain't that inspiring?
Hurrah! Hurrah! We'll join the
Jubilee And that's going some,
 For the Yankees, by gum!

Red, white and blue, I am for you!
 Honest, you're a grand old flag!

You're a grand old flag
 You're a high flying flag
And forever in peace may
 you wave.
You're the **emblem** of
 The land I love,
The home of the free and
 the brave.
Ev'ry heart beats true
'neath the Red, White, and Blue,
Where there's never a boast
 or brag.
But should **auld** acquaintance
 be forgot
Keep your eye on the grand
 old flag.

ANALYZING LITERATURE

1. **Recall and Interpret** What does the American flag represent to Cohan?
2. **Evaluate and Connect** How does Cohan include the South in the song?

Interdisciplinary Activity

Science World War I caused a horrifying number of casualties, partly because of new technology. Research some medical practices and equipment used on the battlefield at the time. Describe these in a report. Photocopy pictures from books and encyclopedias to illustrate your report.

SECTION 5 Searching for Peace

Guide to Reading

Main Idea
Strong opposition greeted President Wilson's plans for peace.

Key Terms
Fourteen Points, League of Nations, reparations

Reading Strategy
Analyzing Information As you read the section, re-create the diagram below and identify these individuals and the role each played in the postwar era.

Individual	Identity and Role
Woodrow Wilson	
David Lloyd George	
Henry Cabot Lodge	

Read to Learn
• what principles Woodrow Wilson proposed as the basis for peace.
• why many Americans opposed the Treaty of Versailles.

Section Theme
Global Connections The end of the war brought changes to many parts of the world and an attempt to establish world peace.

Preview of Events

1919	1920	1921
1919 Paris Peace Conference begins; Treaty of Versailles is signed	**1920** Senate rejects the League of Nations	**1921** U.S. signs separate peace treaty with Central Powers

AN American Story

"We want Wilson," the war-weary crowd roared. "Long live Dr. Wilson!" British students with American flags smiled, tossing flowers in the President's path. Everywhere in Europe the Wilsons visited—Paris, Rome, Milan—the reception was jubilant. Boosted by the cheers of the European crowds, Wilson walked into the Paris Peace Conference at the Palace of Versailles with confidence. He was sure that his plan for a just and lasting peace would win swift approval both in Europe and in America.

After the War

In January 1919, world leaders from 27 nations gathered in Paris, France, for the peace conference following World War I. President Woodrow Wilson led the American delegation. When Wilson arrived in the city, enormous crowds cheered him. Well-wishers threw flowers in his path and unfurled banners that read "Long Live Wilson!" With great hope, Europeans looked to Wilson to help build a better postwar world. Yet enormous problems lay ahead.

Europe lay in ruins. Much of its landscape was devastated, its farms and towns destroyed. The human losses were terrible. France, Russia, Germany, and Austria-Hungary each lost between one and two million people in the fighting. Millions more were wounded. More than 50,000 Americans were killed in battle, while another 60,000 soldiers died from disease. Estimates for the whole war placed the number of soldiers killed worldwide at nearly 9 million. Millions of civilians also lost their lives.

Europe also faced social and political turmoil. Millions of people found themselves homeless and hungry. Civil war raged in Russia. Poles, Czechs, and other peoples struggled to form independent nations out of the collapsed empires of Turkey, Russia, and Austria-Hungary. These problems complicated the search for peace and stability.

Wilson's Fourteen Points

Woodrow Wilson had a vision of a just and lasting peace. Wilson outlined his peace plan in a proposal known as the Fourteen Points. Several of the points concerned the adjustment of boundaries in Europe and the creation of new nations. These points reflected Wilson's belief in **"national self-determination"**—the right of the people to decide how they should be governed.

Wilson also proposed a number of principles for conducting international relations. These included calls for free trade, freedom of the seas, an end to secret treaties or agreements, reductions and limits on arms, and the peaceful settlement of disputes over colonies. *(See page 993 of the Appendix for an excerpt of Wilson's Fourteen Points.)*

League of Nations

Wilson's final point concerned the creation of a League of Nations. The League's member nations would help preserve peace and prevent future wars by pledging to respect and protect one another's territory and political independence.

Wilson's Fourteen Points reflected his strong faith in the ability of governments to resolve their problems fairly. At first many Europeans welcomed Wilson's ideas. Then problems arose when the plan interfered with the competing

Total Mobilized Forces
Allies 42 million
Central Powers 23 million

Military Deaths
Allies 5.1 million
Central Powers 3.4 million

Graph Skills

Analyzing Information Which side had the larger fighting force? More casualties?

interests of the individual nations. Also, some of Wilson's points were vague. They did not propose concrete solutions to difficult questions—such as how to achieve self-determination in regions where many different ethnic groups lived closely together.

✓ **Reading Check** **Explaining** What is "national self-determination"?

The Peace Conference

The victorious Allies dominated the talks at the Paris Peace Conference. The Allies did not invite either Germany or Russia—now ruled by the Bolsheviks—to participate. The major figures in the negotiations were the Big Four—President Wilson, Prime Minister David Lloyd George of Great Britain, Premier Georges Clemenceau of France, and Prime Minister Vittorio Orlando of Italy.

The Allies Disagree

Wilson faced a difficult task. Although Europeans cheered him, their leaders showed little enthusiasm for the Fourteen Points.

While Wilson opposed punishing the defeated nations, the European Allies sought revenge. Clemenceau wanted to make sure that Germany, which had invaded France twice in

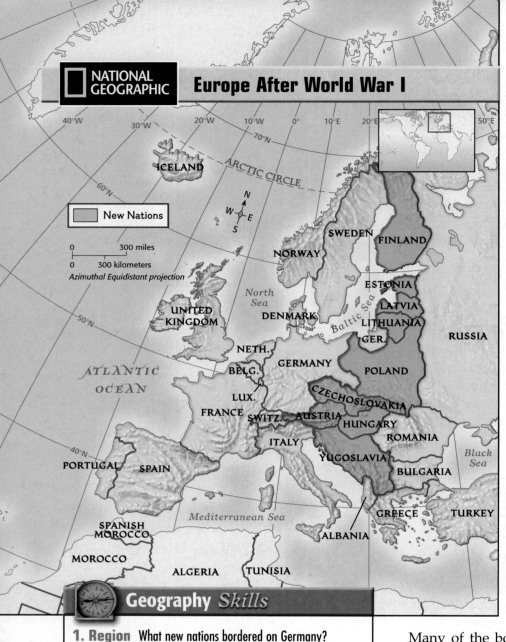

New Nations

0   300 miles
0   300 kilometers
Azimuthal Equidistant projection

ICELAND

ARCTIC CIRCLE

SWEDEN   FINLAND
NORWAY

ESTONIA
North   LATVIA
Sea   LITHUANIA
UNITED   DENMARK
KINGDOM   GER.
                          RUSSIA
NETH.   GERMANY
BELG.   POLAND
LUX.   CZECHOSLOVAKIA
FRANCE   SWITZ. AUSTRIA
                 HUNGARY
         ITALY   ROMANIA
PORTUGAL SPAIN   YUGOSLAVIA
                            BULGARIA   Black
                                        Sea
ATLANTIC
OCEAN

Mediterranean Sea   GREECE TURKEY
SPANISH   ALBANIA
MOROCCO

MOROCCO
         ALGERIA TUNISIA

Geography *Skills*

1. **Region** What new nations bordered on Germany?
2. **Analyzing Information** Which new nations did not have any coastline along a sea or ocean?

Britain, and the United States supported anti-Bolshevik forces fighting for control of Russia. All three countries sent troops to Russia.

The Treaty of Versailles

On June 28, 1919, after months of difficult negotiations, the Allies and Germany signed a treaty at the Palace of Versailles outside of Paris. The harsh terms of the treaty shocked the Germans. In defeat, however, they had no choice but to sign.

Under the terms of the **Treaty of Versailles,** Germany had to accept full responsibility for the war and to pay billions of dollars in reparations to the Allies. Germany also had to disarm completely and give up all its overseas colonies and some territory in Europe.

The treaty carved up the Austro-Hungarian and Russian Empires to create new nations or restore old ones. The emergence of these nations fulfilled part of Wilson's vision of "national self-determination." Many of the borders of the new countries were disputed, however, and this led to future conflicts.

Though disappointed by the rejection of much of his Fourteen Points, Wilson succeeded in having the League of Nations included in the treaty. He believed that the League would correct any mistakes in the rest of the treaty.

Reading Check **Explaining** What provisions about reparations were included in the Treaty of Versailles?

Opposition at Home

Wilson presented the Treaty of Versailles to the United States Senate for ratification in July 1919. "Dare we reject it and break the heart of the world?" he asked. In spite of his plea, a difficult struggle lay ahead.

his lifetime, could never invade his country again. He believed that Germany should be broken up into smaller countries. Both he and Lloyd George demanded that Germany make large reparations, or payments, for the damage Germans caused in the war. Although Wilson struggled to uphold the principles of his Fourteen Points at the Paris meeting, he was forced again and again to compromise or give in to the demands of the other Allies.

At the same time, the Allies had to decide how to deal with the new Bolshevik government of Russia. Fearing the spread of communism, France,

Many Americans had doubts about the treaty. Some thought the treaty dealt too harshly with Germany. A great many Americans worried about participation in the League of Nations, which marked a permanent American commitment to international affairs.

In 1919 the Republicans controlled the Senate, which had to ratify the treaty. Some Republican senators saw the ratification issue as a chance to embarrass President Wilson, a Democrat, and to weaken the Democratic Party before the upcoming elections of 1920. Other senators had sincere concerns about the treaty, particularly the League of Nations. A few senators opposed signing any treaty.

The most powerful opponent of the treaty was **Henry Cabot Lodge** of Massachusetts, head of the Senate Foreign Relations Committee. Lodge, a longtime foe of President Wilson, claimed that membership in the League would mean that

66American troops and American ships may be ordered to any part of the world by nations other than the United States, and that is a proposition to which I, for one, can never assent.99

Lodge delayed a vote on the treaty so that opponents could present their cases. He then proposed a number of reservations that would limit America's obligations under the treaty.

In September, Wilson went on a national speaking tour to rally support for the treaty and the League of Nations. On September 25, Wilson collapsed. The rest of his tour was canceled. Back in Washington Wilson suffered a stroke that left him partially paralyzed. During the president's illness, his wife, Edith Wilson, tried to shield him from the pressures of responsibility and took a leading role in deciding which issues were important enough to raise with him.

The Treaty Is Rejected

In the months following Wilson's stroke, opposition to the treaty grew. In March 1920, when the Senate voted on the treaty with Lodge's changes, Wilson ordered loyal Democrats to vote against it.

Opposed by most Republicans and deserted by former supporters, the Treaty of Versailles—along with the League of Nations—was rejected in the Senate. Wilson hoped the 1920 election would be a "great and solemn referendum" on the League. He even considered running for a third term. In the end, however, Wilson did not run. In 1921 the United States signed a separate peace treaty with each of the Central Powers, and it never joined the League of Nations.

Reading Check **Explaining** How did the Senate vote on the treaty?

SECTION 5 ASSESSMENT

Checking for Understanding

1. **Key Terms** Write a short article about the plans for peace after World War I; use each of these key terms: Fourteen Points, League of Nations, reparations.
2. **Reviewing Facts** What nations were created or restored through the Treaty of Versailles?

Reviewing Themes

3. **Global Connections** How did President Wilson think the League of Nations would help maintain world peace?

Critical Thinking

4. **Analyzing Information** Some Americans thought the Treaty of Versailles was too hard on Germany. What terms would you have proposed for Germany?
5. **Organizing Information** Re-create the diagram below and describe the provisions of the treaty ending World War I.

```
         Treaty of Versailles
        ┌──────┬──────┬──────┐
     ┌─────┐         ┌─────┐
     └─────┘         └─────┘
            ┌─────┐
            └─────┘
```

Analyzing Visuals

6. **Geography Skills** Examine the map on page 690 showing European borders following World War I. Which of the following was not a new nation—Poland, Latvia, or Bulgaria? Was Portugal a new nation?

Interdisciplinary Activity

Geography Compare the map of Europe after World War I to a map of Europe today. Make a list of the significant border changes that have occurred since that time.

Chapter Summary
World War I

1914
- Archduke Franz Ferdinand assassinated
- Austria-Hungary declares war on Serbia
- Germany declares war on Russia and France
- Germany invades Belgium
- Great Britain joins Allies
- Allies turn back German forces at Marne

1915
- Poison gas used for first time in battle
- Submarine warfare begins
- President Wilson declares he will keep America out of war
- *Lusitania* is sunk

1916
- French suffer heavy losses at Battle of Verdun
- President Wilson calls for Germany to stop submarine warfare

1917
- U.S. severs diplomatic relations with Germany
- U.S. declares war on Germany in April
- First American troops reach France in June

1918
- General Pershing leads the American Expeditionary Force in Europe
- Allies turn back Central Powers at Château-Thierry
- U.S. troops drive Germans out of Belleau Wood
- Allies defeat German forces at Second Battle of Marne

1919
- Treaty of Versailles signed, officially ending the Great War

Reviewing Key Terms

Examine the pairs of words below. Then write a sentence explaining what each of the pairs has in common.

1. nationalism, militarism
2. mobilization, convoy
3. Fourteen Points, League of Nations
4. espionage, sabotage

Reviewing Key Facts

5. Why did European nations form alliances?
6. Why did the Zimmermann telegram push the United States toward war?
7. What was the Sussex Pledge?
8. Who won the presidency in the election of 1916?
9. How did Russia's withdrawal affect World War I?
10. In what ways did the war help improve conditions for American workers?
11. Who were the leaders at the Paris Peace Conference?
12. What was Henry Cabot Lodge's greatest concern about the League of Nations?

Critical Thinking

13. **Science and Technology** What advantages did airplanes provide in the war?
14. **Government and Democracy** How did President Wilson use Russia's revolution in March of 1917 to gain support for the war?
15. **Analyzing Information** What four nations dominated the Paris Peace Conference?
16. **Determining Cause and Effect** Re-create the diagram below and explain the causes of the labor shortage in the United States during the war.

Practicing Skills

17. **Outlining** On a separate sheet of paper, prepare an outline of Section 5 of the text.

Geography and History Activity

Study the map below; then answer the questions that follow.

NATIONAL GEOGRAPHIC
The Western Front, 1914–1918

Map legend:
- --- Farthest German advance, 1914
- → Allied offensive, 1918
- ━ Armistice line, 1918
- ✸ Indecisive battle
- ✹ Allied victory

18. **Location** About how far from Paris was the Battle of Amiens?

19. **Movement** In which direction did Allied forces move after the battle of Ypres?

20. **Location** In what country were the battles of Amiens and Verdun fought?

Technology Activity

21. **Using the Internet** Search the Internet to find out more details about the time of the "Great War"—World War I. Use the information you find to create a chart titled "World War I—A Closer Look." Focus on causes of the war, methods of warfare, and the outcome of the war for various countries. Include numbers of casualties and costs of rebuilding.

HISTORY Online

Self-Check Quiz
Visit at taj.glencoe.com and click on **Chapter 23—Self-Check Quizzes** to prepare for the chapter test.

Citizenship Cooperative Activity

22. **Drawing Conclusions** With a partner, research primary and secondary sources about the Espionage Act of 1917. Write a one-page paper to answer these questions: Are restrictive laws necessary during wartime? Why or why not? Share your paper with your classmates.

Economics Activity

23. What effects does war have on a nation's economy? Describe at least one positive and one negative effect.

Alternative Assessment

24. **Expository Writing** Write a paragraph to explain why the League of Nations was so important to President Wilson.

Standardized Test Practice

Directions: Choose the *best* answer to the following question.

The United States did not enter World War I until 1917. Which of the following was the most important factor in convincing the American public to support the war?

A German submarine attacks against American merchant ships

B Continued loss of troops and land by the Russian army

C Failure of the British and French to defeat Germany

D The threat of a German invasion

Test-Taking Tip

This question asks you to remember a *fact* about World War I. Since most Americans favored a policy of isolation, answer **C** is not a strong enough reason to change public opinion.

Creating a Special-Edition Newspaper

How did you learn about the latest exciting national or international event? You probably heard or read about it in the mass media—newspapers, magazines, radio, and television. Throughout history the media have played a major part in shaping the opinions of Americans about national and international events. Imagine you are a news reporter. Create a newspaper that reports the events of World War I to the American public.

The Way It Was

Today almost every American receives information from the mass media. The media did not always grab the public's attention so easily though. Before the late 1800s, newspapers simply reported the news. In the late 1800s, however, newspapers started using sensational headlines. When many Americans picked up their papers and read "LUSITANIA SUNK BY A SUBMARINE, PROBABLY 1,260 DEAD," they felt angry. Many called for revenge and war against the aggressor, which many newspapers claimed was Germany. Eventually this outrage led to America's involvement in World War I. Throughout the war, while American soldiers fought with the Allies in Europe, their friends and family eagerly scanned the newspapers to learn what was happening on the war front. Americans relied on the newspapers to keep them up to date on the latest happenings. Now, create a special edition newspaper to inform Americans of an event or battle of World War I.

Believe It or Not

On November 7, 1918, Americans read in the newspapers that World War I had ended. Instantly people poured into the streets to celebrate. However, in Europe, fighting continued. The newspapers were wrong! The war really ended three days later.

Materials

✓ paper and pen or pencil
✓ access to library and/or Internet resources
✓ newspapers or magazines
✓ tape or paste
✓ a typewriter or PC (optional)

What To Do

After you have organized into groups of three or four, follow the directions below. Decide upon specific tasks for each member.

1 As a group, use your textbook or other sources to research and decide what event, situation, or person(s) will be the focus of your special-edition World War I newspaper.

2 As a group, assign the following roles to group members: historian, journalist, illustrator/cartographer, and biographer.

3 Individually, complete the research that relates to the role you have been assigned. Keep in mind that newspaper reporters focus on answering the "five W" questions when researching their stories: ***Who*** was involved, ***What*** happened, ***When*** it happened, ***Where*** it happened, and ***Why*** it happened.

4 After you complete your research, write one feature story from the viewpoint of your role. (Remember to include the five W's!) Don't forget to include a headline that will catch readers' attention.

5 Provide one another with constructive advice and revise the stories as needed.

6 Combine your final articles into a group newspaper. Work together to choose the best layout for the newspaper. Together, decide if the special-edition newspaper is complete. Is it missing some graphics? Would it look better with a cartoon or photograph? Are some of the stories too long or too short? Revise your newspaper if needed.

7 Distribute your special-edition newspaper to the class.

Project Report

1. What is the subject of your special-edition newspaper? Why did your group select this topic?

2. How did working with a group help you create a better newspaper? How might your newspaper be different if you had worked on it alone?

3. **Analyzing Information** What advice would you give to a younger student who wants to become a newspaper reporter?

Go a Step Further

Turn one of the feature stories in your newspaper into a late-breaking radio broadcast. Before writing your broadcast, consider how an audio story would be different from a written story. Read your broadcast to the class.

UNIT
9
Turbulent Decades

1919–1945

Why It Matters

As you study Unit 9, *you will examine how the Great Depression affected people's lives and the nation as a whole. You will also learn about the causes of World War II. The following resources offer more information about this period in American history.*

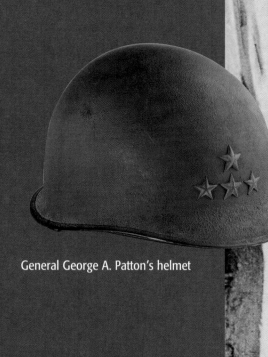

General George A. Patton's helmet

Primary Sources Library

See pages 974–975 for primary source readings to accompany Unit 9.

🖭 *Use the* **American History** **Primary Source Document Library** **CD-ROM** *to find additional primary sources about the Great Depression and World War II.*

People of Palermo, Sicily, welcome American forces, July 1943

"*The only thing we have to fear is fear itself.*"

—Franklin Delano Roosevelt, 1933

CHAPTER 24

The Jazz Age

1919–1929

Why It Matters

People called the 1920s the Jazz Age—in part because of the popular new music— but also because of the restless, carefree spirit of the time. The economy boomed and many Americans prospered. Many Americans, however, did not share in the economic gains of this era.

The Impact Today

The 1920s produced striking new changes in American society. New forms of entertainment such as radio and film remain popular today. The automobile forever changed the American way of life. It helped shift homes, shops, and factories from the inner cities to the suburbs.

 The American Journey *Video* *The chapter 24 video, "The Jazz Age," explores the development of jazz music in American culture.*

1920
* Prohibition begins
* Nineteenth Amendment grants woman suffrage

1923
* Duke Ellington forms Washingtonians

1924
* National Origins Act passed

1925
* Scopes Trial

United States
PRESIDENTS

Harding 1921–1923

Coolidge 1923–1929

1921

1923

1925

World

1922
* Joyce's *Ulysses* published
* Mussolini becomes prime minister of Italy

Safety Last Actor Harold Lloyd's movie adventures symbolized the thrills and excitement of the Jazz Age.

FOLDABLES™
Study Organizer

Explaining Vocabulary Study Foldable
To fully understand what you read you must be able to identify and explain key vocabulary terms. Use this foldable to identify, define, and use important terms in Chapter 24.

Step 1 Fold a sheet of notebook paper in half from side to side.

Step 2 On one side, cut along every third line.

Tabs will form as you cut.

Step 3 Label your foldable as you read the chapter. The first vocabulary term is labeled in the model below.

Usually forms 10 tabs.

Reading and Writing As you read the chapter, write key vocabulary terms on the front tabs of your foldable. Then write the definition of each term under the tab and write a sentence using each term correctly.

1927
- Lindbergh flies across Atlantic
- Babe Ruth hits 60 home runs
- *The Jazz Singer,* the first movie with sound, premiers

1927 *1929*

1927
- Working model of television demonstrated
- Lemaitre proposes big bang theory

1928
- Kellogg-Briand Pact signed by 15 nations
- Fleming discovers penicillin

1929
- Hubble proposes theory of expanding universe
- U.S. stock market crash triggers global depression

HISTORY Online

Chapter Overview
Visit taj.glencoe.com and click on **Chapter 24—Chapter Overviews** to preview chapter information.

Time Of Turmoil

Main Idea

World War I made some Americans intolerant—not willing to respect the beliefs or practices of others.

Key Terms

capitalism, anarchist, deport

Reading Strategy

Analyzing Information As you read the section, re-create the diagram below and answer the question for each blank.

	What was it?
The Red Scare	
Sacco-Vanzetti trial	
UNIA	

Read to Learn

- what factors contributed to prejudice toward foreigners.
- how the labor and racial unrest of the 1920s affected the nation.

Section Theme

Continuity and Change After World War I, conflicts came to the surface, especially among workers and different races.

Preview of Events

♦1910	♦1915	♦1920	♦1925
1914 Marcus Garvey founds Universal Negro Improvement Association	**1917** Bolsheviks seize control of Russia	**1920** Thousands arrested during Palmer raids	**1921** Sacco and Vanzetti declared guilty

AN
American Story

On a hot summer day in 1920, about 50,000 African Americans marched through the streets of Harlem in New York City. Thousands more lined the sidewalks, cheering the marchers. Their leader, Marcus Garvey, stirred new hope in African Americans, saying: "We are descendants of a people determined to suffer no longer." A participant at the march later recalled, "It was the greatest demonstration of [African American unity] in American history. . . ."

Fear of Radicalism

Most of the 1920s was anything but unified. During World War I, the United States government had taken away some of the liberties of American citizens. Many people who opposed the nation's role in the war were arrested. After the war an atmosphere of distrust remained. Tired of war and world responsibilities, Americans were eager to return to normal life. They grew more and more suspicious of foreigners, foreign ideas, and those who held views different from their own.

In 1919 Wilson and the world leaders attending the peace conference signed the **Treaty of Versailles.** Despite Wilson's efforts, however, the Senate refused to ratify the treaty.

At about the same time, the Russian Revolution deeply disturbed some Americans. As you read in Chapter 23, the Bolsheviks took control of Russia in November 1917 and began establishing a Communist state. They encouraged workers around the world to overthrow capitalism—an economic system based on private property and free enterprise—anywhere it existed. Many Americans feared that "bolshevism" threatened American government and institutions.

Fanning those fears were the actions of anarchists—people who believe there should be no government. A series of anarchist bombings in 1919 frightened Americans. A number of public officials—mayors, judges, and the attorney general of the United States—received packages containing bombs. One bomb blew off the hands of the maid of a United States senator. Many of the anarchists were foreign-born, which contributed to the fear of foreigners that was sweeping the country.

The Red Scare

This wave of fear led to the **Red Scare,** a period when the government went after "Reds"—as Communists were known—and others with radical views. In late 1919 and early 1920, Attorney General **A. Mitchell Palmer** and his deputy, J. Edgar Hoover, ordered the arrest of people suspected of being Communists and anarchists. Palmer and Hoover also staged raids on the headquarters of various "suspicious" groups. In the raids, the government arrested a few thousand people, ransacked homes and offices, and seized records. They did not find the large stockpiles of weapons and dynamite they claimed they were seeking.

Palmer said the raids were justified. "The blaze of revolution was sweeping over every American institution of law and order," he declared, "burning up the foundations of society." The government deported—expelled from the United States—a few hundred of the aliens it had arrested but quickly released many others for lack of evidence. In time people realized that the danger of revolution was greatly exaggerated. The Red Scare passed—but the fear underlying it remained.

Sacco and Vanzetti

Fear of immigrants and radical ideas surfaced in a criminal case in Massachusetts in 1920. Two men robbed a shoe factory in South Braintree, Massachusetts, shooting and killing a guard and

Picturing **History**

Nicola Sacco and Bartolomeo Vanzetti enter a Massachusetts courtroom, while immigrant protesters in New York City demand the freedom of the two men. **What did the Sacco and Vanzetti case reveal about the feelings of many Americans?**

Strikes, such as the 1919 steel strike, lessened public support for labor unions.

paymaster. Soon afterward the police arrested Italian immigrants **Nicola Sacco** and **Bartolomeo Vanzetti** for the crime. The two men were tried and convicted in July 1921 and were sentenced to death.

The Sacco and Vanzetti case created a furor. Neither man had a criminal record. Both men were anarchists, and Sacco owned a pistol similar to the murder weapon. Future Supreme Court justice Felix Frankfurter wrote a defense of the two men. Chief Justice William Howard Taft attacked Frankfurter for "vicious propaganda."

Many Americans demanded that the death sentence be carried out. In 1927 a special commission appointed by the governor of Massachusetts upheld the verdict. Sacco and Vanzetti—proclaiming their innocence—were executed. While historians continue to debate the verdict, the case suggested the depth of feelings against foreigners and radicals in the United States in the 1920s.

✓ Reading Check **Explaining** What is capitalism based on?

Labor Unrest

During the war years, labor and management had put aside their differences. A sense of patriotism, high wages, and wartime laws kept conflict to a minimum. When the war ended, conflict flared anew. American workers demanded increases in wages to keep up with rapidly rising prices. They launched more than 2,500 strikes in 1919. The wave of strikes fueled American fears of Bolsheviks and radicals, whom many considered to be the cause of the labor unrest.

Strikes Sweep Country

A long and bitter strike—the largest in American history to that point—occurred in the steel industry. Demanding higher wages and an eight-hour workday, about 350,000 steelworkers went on strike in September 1919. Using propaganda techniques learned during the war, the steel companies started a campaign against the strikers. In newspaper ads they accused the strikers of being "Red agitators." Charges of communism cost the strikers much needed public support and helped force them to end the strike—but not before violence had occurred on both sides. Eighteen strikers had died in a riot in Gary, Indiana.

In September 1919, police officers in **Boston** went on strike, demanding the right to form a union. This strike by public employees angered many Americans, and they applauded the strong stand Massachusetts governor **Calvin Coolidge** took against the strikers. Coolidge said,

❝ There is no right to strike against the public safety by anybody, anywhere, any time. **❞**

When the strike collapsed, officials fired the entire Boston police force. Most Americans approved of the decision.

Workers found themselves deeper in debt because of rising prices and unchanged wages. Still labor unions failed to win wide support among working families. Many Americans connected unions with radicalism and bolshevism. A growing feeling against unions, together with strong pressure from employers and the government not to join unions, led to a sharp drop in union membership in the 1920s.

During this period of union decline, a dynamic African American, **A. Philip Randolph,** started the Brotherhood of Sleeping Car Porters. Made up mostly of African Americans, this union of railroad workers struggled during its early years but began to grow in the 1930s, when government policy encouraged unions. In the 1950s and the 1960s, Randolph would emerge as a leader of the civil rights movement.

☑ **Reading Check** **Summarizing** What was the outcome of the Boston police strike?

Racial Unrest

During World War I, more than 500,000 African Americans had left the South for new jobs in the North. Many Northern whites resented African American competition for jobs.

In 1919 rising racial tensions led to violence. In the South more than 70 African Americans were lynched. In Chicago a violent riot broke out after a group of whites stoned an African American youth who was swimming in Lake Michigan. The youth drowned, and the incident set off rioting. For two weeks African American and white gangs roamed city streets, attacking each other and burning buildings. The riot left 15 whites and 23 African Americans dead and more than 500 people injured.

Many African Americans turned to **Marcus Garvey** for answers. Marcus Garvey was born to a poor family in Jamaica, the youngest of 11 children. Educated as a journalist and filled with ambition, Garvey arrived in New York City at the age of 28. A powerful leader with a magnetic personality, Garvey opposed integration. Instead he supported a "back-to-Africa" movement, urging African Americans to establish their own country in Africa. Garvey founded the **Universal Negro Improvement Association** (UNIA) in 1914 to promote racial unity and pride.

During the 1920s Garvey gained an enormous following and great influence, especially among the urban poor. Garvey told audiences that "to be a Negro is no disgrace, but an honor." With branches in many states, the UNIA organized rallies and parades to build pride and confidence among African Americans. It helped African Americans start businesses. One African American newspaper summed up Garvey's achievements: "He taught [African Americans] to admire and praise black things and black people."

☑ **Reading Check** **Explaining** Did Marcus Garvey support or oppose integration? Explain.

SECTION 1 ASSESSMENT

Checking for Understanding

1. **Key Terms** Define each of the following terms: capitalism, anarchist, deport.
2. **Reviewing Facts** Who were Sacco and Vanzetti? Explain how the fear of radicals and foreigners affected the outcome of the Sacco and Vanzetti trial.

Reviewing Themes

3. **Continuity and Change** Why was there a sharp drop in union membership during the 1920s?

Critical Thinking

4. **Drawing Conclusions** Suppose you are making a video about the life of Marcus Garvey. If he could speak to American youth today, what statement might he make?
5. **Making Generalizations** Re-create the diagram below and list the reasons organized labor had for demanding better wages after the war.

Reasons for demanding better wages

Analyzing Visuals

6. **Picturing History** Compare the photographs of the demonstrators on pages 701 and 702. What are the purposes of the demonstrations? In what ways are the photos similar? Different?

Interdisciplinary Activity

Descriptive Writing Make a list of three to five adjectives that you think describe the mood of the country during this era. Draw or paint these adjectives on poster board in a way that expresses the words' meanings.

SECTION 2 Desire for Normalcy

Guide to Reading

Main Idea
The Harding and Coolidge administrations stressed a return to government as it had been before progressivism and World War I.

Key Terms
lease, isolationism

Reading Strategy
Organizing Information As you read the section, re-create the diagram below and describe the policies the Harding and Coolidge administrations followed.

Administration policies	
Domestic affairs	Foreign affairs

Read to Learn
• what problems faced the Harding presidency.
• what policies Presidents Harding and Coolidge followed in business and foreign affairs.

Section Theme
Continuity and Change Presidents Harding and Coolidge promised to return America to normalcy after the war.

Preview of Events

◆1920		◆1925		◆1930

1920
Warren G. Harding is elected president

1922
Senate investigates Teapot Dome lease

1923
Calvin Coolidge becomes president

1928
Kellogg-Briand Pact aims to outlaw war

AN American Story

Warren G. Harding attracted attention with his friendly personality, fine voice, and handsome appearance. These glowing assets could easily make Harding president, thought political strategist Harry Daugherty. As Harding's campaign manager, Daugherty took credit for prodding Harding into the 1920 presidential race: "I found him sunning himself, like a turtle on a log, and I pushed him into the water."

The Harding Presidency

In the summer of 1920, the Republicans gathered in Chicago to nominate a candidate for president. Although confident of victory in the upcoming election, they had no outstanding leaders to head the party ticket. As one Republican noted, "There ain't any first raters this year." So party bosses chose "the best of the second raters" as their presidential candidate—Senator **Warren G. Harding** of Ohio. Harding had earned a reputation as a loyal Republican, and Ohio political boss Harry Daugherty pushed through his nomination.

Sensing Americans' longing for calm and stability after decades of progressive reform and world war, Harding declared in his campaign that "America's present need is not heroics, but healing." He promised a return to "normalcy." What Harding meant by "normalcy" was not really clear, but the word sounded reassuring to those Americans who wanted an end to foreign involvement and domestic turmoil.

As Harding's running mate, the Republicans nominated Massachusetts governor **Calvin Coolidge,** who was recognized for his firm stand in the Boston police strike. The Harding-Coolidge ticket won a landslide victory in November 1920—the first presidential election in which women could vote. The Republicans defeated the Democratic candidate, Governor **James Cox** of Ohio, and his young running mate, **Franklin Delano Roosevelt** of New York. The Republicans also made large gains in Congress.

Harding admitted having doubts about his qualifications for the presidency. He reportedly told a friend, "I knew that this job would be too much for me." He tried to compensate by appointing several talented people to the cabinet—**Charles Evans Hughes,** a former Supreme Court justice, as secretary of state; **Andrew Mellon,** a prominent Pittsburgh banker and financier, to head the Treasury Department; and **Herbert Hoover,** a talented organizer, as secretary of commerce.

The "Ohio Gang"

President Harding also gave jobs in government to many of his friends and political supporters—the so-called **Ohio Gang.** He appointed **Harry Daugherty** attorney general. He named Senator **Albert Fall** of New Mexico, a close friend, secretary of the interior. **Charles Forbes,** another friend, became head of the Veterans Bureau. Other friends of Harding filled offices throughout the administration.

Many of these appointees were unqualified; some turned out to be corrupt. By 1922 Washington buzzed with rumors of scandals within the Harding administration. Forbes, convicted of stealing funds from the Veterans Bureau, fled to avoid imprisonment. Daugherty was accused of receiving bribes but refused to resign.

Teapot Dome Scandal

The biggest scandal of the Harding administration involved Albert Fall. In 1922 Fall secretly leased, or rented, government oil reserves in Elk Hills, California, and Teapot Dome, Wyoming, to the owners of two oil companies. In exchange Fall received more than $400,000. After the scandal became public, Fall was convicted of bribery and sent to prison, becoming the first cabinet officer ever to go to jail. **Teapot Dome** became a symbol of the corruption in the Harding administration and of government corruption and scandal in general.

Harding himself was not directly involved in any scandals, but as the rumors spread, he grew increasingly distressed. "I have no trouble with my enemies," he said. "But my friends . . . they're the ones that keep me walking the floor nights!"

Warren G. Harding conducted a successful "front porch" campaign for the presidency in 1920.

Analyzing *Political Cartoons*

The cartoonist uses familiar images of the 1920s. "Big Business", portrayed as a carefree "flapper" girl, dances to jazz music played by President Coolidge. **What was the relationship between government and business during Coolidge's presidency?**

Although Coolidge and Harding differed in style, they held similar political views. Coolidge believed that the best government was the least government and that government should not interfere in the life of the nation. He once said approvingly, "If the federal government should go out of existence, the common run of the people would not detect the difference for a considerable length of time."

In the summer of 1923, before the full story of the scandals came out, Harding escaped the stresses of Washington, D.C., by taking a trip west. During the trip he became ill, suffered a heart attack, and died.

Vice President Calvin Coolidge was visiting his father in Vermont when he was awakened in the early morning hours of August 3, 1923, with the news of President Harding's death. Coolidge's father, a justice of the peace, administered the presidential oath of office. Then the new president—in characteristic Coolidge fashion—calmly turned off the lights and went back to bed.

Honesty Returns to the White House

Calvin Coolidge was in many ways the complete opposite of Harding. While Harding loved to talk and meet people, Coolidge said very little and earned the name "Silent Cal." In addition, Coolidge had a reputation for honesty. After becoming president, he allowed the investigations into the Harding scandals to proceed without interference. He fired Daugherty and replaced the remaining members of the Ohio Gang with honest officials.

A Friend to Business

Under President Coolidge the government took an active role in supporting business. As the president explained, "The chief business of the American people is business. . . . The man who builds a factory builds a temple."

Coolidge and the Republican-dominated Congress aimed to create a favorable climate for business to promote the nation's economic prosperity. The government lowered income tax rates on the wealthiest Americans and on corporate profits and cut government spending. It also raised tariffs to protect American business and overturned laws regulating child labor and wages for women.

A New Term

Coolidge seemed to be exactly what the country wanted. At the Republican national convention in 1924, the president was nominated without opposition. The Democrats took more than 100 ballots to nominate a little-known lawyer, John W. Davis of West Virginia, as their presidential candidate. Wisconsin senator Robert La Follette led a third party, the Progressives, in the race. Coolidge swept the 1924 presidential election with 54 percent of the popular vote. For the first time in America's history, women won governors' races—**Nellie Tayloe Ross** in Wyoming and **Miriam Ferguson** in Texas.

✓ **Reading Check** **Comparing** Do you think Coolidge followed Harding's policies about business? Explain.

Foreign Policy

Harding and Coolidge both favored a limited role for the nation in world affairs. They desired world peace but did not want the nation to join the League of Nations or become involved in international disagreements. Harding had promised the American people that he would not lead them into the League "by the side door, back door, or cellar door." Many Americans supported this policy of isolationism.

Promoting Peace

The Harding administration made serious efforts to promote peace. After the war the United States, Great Britain, and Japan began a naval arms race. In 1921 Secretary of State Hughes invited Japan and Britain to Washington, D.C., to discuss the problem. In February 1922 the three nations, along with France and Italy, signed the **Five-Power Treaty** to limit the size of the nations' navies. The treaty marked the first time in modern history that world powers agreed to disarm.

The United States continued working for peace. In August 1928, it joined 14 other nations in signing the **Kellogg-Briand Pact,** which called for outlawing war. Within a few years, 48 other nations had signed the pact, but it lacked any means of enforcing peace.

A More Friendly Neighbor

The United States had intervened in Latin American countries several times in the early 1900s to support American business interests. When Harding took office, American troops were stationed in Haiti, the **Dominican Republic,** and **Nicaragua,** and relations with Mexico were tense.

After the Dominican Republic and Nicaragua held elections in the mid-1920s, the United States withdrew its troops from those countries.

At about the same time, American investors asked President Coolidge to send troops into Mexico when its government threatened to take over foreign-owned oil and mining companies. Coolidge chose to negotiate instead, and the United States reached a settlement with Mexico.

✓ **Reading Check** **Explaining** Why would the Kellogg-Briand Pact prove to be ineffective?

SECTION 2 ASSESSMENT

Checking for Understanding

1. **Key Terms** Use the terms lease and isolationism in separate sentences that will help explain their meanings.
2. **Reviewing Facts** Where was Teapot Dome? What did Teapot Dome come to symbolize?

Reviewing Themes

3. **Continuity and Change** What actions did the United States take to promote world peace in the 1920s?

Critical Thinking

4. **Comparing** What role did Harding and Coolidge think the government should play in people's lives?
5. **Making Generalizations** Re-create the diagram below and list two ways the United States government worked to promote American business.

Analyzing Visuals

6. **Political Cartoons** Study the cartoon on page 706. Who do the figures represent? What image of the Federal government does the cartoon portray?

Interdisciplinary Activity

Art Draw a political cartoon that illustrates an example of an event that took place during the Harding presidency. Make sure to include a caption with your cartoon.

Critical Thinking SKILLBUILDER

Making Generalizations

Why Learn This Skill?

If you say "We have a great football team," you are making a generalization, or general statement, about your team. If you go on to say that your team has not lost a game this season and is the top-ranked team, you are providing evidence to support your generalization. When you are studying history, it is often necessary to put together pieces of information, called supporting statements, to arrive at a full picture.

Learning the Skill

In some cases, authors provide only supporting statements, and you need to make the generalizations on your own.

To make generalizations, follow these steps:
- Identify the subject matter.
- Gather facts and examples related to it.
- Identify similarities or patterns among these facts.
- Use these similarities or patterns to form some general ideas about the subject.

Practicing the Skill

Read the passage and the generalizations. Then answer the questions that follow.

By 1927, 4 out of 5 cars had closed tops, compared with only 1 in 10 in 1919. Now protected from the weather, many families hopped into their cars for short day trips. Many city workers moved to houses in the new suburbs. Car owners now traveled easily to once-distant places, bringing far-flung Americans together for the first time.

Generalizations About the Automobile
a. Automobiles were too expensive to buy.
b. The automobile changed American culture in many ways.
c. Many businesses arose from the need to service the newly mobile nation.
d. Suburbs grew as a result of the automobile.

1 Which of the generalizations above are supported by the details in this passage?

2 Write one or two statements that support each of these generalizations.

3 Which of the generalizations are not supported by the passage? Explain.

Applying the Skill

Making Generalizations Make a general statement about your class that describes it. Then write three or four supporting details for that generalization.

GO TO

Glencoe's **Skillbuilder Interactive Workbook CD-ROM, Level 1,** provides instruction and practice in key social studies skills.

Traffic jam, 1920s

A Booming Economy

Guide to Reading

Main Idea

The United States experienced periods of prosperity and economic expansion during the 1920s.

Key Terms

recession, gross national product, productivity, installment buying

Reading Strategy

Analyzing Information As you read the section, re-create the diagram below and describe how these ideas affected the American economy.

	Effect on economy
Scientific management	
Assembly line	
Installment buying	

Read to Learn

• how the prosperity of the 1920s affected the nation and the American people.
• what impact the automobile had on American life.

Section Theme

Economic Factors After a brief postwar recession, the American economy began a steady growth that lasted for most of the 1920s.

Preview of Events

♦1920 ♦1925 ♦1930

1920s Stock market booms

1922 GNP reaches $70 billion

1924 Model T sells for less than $300

1929 Electricity runs 70 percent of factories

AN American Story

During the "golden age of the automobile" in the 1920s, the car became a vital part of many Americans' lives. A mother of nine children said that her family "would rather do without clothes than give up the car." In the past, they had wanted to visit her sister-in-law, but by the time the children were "shoed and dressed" there wasn't any money left to pay for trolley fare. "Now no matter how [the children] look, we just poke 'em in the car and take 'em along."

Growth in the 1920s

After World War I, the American economy experienced problems readjusting to peacetime. Millions of soldiers returned, entering the labor force and competing for jobs. Government orders for wartime goods came to a halt, forcing many companies to lay off workers. Other companies went bankrupt. Prices rose, making it hard for workers to make ends meet. This economic downturn, or recession, lasted about two years. The economy then began a steady growth that lasted most of the decade. In 1922 the nation's gross national product

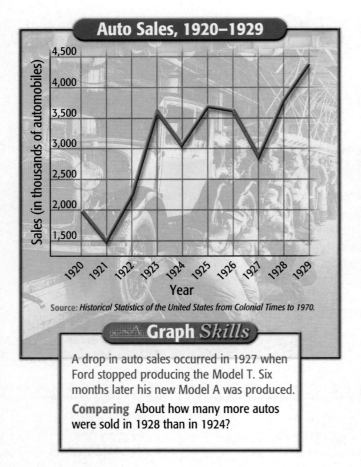

Auto Sales, 1920–1929

Sales (in thousands of automobiles)

Year

Source: *Historical Statistics of the United States from Colonial Times to 1970.*

Graph Skills

A drop in auto sales occurred in 1927 when Ford stopped producing the Model T. Six months later his new Model A was produced.

Comparing About how many more autos were sold in 1928 than in 1924?

(GNP)—the total value of all goods and services produced—was $70 billion. By 1929 it had risen to $100 billion!

Technology made rapid industrial growth possible, and electricity powered American industry. Before World War I, only 30 percent of factories were run by electricity. By 1929 this figure had risen to 70 percent. Electricity was cheaper than steam power. By cutting costs, businesses could lower prices and increase profits.

Scientific Management

New ways of managing operations contributed to economic growth as well. Many employers used **scientific management**—hiring experts to study how goods could be produced more quickly. By adopting new work methods, businesses tried to lower costs and increase productivity—the amount of work each worker could do.

Many businesses adopted mass production techniques using the **assembly line,** which was first introduced in Henry Ford's automobile factories. Assembly line methods increased productivity and cut production costs.

Worker Relations

Businesses tried to build better relations with workers. Many companies set up safety programs that lowered the risk of death or injury on the job. Some began to provide health and accident insurance. Many companies encouraged workers to buy stock in the company. These steps—known as **welfare capitalism**—were designed to link workers more closely to the company they worked for. Business also adopted these steps to discourage workers from joining independent unions.

The Consumer Economy

American industry changed in another way as well. As electricity became more available, demand grew for appliances using electric power. By the 1920s, more than 60 percent of American households had electricity. Consumers eagerly acquired refrigerators, stoves, vacuum cleaners, fans, and radios. As demand for these items grew, more and more of them were produced, leading to reduced production costs and lower prices. Between 1920 and 1929, for example, the cost of a refrigerator dropped from $600 to $300.

These appliances transformed daily life. People did not have to spend as much time on household chores. Now they had more leisure time.

In the 1920s successful companies joined with or purchased competitors. Three companies—Ford, General Motors, and Chrysler—dominated the auto industry. One grocery chain—the Great Atlantic and Pacific Tea Company (A&P)—had more than 15,000 stores across the country. Businesses became national as the products of many local companies were replaced by national brands.

To market those national brands, businesses spent more and more money on advertising. Propaganda techniques learned during World War I were now used to persuade consumers to buy a particular brand of toothpaste, clothing, or soap. Newspapers and magazines were filled with ads, and with the spread of radio a new advertising form—the commercial announcement—was born.

Spurred by ads to buy more and more, consumers found a new way to make those purchases—installment buying. Consumers could now buy products by promising to pay small, regular amounts over a period of time. One critic of installment buying called the system "a dollar down and a dollar a week forever." The installment method of buying boosted consumer spending.

✓ **Reading Check** **Explaining** Why did the price of some consumer goods decrease?

The Automobile Age

More often than not, people used the installment plan to buy a new car. During the 1920s, automobile registrations jumped from 8 million to 23 million. America quickly became a "car culture," in which people's lives revolved around the automobile. The nation's economy, too, revolved around the automobile. Almost four million Americans worked for auto companies or in related jobs. **Detroit, Michigan,** became the automobile manufacturing center of the world.

Henry Ford was a pioneer in the manufacture of affordable automobiles with his **Model T,** which was built using assembly line methods. The car was sturdy, reliable, inexpensive, and available only in black. In 1914 Ford stunned the auto industry—and all corporate leaders, for that matter—by announcing that he would pay his workers the high wage of $5 per day. Workers were happy, and Ford had more potential customers as he steadily dropped the price of his Model T. By 1924 the car sold for less than $300. With the average industrial worker earning about $1,300 a year, many families could afford to buy a Model T.

TECHNOLOGY *& History*

Henry Ford's Assembly Line

The industrial boom of the 1920s owed much to the assembly line Henry Ford first used in 1913–1914. Parts moved on a conveyor belt. Workers attached the parts to cars moving past them at a steady speed of six feet per minute.

How large was Ford's plant?

Henry Ford

1 **Tires** are put on the **wheels** and dropped down rollways.

2 **Tanks** filled with one gallon of gas slide from the "Tank Bridge."

3 **Engines** built on the third floor are lowered onto the chassis.

4 **Radiators** arrive from the far end of the 60-acre factory.

5 Auto **bodies** are assembled on the second floor, then lowered through the ceiling onto the moving chassis.

By the mid-1920s,
other automobile models
challenged the Model T.
General Motors cut into
Ford's sales by offering a
line of cars in a range of
colors and with features
to improve passenger
comfort. In 1927 Ford
responded with the **Model A,** which had better
engineering and came in several colors. Out of
this competition came the practice of introducing
new car models each year.

Effect on Other Industries

The automobile had a tremendous impact on
other American industries. Americans' love of
driving called for new roads and highways.
Highways, in turn, needed gas stations and rest
stops. Businesses along major roads profited
from the millions of people now traveling around
the country by car. Tourism grew dramatically.

The car boom affected industries that made
products used in cars. The steel, rubber, and
glass industries grew. During the 1920s the oil
industry shifted from producing lubricants to
refining gasoline for automobiles.

The automobile dramatically changed the
lives of many Americans. Travel for pleasure
became a regular part of American life. People
could now go wherever they wished. Cars also

contributed to the spread of suburbs. Because
people could now drive to work, they could live
in a suburb and still hold a job in the city.

Those Left Behind

Despite all the signs of prosperity, many
Americans did not share in the boom of the
1920s. Farmers had an especially difficult time.
During the war, the federal government had
purchased wheat, corn, and other products, and
farmers had prospered from higher prices.
When the war ended, farmers had to compete
with European agriculture again. Food prices
fell, and farm income plummeted. Unable to pay
their debts, many farmers lost their farms.

Farmers were not the only ones feeling the
pinch. Those who worked in the railroad and coal
mining industries had a difficult time as trucks
took business from railroads and electricity
replaced coal as a power source. Americans now
were buying less cotton and more clothes made
of synthetic fibers. As cotton prices plunged,
many textile factories were forced to shut down.
Wages rose slightly for most workers, but the cost
of living rose more. By 1929 nearly three-fourths
of families had incomes below $2,500, the
accepted level necessary for a comfortable life.

✓ Reading Check **Explaining** What action did Henry
Ford take when other auto manufacturers offered new lines
of cars?

SECTION 3 ASSESSMENT

Checking for Understanding

1. **Key Terms** Define each of the following terms: recession, gross
national product, productivity,
installment buying.
2. **Reviewing Facts** Describe the economic problems that existed in
America after World War I.

Reviewing Themes

3. **Economic Factors** How did the auto
industry help boost other industries?

Critical Thinking

4. **Drawing Conclusions** How did welfare capitalism discourage people
from joining unions?
5. **Organizing Information** Re-create
the diagram below and identify three
factors that helped to bring about a
strong economy.

Analyzing Visuals

6. **Graph Skills** Study the graph on
page 710. In which year did auto
sales first pass three million?

Interdisciplinary Activity

Math Research the total auto sales
for a recent 10-year period. Compare your findings with the graph
on page 710. Write a paragraph
comparing the two sets of figures.
Include any conclusions you reach.

SECTION 4 The Roaring Twenties

Guide to Reading

Main Idea
Many Americans favored traditional values, while others favored change.

Key Terms
flapper, mass media, expatriate, Prohibition, nativism, quota system, evolution

Reading Strategy
Organizing Information As you read the section, re-create the diagram below and describe the accomplishments of these individuals.

	Accomplishments
Charles Lindbergh	
Bessie Smith	
Langston Hughes	
Ernest Hemingway	

Read to Learn
• how lifestyles in America changed in the 1920s.
• what cultural clashes occurred in the United States in the 1920s.

Section Theme
Continuity and Change The Roaring Twenties were a time of changing attitudes and clashing cultures.

Preview of Events

♦1920   ♦1925   ♦1930

1920
Nineteenth Amendment grants woman suffrage

1924
Congress passes National Origins Act

1927
Lindbergh flies solo across the Atlantic

1928
Herbert Hoover is elected president

AN American Story

On the evening of May 19, 1927, a young pilot named Charles Lindbergh learned that, although it was drizzling on Long Island, the weather reports predicted fair skies for his miraculous trip. He decided to get ready. Throughout a sleepless night, Lindbergh made the final preparations for takeoff. Shortly before 8:00 A.M., Lindbergh climbed into his aircraft and took off for Paris. With the news of his departure "flashing along the wires," the American people were united in "the exaltation of a common emotion." All minds and hearts were focused on the brave pilot who was crossing the vast Atlantic Ocean.

New Directions

In May 1927, aviator **Charles Lindbergh** became the first person to fly alone across the Atlantic Ocean. He did so in a tiny, single-engine plane named the *Spirit of St. Louis*. Americans went wild and hailed a new hero. Cities across the nation held parades to honor Lindbergh—in New York City well-wishers threw

CHAPTER 24   The Jazz Age   **713**

started professional careers, and more women worked after marriage. But the vast majority of married women remained within the home, working as homemakers and mothers.

The flapper symbolized the new "liberated" woman of the 1920s. Pictures of flappers—carefree young women with short, "bobbed" hair, heavy makeup, and short skirts—appeared in magazines. Many people saw the bold, boyish look and shocking behavior of flappers as a sign of changing morals. Though hardly typical of American women, the flapper image reinforced the idea that women now had more freedom. Prewar values had shifted, and many people were beginning to challenge traditional ways.

✔ Reading Check Describing What did the Nineteenth Amendment guarantee?

Flappers reflected the modern spirit of the Jazz Age.

Movie poster, 1926

1,800 tons of paper streamers—and newspapers reported on his every move. The national embrace of Lindbergh showed what one historian called a "delighted concern over things that were exciting but didn't matter profoundly."

Changes for Women

The 1920s did bring profound changes for women. One important change took place with the ratification of the **Nineteenth Amendment** in 1920. The amendment guaranteed women in all states the right to vote. Women also ran for election to political offices. 📖 *(See page 249 for the text of the Nineteenth Amendment.)*

Throughout the 1920s the number of women holding jobs outside the home continued to grow. Most women had to take jobs considered "women's" work, such as teaching and working in offices as clerks and typists. At the same time, increasing numbers of college-educated women

Entertainment

Changes in attitudes spread quickly because of the growth of mass media—forms of communication, such as newspapers and radio, that reach millions of people. Laborsaving devices and fewer working hours gave Americans more leisure time. In those nonworking hours, they enjoyed tabloid-style newspapers, large-circulation magazines, phonograph records, the radio, and the movies.

The Movies and Radio

In the 1920s the motion picture industry in **Hollywood,** California, became one of the country's leading businesses. For millions of Americans, the movies offered entertainment and escape.

The first movies were black and white and silent, with the actors' dialog printed on the screen and a pianist playing music to accompany the action. In 1927 Hollywood introduced movies with sound. The first "talkie," _The Jazz Singer,_ created a sensation.

The radio brought entertainment into people's homes in the 1920s. In 1920 the first commercial radio broadcast, which carried the presidential election returns, was transmitted by station KDKA in Pittsburgh. In the next three years nearly 600 stations joined the airwaves.

The networks broadcast popular programs across the nation. The evening lineup of programs included something for everyone—news, concerts, sporting events, and comedies. Radio offered listeners a wide range of music—opera, classical, country and western, blues, and jazz. *Amos 'n' Andy* and the *Grand Ole Opry* were among the hit shows of the 1920s. Families sat down to listen to the radio together.

Businesses soon realized that the radio offered an enormous audience for messages about their products, so they began to help finance radio programs. Radio stations sold spot advertisements, or commercials, to companies.

Sports and Fads

Among the favorite radio broadcasts of the 1920s were athletic events. Baseball, football, and boxing soared in popularity. Americans flocked to sporting events, and more people participated in sports activities as well.

Sports stars became larger-than-life heroes. Baseball fans idolized **Babe Ruth,** the great outfielder, who hit 60 home runs in 1927—a record that would stand for 34 years. Football star Red Grange, who once scored four touchdowns in 12 minutes, became a national hero. Golfer Bobby Jones and Gertrude Ederle, the first woman to swim the English Channel, became household names.

In the 1920s Americans took up new activities with enthusiasm, turning them into fads. The Chinese board game *mah-jongg* (mah•ZHAHNG) and crossword puzzles were all the rage. Contests such as flagpole sitting and dance marathons—often lasting three or four days—made headlines. Americans also loved the Miss America Pageant, which was first held in 1921.

✓ **Reading Check** **Comparing** What fads were popular in the 1920s? What are two comparable fads today?

The Jazz Age

During the 1920s people danced to the beat of a new kind of music called jazz. Jazz captured the spirit of the era so well that the 1920s is often referred to as the **Jazz Age.**

Jazz had its roots in the South in African American work songs and in African music. A blend of ragtime and blues, it uses dynamic rhythms and **improvisation**—new rhythms and melodies created during a performance. Among the best-known African American jazz musicians were trumpeter **Louis Armstrong,** pianist and composer **Duke Ellington,** and singer **Bessie Smith.** White musicians such as Paul Whiteman and Bix Biederbecke also played jazz and helped bring it to a wider audience.

Interest in jazz spread through radio and phonograph records. Jazz helped create a unique African American recording industry. Equally important, jazz gave America one of its most distinctive art forms.

Harlem Renaissance

The rhythm and themes of jazz inspired the poetry of **Langston Hughes,** an African American writer. In the 1920s, Hughes joined the growing number of African American writers and artists who gathered in **Harlem,** an African American section of New York City. Hughes described his arrival in Harlem:

❝I can never put on paper the thrill of the underground ride to Harlem. I went up the steps and out into the bright September sunlight. Harlem! I stood there, dropped my bags, took a deep breath and felt happy again.❞ *Langston Hughes*

Harlem witnessed a burst of creativity in the 1920s—a flowering of African American culture called the **Harlem Renaissance.** This movement instilled an interest in African culture and pride in being African American.

During the Harlem Renaissance, many writers wrote about the African American experience in novels, poems, and short stories. Along with Hughes were writers like James Weldon Johnson, Claude McKay, Countee Cullen, and Zora Neale Hurston.

Bessie Smith

Jazz record label

"MA" RAINEY'S
Dream Blues
with Two Guitar Accompaniment
by The Pruit Twins
Paramount
12098

Based in New Orleans, King Oliver's Creole Jazz Band was one of the best and most important bands in early jazz.

A Lost Generation of Writers

At the same time that the Harlem Renaissance blossomed, other writers were questioning American ideals. Disappointed with American values and in search of inspiration, they settled in Paris. These writers were called expatriates—people who choose to live in another country. Writer **Gertrude Stein** called these rootless Americans "the lost generation."

Novelist **F. Scott Fitzgerald** and his wife, Zelda, joined the expatriates in Europe. In *Tender Is the Night*, Fitzgerald wrote of people who had been damaged emotionally by World War I. They were dedicated, he said,

❝to the fear of poverty and the worship of success.❞

Another famous American expatriate was novelist **Ernest Hemingway,** whose books *The Sun Also Rises* and *A Farewell to Arms* reflected the mood of Americans in postwar Europe.

While some artists fled the United States, others stayed home and wrote about life in America. Novelist **Sinclair Lewis** presented a critical view of American culture in such books as *Main Street* and *Babbitt*. Another influential American writer was **Sherwood Anderson.** In his most famous book, *Winesburg, Ohio*, Anderson explored small-town life in the Midwest.

✓ **Reading Check** **Describing** What type of music did Louis Armstrong play?

Prohibition

During the 1920s the number of people living in cities swelled, and a modern industrial society came of age. Outside of the cities, many Americans identified this new, urban society with crime, corruption, and immoral behavior. They believed that the America they knew and valued—a nation based on family, church, and tradition—was under attack. Disagreement grew between those who defended traditional beliefs and those who welcomed the new.

The clash of cultures during the 1920s affected many aspects of American life, particularly the use of alcoholic beverages. The temperance movement, the campaign against alcohol use, had begun in the 1800s. The movement was rooted both in religious objections to drinking alcohol and in the belief that society would benefit if alcohol were unavailable.

The movement finally achieved its goal in 1919 with the ratification of the **Eighteenth Amendment** to the Constitution. This amendment established Prohibition—a total ban on the manufacture, sale, and transportation of liquor throughout the United States. Congress passed the **Volstead Act** to provide the means of enforcing the ban. In rural areas in the South and the Midwest, where the temperance movement was strong, Prohibition generally succeeded. In the cities, however, Prohibition had little support. The nation divided into two camps: the "drys"—those who supported Prohibition—and the "wets"—those who opposed it.

Consequences of the Ban

A continuing demand for alcohol led to widespread lawbreaking. Some people began making wine or "bathtub gin" in their homes. Illegal bars and clubs, known as speakeasies, sprang up in cities. Hidden from view, these clubs could be entered only by saying a secret password.

With only about 1,500 agents, the federal government could do little to enforce the Prohibition laws. By the early 1920s, many states in the East stopped trying to enforce the laws.

Prohibition contributed to the rise of organized crime. Recognizing that millions of dollars could be made from **bootlegging**—making and selling illegal alcohol—members of organized crime moved in quickly and took control. They used their profits to gain influence in businesses, labor unions, and governments.

Crime boss Al "Scarface" Capone controlled organized crime and local politics in Chicago. Defending his involvement in illegal alcohol, Capone said,

❝I make my money by supplying a popular demand. If I break the law, my customers are as guilty as I am.❞

Eventually, Capone was arrested and sent to prison.

Al Capone

Over time many Americans realized that the "noble experiment," as Prohibition was called, had failed. Prohibition was repealed in 1933 with the **Twenty-first Amendment.** 📖 *(See pages 249 and 250 for the text of the Eighteenth and Twenty-first Amendments.)*

✔️ **Reading Check** **Analyzing** Why was Prohibition difficult to enforce?

Nativism

The anxieties many native-born Americans felt about the rapid changes in society contributed to an upsurge of nativism—the belief that native-born Americans are superior to foreigners. With this renewed nativism came a revival of the **Ku Klux Klan.**

As you read in Chapter 17, the first Klan had been founded in the 1860s in the South to control newly freed African Americans through the use of threats and violence. The second Klan, organized in 1915, still preyed on African Americans, but it had other targets as well—Catholics, Jews, immigrants, and other groups believed to represent "un-American" values.

In the 1920s the new Klan spread from the South to other areas of the country, gaining considerable power in such states as Indiana and Oregon and in many large cities. For the most part, the Klan used pressure and scare tactics to get its way, but sometimes Klan members whipped or lynched people or burned property.

The Klan began to decline in the late 1920s, however, largely as a result of scandals and power struggles involving Klan leaders. Membership shrank, and politicians who had been supported by the Klan were voted out of office.

The concerns of the Red Scare days had not completely disappeared. Some Americans feared foreign radicals would overthrow the government. Others believed foreigners would take away their jobs. This anti-immigrant prejudice was directed mainly at southern and eastern Europeans and Asians.

People In History

Will Rogers 1879-1935

Part Native American, Will Rogers grew up in the West roping cattle and riding on the range. He landed jobs with Wild West shows and soon perfected his riding and trick-roping act, which, along with his personality and sense of humor, made him a star.

By 1920 Will Rogers was starring on both stage and screen. A daily newspaper column he started in 1926 spread his humorous views on life and politics. Claiming "I don't make jokes—I just watch the government and report the facts," he poked fun in a light-hearted way and was never hostile. One of his favorite sayings was "I never met a man I didn't like."

By the late 1920s, audiences were listening to his commentary on the radio. To Americans, Rogers had become a national treasure. They mourned when Rogers died in a plane crash near Point Barrow, Alaska, in August 1935.

In 1921 Congress responded to nativist fears by passing the **Emergency Quota Act.** This law established a quota system, an arrangement placing a limit on the number of immigrants from each country. According to the act, only 3 percent of the total number of people in any national group already living in the United States would be admitted during a single year. Because there had been fewer immigrants from southern and eastern Europe than from northern and western Europe at that time, the law favored northern and western European immigrants.

Congress revised the immigration law in 1924. The **National Origins Act** reduced the annual country quota from 3 to 2 percent and based it on the census of 1890—when even fewer people from southern or eastern Europe lived in America. The law excluded Japanese immigrants completely. An earlier law, passed in 1890, had already excluded the Chinese.

These quota laws did not apply to countries in the Western Hemisphere. As a result, immigration of Canadians and Mexicans increased. By 1930 more than one million Mexicans had come to live in the United States.

✓ Reading Check **Describing** What is a quota system?

The Scopes Trial

Another cultural clash in the 1920s involved the role of religion in society. This conflict gained national attention in 1925 in one of the most famous trials of the era.

In 1925 the state of Tennessee passed a law making it illegal to teach evolution—the scientific theory that humans evolved over vast periods of time. The law was supported by Christian fundamentalists, who accepted the biblical story of creation. The fundamentalists saw evolution as a challenge to their values and their religious beliefs.

A young high school teacher named John Scopes deliberately broke the law against teaching evolution so that a trial could test its legality. Scopes acted with the support of the American Civil Liberties Union (ACLU). During the sweltering summer of 1925, the nation followed day-to-day developments in the **Scopes trial** with great interest. More than a hundred journalists from around the country descended on Dayton, Tennessee, to report on the trial.

Two famous lawyers took opposing sides in the trial. **William Jennings Bryan,** Democratic candidate for president in 1896, 1900, and 1908 and a strong opponent of evolution, led the prosecution. **Clarence Darrow,** who had defended many radicals and labor union members, spoke for Scopes.

Although Scopes was convicted of breaking the law and fined $100, the fundamentalists lost the larger battle. Darrow's defense made it appear that Bryan wanted to impose his religious beliefs on the entire nation. The Tennessee Supreme Court overturned Scopes's conviction, and other states decided not to prosecute similar cases.

The Scopes case may have dealt a blow to fundamentalism, but the movement continued to thrive. Rural people, especially in the South and Midwest, remained faithful to their religious beliefs. When large numbers of farmers migrated to cities during the 1920s, they brought fundamentalism with them.

✓ **Reading Check** **Explaining** What law did Scopes challenge?

The Election of 1928

In 1927 President Coolidge shocked everyone by announcing that he would not run for a second full term. **Herbert Hoover** declared his candidacy for the Republican nomination.

During World War I, Hoover had won respect as the head of a committee providing food relief for Europe. He showed such a gift in the role that "to Hooverize" came to mean "to economize, to save and share." Later, Hoover served Presidents Harding and Coolidge as secretary of commerce.

Hoover worked tirelessly to promote cooperation between government and business. A symbol of the forward-looking middle class, he easily won the Republican nomination.

The Democrats chose a far different kind of candidate—**Alfred E. Smith,** governor of New York. The son of immigrants and a man of the city, Smith opposed Prohibition and championed the poor and the working class. As the first Roman Catholic nominee for president, Smith was the target of anti-Catholic feeling. Hoover won the election by a landslide due to both the Republican prosperity of the 1920s and the prejudice against Smith. The contest reflected many of the tensions in American society—rural versus urban life, nativism versus foreign influences, "wets" versus "drys," Protestants versus Catholics, traditional values versus modern values.

✓ **Reading Check** **Identifying** Who was elected president in 1928?

SECTION 4 ASSESSMENT

Checking for Understanding

1. **Key Terms** Use each of these terms in a sentence that will help explain its meaning: flapper, mass media, expatriate, Prohibition, nativism, quota system, evolution.
2. **Reviewing Facts** What was the Harlem Renaissance? Name two writers associated with it.

Reviewing Themes

3. **Continuity and Change** How did the Scopes trial reflect the desire of many Americans to return to traditional values?

Critical Thinking

4. **Making Generalizations** Why do you think Gertrude Stein referred to many American writers as "the lost generation"?
5. **Drawing Conclusions** Re-create the diagram below and describe how each person contributed to his or her field.

	Contribution
Sherwood Anderson	
Countee Cullen	
Louis Armstrong	

Analyzing Visuals

6. **Picturing History** Study the photos on page 716. What does the mood of the country seem to be at this time? Write a short paragraph in which you explain your analysis.

Interdisciplinary Activity

Reading Find and read a poem by a writer who interests you. Find illustrations and photographs that help to communicate the meaning of the poem. Display the poem and illustrations on poster board.

Chapter Summary

The Jazz Age

Time of Turmoil

- Fear of communism grows.
- Labor strikes occur.
- Racial tensions grow.
- Voters elect leaders who promise isolation.
- Harding's administration is marred by scandal.
- Coolidge continues Harding's pro-business economic policies.

A Booming Economy

- Demand grows for products.
- Installment buying boosts consumer spending.
- The auto industry brings benefits and changes.

The Roaring Twenties

- Women gain the right to vote through the Nineteenth Amendment.
- Mass media grows.
- Entertainment industry grows.
- Harlem Renaissance instills interest in African culture.

Clashing Cultures

- The Eighteenth Amendment establishes Prohibition. The Twenty-first Amendment repeals Prohibition.
- Nativism helps revive the Ku Klux Klan.
- Congress passes quota laws to limit immigration.
- The Scopes trial symbolizes the tensions of the 1920s.

Reviewing Key Terms

On a sheet of paper, use the following vocabulary words to write two paragraphs about the decade of the 1920s.

1. isolationism
2. gross national product
3. installment buying
4. Prohibition
5. quota system

Reviewing Key Facts

6. What is capitalism?
7. How did Calvin Coolidge respond to the 1919 Boston police strike?
8. Who were the presidential candidates in 1920?
9. What did the Five-Power Treaty limit?
10. What is installment buying?
11. What did Charles Lindbergh accomplish?
12. Name three important jazz musicians.

Critical Thinking

13. **Determining Cause and Effect** How was the Red Scare used to turn the public against unions?
14. **Reviewing Themes: Global Connections** How did President Harding feel about the League of Nations?
15. **Analyzing Information** What new forms of entertainment were available to the American people in the 1920s as a result of new technology?
16. **Economic Factors** Re-create the diagram below and describe what you think are the advantages and disadvantages of scientific management.

Scientific management	
Advantages	Disadvantages

Citizenship Cooperative Activity

17. **The Political Process** With a partner, find out how political parties in your state nominate candidates for office. Then interview neighbors who are active in a political party. If any of them have participated in the nominating process, ask them about their experiences. Prepare a brochure on the nominating process to distribute in your neighborhood.

Geography and History Activity

Study the graph below; then answer the questions that follow.

Self-Check Quiz
Visit **taj.glencoe.com** and click on **Chapter 24—Self-Check Quizzes** to prepare for the chapter test.

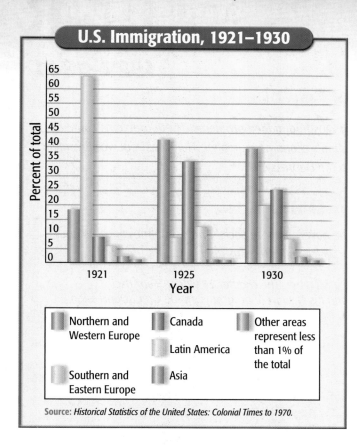

U.S. Immigration, 1921–1930

Percent of total

Year — 1921, 1925, 1930

- Northern and Western Europe
- Southern and Eastern Europe
- Canada
- Latin America
- Asia
- Other areas represent less than 1% of the total

Source: *Historical Statistics of the United States: Colonial Times to 1970.*

18. What information is presented on the graph?

19. What percentage of emigrants came from Asia in 1925?

20. During which year shown was emigration from Canada the highest?

21. From what region was emigration the highest in 1921?

22. Use information presented in the graph to confirm or disprove this generalization: The percentage of emigrants from Canada remained constant throughout the decade.

Practicing Skills

23. **Making Generalizations** Over a period of weeks, read the editorials in your local newspaper. Then write a list of generalizations about the newspaper's position on issues such as politics or crime.

Economics Activity

24. Working with a partner, contact your local chamber of commerce to learn about some of the major businesses or industries in your area. Next conduct a business survey in your neighborhood. Find out where people work, what type of work they do, and how long they have worked. Encourage the people you survey to learn more about local businesses.

Alternative Assessment

25. **Portfolio Project** Research the lives of people who were teenagers during the 1920s. Your local history museum or back issues of newspapers may be helpful. Try to learn about some of the following topics: education, styles of clothing, forms of recreation, and music. Look for pictures that record styles of clothing, hairdos, and social events of the period. Report your findings orally to the class. Then file your written summary in your portfolio.

Standardized Test Practice

Directions: Choose the *best* answer to the following question.

In 1920, women won an important victory when the Nineteenth Amendment was ratified. What did this amendment accomplish?

F It required colleges to accept women.

G It guaranteed equal wages for equal work.

H It banned discrimination in the workplace.

J It granted women the right to vote.

Test-Taking Tip

Eliminate answers that don't make sense. For example, choice **F** is unlikely because the Nineteenth Amendment did not require colleges to accept women. Use the process of elimination to find the right answer.

CHAPTER 25

The Depression and FDR

1929–1941

Why It Matters

The prosperous times of the 1920s had hidden problems. These problems came out in the open in 1929 when the nation's economy crumbled. The New Deal was President Roosevelt's way of dealing with the Depression.

The Impact Today

The New Deal actively involved the government in social and economic concerns and created the Social Security system, which still affects us all.

The American Journey Video *The chapter 25 video, "Fear Itself," examines the impact of FDR and his New Deal programs on the Great Depression.*

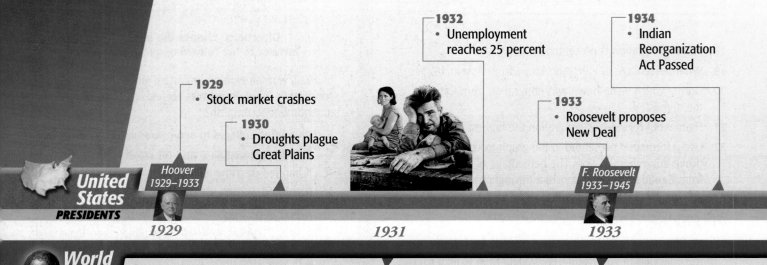

1932
• Unemployment reaches 25 percent

1934
• Indian Reorganization Act Passed

1929
• Stock market crashes

1930
• Droughts plague Great Plains

1933
• Roosevelt proposes New Deal

United States PRESIDENTS

Hoover 1929–1933

F. Roosevelt 1933–1945

1929   1931   1933

World

1931
• Japan invades Manchuria

1933
• Hitler comes to power in Germany

Work for the Unemployed Programs like the Works Progress Administration provided jobs during the Great Depression.

1935
• Social Security Act Passed

1939
• *Gone With the Wind* premieres

1935   *1937*   *1939*

1935
• Italy invades Ethiopia

1936
• Spanish Civil War begins
• German Jews lose right to vote

1939
• Hitler invades Poland; World War II begins

HISTORY
Online

Chapter Overview
Visit taj.glencoe.com and click on **Chapter 25—Chapter Overviews** to preview chapter information.

The Great Depression

Guide to Reading

Main Idea
The Great Depression was a world-wide business and economic slump that lasted through the 1930s.

Key Terms
stock exchange, on margin, default, relief, public works

Reading Strategy
Organizing Information As you read the section, re-create the diagram below and explain how the Great Depression affected each of these groups.

Effects of the Great Depression

industrial workers	farmers	home-owners

Read to Learn
- what caused the stock market crash.
- how the Great Depression plunged many Americans into poverty.
- how Hoover reacted to the Great Depression.

Section Theme
Economic Factors Many factors contributed to the economic crisis known as the Great Depression.

Preview of Events

♦1928   ♦1930   ♦1932

1928
Herbert Hoover is elected president

1929
Stock market crashes

1930s
The Great Depression strikes

1932
Bonus Army marches on Washington, D.C.

AN American Story

The bubble of American prosperity burst when the New York stock market collapsed in October 1929. Thousands of investors lost all their savings. Wall Street—the nation's financial center—was in a state of shock. Many Americans suddenly found themselves out of work. In 1932 the popular actor and humorist Will Rogers remarked: "We'll hold the distinction of being the only nation in the history of the world that ever went to the poorhouse in an automobile."

The Stock Market

In the booming economy of the 1920s, confident business and government leaders said the nation had entered a new era of prosperity for all. The chairman of General Motors advised people to invest money in the stock market every month—and many followed his advice. "Grocers, motormen, plumbers, seamstresses, and . . . waiters were in the market," reported writer Frederick Lewis Allen. The "market had become a national mania."

Suddenly, in October 1929, everything changed. Almost overnight the value of stocks plunged. Millionaires lost fortunes, and thousands of less wealthy investors lost their savings. The United States was about to enter its worst domestic crisis since the Civil War.

The Boom

A **stock exchange** is an organized system for buying and selling shares, or blocks of investments, in corporations. In the late 1920s, the value of stocks on the New York Stock Exchange climbed to dizzying heights, reaching record levels in September 1929.

Because many investors lacked the money to continue purchasing stock, they bought **on margin.** This means they paid only a fraction of the stock price and borrowed the rest from their brokers. Brokers, in turn, borrowed their money from banks. As long as the value of stocks continued to rise, the buyer could sell later, pay back what had been borrowed, and make a profit. If that value fell, though, investors and brokers would not have enough cash to pay off the loans.

The Crash

Fearing that the boom market would end, some investors began selling their stocks in late September. These sales made stock prices fall. Brokers began to demand repayment of loans, forcing investors who had bought on margin to sell their stock.

Prices declined steadily until October 21, but most financial experts thought the market was experiencing nothing more than a "period of readjustment." Then, for three straight days, stock prices plunged as investors sold millions of shares each day. Panicked traders sold almost 13 million shares on October 24, a day that became known as **"Black Thursday."**

Following a few days of calm, the decline and confusion continued on Monday. On Tuesday, October 29, the crisis worsened. By the end of the day, more than 16 million shares had changed hands and stock prices had plummeted. Journalist Jonathan Norton Leonard described the scene:

❝The selling pressure was . . . coming from everywhere. The wires to other cities were jammed with frantic orders to sell. So were the cables, radio, and telephones to Europe and the rest of the world. Buyers were few, sometimes wholly absent.❞

The New York Stock Exchange closed for a few days to prevent more panic selling. Shock spread across the country.

✓ **Reading Check** **Explaining** What is buying stock "on margin"?

The Great Depression

During the next two years, the United States slid into a severe economic crisis called the **Great Depression.** The nation's total economic output dropped 43 percent in three years, from $104 billion in 1929 to $58 billion in 1932.

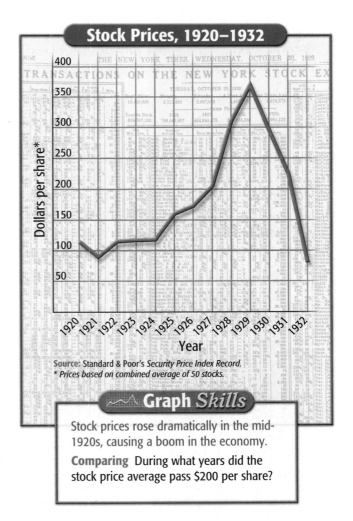

Stock Prices, 1920–1932

Source: Standard & Poor's *Security Price Index Record.*
* Prices based on combined average of 50 stocks.

Graph Skills

Stock prices rose dramatically in the mid-1920s, causing a boom in the economy.

Comparing During what years did the stock price average pass $200 per share?

While the stock market crash shook people's confidence in the economy, it did not cause the Depression. Other factors, working together, sent the economy into a long tailspin.

An Unbalanced Economy

The problems that led to the Great Depression began to give out warning signals in the early 1920s. Farm income shrank throughout the decade. Industries also declined. In the months before the stock market crash, the automobile and construction industries suffered from lagging orders. As a result, employers cut wages and laid off workers. With their incomes slashed, many Americans could no longer afford the consumer goods that the nation's industries had been churning out.

Another factor that fueled the Depression was the growing gap in wealth between rich people and most Americans. The prosperity of the 1920s did not help all Americans equally. In 1929 less than 1 percent of the population owned nearly one-third of the country's wealth. At the same time, about 75 percent of American families lived in poverty or on the very edge of it.

Credit Crisis

Borrowed money fueled much of the economy in the 1920s. Farmers bought land, equipment, and supplies on credit. Consumers used credit to buy cars. Investors borrowed to buy stocks. Many small banks suffered when farmers defaulted, or failed to meet loan payments. Large banks, which had bought stocks as an investment, suffered huge losses in the stock market crash. These losses forced thousands of banks across the nation to close between 1930 and 1933; millions of depositors lost their money.

International Depression

Weaknesses in the American economy also sapped the strength of foreign economies. European countries needed to borrow money from American banks and to sell goods to American consumers in order to repay their World War I debts to the United States. During the late 1920s, bank funds for loans dried up. International trade slowed down because, without American loans, other nations had less money to spend.

Joblessness and Poverty

As the Depression tightened its grip on the United States, millions lost their jobs. In 1932, 25 percent of American workers were out of work. The unemployment rate remained near 20 percent throughout the decade. Industrial cities were hardest hit. Workers who managed to keep their jobs worked only part-time or for reduced wages.

The newly unemployed felt devastated. New Yorker Sidney Lens, who lost his job, wrote about developing

❝ a feeling of worthlessness—and loneliness; I began to think of myself as a freak and misfit.❞

Long lines of hungry people snaked through the streets of the nation's cities. They waited for hours to receive a slice of bread, a cup of coffee, or a bowl of soup from soup kitchens run by local governments or charities.

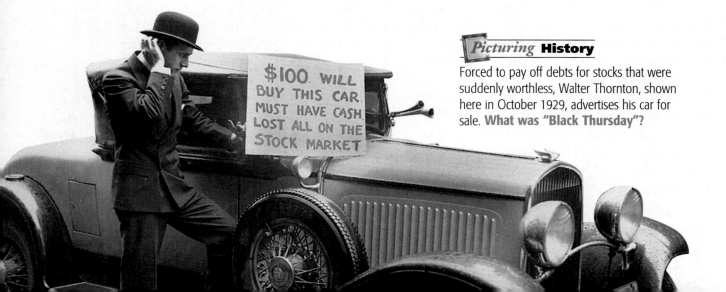

Picturing **History**

Forced to pay off debts for stocks that were suddenly worthless, Walter Thornton, shown here in October 1929, advertises his car for sale. **What was "Black Thursday"?**

$100. WILL BUY THIS CAR. MUST HAVE CASH. LOST ALL ON THE STOCK MARKET

MORE ABOUT...

Brother Can You Spare a Dime?

"Brother Can You Spare a Dime?" was a popular song in the 1930s during the Great Depression. In those days, prices were so low that if you were lucky enough to have a dime, you could actually buy something with it.

WORK-IS-WHAT-I WANT-AND-NOT-CHARITY. WHO-WILL-HELP-ME-GET-A-JOB-7 YEARS-IN-DETROIT. NO MONEY SENT AWAY. FURNISH-BEST-OF-REFERENCES PHONE RANDOLPH 8391 Room #35.

Prices During 1932–1934	
Sirloin steak (per pound)	$0.29
Chicken (per pound)	.22
Bread (20-ounce loaf)	.05
Potatoes (per pound)	.02
Bananas (per pound)	.07
Milk (per quart)	.10
Cheese (per pound)	.29
Tomatoes (16-ounce can)	.09
Oranges (per dozen)	.27
Cornflakes (8 ounces)	.08

The Great Depression saw "Hoovervilles," such as this one in New York City, and unemployed workers standing on street corners pleading for jobs.

Listed here are Depression-era prices for selected foods. Read the list to see how far that "dime" from your "brother" would go.

Unemployed people tried to earn a few cents by shining shoes or selling apples on street corners. Those who had lost their homes built shelters out of old boxes and other debris, sometimes grouped together in pitiful "shantytowns." Some referred bitterly to the shantytowns as **Hoovervilles** because of President Hoover's failure to act. Across the country Americans wondered why the president did nothing to end the suffering. 📖 *(See page 974 of the Primary Sources Library for one account of life during the Depression.)*

✓ **Reading Check** **Describing** What percentage of American workers were out of work in 1932?

Hoover and the Crisis

President Hoover thought the economic crisis was only temporary and that prosperity was "just around the corner." He also believed that the "depression cannot be cured by legislative action or executive pronouncement." Instead, Hoover called on business leaders not to cut wages or production of goods and on charities to do their best for the needy. Voluntary action by private citizens and local governments, Hoover said, would pull the nation through tough times.

Charities, churches, and volunteers worked heroically to provide relief—aid for the needy. So did state and local governments. Some cities withheld part of city workers' wages—already reduced—to fund soup kitchens. But the number who needed help was simply overwhelming.

Government Action

Eventually Hoover recognized that the federal government had to take steps to combat the Depression. In 1931 he authorized additional federal spending on public works—projects such as highways, parks, and libraries—to create new jobs. State and local governments ran out of money, however, and the combined spending by all three levels of government declined.

Bonus Army set up its camp near the Capitol.

Hoover tried a different measure in January 1932, when he asked Congress to create the **Reconstruction Finance Corporation** (RFC). The RFC lent money to businesses. It also provided funds for state and local programs providing relief. However, the RFC's directors were reluctant to make risky loans, and much of its budget remained unspent.

The Bonus Army

The march on Washington by the **Bonus Army** turned many Americans, who were already blaming Hoover for the Depression, firmly against the president. Congress had agreed to give each veteran of World War I a $1,000 bonus in 1945. Jobless veterans wanted the bonuses right away. In the summer of 1932, they formed the Bonus Army and marched to **Washington, D.C.,** to demand their money. At its peak the Bonus Army included about 20,000 veterans. Congress and the president turned the veterans down. Most of the veterans left, but about 2,000, joined by their families, vowed to remain until the bonuses were paid. When the police tried to disband the veterans' camp, conflict broke out and two people were killed.

Hoover responded by calling in the army. With tanks, machine guns, and cavalry, troops led by Army chief of staff General **Douglas MacArthur** and his aide **Dwight D. Eisenhower** entered the protesters' camp. Veterans and their families fled in terror as the troops burned their camp.

Hoover announced that "a challenge to the authority of the United States government has been met." Many Americans were horrified that the government had attacked its own citizens, particularly war veterans. Hoover seemed cold, distant, and out of touch with ordinary people. Many people thought the time had come for a change in government.

Reading Check **Explaining** What did the Reconstruction Finance Corporation provide?

SECTION 1 ASSESSMENT

Checking for Understanding

1. **Key Terms** Write a conversation between two friends at the time of the Great Depression. Include these terms in your writing: stock exchange, on margin, default, relief, public works.

2. **Reviewing Facts** What did the Bonus Army want? Where did it set up camp?

Reviewing Themes

3. **Economic Factors** How did buying stocks on margin contribute to the stock market crash?

Critical Thinking

4. **Drawing Conclusions** Do you think President Hoover followed the proper course in his handling of the Great Depression?

5. **Determining Cause and Effect** Recreate the diagram below and identify four major factors that led to the Great Depression.

Analyzing Visuals

6. **Graph Skills** Study the graph on page 725. When did the average price of stocks reach its peak? During what years did the average drop below $100 per share?

Interdisciplinary Activity

Economics Using the food prices on page 727, make a grocery list of what you could buy on a budget of $3.00 a week. Make another list of which of the same items you could buy today if you only had $3.00 a week.

Roosevelt's New Deal

Guide to Reading

Main Idea

President Franklin Roosevelt promised to take action to get America out of the Great Depression.

Key Terms

Hundred Days, New Deal, work relief, subsidy

Reading Strategy

Classifying Information As you read the section, re-create the diagram below and identify each of the listed items.

	What is it?
The New Deal	
TVA	
CCC	
FDIC	

Read to Learn

• how Roosevelt tried to restore the confidence of the American people.
• what programs were created in FDR's first 100 days.

Section Theme

Government and Democracy New Deal legislation affected banking, the stock market, industry, agriculture, and welfare.

Preview of Events

◆1932	◆1933	◆1934
1932 Franklin Roosevelt is elected president	**1933** Programs during the Hundred Days improve the economy	**1934** Securities and Exchange Commission is created

AN American Story

Washington, D.C., was dark and dreary on March 4, 1933. President Franklin D. Roosevelt stood bareheaded in the chilly wind, tightly gripping the sides of the reading stand in front of him. His face was stern as he began his Inaugural Address. "This nation asks for action and action now!" he cried.

As Roosevelt spoke, his voice had an electric effect on the masses of people before him. The crowd shouted back its approval. To millions of despairing Americans, Roosevelt's voice was the symbol of hope. It seemed that the gloom was starting to lift.

Franklin D. Roosevelt

With the nation's economy crumbling, the Democrats believed they had a good chance of winning the presidency. Meeting in Chicago in June 1932, the Democrats chose Governor **Franklin D. Roosevelt** of New York as their candidate. Roosevelt—or FDR, as he was called—seemed to bring a fresh approach to politics.

Franklin Roosevelt, who was paralyzed by polio as a young man, is shown with Ruth Bie, the daughter of the caretaker at FDR's estate.

When Roosevelt learned that he had been nominated, he flew to Chicago to deliver the first acceptance speech ever made at a convention. He told the Democrats—and the nation—"I pledge you, I pledge myself, to a new deal for the American people."

As the Republicans and Democrats held their conventions in 1932, the Depression grew worse. The Republicans met in Chicago and nominated President Hoover for reelection. With the country's economy in trouble, Hoover's chances for winning reelection looked poor.

Early Years of Promise

Franklin D. Roosevelt, a distant cousin of former president Theodore Roosevelt, came from a wealthy family. Ambitious and charming, FDR decided on a career in politics. In 1905 he married Theodore Roosevelt's niece, **Eleanor Roosevelt,** and she became a tireless partner in his public life.

FDR's political career began with his election to the New York state senate in 1910. In 1913 he became assistant secretary of the navy, and in 1920 the Democrats chose him as their candidate

for vice president. The Democrats lost the election to Warren G. Harding, but Franklin Roosevelt's political future seemed bright.

Then in 1921 polio struck Roosevelt, paralyzing both his legs. Yet FDR's will remained strong. "Once I spent two years lying in bed trying to move my big toe," he said later. "After that, anything else seems easy."

Return to Politics

After a few years, FDR decided to return to politics. He never publicly mentioned his paralyzed legs, and he asked journalists not to photograph his leg braces or wheelchair. Elected governor of New York in 1928 and reelected in 1930, Roosevelt earned a national reputation as a reformer. He drew on the advice of a group of progressive lawyers, economists, and social workers—known as the **Brain Trust**—to develop relief programs for the state. When he decided to run for president, he counted on the Brain Trust to help him guide the nation to recovery.

During the 1932 campaign, Roosevelt declared that "the country needs and . . . demands bold, persistent experimentation." He also spoke of trying to help "the forgotten man at the bottom of the economic pyramid."

✔ **Reading Check** **Identifying** Who were the Republican and Democratic candidates for president in 1932?

FDR Takes Charge

The American people were charmed by Roosevelt's confidence and his promise of action. On November 8, they went to the polls and elected Roosevelt in a landslide. He captured all but six states and received 472 of the 531 electoral votes. Democrats won important victories in Congress, also. People clearly wanted a change.

In the months before Roosevelt took office, the economy worsened. Protests in some cities erupted into violence. Meanwhile the banking system was collapsing. As more people rushed to withdraw their deposits, more and more banks went out of business. People became desperately afraid.

At his inauguration on March 4, 1933, Roosevelt told the nation that "the only thing we have to fear is fear itself—nameless, unreasoning, unjustified terror." He reassured people and pointed out that the "greatest primary task is to put people to work." He also promised immediate action on the banking crisis.

Restoring Confidence in Banks

Two days after the inauguration, Roosevelt ordered all banks closed for four days. He also called Congress to a special session, at which he presented the administration's plan for handling the banking problem. About seven hours later, Congress had passed and Roosevelt had signed the **Emergency Banking Relief Act.** The act proposed a wide range of presidential powers over banking and set up a system by which banks would open again or be reorganized. By mid-March half of the nation's banks had reopened.

Flood victims stand in line waiting for food and clothing. They are a sharp contrast to the happy family on the billboard.

At the end of his first week in office, FDR assured Americans in a radio broadcast "that it is safer to keep your money in a reopened bank than under the mattress." The next day deposits far exceeded withdrawals. The banking crisis had ended.

The president's radio talk was the first of many. He called these informal talks **fireside chats** because he sat next to a fireplace in the White House as he spoke. These fireside chats helped FDR gain the public's confidence.

The Hundred Days

After solving the banking crisis, President Roosevelt quickly tackled other areas of national concern. He sent Congress a stack of proposals for new programs to deal with the nation's economic problems. In all Roosevelt sent 15 proposals to Congress, and Congress approved every one of them.

Lasting about three months, the special session of Congress that Roosevelt called to launch his programs came to be called the Hundred Days. It was an amazingly productive time. Optimism swept through the capital. Journalist Thomas Stokes recalled, "The gloom, the tenseness, the fear of the closing months of the Hoover administration had vanished."

✓ **Reading Check** **Identifying** What law set up a plan to reorganize the nation's banks?

The New Deal

First New Deal Program	Initials	Begun	Purpose
Civilian Conservation Corps	CCC	1933	Provided jobs for young men to plant trees and build bridges
Tennessee Valley Authority	TVA	1933	Built dams to provide cheap electric power to seven Southern states; set up schools and health centers
Federal Emergency Relief Administration	FERA	1933	Gave relief to unemployed and needy
Agricultural Adjustment Administration	AAA	1933	Paid farmers not to grow certain crops
National Recovery Administration	NRA	1933	Helped set standards for production, prices, and wages
Public Works Administration	PWA	1933	Built ports, schools, and aircraft carriers
Federal Deposit Insurance Corporation	FDIC	1933	Insured savings accounts in banks approved by the government
Second New Deal Program			
Rural Electrification Administration	REA	1935	Loaned money to extend electricity to rural areas
Works Progress Administration	WPA	1935	Employed men and women to build hospitals, schools, parks, and airports; employed artists, writers, and musicians
Social Security Act	SSA	1935	Set up a system of pensions for the elderly, unemployed, and people with disabilities
Farm Security Administration	FSA	1937	Lent money to sharecroppers; set up camps for migrant workers
Fair Labor Standards Act	FLSA	1938	Established minimum wages and maximum hours for all businesses engaged in interstate commerce

📈 **Chart** *Skills*

Under the Roosevelt New Deal during the 1930s, the federal government assumed responsibility for the welfare of many citizens.

Analyzing Information Why did setting up the FDIC help all Americans?

The New Deal Takes Shape

The new laws that Congress passed during the Hundred Days—and in the months and years that followed—came to be called the New Deal. New Deal laws and regulations affected banking, the stock market, industry, agriculture, public works, relief for the poor, and conservation of resources. These laws changed the face of America dramatically.

Frances Perkins, Roosevelt's secretary of labor, later recalled those early, exciting days of the New Deal:

> 66In March 1933, the New Deal was not a plan. . . . It was a happy phrase [FDR] had coined during the campaign. . . . It made people feel better, and in that terrible period of depression they needed to feel better.99

$ Economics

Jobs and Relief

Roosevelt gave high priority to creating jobs. He planned to help the unemployed with work relief programs, giving needy people government jobs. During his first month in office, FDR asked Congress to create the **Civilian Conservation Corps** (CCC). Over the next 10 years, the CCC employed about 3 million young men to work on projects that benefited the public, planting trees to reforest areas, building levees for flood control, and improving national parks.

Roosevelt made aid to the poor and suffering another priority. FDR established the **Federal Emergency Relief Administration** (FERA) to give money to the states for use in helping people in need. Roosevelt appointed **Harry Hopkins,** a New York social worker, to lead the FERA. Hopkins became one of FDR's closest advisers and got involved in several other New Deal programs.

Roosevelt did not forget agriculture. On May 12, Congress passed the **Agricultural Adjustment Act** (AAA). The act had two goals: to raise farm prices quickly and to control production so that farm prices would stay up over the long term.

In the AAA's first year, though, the supply of food outstripped demand. The AAA could raise prices only by paying farmers to destroy crops, milk, and livestock. To many it seemed shocking to throw food away when millions of people went hungry. The New Dealers claimed the action was necessary to bring prices up.

To control production and farm prices, the AAA paid farmers to leave some of their land uncultivated. If market prices of key farm products such as wheat and cotton fell below a certain level, the AAA would pay farmers subsidies—grants of money—to make up the difference. In the first three years of the New Deal, farmers' incomes rose by about 50 percent. The Supreme Court ruled that the AAA was unconstitutional in *United States* v. *Butler* (1936) for invading the reserved powers of the states.

Rebuilding a Region

One of the boldest programs launched during the Hundred Days was the **Tennessee Valley Authority** (TVA). The TVA aimed to control flooding, promote conservation and development, and bring electricity to rural areas along the **Tennessee River.** By building new dams and improving others, the TVA ended the region's disastrous floods. And with hydroelectric power generating affordable electricity, thousands of farms and homes in some Southern states were wired for electricity for the first time.

Some critics charged that funds for the TVA should be used to support programs nationwide. Power companies also attacked the program as unfair and communistic. When the spring rains came in 1937, however, the system worked—the dams prevented the Tennessee River from flooding. In the end, most observers agreed that the TVA was an example of successful social and economic planning.

Driller, Fort Loudon Dam, Tennessee

Helping Business and Labor

On the last day of the Hundred Days, Congress passed the **National Industrial Recovery Act** (NIRA), which Roosevelt called "the most important and far-reaching legislation" ever passed in the United States. The NIRA aimed to boost the economy by helping business regulate itself.

The NIRA created the **National Recovery Administration** (NRA), which encouraged businesses to set a minimum wage and abolish child labor. In addition the NRA tried to set up codes governing pricing and other practices for every industry. **Hugh Johnson,** a former general named to head the NRA, launched a campaign to promote the agency. Before long the agency's blue eagle symbol and slogan—"We Do Our Part"—appeared everywhere.

The Blue Eagle, symbol of the NRA

Another program that the NIRA launched was the **Public Works Administration** (PWA). Its goal was to stimulate the economy through the building of huge public works projects that needed large numbers of workers. The agency employed people to work on the construction of roads, shipyards, hospitals, city halls, and schools. Many PWA projects—such as New York City's Lincoln Tunnel and Kentucky's Fort Knox—still stand. The PWA spent its funds slowly, though, and did not have much immediate impact on unemployment.

To avoid future banking crises, Roosevelt called for reform of the nation's financial system. Congress established the **Federal Deposit Insurance Corporation** (FDIC) to insure bank deposits. The government guaranteed that money placed in a bank insured by the FDIC would not be lost if the bank failed.

Congress also passed a law regulating the sale of stocks and bonds and created the **Securities and Exchange Commission** (SEC). This 1934 law gave the SEC the power to punish dishonest stockbrokers and speculators.

Assessing the Early New Deal

The New Deal did not cure the nation's ills. The Depression dragged on, bringing continued hardship. Farmers continued to lose their land. Unemployment remained at high levels. Many people still struggled to survive and to make ends meet.

Yet the darkest days had passed. The panic of 1932 and 1933 had receded, and the flurry of activity from the nation's capital had restored some measure of confidence.

✓ Reading Check **Describing** What were the goals of the Agricultural Adjustment Act?

SECTION 2 ASSESSMENT

Checking for Understanding

1. **Key Terms** Write sentences about the New Deal; use these vocabulary terms: **Hundred Days, work relief, subsidy.**

2. **Reviewing Facts** For what region did the Tennessee Valley Authority provide electricity?

Reviewing Themes

3. **Government and Democracy** Describe the actions that Roosevelt took to restore confidence in banks and in the stock exchange.

Critical Thinking

4. **Comparing** Compare Hoover's and Roosevelt's programs to combat the Depression.

5. **Organizing Information** Re-create the diagram below and list three New Deal programs that Roosevelt established to create jobs or aid society as a whole.

Analyzing Visuals

6. **Chart Skills** Examine the table on page 732. Which programs were set up primarily to help farmers and rural areas? What was the purpose of the TVA?

Interdisciplinary Activity

Government Create a table that lists the positive and negative aspects of the New Deal farm program. Summarize in a brief paragraph what conclusions you can draw from your table.

SECTION 3 Life During the Depression

Guide to Reading

Main Idea
The Depression was a difficult time for Americans because many faced unemployment and the loss of land and other property.

Key Terms
Dust Bowl, migrant worker

Reading Strategy
Classifying Information As you read the section, re-create the diagram below and describe how different groups of people coped with difficult times.

Effects of the Great Depression		
Hispanic Americans	Great Plains farmers	African Americans

Read to Learn
• how the Depression affected minority groups.
• what radical political movements gained influence.

Section Theme
Economic Factors The Depression made life difficult for all Americans, and many migrated to other regions hoping for a better life.

Preview of Events

♦1930 ——————————— ♦1935 ——————————— ♦1940

1932
Hattie Caraway is elected first woman senator

1934
Indian Reorganization Act is passed

1939
Gone With the Wind film is released

AN American Story

"They hung around street corners and in groups. . . . They felt despised, they were ashamed of themselves. They cringed, they comforted one another. They avoided home." With these words, a social worker described unemployed Pennsylvania coal miners. Their pain was echoed across America by countless men, women, and children whose hopes were being crushed by the Depression.

Hard Times in America

Not every worker lost a job during the Depression. Not every family needed aid. Most Americans, however, had to make do with less: less income, less food, and less security.

Some families survived the Depression by pulling together. Parents and children shared homes with grandparents or other relatives to save money. Although the birthrate had decreased, school enrollment actually increased; because fewer young people could find work, they remained in school.

CHAPTER 25   The Depression and FDR   **735**

The strain shattered other families, however. Nearly two million men—and a much smaller number of women—abandoned their homes. They took to the road, drifting to warm places such as Florida and California.

Women Go to Work

Many people thought that women should not hold jobs as long as men were unemployed. Despite such prejudices, desperation drove a large number of women into the workforce. Many families survived on a woman's income—even though American women earned less than men.

Women also worked harder at home to make ends meet. Instead of buying clothes or groceries, they sewed their own clothing, baked their own bread, and canned their own vegetables. Some women started home businesses such as laundries or boardinghouses.

The New Deal era opened doors for women in public life. President Roosevelt appointed the first woman ever to serve in the cabinet, **Frances Perkins.** He also named more than 100 other women to federal posts. One—Ellen Sullivan Woodward—started a program to give jobs to women. In 1932 **Hattie Caraway** of Arkansas became the first woman to be elected to the United States Senate.

The best-known woman in American public life was **Eleanor Roosevelt,** who often acted as her husband's "eyes and ears." She made many fact-finding trips for the president because polio had limited his mobility. Mrs. Roosevelt campaigned vigorously for women and minorities and other humanitarian concerns. She wrote a daily newspaper column and used her boundless energy to meet people all over the country.

✔ **Reading Check** **Identifying** Who was the first woman to serve in a president's cabinet? How many other women were appointed to federal posts at this time?

The Dust Bowl

To make matters worse, the southern Great Plains suffered an environmental disaster during the 1930s. Hardest hit were western Kansas and Oklahoma, northern Texas, and eastern Colorado and New Mexico—the region dubbed the Dust Bowl.

People In History

Charles Drew 1904–1950

African American Charles Drew was born and raised in the segregated city of Washington, D.C., and refused to let racial prejudice stop him. His early interests were in education, particularly in medicine, but he was also an outstanding athlete. He starred at Dunbar High School in football, baseball, basketball, and track and field.

He graduated from Amherst College in Massachusetts and earned his medical degree at Canada's McGill University. In the 1930s Drew conducted pioneering research on blood plasma, and he created the model for blood and plasma storage that is used by the Red Cross today. When the United States entered World War II, Drew was in charge of the military's blood plasma program.

Drew's research changed transfusion methods so that stored plasma could be given to soldiers wounded on the battlefield—a medical advance that saved many lives. Drew later resigned to protest the military's decision to maintain racially segregated blood banks.

★ Geography

What Caused the Dust Bowl?

Using new technology such as tractors and disc plows, farmers had cleared millions of acres of sod for wheat farming. They did not realize that the roots of the grass had held the soil in place. When a severe drought struck in 1931, crops died and the soil dried out. Strong prairie winds simply blew the soil away.

Each storm stripped away more soil. One storm in 1934 carried about 300 million tons of soil, depositing some of it on ships 300 miles out in the Atlantic Ocean. The drought—and the storms—continued for years.

People called the storms "black blizzards." A Texas boy wrote:

> 66These storms were like rolling black smoke. We had to keep the lights on all day. We went to school with headlights on, and with dust masks on.99

Thousands of Dust Bowl farmers went bankrupt and had to give up their farms. About 400,000 farmers migrated to California and became **migrant workers,** moving from place to place to harvest fruits and vegetables. So many came from Oklahoma that people called them "Okies." One observer described their arrival:

> 66They came in decrepit [broken-down], square-shouldered [cars] . . . that looked like relics of some antique culture . . . piled high with mattresses and cooking utensils and children, with suitcases, jugs and sacks strapped to the running boards.99

✓ **Reading Check** **Explaining** Where did many families move to escape the Dust Bowl?

The Plight of Minorities

The Depression fell especially hard on the minority groups who were already on the lower rungs of the American economic ladder. These groups included African Americans, Native Americans, and Hispanic Americans.

Dorothea Lange photographed a homeless Oklahoma family during Dust Bowl days.

African Americans

In the South more than half of the African American population had no jobs. African Americans who lived and worked in Southern cities found their jobs taken by white people who had lost theirs. The collapse of farm prices crushed African American farmers.

Seeking more opportunity, about 400,000 African American men, women, and children migrated to Northern cities during the decade of the 1930s. These migrants did not fare much better there, however. The jobless rate for African Americans remained high.

African Americans did make some political gains during the Depression. President Roosevelt appointed a number of African Americans to federal posts. He had a group of advisers, known as the Black Cabinet, that included Robert Weaver, a college professor, and **Ralph Bunche,** who worked for the State Department. **Mary McLeod Bethune,** who established Bethune-Cookman College in Florida, also served as an adviser.

African Americans continued to fight against prejudice. In 1939 opera singer Marian Anderson was denied permission to sing in Constitution Hall because she was black. Mrs. Roosevelt helped arrange for Anderson to give a historic concert at the Lincoln Memorial.

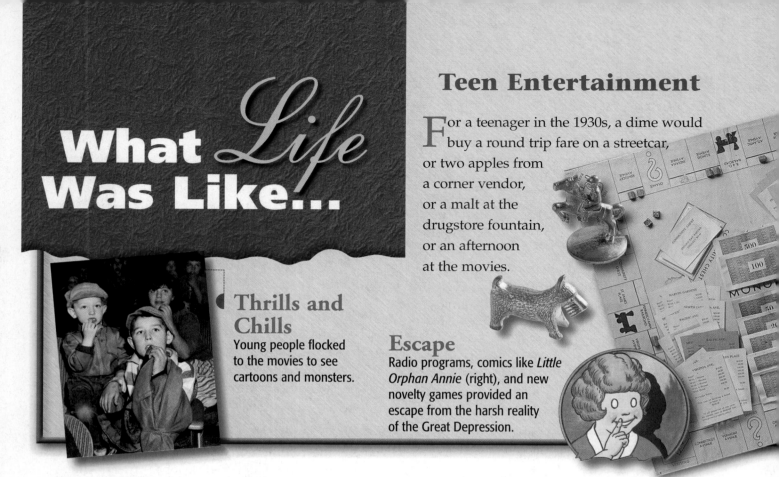

What *Life* Was Like...

Teen Entertainment

For a teenager in the 1930s, a dime would buy a round trip fare on a streetcar, or two apples from a corner vendor, or a malt at the drugstore fountain, or an afternoon at the movies.

Thrills and Chills
Young people flocked to the movies to see cartoons and monsters.

Escape
Radio programs, comics like *Little Orphan Annie* (right), and new novelty games provided an escape from the harsh reality of the Great Depression.

Native Americans

The 1930s did bring some benefits to Native Americans. The new head of the Bureau of Indian Affairs, **John Collier,** introduced a set of reforms known as the Indian New Deal.

Collier halted the sale of reservation land, got jobs for 77,000 Native Americans in the Civilian Conservation Corps, and obtained Public Works Administration funds to build new reservation schools. Most important, he pushed Congress to pass the **Indian Reorganization Act** of 1934. This law restored traditional tribal government and provided money for land purchases to enlarge some reservations.

Hispanic Americans

At the beginning of the 1930s, about two million people of Hispanic descent lived in the United States, mostly in California and the Southwest. Many had emigrated from Mexico. They worked as farmers, migrant workers, and laborers. As the Great Depression deepened, resentment against Mexican Americans grew. Many lost their jobs. Politicians and labor unions demanded that Mexican Americans be forced to leave the United States.

The government encouraged Mexican immigrants to return to Mexico. Authorities gave them one-way train tickets to Mexico or simply rounded them up and shipped them south across the border. More than 500,000 Mexican Americans left the United States during the early years of the Depression, often involuntarily.

Reading Check **Explaining** What was the purpose of the Indian Reorganization Act?

Radical Political Movements

Hard times helped **radical** political groups gain ground in the United States during the 1930s. Radical groups advocate extreme and immediate change. Socialists and Communists viewed the Depression not as a temporary economic problem but as the death of a failed system. They proposed sweeping changes.

Communism attracted workers, minority-rights activists, and intellectuals with promises to end economic and racial injustice. Although both socialism and communism had significant influence, neither became a major political force in the United States.

Another political development that caught the attention of many Americans was the rise of **fascists** in Germany and Italy. Fascism is a political philosophy that holds the individual second to the nation and advocates government by dictatorship. In 1936 the **Spanish Civil War** began. Germany and Italy supported fascists who were trying to take over the Spanish government. Although the United States remained neutral, more than 3,000 Americans went to Spain to fight the fascists.

✓**Reading Check** **Explaining** What is fascism?

Entertainment and the Arts

The Depression produced two separate trends in entertainment and the arts. One was escapism—light or romantic entertainment that helped people forget about their problems. The other was social criticism—portraits of the injustice and suffering of Depression America.

Radio became enormously popular during the 1930s. Daytime dramas sponsored by laundry detergents earned the nickname "soap operas." Adventure programs such as *Dick Tracy, The Lone Ranger,* and *Superman* had millions of listeners, as did variety shows featuring comedians George Burns, Gracie Allen, and Jack Benny.

At the Movies

Every week about 85 million people went to movie theaters, usually to escape their cares and worries. Some movies did explore serious topics. For example, *The Grapes of Wrath* (1940) was a screen version of John Steinbeck's powerful novel about farm families fleeing the Dust Bowl. The 1939 film of Margaret Mitchell's novel, *Gone With the Wind,* set in the Civil War era, also portrayed people coping with hard times.

Images of the Times

Many writers and painters portrayed the grim realities of Depression life. Richard Wright's novel *Native Son* told the story of an African American man growing up in Chicago. Writer James Agee and photographer Walker Evans depicted poor Southern farm families in *Let Us Now Praise Famous Men.*

Photographer Margaret Bourke-White also recorded the plight of American farmers, and Dorothea Lange took gripping photographs of migrant workers. Painters such as Grant Wood and Thomas Hart Benton showed ordinary people confronting the hardships of Depression life.

✓**Reading Check** **Analyzing** Would you consider *Gone With the Wind* social criticism or escapism? Explain.

SECTION 3 ASSESSMENT

Checking for Understanding

1. **Key Terms** Define Dust Bowl and migrant worker.
2. **Reviewing Facts** Describe three of the benefits that Native Americans received from the Indian New Deal including the Indian Reorganization Act.

Reviewing Themes

3. **Economic Factors** Why did many African Americans migrate from the South to the North during the 1930s?

Critical Thinking

4. **Determining Cause and Effect** Why did radical political movements gain popularity during the 1930s?
5. **Classifying Information** Re-create the diagram below and list the accomplishments of three individuals discussed in Section 3.

Individual	Accomplishments
1.	
2.	
3.	

Analyzing Visuals

6. **Picturing History** Look at the photograph by Dorothea Lange on page 737. Write a paragraph in which you describe why the family is leaving its home and where they are going.

Interdisciplinary Activity

Descriptive Writing Think of a modern story idea that would be considered social criticism. Using the outline of the story, write a short scene in which the characters point out a flaw in their society.

GEOGRAPHY & HISTORY

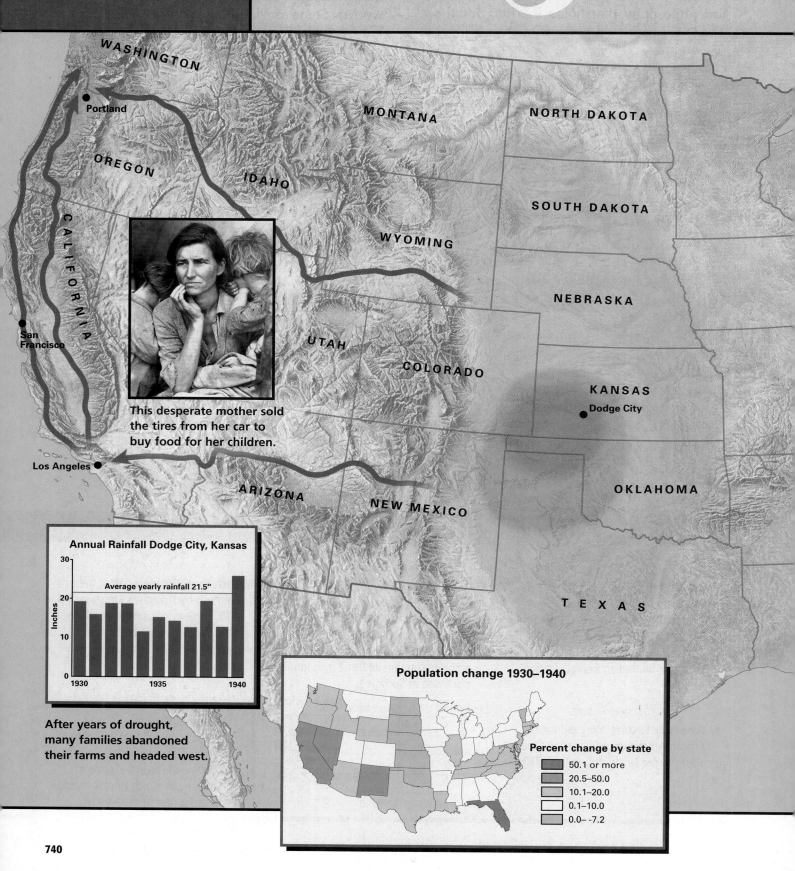

This desperate mother sold the tires from her car to buy food for her children.

Annual Rainfall Dodge City, Kansas

Average yearly rainfall 21.5"

Inches

30	
20	
10	
0	

1930   1935   1940

After years of drought, many families abandoned their farms and headed west.

Population change 1930–1940

Percent change by state

- 50.1 or more
- 20.5–50.0
- 10.1–20.0
- 0.1–10.0
- 0.0– -7.2

WASHINGTON

Portland

OREGON

IDAHO

MONTANA

NORTH DAKOTA

SOUTH DAKOTA

WYOMING

CALIFORNIA

San Francisco

UTAH

COLORADO

NEBRASKA

KANSAS

Dodge City

Los Angeles

ARIZONA

NEW MEXICO

OKLAHOMA

TEXAS

DUST BOWL

DURING THE 1930s, dust storms ravaged the Great Plains. This area was labeled the "Dust Bowl." Dust storms, dubbed "dusters" or "black blizzards" swept across the region darkening the sky and burying fences, fields, and even houses and barns.

Dust storm in Hugoton, Kansas

Dust Bowl

← Migration route

☐ Damage

☐ Severe damage

☐ Most severe damage

0   200 miles

0   200 kilometers

These "Dust Bowl refugees" were stranded on the highway when their truck broke down in New Mexico.

LIVING ON THE PLAINS

Settlers had flocked to the plains and plowed up the grasses to plant wheat and other crops. Repeated deep plowing destroyed the protective root layer of the tough grasses and sod that held moisture and anchored the soil.

DARK CLOUDS

In the early 1930s a severe drought struck the region and the wind began to blow the fine-grained soil away. The drought lasted for years and caused many dust storms. Sometimes the storms lasted for weeks. High winds blew topsoil all the way to the Atlantic Ocean. Desperate farmers watched their crops shrivel and blow away.

HEADING WEST

Many families lost their jobs and their farms. They finally crammed their belongings into their old jalopies and headed west. During the 1930s half a million migrants traveled west searching for jobs. The migrants, many of them living out of their cars, would travel from farm to farm hoping to find work picking fruit, vegetables, or cotton.

RELIEF

New Deal programs finally brought relief to victims of the Dust Bowl. In addition to helping migrants, the federal government taught farmers in the Dust Bowl new conservation measures to preserve their land. Rains eventually fell, but true prosperity did not return to America until factories geared up production for World War II.

LEARNING from GEOGRAPHY

1. Which states suffered the most severe damage?

2. What states grew by more than 20 percent in population during 1930s? Why do you think these states experienced the greatest growth?

SECTION 4 Effects of the New Deal

Guide to Reading

Main Idea
As the Great Depression continued and the administration became the target of increasing criticism, Roosevelt launched the Second New Deal.

Key Terms
pension, Second New Deal, Social Security Act, unemployment insurance

Reading Strategy
Classifying Information As you read the section, re-create the diagram below and describe the aims of the programs and laws listed.

Program	Aims
Works Progress Administration	
Social Security Act	
Fair Labor Standards Act	

Read to Learn
- why people criticized Roosevelt and the New Deal.
- how the Second New Deal created new economic and social roles for government.

Section Theme
Government and Democracy Roosevelt continued to launch new programs to improve the economy.

Preview of Events

♦1934　　　♦1935　　　♦1936　　　♦1937

1935
FDR launches the Second New Deal

1936
FDR wins reelection

1937
Sit-down strike occurs in Flint, Michigan

AN American Story

Support for Franklin D. Roosevelt's efforts to end the Great Depression was far from unanimous. Many wealthy and conservative people attacked the president's "radical" policies. A political cartoon of the 1930s showed a boy writing the word *ROOSEVELT* on the sidewalk in front of his rich family's house. His sister calls out, "Mother, Wilfred wrote a bad word!"

New Deal Opponents

In the early days of his presidency, FDR counted on big business to support his efforts to revive the economy. The National Recovery Administration, for example, invited participation from the business community. In general, however, the business world opposed the New Deal.

Business leaders accused Roosevelt of spending too much government money and of trying to destroy free enterprise. In 1934 some of these conservative critics formed the Liberty League to "defend and uphold the Constitution." The League wanted government to let business alone and play a less active role in the economy. Although the Liberty League did not win widespread support, its existence convinced FDR that big business was against him.

Demanding More Reform

At the same time, Roosevelt drew fire from liberal critics. They wanted a more active government. Three men gained wide popularity with schemes to help the average American.

One of Roosevelt's critics was Father **Charles Coughlin,** a Detroit priest who reached millions of listeners through his weekly radio program. Coughlin, once a Roosevelt supporter, attacked FDR for not dealing firmly enough with big business, calling him "Franklin Double-Crossing Roosevelt." Coughlin used his radio show to attack bankers, Jews, Communists, and labor unions, as well as the New Deal. In time Coughlin lost support because of his extreme views.

Francis Townsend, a California doctor, rose to fame with his plan for a monthly pension, or payment, for older people. Older workers who quit their jobs, making them available to younger people, would receive a pension. Townsend's plan received little support from Congress. It did, however, force many Americans to think about the plight of the elderly poor and the needs of retired people.

Of greatest concern to Roosevelt, however, was Senator **Huey Long** of Louisiana. When he was governor of Louisiana, Long had won wide support with public works projects and attacks on big businesses.

In 1932 Long supported FDR, but within a year, the two men had split. One of Long's major complaints against the president was that he had not taken steps to redistribute wealth in the United States. By 1934 Long had developed his own plan for doing so. His "Share Our Wealth Plan" called for taxing the rich heavily, then using that money to give every American a home and $2,500 a year. As his appeal spread, Long became a threat to Roosevelt. Polls indicated that in 1936 he might receive as many as four million votes on a third-party ticket. But in 1935 he was assassinated.

✓ **Reading Check** **Describing** What group was Townsend's pension plan designed to help?

$ Economics
The Second New Deal

By the mid-1930s the economy had improved slightly, but the Depression was far from over. FDR took bolder steps.

FDR's critics: Huey Long (left) and Father Coughlin (right)

To bring in more government funds, Roosevelt pushed Congress to pass the **Revenue Act** of 1935. The act raised taxes on wealthy people and corporations. Critics accused him of "soaking the rich" to pay for his programs, but many Americans cheered.

In 1935 President Roosevelt launched a new set of programs and reforms, often called the Second New Deal. The laws passed at this time changed American life even more than the Hundred Days had done.

Creating Jobs

Millions of people—20 percent of the workforce—were still unemployed in 1935. In April Congress created the **Works Progress Administration** (WPA) to give people jobs and help the country. Led by Harry Hopkins, the WPA kept about two million people employed between 1935 and 1941. WPA workers built or repaired about 800 airports, 125,000 public buildings, 75,000 bridges, and 650,000 miles of roads.

The WPA also found work for unemployed writers, artists, and musicians. WPA painters decorated the new public buildings with murals. Writers and photographers documented life throughout America. The writers produced *Life in America,* 150 volumes that recorded folktales and songs, African American narratives, and Native American traditions.

Help for Those in Need

Before the Second New Deal, America was the only advanced industrial nation without a national government program to help the needy. In August 1935 Congress passed the Social Security Act.

The Social Security Act created a tax on workers and employers. That money provided monthly pensions for retired people. Another tax, on employers alone, funded unemployment insurance payments to people who lost their jobs. In addition, Social Security helped people with disabilities, the elderly poor, and children of parents who could not support them.

With the Social Security Act, the federal government took responsibility for the welfare of all citizens. It launched the American welfare system.

Reading Check **Explaining** How did the government raise money for Social Security?

HISTORY Online

Student Web Activity
Visit taj.glencoe.com and click on **Chapter 25— Student Web Activities** for an activity about living during the Great Depression.

The Labor Movement

Labor unions grew stronger as workers battled the Depression. In 1937 workers at the General Motors plant in **Flint, Michigan,** used a new technique—the sit-down strike. Strikers continuously occupied the plant and refused to work until management agreed to negotiate with them about their demands. For 44 days families

Picturing **History**
The glass sign was hand-painted by a member of the United Mine Workers Union. **How did workers benefit from the New Deal?**

and friends of the Flint strikers brought them food. Finally, the strikers won the right to organize their union.

The most influential labor leader during the 1930s was **John L. Lewis,** head of the United Mine Workers. To increase labor's power, Lewis strived to unite workers in every industry in a single union. Most unions in the American Federation of Labor (AFL) represented only skilled workers. Lewis called for industrial unions to include unskilled workers—the largest group in the labor force.

In 1935 Lewis formed a new union called the **Congress of Industrial Organizations** (CIO), which helped create industrial unions. By 1938 the CIO had four million members, including large numbers of women and African Americans.

Unions found support in the New Deal. The 1935 **National Labor Relations Act**—also called the **Wagner Act** after its sponsor, Senator Robert Wagner of New York—guaranteed workers the right to form unions to bargain collectively with employers. The act also created the National Labor Relations Board to enforce its provisions. In 1938 Congress passed the **Fair Labor Standards Act** (FLSA), which banned child labor and set a minimum wage of 40 cents an hour. The FLSA and the Wagner Act form the basis of American labor rights today.

Reading Check **Comparing** How did the CIO differ from the AFL?

The Supreme Court

Those who opposed the New Deal challenged many of its laws in the courts, claiming that they were unconstitutional. Several important cases reached the Supreme Court.

In May 1935, the Supreme Court ruled that the National Industrial Recovery Act was unconstitutional. In the opinion of the Court, Congress had exceeded its lawful power to regulate interstate commerce. In January 1936, the Supreme Court struck down the Agricultural Adjustment Act. Cases were also pending against the Wagner Act, the Social Security Act, and the Tennessee Valley Authority. It seemed as though the Supreme Court might destroy the New Deal.

A Second Term

The presidential campaign of 1936 was based on a single issue: Did the American people support FDR and the New Deal?

To run against Roosevelt, the Republicans nominated **Alfred M. Landon,** governor of Kansas. Landon attracted dissatisfied Democrats as well as Republicans. FDR campaigned as the champion of the average American. He denounced big business and the rich, who "are unanimous in their hate for me—and I welcome their hatred."

On Election Day FDR received 61 percent of the popular vote, the biggest landslide in an American presidential election to that time. Roosevelt's support came from progressives and liberals, the poor and unemployed, urban workers, and African Americans. These groups would form the core of the Democratic Party for decades to come.

Roosevelt's "Court-Packing" Plan

Soon after his reelection, FDR took action to prevent the Supreme Court from undoing the New Deal. He asked Congress to increase the number of justices on the Court from 9 to 15, saying that the 9 justices were overworked and needed additional help. FDR would appoint the 6 new justices—selecting, of course, justices who would uphold the New Deal.

The proposal aroused bitter opposition. Critics accused the president of trying to "pack" the Court and ruin the system of checks and balances set up in the Constitution. The issue died when the Court ruled in favor of the Wagner Act and the Social Security Act. The New Deal was no longer in serious danger from the Court. The unpopularity of the court-packing plan, however, cost Roosevelt a great deal of support and triggered a split in the Democratic Party.

The Roosevelt Recession

By the summer of 1937, the national income had nearly returned to its 1929 level. Believing that the Depression was finally over, Roosevelt tried to reduce the government's debt by cutting spending on relief and job programs.

The economy faltered immediately. Farm prices dropped. Four million people lost their jobs. Times nearly as hard as 1932–1933 returned. The new economic downturn, known to some as the **Roosevelt Recession,** lasted into 1938. Roosevelt helped to reverse it with a flood of government spending on public works.

The End of the New Deal

The court-packing fight and the Roosevelt Recession cost FDR support in Congress. The economy had not fully recovered, in spite of the wide-ranging New Deal programs. As the 1930s drew to a close, however, world events caused Americans to turn their attention from domestic to foreign affairs. Dangerous forces were on the rise in Asia and Europe.

Reading Check **Explaining** Why was Roosevelt's plan to change the Supreme Court criticized?

SECTION 4 ASSESSMENT

Checking for Understanding

1. **Key Terms** Write sentences about the Second New Deal; use these vocabulary terms: **pension, Social Security Act, unemployment insurance.**
2. **Reviewing Facts** Summarize the economic plan of Huey Long.

Reviewing Themes

3. **Government and Democracy** What was the aim of Social Security and exactly whom did it help?

Critical Thinking

4. **Making Generalizations** Why did many business leaders oppose Roosevelt's New Deal?
5. **Determining Cause and Effect** Why did Roosevelt propose to change the number of justices on the Supreme Court? Re-create the diagram below and list one cause and two effects of FDR's proposal.

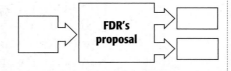

Analyzing Visuals

6. **Political Cartoons** Review the cartoon "Packing the Court" on page 745. Does the cartoon show support for or opposition to the plan? How can you tell?

Interdisciplinary Activity

Government Research the effect of the New Deal in your community. Find out if the federal government in the 1930s supported any local projects in conservation, construction, or the arts.

Social Studies
SKILLBUILDER

Analyzing News Media

Why Learn This Skill?

Every citizen needs to be aware of current issues and events to make good decisions when exercising citizenship rights.

Learning the Skill

To get an accurate profile of current events, you must learn to think critically about the news. The steps below will help you think critically.

- First, think about the source of the news story. Reports that reveal sources are more reliable than those that do not. If you know the sources, you can evaluate them. Can all facts be verified?
- Many news stories also interpret events. Such analyses may reflect a reporter's biases. Look for biases as you read or listen to news stories.
- Ask yourself whether the news is even-handed and thorough. Is it reported on the scene or secondhand? Does it represent both sides of an issue? The more sources cited for a fact, the more reliable it usually is.

Practicing the Skill

On this page is an excerpt from the New York Times *newspaper of February 6, 1937. Read the excerpt; then answer the following questions.*

❶ What point is the article trying to make?

❷ Is the article reporting something on the scene or secondhand?

❸ Does the article reflect bias or strong opinion about the news item?

❹ Is only one side of the issue presented? Explain.

AIM TO PACK COURT, DECLARES HOOVER

President Roosevelt's message to Congress asking for authority to appoint new Federal judges whenever existing ones were over 70 years old was characterized last night by Herbert Hoover, his predecessor in the White House, as a proposal for "packing" the Supreme Court to get through New Deal measures. . . .

"The Supreme Court has proved many of the New Deal proposals as unconstitutional. Instead of the ample alternatives of the Constitution by which these proposals could be submitted to the people through constitutional amendment, it is now proposed to make changes by 'packing' the Supreme Court. It has the implication of subordination of the court to the personal power of the Executive."

Applying the Skill

Analyzing News Media Think of an issue in your community on which public opinion is divided. Read newspaper features and editorials about the issue and listen to television reports. Can you identify biases? Which reports more fairly represent the issue and the solutions? Which reports are the most reliable?

 Glencoe's **Skillbuilder Interactive Workbook CD-ROM, Level 1,** provides instruction and practice in key social studies skills.

Chapter Summary
The Depression and FDR

Causes

- Income gap between rich and poor grows
- High tariffs and war debts
- Overuse of credit to make purchases
- Industry and agriculture supply exceeds demand
- Sales lag
- International market falters
- Stock market crash; financial panic

The Great Depression

Effects

- Millions lose jobs, poverty is widespread
- Businesses and banks close
- Depression spreads to other countries
- Roosevelt wins presidency
- New Deal legislation enacted
- Despite periods of economic upturn, the Depression remains

Reviewing Key Terms

On a sheet of paper, use at least six of the following terms to write a paragraph on the Great Depression or the New Deal.

1. default, relief, public works, Hundred Days, New Deal, Dust Bowl, migrant worker, pension, Social Security Act, subsidy, unemployment insurance

Reviewing Key Facts

2. What did the Bonus Army want the government to do?
3. What was the New Deal?
4. How did the CCC benefit the unemployed as well as the nation?
5. In what region was the Dust Bowl centered?
6. Summarize the advances made by African Americans and women during the Great Depression.
7. What was the purpose of the Social Security Act?
8. Describe two laws passed during the Second New Deal that helped workers and unions.

Critical Thinking

9. **Economic Factors** How did the trend of buying on credit in the 1920s affect banks during the Depression?
10. **Determining Cause and Effect** How did new technology help cause the Dust Bowl disaster?
11. **Reviewing Themes: Government and Democracy** Re-create the diagram below and list two ways the federal government changed during Roosevelt's administration.

Practicing Skills

12. **Analyzing News Media** Find two articles, one in a current newspaper and the other in a newsmagazine, on a topic involving the economy. Compare the articles. Did either of the articles show any biases? List any unsupported claims.

Geography and History Activity

Study the map below and answer these questions.

NATIONAL GEOGRAPHIC

The Tennessee Valley Authority

Area supplied with power from the TVA
— Dam
■ Steam power plant

0   100 miles
0   100 kilometers
Lambert Equal-Area projection

13. Place What physical feature made Tennessee particularly suited for the Tennessee Valley Authority project?

14. Region Which states were supplied with power from the TVA?

15. Location On the map, what dams are located along the Tennessee River?

Economic Activity

16. Use the Internet and other resources to research the various types of credit available to consumers today. Assess the advantages and disadvantages of each type of credit. Do you think consumer credit today could contribute to an economic depression like that of the 1930s?

HISTORY Online

Self-Check Quiz
Visit **taj.glencoe.com** and click on **Chapter 25— Self-Check Quizzes** to prepare for the chapter test.

Citizenship Cooperative Activity

17. Research Work with members of your group to prepare a photo essay to document the hardships of the Depression. Photocopy some of the photos and display them in an interesting way on a sheet of cardboard. Write captions for each photo, provide photo credits, and write a title for your essay. Then, with the rest of the class, create a walk-through gallery to display all the photo essays.

Alternative Assessment

18. Portfolio Writing Activity Both Eleanor and Franklin Roosevelt received many letters from the public during the Depression asking for jobs, money, food, and clothing. Write a letter from either of the Roosevelts responding to a plea for help. Explain in your letter what you can or cannot do for this person. Use what you have learned about the Roosevelts' personalities to make your letters realistic.

Standardized Test Practice

Directions: Choose the *best* answer to the following question.

All of the following programs were created by Roosevelt in the First New Deal EXCEPT the

A Agricultural Adjustment Act (AAA).

B Civilian Conservation Corps (CCC).

C Fair Labor Standards Act (FLSA).

D Tennessee Valley Authority (TVA).

Test-Taking Tip.

Be careful when you see the word EXCEPT in a question. Read carefully all the answer choices and choose the one that *doesn't* fit with the question. Many times there are specific words in the question that tell you something specific. Here, the question asks about the First New Deal, not the Second New Deal.

CHAPTER 26

World War II

1939–1945

Why It Matters

World War II, the most destructive war in history, resulted in the deaths of more than 40 million people. More than half of the deaths were civilians, including about six million Jews and many others that were killed in the Holocaust. At the end of the war, the United States emerged as the strongest nation in the world and the possessor of a powerful weapon—the atomic bomb.

The Impact Today

World War II marked the beginning of the nation's role as a superpower. The war also transformed the American economy into an enormously productive and enduringly prosperous economy.

 The American Journey Video The chapter 26 video, "War on the Home Front," discusses what life was like in America during World War II.

1942
- Japanese Americans sent to internment camps
- U.S. joins Allies in World War II

1940
- Selective Training and Service Act passed

1941
- U.S. enters the war
- Lend-Lease Act passed

 United States PRESIDENTS

 F. Roosevelt 1933–1945

1940   *1941*   *1942*

 World

1939
- Germany seizes Czechoslovakia

1940
- German troops occupy Paris
- Germany bombs Britain

1941
- Germany attacks the Soviet Union

Sequencing Events Study Foldable Make this foldable to describe and sequence the events of World War II.

Step 1 Collect 3 sheets of paper and place them about 1 inch apart.

Keep the edges straight.

Step 2 Fold up the bottom edges of the paper to form 6 tabs.

This makes all tabs the same size.

Step 3 When all the tabs are the same size, fold the paper to hold the tabs in place and staple the sheets together. Turn the paper and label each tab as shown.

World War II
Road to War
War Begins
On the Home Front
War in Europe and Africa
War in the Pacific

Staple together along the fold.

Reading and Writing As you read the chapter, identify, sequence, and briefly describe the key events that belong under each heading on your foldable. Write information under each tab.

Mission Over Normandy by **William S. Phillips** During World War II, the Army Air Corps fought enemy aircraft, bombed targets, and transported soldiers.

1945
• U.S. drops atomic bombs on Hiroshima and Nagasaki

1943   *1944*   *1945*

1944
• D-Day: Allies land in Normandy

1945
• Concentration camps found where Nazis killed millions
• World War II ends

HISTORY Online

Chapter Overview
Visit taj.glencoe.com and click on **Chapter 26— Chapter Overviews** to preview chapter information.

Guide to Reading

Main Idea
As dictators threatened world peace, the United States tried to follow a policy of neutrality.

Key Terms
dictator, fascism, anti-Semitism, totalitarian, appeasement

Reading Strategy
Organizing Information As you read Section 1, re-create the diagram below and list three dictators and the countries they ruled in the 1920s and 1930s.

Dictators

Read to Learn
• why dictators came to power around the world.
• what actions led to the outbreak of World War II.

Section Theme
Global Connections Europe tried to avoid war by a policy of appeasement.

Preview of Events

✦1930   ✦1935   ✦1940

1931
Japan invades Manchuria

1933
Hitler becomes chancellor of Germany

1935
Italian forces invade Ethiopia

1939
Germany seizes Czechoslovakia

★ ★ ★ ★ ★ ★ ★ ★ ★
AN
American Story

Many people underestimated Adolf Hitler's influence, but not American journalist William Shirer. He described a rally for Hitler at Nuremberg in September 1934: "Like a Roman emperor Hitler rode into this medieval town. . . . The streets, hardly wider than alleys, are a sea of brown and black uniforms. . . . [W]hen Hitler finally appeared on the balcony for a moment . . . [people] looked up at him as if he were a Messiah, their faces transformed into something positively inhuman." The passion of the Nazis shocked Shirer, and soon it would shock the rest of the world.

The Rise of Dictators

In the late 1920s, Adolf Hitler achieved wide popularity in Germany. In his book *Mein Kampf* (My Struggle), Hitler set forth his political views.

❝He who wants to live must fight, and he who does not want to fight in this world, where eternal struggle is the law of life, has no right to exist.❞

When Hitler became the leader of Germany, he put his strong words into action. Hitler was among other ruthless leaders to rise to power in the 1920s and 1930s by taking advantage of people's anger and suffering. Some Europeans resented the terms of the Treaty of Versailles, signed in 1919, which ended World War I. When a world-wide economic depression hit in the 1930s, frustration and fear added to this anger.

Hitler and other leaders promised a better life. They described a glorious future to people humiliated by losing a war. Once they gained political power, these men became dictators—leaders who control their nations by force.

Italy

Benito Mussolini rose to power by appealing to the resentment of many Italians who felt they had not won enough in the Versailles treaty. Mussolini made fascism—extreme nationalism and racism—popular in Italy. By 1922 his **Fascist Party** had gained enough strength to force the king of Italy to declare Mussolini the head of the government. Within a few years, Mussolini had banned all political parties except his Fascist Party.

Known as *Il Duce* (the leader), Mussolini quickly put an end to democratic rule in Italy. Civil liberties and the free press ceased to exist. Boys and girls of all ages were enrolled in military organizations that taught them loyalty to the new government. Mussolini built up Italy's military and vowed to recapture the glory of the ancient Romans.

In 1935 Mussolini sent Italian forces to invade the African nation of **Ethiopia,** which it annexed—took over as its own territory. Ethiopian emperor Haile Selassie appealed to the League of Nations for help: "God and history will remember your judgment. It is us today. It will be you tomorrow." The League responded by banning trade in weapons and certain other materials with Italy, but it lacked the power to enforce the ban. Italy withdrew from the League and continued its aggressive policies, attacking and annexing its neighbor Albania in 1939.

Germany

The Great Depression had hit Germany extremely hard. Millions of people had lost their jobs, and its economy teetered on the edge of collapse. Germans rallied around Adolf Hitler, a shrewd politician and a spellbinding speaker. Hitler gained popularity by exploiting people's concern about unchecked inflation and severe unemployment. Hitler also played upon bitterness over the Versailles treaty. The treaty had forced Germany to give up some of its territory and to make heavy payments to the victors.

In 1921 Hitler became chairman of the National Socialist German Workers' Party, or the **Nazi Party.** Openly racist, Hitler and the Nazis portrayed the German people as superior to all others. They directed much of their anger against Jews, whom Hitler blamed for Germany's problems. His extreme anti-Semitism—hatred of the Jews—would later lead to unspeakable horrors.

Soon after he became chancellor, or chief minister, of Germany in 1933, Hitler ended all democracy and established totalitarian rule. In a

Analyzing *Political Cartoons*

This American cartoon of Mussolini portrays him with a short body, small hands, a huge belly, and fear in his eyes. Mussolini's arm is raised in a familiar fascist salute. **What is the artist saying about Mussolini and fascism?**

TWO VIEWPOINTS

Should We Intervene or Remain Neutral?

As Adolf Hitler's German army conquered parts of Europe, Americans debated their involvement. Should the United States stand back while the aggression continued and avoid the horrors of a war that was not its war? Or, should it help allies like Great Britain put an end to the destructive ambitions of Nazi Germany?

Petition Sent From the Fight for Freedom National Offices, 1940

We are not neutral. As freedom-loving citizens of the United States, we recognize that our liberty, that democracy everywhere will be ended unless the menace [threat] of Hitler is smashed. We, therefore, petition the Congress of the United States TO REPEAL OUR SUICIDAL, HYPOCRITICAL AND DANGEROUS NEUTRALITY ACT, to remove the prohibition against arming our merchant ships, and dissolve the ban which prevents vessels flying the American flag from sailing the seven seas. American policy has traditionally been that of freedom of the seas. Our Congress must reassert and uphold that right. Our Congress has pledged our resources to those nations fighting Axis aggression, and must reinforce that pledge by guaranteeing that our goods arrive at their destination in the hands of our allies.

Robert M. Hutchins, President of the University of Chicago, January 23, 1941

How can the United States better serve suffering humanity everywhere: by going into this war, or by staying out? I hold that the United States can better serve suffering humanity everywhere by staying out....

If we go to war, we cast away our opportunity and cancel our gains. For a generation, perhaps for a hundred years, we shall not be able to struggle back to where we were. In fact, the changes that total war will bring may mean that we shall never be able to struggle back. Education will cease. Its place will be taken by vocational and military training. The effort to establish a democratic community will stop. We shall think no more of justice, the moral order, and the supremacy of human rights. We shall have hope no longer.

Learning From History

1. What did the members of Fight for Freedom want the U.S. Congress to do?
2. According to Robert Hutchins, what would happen to Americans if the United States entered World War II?
3. How strongly do each of these sides seem to feel about its opinions?

---

totalitarian state, a single party and its leader suppress all opposition and control all aspects of people's lives.

Hitler claimed that Germany had a right to expand its territory. Germany's neighbors watched uneasily as he rebuilt Germany's military strength in defiance of the Versailles treaty. To gain support in his expansion plans, Hitler formed an alliance with Italy in 1936.

Japan

During the Depression many Japanese grew frustrated with their government's failure to solve economic problems. As a result, military leaders rose to power in the early 1930s. These leaders thought they would solve Japan's problems by expanding Japanese power in Asia.

In September 1931, Japan launched an attack on the province of **Manchuria** in northeastern China. The League of Nations condemned the attack, but it took no action.

Left unchallenged, Japan set up a government in Manchuria. In 1937 Japan invaded northern China, moving southward until it occupied most of the country. Three years later Japan signed a pact of alliance, known as the "Axis," with Germany and Italy.

Soviet Union

In the late 1920s, **Joseph Stalin** rose to power as the Communist leader of the Soviet Union. Stalin demanded complete obedience from the people he ruled and got it through the use of force. Stalin executed his rivals, ordered the deaths of thousands suspected of supporting his rivals, and sent millions of Russians to labor camps. He also reorganized the nation's economy, forcing millions of people onto government-owned farms.

American Neutrality

While dramatic changes were taking place in the world, most Americans wanted to avoid involvement. To keep the nation out of future wars, Congress passed a series of **Neutrality Acts** between 1935 and 1937, which banned the sale of weapons to nations at war. The laws also allowed trade only to nations that could pay cash for goods and transport the goods in their own ships. Many American loans to European countries from World War I remained unpaid, and Congress wanted to prevent more debts.

✓ **Reading Check** **Explaining** What is fascism?

Germany on the March

Hitler began moving forward with his plans for expansion. In March 1936, he ordered troops into the **Rhineland.** The Treaty of Versailles had declared the Rhineland, a German territory west of the Rhine River, a neutral zone.

Hitler's next victim was **Austria.** Hitler insisted that Germany should be unified with Austria, a German-speaking nation. In March 1938, he sent troops into Austria and annexed it.

Hitler turned next to the **Sudetenland,** an area of Czechoslovakia where many German-speaking people lived. Falsely claiming that these people were being persecuted, Hitler announced Germany's right to annex the Sudetenland.

Czechoslovakia was prepared to fight to keep the Sudetenland. Britain and France, fearing a full-fledged war in the region, sought a peaceful solution to the crisis. In September 1938, European leaders met in Munich, Germany.

Britain and France thought that they could avoid war by accepting Germany's demands—a policy later known as appeasement. At the **Munich Conference,** the leaders agreed to turn the Sudetenland over to Germany. Hitler, in turn, promised not to expand Germany's territory further. The British prime minister, **Neville Chamberlain,** returned home to cheering crowds, declaring that the agreement had preserved "peace for our time."

Hopes for peace were shattered the following spring. In March 1939, Hitler's army seized the rest of Czechoslovakia. Now even Chamberlain realized that Hitler could not be trusted.

Meanwhile, Hitler was making plans to invade **Poland.** He worried, however, that such an attack would anger Stalin because Poland bordered the Soviet Union. Though bitter enemies, Hitler and Stalin signed a treaty called the **Soviet-German Non-Aggression Pact** in August 1939. The pact freed Hitler to use force against Poland without fear of Soviet intervention. The Nazi-Soviet pact shocked the leaders of Europe.

✓ **Reading Check** **Explaining** Did the policy of appeasement work? Explain.

SECTION 1 ASSESSMENT

Checking for Understanding

1. **Key Terms** Use each of these terms in a sentence that will help explain its meaning: dictator, fascism, anti-Semitism, totalitarian, appeasement.
2. **Reviewing Facts** What actions did Stalin use to gain obedience from the Russian people?

Reviewing Themes

3. **Global Connections** What was the aim of the policy of appeasement? Did it work?

Critical Thinking

4. **Comparing** What goals did the leaders of the nations of Germany, Italy, and Japan share in the 1930s?
5. **Sequencing Information** Re-create the time line below and list the major events in Hitler's rise to power in Germany.

1921	1933	1936	1938	1939
☐	☐	☐	☐	☐

Analyzing Visuals

6. **Analyzing Political Cartoons** Examine the cartoon on page 753. What do you think Mussolini's shadow represents? What word or phrase would you use to describe Mussolini's appearance?

Interdisciplinary Activity

Expository Writing Write newspaper headlines about three important events covered in Section 1.

What were people's lives like in the past?

What—and whom—were people talking about? What did they eat? What did they do for fun? These two pages will give you some clues to everyday life in the U.S. as you step back in time with TIME Notebook.

Star Quality

Apparently no one has told **SHIRLEY TEMPLE** *that this is 1934 and there is a Depression going on. Believe it or not, this six-year-old will earn $400,000 this year. What makes the young movie star such a success? Here is what the group who presented Temple with a special Academy Award said:*

"SHIRLEY TEMPLE BROUGHT MORE happiness to millions of children and grown-ups than any child of her years in the history of the world…."

Shirley Temple

ARCHIVE PHOTOS

Movies

Snow What and the Seven Who? Just in time for the holidays! On December 21, 1937, Disney movie studio has released *Snow White and the Seven Dwarfs*, the first animated full-length feature film. Snow White is joined by Happy, Sleepy, Dopey, Grumpy, Sneezy, Bashful, and Doc.

Snow White

© THE WALT DISNEY COMPANY/PHOTOFEST

Headlines from the Time

MISSING — Lindbergh Baby Search Still On Nearly two months have passed since famed flyer Charles Lindbergh and his wife Anne's baby boy was kidnapped in March 1932. A ladder leading up to the baby's window, muddy footprints, and a ransom note demanding $50,000 are the three clues that have been studied by over 5,000 FBI agents. About 100,000 police and volunteers have combed the horror-stricken country, searching for the baby.

Charles Lindbergh

TIME INC. PICTURE COLLECTION

❝ While I still have got breath in my lungs, I will tell you what a dandy car you make. I [have driven] Fords exclusively when I could get away with one. ❞

CLYDE BARROW,
(half the team of bank robbers Bonnie and Clyde) in a 1934 letter to Henry Ford

❝ I pledge you, I pledge myself, to a new deal for the American people. Let all us here assembled constitute ourselves prophets of a new order of competence and courage ❞

FRANKLIN D. ROOSEVELT,
accepting the Democratic presidential nomination in 1932

BROWN BROTHERS

❝ When these winds hit us, we and our misery were suddenly covered with dust.… If the wind blew one way, here came the dark dust from Oklahoma. Another way and it was the gray dust from Kansas. Still another way, the brown dust from Colorado and New Mexico. ❞

TEXAS FARMER,
in 1934, describing the worst agricultural disaster in U.S. history, the Dust Bowl. Dust has covered an area of 150 million square miles and has displaced more than 750,000 people

BETTMANN/CORBIS

AMERICAN SCENE

Depression Figures

Americans are truly suffering during this Great Depression. It is a time of enormous financial problems for millions of people—not just in the United States, but around the world. Banks are failing, people are losing their life savings, and businesses are closing their doors. The graphs on this page give an idea of this difficult time.

DEPRESSION INCOMES

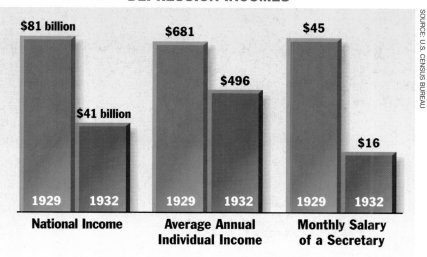

SOURCE: U.S. CENSUS BUREAU

	National Income	Average Annual Individual Income	Monthly Salary of a Secretary
1929	$81 billion	$681	$45
1932	$41 billion	$496	$16

UNEMPLOYMENT IN THE U.S.

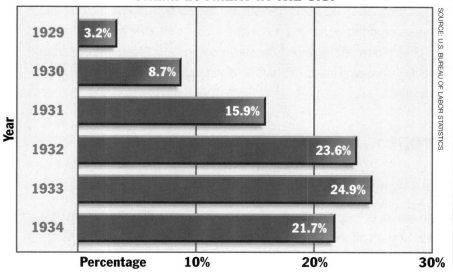

SOURCE: U.S. BUREAU OF LABOR STATISTICS

Year	Percentage
1929	3.2%
1930	8.7%
1931	15.9%
1932	23.6%
1933	24.9%
1934	21.7%

Percentage — 10% — 20% — 30%

Number One *Gone With the Wind* wins the Pulitzer Prize for 1937. Millions of readers set aside their worries as they experienced the epic drama, defeat, and triumphs of Mitchell's cast of characters.

Two is a charm for President Roosevelt, sworn in for the second time on January 20, 1937. FDR turned down a ride in a closed limousine—even though it was raining. He pointed toward the thousands of wet people who lined the streets of Washington, D.C., hoping to catch a glimpse of him, and said, "I'll ride in the open limo. If they can take it, I can!"

TIME INC. PICTURE COLLECTION

President Roosevelt

Three hundred miles per hour — on September 3, 1935, the Bluebird Special made history. This sleek car is the first land vehicle to top 300 mph (500 km).

Four gold medals. Adolf Hitler, Germany's Fascist leader, invited the world to Berlin for the 1936 Olympic Games. Hitler had hoped to prove the supposed "inferiority" of non-Aryan races. No one told that to U.S. superstar Jesse Owens, an African American athlete who won four gold medals in track and field events.

Guide to Reading

Main Idea
Many nations were drawn into the conflict, largely because of political alliances and economic relationships.

Key Terms
blitzkrieg, lend-lease, disarmament

Reading Strategy
Classifying Information As you read Section 2, re-create the diagram shown below and explain the importance of each event.

	Importance
The Battle of Britain	
Signing the Atlantic Charter	
Attack on Pearl Harbor	

Read to Learn
- which European nations fell to Germany in 1939 and 1940.
- how the United States responded to the war in Europe.

Section Theme
Global Connections The war expanded rapidly as nations became more involved and were drawn into the conflict.

Preview of Events

♦1939	♦1940	♦1941	♦1942
September 1939 Germany invades Poland	**August 1940** Britain is bombed by Germany	**June 1941** Hitler attacks the Soviet Union	**December 1941** Japan bombs Pearl Harbor

AN American Story

Sixteen-year-old John Garcia, like others who witnessed the attack on Pearl Harbor, never forgot it: "My grandmother . . . informed me that the Japanese were bombing Pearl Harbor. I said, 'They're just practicing.' She said, no, it was real and the announcer is requesting that all Pearl Harbor workers report to work. . . . I was asked . . . to go into the water and get sailors out that had been blown off the ships. Some were unconscious, some were dead. So I spent the rest of the day swimming inside the harbor, along with some other Hawaiians. . . . We worked all day at that."

War in Europe

In a speech in 1937, President Franklin Roosevelt expressed the feeling of many Americans toward the growing "epidemic of world lawlessness":

&&We are determined to keep out of war, yet we cannot insure ourselves against the disastrous effects of war and the dangers of involvement.99

On September 1, 1939, Hitler sent his armies into **Poland.** Two days later Great Britain and France declared war on Germany. World War II had begun.

The German attack on Poland was swift and fierce. German planes bombed and machine-gunned targets, German tanks blasted holes in Polish defenses, and thousands of soldiers poured into Poland. The Germans called the offensive a blitzkrieg, or "lightning war." Then Soviet troops moved into and occupied eastern Poland, acting on the Soviet agreement with Germany to divide Poland.

Great Britain and France could do little to help Poland because its defeat came so quickly. In late September 1939, the conquered country was split in half by Hitler and Stalin. Stalin also forced the **Baltic** republics of Latvia, Lithuania, and Estonia to accept Soviet military bases. When he tried to do the same with **Finland,** war broke out between the two nations. The Finns held out heroically until March 1940, when the Soviets forced them to surrender.

The War Expands

All through the winter of 1939–1940 the western front was quiet. British and French forces settled in at the **Maginot Line,** a string of steel-and-concrete bunkers along the German border from Belgium to Switzerland. In the spring the fighting began again. In April Hitler attacked **Denmark** and **Norway** to the north, and the following month he turned west to invade the **Netherlands** and **Belgium.** The Netherlands and Belgium immediately asked for help from Great Britain and France—the **Allies.** After terrible bombing raids in the Netherlands, the Dutch surrendered. The Belgians fought courageously, but they too were overwhelmed.

With the collapse of Belgium, Allied troops retreated to the port of **Dunkirk** in the northwest corner of France on the **English Channel.** They were now trapped between the advancing Germans and the French coast. In a daring move, more than 800 British ships—warships, ferries, and fishing boats—joined an operation to rescue the troops. Crossing the Channel again and again, the boats evacuated more than 300,000 French and British troops to safety.

In June the Germans crossed the Somme River and continued their sweep into France. Italy joined the war on the side of Germany

History *Through Art*

The Withdrawal from Dunkirk, June 1940 by Charles R.A. Cundall Boats crossed the English Channel to bring Allied troops from France back to safety in England. **Why did Allied forces retreat?**

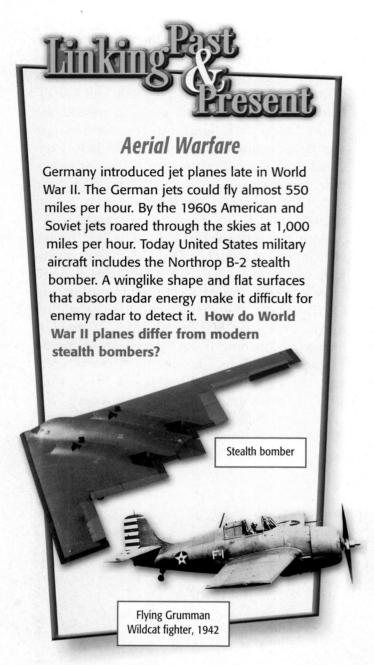

Linking Past & Present

Aerial Warfare

Germany introduced jet planes late in World War II. The German jets could fly almost 550 miles per hour. By the 1960s American and Soviet jets roared through the skies at 1,000 miles per hour. Today United States military aircraft includes the Northrop B-2 stealth bomber. A winglike shape and flat surfaces that absorb radar energy make it difficult for enemy radar to detect it. **How do World War II planes differ from modern stealth bombers?**

Stealth bomber

Flying Grumman Wildcat fighter, 1942

and attacked France from the southeast. Germany and Italy—and later Japan—formed the **Axis Powers.** On June 14, 1940, German troops marched victoriously into Paris. The French surrendered a week later, stunned by the German blitzkrieg.

The Battle of Britain

All that stood between Hitler's domination of Western Europe was Great Britain. In August 1940, the Germans bombed British shipyards, industries, and cities, destroying entire neighborhoods of London and killing many civilians.

Hitler's goal was to break British morale before invading Britain. The British people endured, however, in part because of the inspiration of Prime Minister **Winston Churchill.** When Hitler called for Britain to surrender, Churchill responded defiantly:

> ❝We shall defend our island, whatever the cost may be. We shall fight on the beaches, we shall fight on the landing grounds, we shall fight in the fields and in the streets, we shall fight in the hills; we shall never surrender.❞

Although the **Battle of Britain** continued until October, the Germans never gained control of the skies over Britain. The British Royal Air Force (RAF) mounted a heroic defense and inflicted heavy losses on the German air force. Finally, Hitler ended the air attacks.

Germany Turns East

Frustrated by his failure in Britain, Hitler decided to realize one of his oldest dreams—to destroy the Soviet Union. Ignoring the pact he had made with Stalin, Hitler launched an attack on the Soviet Union in June 1941. Within months German armies had moved into Soviet territory. The Soviet Union joined the Allies in their fight against the Axis Powers.

Reading Check **Examining** Why did Hitler bring the invasion of Britain to an end?

America and the War

The United States watched the war in Europe with growing concern. Although most Americans sympathized with the Allies, they were determined to avoid war. Isolationists banded together to form the **America First Committee.** Its members thought the United States should keep out of Europe's business. Among those who led this group were aviation hero Charles Lindbergh and automaker Henry Ford.

While vowing to remain neutral, Roosevelt took steps to prepare for war. In 1938, at his request, Congress voted to strengthen the navy. In 1939 the president asked Congress to pass a new Neutrality Act that allowed the United States to sell weapons to other countries on a "cash and carry" basis. In 1940 FDR signed the Selective Training and Service Act, the first peacetime draft in United States history. The law applied to American men between the ages of 21 and 35.

The 1940 Election

With the world in crisis, President Roosevelt decided to run for a third term, breaking the tradition set by George Washington. The Republicans chose as their candidate a former Democrat—business leader Wendell L. Willkie of Indiana. Willkie approved almost all of Roosevelt's New Deal reforms and generally agreed with his foreign policy. Public sentiment to stay out of the war was so strong that Roosevelt promised the American people, "Your boys are not going to be sent into any foreign wars." Roosevelt won an easy victory.

U.S. Involvement Grows

With the election won, Roosevelt moved to support the Allies openly. At Roosevelt's urging, Congress approved the Lend-Lease Act in March 1941. The Lend-Lease Act allowed America to sell, lend, or lease arms or other war supplies to any nation considered "vital to the defense of the United States." Britain, which was running out of cash, was the first to use lend-lease. Isolationists opposed the Lend-Lease Act, arguing that it would increase American involvement in the war.

German submarines in the Atlantic Ocean had been sinking British ships, including those carrying supplies from the United States. In mid-1941, American ships began escorting convoys of British merchant ships. After the Germans began firing on American destroyers, Roosevelt issued a "shoot-on-sight" order to American naval vessels that found German and Italian ships in certain areas.

The Atlantic Charter

In August 1941, President Roosevelt and British prime minister Churchill met and drew up the **Atlantic Charter.** While Roosevelt made no military commitments, he joined Churchill in setting goals for a world after "the final destruction of the Nazi tyranny." The two nations pledged that the people of every nation would be free to choose their own form of government and live free of "fear and want." They urged disarmament—giving up military weapons—and the creation of a "permanent system of general security."

✓ **Reading Check** **Explaining** What did the Lend-Lease Act allow the United States to do?

The bombing of London caused much ruin. The Royal Air Force (inset) forced Hitler to abandon his invasion plans.

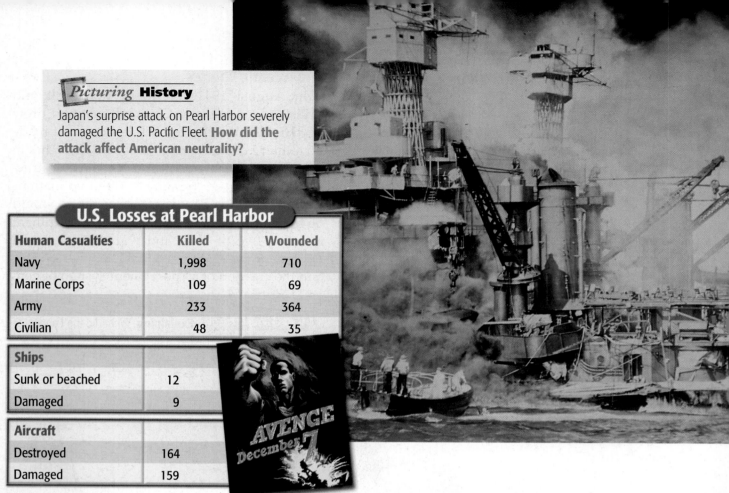

Picturing **History**

Japan's surprise attack on Pearl Harbor severely damaged the U.S. Pacific Fleet. **How did the attack affect American neutrality?**

U.S. Losses at Pearl Harbor		
Human Casualties	**Killed**	**Wounded**
Navy	1,998	710
Marine Corps	109	69
Army	233	364
Civilian	48	35
Ships		
Sunk or beached	12	
Damaged	9	
Aircraft		
Destroyed	164	
Damaged	159	

Source: USS *Arizona* Memorial.

The Japanese Threat

While Hitler and Mussolini were waging war in Europe, the Japanese were making military conquests in the Far East. After seizing much of China in the 1930s, the Japanese continued their expansion. After the fall of France in 1940, they seized the French colony of **Indochina** in Southeast Asia. Japan also planned to take the Dutch East Indies, British Malaya, and the American territory of the Philippines, primarily to acquire badly needed rubber and oil.

The United States Responds

The United States responded to Japan's aggression by applying economic pressure. Roosevelt froze all Japanese assets in American banks, preventing the Japanese from obtaining funds they had in the United States. He also stopped the sale of oil, gasoline, and other natural resources that Japan lacked. The action outraged the Japanese.

In October 1941, the Japanese prime minister, Fumimaro Konoye, resigned. Konoye had been willing to negotiate with the United States because he did not believe Japan could defeat America in a war. The new prime minister, General **Hideki Tōjō,** did not share Konoye's views. Still, on November 20, negotiations were opened in Washington between the United States and Japan. At the same time, confident of Japan's military might, the Tōjō government began planning an attack on the United States.

Attack on Pearl Harbor

At 7:55 A.M. on Sunday, December 7, 1941, Japanese warplanes attacked the American military base at **Pearl Harbor,** Hawaii. The American installations at Pearl Harbor could not have been more vulnerable to attack. Ships were anchored in a neat row and airplanes were grouped together on the airfield, easy targets for a Japanese air attack. The Americans at Pearl Harbor were taken completely by surprise. According to Rear Admiral William R. Furlong,

66 In the Navy housing areas around Pearl Harbor, people couldn't imagine what was wrecking Sunday morning. Captain Reynolds Hayden, enjoying breakfast at his home on Hospital Point, thought it was construction blasting. . . . Lieutenant C. E. Boudreau, drying down after a shower, thought an oil tank had blown up near his quarters . . . until a Japanese plane almost grazed the bathroom window. Chief Petty Officer Albert Molter, puttering around his Ford Island flat, thought a drill was going on until his wife Esther called, 'Al, there's a battleship tipping over.' 99

The attack devastated the American fleet, destroying many battleships, cruisers, and other vessels. Hundreds of planes were destroyed or damaged. More than 2,300 soldiers, sailors, and civilians were killed.

Fortunately, at the time of the attack, the navy's three aircraft carriers were at sea. Their escape from destruction provided the only good news that day.

Grace Tully, one of the president's secretaries, received an urgent call to report to the White House. She later recalled:

AVENGE PEARL HARBOR

OUR BULLETS WILL DO IT

66 Most of the news on the . . . attack was then coming to the White House by telephone from Admiral Stark, Chief of Naval Operations, at the Navy Department . . . each report more terrible than the last, and I could hear the shocked unbelief in Admiral Stark's voice. 99

Pearl Harbor was the worst defeat in United States military history. Yet Pearl Harbor also united Americans. All debate about involvement in the war ended. On the day after Pearl Harbor, President Roosevelt asked Congress for a declaration of war, calling December 7 "a date which will live in infamy." Congress quickly approved the president's request to declare war on Japan.

On December 11, Germany and Italy, Japan's allies, declared war on the United States. Congress then declared war on them as well. The United States had joined the Allied nations—including Great Britain, France, China, and the Soviet Union—against the Axis Powers—Germany, Italy, and Japan—in World War II.

✓ Reading Check Explaining Why did the United States enter World War II?

SECTION 2 ASSESSMENT

Checking for Understanding

1. **Key Terms** Define the following key terms: blitzkrieg, lend-lease, disarmament.
2. **Reviewing Facts** What nations formed the Axis Powers?

Reviewing Themes

3. **Global Connections** What diplomatic actions did the United States take to prevent Japan from taking over nations in Asia?

Critical Thinking

4. **Predicting Consequences** Do you think the United States would have eventually joined the war even if Japanese forces had not attacked Pearl Harbor? Explain.
5. **Sequencing Information** Re-create the time line below and identify the important events.

Sept. 1, 1939	Mar. 1940	Jun. 14, 1940	Dec. 7, 1941
☐	☐	☐	☐

Analyzing Visuals

6. **Analyzing Art** Look at the painting on page 759. What event does the painting show? Why do you think the artist decided to portray this event in such a large view?

Interdisciplinary Activity

Descriptive Writing Write and record a 15-second radio news bulletin announcing the Japanese bombing of Pearl Harbor.

SECTION 3 On the Home Front

Guide to Reading

Main Idea
Demand for war goods created new industries and new jobs.

Key Terms
mobilization, ration, internment camp

Reading Strategy
Organizing Information As you read the section, re-create the diagram below and identify three ways Americans on the home front helped the war effort.

Read to Learn
- what steps the United States took to prepare for fighting the war.
- how the war affected Americans.

Section Theme
Economic Factors The United States had to switch rapidly from a peacetime economy to a wartime economy—providing arms and other supplies for thousands of troops.

Preview of Events

1941
FDR establishes Fair Employment Practices Commission

1942
Revenue Act raises taxes to finance the war; Office of War Information promotes patriotism

1943
Navajo soldiers develop unbreakable radio code

AN American Story

He wanted to join the Marines, but at 5 feet five inches tall he was too short. The Navy also turned him down. Reluctantly, Audie Murphy, the orphaned son of Texas sharecroppers, enlisted in the Army. By the end of the war, Murphy was the most decorated combat soldier of World War II. When victory was declared in Europe in May 1945, Murphy had still not reached his twenty-first birthday. Today, through the Audie Murphy Club, the Army honors noncommissioned officers who best represent Audie Murphy's motto, "You lead from the front."

America Prepares

The Japanese attack on Pearl Harbor united the American people as nothing else could. With astonishing speed the nation's economy and its people prepared to fight the war. Even before Pearl Harbor, the United States had begun raising an army under the Selective Service acts of 1940 and 1941. More than 15 million Americans joined the armed forces during the war, both as draftees and as volunteers.

For the first time, large numbers of women served in the military. About 250,000 women served in the **WACs** (Women's Army Corps), the **WAVES** (Women Appointed for Volunteer Emergency Service in the Navy), and women's units in the marines, Coast Guard, and army air corps. These women did not fight in combat—most performed clerical tasks or worked as nurses—but they played important roles in the war effort.

Equipping the troops and providing arms and other war materials required changes in the nation's economy. To speed up mobilization—military and civilian preparations for war—the American government created a number of new government agencies.

The **War Production Board** supervised the conversion of industries to war production. Under its guidance, automakers shifted from building cars to producing trucks and tanks. The **Office of Price Administration** set limits on consumer prices and rents to prevent inflation. The **National War Labor Board** helped resolve labor disputes that might slow down war production.

Financing the War

From 1941 to the end of World War II, the United States spent more than $320 billion on the war effort—10 times the amount spent in World War I. Much of this money was raised through taxes. The **Revenue Act of 1942** raised corporate taxes and required nearly all Americans to pay income taxes. Congress approved a system for withholding taxes from workers' paychecks—a practice still in effect.

The government also borrowed money to finance the war. As in World War I, the government sold war bonds. Movie stars and other celebrities urged people to buy bonds to support the war.

✓ Reading Check Explaining
What was the purpose of the Revenue Act of 1942, and what did it do?

Wartime America

During the war, industry soared. Factories produced more than 70,000 ships, almost 100,000 tanks and airplanes, and millions of guns. Production speed increased as well. Some cargo ships were built in a matter of weeks.

Those who remained at home had to provide food and shelter for all those in uniform. Civilians also provided training, equipment, transportation, and medical care.

Wartime production helped restore prosperity to the nation after the long years of the Depression. Incomes rose and prices remained fairly stable.

Making Sacrifices

With the war effort came many sacrifices. For millions of American families, the war meant separation from loved ones serving overseas. Those at home lived in dread of receiving a telegram announcing that a family member had been killed, wounded, or captured.

With industries making war materials, Americans faced shortages of many consumer goods. After 1942, for example, automakers

About 2,000 women were accepted into the Women's Air Force Service Pilots.

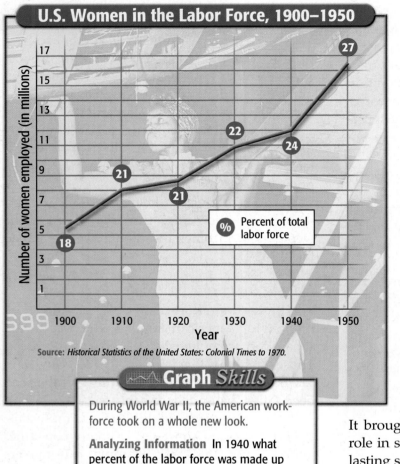

U.S. Women in the Labor Force, 1900–1950

Number of women employed (in millions)

17
15
13
11
9
7
5
3
1

18   21   21   22   24   27

% Percent of total labor force

1900   1910   1920   1930   1940   1950
Year

Source: *Historical Statistics of the United States: Colonial Times to 1970.*

Graph *Skills*

During World War II, the American workforce took on a whole new look.

Analyzing Information In 1940 what percent of the labor force was made up of women?

Many people joined in **civil defense**—protective measures in case of attack. For example, volunteer spotters scanned the skies for enemy aircraft that might try to approach America. Coastal cities enforced blackouts at night so that lights could not serve as beacons for enemy pilots.

The **Office of War Information,** established by the government, promoted patriotism and helped keep Americans united behind the war effort. It also broadcast messages all over the world. 📖 *(See page 975 for another way Americans were asked to contribute to the war effort.)*

(See page 975 for another way Americans were asked to contribute to the war effort.)

✓ **Reading Check** **Explaining** Why were many consumer goods in short supply?

Women and Minorities

The war had a tremendous impact on the lives of women and minorities. It brought opportunity for new jobs and a new role in society. Yet for some, unfair treatment left lasting scars.

As millions of men joined the armed forces, more women than ever before entered the labor force. In factories women worked as welders and riveters and in other jobs previously held by men. An advertising campaign featuring a character called **Rosie the Riveter** encouraged women to take factory jobs. For many women it was their first opportunity to work outside the home.

Although women had new job opportunities, they usually earned less than men. Moreover, when the war ended and the troops returned home, most women would lose their jobs. Still, the war opened new fields to women and changed public opinion about women's right to work.

African Americans During the War

About one million African American men and women served in the armed forces during the war. At first most were given low-level assignments and kept in segregated units. Gradually, military leaders assigned them to integrated

stopped making new cars and turned instead to making tanks, planes, and trucks. Women could not buy stockings—silk imports from war-torn Asia had halted, and nylon was needed to make parachutes.

In addition many resources and goods needed for the war effort were rationed—consumers could buy only limited numbers of them. Americans used government-issued books of ration coupons to purchase certain items, such as shoes, gasoline, tires, sugar, and meat. When people ran out of coupons, they did without the rationed items.

Helping the War Effort

People found other ways to help the war effort. Many planted "victory gardens" to grow vegetables, which were in short supply. Children collected scrap metal for use in industry.

units. In 1942 the army began training whites and African Americans together in officer candidate school. Finally, African Americans were allowed to take combat assignments. The 332nd Fighter Group, known as the **Tuskegee Airmen,** shot down more than 200 enemy planes. **Benjamin Davis, Jr.,** who trained at the Tuskegee flying school, became the first African American general in the United States Air Force. His father, Benjamin Davis, Sr., had been the first African American general in the army.

In civilian life African Americans sought change. In the summer of 1941, labor leader **A. Philip Randolph** demanded that the government ban discrimination against African Americans in defense industries. He planned a large demonstration in Washington in support of his demands. President Roosevelt persuaded Randolph to call off the march by establishing the Fair Employment Practices Commission to combat discrimination in industries that held government contracts. The president announced that

66. . . there shall be no discrimination in the employment of workers in defense industries or government because of race, creed, color, or national origin.99

The war accelerated the population shift that had begun during World War I. Large numbers of African Americans moved from the rural South to industrialized cities in the North and the West in search of work. In some cities, racial tensions erupted in violence. The violence sometimes resulted in death. The riots inspired the African American poet **Langston Hughes** to write:

66Yet you say we're fightin' for democracy.
Then why don't democracy
Include me?99

Native Americans

Many Native Americans left reservations to work in defense industries. Thousands of Native Americans served in the armed forces. **Ira Hayes** became a hero in the battle for Iwo Jima in the Pacific. A special group of Navajo formed the "code talkers." Many of the American radio communications about troop movements and battle plans were being intercepted by the Japanese. The "code talkers" used a special code based on the Navajo language to send messages—a code that the Japanese never broke.

Hispanic Americans

More than 250,000 Hispanic Americans served in the armed forces. The Medal of Honor, the nation's highest military medal, was awarded to 12 Mexican Americans. **Mercedes Cubría** of Cuba became the first Hispanic woman officer in the Women's Army Corps. **Horacio Rivero** of Puerto Rico became the first Hispanic four-star admiral since David Farragut to serve in the United States Navy.

Prompted by the wartime need for labor, United States labor agents recruited thousands of farm and railroad workers from Mexico. This program, called the **bracero** program, stimulated emigration from Mexico during the war years.

Tuskegee Airmen in Italy

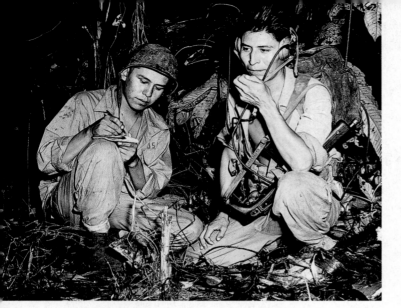

The United States Marines recruited Navajo soldiers to develop a military code that the Japanese could not break.

Like African Americans, Mexican Americans suffered from discrimination, and their presence created tensions in some cities. In 1943, for example, a four-day riot started in **Los Angeles** when white sailors attacked Mexican American teens.

Japanese Americans

After the Japanese bombed Pearl Harbor, Japanese Americans were feared and hated by many other Americans. About two-thirds of Japanese Americans were **Nisei**—American citizens who had been born in the United States. But this fact made little difference to some who questioned the loyalty of Japanese Americans.

Military and political leaders worried about the loyalty of Japanese Americans if Japanese forces invaded the United States. The president directed the army to relocate more than 100,000 West Coast Japanese Americans to detention centers. Located mostly in desert areas, these internment camps were crowded and uncomfortable. Conditions were harsh.

With only days to prepare for the move, most Japanese Americans left valuable possessions behind. Many abandoned their homes and businesses or sold them at a loss. Most had to stay in internment camps for the next three years.

Peter Ota and his family were sent to a camp in Colorado. His father had come to California in 1904 and built up a successful fruit and vegetable business. After the war Ota remembered how his father had suffered.

❝After all those years, having worked his whole life to build a dream—having it all taken away. . . . He died a broken man.❞

In 1944, in *Korematsu* v. *United States,* the Supreme Court upheld the order providing for the relocation of Japanese Americans. In 1988 Americans acknowledged the injustice of relocation. Congress issued a formal apology and agreed to give each survivor $20,000, a token of the nation's regret. 📖 *(See page 998 for a summary of the* Korematsu *case.)*

Reading Check **Identifying** Who were the Nisei?

SECTION 3 ASSESSMENT

Checking for Understanding

1. **Key Terms** Define the following key terms: mobilization, ration, internment camp.
2. **Reviewing Facts** List two ways the United States financed the war effort.

Reviewing Themes

3. **Economic Factors** How did wartime industrial production help the American economy recover from the Depression?

Critical Thinking

4. **Drawing Conclusions** Why did many Americans move to industrialized cities during the war?
5. **Organizing Information** Re-create the diagram below and explain how each of these actions helped the war effort.

Helping the war effort		
Civil defense	Bracero program	Rationing

Analyzing Visuals

6. **Graph Skills** Examine the graph on page 766. When did the number of women employed pass 10 million?

Interdisciplinary Activity

Writing Suppose you are a woman working in a defense factory during the war. This is the first job you have had outside of your home. Write a journal entry describing your first day on the job.

America's LITERATURE

Yoshiko Uchida (1921–1992)

Yoshiko Uchida grew up in California in the 1930s. As a Japanese American, she sometimes felt very different from the people around her. She wanted to be a "typical" American and often resented the Japanese ways of her family. Eventually Uchida learned to value the "invisible thread" that linked her to her heritage.

READ TO DISCOVER

During the war, the American government relocated to camps those Japanese people living in the West. How did Yoshiko and her sister, Kay, spend their time in the internment camp?

READER'S DICTIONARY

Tanforan: horse racing park used as a camp for Japanese Americans

mess hall: military-style dining area

canteen: a general store at a military camp

contraband: forbidden items

diversion: entertainment

The Invisible Thread

Gradually we became accustomed to life in **Tanforan**, especially to standing in long lines for everything. We lined up to get into the **mess hall** or to use a laundry tub or to buy something at the **canteen** (finding only shoelaces when we got in) or to get into the occasional movies that were shown.

We got used to rushing back to our stall after dinner for the 6:00 P.M. head count (we were still in bed for the morning count), and to the sudden unexpected campwide searches for **contraband** by the FBI when we were confined to our stalls for several hours.

For **diversion** we could also go to talent shows, recorded concerts, discussion groups, Saturday night dances, softball games, art classes, and hobby shows. . . .

Representatives from the university, the YMCA and YWCA, and various church groups also came to give us their support and help. They were working on arrangements to get students out of camp and back into schools as soon as possible.

One day our neighbor Mrs. Harpainter came to see us, bringing all sorts of snacks along with flowers from her garden for Mama. Her boys, however, were not allowed inside because they were under sixteen.

When Kay and I heard they were waiting outside the gate, we hurried to the fence to talk to them.

"Teddy! Bobby!"

We ran to greet them, squeezing our fingers through the chain links to touch their hands.

But an armed guard quickly shouted, "Hey, you two! Get away from the fence!"

FBI agent searches family's belongings

ANALYZING LITERATURE

1. **Recall and Interpret** Why did representatives from churches and other groups visit the camp?

2. **Evaluate and Connect** How do you think you would have felt in Uchida's place in the internment camp?

Interdisciplinary Activity

Art Draw plans for a community memorial suitable for remembering Japanese Americans treated unfairly during World War II.

SECTION 4 War in Europe and Africa

Guide to Reading

Main Idea
To win the war, the Allies had to regain control of North Africa and most of Europe.

Key Terms
D-Day, genocide, Holocaust

Reading Strategy
Sequencing Information As you read the section, re-create the time line below and identify important events during the war.

Nov. 1942	May 1943	Jun. 1944

Read to Learn
- what important battles took place in North Africa, Italy, and the Soviet Union between 1942 and 1944.
- what factors contributed to the Allied victory in Europe.

Section Theme
Global Connections The horrors of war continued as the Allies attempted to defeat the Axis Powers.

Preview of Events

♦1942 ♦1944 ♦1946

January 1942
U.S. joins Allies

June 1944
Allied ships land
at Normandy

December 1944
Battle of the Bulge
takes 75,000 lives

May 1945
Germany
surrenders

AN American Story

Ernie Pyle, a war correspondent, described the life of the World War II American soldier: "In the magazines war seemed romantic and exciting, full of heroics and vitality. . . . I saw instead men suffering and wishing they were somewhere else. . . . All of them desperately hungry for somebody to talk to besides themselves . . . cold and fairly dirty, just toiling from day to day in a world full of insecurity, discomfort, homesickness and a dulled sense of danger."

North African Campaign

On January 1, 1942—three weeks after Pearl Harbor—the United States joined Britain, the Soviet Union, and 23 other Allied nations in vowing to defeat the Axis Powers. Although the Japanese were conquering vast areas in the Pacific, the Allied leaders decided to concentrate first on defeating Hitler before dealing with Japan. The situation in Europe was desperate. German forces occupied almost all of Europe and much of North Africa. If the Germans defeated the Soviets, Germany might prove unstoppable.

Stalin and many American military leaders wanted the Allies to launch a major attack on continental Europe across the English Channel. Such an attack would force the Germans to defend the heart of their own empire. Churchill, however, argued that such an assault would be too difficult because of the German military presence in the area. FDR concluded that Churchill was right. The Allies made plans to attack North Africa instead. The Axis forces

there were under the command of German general **Erwin Rommel,** known as the "Desert Fox" because of his success in desert warfare.

In November 1942, the British turned Rommel back at El Alamein. The victory prevented the Germans from capturing the Suez Canal, linking the Mediterranean and the Red Sea.

Landing in Algeria and Morocco on November 8, American, British, and Canadian troops under American general **Dwight D. Eisenhower**

NATIONAL GEOGRAPHIC — World War II in Europe and Africa

Allied Forces →
Major Axis powers
Greatest extent of Axis control
Allied or Ally-controlled
Neutral nations

0   500 miles
0   500 kilometers
Lambert Azimuthal Equal-Area projection

D-Day June 6, 1944

FINAL SOVIET DRIVE July-Aug., 1944

Aug. 15, 1944

Nov. 8, 1942

July 10, 1943

1942 - The British defeat the German tank division at El Alamein.

Geography *Skills*

1. **Place** Where did the Allied forces land on D-Day?
2. **Analyzing Information** When did Allied forces invade Sicily?

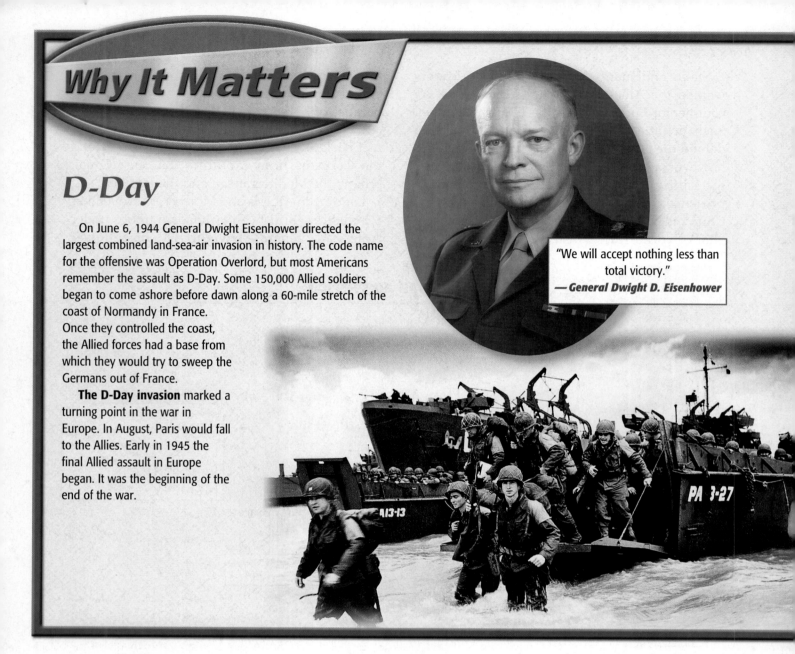

Why It Matters

D-Day

On June 6, 1944 General Dwight Eisenhower directed the largest combined land-sea-air invasion in history. The code name for the offensive was Operation Overlord, but most Americans remember the assault as D-Day. Some 150,000 Allied soldiers began to come ashore before dawn along a 60-mile stretch of the coast of Normandy in France. Once they controlled the coast, the Allied forces had a base from which they would try to sweep the Germans out of France.

The D-Day invasion marked a turning point in the war in Europe. In August, Paris would fall to the Allies. Early in 1945 the final Allied assault in Europe began. It was the beginning of the end of the war.

"We will accept nothing less than total victory."
— *General Dwight D. Eisenhower*

advanced eastward swiftly. The inexperienced Americans met defeat in Tunisia. With the backing of British air and naval power, however, American general **George Patton** closed in on Rommel. The Allies drove the Germans out of North Africa in May 1943.

The Invasion of Italy

The Allies used bases in North Africa to launch an invasion of southern Europe. They took the island of **Sicily** in the summer of 1943 and landed on the Italian mainland in September. As the Allies advanced, the Italians overthrew dictator Benito Mussolini and surrendered. However, German forces in Italy continued to fight.

In the winter of 1943, the Allies met fierce resistance at the monastery town of **Monte Cassino** in central Italy, and their advance faltered. The next January the Allies landed farther north at **Anzio,** a seaport near Rome. German forces kept the Allies pinned down on the beaches at Anzio for four months. The Allies finally broke through the German lines in May and advanced toward **Rome.** They liberated Rome in June 1944.

Air War Over Germany

While fighting raged in North Africa and Italy, the Allies launched an air war against Germany. In the summer of 1942, British and American air forces began a massive bombing campaign

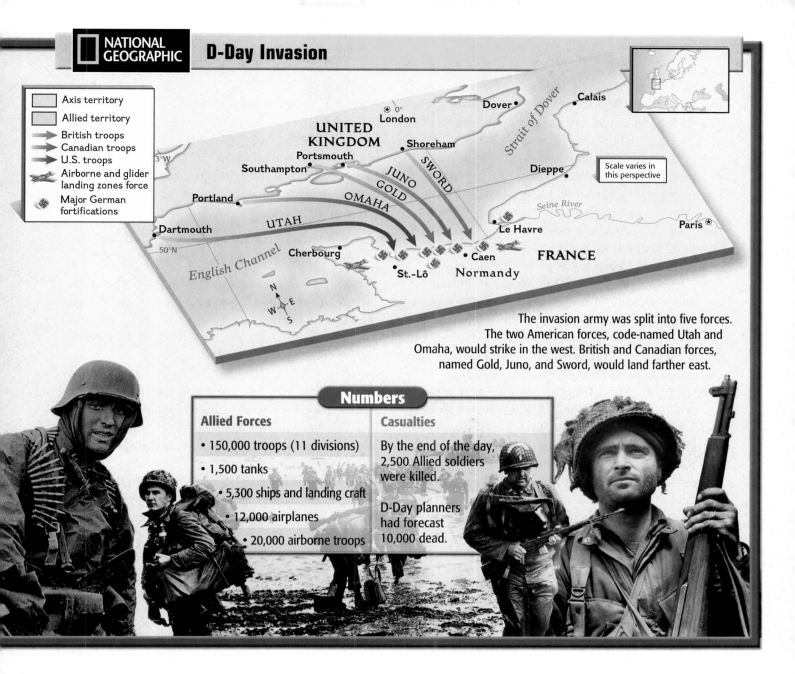

NATIONAL GEOGRAPHIC — D-Day Invasion

Legend:
- Axis territory
- Allied territory
- British troops
- Canadian troops
- U.S. troops
- Airborne and glider landing zones force
- Major German fortifications

Scale varies in this perspective

The invasion army was split into five forces. The two American forces, code-named Utah and Omaha, would strike in the west. British and Canadian forces, named Gold, Juno, and Sword, would land farther east.

Numbers

Allied Forces
- 150,000 troops (11 divisions)
- 1,500 tanks
- 5,300 ships and landing craft
- 12,000 airplanes
- 20,000 airborne troops

Casualties

By the end of the day, 2,500 Allied soldiers were killed.

D-Day planners had forecast 10,000 dead.

---

against Germany. Each day hundreds of American bombers pounded German factories and cities. Each night British bombers battered the same targets. The bombing caused massive destruction and killed thousands of German civilians. In July 1943 a week-long series of bombing raids on the port of Hamburg created a whirling tower of fire that engulfed the city. More than 30,000 people died in the raids. Yet the attacks failed to crack Germany's determination to win the war.

✓ Reading Check **Explaining** Why did the Allies decide to attack North Africa rather than launch an attack on continental Europe?

The Tide Turns in Europe

Meanwhile, the Soviets and the Germans were locked in ferocious combat. For months the Soviet Union bore the main force of Germany's European war effort.

The Eastern Front

After invading the Soviet Union in June 1941, German troops had moved quickly into the nation's interior. By September the Germans surrounded **Leningrad** and began a **siege,** or military blockade, that lasted nearly 900 days. The German attack continued, but Leningrad did not fall. As food ran out, the people of the city ate horses, cats, and dogs—even bread made from wallpaper paste. Thousands died. The Germans could not take the city, however, and in early 1944 the siege was broken.

German forces also attacked other Soviet cities. In 1941 the Germans tried to capture the Soviet capital of **Moscow.** Heavy losses and bad weather slowed their advance, but the Germans reached Moscow's outskirts by December. When all seemed lost, the Soviets staged a counterattack and forced a German retreat.

In the spring of 1942, Germany launched another offensive. A major target was the city of **Stalingrad,** key to oil-rich lands to the south. To take the city, the Germans had to fight street by street and house by house. No sooner had the Germans won Stalingrad than Soviet forces surrounded the city, cutting off the German supply lines. Cold and starving, the German troops fought on until February 1943, when the tattered remains of their army finally surrendered.

After Stalingrad, a major Soviet offensive drove the Germans back hundreds of miles. The Germans mounted a counteroffensive in the summer of 1943, but their defeat at Stalingrad marked a major turning point in the war.

Invasion of France

As the Soviets pushed toward Germany from the east, the Allies were planning a massive invasion of France from the west. General Eisenhower, the commander of Allied forces in Europe, directed this invasion, known as **Operation Overlord.** Eisenhower later wrote of the tense days of preparation:

> 66All southern England was one vast military camp, crowded with soldiers awaiting final word to go.99

Eisenhower planned to land his troops on the French coast of **Normandy** on June 5, but rough seas forced him to delay the landing. Finally, on June 6, 1944—D-Day—the Allied ships landed on the coast of Normandy.

After wading ashore the troops faced land mines and fierce fire from the Germans. Many Allied troops were hit as they stormed across the beaches to establish a foothold on high ground. Within a few weeks, the Allies had landed a million troops in France.

From Normandy the Allies pushed across France. On August 25 French and American soldiers marched through joyful crowds and liberated Paris.

People In History

George S. Patton 1885–1945

Unpredictable and flamboyant, George S. Patton was one of the most remarkable U.S. Army commanders and also the leading authority on tank warfare. Patton was a clever planner, which helped make him one of the war's greatest combat commanders.

Patton distinguished himself in various World War II campaigns, including the invasion of North Africa and the capture of Sicily. The controversy that arose after Patton struck a soldier almost cost him his career. Eventually Patton was reassigned to lead the Third Army. After the invasion of Normandy in the summer of 1944, Patton's army swept across Europe. In December, the Third Army helped win the Battle of the Bulge. By the end of the war, the Third Army liberated more than 80,000 square miles of territory and took thousands of prisoners. Patton died in December 1945 from injuries suffered in an automobile accident.

(Left) Polish Jews taken prisoner, 1943; (above) liberated prisoners at concentration camp at Ebensee, Austria in May 1945

Victory in Europe

Germany fought for survival on two fronts. In the east the Soviets pushed the Germans out of eastern Europe. In the west the British and Americans approached the German border.

The Allied advance across France moved so rapidly that some people thought the war would be over by the end of the year. In late 1944, however, the drive came to a halt at the Rhine River, stalled by German defenses and cold weather.

In mid-December the Germans mounted a last, desperate offensive. On December 16, 1944, they launched a surprise attack along a 50-mile front in Belgium. In the **Battle of the Bulge,** the Germans at first drove troops and artillery deep into a bulge in the Allied lines. After several weeks, however, the Allies pushed the Germans back. The battle, which resulted in more than 100,000 casualties, marked the end of serious German resistance.

The final phase of the war in Europe now began. By mid-April 1945, the Soviets had surrounded **Berlin,** the German capital. Hitler, who had spent the final months of the war in an underground bunker there, realized that the situation was hopeless and committed suicide on April 30. Germany signed an unconditional surrender on May 7, ending the war in Europe. The Allies declared May 8 **V-E Day** for "Victory in Europe."

Death of a President

President Roosevelt did not share in the Allied victory celebration. In February 1945, he had traveled to Yalta in the Soviet Union to meet with Churchill and Stalin. After returning home Roosevelt had gone to Warm Springs, Georgia, for a vacation. He died there suddenly on April 12, 1945.

Americans were saddened by the death of the man who had led them for 12 difficult years. When Vice President **Harry S Truman** heard the news, he asked Eleanor Roosevelt if there was anything he could do for her. She replied, "Is there anything *we* can do for *you?* You are the one in trouble now."

Reading Check **Explaining** Why was the Battle of the Bulge an important victory for the Allies?

The Holocaust

As the Allies liberated areas that had been under German control, they found horrifying evidence of Nazi brutality. Hitler had warned in 1939 that another war would result in "the destruction of the Jews in Europe." Nazi leaders developed what they called "the final solution of the Jewish question." Their "solution" was genocide—wiping out an entire group of people.

Ever since Hitler had gained power in 1933, the Nazis had persecuted Jews. This persecution became more deadly as German power spread through Europe. Once the war began, Nazis rounded up thousands of Jews, shooting them and throwing them into mass graves. One man who witnessed a massacre of Russian Jews wrote of the act:

❝I watched a family of about eight persons. . . . [A soldier] instructed them to go behind the earth mound. . . . They went down into the pit, lined themselves up against the previous victims and were shot.❞

Nazi troops crammed thousands more into railroad cars like cattle, depositing them in **concentration camps**—prison camps for civilians. Guards took the prisoners' belongings, shaved their heads, and tattooed camp numbers on their arms. Forced to live in horrible conditions, the prisoners often had only a crust of bread or watery soup to eat. Thousands became sick and died.

In the early 1940s, the Nazis embarked on their "final solution" to destroy the Jews. They built death camps where they killed thousands of people a day in gas chambers, then burned their bodies in ovens. At the largest camp—**Auschwitz** in Poland—the Nazis killed between 1 and 2 million people. As many as 6 million Jews died in what has become known as the **Holocaust.** Millions of others, including Soviet prisoners of war, Poles, Gypsies, and people with handicaps—were also ruthlessly killed.

As Allied forces moved through Germany and Poland after V-E Day, they saw firsthand the unspeakable horrors of the camps. R.W. Thompson, a British reporter, wrote about one such camp:

❝Across the sandy clearing is the incinerator, but it ran out of [fuel]. A rough record by the chief burner of bodies records 17,000 burned last month. They say each body was roughly clubbed as it went in.❞

People around the world were stunned by this terrible result of Nazi tyranny.

In Remembrance

The United States Holocaust Memorial Museum is located near the National Mall in Washington, D.C. This memorial provides a national mark of respect for all victims of Nazi persecution. In 2001 Congress passed legislation to approve construction of the National World War II Memorial on a site on the National Mall. This is the first national memorial dedicated to all who served during the war.

✔ **Reading Check** **Identifying** What groups of people were victims of the Holocaust?

SECTION 4 ASSESSMENT

Checking for Understanding

1. **Key Terms** Define D-Day, genocide, **and** Holocaust.
2. **Reviewing Facts** In what region did the Allies launch an invasion after they drove the German forces out of North Africa?

Reviewing Themes

3. **Global Connections** When the United States joined the Allies, why did the Allies concentrate first on defeating Hitler?

Critical Thinking

4. **Drawing Conclusions** Why do you think Hitler felt threatened by Jews and other minorities?
5. **Organizing Information** Re-create the diagram below and describe the significance of these events.

Significance	
D-Day	V-E Day

Analyzing Visuals

6. **Geography Skills** Examine the map on page 771. When did the Allied forces launch an attack on German forces in North Africa?

Interdisciplinary Activity

Geography Draw a map of the former Soviet Union and use symbols to show the outcome of the battles between German and Soviet forces.

War in the Pacific

Main Idea
Japan's surrender ends World War II.

Key Terms
island hopping, kamikaze

Reading Strategy
Classifying Information As you read the section, re-create the diagram below and explain the importance of each subject.

	Importance
Island hopping	
Manhattan Project	
V-J Day	

Read to Learn
- how the United States planned to gain control of the Pacific region.
- what role the atomic bomb played in ending the war.

Section Theme
Global Connections When Japanese leaders would not surrender, President Truman ordered the use of the atomic bomb.

Preview of Events

♦1942   ♦1944   ♦1946

April 1942
Allies surrender Bataan

March 1945
Americans seize Iwo Jima

August 1945
Atomic bomb is dropped on Hiroshima

September 1945
Japan surrenders; World War II ends

AN American Story

Bob Krell, a soldier in World War II, felt a need to describe his life in the war: "At night before a big airborne operation you crawl deeper in your sack, but you can't get away from the noise. Over the roar of engines, somebody is shouting a bunch of names. . . . [W]e will climb into our parachutes as dawn breaks. We will trudge out to the planes and climb in, not saying much of anything about anything. . . ." Bob Krell was killed in action 12 hours after he wrote these words.

The Pacific Front

On December 7, 1941, the same day the Japanese attacked Pearl Harbor, Japanese bombers struck American airfields in the **Philippines** and on the islands of **Wake** and **Guam**—key American bases in the Pacific. In the following days, the Japanese intensified their campaign in the Pacific. They invaded Thailand and Malaya and captured Guam, Wake Island, and the British colony of Hong Kong.

Japanese troops had landed in the Philippines in mid-December and quickly taken the capital of Manila. The defending forces—Filipino and American troops commanded by American general **Douglas MacArthur**—were forced to retreat to the rugged **Bataan** Peninsula west of Manila and the small island fortress of **Corregidor.**

The Philippines Fall

After months of fierce fighting, the exhausted Allied troops defending Bataan surrendered on April 9, 1942. The forces on Corregidor held out for another month. The Japanese forced their Bataan prisoners—many sick and near starvation—to march to a prison camp more than 60 miles away. Only much later did the public learn

World War II in the Pacific

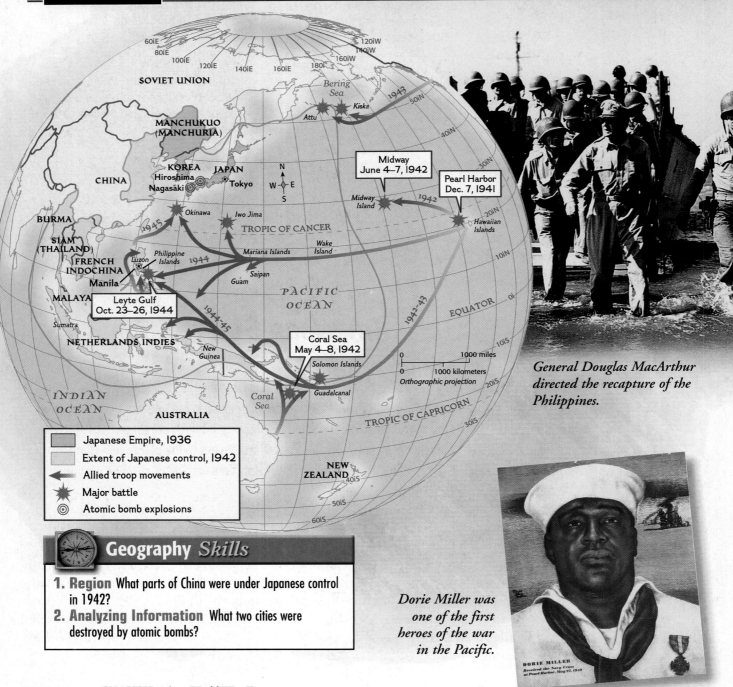

General Douglas MacArthur directed the recapture of the Philippines.

Japanese Empire, 1936
Extent of Japanese control, 1942
Allied troop movements
Major battle
Atomic bomb explosions

Geography *Skills*

1. **Region** What parts of China were under Japanese control in 1942?
2. **Analyzing Information** What two cities were destroyed by atomic bombs?

Dorie Miller was one of the first heroes of the war in the Pacific.

what these prisoners endured. About 76,000 prisoners started out, but only about 54,000 of those on the **Bataan Death March** reached the camp. As one survivor recalled:

> ❝Anybody that could walk, they forced 'em into line. . . . If you fell out to the side, you were either shot by the guards or you were bayoneted [stabbed] and left there.❞

Two months before the surrender, General MacArthur had left for Australia to take command of Allied forces in the Pacific. MacArthur promised the Filipinos, "I shall return."

Island Hopping

With Japan's string of quick victories, American morale was low. Then, in April, 16 American bombers, launched from an aircraft carrier in the Pacific, bombed **Tokyo.** This daring raid led by James Doolittle had little military importance, but it lifted Americans' spirits.

In May, American and Japanese fleets clashed in the Coral Sea northeast of Australia. American ships were heavily damaged, but the Japanese suffered crippling losses. The **Battle of the Coral Sea** was a strategic victory because it halted the Japanese advance on Australia.

An even greater victory followed in June 1942. In the **Battle of Midway,** northwest of Hawaii, the navy destroyed four Japanese aircraft carriers and hundreds of airplanes. This was the first major Japanese defeat.

The United States was now ready to go on the offensive against Japan. The commanders—General MacArthur and Admiral **Chester Nimitz**—adopted a strategy known as island hopping. This called for attacking and capturing certain key islands. The United States then used these islands as bases for leapfrogging to others, moving ever closer to the Philippines—and to Japan.

Between August 1942 and February 1943, American forces engaged in one of the most vicious campaigns of the war for the control of **Guadalcanal,** one of the Solomon Islands. Although the Japanese put up fierce resistance, the Americans finally secured the island.

In June 1944, American forces captured Guam and other islands nearby. Guam provided a base for launching bombing strikes on Japan. In October, American ships destroyed most of the Japanese fleet at the **Battle of Leyte Gulf** in the Philippines, the biggest naval battle in history—in all, 282 ships took part. MacArthur had fulfilled his promise to return to the Philippines.

The Advance on Japan

American forces now closed in on Japan itself. In March 1945, they seized the island of **Iwo Jima** and in June the island of **Okinawa.** The Japanese fought fiercely to defend these islands so near to Japan. Thousands of Americans died in the battles, and many thousands more were wounded.

With most of Japan's air force and navy destroyed, American bombers pounded Tokyo and other Japanese cities. The raids killed thousands of civilians and crippled Japan's economy. In desperation, the Japanese unleashed a corps of suicide pilots known as kamikazes. They crashed planes loaded with explosives into American ships. Kamikaze pilots sank several destroyers during the battle for Okinawa.

☑ **Reading Check** **Explaining** What is significant about the Battle of Midway?

HISTORY Online

Student Web Activity
Visit taj.glencoe.com and click on **Chapter 26— Student Web Activities** for an activity on World War II.

The Atomic Bomb

Although the Japanese faced certain defeat, they continued to fight. Their refusal to surrender led the United States to use a powerful new weapon: the atomic bomb.

In 1939 the German-born physicist **Albert Einstein** had written to President Roosevelt warning him that the Nazis might try to use the energy of the atom to build "extremely powerful bombs." Wanting to develop such weapons first, Roosevelt created a top-secret operation, the **Manhattan Project.** After years of work, scientists tested the atomic bomb in the New Mexico

Raising the U.S. flag at Iwo Jima

desert on July 16, 1945. Truman now had to decide whether to use the bomb against Japan.

The Allies issued the **Potsdam Declaration,** warning that if Japan did not surrender, it faced "prompt and utter destruction." The Japanese leaders did not surrender, and Truman ordered the use of the bomb.

On August 6, 1945, an American B-29 bomber, the *Enola Gay,* dropped an atomic bomb on the Japanese city of **Hiroshima.** Three days later, a second bomb was dropped on the city of **Nagasaki.** The atomic bombs caused immense destruction. The first bomb leveled Hiroshima and killed about 70,000 people; the Nagasaki bomb killed about 40,000. Thousands more were injured, and many died later from radiation.

Reading Check **Identifying** On what Japanese cities were atomic bombs dropped?

The War Ends

After the bombings, the Japanese government agreed to surrender. August 15, 1945, was proclaimed **V-J Day,** for "Victory over Japan." All around America, people expressed happiness and relief. Japan signed the formal surrender on September 2 aboard the battleship the U.S.S. *Missouri.* World War II had finally ended.

In the years immediately after the war, Allied authorities put the top Nazi and Japanese leaders on trial. They were accused of war crimes and crimes against humanity. The Allies held the trials in Nuremberg, Germany, and in Tokyo.

The Cost of the War

World War II was the most destructive conflict in history. More than 40 million people died during the war; more than half of these were civilians killed by bombing, starvation, disease, torture, and murder. American casualties—about 322,000 dead and 800,000 injured—were high, but light compared with those of other nations. The Soviet Union suffered more than 20 million deaths. Those who survived faced the huge task of trying to rebuild their lives and their countries. Nationalist movements grew, particularly in colonial nations that had suffered invasions by the warring powers. Many colonies began to seek independence in the postwar years.

Reading Check **Describing** Who was brought to trial at the Nuremberg trials?

SECTION 5 ASSESSMENT

Checking for Understanding

1. **Key Terms** Use each of these terms in a sentence that will help explain its meaning: island hopping, kamikaze.

2. **Reviewing Facts** Explain the significance of the Battle of Leyte Gulf.

Reviewing Themes

3. **Global Connections** Why did kamikaze missions pose such a deadly threat to Allied forces?

Critical Thinking

4. **Identifying Central Issues** If you had been president, would you have ordered the attacks on Hiroshima and Nagasaki? Why or why not?

5. **Sequencing Information** Re-create the time line below and list important events in the Pacific in 1945.

Mar. 1945	July 1945	Aug. 1945	Sept. 1945

Analyzing Visuals

6. **Geography Skills** Examine the map of World War II in the Pacific on page 778. What naval battle took place in May 1942? In June 1942?

Interdisciplinary Activity

Math Make a bar graph that compares the number of people killed during the war in the major Axis and Allied countries.

Study & Writing
SKILLBUILDER

Writing a Paragraph

Why Learn This Skill?

Paragraphs are the building blocks of an essay or other composition. Each paragraph is a unit—a group of sentences about a single topic or idea.

Learning the Skill

Most well-written paragraphs share four characteristics.

- First, a paragraph expresses one main idea or is about one subject. A topic sentence states that main idea. The topic sentence may be located at the beginning, the middle, or the end of a paragraph.
- Second, the rest of the sentences in a paragraph support the main idea. The main idea may be developed by facts, examples, or reasons.
- Third, the sentences are arranged in a logical order.
- Fourth, transitional words link sentences within the paragraph. These words can also link one paragraph with the next. Examples include *next, then, finally, also, because, however,* and *as a result.*

Practicing the Skill

Use the following sentences to build a paragraph containing a topic sentence and other sentences that give supporting details. Put the sentences in a logical order and add transitional words if you need to. Underline your topic sentence.

1. Three days later an American plane dropped another bomb on Nagasaki.

2. The bomb killed about 70,000 people.

3. This second bomb killed nearly 40,000 people instantly and many more later.

Hiroshima after the atomic bomb

4. On August 6, 1945, the United States dropped an atomic bomb on Hiroshima, Japan.

5. About 100,000 others died later from the effects of radiation.

6. When the bomb exploded, a sheet of flame spread over the city.

Applying the Skill

Writing a Paragraph Choose a topic from the World War II era and write a paragraph about it. Then rewrite the paragraph with its sentences out of order. Exchange papers with a classmate. Can he or she find the topic sentence? Does it work logically?

GO TO

Glencoe's **Skillbuilder Interactive Workbook CD-ROM, Level 1,** provides instruction and practice in key social studies skills.

Chapter Summary
World War II

1931
- Japan invades Manchuria

1933
- Hitler becomes chancellor of Germany

1935
- Italian forces invade Ethiopia

1939
- Germany seizes Czechoslovakia
- Germany invades Poland

1940
- Germany bombs Britain

1941
- Hitler attacks the Soviet Union
- FDR establishes Fair Employment Practices Commission
- Japan bombs Pearl Harbor

1942
- Revenue Act raises taxes to finance the war
- Office of War Information promotes patriotism
- U.S. joins Allies
- Allies surrender Bataan

1943
- Navajo soldiers develop unbreakable radio code

1944
- Allied ships land at Normandy
- Battle of the Bulge

1945
- Germany surrenders
- Americans seize Iwo Jima
- Atomic bomb is dropped on Hiroshima
- Japan surrenders
- World War II ends

Reviewing Key Terms

Examine the pairs of words below. Then write a sentence explaining what the words in each pair have in common.

1. fascism, dictator
2. genocide, Holocaust
3. island hopping, blitzkrieg

Reviewing Key Facts

4. How did Britain and France try to prevent war with Germany?
5. When did Japan attack Pearl Harbor?
6. What did the government do to ensure that industries produced enough war materials?
7. What was Operation Overlord?
8. Who succeeded Franklin Roosevelt as president?
9. What actions by the Japanese convinced the United States to use the atomic bomb?

Critical Thinking

10. **Drawing Conclusions** Explain the importance to Hitler of Germany's 1939 non-agression treaty with the Soviet Union. Why do you suppose the Soviet Union signed it?
11. **Reviewing Themes: Economic Factors** Why did the government require rationing during the war?
12. **Drawing Conclusions** Why did the Allies focus first on the war in Europe rather than on the war in the Pacific?
13. **Comparing** Re-create the diagram below and compare the roles that the United States played in world affairs during the 1930s and 1940s.

	Role in world affairs
The U.S. in the 1930s	
The U.S. in the 1940s	

Technology Activity

14. **Using the Internet** Search the Internet for a World War II site that includes memoirs or excerpts from veterans and/or civilians. Copy or print a part of the memoirs that you find interesting. Post the excerpts on the classroom bulletin board under the heading "Voices of World War II."

Geography and History Activity

The map below shows the attack on Pearl Harbor. Study the map and answer the questions that follow.

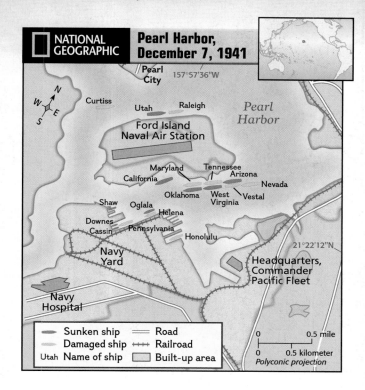

Pearl Harbor, December 7, 1941

NATIONAL GEOGRAPHIC

Pearl City 157°57'36"W

Curtiss
Utah   Raleigh   *Pearl Harbor*

Ford Island
Naval Air Station

Maryland   Tennessee
California   Arizona
                        Nevada
Oklahoma   West   Vestal
Shaw   Oglala   Virginia
            Helena
Downes
Cassin   Pennsylvania
            Honolulu
Navy   21°22'12"N
Yard
                  Headquarters,
                Commander
                Pacific Fleet
Navy
Hospital

Legend	
▬ Sunken ship	═ Road
▭ Damaged ship	+++ Railroad
Utah Name of ship	▭ Built-up area

0   0.5 mile
0   0.5 kilometer
Polyconic projection

15. Location What ships are located along the eastern side of Ford Island?

16. Location What ships were nearest the *Nevada?*

17. Location What happened to the *Raleigh* during the attack?

Practicing Skills

Writing a Paragraph *Write a short paragraph for each of the topic sentences that follow. Each paragraph must have at least three sentences supporting the topic and arranged in a logical way. Use transitional words or phrases to connect your ideas smoothly.*

18. The leaders of Italy, Germany, and Japan attempted to restore their nations to their former greatness through the use of the military.

19. Minority groups played vital roles in World War II, both in the armed forces and at home.

Self-Check Quiz
Visit taj.glencoe.com and click on **Chapter 26— Self-Check Quizzes** to prepare for the chapter test.

Cooperative Citizenship Activity

20. Foreign Policy Goals With a partner, check current newspapers and newsmagazines for articles about United States relations with foreign nations. Clip the articles and build a table categorizing these relations under these headings: *Maintaining national security, Promoting world peace, Protecting free trade, Supporting democratic governments, and Promoting humane treatment of people.*

Economics Activity

21. How might rationing have changed the way families lived? Write a one-page paper in which you describe three ways rationing affected individuals and families during World War II.

Alternative Assessment

22. Portfolio Writing Activity Choose a person discussed in this chapter, and research his or her life and accomplishments before, during, and after World War II. Write a one-page biography based on your findings. Make sure your paper is complete and clear.

Standardized Test Practice

Directions: Choose the *best* answer to the following question.

Which of the following was a turning point in Europe during World War II?

A The Treaty of Paris

B The election of Roosevelt

C The bombing of Pearl Harbor

D The German defeat at Stalingrad

Test-Taking Tip

Eliminate answers that you know are wrong. For example, choice **A,** the Treaty of Paris, was not made in World War II.

UNIT
10 Turning Points

1945–1975

Why It Matters

As you study Unit 10, you will learn
about the changes that came after
World War II. Out of the war came
a new sense of global responsibility as
the United States made every effort to
protect Western democracy. Many
Americans pressed for social reform
and equal rights. In addition, the use
of new technology changed the way
Americans lived and worked.

Primary Sources Library

See pages 976–977 for primary source
readings to accompany Unit 10.
Use the American history
**Primary Source Document Library
CD-ROM** to find additional primary
sources about the Cold War, the civil
rights movement, and the Vietnam era.

American soldier in
Vietnam, 1966

**The Problem We All Live With
by Norman Rockwell**

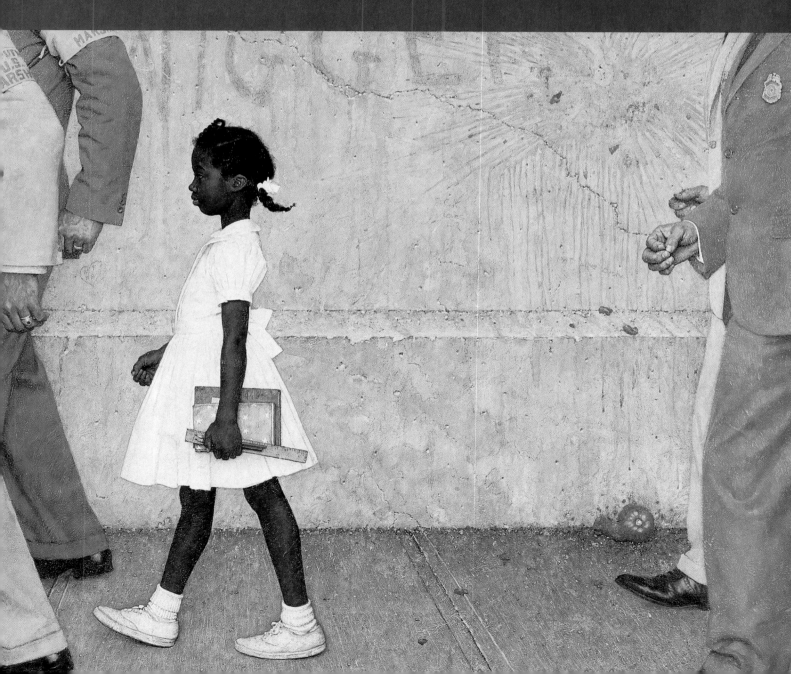

CHAPTER 27

The Cold War Era

1945–1954

Why It Matters

After the end of World War II, the United States and the Soviet Union entered into a bitter rivalry. Each side tried to gain allies and prove that its system—democracy and free enterprise or communism—was better.

The Impact Today

The rivalry between the United States and the Soviet Union shaped much of the modern world. The collapse of the Soviet Union in 1991 marked the end of the Cold War era.

The American Journey Video The chapter 27 video, "The Wall and the Berlin Airlift," details the Berlin blockade and the effects of the Berlin airlift.

1945
• Conference at Yalta; United Nations formed

Truman 1945–1953

United States PRESIDENTS

1947
• Truman Doctrine proposed

1948
• Marshall Plan enacted

1944   1946   1948

World

1946
• Churchill's "Iron Curtain" speech marks beginning of Cold War

1948
• Soviets blockade West Berlin
• State of Israel formed

Conflict in Korea United Nations troops fight in the streets of Seoul, South Korea, September 1950.

FOLDABLES™
Study Organizer

Compare-Contrast Study Foldable Organize and compare information about the rivalry that shaped the Cold War era by making and using this foldable.

Step 1 Fold a sheet of paper from side to side, leaving a 2-inch tab uncovered along the side.

> Fold it so the left edge lies 2 inches from the right edge.

Step 2 Turn the paper and fold it in half.

Step 3 Unfold and cut along the inside fold line.

> Cut along the fold on the front flap to make 2 tabs.

Step 4 Label the foldable as shown.

The Cold War
Democracy | Communism

Reading and Writing As you read about this period of time, write what you learn about democracy and communism under the tabs of your foldable. Compare the two sides and use what you learn to explain how the Cold War started.

1949
- NATO pact signed

1950
- General MacArthur leads troops into Korea

1954
- Senator Joseph McCarthy censured

Eisenhower 1953–1961

1950   1952   1954

1950
- North Korea invades South Korea

1953
- Korean War ends

1949
- Communist victory in China under Mao Zedong

HISTORY *Online*

Chapter Overview
Visit taj.glencoe.com and click on **Chapter 27— Chapter Overviews** to preview chapter information.

SECTION 1 Cold War Origins

Guide to Reading

Main Idea
The United States struggled to prevent the spread of communism.

Key Terms
iron curtain, containment, airlift, cold war

Reading Strategy
Sequencing Information As you read the section, re-create the time line below and list important events in the Cold War.

June 1945	June 1947	June 1948	May 1949

Read to Learn
- how the United States attempted to stop the spread of communism.
- how foreign policy changed as a result of the Cold War.

Section Theme
Global Connections Soviet expansion led to a cold war between the forces of democracy and communism.

Preview of Events

♦1945   ♦1947   ♦1949

February 1945
Conference at Yalta is held

April 1945
Harry S Truman succeeds FDR

May 1948
Jewish leaders proclaim new state of Israel

June 1948
Soviets blockade West Berlin

October 1949
Mao Zedong forms Communist China

AN American Story

The three most powerful men in the world met in Yalta to discuss the fate of the postwar world. President Roosevelt hoped to promote his vision of postwar cooperation. Prime Minister Churchill spoke elegantly and forcefully. Soviet leader Stalin remained stubbornly opposed to much of what was proposed. Stalin stated to his aides, "They want to force us to accept their plans on Europe and the world. Well, that's not going to happen." As the Allies discovered, Stalin had his own plans.

Wartime Diplomacy

While fighting a common enemy during World War II, Western democracies and Soviet leaders had set aside their differences. As the Allies moved toward victory in 1945, questions about the organization of the postwar world arose. Soviet forces had pushed back German armies and occupied much of Eastern and Central Europe. Should these areas—including Poland, Hungary, and Czechoslovakia—remain in Soviet hands?

In February 1945, the "Big Three" Allied leaders—**Franklin D. Roosevelt, Winston Churchill,** and **Joseph Stalin**—met at Yalta, a Soviet port on the Black Sea. They came to discuss issues affecting the postwar world. Out of this meeting came the Yalta agreement, in which the Soviet Union agreed to enter the war against Japan. In return, the Soviets received some territories in Asia.

Reaching an agreement on postwar arrangements proved more difficult. Roosevelt and Churchill feared the Soviet domination of Eastern Europe and the spread of communism. Stalin, on the other hand, wanted to keep a large area of land between the Soviet Union and its potential enemies in the West. Germany presented a special problem. The Allies finally agreed to divide Germany into four zones until elections could be held to determine its future. The Soviet Union, the United States, Britain, and France would each control a zone.

Stalin agreed to allow free elections in occupied Eastern Europe and to cooperate in planning for the new international organization proposed by the United States and Britain. Roosevelt and Churchill felt encouraged about a peaceful postwar world. Their hopes went unfulfilled.

NATIONAL GEOGRAPHIC

Europe After World War II

Legend:
- Communist control
- Divided nation
- NATO member
- Neutral nation
- ⊙ Jointly-occupied city

Geography *Skills*

1. **Place** What nations of Europe remained neutral?
2. **Region** Were most of the nations of Eastern Europe NATO members or under Communist control?

0 — 500 miles
0 — 500 kilometers
Lambert Azimuthal Equal-Area projection

The United Nations

President Roosevelt died suddenly on April 12, 1945. Vice President **Harry S Truman** succeeded him. Facing the enormous responsibilities of the presidency, Truman told reporters, "When they told me yesterday [of Roosevelt's death], I felt like the moon, the stars, and all the planets had fallen on me."

One of Truman's first decisions as president was to go ahead with the meeting to form the new international organization discussed at Yalta. On June 26, in San Francisco, California, 50 nations—including the Soviet Union—signed the charter creating the **United Nations** (UN). The members hoped the UN could settle disputes between nations and prevent future wars.

✓ Reading Check **Describing** How did the Allies agree to divide Germany?

✦Geography

Soviet Expansion in Europe

The uneasy wartime alliance between the Western nations and the Soviet Union did not last. Stalin did not keep his promise to hold free elections in Eastern Europe. Instead the Soviets set up Communist governments in these countries, and Soviet forces remained in the region.

Developments in Eastern Europe led to a growing distrust between the Soviet Union and Western nations. Europe split into two camps—the Soviet-controlled Communist governments of the East and the capitalist democracies.

The Iron Curtain

Winston Churchill believed that the division between East and West was permanent. In 1946 he declared in a speech in Fulton, Missouri, that an "iron curtain" had descended on Europe. Churchill meant that the Soviets had cut off Eastern Europe from the West. Behind this iron curtain, he said, lay the countries of Eastern Europe "in what I must call the Soviet sphere, and all are subject to a very high . . . measure of control from Moscow."

Churchill warned that the Soviets would eventually look beyond Eastern Europe and try to gain control of other parts of the world. This idea alarmed Americans, who had feared the spread of communism ever since the Russian Revolution in 1917.

Civil war raged in **Greece,** as Communist rebels armed by the Soviet Union attempted to overthrow the Greek king and his pro-Western government. At the same time, the Soviets put enormous pressure on **Turkey** to give them naval bases on the straits leading to the Mediterranean Sea.

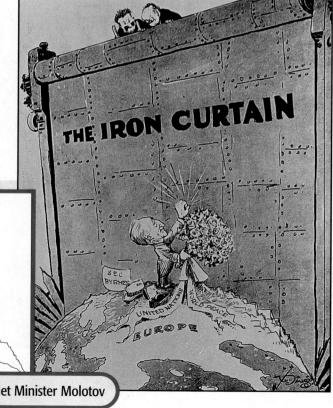

🎩 Analyzing *Political Cartoons*

The iron curtain represented a barrier to the free exchange of ideas between countries under Soviet control and the rest of the world. The iron curtain often appeared in cartoons about the Cold War. **What does the cartoon say about the attitude of Secretary of State Byrnes toward the Soviet leaders?**

Ⓐ Secretary of State Byrnes   Ⓑ Joseph Stalin   Ⓒ Soviet Minister Molotov

Containing the Soviets

Seeking ways to counter Soviet expansion, President Truman drew from the ideas of **George F. Kennan,** an American diplomat and an expert on Soviet history and culture. Kennan argued that the United States and the Soviet Union could not cooperate and that the United States must take forceful steps to stop Soviet expansion. His ideas led to the policy of containment. The United States would try to "contain" Soviet expansion through limited military means and nonmilitary means in areas of the world that were of strategic importance to the United States. Kennan defined these areas narrowly—mostly Western Europe and Japan. But other U.S. officials gradually expanded their view of what was of strategic importance to the country and its future.

The Truman Doctrine

The policy of containment soon went into effect. Speaking to Congress in March 1947, the president proposed a policy that became known as the **Truman Doctrine,** a commitment to help nations threatened by communism and Soviet expansion.

> **❝**I believe that it must be the policy of the United States to support free peoples who are resisting attempted subjugation [conquest] by armed minorities or by outside pressures.**❞**

Congress voted to give military and economic assistance to Greece and Turkey to hold back the Soviet threat.

The Marshall Plan

At the end of World War II, much of Europe lay in ruins. Bombing had destroyed countless houses, factories, bridges, and roads. Many people lacked homes and jobs, and they often did not have enough food. Their war-ravaged societies provided fertile ground for communism, with its promises of housing and employment for all.

George Marshall, the U.S. secretary of state, saw Western Europe as strategically important to the United States. He believed that the best way to keep the countries of Western Europe free of communism would be to help restore their economies. In June 1947, Marshall proposed a plan to provide massive economic aid to Europe. At first his plan met some resistance in Congress. After Soviet-supported Communists took over the government of **Czechoslovakia** in February 1948, however, this resistance disappeared.

Congress approved the Marshall Plan, a program of economic aid for Europe that became a vital part of the policy of containment. Between 1948 and 1951, the Marshall Plan contributed nearly $13 billion to the rebuilding of the countries of Western Europe. As Marshall had predicted, no Western government in the region fell to a communist revolution.

✓ Reading Check **Explaining** How was the Marshall Plan supposed to check communist expansion?

Crisis in Berlin

The Allied leaders at Yalta had divided Germany into four occupation zones. The Soviet Union controlled the eastern part of the country, while the United States, Britain, and France divided the western part. The German capital of **Berlin,** located deep within Soviet-controlled East Germany, was also divided among the four nations.

President Truman believed that a reunited Germany was essential to the future of Europe. Stalin, on the other hand, feared that a reunited Germany would once again pose a threat to the Soviet Union. He sought to maintain Soviet influence in a divided Germany. Tensions over the German issue led to a serious crisis in 1948.

The Berlin Blockade

On June 7, 1948, the United States, Britain, and France announced that they were uniting their zones to form a new West German republic. Each nation's section of Berlin would be included in this republic as well, even though the city lay within Soviet-held East Germany.

The **Berlin blockade** was Stalin's answer to the West's plans for West Germany. On June 24, 1948, Soviet troops rushed into position around the edge of West Berlin. Almost overnight they created a blockade, stopping traffic on all highway,

Why It Matters

Berlin Airlift

In June 1948, the Soviet Union halted all traffic by land or water into or out of Western-controlled Berlin. Allied Powers began supplying the city's 2.5 million residents with the necessities of life—by air. Night and day for more than 10 months, British and United States cargo planes carried food, medicine, clothing, raw materials, and even coal to Berlin. World opinion turned against the Soviet Union and its tactics of starving innocent people to achieve its goals. Berlin became a symbol of America's fight against communism.

The effort—some 278,000 flights delivering 2 million tons of supplies—melted the hatred between former American and German enemies. In May 1949, the Soviet Union finally lifted its blockade.

> *A West Berlin taxi driver explained how the airlift boosted the morale of the people of Berlin.*
> "There. You hear? There is another plane. And there's another. Our faith doesn't come from our hearts or our brain anymore. It comes through the ears."

railroad, and water routes through East Germany to West Berlin. As a result, West Berlin and its two million citizens were cut off from vital supplies. The Soviets hoped this blockade would drive the West out of Berlin.

The Berlin Airlift

President Truman refused to give in to the Soviets. "We stay in Berlin, period," he declared, but he did not want to risk war by using military force to end the blockade. Instead he organized a massive airlift to save the city. American and British cargo planes began flying food, fuel, and other supplies into West Berlin.

The **Berlin airlift** continued day and night for more than 10 months, delivering tons of supplies to West Berlin. Realizing that the Western powers intended to stay in the city, Stalin ended the Berlin blockade in May 1949. Despite the success of the airlift, Berlin and Germany remained divided. In October 1949, the division of Germany into two

nations—the **Federal Republic of Germany,** or West Germany, and the **German Democratic Republic,** or East Germany—became official.

✔ **Reading Check** **Analyzing** How did the Soviet Union respond to plans to form a new West German republic?

Two Armed Camps

The crisis in Berlin confirmed that the United States and the Soviet Union were locked in a cold war—a war in which the two enemies did not actually fight each other. Instead each nation began building up its military forces and arms to intimidate the other. European nations began to take sides in this mounting cold war.

The United States and the countries of Western Europe agreed that the best way to contain the Soviets was through mutual defense. In

NATIONAL GEOGRAPHIC **Berlin: A Divided City**

EAST GERMANY

Tegel
Spree R.
West Berlin
Gatow
Tempelhof
Berlin Wall
East Berlin

N
W—E
S

0   5 miles
0   5 kilometers
Albers Conic Equal-Area projection

✈ Airports
☐ American sector
☐ British sector
☐ French sector
☐ Soviet sector

Soviet leader Joseph Stalin closed all roads and railways into the Western sections of Berlin, cutting off supplies of food and fuel. All flights were streamed along one of three 20-mile wide air corridors.

April 1949, the United States, Canada, and 10 Western European nations signed a pact establishing the **North Atlantic Treaty Organization** (NATO). The agreement stated that "an armed attack against one or more of [the member nations] shall be considered an attack against all." To defend against a possible Soviet invasion of Western Europe, the NATO countries created a large military force.

In response to NATO, the Soviet Union created an alliance of its own with the Communist governments of Eastern Europe. The alliance, established in 1955 by mutual defense treaties known as the **Warsaw Pact,** had a military force that the Soviet Union controlled. The formation of NATO and the Warsaw Pact divided Europe into two armed camps.

The United States Rearms

After World War II, some of President Truman's foreign policy advisers in the **National Security Council** (NSC) argued that America could not rely on other nations to contain the Soviets and resist the spread of communism. Unlike George Kennan and the supporters of the containment policy, the NSC advisers believed the United States needed to take a more active stand against communism everywhere—not just in strategic locations.

In 1950 the NSC released a report, known as **NSC-68,** which said that the United States must actively

66 foster the seeds of destruction within the Soviet Union 99

and fight communist movements wherever they arose. The United States committed itself to combating communist expansion everywhere in the world.

Germany

Germany is reunified On October 3, 1990, the two parts of Germany finally reunited, and Berlin—rejoined as one city—again became the nation's official capital. The German government's move to Berlin from the West German capital of Bonn is scheduled to be completed in the year 2003.

Independence Movements

As the Cold War grew more bitter in Europe, nations in other parts of the world were undergoing dramatic changes. Many states broke free of colonial rule and established independence.

The Philippines gained independence from the United States in 1946. For years afterward Filipinos struggled with terrible poverty, government corruption, and civil war. In the late 1940s, Asian countries such as India, Pakistan, and Burma broke away from the British Empire to form new nations. During the 1950s and the early 1960s, more than 25 African nations gained independence from European colonial powers. The path to independence in Africa was often bloody. Once free, the new nations faced the enormous task of building modern societies.

In the Middle East, Jews and Arabs both claimed the region of **Palestine,** an area the British had controlled. In 1947 the United Nations proposed dividing Palestine into independent Jewish and Arab states with Jerusalem as an international city. The Jews accepted the plan, but the Arab states did not. After declaring its independence, the new Jewish state of **Israel** was attacked by Arab armies in the first of six major wars between the Arabs and Israel.

Communism in China

Perhaps the most threatening change of the postwar period occurred in **China,** the largest country in Asia. In 1949 a long civil war ended with the victory of Chinese Communist forces led by **Mao Zedong** (MAU ZUH•DUNG) over the armies commanded by **Chiang Kai-shek** (JEE•AHNG KY•SHEHK), the head of the Chinese government. Mao Zedong formed a new Communist state, the People's Republic of China, while Chiang Kai-shek retreated with his forces to the island of **Taiwan** off the southeastern coast of China. The United States recognized the government in Taiwan as the legitimate government of all China.

With Communists in control of mainland China, the Soviet Union had a powerful ally in Asia. It appeared to many people that the entire continent of Asia was in danger of converting to communism.

Reading Check **Identifying** What new nation was formed in the Middle East in the 1940s?

SECTION 1 ASSESSMENT

Checking for Understanding

1. **Key Terms** Write a paragraph in which you use each of the following terms correctly: iron curtain, containment, airlift, cold war.
2. **Reviewing Facts** Did the Berlin blockade force the Western powers to leave the city? Explain.

Reviewing Themes

3. **Global Connections** What was the purpose of the Truman Doctrine?

Critical Thinking

4. **Analyzing Information** Explain why the United States's actions during the Berlin blockade were considered part of a "cold war."
5. **Determining Cause and Effect** Re-create the diagram below and explain how the Marshall Plan helped to contain the spread of communism.

| Marshall Plan | ⟹ | |

Analyzing Visuals

6. **Geography Skills** Examine the map of Europe on page 789. Was Spain a neutral nation? Was Turkey a NATO member?

Interdisciplinary Activity

Geography Compare a map of Africa after World War II to a map of Africa today. Photocopy or draw a modern map and indicate five countries that have changed their names or boundaries.

Critical Thinking
SKILLBUILDER

Making Inferences

Why Learn This Skill?

Have you heard someone say, "You can't judge him on face value"? It means that people, things you see, or things you read might not be as they appear to be. There might be a double or hidden meaning to what you see or hear.

Learning the Skill

Inferences are ideas that are not directly stated. **Making Inferences** involves reading between the lines to interpret what you are seeing. You call upon some previous knowledge or just use common sense.

Practicing the Skill

First published at the beginning of the Cold War, *Animal Farm* by George Orwell tells the story of a farm taken over by its overworked, mistreated animals. The fable exposes the negative effects that totalitarian government can have on society. Read this passage from George Orwell's novel *Animal Farm*. Then answer the questions that follow.

> Squealer tries to persuade the animals that Napoleon is a good leader, saying, "Do not imagine, comrades, that leadership is a pleasure! On the contrary, it is a deep and heavy responsibility. No one believes more firmly than Comrade Napoleon that all animals are equal. He would be only too happy to let you make your decisions for yourselves. But sometimes you might make the wrong decisions, comrades, and then where should we be? Suppose you had decided to follow Snowball . . . ?"
>
> "He fought bravely at the Battle of the Cowshed," said somebody.
>
> "Bravery is not enough," said Squealer. "Loyalty and obedience are more important . . ."

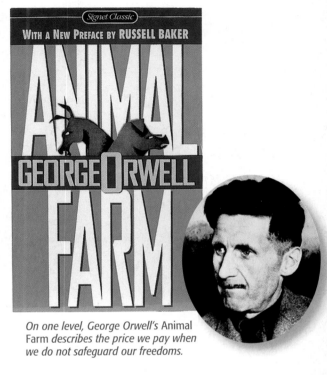

On one level, George Orwell's Animal Farm *describes the price we pay when we do not safeguard our freedoms.*

1. Does Squealer represent the leaders or the common animals?

2. Why does he say that leadership is a "deep and heavy responsibility?"

3. Squealer says that all animals are equal. Does he really believe this? Explain.

Applying the Skill

Making Inferences Choose a poem, or a quote found in a newspaper, that you think has more than one meaning. Share your selection with a classmate to see if they infer a hidden meaning.

 Glencoe's **Skillbuilder Interactive Workbook CD-ROM, Level 1,** provides instruction and practice in key social studies skills.

SECTION 2 Postwar Politics

Guide to Reading

Main Idea
The Truman administration pushed for economic and social reform.

Key Terms
inflation, closed shop

Reading Strategy
Organizing Information As you read the section, re-create the diagram below and identify three measures that were part of Truman's Fair Deal.

The Fair Deal

Read to Learn
• what economic problems Americans faced after World War II.
• what actions President Truman and Congress proposed to deal with the nation's problems.

Section Theme
Economic Factors Americans tried to adjust to a peacetime economy after World War II.

Preview of Events

♦ 1944	♦ 1946		♦ 1948
1944 Congress approves the GI Bill of Rights	**1946** Miners and railroad workers strike	**1947** Taft-Hartley Act limits unions	**1948** Truman wins the presidency

AN American Story

When soldiers returned home after World War II, they came back to a nation facing the difficult task of changing from wartime to peacetime. Would the economy collapse again and another depression sweep the country? President Truman was optimistic: "We are having our little troubles now. Just a blow-up after a little let-down from war." Public concern, however, forced the nation's political leaders into a heated debate over the best way to deal with America's economic problems.

Economics

The Postwar Economy

After World War II, the nation and its economy had to adjust to peacetime life. Industries had to shift from producing war materials to making **consumer goods.** Defense workers had to be retrained to work in consumer industries, and returning soldiers needed jobs.

During the war, government price controls had kept the cost of consumer goods such as food and clothing quite stable. When the government removed these controls, prices began to surge. This rise in prices, or inflation, also resulted from a huge increase in consumer demand and spending. During the war years,

Americans had saved their money because many consumer goods were unavailable or rationed. Now they were eager to spend this money on new consumer products and services.

Workers Seek Higher Wages

As a result of inflation, consumer prices rose at a much faster rate than wages. During the war, workers had accepted government controls on wages and agreed not to strike. Now they would no longer be put off. When employers refused to raise wages, labor unions called for strikes. In 1945 and 1946, millions of steelworkers, railroad workers, and others walked off their jobs, demanding higher wages and better conditions.

Labor unrest and strikes disrupted the nation's economy. When miners went on strike in 1946, many Americans feared that dwindling coal supplies would cause the economy to grind to a halt. At about the same time, a strike by railroad workers caused a total shutdown of the nation's railroads, which were vital to the economy.

Truman Takes Action

Alarmed by the labor unrest, President Truman pressured the striking miners and railroad workers to go back to their jobs. In May 1946, he threatened to draft them into the army if they did not return to work. The president insisted he had the right to take such steps to keep vital industries operating.

President Truman finally forced striking miners back on the job by having the government take over the mines. At the same time, however, he persuaded the mine owners to grant many of the workers' demands. Truman also pressured railroad workers to return to work.

✓ **Reading Check** **Describing** What happened to the price of consumer goods when demand grew after the war?

Truman Faces the Republicans

In September 1945, President Truman, a Democrat, presented Congress with a plan of domestic reforms aimed at solving some of the nation's economic problems. Truman later called this program the **Fair Deal.**

Truman proposed to raise the minimum wage, expand Social Security benefits, increase federal spending to create jobs, build new public housing, and create a system of national health insurance. However, because of opposition by a coalition of Republicans and Southern Democrats, these measures failed to pass in Congress.

Republicans Control Congress

Many Americans blamed Truman and the Democratic Party for the nation's economic problems. In the congressional elections of 1946, the slogan "Had Enough?" helped Republicans win control of both houses of Congress.

The new Republican Congress moved quickly to create its own plans for the nation. Having rejected Truman's program for reform, the Republicans now set up proposals to enact a program that would limit government spending, control labor unions, reduce government regulation of the economy, and reverse policies adopted in the 1930s under FDR's New Deal.

For many Republicans in Congress, the most important problem facing the nation was labor unrest and the growing power of labor unions. Conservative Republicans favored big business

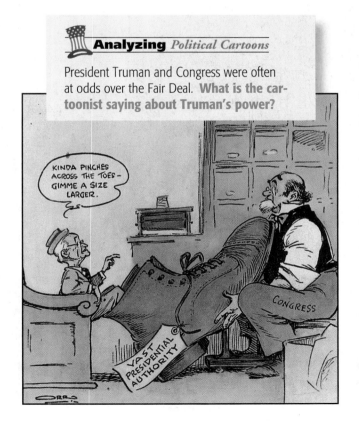

Analyzing *Political Cartoons*

President Truman and Congress were often at odds over the Fair Deal. **What is the cartoonist saying about Truman's power?**

and wanted to limit the power of unions. In the spring of 1947, Congress introduced the **Taft-Hartley bill.** This bill limited the actions workers could take against their employers. It outlawed the closed shop, a workplace that hires only union members. It also allowed the government to temporarily stop any strike that endangered public health or safety. This provision aimed to prevent any future strikes like those of the miners and the railroad workers the year before. Union members and their leaders sharply criticized the Taft-Hartley Act, calling it a "slave labor bill." Although President Truman opposed recent strikes, he also knew that the Democrats needed the support of labor. Truman vetoed the act, but the Republican-controlled Congress overrode his veto.

Government Reorganization

One issue on which Truman and Congress agreed was the need to improve the administration of the federal government, which had greatly expanded since the New Deal. In 1947 Truman appointed a commission headed by former President Herbert Hoover to study ways of improving the efficiency of government. Out of the Hoover Commission's work came plans to create new government departments and agencies.

In 1947 Congress passed the **National Security Act.** It unified the army, navy, marines, and air force under the Department of Defense. A secretary of defense headed the new department. The act also set up a permanent Joint Chiefs of Staff, made up of the heads of each of the armed forces to coordinate military policy. A National Security Council, operating out of the White House, would advise the president on foreign and military matters.

The National Security Act also set up another institution, the **Central Intelligence Agency (CIA).** The CIA aids American foreign policy by collecting information about what is going on in other countries, evaluating it, and passing it

Trading Weapons for Textbooks

Welcome to Indiana University

The GI Bill

In 1944 Congress passed the Servicemen's Readjustment Act, better known as the GI Bill of Rights. GI stands for government issue. This law provided billions of dollars in loans to help returning GI's—soldiers, sailors, and marines—attend college, receive special training, set up businesses, or buy homes. It also provided unemployment and health benefits for the GI's as they looked for jobs.

By making it possible for millions of GI's to go to college, the GI Bill changed U.S. higher education forever. University education was now open to people from every income level.

on to the president and other foreign-policy decision makers. The CIA uses its own secret agents, paid informers, and friendly governments to collect such information.

Many Americans feared that the CIA would be used to spy on American citizens. Truman, however, promised that the new agency would operate only in foreign lands and would not bring "police state methods" into American society. The CIA was so successful that in 1949 Congress gave that agency the right to receive, exchange, and spend money without giving account to Congress.

The Election of 1948

As the 1948 presidential election approached, Truman appeared to be the underdog. Continuing economic problems made the president unpopular with many Americans, and his lack of success in winning passage of domestic reforms made Truman's administration look weak and ineffective.

Divisions within the Democratic Party also increased the chances of an easy Republican victory. At the party's national convention, a group of Southern Democrats walked out to protest Truman's support for civil rights legislation. The Southern Democrats formed the States' Rights Democratic Party, or Dixiecrats, and nominated Governor **Strom Thurmond** of South Carolina for president. At the same time, some liberal members of the Democratic Party left to form the Progressive Party, with **Henry Wallace** as their nominee for president. Wallace opposed Truman's foreign policy and called for closer ties between the United States and the Soviet Union.

Dewey Leads Polls

With the Democrats badly divided, it looked as though Governor **Thomas Dewey** of New York, the Republican nominee, would surely win the election. Opinion polls showed Dewey with a huge lead. One pollster remarked: "Mr. Dewey is still so clearly ahead that we might just as well get ready to listen to his inaugural."

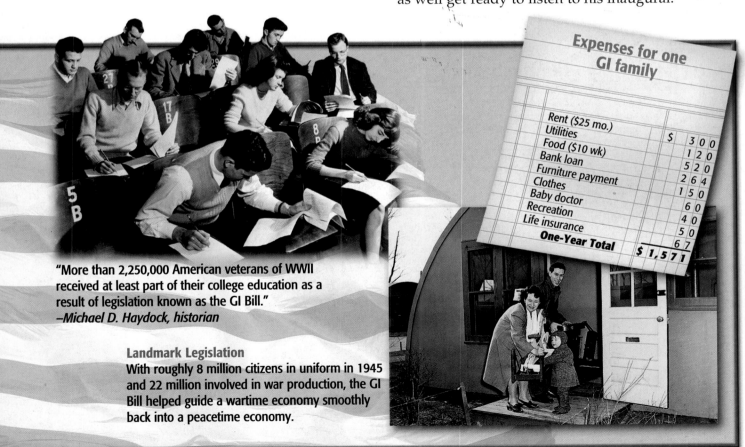

Expenses for one GI family

Rent ($25 mo.)	$	3 0 0
Utilities		1 2 0
Food ($10 wk)		5 2 0
Bank loan		2 6 4
Furniture payment		1 5 0
Clothes		6 0
Baby doctor		4 0
Recreation		5 0
Life insurance		6 7
One-Year Total		**$ 1,5 7 1**

"More than 2,250,000 American veterans of WWII received at least part of their college education as a result of legislation known as the GI Bill."
–Michael D. Haydock, historian

Landmark Legislation
With roughly 8 million citizens in uniform in 1945 and 22 million involved in war production, the GI Bill helped guide a wartime economy smoothly back into a peacetime economy.

Truman campaigned aggressively. Traveling more than 30,000 miles (48,000 km) by train on a "whistle-stop" tour of the country, he gave some 250 speeches along the way. In town after town, he sharply attacked what he called "that do-nothing, good-for-nothing, worst Congress" for rejecting his Fair Deal legislation.

Truman Stages an Upset

On Election Day experts still expected Dewey to win. Expectations for a Republican victory were so great that on the evening of the election—before many votes were counted—the *Chicago Daily Tribune* newspaper issued a special edition announcing "Dewey Defeats Truman."

The nation was in for a great surprise. When all the ballots were counted, Truman had edged out Dewey by more than two million votes in a narrow upset victory. Democrats also regained control of both the House of Representatives and the Senate in the election.

✓ **Reading Check** **Analyzing** Why was the outcome of the 1948 presidential election a surprise?

A Fair Deal for Americans

Truman took the election results as a sign that Americans wanted reform. He quickly reintroduced the **Fair Deal** legislation he had presented to Congress in 1945. Some of these reform measures passed, but his plan lacked broad support, and Congress defeated most of the measures. Congress did pass laws to raise the minimum wage, expand Social Security benefits for senior citizens, and provide funds for housing for low-income families.

🗣 Citizenship
A Stand on Civil Rights

In a message to Congress in 1948, President Truman declared:

❝We shall not, however, finally achieve the ideals for which this nation was founded so long as any American suffers discrimination as a result of his race, or religion, or color, or the land of origin of his forefathers.❞

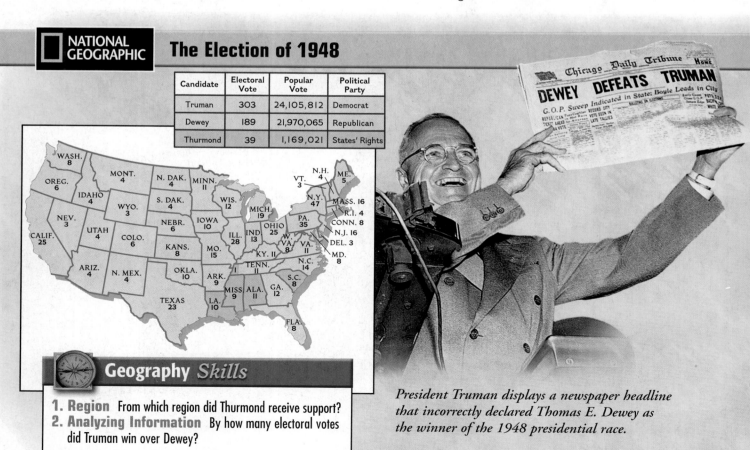

NATIONAL GEOGRAPHIC **The Election of 1948**

Candidate	Electoral Vote	Popular Vote	Political Party
Truman	303	24,105,812	Democrat
Dewey	189	21,970,065	Republican
Thurmond	39	1,169,021	States' Rights

Geography *Skills*

1. **Region** From which region did Thurmond receive support?
2. **Analyzing Information** By how many electoral votes did Truman win over Dewey?

President Truman displays a newspaper headline that incorrectly declared Thomas E. Dewey as the winner of the 1948 presidential race.

Picturing **History**

African Americans welcome Truman to Harlem during his 1948 presidential campaign. **How was Truman successful in advancing civil rights?**

1948 civil rights button

and ordered the armed forces to **desegregate**—to end the separation of races. The president also instructed the Justice Department to actively enforce existing civil rights laws. When Truman proposed his domestic agenda to Congress in 1949, he proclaimed that "every segment of our population and every individual has a right to expect from our government a fair deal." Truman asked for the clearance of slums, government-backed medical insurance, higher minimum wages, and more federal money for public schools. Although much of the president's Fair Deal vision went unfulfilled, he made an important start toward improving the lives of millions of Americans.

Although Truman championed ending such discrimination, he was unable to persuade Congress to pass legislation that would protect the voting rights of African Americans, abolish the poll tax, and make lynching a federal crime. Still, President Truman did take serious steps to advance the civil rights of African Americans. He ordered federal departments and agencies to end job discrimination against African Americans

SECTION ASSESSMENT

Checking for Understanding

1. **Key Terms** Use the terms inflation and closed shop in sentences that will help explain their meaning.
2. **Reviewing Facts** What actions did President Truman take in order to advance the civil rights of African Americans?

Reviewing Themes

3. **Economic Factors** What factors caused inflation of prices after World War II?

Critical Thinking

4. **Determining Cause and Effect** How did the Taft-Hartley Act affect business and unions?
5. **Organizing Information** Complete a diagram like the one shown by describing the adjustments made in the United States to convert from a wartime to a peacetime economy.

Analyzing Visuals

6. **Geography Skills** Examine the election map on page 800. Was the total number of votes cast for Dewey and Thurmond greater than Truman's total?

Interdisciplinary Activity

Economics View copies of newspapers published five years ago. Compare the prices of three items advertised at that time to the same items today. Calculate the percent of increase (or decrease) in price for each of the products.

SECTION 3 The Korean War

Guide to Reading

Main Idea
Americans under the United Nations flag fought to stop a Communist takeover of the Korean peninsula.

Key Terms
stalemate, demilitarized zone

Reading Strategy
Sequencing Information As you read the section, re-create the time line below and list key events in the Korean War.

June 25, 1950	Oct. 19, 1950	Nov. 26, 1950	April 11, 1951	July 27, 1953

Read to Learn
• what events led to the Korean War.
• how America's war aims changed during the war.

Section Theme
Global Connections The United States fought in Korea to stop Communist expansion.

Preview of Events

♦1950   ♦1952   ♦1954

June 1950
North Korea invades South Korea

April 1951
Truman fires General MacArthur

July 1953
Cease-fire agreement is signed

AN American Story

The bitter wind stung the raw faces of 12 U.S. Marine officers. They had just fought for five bloody days to lead their troops out of a Chinese trap in the icy wastes of northeast Korea. Now they listened to the words of their commander: "We are going to come out of this as Marines, not as stragglers. We're going to bring out our wounded and our equipment. We're coming out . . . as Marines or not at all." Two more days of fighting followed, as the tired but determined Marines held off fierce enemy attacks. With the arrival of air cover on the third day, the Marines were able to push back the Chinese and make their escape.

Conflict in Korea

Before June 1950, few Americans knew much about **Korea,** a small east Asian country located on the Korean Peninsula west of Japan. In 1945 Korea was a colony of Japan. At the end of World War II, Japan was stripped of its territorial possessions. The United States and the Soviet Union both sent troops into Korea and agreed to occupy it temporarily. They divided the peninsula in half along the **38th parallel** of latitude, with the Soviets controlling North Korea and the Americans controlling South Korea.

The Soviet Union and the United States could not agree on how to unify Korea. When these two nations removed their forces in 1949, Korea remained divided. Tensions between the two Koreas were high.

On June 24, 1950, President Truman flew to his home in Independence, Missouri, for a brief vacation. While sitting on his porch on a hot summer night, the president received a telephone call from Secretary of State Dean Acheson. "Mr. President," Acheson said in a grim tone, "I have very serious news. The North Koreans have invaded South Korea." Truman knew this meant only one thing: the United States soon would be involved in military action in Asia.

The Invasion of South Korea

After the American troops pulled out of South Korea, North Korea decided to unify the country by force. On June 25, 1950, the armies of North Korea crossed the 38th parallel into South Korea. Poorly armed, the South Koreans were no match for the North. Within days the Communist forces had gained control over much of South Korea, including **Seoul,** the capital city.

President Truman reacted quickly to the Korean invasion, which he believed was supported by the Soviet Union. Without asking Congress to actually declare war, Truman ordered the use of limited American air and sea forces in Korea. He called this "police action" necessary to carry out America's policy of containment. Truman said:

> **❝**Korea is the Greece of the Far East. If we are tough enough now, if we stand up to them like we did in Greece three years ago, they won't take any next steps.**❞**

United Nations Responds

At the same time, President Truman asked the UN to send forces to defend the South Koreans. The United Nations condemned the invasion of South Korea and agreed to send a special force to the region under the United States's direction. President Truman quickly appointed General **Douglas MacArthur,** a hero of World War II, to command the UN forces.

On June 30, just days after the North Korean invasion, General MacArthur led American troops into Korea to stop the Communist advance. By the end of 1950, other nations were supplying troops or other assistance to the American-led war effort. Even so, Americans made up the majority of troops throughout the Korean War.

The United Nations had a clear but difficult goal—push the North Koreans back across the 38th parallel. When China intervened in the conflict, this goal changed, causing Truman and MacArthur to clash over military strategy.

NATIONAL GEOGRAPHIC

The Korean War, 1950–1953

⊛ Capital city

— Truce line, July 1953

PEOPLE'S REPUBLIC OF CHINA

Yalu R.

SOVIET UNION

NORTH KOREA
⊛ Pyongyang

Panmunjom

❷

Inchon

⊛ Seoul

Sea of Japan (East Sea)

SOUTH KOREA

❶ Pusan

JAPAN

❶ Farthest advance of North Koreans **Sept. 1950**

❷ UN landing **Sept. 1950**

❸ Farthest advance of UN forces **Nov. 1950**

❹ Farthest advance of North Koreans and Chinese **Jan. 1951**

134°E
42°N
38°N
122°E
34°N

0   100 miles
0   100 kilometers
Lambert Azimuthal Equal-Area projection

Geography *Skills*

The Korean War raged along the Korean Peninsula.
1. Place What city is located along the 38th parallel?
2. Analyzing Information Whose forces landed at Inchon in September 1950?

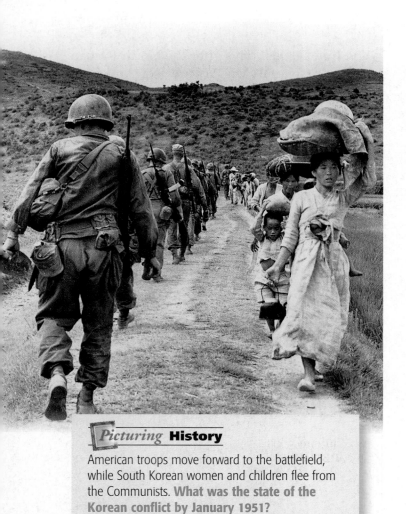

American troops move forward to the battlefield, while South Korean women and children flee from the Communists. **What was the state of the Korean conflict by January 1951?**

Early Phases of the War

By September 1950, North Korean forces had pushed all the way to the southern tip of the Korean Peninsula. Only a small area in the southeast around the port city of **Pusan** was still held by the South Korean army.

After joining the South Koreans, General MacArthur designed a bold counterattack against North Korea. In September, United Nations forces made a daring landing midway on the Korean Peninsula near the port of **Inchon**. They took that strategic city and moved on to recapture Seoul.

Meanwhile American and UN troops began pushing north from Pusan. By October 1 the North Koreans, caught between UN forces advancing from both Seoul and Pusan, were forced to retreat north across the 38th parallel. South Korea now came under the control of the United Nations forces.

Taking the Offensive

Encouraged by this success, General MacArthur urged President Truman to order an invasion of North Korea. He assured Truman that neither **China** nor the Soviet Union would enter the war to help North Korea, and he promised to have troops "home by Christmas." Truman sought and received approval from the United Nations to cross the 38th parallel, invade the North, and create "a unified, independent and democratic Korea"—a new goal for the war.

After receiving these new orders, MacArthur moved his forces northward. The UN forces captured **Pyongyang,** the North Korean capital, on October 19, and then moved north toward the **Yalu River,** part of North Korea's border with China. Total victory seemed just days away.

As the UN forces advanced, the United States received a warning from the Chinese. If the invasion of North Korea continued, China would send in its army to support the North Koreans. Believing the Chinese warning was a bluff, President Truman allowed MacArthur to continue moving north.

The Chinese were not bluffing, however. By late October, thousands of Chinese troops began massing along the border, and some crossed the Yalu River southward into North Korea. On November 26, huge numbers of Chinese troops launched an attack on United Nations forces. Badly outnumbered, the UN forces retreated south back across the 38th parallel. Within weeks, the Communists had recaptured Seoul.

✓Reading Check **Describing** What line separated North from South Korea?

American Leadership Divided

By January 1951, United Nations forces managed to stop their retreat. Launching a counteroffensive, they retook Seoul and pushed the Communists back across the 38th parallel. The war now became a stalemate, a situation in which neither side was able to gain much ground or achieve a decisive victory. The stalemate lasted for almost two years, with much bitter fighting along the 38th parallel.

Truman and MacArthur Disagree

As the stalemate dragged on, President Truman began to consider negotiating an end to the fighting. General MacArthur, however, argued that the UN forces should now attack China, either by invading the country or by bombing Chinese troops stationed in North Korea. Truman opposed MacArthur's plan, fearing that such actions would lead to a larger war with China or escalate into another world war.

In a letter to a member of Congress, MacArthur complained that he was being kept from doing his job. "We must win," he wrote. "There is no substitute for victory."

On April 11, 1951, President Truman relieved General MacArthur of his command in Korea. "I could do nothing else and still be president of the United States," Truman concluded. He wrote:

> ❝If I allowed him to defy the civil authorities in this manner, I myself would be violating my oath to uphold and defend the Constitution.❞

MacArthur's firing created a storm of protest in the United States. The general was extremely popular, and polls showed that a majority of Americans supported him against the president. Moreover, MacArthur did not go quietly. After receiving a hero's welcome on his return to the United States, he delivered a farewell speech to Congress. "Old soldiers never die," he said, "they just fade away."

Ending the Conflict

The two sides in the Korean War began negotiations in July 1951. The talks lasted for two years before a cease-fire agreement was signed on July 27, 1953, during the presidency of Dwight Eisenhower. This agreement ending the war created a demilitarized zone—a region where military forces could not enter—between North and South Korea. The zone extended roughly a mile and a half on either side of the 38th parallel.

The Korean War ended with neither side achieving victory and almost no change in territory. Losses had been great. More than 54,000 Americans died in the war, and another 103,000 were wounded. Nearly two million Koreans and Chinese lost their lives, and large portions of North and South Korea were devastated.

America's involvement in the Korean War sent a clear message to the Soviet Union: The United States was committed to fighting Communist expansion with money, arms, and even lives. At the same time, the inability of the United States to win a clear victory contributed to uncertainty at home about the nation's foreign policy.

✔ **Reading Check** **Comparing** How did Truman's view on the Korean War differ from General MacArthur's view?

HISTORY Online

Student Web Activity
Visit taj.glencoe.com and click on **Chapter 27— Student Web Activities** for an activity on the Korean War.

SECTION 3 ASSESSMENT

Checking for Understanding

1. **Key Terms** Define the following terms: stalemate, demilitarized zone.
2. **Reviewing Facts** How did the Korean War begin?

Reviewing Themes

3. **Global Connections** How did American goals change during the course of the Korean War?

Critical Thinking

4. **Identifying Central Issues** Do you think Truman should have allowed MacArthur to attack China? Why or why not?
5. **Organizing Information** Re-create the diagram below and provide two reasons for the Korean War ending in a stalemate.

Analyzing Visuals

6. **Geography Skills** Examine the map on page 803. When did UN forces make their farthest advance?

Interdisciplinary Activity

Persuasive Writing Write a one-page editorial in which you argue whether a U.S. military leader should or should not be able to override a president's decision.

The Red Scare

Guide to Reading

Main Idea
Life in Cold War America was marked by a search for security.

Key Terms
subversion, blacklist, perjury, allege, censure

Reading Strategy
Classifying Information As you read the section, re-create the diagram below and explain why these individuals are important.

	Historical significance
Alger Hiss	
Ethel Rosenberg	
Joseph McCarthy	

Read to Learn
• what effect Cold War fears had on domestic politics.
• how McCarthyism affected the nation.

Section Theme
Government and Democracy Americans of the postwar era took steps to combat the spread of communism within the United States.

Preview of Events

♦1945   ♦1950   ♦1955

1947
House Un-American Activities Committee holds hearings

1950
Congress passes the McCarran Act

1953
The Rosenbergs are executed as spies

1954
McCarthy is censured

AN
American Story

In 1947, a congressional committee held public hearings on the alleged communist influence in the Hollywood film industry. Many witnesses called before the committee were asked the same questions: "Are you now or have you ever been a member of the Communist Party?" Two witnesses denied having communist ties, but 10 others refused to give a straight "yes" or "no" answer. In dramatic moments worthy of the movies, these "Hollywood Ten" challenged the committee's right to ask about their political beliefs. One of the accused yelled, "This is the beginning of an American concentration camp!"

Cold War Fears

The Cold War intensified Americans' fears of communist subversion, or sabotage. Stories of stolen government documents and spy rings gripped the country in the late 1940s. Then in 1949 Americans learned that the Soviet Union had built its own atomic bomb.

Many Americans worried that Communist spies and sympathizers—people friendly to Communists, or "Reds" as they were known—had penetrated all levels of American society and were attempting to weaken the government.

This **Red Scare** dominated the nation's politics for years and led to a massive hunt to uncover Communists. In this climate of fear, few Americans were safe from accusations of disloyalty—not even the president.

Republican critics began accusing President Truman of being too easy on Communists. In 1947 Truman responded by ordering an investigation into the loyalty of all federal employees. Millions of government workers had to undergo security checks, and thousands were investigated by the FBI. Although the investigations found little evidence of espionage, many federal employees lost their jobs.

Loyalty Oaths and Investigations

Many state and local governments, colleges, and businesses began similar campaigns to uncover communist subversion. Some organizations required individuals to sign oaths swearing their loyalty to the United States. Those who refused risked losing their jobs.

In 1950 Congress passed the **McCarran Act,** which required all Communist organizations to register with the government and to provide lists of members. President Truman vetoed the act. "In a free country, we punish men for crimes they commit," he said, "but never for the opinions they hold." Congress overrode his veto.

In 1947 a congressional committee, the **House Un-American Activities Committee** (HUAC), began investigating communist subversion in the nation. In widely publicized hearings, the committee questioned people about their knowledge of Communists or Communist sympathizers. Individuals came under suspicion because of the beliefs of their friends or coworkers—guilt by association. The committee's activities fueled an anti-Communist hysteria in the nation.

HUAC launched a sensational investigation of the Hollywood film industry, rumored to be full of Communists. A number of those who were summoned refused to testify, and several screenwriters and directors—the "Hollywood Ten"—went to jail for refusing to answer questions about their political beliefs or those of their colleagues. Reacting to public and government pressure, film companies created blacklists— lists of individuals whose loyalty was suspicious—that barred people from working in Hollywood's film industry.

American Spies Revealed

In 1948 **Whittaker Chambers,** a magazine editor, volunteered to testify before HUAC. After admitting that he had spied for the Soviet Union in the 1930s, Chambers accused **Alger Hiss,** a former State Department official, of giving him secret government documents in 1937 and 1938 to pass on to the Soviets.

Chambers produced secret State Department papers he claimed were written by Hiss and microfilm of other secret documents. Chambers swore that he had received the microfilm (which was hidden in a pumpkin) from Hiss. Investigators could not prosecute Hiss for spying because too much time had passed since the events had occurred. However, he was found guilty of perjury, or lying, and sent to prison.

Causes and Effects of the Cold War

Causes

- The Soviet Union expands into Eastern Europe.
- Communism extends into Western Europe, the Middle East, and Asia.
- Western governments fear Soviet aggression.

Effects

- The United States aids anti-Communist forces.
- Western powers form NATO.
- The Korean War erupts.
- A U.S.–Soviet arms race develops.

Graphic Organizer *Skills*

The Cold War pitted the Soviet Union and its allies against the United States and its allies.

Analyzing Information What organization did the Western powers form?

People In History

Margaret Chase Smith 1897–1995

Margaret Chase Smith of Maine was the first woman to be elected to both houses of Congress.

First elected to the House in 1940, Smith made many contributions during her four terms. During World War II, she worked to improve the position of women in the military. She played a major role in the passage of a new law, the Women's Armed Services Integration Act (1948), that allowed women to serve as permanent, regular members of the nation's military forces.

Smith also served four terms in the Senate. Never afraid to speak out on the issues, she was one of the first to condemn the tactics used by Senator Joseph McCarthy in his crusade against communism.

In 1964 Smith was one of the presidential nominees at the Republican National Convention, making her the first woman to have her name placed in nomination by a major political party.

The most dramatic spy case to come before HUAC involved the atomic bomb. **Julius** and **Ethel Rosenberg,** a New York couple who were members of the Communist Party, were accused of plotting to pass secret information about the atomic bomb to the Soviet Union. Brought to trial in 1951, the Rosenbergs were convicted and sentenced to death. The judge in the case declared their crime "worse than murder."

Groups around the world protested the sentence as a gross injustice, but higher courts upheld the death sentence decision. Executed in 1953, the Rosenbergs maintained their innocence to the end and claimed that they were persecuted because of their political beliefs.

✓ **Reading Check** **Explaining** What did the McCarran Act require?

McCarthyism

From 1950 to 1954, the hunt for Communists in America was dominated by Senator **Joseph McCarthy** of Wisconsin. During those years, McCarthy publicly attacked many people alleged—declared without proof—to be Communists. His unfounded accusations destroyed the careers of many innocent Americans and heightened the atmosphere of anti-Communist hysteria in the country. A new word was coined, McCarthyism, which came to mean the use of unproved accusations against political opponents.

Joseph McCarthy rose to national attention almost overnight. In a speech in Wheeling, West Virginia, in February 1950, he announced that America had been betrayed by the "traitorous actions" of certain individuals. Raising a sheet of paper, he claimed to have in his hand a list of 205 State Department employees who were members of the Communist Party. Millions of Americans believed McCarthy's charges.

During the next four years, McCarthy continued to accuse government officials and others of being Communists. His congressional subcommittee attacked and bullied the people it called to testify. Many federal employees resigned or were dismissed as a result of McCarthy's investigations.

Even the most powerful government officials hesitated to oppose him. McCarthy often targeted Democrats. He and his Republican colleagues in

Congress saw anticommunism as an important issue to use against the Democratic Party. Some Republican candidates for Congress, including **Richard Nixon,** successfully smeared their opponents with charges of being soft on communism. Such tactics worked because so many Americans feared the threat of communism.

McCarthy's Downfall

In 1954 McCarthy launched an investigation of the United States Army. He made alarming claims that Communists had infiltrated the military. In a series of televised hearings watched by millions of Americans, McCarthy hurled wild accusations at highly respected army officials.

The televised Army-McCarthy Hearings proved the turning point in the McCarthy investigations. For weeks Americans witnessed McCarthy's sneering and cruel attacks. Toward the end of the hearings, **Joseph Welch,** an attorney for the army, said to McCarthy:

❝Until this moment, Senator, I think I never really gauged your cruelty or your recklessness. . . . Have you left no sense of decency?❞

Many Americans now came to view McCarthy as a cruel bully who had little basis for his accusations. Congress also turned against McCarthy. In December 1954, the Senate voted to censure, or formally criticize, him for "conduct unbecoming a senator." Censure and the

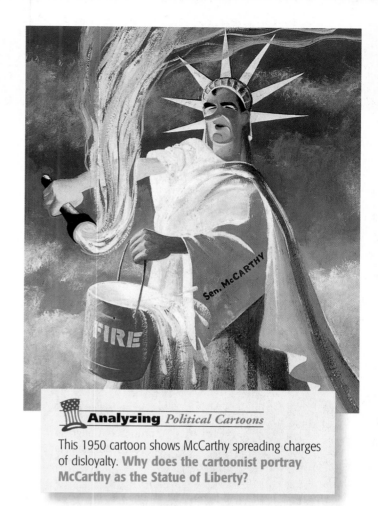

Analyzing *Political Cartoons*

This 1950 cartoon shows McCarthy spreading charges of disloyalty. **Why does the cartoonist portray McCarthy as the Statue of Liberty?**

loss of public support ended McCarthy's influence. Yet during the years when fears of communism had raged in the country, McCarthyism had damaged the lives of many innocent people.

Reading Check **Describing** What claims did McCarthy make against the United States Army?

SECTION 4 ASSESSMENT

Checking for Understanding

1. **Key Terms** Define the following terms: subversion, blacklist, perjury, allege, censure.
2. **Reviewing Facts** Describe the aim of loyalty oaths.

Reviewing Themes

3. **Government and Democracy** What negative effects did McCarthy's anti-Communist actions have on American society?

Critical Thinking

4. **Drawing Conclusions** How do you think television affected the outcome of the Army-McCarthy hearings?
5. **Organizing Information** Re-create the diagram below and give two examples of the government's response to growing fears of communism.

Government response

Analyzing Visuals

6. **Graphic Organizer Skills** Examine the cause-and-effect chart on page 807. Into what areas did the Soviet Union expand? What was one effect of the Cold War?

Interdisciplinary Activity

Art Draw a political cartoon that describes the effect you think Joseph McCarthy had on the American people. Make sure you include a caption with your cartoon.

Chapter Summary
The Cold War Era

Soviet Union

United States

Soviets occupy much of Eastern and Central Europe

THE MARSHALL PLAN
A Program of International Cooperation

Truman Doctrine proposed; Congress approves Marshall Plan

U.S., Britain, and France unite to form West German Republic

Berlin blockade

Berlin airlift

NATO Pact

With UN, U.S. fights in Korean War

Warsaw Pact

U.S. builds largest military force

Reviewing Key Terms

On graph paper, create a word search puzzle using the following terms. Crisscross the terms vertically and horizontally, then fill in the remaining squares with extra letters. Use the terms' definitions as clues to find the words in the puzzle. Share your puzzle with a classmate.

1. iron curtain
2. containment
3. airlift
4. cold war
5. inflation
6. closed shop
7. perjury
8. allege

Reviewing Key Facts

9. Who coined the phrase "iron curtain"? What did it represent?
10. What did the Marshall Plan provide?
11. What is a "cold war"?
12. Why did many labor unions strike after the war?
13. What did the GI Bill provide?
14. Who did the major parties nominate for the presidency in 1948? Who won the election?
15. What was the outcome of the conflict in Korea?
16. What was the purpose of the House Un-American Activities Committee?

Critical Thinking

17. **Analyzing Themes: Global Connections** What was the strategy behind the Marshall Plan?
18. **Analyzing Information** How did Truman exercise his power as commander in chief of the United States military during the Korean War?
19. **Drawing Conclusions** In addition to fighting communism, what other motivation do you think Senator McCarthy had for his actions?
20. **Determining Cause and Effect** Re-create the diagram below and identify two ways the United States used its position as the strongest and wealthiest nation in the world to shape economic recovery in Europe.

Shaping European recovery

Practicing Skills

Making Inferences *Examine the photograph that appears on pages 784 and 785. Then, answer the questions that follow.*

21. Describe the details in the painting.
22. What feelings does the face of the young girl express?
23. What do you know about the movement to integrate schools during the 1950s?
24. Putting all this together, what do you infer as the reason for the girl's expression?
25. Find a newspaper or magazine photograph and write at least three inferences based on the photo.

 Geography and History Activity

Study the map on page 793. Then answer the questions that follow.

26. **Region** Among what four countries was Germany divided?
27. **Place** What country or countries occupied East Berlin?
28. **Place** What country or countries occupied West Berlin?
29. **Location** What is unusual about the location of the airports in Berlin? Explain your reasoning.

Citizenship Cooperative Activity

30. **Military Service** The GI Bill provided many benefits to soldiers returning from World War II. Through these benefits Americans who thought they could never go to college or own their own homes could now achieve these goals. Organize into four groups to explore the incentives offered today for people who join the United States Army, Navy, Marines, and Coast Guard. Use the list of questions that follow to guide your group's research.

   - Is attending college or another institution of extended learning still an option?
   - What kinds of economic incentives are offered to recruits?
   - What advantages are awarded to those joining the armed services today that were not available at the end of World War II?

   Use your information to design a recruitment plan to attract people to a particular branch of the service. Include all forms of media in your plan such as billboards, newspaper ads, radio, and television.

 Self-Check Quiz
Visit **taj.glencoe.com** and click on **Chapter 27— Self-Check Quizzes** to prepare for the chapter test.

 Technology Activity

31. **Using the Internet** Search the Internet for information about how the United Nations is organized. Design a flowchart or graphic organizer that shows the names of each of the main bodies of the UN and how they are related to each other.

 Alternative Assessment

32. **Portfolio Writing Activity** The United States government was anxious to avoid military conflict after World War II. Review the chapter and make a list of examples of how the United States government used negotiation and other nonviolent means to resolve international problems without resorting to war.

Standardized Test Practice

Directions: Choose the *best* answer to the following question.

The United States started the Marshall Plan as a way to prevent an economic collapse in Europe that would open the door to communism. Which of the following was another purpose of the Marshall Plan?

A To shift the balance of power away from Asian nations

B To encourage European Allied efforts in World War II

C To build a strong Europe on which American economic security could depend

D To prevent the Soviet Union from becoming a major military power

Test-Taking Tip

This question requires you to remember a fact about the Marshall Plan. Remember that the plan was an economic program—that is it provided money to help rebuild European economies. Which answer fits best with this information?

CHAPTER 28

America in the 1950s

1953–1960

Why It Matters

The election of Dwight Eisenhower to the presidency ushered in one of the most prosperous periods in American history. Economic growth resulted in increased employment and higher wages throughout the 1950s.

The Impact Today

The prosperity of the 1950s raised questions that remain important in American society today. Can a period of economic growth bring benefits to all Americans—or are some groups likely to be excluded? Can the nation's economic growth be guided by cultural and social values—or does growth occur at the expense of those values? Americans still debate these issues today.

The American Journey Video *The chapter 28 video, "The Fifties Dream," explores popular culture and ideals during the 1950s.*

1953
• Results of polio vaccine tests published

1956
• Federal Highway Act passed

1950s
• Baby boom increases U.S. population by over 20 percent

1955
• Eisenhower meets with Khrushchev at Geneva summit

Eisenhower
1953–1961

United States
PRESIDENTS

1952   *1954*   *1956*

World

1950s
• Abstract expressionism grows in popularity

1953
• Watson, Crick, and Franklin discover DNA structure

1955
• Warsaw pact signed

1956
• Egypt takes control of Suez Canal
• Uprising in Hungary is defeated by Soviet troops

Red Spy Hunt by Thomas Maitland Cleland The 1950s transformed our culture and shaped the way we live today.

FOLDABLES™
Study Organizer

Know-Want-Learn Study Foldable Make this foldable to determine **what you already know,** to identify **what you want to know,** and to record **what you learn** about America in the 1950s.

Step 1 Fold a sheet of paper into thirds from top to bottom.

Step 2 Turn the paper horizontally, unfold, and label the three columns as shown.

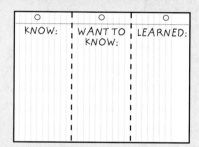

KNOW: | WANT TO KNOW: | LEARNED:

Reading and Writing Before you read the chapter, write what you already know about the 1950s in the "Know" column. Write what you want to know about the 1950s in the "Want to Know" column. Then, as you read the chapter, write what you learn in the "Learned" column. Then check to see if you have learned what you wanted to know (from the second column).

1957
• Kerouac's *On the Road* published

1958
• The United States launches *Explorer*

1959
• Alaska and Hawaii become states

1958   *1960*

1957
• Soviet Union launches *Sputnik*

1959
• Mary and Louis Leakey uncover hominid fossils

HISTORY
Online

Chapter Overview
Visit taj.glencoe.com and click on **Chapter 28— Chapter Overviews** to preview chapter information.

Eisenhower in the White House

Guide to Reading

Main Idea
President Eisenhower promoted policies to compete with the Soviet Union for military and space leadership.

Key Terms
moderate, surplus, arms race, domino theory, summit, peaceful coexistence

Reading Strategy
Organizing Information As you read the section, re-create the diagram below and list examples of actions the United States took to solve problems in world affairs.

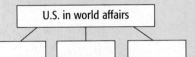

U.S. in world affairs

Read to Learn
- what beliefs and policies characterized the Eisenhower presidency.
- what foreign policy challenges the Eisenhower administration faced.

Section Theme
Science and Technology The United States worked to develop space technology and compete with the Soviets in space.

Preview of Events

♦ 1950   ♦ 1955   ♦ 1960

1952
Eisenhower elected president

1953
Oveta Culp Hobby heads HEW

1957
The Soviets launch *Sputnik*

1959
Alaska and Hawaii enter the Union

AN
American Story

"He merely has to smile at you, and you trust him at once." These words were used to describe Dwight D. Eisenhower, Republican presidential candidate in 1952. Eisenhower had an appeal that went far beyond his party label. His performance in World War II had made him an unquestioned hero in the eyes of almost every American. Above all, his personality and political style made many people feel safe, comfortable, and confident.

Republican Revival

By 1952 Harry S Truman faced widespread dissatisfaction with his presidency. Many Americans were frustrated over the stalemated war in Korea and worried about reports of communist subversion in government. To the Democrats' relief, Truman decided not to run for reelection. The Democrats nominated the respected governor of Illinois, **Adlai E. Stevenson,** for president and Senator John J. Sparkman of Alabama as his running mate.

To head their presidential ticket, the Republicans chose General **Dwight D. Eisenhower,** the popular World War II hero. For vice president, the Republicans selected **Richard M. Nixon,** a young senator from California who had won fame as a tough opponent of communism.

The Campaign

Born in Texas and raised in rural Kansas, Dwight D. Eisenhower graduated from the United States Military Academy at West Point. He rose steadily through the army to become supreme commander of the Allied forces in Europe during World War II. People called him Ike—and they trusted him. His warmth and sincerity attracted many voters.

Eisenhower's steadiness made Americans feel secure. He won wide support with his pledge to bring the Korean War to an "early and honorable end." "If that job requires a personal trip to Korea," he declared, "I shall make that trip."

The Republicans faced a brief crisis during the presidential campaign when the story broke that Richard Nixon had accepted political gifts from supporters. Nixon went on television to defend himself in what came to be known as the "Checkers" speech. He proclaimed that he had done nothing wrong and had kept only one gift—his family dog, Checkers. The speech won broad support for Nixon, persuading Eisenhower to keep him on the ticket.

Landslide Republican Victory

In November 1952, Americans elected Eisenhower to the presidency in a landslide victory—the first Republican to win the White House since 1928. Far more people voted in 1952 than in any previous presidential election. Eisenhower collected over six million popular votes more than Stevenson and carried the electoral college 442 to 89. The Republicans also won control of Congress. The election seemed to usher in a new era in national politics.

✓ Reading Check **Identifying** Who was the candidate for vice president on Eisenhower's ticket?

Domestic Policy

Although Eisenhower had little political experience, he proved to be an effective politician. During his two terms in office, Eisenhower followed a moderate, or middle-of-the-road, approach to domestic policy. He described himself as "conservative when it comes to money and liberal when it comes to human beings."

Eisenhower helped steer the country on a steady course. He avoided ambitious new government programs, but resisted the pressure to abolish popular older ones, and sometimes he even expanded them. As he once told reporters:

> ❝I feel pretty good when I'm attacked from both sides. It makes me more certain I'm on the right track.❞

President Eisenhower wanted to make the federal government "smaller rather than bigger." He supported economic policies aimed at limiting government spending and encouraging private enterprise. With the support of Republicans and conservative Democrats in Congress, the president removed the wage and price controls that the Truman administration had established during the Korean War. He also managed to transfer some authority in financial matters to the states and to make some cuts in government spending. When he left office in 1961, the federal budget had a surplus, or excess, of $300 million.

The nation's 34th president, Dwight Eisenhower, served in the military for more than 30 years.

The Nation Expands

The greatest domestic program of the Eisenhower presidency involved building a network of interstate highways. In June 1956 Congress passed the **Federal Highway Act.** The law funded the construction of more than 40,000 miles (64,000 km) of highways that tied the nation together. The highway program—the largest public works program in the nation's history—also spurred growth in many areas of the nation's economy, including the automobile and oil industries, while improving military mobility in case of an attack.

The nation itself also grew during Eisenhower's presidency. In 1959 **Alaska** and **Hawaii** entered the Union, bringing the number of states to 50. Alaska and Hawaii became the only states not bordering on the other states.

Social Programs

Eisenhower believed that government should protect the basic welfare of Americans. He refused to tamper with Social Security and other New Deal social programs. During his presidency, Eisenhower agreed to extend Social Security benefits to 10 million more people and to provide unemployment insurance to 4 million more. He also approved greater funding for public housing and, in 1955, agreed to an increase in the minimum wage from 75 cents an hour to $1.00.

The creation of the **Department of Health, Education, and Welfare** (HEW) in 1953 confirmed the government's role in helping Americans meet their basic social needs. Eisenhower named **Oveta Culp Hobby** as the first secretary of the new department. Hobby, only the second woman in American history to hold a cabinet post, had organized the Women's Army Corps (WACs) in World War II.

Eisenhower's moderation and leadership won the approval of a majority of Americans. In the 1956 presidential election, he ran against Democrat Adlai Stevenson again. This time Eisenhower won by an even bigger margin, receiving more than 57 percent of the popular vote.

✓ Reading Check **Describing** How did the highway program affect the economy?

Eisenhower and the Cold War

On October 4, 1957, millions of Americans heard the startling news: the Soviets had sent into space the world's first artificial satellite, called *Sputnik.* Within a month, the Soviets successfully launched a second satellite. Americans were both horrified and in awe. They feared that the nation was lagging behind the Soviets. They also feared that the Soviets could launch atomic weapons from space.

Worry turned to embarrassment in December 1957, when the United States tried to launch its own space satellite—*Vanguard.* Hundreds of reporters and spectators watched the rocket rise a few feet off the launching pad—and then explode. The foreign press made fun of the launch, calling it "Flopnik" and "Stayputnik." America's status declined.

United States–Soviet Rivalry

During the 1950s the United States–Soviet rivalry kept the Cold War at the center of American foreign policy. The Eisenhower administration continued to oppose the spread of communism. At the same time, the president looked for ways to keep American–Soviet tensions from erupting into open conflict.

Secretary of State **John Foster Dulles** became Eisenhower's most important foreign policy adviser. Dulles condemned the containment policy of the Truman administration. Eisenhower and Dulles proposed a new, bolder policy. If the Soviet Union attacked any nation, the United States would launch a **massive retaliation**—an instant attack using nuclear weapons. Vice President Nixon explained:

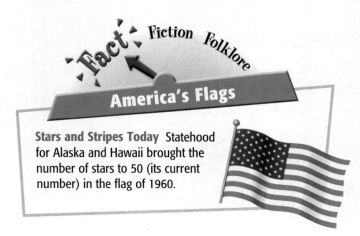

Fact · Fiction · Folklore

America's Flags

Stars and Stripes Today Statehood for Alaska and Hawaii brought the number of stars to 50 (its current number) in the flag of 1960.

> ❝Rather than let the Communists nibble us to death all over the world in little wars, we will rely in the future on massive mobile retaliatory [attacking] powers.❞

Dulles believed that the United States had to use threats to push the Soviets to the brink of war before they would agree to anything. Critics called this tough stance "brinkmanship."

By relying more on nuclear weapons, the Eisenhower administration could reduce the size of the army and the arsenal of **conventional,** or non-nuclear, weapons. These reductions would allow Eisenhower to cut the military budget. As Secretary of Defense Charles Wilson explained, nuclear weapons gave the United States "more bang for the buck."

The Arms Race

Despite Eisenhower's intentions, defense spending increased again. The policy of massive retaliation—and Soviet efforts to counter it—produced a nuclear arms race. Both nations built more and more weapons.

The superpowers built immensely destructive hydrogen bombs—nuclear weapons that were much more powerful than atomic bombs. They developed a variety of guided missiles capable of delivering nuclear warheads. The **intermediate-range ballistic missile** (IRBM) could reach targets up to 1,500 miles (2,414 km) away. The **intercontinental ballistic missile** (ICBM) had a range of many thousands of miles. Soon both sides had massive nuclear arsenals capable of destroying the other side many times over.

As the arms race continued, Americans began preparing for a nuclear attack. The **Civil Defense Administration** educated the public with pamphlets and radio and television messages. Some families built air-raid shelters in their basements or backyards. Schools held air-raid drills. One student described his school's drill: "Students lie on the floor and stick their heads under the lockers." He recalled that he believed this would make him safe during a nuclear attack. 📖 *(See page 976 for an article* LIFE *magazine published on what to do during a nuclear attack.)*

Linking Past & Present

The Space Race

The launch of *Sputnik* shifted the space race into high gear. Nearly 12 years later, a spacecraft from *Apollo 11* landed on a level plain in the Sea of Tranquility on the moon. The long-lived dream of landing on the moon had come true.

At the end of the Cold War, the United States and Russia agreed to build a space station and cooperate on other projects in space. A rivalry that began in fear has become a partnership.

Astronaut on the moon

Competing in Space

The Soviet launch of *Sputnik* and the *Vanguard* failure led America to develop its own space program. Federal money poured into the **National Aeronautics and Space Administration (NASA),** the new government agency in charge of the space program. When the United States succeeded in launching the *Explorer* satellite in January 1958, the Associated Press reported:

> ❝The missile took off in a beautiful launching. It rose slowly at first in a huge splash of flame with a roar that could be heard for miles. . . .❞

The **space race** had begun, and the United States soon began pulling ahead. **Project Mercury** was the nation's first program to put an astronaut in space. Along with its commitment to space exploration and scientific research, the government also encouraged science education by providing more funds for the teaching of science and technology in the nation's schools.

✓ **Reading Check** **Explaining** What is massive retaliation?

Foreign Policy Challenges

With the stakes in the nuclear arms race so high, the United States and the Soviet Union had to act carefully. A minor crisis, badly managed, could lead to all-out war.

Crisis in the Middle East

Trouble arose first in the Middle East. Arab states had attacked Israel soon after its founding in 1948, and tensions there had remained high ever since. Because the United States backed Israel, while the Soviet Union maintained ties

Analyzing *Political Cartoons*

Many cartoons used a bear to stand for the Soviet Union and an eagle to represent the United States. **What do you think the cartoonist was saying by showing the subjects on the edge of a cliff?**

with the Arab states, a Middle East conflict threatened to involve the superpowers as well as their allies.

Fighting did break out in the Middle East in 1956, when Egyptian president **Gamal Abdel Nasser** nationalized, or brought under government control, the **Suez Canal** from British control. Great Britain and France feared that Nasser might close the canal and cut off oil shipments to Europe. In October, the two European powers attacked Egypt. Great Britain and France hoped to overthrow Nasser and seize the canal. Israel, angered by repeated Arab attacks along its borders, agreed to help by invading Egypt.

The United States sponsored a United Nations resolution calling for an immediate truce. The Soviets threatened rocket attacks on British and French cities. In the face of this pressure, the three nations pulled out of Egypt.

Uprising in Hungary

Another crisis erupted in Europe. In October 1956, students and workers demonstrated in **Budapest,** the capital of **Hungary,** for changes in the government. Strikes and riots soon spread. A new government came to power and demanded withdrawal of Soviet troops. In early November, Soviet tanks and troops poured into Hungary and crushed the revolt. Hungarian rebels appealed to the United States for help. President Eisenhower condemned the Soviet crackdown but did not intervene.

War in Southeast Asia

Yet another trouble spot appeared in Southeast Asia, in France's former colony of **Vietnam.** In the early 1950s, the United States gave France billions of dollars in military aid to help it fight the **Vietminh,** nationalist rebels led by Communist leader **Ho Chi Minh.**

In spite of American aid, the French soon faced defeat. In March 1954, Vietminh forces trapped 13,000 French troops at the French base of **Dien Bien Phu.** The French pleaded with the United States to send forces, but Eisenhower refused. The Korean War was still fresh in his memory. "I can conceive of no greater tragedy," he said, "than for the United States to become engaged in all-out war in Indochina."

The Language of the Cold War

These terms were first used during the Cold War era.

Fallout shelter Underground building designed to hold up against fallout from a nuclear attack

Hot line Direct phone line between U.S. and Soviet leaders established after the Cuban missile crisis

Hydrogen bomb Nuclear weapon hundreds of times more powerful than the atomic bombs dropped on Hiroshima and Nagasaki; first tested in 1952

Iron Curtain Term used to describe the separation between communist and democratic nations in Europe

Massive retaliation Policy that promised U.S. attacks in answer to Soviet expansion

Missile Gap Claim that the U.S. had fallen behind the Soviets in producing nuclear missiles

Space Race Rivalry for supremacy in outer space

Sputnik First artificial earth satellite, launched by USSR in 1957 (pictured above)

U-2 Spy plane with ability to take pictures from as high as 80,000 feet (24,400 m)

Intercontinental ballistic missile

Without American troops, the French were forced to surrender in May. Soon after, French and Vietminh representatives in **Geneva, Switzerland,** negotiated a cease-fire agreement. The agreement, known as the **Geneva Accords,** temporarily divided Vietnam. The Vietminh controlled the north, while other Vietnamese—more friendly to the French—held the south. The accords also arranged for the withdrawal of all French troops and called for free elections in a reunited Vietnam in 1956.

Eisenhower believed that if one nation in Asia fell to the Communists, others would also fall, one after the other. He described the danger in what came to be called the domino theory:

You have a row of dominoes set up. You knock over the first one, and what will happen to the last one is that it will go over very quickly.

To keep South Vietnam from becoming the first domino, the United States aided its anti-Communist government. In another step to defend against Communist aggression, the United States helped to create the **Southeast Asia Treaty Organization** (SEATO) in 1954. The United States, Great Britain, France, New Zealand, Australia, the Philippines, Pakistan, and Thailand made up the alliance. The nations pledged joint action against any aggressor.

Troubles in Latin America

The Eisenhower administration also faced communist challenges in Latin America. In 1954 the **Central Intelligence Agency** (CIA) helped overthrow the government of **Guatemala,** which some American leaders feared was leaning toward communism. Latin Americans resented the intervention in Guatemala.

Anti-American feeling became a part of the growing revolutionary movement in **Cuba.** Following the overthrow of dictator Fulgencio Batista (buh•TEES•tuh), rebel leader **Fidel Castro** formed a new government in January 1959. The United States supported Castro at first and welcomed his promise of democratic reforms. But Castro angered Americans when he seized foreign-owned property. His government became a dictatorship and formed close ties with the Soviet Union. During the last days of his presidency in 1961, Eisenhower cut diplomatic ties with Cuba. Relations between the two nations have remained strained ever since.

Cold War "Thaws"

After Soviet dictator Joseph Stalin died in 1953, **Nikita Khrushchev** (krush•CHAWF) emerged as the dominant leader. By the mid-1950s, both American and Soviet leaders were interested in easing Cold War tensions.

In July 1955, Eisenhower, NATO leaders, and Soviet officials met at a summit conference in Geneva, Switzerland. A summit is a meeting of heads of government. The leaders discussed disarmament and German reunification. The friendly atmosphere, promptly called the "Spirit of Geneva," renewed hopes for peace.

After the Geneva summit, a policy of peaceful coexistence began to emerge. This meant that the two superpowers would compete with one another but would avoid war. Khrushchev proposed to Eisenhower that the two leaders visit each other's country and attend another summit in **Paris** in 1960. Eisenhower agreed.

Khrushchev's 10-day trip to the United States in 1959 captured world headlines. As the leaders made plans for their next meeting in Paris, Eisenhower hoped to reach agreements on arms control and nuclear test bans.

The U-2 Incident

Hopes of peace fell to earth with an American plane. For years American pilots had flown high-altitude spy planes—**U-2s**—over Soviet territory to photograph Soviet nuclear sites and military bases.

When the Soviets shot down a U-2 plane on May 1, 1960, and captured its pilot, Francis Gary Powers, Khrushchev denounced the United States for invading Soviet airspace. Although the Paris summit began as scheduled on May 16, the mood had changed. The summit broke up the next day. The brief "thaw" in the Cold War had ended.

Eisenhower's Warning

In his January 1961 Farewell Address to the nation, President Eisenhower issued a warning about the influence of the military. The military budget had grown dramatically, he said, and military leaders had allied with business to seek bigger and more expensive weapons. Eisenhower feared that this alliance—a **"military-industrial complex"**—heated the arms race and could "endanger our liberties or democratic processes." In a twist of history, this former army general warned the nation of the close involvement of government and industry in preparing for war.

✓ Reading Check **Describing** How did relations between the superpowers change after the Geneva summit?

SECTION 1 ASSESSMENT

Checking for Understanding

1. **Key Terms** Use the following terms to write an article about life during the Cold War: arms race, domino theory, peaceful coexistence.
2. **Reviewing Facts** What two states were added to the Union during Eisenhower's presidency?

Reviewing Themes

3. **Science and Technology** How did the Soviet launch of *Sputnik* affect science and technology in the United States?

Critical Thinking

4. **Identifying Central Issues** Why was President Eisenhower willing to send aid to Vietnam?
5. **Comparing** Re-create the diagram below and describe how Eisenhower's view on foreign policy differed from Truman's view.

Foreign policy	
Eisenhower	Truman

Analyzing Visuals

6. **Analyzing Political Cartoons** Study the cartoon on page 818. Who do the figures in the cartoon represent? What idea do you think the cartoonist is presenting?

Interdisciplinary Activity

Science Make a two-level time line with the heading "United States" and "Soviet Union." Track the achievements of these two countries in space from 1957 to 1967.

1950s Prosperity

Guide to Reading

Main Idea
Economic growth changed the social and cultural life of Americans.

Key Terms
productivity, standard of living, affluence, baby boom

Reading Strategy
Organizing Information As you read Section 2, re-create the diagram below and describe three changes that occurred in American life as a result of the strong economy or the growth of technology.

Changes in American life

Read to Learn
• what factors helped the economy grow during the 1950s.
• how the era's prosperity affected American society and culture.

Section Theme
Continuity and Change The economic growth of the 1950s brought great changes to the nation.

Preview of Events

♦1945	♦1950	♦1955	♦1960

1947
William Levitt starts first suburban development

1955
Polio vaccine given to school children

1956
Elvis Presley gains national popularity

AN American Story

During the prosperous 1950s, many Americans left the cities to settle in the suburbs, hoping for a better life for themselves and their children. "Suburbia"—with its great distances between home, school, shopping areas, and downtown—gradually became not only a place but also a lifestyle. One suburban resident observed: "Before we came here, we used to live pretty much to ourselves. . . . Now we stop around and visit people or they visit us. I really think [suburban living] has broadened us."

A Booming Economy

After World War II, many experts predicted America's economy would level off or decline as production of war goods decreased. Instead, after a few years of adjustment, the economy began to grow rapidly and steadily. Between 1945 and 1960, the total value of goods and services produced in the United States increased about 250 percent.

Some of this amazing growth resulted from the burst of military spending during the Korean War. Government spending on housing, schools, welfare, highways, and veteran benefits also spurred the rapid economic expansion. Technological advances contributed to economic growth as well. Business, industry, and agriculture adopted new technology and new production methods, resulting in greater productivity—the ability to produce more goods with the same amount of labor. The demand for new technology led to greater investment in research and in the education and training of scientists, engineers, and technicians.

The **computer** was one of the 1950s' technological advances. Unlike today's small personal computers, early computers were immense, weighing tons and filling whole rooms. Although first used only by the military and the government, computers soon appeared in large corporations. By 1955 International Business Machines (IBM) was the leader in the field, with orders for 129 of its big computers.

Higher Incomes

The economic boom of the 1950s raised the standard of living—a measure of people's overall wealth and quality of life—of millions of Americans. Between 1945 and 1960, **personal income**—the average income, earned or unearned, of every individual in the nation—increased from $1,223 to $2,219. By the end of the 1950s, Americans had the highest standard of living in the world.

Prosperity and steady economic growth also led to new optimism. Economists began to think it was possible to maintain prosperity and growth permanently. Americans felt confident that the government could, when necessary, take steps to avoid serious **recessions,** or downturns in the economy.

✓ Reading Check **Comparing** How did the computers of the 1950s differ from modern computers?

A Changing Nation

Economic growth and prosperity brought many changes to America. These included a growth in population, increased affluence, or wealth, suburban expansion, and a greater demand for consumer goods.

The Baby Boom

Like the economy, the family enjoyed great growth during the postwar years. During the 1950s the nation's population rose from 150 million to 179 million, an increase of nearly 20 percent. People called the nation's soaring birthrate a baby boom.

Several factors encouraged the baby boom. Husbands and wives who had postponed having children during the Depression and World War II started having families. With higher incomes, couples felt they could afford to have more children. In addition, better health

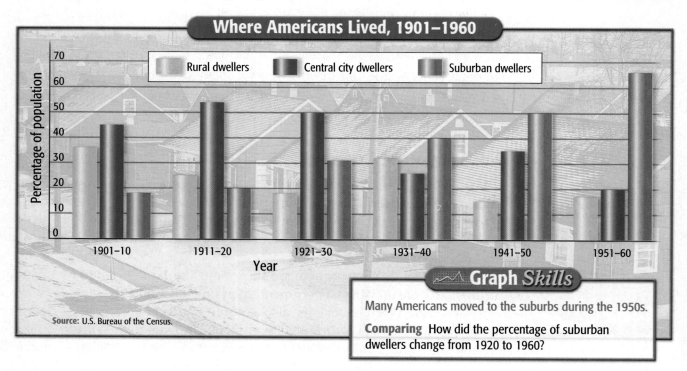

Where Americans Lived, 1901–1960

Rural dwellers   Central city dwellers   Suburban dwellers

Percentage of population

Year: 1901–10, 1911–20, 1921–30, 1931–40, 1941–50, 1951–60

Source: U.S. Bureau of the Census.

Graph Skills

Many Americans moved to the suburbs during the 1950s.

Comparing How did the percentage of suburban dwellers change from 1920 to 1960?

Jonas Salk 1914–1995

By the early 1950s, medical science had made great strides in combating childhood diseases. Antibiotics and vaccines helped control diseases such as diphtheria, influenza, and typhoid fever. A vaccine for polio, however, continued to escape the medical profession. Polio became the era's most dreaded disease because the disease left many of its victims paralyzed for life.

After many years of research, scientist Dr. Jonas Salk developed the first safe and effective vaccine against polio. After it was tested, the Salk vaccine was administered to schoolchildren beginning in 1955. The threat of polio has been almost completely eliminated. Salk was hailed as a hero not only for developing the vaccine, but also for refusing to patent the vaccine. The medical pioneer's last years were spent searching for a vaccine against AIDS.

care, improved nutrition, and medical breakthroughs against disease helped reduce the infant death rate.

The baby boom had a powerful impact on society. Many women left the workforce to stay home and raise their children. The demand for baby products and services grew, stimulating the economy. School enrollment soared as the "baby boomers" reached school age, putting a great strain on the educational system.

Expanding Suburbs

During the 1950s, 75 percent of new home construction took place in the **suburbs.** The new suburbs were usually located on the fringes of major cities.

William Levitt introduced mass-produced housing based on experience he had gained building houses for the navy. He started his first suburban development, called **Levittown,** on Long Island, New York, in 1947. Levittown included more than 17,000 identical houses, built from materials precut and preassembled at a factory and then erected quickly on designated lots. Other builders adopted Levitt's methods or used their own techniques for rapid construction, creating a massive house-building boom.

Suburban housing developments appealed to many Americans. In addition to affordable homes, they offered privacy, isolation from urban problems, space for cars, and a sense of belonging to a community formed by people similar in age, social background, and race.

Though affordable, the suburbs did not offer opportunities for home ownership to everyone. Many American cities had growing populations of middle-class minorities, particularly African American and Hispanic American, who longed to escape the noise and the crime of the cities. However, the developers of the nation's postwar suburbs often refused to sell homes to minorities.

A Nation on Wheels

The car made suburban escape possible. People needed cars to get to work, to go shopping, and to run errands. For suburban families, cars were not a luxury but a necessity.

The construction of thousands of miles of new highways in the 1950s encouraged the spread of suburbs. Suburban America became a "car culture" in which life centered on the automobile. Southern California came to symbolize suburban life and this car culture. In California, the drive-in capital of the nation, a person could go to the movies, eat fast food, do banking, and even attend religious services without leaving the car. One suburban California woman spoke for many other Americans when she explained her need for a car:

> 66 I live in Garden Grove, work in Irvine, shop in Santa Ana . . . my husband works in Long Beach, and I used to be the president of the League of Women Voters in Fullerton. 99

Air Travel

Americans were also finding it easier to travel by air. The jet engine was perfected in the 1950s, and the first jet-powered commercial aircraft began operation. By the early 1950s, the airliner was on the way to replacing the railroad train and the ocean liner as the preferred transportation for long-distance travel.

A Consumer Society

Americans of the 1950s went on a buying spree. Affluence, the growing variety and quantity of products available, and expanded advertising all played a role in the increased demand for consumer goods. Buying goods became easier, too. Many Americans used credit cards, charge accounts, and easy-payment plans to purchase goods.

Consumers eagerly sought the latest products—dishwashers, washing machines, television sets, stereos, and clothes made from synthetic fabrics. The growing market for bigger and better cars prompted automakers to outdo

TECHNOLOGY & History

Jet Travel

The first commercial jet transport, the Boeing 707, made aviation history with its maiden flight December 20, 1957. It could carry more passengers for longer distances than any previous aircraft. *In what ways do you think jet aircraft affected the American economy?*

Jet control panel

On October 26, 1958, Pan American World Airways started the first 707 jet service between New York and Paris.

1 Fuel tanks held up to 21,000 gallons, allowing the 707 to fly for almost 6,000 miles before stopping to refuel.

2 The Boeing 707 could carry up to 181 people in **passenger seating**.

Rudder

Flight deck

Flaps

3 The 4 turbofan **jet engines** powered a cruising speed of 600 mph. (Earlier transports had carried 21 passengers at a speed of 170 mph.)

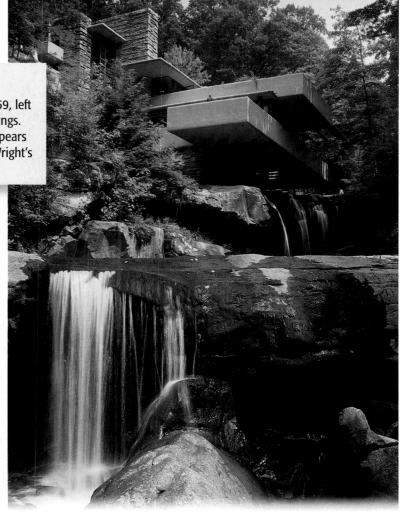

one another by manufacturing bigger, faster, and flashier cars. They came out with new models every year, adding stylish features such as chrome-plated bumpers and soaring tail fins.

The advertising and marketing of products on television, on radio, and in magazines created consumer fads and crazes that swept the nation. In the late 1950s, Americans bought millions of hula hoops—large plastic rings they twirled around their waists. Other popular fads included crew cuts for boys, poodle skirts for girls, and a new snack—pizza.

An American Culture

By 1949 over 900,000 American households had television sets. These large wooden cabinets had small screens that displayed grainy black-and-white images. During the 1950s an average of 6.5 million sets were produced annually. By the end of the decade, most American families had television.

Television profoundly changed American life. It became the main form of entertainment for many people as well as an important source of news and information. Religious leaders helped spread religious commitment with the aid of modern communications. They had their own radio and television programs, best-selling books, and newspaper columns. **Billy Graham,** a popular Protestant minister and preacher, attracted thousands of people throughout the nation and in other parts of the world. **Fulton J. Sheen,** a Roman Catholic bishop, became a television personality through his weekly program. Protestant minister **Norman Vincent Peale** attracted many thousands of followers with his message of

"positive thinking." Another popular religious leader, Jewish rabbi **Joshua Loth Liebman** expressed tolerance for religious differences:

> 66Tolerance is the positive and cordial effort to understand another's beliefs, practices, and habits without necessarily sharing or accepting them.99

Billboards and television commercials proclaimed: "Bring the whole family to church" and "The family that prays together stays together." Messages like these clearly indicated that postwar society was focused on the family.

Millions of Americans watched the same programs. Families gathered to watch quiz shows such as *The $64,000 Question.* Children tuned in to programs such as *The Mickey Mouse Club* and *Howdy Doody.* Teens kept up with the latest hit songs on *American Bandstand.* Families followed weekly episodes of *I Love Lucy, Leave It to Beaver,* and *Father Knows Best.* The images shown in

One of the most popular cars of 1957, the Chevrolet Bel Air sold for about $2,500.

many programs—of happy middle-class families in neat middle-class homes—helped shape Americans' expectations for their own lives.

Finally, television had an important effect on the consumer culture. Television advertising helped create a vast national market for new products and fashions. Some shows—such as the *Philco Television Playhouse*—adopted the names of their sponsors, which brought the sponsors prestige.

A new form of music—rock 'n' roll—achieved great popularity in the 1950s. Many teens rejected the mellow popular music favored by their parents. They preferred the heavily accented beats and simple lyrics of rock 'n' roll.

Rock 'n' roll grew from the rhythm and blues music that African American musicians had created years before. It often had some elements of country music. In rock 'n' roll, the tempo was quicker, and electrically amplified instruments—mostly guitars—were used.

One of the first rock hits, reaching number one in 1955, was Bill Haley and the Comets' *Rock Around the Clock*. Adapting the style of African American performers such as Chuck Berry and Little Richard, **Elvis Presley** burst on the national scene in 1956. Presley quickly became known as the king of rock 'n' roll and was an idol to millions of young Americans. Many young men copied his ducktail haircut and swaggering mannerisms.

For teenagers, the shared experience of listening to the music helped forge a common identity and bond. The differing attitudes of the older and younger generations toward music, as well as other forms of popular culture, later came to be known as the **generation gap.**

✓**Reading Check** **Analyzing** Why did suburban life appeal to many Americans?

SECTION 2 ASSESSMENT

Checking for Understanding

1. **Key Terms** Use each of these terms in a sentence that will help explain its meaning: productivity, standard of living, affluence, baby boom.
2. **Reviewing Facts** How did Americans' per capita income change during the 1950s?

Reviewing Themes

3. **Continuity and Change** Describe the link between television and consumer spending in the 1950s.

Critical Thinking

4. **Compare and Contrast** Think about the ways television and the automobile changed the way Americans lived during the 1950s. How would your life be different without them?

5. **Analyzing Information** Re-create the diagram below and identify factors that stimulated economic growth in the 1950s.

Economic growth

Analyzing Visuals

6. **Graph Skills** Examine the graph on page 822. How did the percentage of rural dwellers change from 1920 to 1960?

Interdisciplinary Activity

Music Paste photographs or drawings on poster board of the musicians that you think represent the best of modern music. Write captions that include your explanation of why music is an important part of American culture.

Critical Thinking
SKILLBUILDER

Analyzing Information

Why Learn This Skill

Have you ever heard someone say, "Don't believe everything you read"? To be an informed citizen, you have to analyze information carefully as you read to make sure you understand the meaning and the intent of the writer.

Learning the Skill

1. Identify the subject or topic of the information.

2. How is the information organized? What are the main points?

3. Think about how reliable the source of the information is.

4. Summarize the information in your own words. Does the information agree with or contradict something you already know?

Practicing the Skill

In this chapter you read about new trends in music and the influence of Elvis Presley. The information that follows is from a biography of Presley. Analyze the paragraph and answer the questions that follow.

Elvis Presley may be the single most important figure in American twentieth-century popular music. Not necessarily the best, *and certainly not the most consistent. But no one could argue that he was not the musician most responsible for popularizing rock and roll. His 1950s recordings established the basic language of rock and roll; his explosive stage presence set standards for the music's visual image; his vocals were incredibly powerful and versatile.*

1. Was the information easy to understand? Explain.

2. Consider the source of the information. Does that make it seem more valid or less valid? Why?

Elvis Presley in a 1956 performance

3. Summarize the paragraph in a sentence of your own.

4. Do you think the writer admired or did not admire Presley? Why?

Applying the Skill

Analyzing Information Choose an article from a newsmagazine. Read it and analyze the information. Answer questions one, two, and three, as they apply to the article.

 Glencoe's **Skillbuilder Interactive Workbook CD-ROM, Level 1,** provides instruction and practice in key social studies skills.

Problems in a Time of Plenty

AN American Story

Picture postcards of Washington, D.C. in the 1950s showed the Capitol and other government buildings. Hidden behind the tall buildings was a very different United States, however. It was a nation of crumbling streets and rat-infested tenements, hungry and, sometimes, homeless people. The "invisible poor" lived in a nation not of affluence and plenty, but of desperate need.

Poverty

In the 1950s more than 20 percent of Americans lived in poverty. Millions more struggled to survive on incomes only slightly above the poverty level. Such poverty marred the landscape of the affluent society.

Many farmers did not share in the prosperity of the 1950s. Huge crop surpluses during those years caused the prices of farm products—and thus farm income—to decline dramatically. Large business enterprises bought vast areas of available farmland. They used large sums of money to transform agriculture into a thriving business. New machines and chemicals helped produce an abundance of food for American and foreign consumers. While some farmers benefited from these changes, others suffered. Because small farms could not compete with large farms, many small-farm families sold their land and migrated to urban areas. Thousands of small farmers who remained in agriculture struggled to stay out of poverty.

Farmworkers suffered as well. In the South, African American sharecroppers and tenant farmers had always struggled to survive. Their problems increased when mechanized cotton pickers replaced workers. The popularity of synthetic fibers reduced the demand for cotton. Southern farmworkers lost their jobs, cotton production fell, and thousands of farmers lost their land.

Migrant farmworkers in the West and the Southwest—mostly Mexican Americans and Asian Americans—also suffered. They toiled long hours for very low wages and lived in substandard housing.

Rural poverty did not always come from agricultural problems. In **Appalachia,** a region stretching along the Appalachian Mountains through several states, the decline of the coal industry plunged thousands of rural mountain people into desperate poverty.

Urban Poverty

As increasing numbers of middle-class Americans moved to the suburbs in the 1950s, they left the poor behind. The inner cities became islands of poverty. To these islands people still came looking for work. Continuing their migration from rural areas of the South, more than three million African Americans moved to cities in the North and the Midwest between 1940 and 1960. Many poor Hispanics—Puerto Ricans in the East and Mexicans in the Southwest and the West—also moved to American cities.

The migration of poor African Americans and Hispanics to Northern cities hastened the departure of whites to the suburbs. This "white flight"

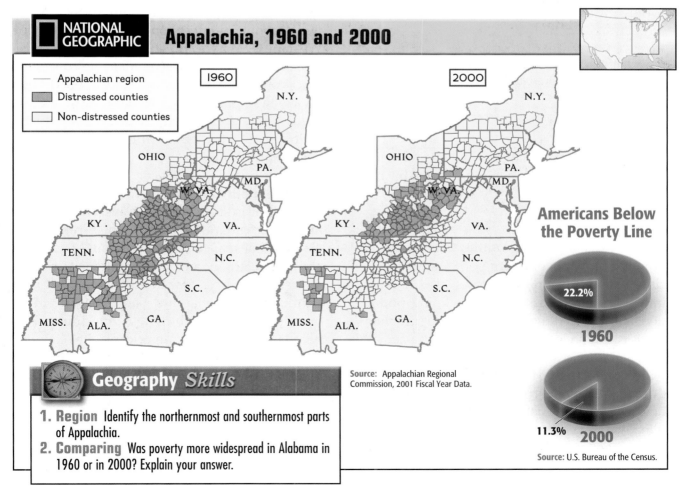

NATIONAL GEOGRAPHIC

Appalachia, 1960 and 2000

- Appalachian region
- Distressed counties
- Non-distressed counties

1960

2000

N.Y. OHIO PA. MD. W. VA. KY. VA. TENN. N.C. S.C. MISS. ALA. GA.

Source: Appalachian Regional Commission, 2001 Fiscal Year Data.

Americans Below the Poverty Line

22.2% 1960

11.3% 2000

Source: U.S. Bureau of the Census.

Geography *Skills*

1. **Region** Identify the northernmost and southernmost parts of Appalachia.
2. **Comparing** Was poverty more widespread in Alabama in 1960 or in 2000? Explain your answer.

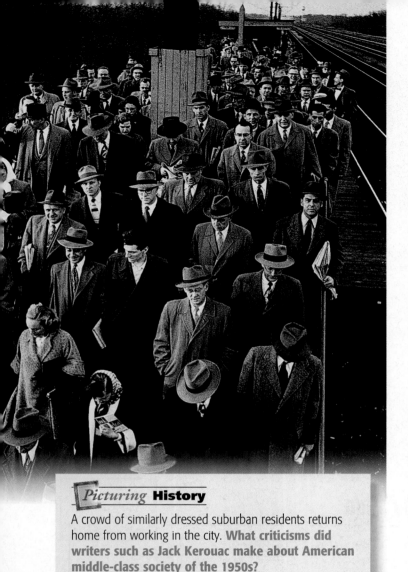

turned some areas of cities into ghettos—neighborhoods that were inhabited mainly by poor minority groups.

Urban Unemployment

Few good job opportunities existed for the growing numbers of urban poor. As whites fled cities, factories and businesses also relocated into suburban areas. With a declining population, cities faced growing financial problems. Taxes could no longer keep up with the demand for such services as public transportation and police protection. Moreover, automation—producing goods using mechanical and electronic devices—reduced jobs in the industries that remained. It became more and more difficult for the urban poor to rise from poverty and improve their lives.

The urban poor struggled not only with poverty but also with racial discrimination in employment, housing, and education. Crime and violence often grew out of inner-city poverty, especially among young people who saw no hope for escape from life in the ghetto.

Reading Check **Explaining** What effect did automation have on factory jobs?

Voices of Dissent

Changes in American society in the 1950s caused some people to question the values that were emerging. Some critics charged that the sameness of suburban and corporate life had a cost—the loss of individuality. Others condemned American materialism—a focus on accumulating money and possessions rather than an interest in spiritual matters.

Social Critics

During the 1950s, leading social critics examined the complexity of modern society. Many wrote about its effects on individual behavior. **William H. Whyte, Jr.,** studied American business life in *The Organization Man.* He concluded that young executives who abandoned their own views to "get along" were the most likely to succeed. He drew a somber picture of "organization men" who "have left home spiritually as well as physically."

In his book *The Affluent Society*, economist **John Kenneth Galbraith** wrote of the prosperous American society of the 1950s. However, not all Americans shared in this prosperity. Galbraith described a suburban family, comfortably installed in an "air-conditioned, power-steered and power-braked automobile," driving "through cities that are badly paved, made hideous by litter, blighted buildings, billboards." Prosperous Americans, he claimed, often ignored the problems and hardships faced by other Americans.

The Beat Generation

A group of writers called the Beats had even sharper criticism of American society. The term "Beat," said novelist **Jack Kerouac,** meant "weariness with all forms of the modern industrial state." Kerouac, poet **Allen Ginsberg,** and other Beats rebelled against American culture.

Kerouac's novel *On the Road,* the most influential book of the Beats, described the wild adventures of friends who drove aimlessly around the country. Its main character was

> ❝mad to live, mad to talk, mad to be saved, desirous of everything at the same time.❞

The novel made Kerouac an instant celebrity.

Millions of young Americans read the works of Beat writers. Some adopted Beat attitudes of rebellion and isolation from society.

Questioning Roles

With society changing, women and African Americans began questioning their roles. In the 1950s both groups strived to gain greater freedom and equality.

"The suburban housewife was the dream image of the young American woman," wrote **Betty Friedan,** herself a suburban wife and mother. "She was healthy, beautiful, educated, [and] concerned only about her husband, her children, and her home." Television, advertising, and magazines reinforced this image of women as perfect wives and mothers and presented the idea of suburban life as the path to a full and happy life.

As Friedan discovered, however, many suburban housewives were dissatisfied with this role and longed to express their individuality. Her book, *The Feminine Mystique,* described the frustration and unhappiness of these women.

African Americans also questioned their place in society in the 1950s. After years of struggling for their rights, African Americans became increasingly impatient for change and less willing to accept their status as second-class citizens. They launched a new campaign for full civil rights.

Three events in the 1950s proved especially important for African Americans. First, the Court decision in *Brown* v. *Board of Education of Topeka* (1954) declared racial segregation in public schools to be unconstitutional. Second, African Americans staged a successful boycott of segregated buses in Montgomery, Alabama. Third, President Eisenhower sent troops to Little Rock, Arkansas, to enforce a court order to integrate a high school. These three events, which you will learn more about in Chapter 29, paved the way for the successes of the civil rights movement in the 1960s.

✓ **Reading Check** **Describing** What criticisms were made about suburban and corporate life?

HISTORY Online

Student Web Activity
Visit taj.glencoe.com and click on **Chapter 28— Student Web Activities** for an activity on life in the 1950s.

SECTION 3 ASSESSMENT

Checking for Understanding

1. **Key Terms** Write a short paragraph in which you use the following terms: ghetto, automation, materialism.
2. **Reviewing Facts** Problems in what industry led to unemployment and economic woes in Appalachia?

Reviewing Themes

3. **Continuity and Change** How were American inner cities changing during the 1950s?

Critical Thinking

4. **Drawing Conclusions** Why do you think some women were dissatisfied with their roles during the 1950s?
5. **Determining Cause and Effect** Re-create the diagram below and explain how automation affected each of the following groups.

Effects of Automation		
Factory owner	Small farmer	Industrial worker

Analyzing Visuals

6. **Picturing History** Examine the photographs in this section. Write a caption for each of the photographs in which you describe what the subjects are doing.

Interdisciplinary Activity

Descriptive Writing Write a poem at least 12 lines long that might have been written by a social critic of the 1950s.

TIME NOTEBOOK

What were people's lives like in the past?

What—and whom—were people talking about? What did they eat? What did they do for fun? These two pages will give you some clues to everyday life in the U.S. as you step back in time with TIME Notebook.

CULVER PICTURES

Profile

On July 20, 1969, **NEIL ARMSTRONG** *became the first human to walk on the moon. There he spoke the famous words "That's one small step for a man, one giant leap for mankind." Later, Armstrong reflected on his voyage and the "spaceship" we call Earth.*

"FROM OUR POSITION HERE ON THE EARTH, IT IS DIFFICULT to observe where the Earth is, and where it's going, or what its future course might be. Hopefully by getting a little farther away, both in the real sense and the figurative sense, we'll be able to make some people step back and reconsider their mission in the universe, to think of themselves as a group of people who constitute the crew of a spaceship going through the universe. If you're going to run a spaceship you've got to be pretty cautious about how you use your resources, how you use your crew, and how you treat your spacecraft."

—*from the book* First on the Moon

BETTMANN/CORBIS

Neil Armstrong

WHAT'S IN & WHAT'S OUT

ADAM SCULL/ GLOBE PHOTOS

Kermit

TV GUIDE
Weekly magazine has circulation of about 6.5 million by 1959.

KERMIT
It's easy being green – when you're a hot Muppet on the hit show *Sesame Street* that first aired in 1969.

MINI SKIRTS
Skirts in 1964 reach new heights.

COLLIER'S
The respected magazine loses readership, publishing its final edition on Jan. 4, 1957.

TV'S BEAVER
After 234 episodes, *Leave It to Beaver* goes off the air in 1963.

POODLE SKIRTS
1950s girls wear these long skirts with a puffy crinoline underneath.

Leave It to Beaver

GLOBE PHOTOS

American Scene 1950–1960

	Bowling Lanes (thousands)	Little Leagues	Hot Dog Production (estimated millions of pounds)	Potato Chip Production (estimated millions of pounds)	Encyclopedia Sales (millions of dollars)
1950	52.5	776	750	320	72
1960	108.0	5,700	1,050	532	300

Be Prepared

"Know the Bomb's True Dangers. Know the Steps You Can Take to Escape Them!—You Can Survive."
Government pamphlet, 1950

ARE YOU DIGGING YOUR OWN bomb shelter? Better go shopping. Below is a list of items included with the $3,000 Mark I Kidde Kokoon, designed to accommodate a family of five for a three- to five-day underground stay.

- 3-way portable radio
- air blower
- radiation detector
- protective apparel suit
- face respirator
- radiation charts (4)
- hand shovel combination (for digging out after the blast)
- gasoline-driven generator
- gasoline (10 gallons)
- chemical toilet
- toilet chemicals (2 gallons)
- bunks (5)
- mattresses and blankets (5)
- air pump (for blowing up mattresses)
- incandescent bulbs (2) 40 watts
- fuses (2) 5 amperes
- clock—non-electric
- first aid kit
- waterless hand cleaner
- sterno stove
- canned water (10 gallons)
- canned food (meat, powdered milk, cereal, sugar, etc.)
- paper products

Bomb Shelter

BETTMANN/CORBIS

NUMBERS 1957

3¢ First class postage stamp

19¢ Loaf of bread

25¢ Issue of *Sports Illustrated*

35¢ Movie ticket

50¢ Gallon of milk (delivered)

$2.05 Average hourly wage

$2,845 Average cost of a new car

$5,234 Median income for a family of four

POPPERFOTO/ARCHIVE PHOTO

WORD AND MUSIC
Translation, Please!

Match the jazz or bebop word to its meaning.

1. crazy — a. become enthusiastic
2. dig — b. wonderful, great
3. flip — c. understand, appreciate
4. hip — d. aware

answers: 1. b; 2. c; 3. a; 4. d

833

Chapter Summary

America in the Fifties

Eisenhower's Domestic Policy

- Attempts to limit government spending
- Federal Highway Act
- Extends social programs

The Cold War

- American leaders adopt policy of massive retaliation
- NASA is created
- Crisis in the Middle East
- Uprising in Hungary
- War in Southeast Asia
- Troubles in Latin America
- Geneva Summit encourages peaceful coexistence
- U-2 incident rekindles Cold War

Prosperity

- Productivity increased
- Per capita income and the standard of living increased
- The baby boom increases population
- Suburban housing developments boom
- Car culture grows
- Consumerism grows
- Television viewing increases

Problems and Issues

- Growing competition hurts small farmers
- Decline in coal industry increases poverty in rural areas
- Inner cities decay as businesses and residents relocate
- Social critics question conformity
- Women question their roles in society
- African Americans challenge segregation

Reviewing Key Terms

Examine the groups of words below. Then write a sentence explaining what each group has in common.

1. automation, productivity
2. affluence, standard of living
3. domino theory, arms race
4. summit, peaceful coexistence

Reviewing Key Facts

5. What states entered the Union in 1959?
6. Name three foreign policy challenges the Eisenhower administration faced.
7. What was the goal of Project Mercury?
8. How did the Geneva summit help to ease Cold War tensions?
9. Who formed a new government in Cuba in 1959?
10. Identify technological advances of the 1950s.
11. What are downturns in the economy called?
12. What medical breakthrough did Dr. Jonas Salk make?
13. Identify three religious leaders who influenced Americans in the 1950s.
14. How did the mass movement to the suburbs affect inner cities?

Critical Thinking

15. **Analyzing Information** What general economic policies did the Eisenhower administration support?
16. **Determining Cause and Effect** Why would the development of nuclear weapons have allowed Eisenhower to cut the military budget?
17. **Analyzing Themes: Continuity and Change** Why was there such a great demand for automobiles in the 1950s?
18. **Determining Cause and Effect** Re-create the diagram below and explain how these two factors created problems for farmers and farm workers.

Farm problems	
Crop surpluses	Synthetic fiber industry

Practicing Skills

Analyzing Information Reread the "People in History" feature on page 823 and answer the questions that follow.

19. Who is the subject of the feature?

20. How did polio affect its victims?

21. What effect did the use of the polio vaccine have?

 Geography and History Activity

Study the maps on page 829; then answer the questions that follow.

22. Region How many states are included in the Appalachia region?

23. Location In which states did poverty strike the hardest in 1960?

24. Comparing Maps Was poverty in the Appalachian region more widespread in 1960 or in 2000? How can you tell?

Citizenship Cooperative Activity

25. Analyzing Social Issues Throughout history social critics have tried to draw attention to the injustices of society. Working in groups of three, research to find three poems written by modern poets that deal with current social problems. Social problems might include, for example, poverty, prejudice, and the prevalence of violence. Mount each of your poems on an 8½" x 11" sheet of paper and use photographs or drawings to illustrate each. Your group might also want to include short descriptions or captions to identify your photographs or drawings. Combine your poems with those of other groups to create a poetry collection titled "A Decade of Dissent."

Economics Activity

26. Math Practice The Bureau of Labor Statistics issued these statistics on workers between the ages of 16 and 24 who were employed in July 1998. Use the statistics to create a bar graph showing the numbers of people working in the different economic sectors.

About 7 in 8 employed youth worked in private business this summer. The largest employers were retail trade (7.4 million) and services (5.8 million). There were also large numbers of youth employed in manufacturing (2.2 million) and construction (1.2 million). Government employed a total of 1.5 million young people in July. Nearly 3 in 5 of the young people with government jobs worked in local government.

Self-Check Quiz
Visit **taj.glencoe.com** and click on **Chapter 28— Self-Check Quizzes** to prepare for the chapter test.

 Technology Activity

27. Using the Internet In the 1950s it would have been hard to imagine the role computers would play in our lives today. One by-product of the computer revolution is the hundreds of new computer-related words we have added to our language. Words such as *surfing* and *megabyte* describe computers and how we use them. Do an internet search and compile a list of words that probably did not exist before computers were invented in the 1950s. Share your findings with the class.

 Alternative Assessment

28. Portfolio Writing Activity Talk to a friend or relative who is a baby boomer. How is life different for people of your generation? What do you think will be the effect on society when baby boomers retire? Write a report that focuses on these questions. Place it in your portfolio.

Standardized Test Practice

Directions: Choose the *best* answer for this multiple choice question.

The Cold War between the United States and the former Soviet Union was a rivalry between what two forms of government?

A communism and socialism

B communism and dictatorship

C communism and democracy

D democracy and monarchy

Test-Taking Tip

To answer this question, you need to remember various systems of government are defined. Did either the United States or the former Soviet Union live under a monarchy—rule by a king or queen? Since they did not, you know that answer **D** is incorrect.

CHAPTER 29

The Civil Rights Era

1954–1973

Why It Matters

In the 1950s, a tide of protest began to rise in America against deeply rooted attitudes of racism and discrimination. The campaign for equality grew and gained momentum in the 1960s. Although the civil rights movement could not overcome all the obstacles, it achieved some great and long-lasting successes.

The Impact Today

Inspired by the movements of the 1950s and 1960s, many Americans work to secure full rights for all citizens.

The American Journey Video *The chapter 29 video, "Beyond Prejudice," examines what it was like to be a young adult during the civil rights movement.*

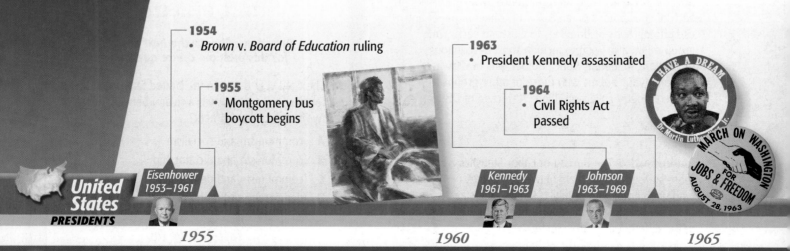

1954
• *Brown v. Board of Education* ruling

1955
• Montgomery bus boycott begins

1963
• President Kennedy assassinated

1964
• Civil Rights Act passed

United States PRESIDENTS

Eisenhower 1953–1961

Kennedy 1961–1963

Johnson 1963–1969

1955   *1960*   *1965*

World

1954
• French forced out of Vietnam

1959
• Fidel Castro seizes power in Cuba

1962
• Algeria gains independence from France

1964
• Nelson Mandela receives life sentence in South Africa

I HAVE A DREAM
Dr. Martin Luther King, Jr.

MARCH ON WASHINGTON
FOR JOBS & FREEDOM
AUGUST 28, 1963

March on Washington On August 28, 1963, more than 200,000 people gathered to urge support for civil rights legislation.

1968
- Dr. Martin Luther King, Jr., assassinated
- Indian Civil Rights Act passed

1970
- Grape workers gain increased pay and better conditions

Nixon
1969–1974

1971
- Floppy disk introduced

1970   *1975*

1967
- First heart transplant performed in South Africa

1972
- Britain imposes direct rule on Northern Ireland
- Terrorists kill Israeli Olympic athletes

HISTORY
Online

Chapter Overview
Visit taj.glencoe.com and click on **Chapter 29—Chapter Overviews** to preview chapter information.

The Civil Rights Movement

Guide to Reading

Main Idea
Despite obstacles, African Americans pressed for equal rights.

Key Terms
segregation, integrate, boycott, civil disobedience

Reading Strategy
Classifying Information As you read the section, re-create the diagram below and describe the roles these people played in the civil rights movement.

	Roles
Linda Brown	
Rosa Parks	
Martin Luther King, Jr.	

Read to Learn
• how a Supreme Court decision helped African Americans in their struggle for equal rights.
• why Dr. Martin Luther King, Jr., emerged as a leader.

Section Theme
Civic Rights and Responsibilities African Americans organized in an effort to secure equal rights.

Preview of Events

♦1954   ♦1955   ♦1956   ♦1957

1954
Supreme Court strikes down segregation in education

1955
Rosa Parks is arrested; Montgomery bus boycott begins

1957
Dr. Martin Luther King, Jr., heads SCLC; Federal troops help integrate a Little Rock high school

AN
American Story

Jackie Robinson could do everything on a baseball field—hit singles, slam home runs, and speed from base to base. Robinson was the first African American to play major league baseball. When his team, the Brooklyn Dodgers, reached the World Series in 1947, Robinson recalled, "I experienced a completely new emotion when the National Anthem was played. This time, I thought, it is being played for me, as much as for anyone else."

Equality in Education

African Americans had suffered from racism and discrimination in the United States since colonial times. As the nation entered the second half of the twentieth century, many African Americans believed that the time had come for them to enjoy an equal place in American life. They fought for equal opportunities in jobs, housing, and education. They also fought against segregation—the separation of people of different races.

The *Brown* Decision

The **NAACP** (National Association for the Advancement of Colored People) had worked on behalf of African Americans since its founding in 1909. In the 1950s, NAACP lawyers searched for cases they could use to challenge the laws allowing the segregation of public education.

The Supreme Court had upheld segregation laws in the past. In 1896 in *Plessy v. Ferguson,* it had ruled that "separate but equal" public facilities were legal. **Thurgood Marshall,** the chief lawyer for the NAACP, decided to challenge the idea of "separate but equal." The NAACP began to decide which among the nation's segregated school districts to bring before the Court. Seven-year-old African American Linda Brown was not permitted to attend an all-white elementary school just blocks from her house. The Brown family sued the school system but lost. Marshall and the NAACP appealed the case all the way to the Supreme Court.

The case of **Brown v. Board of Education of Topeka, Kansas,** combined with several similar cases, reached the Supreme Court in December 1952. Marshall argued that segregated schools were not and could not be equal to white schools. For that reason segregated schools violated the Fourteenth Amendment.

On May 17, 1954, the Court unanimously ruled in *Brown* v. *Board of Education of Topeka, Kansas,* that it was unconstitutional to separate schoolchildren by race. The *Brown* decision reversed the Court's decision in *Plessy* v. *Ferguson.* 📖 *(See page 997 for a summary of the* Brown *decision.)*

NATIONAL GEOGRAPHIC

Segregation in United States Schools, 1950

CANADA

WASH.
OREGON
MONTANA
NORTH DAKOTA
MINN.
IDAHO
SOUTH DAKOTA
WIS.
WYOMING
MICH.
NEVADA
NEBRASKA
IOWA
UTAH
ILL. IND. OHIO
CALIF.
COLORADO
KANSAS
MO.
W. VA. VA.
KY.
ARIZONA
NEW MEXICO
OKLA.
ARK.
TENN.
N.C.
S.C.
MISS. ALA. GA.
TEXAS
LA.
FLA.

N.H. MAINE
VT.
N.Y. MASS.
R.I.
PA. CONN.
N.J.
DEL.
MD.

PACIFIC OCEAN
MEXICO
ATLANTIC OCEAN
Gulf of Mexico

40°N
30°N
90°W 80°W

	Segregated by law
	Local districts decided
	Segregation prohibited
	No specific legislation

0 — 500 miles
0 — 500 kilometers
Azimuthal Equidistant projection

Geography *Skills*

School segregation was treated differently in various parts of the United States.

1. Region In how many states were schools segregated by law?

2. Analyzing Information In what region was segregation predominant?

Integrating the Schools

The Court's decision in *Brown* v. *Board of Education* called on school authorities to make plans for integrating—bringing races together—in public schools. The Court also ordered that integration was to be carried out "with all deliberate speed"—as fast as reasonably possible.

Some school systems integrated quickly. However, in parts of the South, local leaders vowed to keep African American children out of white schools. A clash between the federal government and these states seemed unavoidable.

Confrontation in Little Rock

In 1957 a federal judge ordered Central High School in **Little Rock, Arkansas,** an all-white school, to admit African American students. Arkansas governor **Orval Faubus** opposed integration. In September he called out the state's National Guard to prevent African Americans from entering the high school.

On the first day of classes, armed members of the National Guard blocked the school's entrance and turned away nine African American students.

One of them, 15-year-old **Elizabeth Eckford,** recalled that when she tried to squeeze past a member of the guard,

> 66He raised his bayonet, and then the other guards moved in and raised their bayonets.99

For the first time since the Civil War, a Southern state had defied the authority of the federal government. Although Eisenhower had some doubts about the *Brown* decision, he believed it was his duty to enforce the law. The president warned Faubus that, if the governor did not admit the students, the federal government would act.

When a federal judge ruled that the governor had violated federal law, Faubus removed the National Guard. Eisenhower sent hundreds of soldiers to Little Rock to patrol the school grounds and protect the students. Shielded by the federal troops, the nine African American students entered the school.

Reading Check **Explaining** What did the Supreme Court rule in *Brown* v. *Board of Education*?

Picturing **History**

Elizabeth Eckford (center) braves the insults of white citizens to enter Central High School in Little Rock, Arkansas. **How did President Eisenhower respond to the crisis in Little Rock?**

Dr. Martin Luther King, Jr. 1929–1968

After the Montgomery bus boycott, Dr. Martin Luther King, Jr., emerged as the leader of the African American protest movement. What drove him into this demanding role in history?

The son of a Baptist minister, King attended Morehouse College, and when he was 18 years old decided on a career in the ministry. By the time he first arrived in Montgomery in September 1954 as pastor of the Dexter Avenue Baptist Church, he had also met and married Coretta Scott.

From the beginning of the Montgomery bus boycott, King encouraged his followers to use nonviolent resistance. This meant that those who carried out the demonstrations should not fight with authorities. In spite of his stand on nonviolence, King often became the target of violence.

In April 1968, King was in Memphis, Tennessee, to support a strike of sanitation workers. There, the minister was shot while standing on a motel balcony.

Gains on Other Fronts

While school integration continued, African Americans made other advances in securing their rights. More and more took part in a movement dedicated to securing fair and equal treatment.

The Montgomery Bus Boycott

On the evening of December 1, 1955, **Rosa Parks** boarded a bus in downtown **Montgomery, Alabama.** Parks, a seamstress, was secretary of the local chapter of the NAACP. She found an empty seat in the section reserved for whites.

When white passengers entered the bus, the driver told Parks, an African American, to move to the rear of the bus. Parks refused. At the next bus stop, she was taken off the bus by police, arrested for breaking the law, and fined $10. The episode could have ended there—but it did not.

Rosa Parks's arrest led African Americans in Montgomery to organize a boycott—a refusal to use—the city's buses. The boycott organizers hoped to hurt the city financially and force it to alter its policies. They had strength in numbers—almost 75 percent of the bus company's riders were African American.

At a boycott meeting, a young Baptist minister came forward to speak. Not widely known at the time, **Dr. Martin Luther King, Jr.,** made an impact on the crowd. He declared:

> ❝We're here because, first and foremost, we are American citizens, and we are determined to acquire our citizenship to the fullness of its meaning. We are tired—tired of being segregated and humiliated, tired of being kicked about by the brutal feet of oppression.❞

The boycott upset many people's daily lives, but the African Americans of Montgomery pulled together to make it work. Students hitchhiked to school; workers walked or rode bikes to their jobs. King helped organize car pools to shuttle people from place to place.

The bus boycott lasted for more than a year. City officials arrested King and other leaders at different times, but African Americans held firm. The local bus company lost thousands of dollars in fares, and downtown businesses lost customers. Finally, the Supreme Court settled the matter by ruling that the Montgomery bus segregation law was unconstitutional. In December 1956, the boycott ended.

Causes and Effects of the Move Toward Equality

Causes
- 1955, Rosa Parks is arrested
- 1955, Montgomery bus boycott begins
- 1957, Conflict at Little Rock
- 1957, SCLC is organized
- 1960, Students stage sit-ins
- 1963, March on Washington, D.C.

Effects
- 1962, James Meredith enrolls at University of Mississippi
- 1967, Thurgood Marshall appointed to Supreme Court
- 1968, Shirley Chisholm elected to House of Representatives
- 1972, Barbara Jordan elected to Congress

Graphic Organizer → Skills

African Americans faced many obstacles in their struggle for equal rights.

Analyzing Information What protest followed the arrest of Rosa Parks?

Nonviolent Protest

With the victory in Montgomery, King became a leader of the civil rights movement. He followed the tactics of **A. Philip Randolph,** the nation's most prominent African American labor leader. King was also strongly influenced by **Mohandas Gandhi,** who had used nonviolent protest to help India gain independence from Great Britain. In keeping with his beliefs, Gandhi used protest methods based on civil disobedience, or the refusal to obey laws that are considered unjust.

In January 1957, King and 60 other ministers started a new organization called the **Southern Christian Leadership Conference** (SCLC). SCLC leaders emphasized nonviolent protest. They showed civil rights workers how to protect themselves from violent attacks. The SCLC also discussed how to identify targets for protests and how to organize people for support. In taking these steps, the SCLC prepared African Americans for the struggle for equal rights.

✓**Reading Check** **Describing** How did the Montgomery bus boycott begin?

SECTION 1 ASSESSMENT

Checking for Understanding

1. **Key Terms** Use these terms in sentences that explain important events in the civil rights movement: segregation, integrate, boycott, civil disobedience.
2. **Reviewing Facts** Name the Supreme Court decision that banned segregation in education.

Reviewing Themes

3. **Civic Rights and Responsibilities** How did the Montgomery bus boycott end?

Critical Thinking

4. **Drawing Conclusions** Why do you think Dr. Martin Luther King, Jr., believed nonviolent protest was the most effective course to gain civil rights?
5. **Sequencing Information** Re-create the time line below and list important events in the civil rights movement in the 1950s.

May 1954	Dec. 1955	Jan. 1957	Sept. 1957
☐	☐	☐	☐

Analyzing Visuals

6. Examine the map on page 839. In what states did local school districts decide whether schools were integrated or not? In what states in the far northwest was segregation prohibited?

Interdisciplinary Activity

Descriptive Writing Write a song to be sung at a civil rights march. Base your lyrics on the story of Rosa Parks and her courage the night of her arrest.

America's LITERATURE

Maya Angelou (1928–)

Maya Angelou, born in 1928, has written poetry, fiction, and plays. Born Marguerite Johnson, Angelou and her brother, Bailey, were raised by their grandmother, Annie Henderson, the owner of a general store in Stamps, Arkansas.

READ TO DISCOVER

In the following excerpt from Angelou's autobiography, she is about 10 years old. Bright but painfully self-conscious, she has become withdrawn and refuses to speak to anyone. As you read, pay attention to the actions of the characters.

READER'S DICTIONARY

familiar: close friend or associate

Her World *by*
Philip Evergood

I Know Why the Caged Bird Sings

Mrs. Bertha Flowers was the aristocrat of Black Stamps. She had the grace of control to appear warm in the coldest weather, and on the Arkansas summer days it seemed she had a private breeze which swirled around, cooling her. . . .

She was one of the few gentlewomen I have ever known, and has remained throughout my life the measure of what a human being can be.

Momma had a strange relationship with her. Most often when she passed on the road in front of the Store, she spoke to Momma in that soft yet carrying voice, "Good day, Mrs. Henderson." Momma responded with "How you, Sister Flowers?"

Mrs. Flowers didn't belong to our church, nor was she Momma's **familiar.** Why on earth did she insist on calling her Sister Flowers? Shame made me want to hide my face. Mrs. Flowers deserved better than to be called Sister. Then, Momma left out the verb. Why not ask, "How *are* you, *Mrs.* Flowers?" With the unbalanced passion of the young, I hated her for showing her ignorance to Mrs. Flowers. It didn't occur to me for many years that they were as alike as sisters, separated only by formal education. . . .

Occasionally, though, Mrs. Flowers would drift off the road and down to the Store and Momma would say to me, "Sister, you go on and play." As I left I would hear the beginning of an intimate conversation. Momma persistently using the wrong verb, or none at all. . . .

I heard the soft-voiced Mrs. Flowers and the textured voice of my grandmother merging and melting. They were interrupted from time to time by giggles that must have come from Mrs. Flowers. . . .

She acted just as refined as whitefolks in the movies and books and she was more beautiful, for none of them could have come near that warm color without looking gray by comparison.

From *I Know Why the Caged Bird Sings*, by Maya Angelou. Copyright © 1969 by Maya Angelou. Reprinted by permission of Random House, Inc.

ANALYZING LITERATURE

1. **Recall and Interpret** Describe the relationship between Momma and Mrs. Flowers.

2. **Evaluate and Connect** Do you think you would like Mrs. Flowers? Explain.

Interdisciplinary Activity

Informative Writing Write a one-page sketch describing an encounter you had with a person who influenced your life in a positive way.

Kennedy and Johnson

Guide to Reading

Main Idea
John Kennedy's New Frontier and Lyndon Johnson's Great Society were government programs to fight poverty, help cities and schools, and promote civil rights.

Key Terms
poverty line, Medicare, Medicaid

Reading Strategy
Organizing Information As you read the section, re-create the diagram below and list four programs that were part of the War on Poverty.

War on Poverty

Read to Learn
- what the goals were for Kennedy's New Frontier.
- what new programs were created as part of the Great Society.

Section Theme
Government and Democracy Presidents Kennedy and Johnson proposed increased spending on social programs.

Preview of Events

♦1960	♦1962	♦1964	♦1966
Jan. 1961 John F. Kennedy takes office as president	**Nov. 1963** Kennedy is assassinated	**Jan. 1964** President Johnson announces war on poverty	**July 1964** Civil Rights Act of 1964 is passed

AN American Story

They stood together on the inaugural platform: 43-year-old John F. Kennedy—tanned, vigorous, and coatless despite the subfreezing weather—and 70-year-old Dwight D. Eisenhower, wearing a muffler, looking like a tired general. The appearances of the two men, a generation apart in age, symbolized the change of leadership. Kennedy's speech promised so much: "Let every nation know . . . that we shall pay any price, bear any burden, meet any hardship, support any friend, oppose any foe to assure the survival and the success of liberty. . . ."

Election of 1960

By 1960, the crusade for civil rights had become a national movement. Against this background, the nation prepared for a presidential election. The Republican candidate, Vice President **Richard M. Nixon,** pledged to continue the policies of President Eisenhower. The Democratic candidate, **John F. Kennedy,** promised new programs to "get the country moving again."

For much of the campaign, polls showed Nixon in the lead. One reason for this was the fact that Kennedy was Roman Catholic. No Catholic had ever been president, and many Americans feared that if Kennedy won he might show more loyalty to his church than to his country. Kennedy answered by stressing his belief in the separation of church and state.

John F. Kennedy

Kennedy came from one of the country's wealthiest and most powerful families. His father, Joseph P. Kennedy, was a successful business leader and the American ambassador to Britain at the start of World War II.

John Kennedy joined the United States Navy during World War II and was assigned to active duty in the Pacific. When the Japanese sank the PT (patrol torpedo) boat he commanded, Kennedy saved the life of a crew member by swimming to shore with the injured man on his back. The rescue effort led to navy and marine medals for Kennedy but also aggravated an old back injury he had. The story of the rescue was later described in Robert Donovan's book *PT 109.*

Kennedy's political career began in 1946 when he won a seat in Congress from Massachusetts. Six years later, he was elected to the United States Senate. The young senator wrote a book, *Profiles in Courage,* which described difficult political decisions made by past United States senators. The book became a best-seller and received a Pulitzer Prize. After easily winning reelection to the Senate in 1958, Kennedy campaigned for the presidency in 1960.

A New President

The turning point in the 1960 election came when the candidates took part in the first televised presidential debates. Kennedy appeared handsome and youthful. Nixon, who was recovering from an illness, looked tired and sick. Kennedy spoke with confidence about the future. Many viewers thought that Kennedy made a better impression.

In November, nearly 70 million voters turned out to choose between Nixon and Kennedy. For the first time, the people of Alaska and Hawaii took part in a presidential election. The results were extremely close. In the popular vote, Kennedy won 49.7 percent, while Nixon received 49.5 percent. In the electoral vote, Kennedy gained a greater margin over Nixon—303 to 219 votes.

✓ **Reading Check** **Identifying** Who were the presidential candidates in 1960?

The New Frontier

On January 20, 1961, snow covered Washington, D.C., and icy winds whipped through the city. Still, thousands of people streamed to the Capitol to see John Fitzgerald Kennedy become the thirty-fifth president of the United States. 📖
(See page 995 for part of President Kennedy's Inaugural Address.)

Richard Nixon and John Kennedy took part in the first televised presidential debates in 1960.

In 1960 for the first time, radio and television played a major factor in a presidential campaign. This advertisement for television sets focuses on the televised presidential debates.

He offered the nation youth, energy, and hope. In his Inaugural Address, Kennedy spoke of a new era:

> 66Let the word go forth from this time and place . . . that the torch has been passed to a new generation of Americans.99

The young president promised to face the nation's challenges with determination. In closing, Kennedy roused the American people to action:

> 66And so, my fellow Americans: ask not what your country can do for you—ask what you can do for your country.99

Domestic Policies

Kennedy drew up plans for the **New Frontier,** a group of proposals involving social programs. One bill he sent to Congress called for more federal funds for education. Another bill aimed to help poor people get jobs. Reluctant to commit to Kennedy's expensive programs, Congress failed to pass most of these bills.

Another area of concern for Kennedy was civil rights. The president wished to help African Americans in their fight for equal rights. At the same time he worried that moving too quickly would anger Southern Democrats in Congress, whose support he needed to enact legislation.

Lyndon Johnson takes the oath of office aboard Air Force One after the assassination of President Kennedy.

In 1963 Kennedy decided to ask Congress to pass a bill guaranteeing civil rights. The House approved the measure, but it stalled in the Senate. Meanwhile, the president left for a campaign trip to Dallas, Texas.

Kennedy Assassinated

On November 22, 1963, Kennedy arrived in Dallas with his wife, Jacqueline. As the president and the First Lady rode through the streets in an open car, several shots rang out. Kennedy slumped against his wife. The car sped to a hospital, but the president was dead. Shortly afterward, Vice President **Lyndon B. Johnson** took the oath of office as president.

The assassination stunned the nation. Television networks broadcast the news almost without interruption for the next few days. Millions of Americans numbly watched the funeral.

In the midst of the grief came another shock. The day of Kennedy's shooting, Dallas police had arrested **Lee Harvey Oswald** and charged him with killing the president. Two days later, as police moved Oswald from one jail to another, Jack Ruby jumped through the circle of police officers and journalists and shot and killed Oswald.

Rumors that a group of enemies had plotted the assassination swirled around the country. Soon afterward, President Johnson appointed **Earl Warren,** chief justice of the United States, to head a commission to investigate the Kennedy shooting. After months of study, the **Warren Commission** issued its report. Oswald had acted on his own, it said. The report did not satisfy everyone, however. Many people believed the assassination was a conspiracy, or secret plot.

✓ **Reading Check** **Describing** What happened on November 22, 1963?

The "Great Society"

Soon after becoming president, Lyndon B. Johnson outlined a set of programs even more ambitious than Kennedy's New Frontier. He called his proposals the **"Great Society."** In a speech he explained his vision of America:

> ❝In a land of great wealth, families must not live in hopeless poverty. In a land rich in harvest, children must not go hungry. . . . In a great land of learning and scholars, young people must be taught to read and write.❞

Johnson had acquired great skill as a legislator during his 22 years in Congress. He used this skill to persuade Congress to launch programs that would make the Great Society real.

The War on Poverty

In January 1964, President Johnson declared "an unconditional war on poverty in America." The first part of his plan for a Great Society consisted of programs to help Americans who lived below the poverty line—the minimum income needed to survive. A program called **Head Start** provided preschool education for the children of poor families. **Upward Bound** helped poor students attend college. The **Job Corps** offered training to young people who wanted to work. **Volunteers in Service to America** (VISTA) was a kind of domestic peace corps of citizens working in poor neighborhoods.

Among the most important laws passed under Johnson were those establishing Medicare and Medicaid. Medicare helped pay for medical care for senior citizens. Medicaid helped poor people pay their hospital bills.

Helping Cities and Schools

Other parts of the Great Society targeted the nation's crumbling cities. In 1966 President Johnson established the **Department of Housing and Urban Development** (HUD), which helped fund public housing projects. Another program, Model Cities, provided money to help rebuild cities. Schools received a boost from the Elementary and Secondary Education Act of 1965, which greatly increased spending for education.

Civil Rights

Although raised in the South, Lyndon Johnson was not a segregationist. He believed that the nation must protect the rights of all American citizens. When Johnson took office, he vowed to turn the civil rights bill Kennedy had proposed into law. In early 1964 he warned Congress that: "We are going to pass a civil rights bill if it takes all summer."

With growing support across the nation for the goals of the civil rights movement, Congress passed the **Civil Rights Act of 1964** in July. The act prohibited discrimination against African Americans in employment, voting, and public accommodations. It banned discrimination not only by race and color, but also by sex, religion, or national origin.

✓ **Reading Check** **Comparing** What did Medicare and Medicaid do?

SECTION 2 ASSESSMENT

Checking for Understanding

1. **Key Terms** Use each of the following words in sentences about the Great Society: poverty line, Medicare, Medicaid.
2. **Reviewing Facts** What was the purpose of the Job Corps?

Reviewing Themes

3. **Government and Democracy** Describe Johnson's policies toward civil rights.

Critical Thinking

4. **Drawing Conclusions** Should televised debates influence how Americans choose their president? Explain your reasoning.
5. **Organizing Information** Re-create the diagram below and identify three proposals that Kennedy asked Congress to act on.

```
      Kennedy proposals
     /        |        \
 (  )       (  )      (  )
```

Analyzing Visuals

6. **Analyzing Artifacts** Examine the campaign items on page 844. What are the ideas that each is trying to present to voters? Compare these items to current campaign buttons and posters you have seen.

Interdisciplinary Activity

Citizenship Choose one of President Kennedy's or President Johnson's programs and create a poster supporting or opposing it.

The Struggle Continues

Guide to Reading

Main Idea
New leaders emerged as growing numbers of African Americans became dissatisfied with the slow progress of civil rights.

Key Terms
sit-in, interstate

Reading Strategy
Classifying Information As you read the section, re-create the diagram below and describe the roles these people played in the civil rights movement.

	Roles
James Meredith	
Malcolm X	
Stokely Carmichael	

Read to Learn
- what actions African Americans took in the early 1960s to secure their rights.
- how tensions erupted in violence in many American cities.

Section Theme
Continuity and Change New African leaders, such as Malcolm X, called for changes in strategies and goals.

Preview of Events

♦1960	♦1965	♦1970

1961 Freedom Riders move through the South

1962 James Meredith enrolls at University of Mississippi

1963 More than 200,000 people march in Washington, D.C.

1968 Dr. Martin Luther King, Jr., is assassinated

AN American Story

On February 1, 1960, four African American students walked into a store in Greensboro, North Carolina. After buying a few items, they sat down at a "whites-only" lunch counter. When a waitress questioned what they were doing, one of the students replied, "We believe since we buy books and papers in the other part of the store, we should get served in this part." They were refused service, and the four sat at the counter until the store closed. By the end of the week, hundreds of students had joined the protest. Angry whites jeered at the students and dumped food on them. The protesters refused to leave or strike back.

The Movement Grows

A new wave of civil rights activity swept across the nation in the 1960s. Early activity targeted segregation in the South. Segregation existed in the North as well. In Northern cities and suburbs, African Americans and whites often lived in different neighborhoods; as a result, their children often attended different schools.

Soon African Americans expanded their goal to fighting discrimination and racism in the North as well as in the South.

High school and college students staged sit-ins in nearly 80 cities. A sit-in is the act of protesting by sitting down. Sit-ins were staged throughout the nation against stores that practiced segregation. Store managers wanted to end the disturbances and the loss of business. Gradually many stores agreed to desegregate.

The sit-ins helped launch a new civil rights group, the **Student Nonviolent Coordinating Committee** (SNCC). Civil rights activist **Ella Baker** was a guiding spirit behind SNCC and one of its organizers. Earlier, Baker had played important roles in both the NAACP and the SCLC. SNCC was a key player in the civil rights movement for several years.

Freedom Rides

The Supreme Court had ruled in 1960 against segregated bus facilities. Another civil rights group, the **Congress of Racial Equality** (CORE), decided to see whether the ruling was being enforced. On May 4, 1961, a group of African American and white CORE members left Washington, D.C., on two buses bound for New Orleans. They called themselves **Freedom Riders.**

The bus trip went smoothly until it reached Alabama, where angry whites stoned and beat the Freedom Riders.

Television and newspapers broadcast reports of the beatings. **Robert Kennedy,** the United States attorney general, asked CORE to stop the Freedom Rides for a "cooling-off period." CORE leader **James Farmer** responded: "We have been cooling off for 350 years. If we cool off any more, we will be in a deep freeze."

Violence and Arrests

The Freedom Riders pressed on, only to meet more violence in Birmingham and Montgomery, Alabama. There were no mobs waiting for the Freedom Riders in Jackson, Mississippi. However, police, state troopers, and Mississippi National Guard units were everywhere. As the Riders stepped off the bus and tried to enter the whites-only waiting room at the bus station, they were arrested for trespassing and jailed.

Despite the violence and the jail sentences, more Freedom Riders kept coming all summer. In the fall the Interstate Commerce Commission took steps to enforce the Supreme Court ruling, issuing new regulations that banned segregation on interstate buses—those that crossed state lines—and in bus stations.

Picturing **History**

Police in Birmingham, Alabama, used high-pressure water hoses against civil rights marchers. Sit-ins were another form of protest. **What was the purpose of the Freedom Rides?**

Integrating Universities

African Americans continued to apply pressure to secure their civil rights. They spurred President Kennedy to take a more active role in the civil rights struggle.

In 1962 a federal court ordered the University of Mississippi to enroll its first African American student, **James Meredith.** However, Mississippi governor **Ross Barnett,** with the aid of state police, prevented Meredith from registering. When President Kennedy sent federal marshals to escort Meredith to the campus, riots erupted. A mob stormed the administration building armed with guns and rocks. The marshals fought back with tear gas and nightsticks. Meredith succeeded in registering but two people were killed. Federal troops were stationed at the university to protect him until he graduated in 1963.

Another confrontation between state and federal power took place in June 1963—this time in Alabama. Governor **George Wallace** vowed he would "stand in the schoolhouse door" to block the integration of the University of Alabama in Tuscaloosa. President Kennedy, acting on the advice of his brother, sent the Alabama National Guard to ensure the entry of African Americans to the university. As a result, Wallace backed down.

Birmingham

In the spring of 1963, Dr. Martin Luther King, Jr., and the SCLC targeted **Birmingham, Alabama,** for a desegregation protest. Police arrested hundreds of demonstrators, including King, but the demonstrations continued. During King's two weeks in jail, he wrote the eloquent "Letter from Birmingham Jail," in which he wrote:

> 66For years now I have heard the word 'Wait!' It rings in the ear of every Negro with piercing familiarity. This 'Wait' has almost always meant 'Never.' We must come to see . . . that 'justice too long delayed is justice denied.'99

What If...

Jackie Robinson Failed to Make the Major Leagues?

Can you imagine major league baseball without such superstars as Sammy Sosa or Ken Griffey, Jr.? Yet these great players may never have had the chance if not for Jackie Robinson. When Robinson first played for the Brooklyn Dodgers on April 15th, 1947, he became the first African American in the twentieth century to play major league baseball. His outstanding play and courage in the face of adversity led to the signing of many more African American players.

Yet what if Robinson had failed? Some sports historians believe that many more years might haved passed before another chance opened for an African American player. Robinson's wife, Rachel, notes, "Jack knew that by breaking the color barrier, he was not only paving the way for minorities in professional sports, but was also providing opportunities in all facets of life. . . ."

Houston Federal Judge David Hittner echoes those sentiments:

66I think the start of the heavy civil rights movement came with the breaking of the color barrier in major league baseball. It was one of the great indications of the impetus of the civil rights movement in the United States. To me, it really was the start. It showed a lot of folks that, here was the concept of equality. It nailed many nails in the coffin, particularly in terms of the perception of inferiority. Jackie Robinson was a pioneer. He had to stand there and take it, just so others could maybe someday get to where he was.99

With Robinson's success came integration in other sports. By the mid-1950s African American athletes had established themselves as a powerful force in almost all professional sports.

National television carried vivid pictures of police setting snarling police dogs on unarmed demonstrators and washing small children across streets with the powerful impact of fire hoses. President Kennedy sent 3,000 troops to restore peace. On June 11, 1963, in Jackson, Mississippi, **Medgar Evers,** state field secretary for the NAACP, was murdered. The murder and the events in Alabama forced President Kennedy to make a decision. Appearing on national television, Kennedy spoke of the "moral issue" facing the nation:

> ❝The heart of the question is whether all Americans are to be afforded equal rights and equal opportunities, whether we are going to treat our fellow Americans as we want to be treated. If an American, because his skin is dark, cannot . . . enjoy the full and free life which all of us want, then who among us would be content to have the color of his skin changed and stand in his place?❞

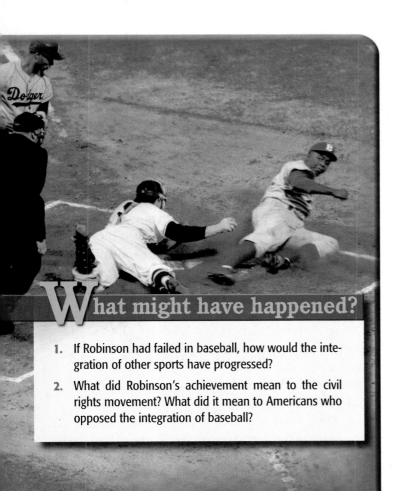

What might have happened?

1. If Robinson had failed in baseball, how would the integration of other sports have progressed?

2. What did Robinson's achievement mean to the civil rights movement? What did it mean to Americans who opposed the integration of baseball?

Days later, the president introduced new legislation giving all Americans the right to be served in public places and barring discrimination in employment.

March on Washington

To rally support for the civil rights bill, Dr. Martin Luther King, Jr., and the SCLC organized a massive march in Washington, D.C., on August 28, 1963. More than 200,000 people, of all colors and from all over the country, arrived to take part. Emily Rock, a 15-year-old African American, described how she felt at the march:

> ❝There was this sense of hope for the future—the belief that this march was the big step in the right direction. It could be heard in the voices of the people singing and seen in the way they walked. It poured out into smiles.❞

About 6,000 police officers stood nearby, but they had nothing to do but direct traffic. There was no trouble. Proceeding with great dignity and joy, the marchers carried signs urging Congress to act. They sang songs, including one that was becoming the anthem of the civil rights movement: "We Shall Overcome." 📖 *(See page 977 of the Primary Sources Library for the words to this song.)*

Late in the afternoon, Dr. Martin Luther King, Jr., spoke to the crowd in ringing words of his desire to see America transformed:

> ❝I have a dream that one day this nation will rise up and live out the true meaning of its creed: 'We hold these truths to be self-evident; that all men are created equal.' . . . When we let freedom ring, . . . we will be able to speed up that day when all of God's children . . . [will] join hands and sing in the words of the old . . . spiritual, 'Free at last! Free at last! Thank God Almighty, we are free at last!'❞
>
> 📖 *(See page 996 for more of this famous speech.)*

Freedom Summer

Congress did not pass Kennedy's civil rights bill until after his death. President **Lyndon B. Johnson,** who succeeded Kennedy, finally this there can be no argument," he said. "Every American citizen must have an equal right to vote." In August Johnson signed the **Voting Rights Act of 1965** into law. The act gave the federal government the power to force local officials to allow African Americans to register to vote.

The act led to dramatic changes in political life in the South. In 1966 about 100 African Americans held elective office in the South. By 1972 that number had increased 10 times.

✔ **Reading Check** **Analyzing** Why were sit-ins an effective strategy against segregation?

persuaded Congress to pass the bill. The Civil Rights Act of 1964 outlawed discrimination in hiring and ended segregation in stores, restaurants, theaters, and hotels. Yet, in many states, African Americans still could not vote. Poll taxes and other discriminatory laws prevented them from exercising this right.

During the summer of 1964, thousands of civil rights workers spread throughout the South to help African Americans register to vote. They called the campaign **Freedom Summer,** but the workers faced strong, sometimes violent, opposition.

The Right to Vote

The next year SNCC organized a major demonstration in **Selma, Alabama,** to protest the continued denial of African Americans' right to vote. Police attacks on the marchers again dramatized the cause.

President Johnson stepped in. On March 15, 1965, in a televised speech, the president urged passage of a voting rights bill. "About

Other Voices

By the mid-1960s, the civil rights movement had won numerous victories. Yet a growing number of African Americans grew tired of the slow pace of change and bitter over white attacks.

Malcolm X, a leader in the Nation of Islam (or Black Muslims), emerged as an important new voice for some African Americans. Malcolm X criticized the civil rights goal of integration, declaring that the best way for African Americans to achieve justice was to separate themselves from whites.

Malcolm X gained increasing support. By 1965, however, he had begun to change his ideas. Instead of racial separation, he called for "a society in which there could exist honest white-black brotherhood." Soon afterwards, he was killed by an assassin from a rival group among the Black Muslims. His fiery words and passionate ideas, contained in his autobiography and other writings, continued to influence the civil rights movement after his death.

Black Power

Other African American leaders embraced more radical approaches. **Stokely Carmichael,** who became the leader of SNCC, advanced the idea of **Black Power.** This was a philosophy of racial pride that said African Americans should create their own culture and political institutions. Carmichael and other radicals called at times for revolution, a complete transformation of society. Although rejected by such groups as the NAACP, the idea of Black Power had a great impact on the civil rights movement.

Violence Erupts

In Oakland, California, a group of young radicals formed the **Black Panther Party.** The Panthers symbolized a growing tension between African Americans and urban police. Large numbers of African Americans in urban areas felt frustrated about poverty and unemployment. The Panthers demanded reforms and armed themselves in opposition to the police. Several armed clashes with the police occurred.

The first major urban riots since the 1940s took place in the summer of 1965 in the **Watts** section of **Los Angeles.** In a week of rioting, 34 people died and much of Watts burned to the ground. National Guard troops were called in to end the uprising. The Watts riot was the first of a series of racial disorders that hit cities in the summers of 1965, 1966, and 1967.

Between the years of 1965 and 1967 rioting broke out in more than 40 Northern cities, including San Francisco, Chicago, and Cleveland. In July 1967, five days of protests, looting, and burning of buildings in Newark, New Jersey, ended with the deaths of 26 people and more than $10 million in damage. The next week, a massive uprising in Detroit shut the city down for several days.

President Johnson named a commission to study the causes of the riots and to suggest steps to improve conditions. The report of this group, the Kerner Commission, warned that "our nation is moving toward two societies, one black, one white—separate and unequal."

The wave of urban riots devastated many African American neighborhoods. The riots ended—but not before one last burst of rage.

King Is Assassinated

On April 4, 1968, racial tension in the United States took another tragic turn. On that night in Memphis, Tennessee, an assassin shot and killed Dr. Martin Luther King, Jr. King's assassination set off angry rioting in more than 100 cities. Fires burned in the nation's capital, just blocks from the Capitol and the White House.

Thousands of people attended King's funeral in Atlanta. Millions more watched on television. All mourned the death of an American hero who, the night before his death, had said God "has allowed me to go up to the mountain, and I've seen the promised land. I may not get there with you. But I want you to know tonight, that we, as a people, will get to the promised land!"

✓ Reading Check **Explaining** Why did some African American leaders criticize the goal of integration?

SECTION 3 ASSESSMENT

Checking for Understanding

1. **Key Terms** Using complete sentences, define the following terms: sit-in, interstate.
2. **Reviewing Facts** What idea did Stokely Carmichael advance?

Reviewing Themes

3. **Continuity and Change** How did the beliefs and strategies of groups such as the Black Panthers differ from the beliefs and strategies of Dr. Martin Luther King, Jr.?

Critical Thinking

4. **Predicting Consequences** What do you think would have happened in the civil rights movement had King not been assassinated?
5. **Analyzing Information** Re-create the diagram below and describe three events of racial unrest that spread to major cities during the summers of 1965–1967.

Racial unrest

Analyzing Visuals

6. **Picturing History** Examine the photographs on page 849. Write a caption that describes what is happening in the pictures. If you were a reporter interviewing these people, what would you ask them?

Interdisciplinary Activity

Expository Writing Choose a civil rights figure from the section. Research this person and write a personal profile. Include copies of photographs, speeches, and so on, as appropriate.

FREEDOM RIDERS

SEGREGATED WAITING ROOMS, restaurants, restrooms, and buses still existed in the South in 1961, despite Supreme Court orders to integrate facilities serving passengers traveling from state to state.

ON THE ROAD

On May 4th, 1961, 13 neatly dressed African-American and white Freedom Riders boarded buses in Washington, D.C. Determined to challenge segregation, these men and women knew they might encounter violence or be arrested as they headed toward New Orleans. The Riders were turned away from a bus station in Danville, Virginia, and police stopped a scuffle in Rock Hill, South Carolina. Despite these incidents, the trip through Virginia, the Carolinas, and Georgia went fairly smoothly.

TROUBLE DEVELOPS

In Alabama, however, trouble started. White mobs ambushed the Riders in Anniston and Birmingham, torching one of the buses. When many of the battered Freedom Riders decided to abandon the buses in Birmingham and fly to New Orleans, new groups took up the cause in Nashville, Tennessee, and other cities. They eventually made it to Jackson, Mississippi, where they were arrested.

ENFORCING THE LAW

Freedom Riders continued these non-violent protests until they got what they wanted. In September 1961 Attorney General Robert Kennedy persuaded the Interstate Commerce Commission to enforce the Supreme Court's ruling prohibiting racial discrimination on buses and in transportation facilities.

LEARNING from GEOGRAPHY

1. **Why do you think the Freedom Riders decided to protest in this region of the United States?**

2. **Where did Freedom Riders encounter the greatest difficulties? Were they successful in reaching their goal?**

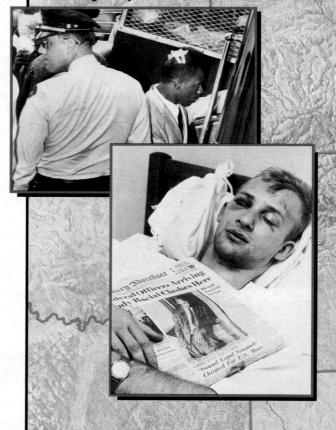

Police arrest Freedom Rider John Lewis (top) in Jackson, Mississippi. Jim Zwerg (below) lies in a hospital bed after beatings by people in favor of segregation at a Montgomery, Alabama, bus terminal.

LOUISIANA

Freedom Riders

← First bus route

← Second bus route

←- Air route

0   50 miles

0   50 kilometers

Angry segregationists ambushed the bus near Anniston, Alabama. Officers finally dispersed the mob, allowing the Freedom Riders to stumble out.

MARYLAND

Annapolis

May 4, 1961
Freedom Riders
begin journey

Washington, D.C.

Fredericksburg

Richmond

VIRGINIA

Farmville

Petersburg

May 5

Danville

May 17, 1961
Second group of Freedom
Riders begins the journey

Greensboro

Raleigh

NORTH CAROLINA

Nashville

Mississippi River

TENNESSEE

Charlotte

Rock Hill

Columbia

Athens

SOUTH
CAROLINA

Atlanta

Tallapoosa

Anniston

May 13

Augusta

Birmingham

ATLANTIC OCEAN

MISSISSIPPI

GEORGIA

Selma

Montgomery

Meridian

May 20

Jackson
May 25

ALABAMA

Alabama National Guardsmen with bayoneted rifles escort Freedom Riders on board a bus near Montgomery, Alabama.

Baton
Rouge

Gulf
of
Mexico

New Orleans
May 17

N
W   E
S

Other Groups Seek Rights

Guide to Reading

Main Idea

In the 1960s and 1970s, growing numbers of women, Hispanic Americans, Native Americans, and disabled Americans entered the struggle for equal rights.

Key Terms

feminist, Hispanic

Reading Strategy

Organizing Information As you read the section, re-create the diagram below and describe the role each person played in the 1960s and 1970s.

	Roles
Phyllis Schlafly	
César Chávez	
Herman Badillo	

Read to Learn

- what steps women and minorities took to improve their lives.
- what new leaders emerged.

Section Theme

Continuity and Change During the 1960s and 1970s, women and minorities used political action to shatter stereotypes and improve their lives.

Preview of Events

◆1960   ◆1965   ◆1970   ◆1975

1963
Congress passes Equal Pay Act; *The Feminine Mystique* is published

1966
National Organization for Women is created

1973
American Indian Movement protests at Wounded Knee, South Dakota

AN American Story

Mexican American farmworker Jesse de la Cruz had labored for decades in the grape and cotton fields of the Southwest. In 1972 she began working for the United Farm Workers Union. Cruz made speaking tours, trying to bring women into the union. "Women can no longer be taken for granted—that we're just going to stay home and do the cooking and cleaning," she told her listeners. "It's way past the time when our husbands could say, 'You stay home! You have to take care of the children! You have to do as I say!'"

Women's Rights

The effects of the civil rights movement reached well beyond the African American community. Women, Hispanics, Native Americans, and people with disabilities all found inspiration in the struggles of African Americans. In 1961 President John F. Kennedy created the Commission on the Status of Women. It reported that women—an ever-growing part of the workforce—received lower pay than men, even for performing the same jobs. In 1963 Kennedy convinced Congress to pass the **Equal Pay Act,** which prohibited employers from paying women less than men for the same work.

Uniting for Action

In 1966 feminists—activists for women's rights—created the **National Organization for Women** (NOW). NOW fought for equal rights for women in all aspects of life—in jobs, education, and marriage.

Among its early successes, NOW helped end separate classified employment ads for men and women, and airline rules that required female flight attendants to retire at age 32. In the 1960s and 1970s, NOW and similar groups worked to increase the number of women entering the professions. Banks, realtors, and department stores were forced to grant loans, mortgages, and credit that they long had denied to female applicants.

In the early 1970s, NOW launched a campaign for an **Equal Rights Amendment** (ERA) to the Constitution. The amendment stated that "equality of rights under the law shall not be denied or abridged by the United States or by any state on account of sex." **Phyllis Schlafly** and other opponents of the ERA warned that the amendment would upset the traditional roles of society and lead to the breakdown of the family. Some people argued that the amendment was unnecessary because the Constitution already provided women with adequate protection. In the end, not enough states ratified the amendment to make it law.

Women Gain Opportunities

Despite the defeat of the Equal Rights Amendment, women progressed in a number of areas in the 1970s. In 1972 the federal government outlawed discrimination against women in educational programs receiving federal funds. This law, along with the efforts of many businesses, helped women begin to make advances in the world of work.

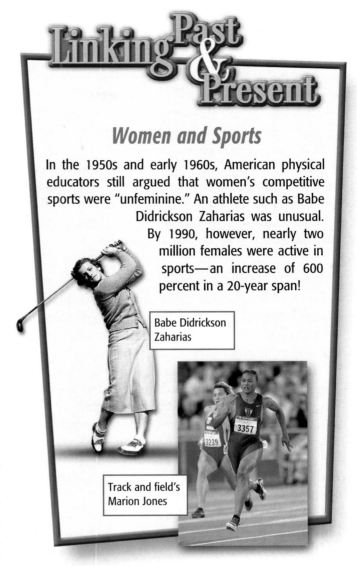

Linking Past & Present

Women and Sports

In the 1950s and early 1960s, American physical educators still argued that women's competitive sports were "unfeminine." An athlete such as Babe Didrickson Zaharias was unusual. By 1990, however, nearly two million females were active in sports—an increase of 600 percent in a 20-year span!

Babe Didrickson Zaharias

Track and field's Marion Jones

Women gained more job opportunities, and more women rose to higher-level jobs in their companies. 📖 *(See page 977 for one woman's struggle to gain equal pay in the work place.)*

Most of the nation's all-male colleges and universities began admitting women. More women than ever entered medical school and law school to become doctors and lawyers.

Women also made progress in the political arena. Many women gained local and state offices. Several women won seats in the Senate and the House of Representatives and appointments to the president's cabinet. In 1981 President Ronald Reagan appointed **Sandra Day O'Connor** as the first female justice of the Supreme Court.

Reading Check **Summarizing** What happened to the Equal Rights Amendment?

Hispanic Americans

In the 1960s the rapidly growing Hispanic population sought equal rights. The term *Hispanic American* refers to those Americans who have come, or are descended from others who have come, to the United States from the countries of Latin America and Spain. From 3 million in 1960, the Hispanic population in the United States rose to 9 million by 1970 and to 15 million by 1980. Although they share the heritage of the Spanish culture and language, Hispanics are a diverse group with different histories.

Farmworkers Organize

By far, the largest Hispanic group in the United States comes from the country of Mexico. By 1980 more than eight million Mexican Americans were living in the United States.

The fight for rights started among Mexican American migrant farmworkers. These people, who planted and harvested a large share of the nation's food supply, faced great hardships. The migrant farmers did backbreaking work, laboring from dawn until dusk for low wages. When one job ended, they had to travel from farm to farm in search of the next job.

In the early 1960s, migrant workers formed unions to fight for better wages and working conditions. Their leader, **César Chávez,** organized thousands of farmworkers into the United Farm Workers (UFW).

The union went on strike and organized nationwide boycotts. Consumers across the country supported the UFW by refusing to buy grapes, lettuce, and other farm produce under boycott. The success of the boycotts enabled the UFW to win higher wages and shorter work hours for many farmworkers.

The union boycott was followed by emerging political power among Hispanic Americans. In the years that followed, Hispanic Americans would join together in an organization called **La Raza Unida** to fight discrimination and to elect Hispanics to government posts. **The League of United Latin American Citizens (LULAC)** won lawsuits in federal court to guarantee Hispanic Americans the right to serve on juries and the right to send their children to unsegregated schools.

Puerto Ricans

Puerto Ricans, another major group of Hispanics, come from the island of Puerto Rico, a commonwealth of the United States. They are American citizens who have made major contributions to the United States.

In 1970 the first representative to Congress of Puerto Rican origin, **Herman Badillo,** was elected from New York City. After four terms, Badillo served as the city's deputy mayor. Baseball all-time great **Roberto Clemente** performed heroically both on and off the baseball diamond. In 1972 Clemente died in a plane crash while delivering relief supplies to earthquake victims in Nicaragua.

Because Puerto Rico is not a wealthy island, many Puerto Ricans have migrated to American cities in search of jobs. By 1970 they made up 10 percent of the population of New York City. As with African Americans, though, they often faced discrimination in their job search, leading to no work or work for low pay. Many of the children and grandchildren of the Puerto Ricans who arrived in New York in the 1960s migrated to neighboring states, but many Puerto Ricans remained in New York City.

Cubans Arrive

César Chávez

After the Cuban Revolution of 1959, dictator Fidel Castro established a Communist government and seized the property of many Cubans. More than 200,000 people opposed to Castro fled to the United States in the 1960s. Thousands more came in the 1980s.

These immigrants settled all over the United States. The largest number of Cubans settled in south Florida, where they have established a thriving community.

In 1975 Hispanic people and other groups won a victory with the extension of voting rights. The new law required that registration and voting be carried out in other languages as well as in English. This was designed to help those citizens who might not read or speak English. Election materials, for example, are available in Spanish and English in many states.

Reading Check Explaining Why did many Cubans flee their homeland in the 1960s?

Native Americans

The years after World War II were a time of transition for Native Americans. Starting in the early 1950s, the federal government urged Native Americans to leave the reservations to work in cities. Federal policy also tried to weaken the power of tribal government.

This policy did not improve the lives of Native Americans. Many could not find jobs in the cities. Those still crowded on reservations enjoyed few jobs or other opportunities. More than one-third of Native Americans lived below the poverty line. Unemployment was widespread—as high as 50 percent in some areas. A 1966 study revealed that Native Americans suffered so much from malnutrition and disease that their life expectancy was only 46 years.

Efforts to Organize

In the 1960s Native Americans organized to combat these problems. They wanted political power and they demanded independence from the United States government. Native Americans also increasingly emphasized their own history, language, and culture in their schools. The **National Congress of American Indians** (NCAI) sought more control over Native American affairs.

In 1961 more than 400 members of 67 Native American nations gathered in Chicago. In a Declaration of Indian Purpose, these delegates

Wounded Knee button

Picturing History
In the 1973 AIM takeover of Wounded Knee, Native American leaders Russell Means (left) and Dennis Banks (right) protested broken treaties and civil rights violations. **Why was Wounded Knee chosen as the place for the AIM protest?**

stated that Native Americans have the "right to choose our own way of life," and maintained that "a treaty, in the minds of our people, is an eternal word."

The federal government recognized the Native Americans' issues. Congress passed the **Indian Civil Rights Act of 1968,** which formally protected the constitutional rights of all Native Americans. At the same time, the new law recognized the right of Native American nations to make laws on their reservations.

A Supreme Court decision in the 1970s reaffirmed the independence of tribal governments. Other court decisions confirmed Native Americans' rights to land granted in treaties.

American Indian Movement

Believing the process of change too slow, some younger Native Americans began taking stronger actions. In 1968 a group established the **American Indian Movement** (AIM), which worked for equal rights and improvement of living conditions.

AIM was founded by Clyde Bellecourt, Dennis Banks, and others. Later, Russell Means became a leader. AIM carried out several protests. In

Picturing History

Since the 1960s, people with physical disabilities have demanded—sometimes through protest—better access to stadiums, restaurants, and other public buildings. **How has Congress responded to their protests?**

November 1969, for example, AIM was one of the Native American groups that took over Alcatraz Island, a former prison in San Francisco Bay. AIM wanted the island to serve as a cultural center. The incident ended in June 1971 when the groups surrendered to U.S. marshals.

In the fall of 1972, AIM members occupied the Bureau of Indian Affairs in Washington, D.C. They demanded the lands and rights guaranteed under treaties with the United States. They surrendered the building after the government agreed to review their complaints.

In February 1973, AIM occupied the small town of **Wounded Knee, South Dakota,** the site of the 1890 massacre of Sioux by federal troops. In the early 1970s, Wounded Knee was part of a large Sioux reservation. The people there suffered from terrible poverty and ill health.

AIM leaders vowed to stay until the government met demands for change and investigated the treatment of Native Americans. The siege ended on May 8, but it focused national attention on the terrible conditions under which Native Americans lived.

Americans With Disabilities

People with physical disabilities also sought equal treatment in the 1960s and the 1970s. Congress responded by passing a number of laws.

One law concerned the removal of barriers that prevented some people from gaining access to public facilities. Another required employers to offer more opportunities for disabled people in the workplace. Yet another asserted the right of children with disabilities to equal educational opportunities. As a result of these actions, people with disabilities enjoy more job opportunities, better access to public facilities, and a greater role in society.

Reading Check **Identifying** What act protects the rights of all Native Americans?

SECTION 4 ASSESSMENT

Checking for Understanding

1. **Key Terms** Use each of these terms in a sentence that will help explain its meaning: feminist, Hispanic.
2. **Reviewing Facts** Who was the first female justice to serve on the Supreme Court?

Reviewing Themes

3. **Continuity and Change** What was the purpose of the American Indian Movement? What rights did Native Americans gain in the 1960s?

Critical Thinking

4. **Analyzing Information** Identify two organizations that Native Americans developed to help them take more control of their own lives.
5. **Drawing Conclusions** Re-create the diagram below and list two reasons why you think people with disabilities felt the need to work for equal treatment in the 1960s and 1970s.

Working for equal treatment

Analyzing Visuals

6. **Political Cartoons** Bring to class a copy of a political cartoon from a recent newspaper or magazine. Try to find a cartoon in which the topic is the rights of people. Explain the cartoonist's viewpoint and the tools used to make the point.

Interdisciplinary Activity

Citizenship Create a poster that might have been used in a march to support or oppose the ERA.

Critical Thinking
SKILLBUILDER

Drawing Conclusions

Why Learn This Skill?

Drawing conclusions allows you to understand ideas that are not stated directly.

Learning the Skill

Follow these steps in learning to draw conclusions:
- Review the facts that are stated directly.
- Use your knowledge and insight to develop some conclusions about these facts.
- Look for information to check the accuracy of your conclusions.

Practicing the Skill

The excerpt on this page was written by Dr. Martin Luther King, Jr., after he was arrested in Birmingham, Alabama, for peaceably demonstrating against segregation. King began writing this letter in response to a newspaper ad in which a group of white ministers called for an end to the demonstrations. King's words attempt to explain to the white ministers his use of civil disobedience.

Dr. Martin Luther King, Jr.

After reading the excerpt, answer the questions, which require you to draw conclusions.

66 We know through painful experience that freedom is never voluntarily given by the oppressor; it must be demanded by the oppressed. . . . For years now I have heard the word 'Wait!' It rings in the ear of every Negro with piercing familiarity. This 'Wait' has almost always meant 'Never.' We must come to see, with one of our distinguished jurists, that 'justice too long delayed is justice denied.' 99

—*Dr. Martin Luther King, Jr.*
"Letter from Birmingham Jail," 1963

1 How does King say that freedom is earned?

2 What were the African Americans "waiting" for?

3 What happens to justice if it is delayed?

4 What conclusions can you draw from King's overall tone in his letter?

5 What evidence could help prove your conclusions?

Applying the Skill

Drawing Conclusions Read a newspaper or newsmagazine article about a criminal court case. Use the facts in the article to draw a conclusion about the innocence or guilt of the accused.

 Glencoe's **Skillbuilder Interactive Workbook CD-ROM, Level 1,** provides instruction and practice in key social studies skills.

Chapter Summary
The Civil Rights Era

African Americans challenge segregation

- Brown v. Board of Education of Topeka, Kansas
- Montgomery bus boycott
- Freedom Riders
- March on Washington
- Civil Rights Act of 1964
- Voting Rights Act of 1965

Hispanic Americans organize

- César Chávez organizes United Farm Workers
- La Raza Unida and LULAC fight discrimination
- Voting rights extended

Native Americans demand rights

- Indian Civil Rights Act of 1968
- NCAI and AIM call attention to problems

Women fight for equal rights

- Equal Pay Act
- National Organization for Women
- ERA brings attention to women's rights

Reviewing Key Terms
Use these key terms to create a newspaper article in which you describe important events during the civil rights era.

1. poverty line
2. integrate
3. segregation
4. boycott
5. sit-in

Reviewing Key Facts

6. What Supreme Court case abolished segregation in schools?
7. Whose arrest sparked the Montgomery bus boycott?
8. What is civil disobedience?
9. What was the main goal of President Kennedy's New Frontier program?
10. What conclusion did the Warren Commission reach?
11. What did the Civil Rights Act of 1964 prohibit?
12. What is significant about James Meredith?
13. Why was the March on Washington organized?
14. What was the goal of Black Power?
15. What did Herman Badillo accomplish?

Critical Thinking

16. **Making Generalizations** Why do you think the civil rights movement gained momentum during this era?
17. **Analyzing Themes: Civic Rights and Responsibilities** According to Thurgood Marshall, what constitutional amendment was violated by allowing school segregation? Explain why Marshall argued that segregated schools were unconstitutional.
18. **Compare and Contrast** How did the idea of Black Power differ from Martin Luther King's goals for the civil rights movement?
19. **Determining Cause and Effect** Re-create the diagram below and describe two impacts that the African American civil rights movement had on other minorities.

Civil rights movement

862

Practicing Skills

Drawing Conclusions *Read the passage below and answer the questions that follow. Remember to review the information and add your own knowledge before drawing any conclusions.*

Malcolm X, a strong African American leader, bitterly and regretfully recalled his youthful efforts at straightening his hair in order to look more like a white person:

> 66 This was my first big step toward self-degradation: when I endured all of that pain, literally burning my flesh to have it look like a white man's hair. I had joined that multitude of Negro men and women in America who are brainwashed into believing that the black people are 'inferior'—and white people 'superior.' 99
>
> —Malcolm X, *Autobiography of Malcolm X,* 1965

20. What reason does Malcolm X give for straightening his hair?

21. As an adult, how did Malcolm X view his youthful actions?

22. What conclusion can you draw about the views of many African American people toward white people at that time?

23. What statement from the passage supports your conclusion?

 Geography and History Activity

Study the map on page 839. Then answer the questions that follow.

24. Location What law regarding segregation did Colorado have in place?

25. Region Explain why you agree or disagree with this statement: Many states in the West had no specific legislation concerning segregation in schools.

Citizenship Cooperative Activity

26. Researching With members of your group research to find out how many people of different ethnic backgrounds live in your county. Make a graph to illustrate your findings. Then choose one of the minority ethnic groups to research. Prepare a written report with illustrations to provide more information about this particular ethnic group in your county. You may want to find out if members of this ethnic

group have settled in one particular area of the county, if they have formed special clubs or organizations, or if they observe any special holidays.

Self-Check Quiz
Visit <u>taj.glencoe.com</u> and click on **Chapter 29—Self-Check Quizzes** to prepare for the chapter test.

 Technology Activity

27. The United Farm Workers are still active today. Search the Internet for information about this organization and create a brochure that explains its goals.

 Alternative Assessment

28. Creating a Time Line Review the chapter for dates important to minority groups. Create a time line that traces the progress of African Americans, Hispanics, Native Americans, and women in their struggle for equal rights during the 1950s and 1960s.

Standardized Test Practice

Directions: Choose the *best* answer to the following question.

In *Brown* v. *Board of Education of Topeka, Kansas,* the Supreme Court ruled that Topeka's school district had engaged in which unconstitutional practice?

A Prohibited school prayer

B Bussed students to schools far away from their homes

C Had set up different schools for white and African American students

D Refused to offer required courses

Test-Taking Tip

The important word in this question is *unconstitutional.* Transporting students great distances seems inconvenient, but it is not specifically banned by the Constitution. Therefore, you can eliminate answer **B.**

CHAPTER
30 The Vietnam Era
1960–1975

Why It Matters

The United States became involved in Vietnam because it believed that if all of Vietnam fell under a Communist government, communism would spread throughout Southeast Asia and beyond. The Vietnam War was the longest war in the nation's history.

The Impact Today

More than 58,000 U.S. troops died in Vietnam. The war damaged people's confidence in their government. Americans grew more willing to challenge the president on military and foreign policy issues after Vietnam. The war also became a yardstick to gauge whether to involve American troops in later crises.

The American Journey *Video* *The chapter 30 video, "The First TV War," explores how televised images brought the Vietnam War into American households and influenced public opinion about the war.*

1962
• Cuban missile crisis

1965
• U.S. involvement in Vietnam grows

United States
PRESIDENTS

Eisenhower 1953–1961

Kennedy 1961–1963

Johnson 1963–1969

1960

1963

1966

World

1959
• Civil war begins in Vietnam

1961
• Berlin Wall erected

1966
• Cultural Revolution in China

Helping a **Comrade** Members of the First Marine Division carry a wounded marine to safety during battle in South Vietnam.

FOLDABLES™
Study Organizer

Sequencing Events Study Foldable Sequence the actions of the United States's presidents during the Vietnam War by making and using this foldable.

Step 1 Fold one sheet of paper in half from side to side.

Step 2 Turn the paper and fold it into thirds.

Step 3 Unfold and label the foldable as shown.

J.F.K. | L.B.J. | Nixon

Step 4 Cut the top layer only along both fold lines.

J.F.K. | L.B.J. | Nixon

This will make three tabs.

Reading and Writing As you read the chapter, record facts about the actions and policies of the presidents in office during the Vietnam era. Be sure to also record the dates of these important events.

1968
• Robert Kennedy assassinated

1969
• Armstrong walks on moon

1973
• Paris peace accords end U.S. involvement in Vietnam

1970
• Kent State shootings

Nixon 1969–1974

Ford 1974–1977

1969   *1972*   *1975*

1968
• North Vietnam launches Tet offensive

1970
• Civil War begins in Cambodia

1975
• Vietnam War ends after fall of Saigon

HISTORY Online

Chapter Overview
Visit taj.glencoe.com and click on **Chapter 30— Chapter Overviews** to preview chapter information.

Kennedy's Foreign Policy

Guide to Reading

Main Idea
In the early 1960s, the nation faced Soviet threats relating to Cuba and to Berlin.

Key Terms
guerrilla warfare, flexible response, executive order, exile, blockade, hot line

Reading Strategy
Organizing Information As you read Section 1, re-create the diagram below and describe the actions the Kennedy administration took in response to these crises.

Response to Crises	
Berlin Wall	Cuban missile crisis

Read to Learn
- how the Kennedy administration handled challenges to foreign affairs.
- what happened during the Cuban missile crisis.

Section Theme
Geography and History The Kennedy administration faced crises in Cuba and Berlin.

Preview of Events

♦1960   ♦1965   ♦1970

1961
Bay of Pigs invasion fails

1962
Cuban missile crisis occurs

1963
Telephone hot line links U.S., Soviet leaders

1969
Neil Armstrong walks on the moon

AN American Story

"In the long history of the world, only a few generations have been granted the role of defending freedom in its hour of maximum danger. I do not shrink from this responsibility—I welcome it." So spoke John F. Kennedy in his Inaugural Address. Although Kennedy talked of approaching this responsibility with "energy" and "devotion," events unfolding around the world—in Cuba, Eastern Europe, and Vietnam—would challenge his determination. The new president and nation soon faced a series of crises.

New Directions

President Kennedy continued the anti–Communist foreign policy begun under Presidents Truman and Eisenhower. In pursuing that policy, though, Kennedy tried some new approaches.

During the presidential campaign, Kennedy led Americans to believe that the nation had fewer nuclear missiles than the Soviet Union. As president, Kennedy increased spending on nuclear arms. At the same time, he tried to convince Nikita Khrushchev, the Soviet leader, to agree to a ban on nuclear testing.

Strength Through Flexibility

Kennedy also worked to improve America's ability to respond to threats abroad. In certain areas of the world, Communist groups fought to take control of their nation's government. Many of these groups received aid from the Soviet Union. They employed guerrilla warfare, or fighting by small bands using tactics such as sudden ambushes.

The United States needed a new approach for fighting guerrilla wars. Kennedy introduced a plan called flexible response, which relied on special military units trained to fight guerrilla wars. One of these units was the Special Forces, known as the **Green Berets.** The Special Forces provided the president with troops ready to fight guerrilla warfare anywhere around the world.

Strength Through Aid

President Kennedy understood that the poverty in Latin America, Asia, and Africa made the Communist promises of economic equality seem attractive. He decided to provide aid to countries in those areas to counteract the appeal of communism. On March 1, 1961, the president signed an executive order creating the **Peace Corps.** An executive order is a rule issued by the chief executive.

Americans who volunteered for the Peace Corps worked in other countries as teachers, health workers, and advisers in farming, industry, and government. By 1963 some 5,000 volunteers were working in more than 40 countries.

To promote Latin America's growth, Kennedy proposed a 10-year development plan called the **Alliance for Progress.** In his Inaugural Address, Kennedy promised Latin American leaders that the United States would "assist free men and free governments in casting off the chains of poverty." He hoped as well to prevent the rise of Communist states in the region.

✔ Reading Check **Explaining** Why did President Kennedy form the Peace Corps?

Cold War Confrontations

In 1961, just a few months after taking office, President Kennedy faced a foreign policy crisis in Cuba. That same year, the United States and the Soviet Union clashed in Europe.

As you read in Chapter 28, **Fidel Castro** had seized power in Cuba in 1959. When Castro formed an alliance with the Soviet Union, Americans felt threatened because Cuba lies only 90 miles (144 km) south of Florida. Late in Eisenhower's presidency, officials in the Central

History *Through Art*

The Peace Corps in Ethiopia, 1966 by Norman Rockwell Volunteers worked in many developing countries in Africa. **Which Kennedy program dealt with Latin America's economy?**

Intelligence Agency (CIA) forged a plan to overthrow Castro. The CIA recruited refugees who had fled Castro's Cuba and settled in the United States. The plan called for these exiles, or persons forced from their homes, to land in Cuba, spark an uprising, and overthrow Castro. Although Kennedy had doubts about the plan, he accepted the advice of military advisers and the CIA and allowed it to go forward.

On April 17, 1961, about 1,500 CIA-trained Cuban exiles landed at the **Bay of Pigs** in southern Cuba. Many blunders occurred, and at a crucial moment, Kennedy refused to provide American air support. Within days Cuban forces crushed the invasion and captured the survivors.

The Bay of Pigs embarrassed Kennedy, who took the blame for the failure. The disaster had three consequences. First, Kennedy never again completely trusted military and intelligence advice. Second, other nations in Latin America lost trust in Kennedy. Third, Soviet premier Khrushchev concluded that Kennedy was not a strong leader and could be bullied.

The Berlin Wall

Though 16 years had passed since the end of World War II, the wartime Allies had still not settled the status of Germany. West Germany gained complete independence in 1949, but the Soviet Union continued to control East Germany.

The location of **Berlin**—fully within Soviet-controlled East Germany—posed special problems. American, British, and French troops still remained in the western part of the city, and they sometimes had difficulty getting into West Berlin and maintaining control there. Meanwhile a steady flow of people fled to West Berlin from Communist East Berlin, hoping to escape economic hardship and find freedom.

At a June 1961 summit conference in Vienna, Austria, Premier Khrushchev told President Kennedy that the West must move out of Berlin, and he insisted on an agreement by the end of the year. Kennedy rejected Khrushchev's demand. To emphasize the West's right to stay in West Berlin, the United States later sent more troops to protect the city.

People In History

Alan Shepard 1923-1998

Alan Shepard became a national hero on May 5, 1961, when he became the first American in space. His flight aboard the tiny *Freedom 7* spaceship lasted 15 minutes and reached an altitude of about 120 miles. Although the flight was brief, it was a key step forward for the United States in its space race with the Soviet Union.

After graduating from the United States Naval Academy in 1944, Shepard served during World War II. After the war, he attended the Naval Test Pilot School. In 1959 Shepard was named one of NASA's original seven astronauts.

Ten years after his flight aboard *Freedom 7*, Shepard commanded the *Apollo 14* moon mission,

during which he spent a record 33.5 hours on the surface of the moon.

In 1974 Shepard retired from both NASA and the Navy and entered private business. He served as the president of the Mercury Seven Foundation, which provides college science scholarships for deserving students.

Later that summer, a large number of East Germans fled to the West. On August 13, the East German government, with Soviet backing, closed the border between East and West Berlin and built a wall of concrete blocks and barbed wire along it. The Soviets posted armed guards along the wall to stop more East Germans from fleeing to the West. The **Berlin Wall** cut communications between the two parts of the city.

The Western Allies continued to support the independence of West Berlin. They could do little, however, to stop the building of the wall, which came to symbolize Communist repression.

✓ Reading Check **Explaining** Why did the Soviet Union build the Berlin Wall?

The Cuban Missile Crisis

The most dangerous Cold War dispute between the Americans and Soviets came in 1962. Once again the dispute involved Cuba.

In mid-October 1962, an American spy plane flying over Cuba made a disturbing discovery. Photographs revealed that the Soviets were building launching sites for nuclear missiles. These missiles could easily reach the United States in a matter of minutes.

For the next week, President Kennedy met secretly with advisers to determine how to deal with the **Cuban missile crisis.** They explored several options, including invading Cuba and bombing the missile sites. New spy photographs showed the bases nearing completion faster than expected. A decision had to be made.

On October 22, President Kennedy, speaking on national television, revealed the "secret, swift, and extraordinary buildup" of missiles in Cuba. Kennedy ordered the navy to blockade, or close off, Cuba until the Soviets removed the missiles. He threatened to destroy any Soviet ship that tried to break through the blockade. The president also declared:

❝It shall be the policy of this nation to regard any nuclear missile launched from Cuba against any nation in the Western Hemisphere as an attack by the Soviet Union on the United States.❞

NATIONAL GEOGRAPHIC — The Cuban Missile Crisis: October 14–28, 1962

Geography Skills

This map shows the range of the Soviet missiles in Cuba. Their accuracy fell off as range increased.
1. **Region** What parts of the United States could intermediate-range missiles reach?
2. **Analyzing Information** What strategy did the United States use to respond to the Soviet threat in Cuba?

The United States would respond, he warned, with a nuclear attack against the Soviet Union.

As the two superpowers neared the brink of nuclear war, people all over the world waited nervously. However, Khrushchev was not ready to back down, and Soviet ships—some carrying missiles—continued to approach Cuba.

Two days after Kennedy's announcement, a breakthrough occurred. Some Soviet ships nearing the blockade turned back.

However, some Soviet ships still headed toward Cuba, and work on the missile bases continued. The president's advisers worked on plans for an air attack on the missile sites—just in case.

After five agonizing days, when the world appeared on the brink of nuclear war, the Soviet ships turned back from the blockade. Soviet leaders also decided to withdraw their missiles from Cuba.

Having come so close to nuclear disaster, the superpowers worked to establish a better relationship. In the summer of 1963, Kennedy and Khrushchev created a direct telephone link, called the hot line, between Moscow and Washington to allow the leaders to communicate instantly in times of crisis.

That same summer, the two nations signed a treaty banning nuclear tests aboveground and underwater.

Rivalry in Space

The United States competed with the Soviet Union in another area during the Kennedy administration—outer space. The space race began when the Soviet Union launched *Sputnik,* the world's first successful satellite, in 1957. In April 1961, Soviet cosmonaut **Yuri Gagarin** (guh•GAHR•uhn) became the first person to orbit the earth. One month later, **Alan Shepard, Jr.,** became the first American to make a spaceflight.

Shortly after Shepard's flight, Kennedy challenged the nation to a great undertaking. In a speech to Congress, he said:

❝I believe that this nation should commit itself to achieving the goal, before this decade is out, of landing a man on the moon and returning him safely to the earth.❞

The president asked Congress for more money for **NASA** (the National Aeronautics and Space Administration), which ran the space program. NASA expanded its launching facility in Florida and built a control center in Houston, Texas.

Astronaut **John Glenn** thrilled the country in February 1962 when he orbited the earth in a spacecraft, the first American to do so. An even greater triumph for the space program came on July 20, 1969, with the **Apollo project.** Awestruck television viewers around the world watched the spacecraft *Eagle* land on the surface of the moon. Hours later, with millions still watching, astronaut **Neil Armstrong** took the first human step on the moon and announced: "That's one small step for a man, one giant leap for mankind." By the end of the Apollo project in 1972, 10 more Americans had landed on the moon.

✓ **Reading Check** **Explaining** Why did President Kennedy order a blockade of the island of Cuba?

SECTION 1 ASSESSMENT

Checking for Understanding

1. **Key Terms** Write a sentence in which you correctly use each of the following terms: guerrilla warfare, flexible response, executive order, exile, blockade, hot line. Below each sentence write the definition of the term used.

2. **Reviewing Facts** Who was the first American to orbit the earth in a spacecraft?

Reviewing Themes

3. **Geography and History** Why did West Berlin's location make it difficult for the allies to defend it?

Critical Thinking

4. **Making Inferences** Why do you think Khrushchev sent missiles to Cuba?

5. **Analyzing Information** Re-create the diagram below and identify strategies that the Kennedy administration considered to stop the buildup of missiles in Cuba.

Cuban missile crisis

Analyzing Visuals

6. **Geography Skills** Examine the map of the Cuban missile crisis on page 869. According to the map, was Washington, D.C., within the range of a medium ballistic missile? Could a medium-range missile reach Los Angeles?

Interdisciplinary Activity

Persuasive Writing Write a speech that President Kennedy might have written to defend his actions during the Cuban missile crisis. Use complete sentences except where fragments are appropriate.

War in Vietnam

Guide to Reading

Main Idea
U.S. military involvement in Vietnam increased steadily throughout the 1960s.

Key Terms
Vietcong, coup, escalate, search-and-destroy mission

Reading Strategy
Organizing Information Re-create the diagram below and fill in the main events that occurred after the Gulf of Tonkin Resolution.

Read to Learn
• how Vietnam became a divided country.
• why America increased its involvement in the Vietnam War.

Section Theme
Global Connections Unable to end the Vietnam War quickly, the United States found itself increasingly drawn into the conflict.

Preview of Events

♦1950	♦1960	♦1970

1954
Geneva Accords divide Vietnam

1959
Civil war in Vietnam begins

1964
Gulf of Tonkin Resolution passed

1968
More than 500,000 U.S. troops are in Vietnam

AN American Story

In March 1967 David Parks, an African American soldier serving in Vietnam, described an enemy attack on his camp: "I was asleep when the first shell exploded. The earth shook and I rolled to the ground as someone hollered, 'Incoming!' . . . I shook like jelly as the shrapnel burst all around our bunker. . . . All we could do was open up with our 50-caliber and small arms. . . . I'm not sure the native people are with us. They smile at us in the daytime and their sons shoot at us at night. It's hard to spot the real enemy."

The U.S. and Vietnam

In the early 1960s, the United States became involved in a fight against communism in Southeast Asia. The war in **Vietnam** did not unfold as Americans had hoped, however. General Maxwell Taylor, who served as American ambassador to Vietnam, reflected on the war in Vietnam years after it had ended:

❝First, we didn't know ourselves. We thought we were going into another Korean war, but this was a different country. Secondly, we didn't know our South Vietnamese allies. We never understood them, and that was another surprise. And we knew even less about North Vietnam.❞

Origins of the War

The roots of the Vietnam conflict can be traced back to World War II, when Japanese forces captured the French colony of Indochina in Southeast Asia. Vietnamese forces led by Communist **Ho Chi Minh** (hoh chee MIHN) fought against the Japanese.

When Japan surrendered at the end of World War II, Ho Chi Minh declared Vietnam's independence. The French, however, were unwilling to give up their empire. Their Indochina colony—the present-day nations of Cambodia, Laos, and Vietnam—was among the richest of France's colonies, supplying such valuable resources as rice, rubber, and tin. Ho Chi Minh and his forces fought the French in a long, bloody war, finally defeating the French in 1954 at Dien Bien Phu.

The Geneva Accords

That same year, diplomats from the United States, France, Great Britain, the Soviet Union, China, and Vietnam met in Geneva, Switzerland, to work out a peace agreement. According to the **Geneva Accords,** Vietnam would be divided temporarily. Ho Chi Minh's Communist nationalists would control the North.

Hanoi served as its capital. Non-Communist forces—supported by the United States—would control the South, with **Saigon** as the capital. Vietnam would be unified in 1956 after national elections.

Neither the United States nor South Vietnam had signed the agreement, but they did not oppose its provisions. At the same time, an American representative warned that the United States reserved the right to step in if Communist North Vietnam moved aggressively against the South.

In 1955 **Ngo Dinh Diem** (NOH DIHN deh •EHM), the French-educated Vietnamese leader, gained control of the government of South Vietnam. The following year, Diem, with American support, refused to hold the elections. Diem's brutal policies and his refusal to hold elections angered many Vietnamese.

Communist supporters of Ho Chi Minh remained in the South after Vietnam was divided. In the late 1950s, Diem launched a campaign to destroy the power of the Communists. In response, the Communists organized themselves as the **National Liberation Front** (NLF)—better known to Americans as the Vietcong. In 1959 the Vietcong, on orders from Ho Chi Minh, began a war against the Diem regime.

Ho Chi Minh

"The helicopter added a new dimension to warfare—mobility. The helicopter took soldiers into battle, supplied them, and evacuated the wounded and the dead."

A Growing American Role

The United States had replaced the French as the dominant foreign power in the South in 1955. If Communists took South Vietnam, President Eisenhower once said, the other countries of Southeast Asia would fall to communism like a row of dominoes—one right after the other. This **domino theory** helped shape American policy in Vietnam for the next 20 years.

To support South Vietnam, the Eisenhower administration sent the country billions of dollars in aid. It also dispatched a few hundred soldiers, who acted as advisers to the South Vietnamese government and army.

Like Eisenhower, President Kennedy saw Vietnam as part of the global struggle in the fight against communism. Kennedy sent more Special Forces troops—the Green Berets—to train and advise South Vietnamese troops. Kennedy also pressured Diem to make political and economic reforms to eliminate the conditions that had allowed communism to take root in the first place. But Diem refused to comply.

Instead of paying for new schools, health clinics, or land reform, American funds often ended up in the pockets of corrupt South Vietnamese officials. At the same time, North Vietnam sent aid and troops to the South to help the Vietcong in a guerrilla war against Diem that began in 1959.

The Diem government lost support throughout the country. His government took rights away from **Buddhists**—the majority of the people in South Vietnam—and favored Catholics, like himself. Buddhists responded with protests, some of which ended in bloodshed when government troops fired into the crowds.

In early 1963 Buddhist monks showed their opposition to Diem's rule by setting themselves on fire on busy streets. Horrifying photographs of monks engulfed in flames appeared in newspapers and on television screens around the world. The Kennedy administration found it difficult to continue to support Diem.

On November 1, 1963, a group of South Vietnamese army officers staged a coup—overthrew the government—and assassinated Diem. The

More than 7,500 American nurses served during the Vietnam conflict.

President Johnson wanted congressional support for expanding the American role in Vietnam. The opportunity to get that support came in August 1964, when North Vietnamese patrol boats allegedly attacked American destroyers in the Gulf of Tonkin near North Vietnam. Congress quickly passed a resolution that allowed the president to "take all necessary measures to repel any armed attack against the forces of the United States." The **Gulf of Tonkin Resolution** gave Johnson broad authority to use American forces in Vietnam.

In 1965 Johnson began to esca-late—gradually increase—United States involvement in Vietnam. The buildup included both ground troops and an air campaign.

United States Marines landed near **Da Nang,** South Vietnam, on March 8, 1965. During the next three years, the number of American troops in Vietnam increased sharply. About 180,000 soldiers were in Vietnam by the end of 1965, almost 400,000 by the end of 1966, and more than 500,000 by 1968.

The United States also unleashed an intense bombing campaign called Operation Rolling Thunder. Some planes attacked the **Ho Chi Minh Trail,** a network of roads, paths, and bridges that wound from North Vietnam through Cambodia and Laos into South Vietnam. North Vietnamese troops used this route to bring equipment south. Other planes targeted bridges, docks, factories, and military bases in the North.

The bombing increased in intensity from 1965 through 1968. By then American planes had dropped more bombs on North Vietnam than they had dropped on Germany, Italy, and Japan during World War II.

Fighting the War

The American troops found fighting a ground war in Vietnam difficult. Dense jungles, muddy trails, and swampy rice paddies hampered troop

Kennedy administration had supported the coup, but not the assassination. After President Kennedy was assassinated later that same month, the question of what to do in Vietnam fell on the shoulders of President **Lyndon B. Johnson.**

✓ **Reading Check** **Analyzing** How did the domino theory affect the decision regarding the conflict in Vietnam?

The Conflict Deepens

At the time of Kennedy's death, the United States had nearly 16,000 American troops in Vietnam as advisers. President Johnson sent Secretary of Defense **Robert McNamara** to Vietnam on a fact-finding mission.

McNamara told the president that South Vietnam could not resist the Vietcong rebels without more help from the United States. In a May 1964 conversation, taped but not made public until 1997, Johnson himself expressed doubts about American commitment. "I don't think it's worth fighting for," he said, "but I don't think we can get out." Nevertheless, as Vietcong attacks continued, the United States moved toward deeper involvement.

movement. The South Vietnamese army did not always fight effectively. As the Vietcong guerrillas blended with the population, American soldiers found it hard to tell friends and enemies apart.

The American forces began to conduct search-and-destroy missions. The goal was to seek out Vietcong or North Vietnamese units and destroy them. The Americans hoped to eventually defeat the Communists or force them to negotiate.

Ground troops coordinated their moves with air support. Patrols on the ground radioed their location, and helicopter gunships roared to the scene to blast the enemy with cannon and machine-gun fire.

Planes bombed areas of South Vietnam in an effort to drive guerrillas from their jungle cover. Both sides used planes to drop napalm, an explosive that burned intensely, to destroy jungle growth. North Vietnamese and Vietcong forces also used napalm in flamethrowers, devices that expel fuel or a burning stream of liquids. To improve visibility, chemical herbicides were sprayed in Vietnam to clear out forests and tall grasses. One herbicide, **Agent Orange,** is believed to have contaminated many Americans and Vietnamese, causing serious health problems.

Frustration Grows

The bombing of the Ho Chi Minh Trail and the North did not stop the constant flow of troops and equipment south. Neither did it break the morale of the North Vietnamese. As one of their leaders later said,

    ❝The Americans thought that the more bombs they dropped, the quicker we would fall to our knees and surrender. But the bombs heightened, rather than dampened, our spirit.❞

Picturing **History**

A wounded American soldier reaches for a fallen comrade. **How many American troops were in Vietnam by late 1967?**

875

Military I.D. tags, commonly called dog tags, included the wearer's name, branch of service, blood type, and religion, if desired by the wearer.

The search-and-destroy missions killed thousands of North Vietnamese and Vietcong troops—but the troops always seemed to be replaced. What Ho Chi Minh had said to the French became true again:

❝You can kill ten of my men for every one I kill of yours. But even at those odds, you will lose and I will win.❞

American troops advanced into rice paddies, jungles, and small villages and killed scores of Vietcong. Yet the next day, the same area had to be attacked again.

American soldiers grew frustrated. Philip Caputo, a young marine lieutenant, recalled the changing attitude:

❝When we marched into the rice paddies on that damp March afternoon, we carried, along with our packs and rifles, the implicit convictions that the Vietcong could be quickly beaten. We kept the packs and rifles; the convictions, we lost.❞

Debate in the White House

Officials in the Johnson administration saw the mounting Communist losses and believed at first that the United States could succeed. As the war dragged on, however, some government officials saw a gloomier situation. Secretary of Defense McNamara began to argue that the ground war and the air attacks had failed and that the war could not be won. Outside the nation's capital, opposition to the war grew. Soon it swelled to anger.

✓ **Reading Check** **Identifying** What is Agent Orange? What are its effects?

SECTION 2 ASSESSMENT

Checking for Understanding

1. **Key Terms** Use the following terms in sentences or short paragraphs: Vietcong, coup, escalate. Relate them by using two or more of the terms in each sentence or paragraph.
2. **Reviewing Facts** How many American troops were in Vietnam by the end of 1965?

Reviewing Themes

3. **Global Connections** How did President Johnson gain congressional approval to use American forces in Vietnam?

Critical Thinking

4. **Making Inferences** Explain how Americans' view of communism influenced policy to support South Vietnam.
5. **Organizing Information** Re-create the diagram below and explain the purpose of the military strategies.

Strategy	Purpose
Search-and-destroy missions	
Operation Rolling Thunder	

Analyzing Visuals

6. **Picturing History** Examine the photograph on page 875. Write a caption expressing what you think the soldier is saying to his fallen comrade.

Interdisciplinary Activity

Research and Sequencing Use books, magazines, and newspapers to learn about the plight of American POWs (prisoners of war) and MIAs (soldiers missing in action) in Vietnam. Make a time line to show what the government and private citizens have done on their behalf.

The Vietnam Years at Home

Guide to Reading

Main Idea
Many Americans opposed the nation's involvement in Vietnam. Many others believed that U.S. leaders were not doing enough to win the war.

Key Terms
counterculture, deferment, dove, hawk, credibility gap, silent majority

Reading Strategy
Organizing Information As you read the section, re-create the diagram below and state how you think people known as doves and hawks differed on these issues.

	The Draft	Escalation
Doves		
Hawks		

Read to Learn
• what factors contributed to the rise of the protest movement.
• how Americans at home responded to the war in Vietnam.

Section Theme
Continuity and Change As the war continued, disagreement over the nation's role in Vietnam grew.

Preview of Events

♦1967   ♦1968   ♦1969

October 1967
War protesters march on Pentagon

April 1968
Dr. Martin Luther King, Jr., is assassinated

June 1968
Robert F. Kennedy is assassinated

November 1968
Richard Nixon wins presidency

AN
American Story

    As the Vietnam War dragged on, Americans became divided over the U.S. presence in that country. Even reporters showed their biases when they covered the antiwar demonstrations at the Pentagon in 1967. On one hand, older reporters, who stood behind the police, wrote about radicals storming the Pentagon. On the other side of the police barricade, younger reporters wrote about the brutality of the U.S. Marshals. Each side of the generation gap firmly believed that its version of the story was correct.

The Youth Protest

    While fighting raged in Vietnam, the American people disagreed sharply over the war. Prowar and antiwar groups attacked each other with mounting anger. Antiwar demonstrators called President Johnson and his supporters "killers." Supporters of the war referred to the protesters as "traitors." The war seemed to split America—and much of the division resulted from what people called the **generation gap.**

As United States involvement in the war increased, so did opposition to it. Some Americans felt that the conflict in Vietnam was a civil war and should not involve the United States. Others were concerned that the cost of America's commitment to Vietnam was hurting domestic programs. All condemned the devastation of the countryside and lives lost during the course of the war.

Many who opposed the war were part of the counterculture, a movement that rejected traditional American values. Some common symbols of the counterculture—torn blue jeans and long hair for males—aroused opposition from parents. Popular music played a role in communicating the ideas of the counterculture.

Other parts of the counterculture represented a more serious challenge to traditional middle-class values. Some young people refused to follow customary social roles of study, work, and family. They aimed to reject aspects of American society—the competition for material goods and personal success.

Opposition to the Draft

Student protests targeted the selective service system—the **draft** that supplied soldiers for the war. The law required all men to register for the draft when they reached age 18. Opposition to the draft had two sources.

Those strongly opposed to American involvement in Vietnam believed that by forcing an end to the draft they could halt the supply of soldiers needed to fight there. Others called the draft unfair. Draft boards had the power to give

Texas business executive H. Ross Perot attempted to deliver food, medicine, mail, and clothing to U.S. prisoners of war in Vietnam.

people deferments that excused them from the draft for various reasons. Full-time students attending college—mostly from the middle class—received such deferments. As a result an increasing percentage of soldiers came from poor or working-class families. Many who opposed the draft argued that deferments discriminated against the poor.

Some protesters became **conscientious objectors,** claiming that their moral or religious beliefs prevented them from fighting in the war. Other protesters showed their opposition by burning their draft cards—their military registration forms. Congress responded with a law making the burning of draft cards a crime.

Doves and Hawks

Students and other opponents of the Vietnam War came to be called doves. Supporters of the war became known as hawks.

Across the nation more and more Americans came to view the war unfavorably. Some thought the United States should not be fighting in Vietnam. Others opposed the way the government conducted the war. Both hawks and doves criticized President Johnson for his handling of the war in Vietnam, and his approval rating declined dramatically.

The War Loses Support

As opposition to the war mounted, the opponents staged larger demonstrations. In October 1967, more than 50,000 people marched to the **Pentagon**—headquarters of the Defense Department—to protest the war.

Attacks by opponents of the war grew sharper and more bitter. The Secret Service, charged with guarding President Johnson, feared for his safety and urged him not to speak in public. He began to appear only before crowds known to be sympathetic.

The president had often urged people to come together to discuss issues calmly. "Let us reason together," he had said. By 1968 Americans showed less willingness to talk reasonably, and violent events often overtook discussion.

✓ Reading Check **Explaining** What are draft deferments? Who received them?

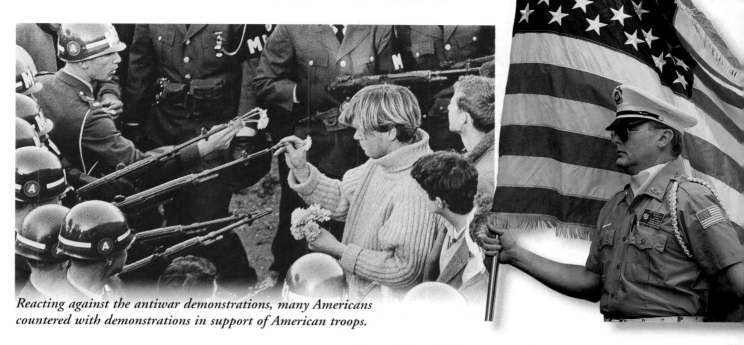

Reacting against the antiwar demonstrations, many Americans countered with demonstrations in support of American troops.

1968—Year of Crisis

The year 1968 opened with a shock for the American people. On January 23, North Korean boats seized the **USS Pueblo,** a navy spy ship cruising in international waters off the coast of Korea. The news that a foreign country had captured an American ship and its crew shocked the nation.

The next week brought another staggering blow as North Vietnam launched a major series of attacks in South Vietnam. As Americans soon learned, 1968 would be a long, dramatic, and very difficult year.

The Tet Offensive

On January 31, 1968, the North Vietnamese and Vietcong launched a series of attacks throughout South Vietnam. The attacks, which began on the Vietnamese new year—Tet—became known as the **Tet offensive.** Tet marked a turning point in the Vietnam War.

The Tet offensive targeted American military bases and South Vietnam's major cities. Vietcong troops raided the United States embassy in **Saigon,** the capital. The Vietcong also struck in **Hue,** the ancient capital of Vietnam, and fought for almost a month.

All across South Vietnam, Americans and South Vietnamese troops fought bravely to retake the cities. They finally drove the Vietcong back and inflicted thousands of casualties. The enormous losses that the Vietcong suffered forced North Vietnam to take over a larger share of the fighting. In military terms, the Americans and the South Vietnamese won the battle.

Impact Back Home

In the United States, however, the Tet offensive turned many more Americans against the war—and against President Johnson. The sight of Vietcong guerrillas killing Americans in the embassy shocked television viewers. The many days needed to defeat the assault on Hue undermined the army's statements about the United States winning the war.

Major newspapers and magazines openly criticized the Johnson administration's conduct of the war. The *Wall Street Journal* wrote, "The American people should be getting ready to accept . . . the prospect that the whole Vietnam effort may be doomed."

Most Americans seemed to agree. Fewer people believed that the army was making progress in the war. More people believed that the army was losing ground. The Johnson administration developed a credibility gap—fewer people trusted its statements about the war.

As opposition to the war grew, President Johnson faced challenges in his own party. In late 1967, Democratic senator **Eugene McCarthy** of Minnesota had announced that he would run for the party's nomination for the presidency as a protest against the war. Not well known, McCarthy seemed to have little chance of winning. In the March 12 primary in New Hampshire, however,

TWO VIEWPOINTS

Should We Be Fighting the Vietnam War?

As the war in Vietnam dragged on, political support for it began to evaporate. While government politicians coaxed Americans to support goals of liberty and democracy, antiwar protesters counted the corpses sent home and argued that the war was useless.

President Johnson addresses the nation, March 31, 1968

Tonight I renew the offer I made in August—to stop the bombardment of North Vietnam. We ask that talks begin promptly, that they be serious talks on the substance of peace. . . .

There is division in the American house now. There is divisiveness among us all tonight. And holding the trust that is mine, as President of all the people, I cannot disregard the peril to the progress of the American people and the hope and the prospect of peace for all peoples. . . .

Accordingly, I shall not seek, and I will not accept, the nomination of my party for another term as your President.

But let men everywhere know, however, that a strong, a confident, and a vigilant America stands ready tonight to seek an honorable peace—and stands ready tonight to defend an honored cause—whatever the price, whatever the burden, whatever the sacrifices that duty may require. . . .

Walter Cronkite, news broadcaster, after the Tet offensive, February 27, 1968

We have too often been disappointed by the optimism of the American leaders, both in Vietnam and Washington, to have faith any longer in the silver linings they find in the darkest clouds. . . . To say that we are closer to victory today is to believe, in the face of evidence, the optimists who have been wrong in the past. To suggest we are on the edge of defeat is to yield to unreasonable pessimism. To say that we are mired in stalemate seems the only realistic, yet unsatisfactory conclusion. . . .

[I]t is increasingly clear to this reporter that the only rational way out then will be to negotiate, not as victors, but as an honorable people who lived up to their pledge to defend democracy, and did the best they could.

Walter Cronkite

Learning From History

1. What does Johnson mean by "division in the American house"?
2. Why might Americans like Walter Cronkite be frustrated with the war?
3. Do the president's words seem realistic? How might Cronkite respond to the president's address?

McCarthy surprised everyone by taking 42 percent of the popular vote. Although Johnson won the primary, McCarthy's strong showing indicated widespread opposition to the war.

Later, another antiwar candidate entered the race. **Robert F. Kennedy,** attorney general during his brother's presidency and now a senator from New York, announced that he, too, would seek the Democratic nomination.

The President Responds

Events in Vietnam and the growing antiwar movement disturbed President Johnson. Following the Tet offensive, the American commander in Vietnam, General **William Westmoreland,** had requested still more troops. Instead of agreeing, the president ordered a reevaluation of the war. He also reevaluated his own campaign for reelection in 1968.

On March 31, 1968, after consulting advisers, President Johnson appeared on television to announce a "new step toward peace"—he would halt the bombing of North Vietnam's cities. He asked North Vietnam for a comparable action so that peace negotiations could begin.

The president concluded his speech with a startling announcement. He said, "I shall not seek, and I will not accept, the nomination of my party for another term as your president."

✓**Reading Check** Identifying What candidates from President Johnson's own party challenged him?

Violence Erupts

A few days after Johnson's withdrawal from the presidential race, tragedy struck the nation. A sniper in Memphis, Tennessee, shot and killed

After Robert Kennedy's death in June 1968, a divided Democratic convention met in Chicago. Chicago mayor Richard Daley had barbed wire set up at the convention hall to keep out antiwar protesters. **How did most Americans react to the violence in Chicago?**

Dr. Martin Luther King, Jr., the leading activist in the civil rights movement.

The King assassination triggered a rash of riots across the country. Army troops were called on to control unruly crowds in various cities. Already saddened by King's death, Americans worried about the renewed urban violence.

While the nation agonized over unrest at home and war abroad, the presidential race picked up speed. Vice President **Hubert H. Humphrey** joined Eugene McCarthy and Robert Kennedy in seeking the Democratic nomination. Kennedy edged out McCarthy in a number of primary elections, but McCarthy rebounded and scored a primary victory in Oregon. Humphrey, meanwhile, avoided the primaries. He gathered support among Democratic Party leaders, who in some states chose the delegates.

In early June 1968, Kennedy and McCarthy faced each other in the primary election in California, the state with the most delegates. That night, after Kennedy won, an assassin shot and killed him—and the nation reeled with the shock of yet another assassination.

The Democratic Convention

By the time the Democrats held their convention in **Chicago,** Humphrey appeared to have enough votes to win the nomination. As a long-time supporter of civil rights and labor causes, Humphrey had considerable backing in his party. As a supporter of Johnson's Vietnam policy, however, Humphrey was linked to the prowar faction of the party.

Antiwar Democrats felt angry and excluded from the convention. Tension filled the air. When trouble broke out, though, it did not occur as much in the convention hall as in the city's streets.

Frustrated by the almost certain victory of Humphrey, thousands of antiwar activists flocked to Chicago to protest. Chicago's mayor, **Richard J. Daley,** feared violence from the demonstrators and had the police out in force. The police made some arrests the first two nights, but no major problems developed.

On the third day, the antiwar protesters planned to march to the convention site to protest Humphrey's nomination. Police blocked the marchers at the hall. When the marchers headed in another direction, the police stopped them again. The protesters began to pelt the police with sticks and bottles. The police threw tear gas and charged in, wielding nightsticks. They pursued those who fled, beating some and arresting many.

Humphrey won the Democratic nomination, but the violence outside and the anger within the hall—all shown on television—had damaged his candidacy. The Democrats appeared unable to control their own convention. Humphrey admitted, "Chicago was a catastrophe."

✓ **Reading Check** **Identifying** What two popular leaders were assassinated in 1968?

Election of 1968

A majority of Americans disapproved of the police action in Chicago, but at the same time, strongly opposed the actions of the protesters. The years of protest and dissent had taken their toll and a backlash had set in. Most Americans fervently wished for a return to "law and order."

The Wallace Candidacy

One presidential candidate who used the "law and order" theme was Governor **George C. Wallace** of Alabama. Running as a third-party candidate, Wallace promised to crack down on "long-hair . . . draft card-burning youth." In addition, he criticized efforts to integrate schools by busing students and ridiculed "pointy-headed" bureaucrats in Washington for telling people how to run their lives.

Wallace's tough stand on law and order and his appeal to racial fears attracted many voters. Some political reporters predicted Wallace could win as much as 20 percent of the vote.

The "Silent Majority"

The Republican presidential nominee, former vice president **Richard M. Nixon,** also tried to tap into voters' growing conservative sentiment. Nixon pledged to represent the "quiet voice" of the "great majority of Americans, the non-shouters, the nondemonstrators." He called these people the "silent majority." Declaring that the "first civil right of every American is to be free from domestic violence," Nixon promised a return to law and order.

Nixon remained vague on his views of Vietnam. He promised that he would achieve "peace with honor," but he would not provide details of his plan.

During the election campaign, Nixon sought to win some of the traditionally Democratic Southern states with the law-and-order issue. This "Southern strategy" paid off. Although Wallace did take five Southern states and 46 electoral votes, Nixon won seven Southern states and their 78 electoral votes.

Nixon Wins

The popular vote was close. Nixon edged out Humphrey by about 500,000 votes—a difference of less than 1 percent. In the electoral vote, however, Nixon won a solid majority—301 votes to Humphrey's 191.

Nixon entered the presidency with the votes of only 43.4 percent of the people. Nixon and Wallace together, however, had won almost 57 percent of the vote. It seemed that a substantial majority of Americans wanted the government to restore order.

✓ Reading Check **Identifying** What presidential candidate provided a strong third-party challenge in 1968?

SECTION 3 ASSESSMENT

Checking for Understanding

1. **Key Terms** Define counterculture, deferment, dove, hawk, credibility gap, silent majority.
2. **Reviewing Facts** What did conscientious objectors declare?

Analyzing Themes

3. **Continuity and Change** What was the result of the 1968 presidential election?

Critical Thinking

4. **Making Inferences** How do you think the credibility gap affected Johnson's ability to be an effective president?
5. **Determining Cause and Effect** Re-create the diagram below and explain why support for war in Vietnam eroded.

Support for the war effort falls

Analyzing Visuals

6. **Picturing History** Look at the photographs on page 879. Write a paragraph to describe what is happening.

Interdisciplinary Activity

Research Interview friends and relatives who lived during the Vietnam War era to see how people in your community reacted to the conflict. Present an oral report of your findings.

Technology SKILLBUILDER

Building a Database

Why Learn This Skill?

Have you ever collected baseball cards or cataloged the CDs in your collection? Have you ever kept a list of the names and addresses of your friends and relatives? If you have collected information and kept some sort of list or file, then you have created a database.

Learning the Skill

An electronic database is a collection of facts that are stored in files on the computer. The information is organized in fields.

A database can be organized and reorganized in any way that is useful to you. By using a database management system (DBMS)—special software developed for record keeping—you can easily add, delete, change, or update information. You give commands to the computer telling it what to do with the information, and it follows your commands. When you want to retrieve information, the computer searches through the files, finds the information, and displays it on the screen.

Practicing the Skill

Richard M. Nixon is one of the presidents discussed in this chapter. Follow these steps to build a database of the political and cultural events that took place during his presidency.

1 Determine what facts you want to include in your database.

2 Follow instructions in the DBMS you are using to set up fields. Then enter each item of data into its assigned field.

Nixon greets well-wishers at a campaign rally.

3 Determine how you want to organize the facts in the database—chronologically by the date of the event, or alphabetically by the name of the event.

4 Follow the instructions in your computer program to place the information in order of importance.

5 Check that the information in your database is all correct. If necessary, add, delete, or change information or fields.

Applying the Skill

Building a Database Bring current newspapers to class. Using the steps just described, build a database of political figures mentioned in the newspapers. Explain to a partner why the database is organized the way it is and how it might be used in this class.

SECTION 4 Nixon and Vietnam

Guide to Reading

Main Idea
President Nixon put a plan in place to train and equip South Vietnamese soldiers to take the place of American troops.

Key Terms
Vietnamization, martial law, MIAs

Reading Strategy
Organizing Information As you read the section, re-create the diagram below and identify three strategies Nixon used to end the war.

Nixon strategies

Read to Learn
• what steps Nixon took to end the war in Vietnam.
• what the costs of the Vietnam War were.

Section Theme
Continuity and Change President Nixon changed the strategy of the conflict that included intense bombing and Vietnamization.

Preview of Events

♦1968   ♦1970   ♦1972   ♦1974

June 1969
Nixon begins to withdraw troops from Vietnam

April 1970
Nixon sends troops to Cambodia

May 1970
Six students killed at Kent State and Jackson State

January 1973
Paris peace accords end U.S. involvement in Vietnam

AN
American Story

President Nixon's inauguration in January 1969 took place on a cold, gloomy day. Hundreds of demonstrators chanting antiwar slogans and holding anti-Nixon posters stood along Pennsylvania Avenue in Washington, D.C. At one point Nixon's limousine was pelted with sticks, stones, and bottles. Offended by this behavior, World War II veterans shouted at the demonstrators, labeling the protesters "communists" and "traitors." This marked the first time an inaugural parade was disrupted in the 180 years of the presidency.

A New Strategy

In his Inaugural Address in January 1969, **Richard M. Nixon** appealed to the American people for calm:

❝We cannot learn from one another until we stop shouting at one another—until we speak quietly enough so that our words can be heard as well as our voices.❞

Nixon had campaigned on a pledge of "peace with honor" in Vietnam. He wanted to pull American forces out of Vietnam, but he did not want American withdrawal to be seen as a sign of defeat. Nixon's strategy of peace with honor had three parts—reform of the selective service system, giving South Vietnam more responsibility in fighting the war, and expanding the bombing campaign.

Under President Nixon the selective service system changed. College students could no longer obtain draft deferments, only 19-year-olds could be called for service in Vietnam, and draftees would be chosen by lottery on the basis of their birthday. Protests against the draft faded with these reforms because the government began calling up fewer young men and because President Nixon promised to eliminate the selective service in the future.

President Nixon started withdrawing American troops from Vietnam in June 1969. He did not, however, want to abandon South Vietnam to the Communists. By the end of the year, Nixon had developed his plan of Vietnamization and announced it to the American people. **Vietnamization** called for the army of South Vietnam to take a more active role in fighting the war—and for Americans to become less involved. While stepping up the training of South Vietnamese soldiers, American ground troops would gradually withdraw from the country.

When Nixon took office in January 1969, more than 540,000 American troops were in Vietnam. By the end of 1970, the number had fallen to 334,000 and by 1971 to about 60,000.

In the third part of his Vietnam policy, Nixon expanded the bombing campaign. Hoping to relieve pressure on troops in South Vietnam, the president ordered the bombing of enemy supply routes and hideouts in neighboring Cambodia and Laos. Although the Nixon administration sought publicity for changes to the draft and the

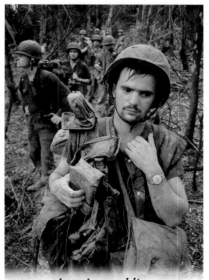

American soldiers on patrol

withdrawal of troops, it kept the bombing of Cambodia secret.

Reading Check **Explaining** Why did the U.S. expand its bombing campaign?

Renewed Opposition at Home

A new round of antiwar demonstrations began in late 1969, reflecting the growing sentiment for ending the war. In October more than 300,000 people took part in an antiwar protest in Washington, D.C.

The government also tried to end the war through peace talks with North Vietnam. **Henry Kissinger,** the president's national security adviser, represented the United States in the Paris talks. The United States had launched the bombing campaign to persuade the North Vietnamese to agree to settlement terms, but the North Vietnamese adopted a wait-and-see attitude. They believed that the strength of the antiwar movement in the United States would force the Americans to withdraw.

The new antiwar protests and North Vietnam's unyielding attitude alarmed President Nixon. In his speech on Vietnamization in November, he appealed to the "silent majority" of Americans for support for his policy. "North Vietnam cannot defeat or humiliate the United States," he said. "Only Americans can do that."

Expanding the War

Further conflict gripped Southeast Asia when Cambodia plunged into a civil war between Communist and non-Communist forces. Nixon decided in April 1970 to send American troops to destroy Communist bases in Cambodia.

The attack aroused outrage in Congress and elsewhere. By sending American troops to Cambodia, critics charged, Nixon invaded a neutral country and overstepped his constitutional authority as president.

December 1972 Giant B-52 bombers, powered by jet engines, were among the aircraft used to fly more than 2,000 missions against North Vietnam in the "Christmas" bombing. It was the most concentrated bombing of the war—and in history.

CHINA

BURMA

Dien Bien Phu

Hanoi
Haiphong

NORTH VIETNAM

Gulf of Tonkin

20°N

LAOS

Invasion of Laos, Feb. 8–March 1971

17th Parallel
Demilitarized Line

17°N

Quang Tri
Khe Sanh

Hue
Da Nang
Chu Lai

My Lai massacre, March 16, 1968

THAILAND

N
W E
S

Invasion of Cambodia, May 1–June 29, 1970

Pleiku

HO CHI MINH TRAIL

Gulf of Thailand

Ban Me Thuot

CAMBODIA

SOUTH VIETNAM

Phnom Penh

Saigon

Can Tho

Mekong Delta

10°N

South China Sea

0   200 miles
0   200 kilometers
Miller Cylindrical projection

110°E

→ Major U.S. and South Vietnamese troop movements

→ Major North Vietnamese supply lines

■ U.S. bases

Geography *Skills*

Throughout the war United States troops and the government of South Vietnam controlled the major cities.

1. Location Along what line of latitude did the demilitarized zone run?

2. Analyzing Information Through which countries did the Ho Chi Minh Trail run?

United States in the Vietnam War

United States Troops in Vietnam, 1965—1973

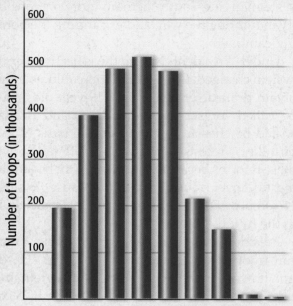

Source: *Statistical Abstract of the United States.*

Opposition to the War

1973 Cease-fire signed

1968 Tet offensive

1969 First withdrawal of U.S. troops

1965 U.S. escalates involvement

Source: *The Gallup Poll: Public Opinion.*

Picturing **History**

A stunned woman kneels beside the body of a student killed at Kent State. **What event sparked the student unrest at Kent State?**

PROTEST!

Kent State

The Cambodian invasion provoked a storm of antiwar protests on campuses across the nation. Most proceeded peacefully. However, two protests ended in tragedy.

At a protest at Kent State University in **Kent, Ohio,** students burned a military building on campus. Ohio's governor declared martial law—emergency military rule—on the campus and ordered 3,000 National Guard troops to Kent.

On May 4 armed troops arrived on campus. Eighteen-year-old Leone Keegan, a freshman, remembered going to class that morning:

> **❝**I saw all these young men in uniforms standing on the street corners with their rifles, and I was thinking, What is this?**❞**

At noon students gathered for a protest rally on the campus lawn. The National Guard members—young, inexperienced, and nervous—told the protesting students to leave. "Evacuate the area. You have no right to assemble," they shouted through bullhorns. The students shouted back, "We don't want your war." Some students threw stones.

The troops shot tear gas toward the students; many students ran. One National Guard unit chased some students between two buildings.

Then—for reasons that are unclear—the troops opened fire. ". . . [T]hey're killing us," screamed one student in disbelief. Four students were dead and at least nine more were wounded.

Jackson State

Violence flared again on May 15 at the nearly all-African American college of **Jackson State** in Mississippi. Following a night of campus violence, two students were shot and killed. Witnesses charged that the police had recklessly blasted the residence hall with shotguns. The police claimed they were protecting themselves from sniper fire.

A wave of student strikes followed the tragedies at Kent State and Jackson State. Hundreds of colleges and universities suspended classes or closed down completely.

The president took a hard line. The Kent State shootings, he said, "should remind us once again that when dissent turns to violence it invites tragedy." A commission that investigated events at Kent State found that the shootings were unjustified. A majority of Americans, however, seemed to agree with the president.

✓ **Reading Check** **Identifying** Who represented the United States in the Paris talks?

The Vietnam Veterans Memorial in Washington, D.C., designed by Maya Lin, carries the names of more than 58,000 Americans who died in Vietnam. **Why do you think this memorial has such an impact on those who see it?**

"Peace Is at Hand"

Meanwhile, the Nixon administration continued to negotiate with representatives of the North Vietnamese government. These talks stalled, however.

In March 1972, the North Vietnamese launched another major offensive in the South. Because the United States had few troops left in Vietnam, Nixon resumed bombing. Nixon ordered American planes to bomb targets near **Hanoi,** the capital of North Vietnam. He also ordered the navy to plant mines in North Vietnamese harbors.

The president stopped insisting that North Vietnam remove all its troops from South Vietnam before a full American withdrawal. Nixon sent Henry Kissinger to negotiate. In the fall of 1972—just before the presidential election in the United States—they reached a tentative agreement. "Peace is at hand," Kissinger announced.

His statement came too soon. The agreement collapsed because the South Vietnamese president objected to allowing North Vietnamese forces to remain in South Vietnam.

Paris Peace Accords

After his reelection, Nixon unleashed American airpower against North Vietnam. In December 1972, the heaviest bombardment of the war fell on North Vietnam's cities, provoking outrage in the United States and abroad.

Nixon stood firm, and North Vietnam returned to the peace talks. The Americans pressured the South Vietnamese to accept the peace terms. On January 27, 1973, the negotiators signed the peace agreement.

The United States agreed to pull its remaining troops out of the country. The North Vietnamese agreed to return all American prisoners of war. While the Paris peace accords ended American involvement in Vietnam, they did not end the conflict.

The War Ends

The North Vietnamese never abandoned their goal of unifying Vietnam under their control. In early 1975 they launched a final major offensive. The weakened South Vietnamese army collapsed suddenly on all fronts. Within a few weeks, North Vietnamese tanks reached the outskirts of Saigon.

As North Vietnamese forces closed in on Saigon, the last Americans scrambled to escape the country, some by helicopter from the roof of the American embassy. Thousands of Vietnamese citizens who had supported or worked for the Americans also fled to the United States. Many more could not escape. In the early hours of April 30, 1975, Saigon fell to the Communists. Soon after, South Vietnam surrendered. The long war was over.

✓ **Reading Check** Analyzing What was the result of the Paris peace agreements?

Legacy of the War

The Vietnam War took a staggering toll of life and suffering. More than one million Vietnamese—civilians as well as soldiers on one side or the other—died between 1965 and the end of the conflict. Vietnam lay in ruins with many villages destroyed.

More than 58,000 Americans were dead; 300,000 were wounded, many of them permanently disabled. The United States had poured more than $150 billion into the war.

About 2.7 million Americans had served in Vietnam. Unlike the veterans of World War II, they found no hero's welcome when they returned home. Many Americans simply wanted to forget the war. They paid little attention to those who had fought and sacrificed in Vietnam.

The relatives of the American soldiers who had been classified as missing in action, or as **MIAs,** continued to demand that the government press the Vietnamese for information. The Vietnamese did allow a number of American groups to search the countryside. As the years passed, however, the likelihood of finding anyone alive faded.

HISTORY Online

Student Web Activity
Visit taj.glencoe.com and click on **Chapter 30— Student Web Activities** for an activity on the Vietnam War.

A Step Toward Healing

The construction of the **Vietnam Veterans Memorial** in Washington, D.C., provided a step toward healing the country's wounds. Designed by **Maya Ying Lin,** the striking memorial is a polished black granite wall in the shape of a private's stripes. It bears the names of all the Americans who died or were missing in action in the conflict.

When they visit the wall, families, friends, and comrades in war seek out the names of those who fought in Vietnam and did not return. Since the memorial was dedicated in 1982, visitors have left thousands of keepsakes and remembrances there. The flowers, letters, poems, and pictures left at the wall pay a proud and moving tribute to the Americans who died in the service of their country.

✓ **Reading Check** Identifying What are MIAs?

SECTION 4 ASSESSMENT

Checking for Understanding

1. **Key Terms** Define Vietnamization, martial law, MIAs.
2. **Reviewing Facts** Why did Nixon's actions in Cambodia anger many people?

Analyzing Themes

3. **Global Connections** Explain the process of Vietnamization. Who proposed this plan?

Critical Thinking

4. **Drawing Conclusions** Do you think Nixon succeeded in attaining "peace with honor"? Explain.
5. **Sequencing Information** Re-create the time line below and identify key dates and events in the Vietnam War during the Nixon presidency.

June 1969   April 1975

Analyzing Visuals

6. **Geography Skills** Examine the map on page 886. Where was the demilitarized zone located?

Interdisciplinary Activity

Expository Writing Imagine you are a reporter during the Vietnam era. Research and write a news story on an aspect of the war that you find interesting. Use creative word choice and expression.

Chapter Summary

The Vietnam Era

1954
- Geneva Accords divide Vietnam

1957
- Soviet Union launches *Sputnik*

1959
- Civil War begins in Vietnam

1961
- Bay of Pigs invasion fails
- Berlin Wall erected

1962
- Cuban Missile crisis occurs

1963
- John F. Kennedy is assassinated
- Lyndon B. Johnson sworn in as president

1964
- Gulf of Tonkin Resolution passed

1967
- More than 500,000 U.S. troops in Vietnam
- War protesters march on Pentagon

1968
- North Korea captures USS *Pueblo*
- North Vietnamese launch Tet offensive
- Dr. Martin Luther King, Jr., is assassinated
- Robert Kennedy is assassinated
- Violence erupts at Democratic convention in Chicago
- Richard Nixon wins presidency

1969
- Neil Armstrong walks on the moon
- Nixon begins to withdraw troops from Vietnam

1970
- Nixon sends troops to Cambodia
- Six students killed at Kent State and Jackson State

1973
- Paris peace accords end U.S. involvement in Vietnam

Reviewing Key Terms

On a sheet of paper, use all of the following terms to write sentences relating to the information in the chapter.

1. flexible response
2. hot line
3. Vietcong
4. domino theory
5. escalate
6. deferment
7. Vietnamization
8. MIAs

Reviewing Key Facts

9. Why did the Soviets build the Berlin Wall?
10. Why did President Kennedy blockade Cuba?
11. In what way did the Gulf of Tonkin Resolution extend President Johnson's power?
12. What is Agent Orange?
13. What was the Tet offensive?

Critical Thinking

14. **Comparing** Why do you think most Americans supported the war effort during World War II, but many did not support the Vietnam War?

15. **Drawing Conclusions** President Johnson made the decision not to run for reelection in 1968. Determine whether you believe that President Johnson's decision was a good one or a bad one for the country. On a diagram like the one shown, write at least three reasons to support your decision.

Reasons why LBJ should or should not run

Practicing Skills

16. **Using a Database** Prepare a database of the major battles of the Vietnam War involving United States troops. At your local library, research to find information about the sites of the battles, who the commanding officer was, how many American soldiers were killed or wounded at the sites, and how many North Vietnamese were killed or wounded. Share your database with the rest of your class.

Geography and History Activity

Study the two maps on this page; then answer the questions that follow.

Self-Check Quiz
Visit taj.glencoe.com and click on **Chapter 30—Self-Check Quizzes** to prepare for the chapter test.

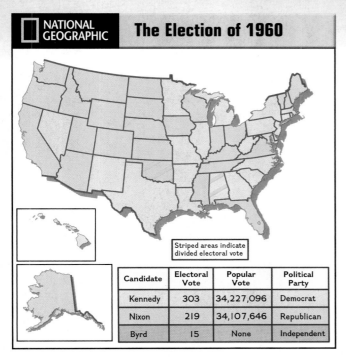

NATIONAL GEOGRAPHIC — **The Election of 1960**

Striped areas indicate divided electoral vote

Candidate	Electoral Vote	Popular Vote	Political Party
Kennedy	303	34,227,096	Democrat
Nixon	219	34,107,646	Republican
Byrd	15	None	Independent

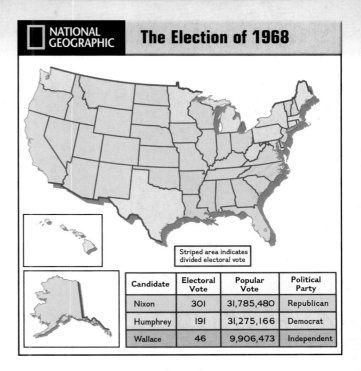

NATIONAL GEOGRAPHIC — **The Election of 1968**

Striped area indicates divided electoral vote

Candidate	Electoral Vote	Popular Vote	Political Party
Nixon	301	31,785,480	Republican
Humphrey	191	31,275,166	Democrat
Wallace	46	9,906,473	Independent

17. Region In what regions of the country did Kennedy receive the strongest support in the 1960 election? In which regions was support for Kennedy weakest?

18. Region What regions supported Nixon in 1960? In 1968?

19. Region Explain why you agree or disagree with the following: The Northeast was Nixon's strongest region in 1968.

Citizenship Cooperative Activity

20. Individual Involvement With two other students, research to find what opportunities exist in your community for individual involvement on issues. For example, does your community have a recycling program? Find out what you might do to assist in these efforts. Report your findings to the class.

 Alternative Assessment

21. Portfolio Writing Activity United States involvement in Vietnam officially ended in 1973. What effects of the war are still part of American life? Write a paragraph discussing what these effects are.

Standardized Test Practice

Directions: Choose the *best* answer to the following question.

What happened in Vietnam after the last American troops left?

A The process of Vietnamization began.

B South Vietnam surrendered to North Vietnam.

C The two sides met at Paris.

D President Johnson decided not to seek a second term.

Test-Taking Tip

Be aware of the order of events asked about in a question. This question asks about events in Vietnam after the United States pulled out. Choice **A** is an event that occurred before the pull out.

UNIT
11

Modern America

1968–Present

Why It Matters

Incredible change marked the last part of the twentieth century. The Cold War came to an end. Faith in government was shaken by presidential scandal. As the United States entered a new century, new challenges emerged. The American people responded to terrorism by looking for new ways to preserve and protect their ideals in a changing world. The following resources offer more information about this period in American history.

Decorative flag, computer art

Primary Sources Library

See pages 978–979 for primary source readings to accompany Unit 11.

Use the American history **Primary Source Document Library CD-ROM** *to find additional primary sources about Modern America.*

The International
Space Station

"*America, at its best, is compassionate.*"

—President George W. Bush,
2001 Inaugural Address

CHAPTER 31

Search for Stability

1968–1981

Why It Matters

During the 1960s and 1970s, the American people's view of the nation and the government changed. Some believed that the United States had lost its position as the economic and political leader of the free world. Yet the American system of constitutional government worked and survived.

The Impact Today

Today many Americans continue to express doubts about the political system. Mistrust of politicians, especially "Washington insiders," has reduced voter turnout in elections. It has also spurred the creation of political movements outside the two major parties.

The American Journey Video *The chapter 31 video, "Watergate," details the events in the Watergate controversy.*

1972
- Nixon visits Beijing
- SALT I signed

1973
- Watergate hearings

1974
- Nixon resigns presidency

United States
PRESIDENTS

Nixon
1969–1974

Ford
1974–1977

1966   1970   1974

 World

1967
- Six-Day Arab-Israeli War

Temporarily...
10 GALLONS
PER CUSTOMER
We appreciate
your business
& cooperation.

1973
- OPEC imposes embargo of oil to U.S.

Celebrating the Bicentennial Fireworks light up the Statue of Liberty during celebration of the nation's 200th birthday on July 4, 1976.

Evaluating Information Study Foldable
Make and use this foldable to organize information about America's search for stability at the end of the twentieth century.

Step 1 Mark the midpoint of a side edge of one sheet of paper. Then fold the outside edges in to touch the midpoint.

Step 2 Fold in half from side to side.

Step 3 Open and cut along the inside fold lines to form four tabs. Label your foldable as shown.

What led to better relations with China?

What happened in Iran in 1979?

Why did President Nixon resign?

Who won the election of 1980?

Cut along the fold lines on both sides.

Reading and Writing As you read the chapter, search for the answers to these four questions. Write answers under each of the tabs.

1977
- Panama Canal treaties signed

1979
- Iranians take 52 U.S. hostages
- Accident at Three Mile Island

1980
- U.S. boycotts Moscow Olympics

1981
- Iranians release U.S. hostages

Carter 1977–1981

Reagan 1981–1989

1978

1982

1975
- 36 nations agree to Helsinki Accords

1978
- First test-tube baby born in London

1979
- Soviet troops invade Afghanistan

1981
- Scientists identify AIDS

HISTORY
Online

Chapter Overview
Visit taj.glencoe.com and click on **Chapter 31— Chapter Overviews** to preview chapter information.

Nixon's Foreign Policy

Guide to Reading

Main Idea
President Nixon tried to ease cold war tensions but pursued active policies in the Middle East and Latin America.

Key Terms
détente, balance of power, embargo, shuttle diplomacy

Reading Strategy
Classifying Information As you read the section, re-create the diagram below and describe the goals of these strategies and policies.

Goals

Détente: | Balance of power: | Shuttle diplomacy:

Read To Learn
• how Richard Nixon changed U.S. political relations with the Soviet Union and China.
• what actions the U.S. took regarding the Middle East and Latin America.

Section Theme
Global Connections Richard Nixon pursued a very active foreign policy.

Preview of Events

♦1970   ♦1972   ♦1974

April 1971
American table-tennis team visits China

February 1972
President Nixon visits Beijing

May 1972
Leaders sign the first Strategic Arms Limitation Treaty

October 1973
Arab countries impose oil embargo on the U.S.

AN American Story

To improve relations with the Communist world, President Richard Nixon made a historic visit to China in February 1972. Nixon later described how he felt upon his arrival in Beijing, the Chinese capital: ". . . 'The Star Spangled Banner' had never sounded so stirring to me as on that windswept runway in the heart of Communist China. . . . As we left the airport, [Chinese leader Zhou Enlai] said, 'Your handshake came over the vastest ocean in the world—twenty-five years of no communication.' "

Easing the Cold War

In his Inaugural Address on January 20, 1969, President Richard M. Nixon told the American people, "The greatest honor . . . is the title of peacemaker." Many Americans wondered whether Nixon fit the role of peacemaker. During his years in Congress, he had gained a reputation as a fierce enemy of communism. Few people imagined that Nixon, the anti-Communist crusader, would introduce policies to improve America's relations with the Communist world.

Behind the Iron Curtain

President Nixon intended to leave his mark on foreign policy. He hoped to build a more stable, peaceful world by reaching out to the Soviet Union and the People's Republic of China. In the summer of 1969, Nixon visited several countries, including Romania—the first time an American president had gone behind the iron curtain. Nixon wanted to find areas of common interest and cooperation with these Cold War opponents.

Détente

To help him in this task, Nixon appointed **Henry Kissinger,** a Harvard University professor, as his national security adviser. Kissinger and Nixon shared a belief in *realpolitik*—policies based on national interests rather than political ideology. They believed that peace among nations would come through negotiation rather than through threats or force. President Nixon formulated a foreign policy plan of détente—attempts at relaxing, or easing, international tensions. As détente replaced confrontation, the United States and Communist states could begin working together to resolve issues that divided them.

Nixon realized that détente would work only if a balance of power existed. A balance of power is a distribution of power among nations to prevent any one nation from becoming too powerful. "It will be a safer world and a better world," he declared,

> ❝if we have a strong, healthy United States, Europe, Soviet Union, China, Japan—each balancing the other, not playing one against the other.❞

Picturing **History**

Henry Kissinger (below) helped President Nixon handle foreign policy matters. Premier Zhou Enlai and President Nixon (right) inspect troops during Nixon's 1972 visit to China. **When did the United States and China establish full diplomatic relations?**

China

Since the Communist takeover of China in 1949, the United States had refused to recognize the **People's Republic of China,** the most populated nation on the earth. Instead the United States recognized the anti-Communist Chinese government under **Chiang Kai-shek** in exile on the island of Taiwan.

By the time Nixon became president, however, each side had good reasons for wanting to improve relations. China distrusted and feared the Soviet Union. The United States hoped that recognition of China would help end the war in Vietnam and drive a deeper wedge between the two Communist powers.

The winds of change began to blow in the fall of 1970 when Nixon told reporters that he wanted to go to China. Noting this change in tone, the Chinese responded by inviting an American table-tennis team to visit the country in April 1971. A week later the United States announced the opening of trade with China.

"Ping-Pong diplomacy" was accompanied by secret talks between American and Chinese officials about forging closer ties between the two nations. After Kissinger made a secret trip to China in July 1971, President Nixon announced that he would visit **Beijing,** the Chinese capital, "to seek the normalization of relations."

In February 1972 Nixon arrived in China for a week-long visit. Nixon and China's premier **Zhou Enlai** agreed to allow greater scientific and cultural exchange and to resume trade. Although formal diplomatic relations were not established until 1979, Nixon's trip marked the first formal contact with China in more than 25 years.

The Soviet Union

Nixon followed his history-making trip to China with a visit to **Moscow,** the Soviet capital, in May 1972. The Soviets eagerly welcomed the thaw in Cold War politics. They wanted to prevent a Chinese-American alliance and to slow the costly arms race. They also hoped to gain access to United States technology and to buy badly needed American grain. Soviet leader **Leonid Brezhnev** remarked,

66 There must be room in this world for two great nations with different systems to live together and work together. 99

While in Moscow, President Nixon signed the Strategic Arms Limitation Treaty, or **SALT I.** This landmark treaty, the result of talks begun in 1969, restricted the number of certain types of nuclear missiles in American and Soviet arsenals. Although SALT I did not end the arms race, it greatly reduced tensions between the United States and the Soviet Union.

The United States and the Soviet Union also agreed to work together in trade and science. Nixon—and the world—hoped that a new era of cooperation would bring greater stability to world affairs.

Reading Check **Identifying** What is détente?

High Lob

Analyzing *Political Cartoons*

"Ping-Pong diplomacy" improved relations between the United States and the People's Republic of China. **What nations do the players represent?**

Picturing **History**

Many Palestinians lived in exile, scattered throughout the Middle East, North Africa, and Europe. **What was the cause of the Yom Kippur War?**

The Middle East

President Nixon's foreign policy aimed to maintain world stability without being drawn into regional disputes. The president wanted to avoid any involvement that might lead to another situation like Vietnam. Nixon stated that the United States would help in "the defense and development of allies and friends" but not take "basic responsibility" for the future of those nations. A crisis soon arose in the Middle East that tested this policy.

Arab-Israeli Tensions

Since the founding of the Jewish state of Israel in 1948, the United States had supported Israel in its struggles against its Arab neighbors. Tensions between Israel and the Arab states had erupted in war in 1948, 1956, and 1967. The Six-Day War of 1967 left Israel in control of east Jerusalem, the **West Bank,** the **Golan Heights** of Syria, and the **Gaza Strip** and **Sinai Peninsula** of Egypt. The 1967 war also increased the number of Arab refugees. Thousands of Palestinians now lived in Israeli-held territory, and thousands more lived in neighboring Arab states. The Palestinians' demand for their own homeland became another source of instability.

Yom Kippur War

War erupted again on October 6, 1973. Egypt and Syria attacked Israel in an attempt to regain territory lost in the Six-Day War. Because the attack occurred on Yom Kippur, a major Jewish holiday, the conflict became known as the **Yom Kippur War.**

The United States pressured Israel to accept a cease-fire. A cease-fire came, but not before the Israelis had regained most of the territory lost in the initial Arab advance. Israel also had taken additional territory from Syria and Egypt.

Angry at the United States for supporting Israel, Arab oil-producing states imposed an embargo—a ban on shipments—of oil to the United States and to other nations not seen as "friendly." The embargo caused an oil shortage in the United States. Long lines of cars formed at gas pumps and Americans became angry as gas prices skyrocketed.

Shuttle Diplomacy

President Nixon sent Kissinger, now secretary of state, to the region to gain the trust of Arab leaders and to negotiate some type of agreement between Israel and its Arab neighbors. During the next two years, Kissinger engaged in shuttle diplomacy—traveling back and forth between the capitals of Israel, Egypt, and Syria trying to resolve the oil crisis and forge a lasting peace.

Early in 1974, **Golda Meir,** the prime minister of Israel, and **Anwar el-Sadat,** the president of Egypt, reached agreements that separated Israeli and Arab forces in the Sinai Peninsula and Golan Heights. Then in March 1974, Kissinger persuaded the Arab nations to end the oil embargo. Kissinger also improved relations with Egypt, the largest and most powerful Arab state, by promising large amounts of foreign aid.

Israeli leader Golda Meir

☑ **Reading Check** **Summarizing** What happened in the U.S. as a result of the oil embargo?

Latin America

The Nixon administration sought to protect its interests in Latin America and to prevent the spread of communism. In 1970 the South American country of **Chile** elected **Salvador Allende** president. Allende was a follower of **Karl Marx,** the founder of communism. When the new Chilean government took over American businesses in Chile, the United States protested. Nixon and his foreign-policy advisers feared an increase in Soviet influence in Chile and the spread of communism in Latin America.

With the backing of the CIA (Central Intelligence Agency), a small group of Chilean military leaders under General **Augusto Pinochet** overthrew the government and killed Allende. The United States immediately recognized the new military dictatorship and restored foreign aid to Chile.

The situation in Chile reflected another aspect of Nixon's foreign policy. Although willing to pursue détente with China and the Soviet Union, the president was still determined to contain the spread of communism—and Soviet influence—in the world.

☑ **Reading Check** **Explaining** Why did the United States oppose Salvador Allende?

SECTION 1 ASSESSMENT

Checking for Understanding

1. **Key Terms** Use each of these terms in a sentence that will help explain its meaning: détente, balance of power, embargo, shuttle diplomacy.
2. **Reviewing Facts** How did Henry Kissinger contribute to Nixon's presidency?

Reviewing Themes

3. **Global Connections** What was Nixon's main foreign policy goal?

Critical Thinking

4. **Drawing Conclusions** Why did Nixon think that improving relations with China would make the Soviet Union more cooperative?
5. **Organizing Information** Re-create the diagram below and identify each leader.

Zhou Enlai ⟶ ◯

Anwar el-Sadat ⟶ ◯

Golda Meir ⟶ ◯

Analyzing Visuals

6. **Sequencing Events** Study the time line that appears on pages 894–895. When did OPEC impose the oil embargo? Who was the nation's president when the Panama Canal treaties were signed?

Interdisciplinary Activity

Current Events Find a newspaper article that discusses the Israeli-Arab relationship today and compare it to the relationship that existed in the 1960s and 1970s.

SECTION 2 Nixon and Watergate

Guide to Reading

Main Idea
Nixon tried to deal with the nation's economic problems, but was forced to resign due to the Watergate scandal.

Key Terms
revenue sharing, affirmative action, stagflation, deficit, impeachment, amnesty, underemployment

Reading Strategy
Organizing Information As you read the section, list three challenges that Nixon faced during his presidency.

Read To Learn
• how Nixon struggled with domestic problems.
• how the Watergate scandal affected politics.

Section Theme
Continuity and Change Economic problems and political scandal marked the 1970s and troubled both Richard Nixon and Gerald Ford.

Preview of Events

◆1972	◆1973	◆1974	◆1975
June 1972 Break-in at Watergate occurs	**1973** OPEC oil embargo reduces U.S. supplies	**August 1974** Nixon resigns the presidency	**December 1974** CIA's secret files revealed

AN American Story

President Nixon had grave concerns about the state of American society. "We live in a deeply troubled and profoundly unsettled time. Drugs, crime, campus revolts, racial discord, draft resistance—on every hand we find old standards violated, old values discarded." Nixon believed that a "silent majority" of middle-class Americans shared his concerns about increasing crime and social disorder. In an ironic twist of events, however, the Nixon administration itself would get caught up in a web of illegal activities.

Nixon's Domestic Program

In his 1968 presidential campaign, Nixon had pledged to bring "law and order" back to American society. He also vowed to reduce government's role in people's lives.

Nixon's drive to restore law and order involved "cracking down on crime" and imposing stiffer penalties on lawbreakers. To strengthen the power of the police Nixon used federal funds to help state and city police forces.

CHAPTER 31   Search for Stability   **901**

The Courts

Nixon thought the federal courts should be tougher on criminals. "As a judicial conservative," he said, "I believe some Court decisions have gone too far in weakening the peace forces against the criminal forces in our society." During his presidency, four vacancies arose on the Supreme Court. Nixon hoped that the justices he appointed—**Warren Burger** as chief justice, and **Harry Blackmun, Lewis Powell,** and **William Rehnquist**—would shift the Court to a more conservative position. The decisions of the new justices did not fully meet the president's conservative goals, however.

New Federalism

Nixon wanted to reduce federal involvement in people's lives and to cut federal spending. He pledged to "reverse the flow of power and resources from the states and communities to Washington and start power and resources flowing back . . . to the people." To accomplish this goal, he introduced a program called the **New Federalism.**

One part of the New Federalism called for giving the states some of the revenue earned from federal taxes for use at the state and local levels. This revenue sharing became law in 1972.

Nixon also sought to end or scale back many Great Society programs begun under President Johnson. He promised to "quit pouring billions of dollars into programs that have failed." He abolished the Office of Economic Opportunity, the agency that had led Johnson's War on Poverty.

On civil rights issues, Nixon took a conservative position aimed at appealing to white voters. For example, Nixon opposed **busing.** Busing was used to promote racial integration by transporting students from mostly white or African American neighborhoods to racially mixed schools.

At the same time, however, his administration worked to carry out federal court orders to integrate schools. The Nixon administration also promoted affirmative action, or preference to minorities in jobs where they had previously been excluded. A practical politician, President Nixon did accept new government programs that had popular support. He approved the creation of two new agencies—the **Occupational Safety and Health Administration** (OSHA) to ensure workers' safety and the **Environmental Protection Agency** (EPA) to protect the environment.

Economics

Economic Problems

While attempting to change the direction of government, President Nixon had to deal with serious economic problems. Industry and manufacturing were declining because of foreign competition. Businesses and consumers struggled with **inflation**—a general rise in the prices of goods and services—fueled by international competition for raw materials and the increasing cost of oil. The United States also faced slow economic growth and high unemployment.

Analyzing *Political Cartoons*

This cartoon reflects how the value of the American dollar declined during the early 1970s. **What does the image of George Washington suggest about the mood of the country?**

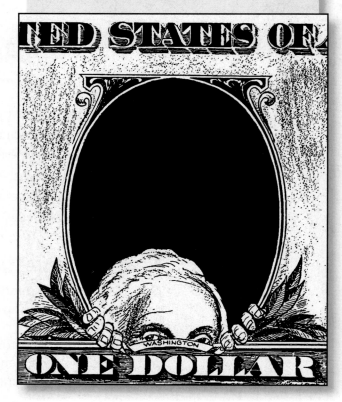

Seeking Economic Stability

President Nixon tried a number of approaches to reduce inflation. He began by cutting federal spending. At the same time, he called for a **tight money policy.** Interest rates were raised so that people would borrow less and spend less. With less money in circulation, prices dropped. However, as demand slowed, business began to cut back and output fell. These steps slowed economic growth and brought on stagflation—a combination of rising prices and a sluggish economy.

Nixon then switched tactics. He temporarily froze wages and prices and issued guidelines for any future increases. This put a brake on inflation, but the economy remained in a recession.

Later, Nixon tried a third approach—increasing federal spending to stimulate the economy. Although this policy helped revive the economy for a short time, it also created a budget deficit in which government spending was greater than government revenue. None of Nixon's policies managed to restore the economy to its previous strength, and economic problems continued to trouble his administration.

✓ **Reading Check** **Analyzing** What was stagflation?

Nixon's Second Term

Looking ahead in 1971 to the presidential campaign of 1972, Nixon had doubts about his chances for reelection. The war in Vietnam had not yet ended, and the easing of tensions with China had not yet occurred. Businesses and consumers had to struggle with the effects of inflation. The president and his supporters wanted to ensure his reelection.

A Campaign Against Enemies

To help plan his campaign strategy, Nixon relied on a small group of loyal aides. The aides closest to the president were **John Ehrlichman,** his chief domestic adviser, and **H.R. Haldeman,** his chief of staff.

In their drive to win reelection, the president and his closest advisers, it was later revealed, stretched, and sometimes crossed, the bound-

aries of the law. In 1971, for example, Nixon asked his aides for an "enemies list" of people considered unfriendly to the administration. He then ordered the FBI and the Internal Revenue Service (IRS) to investigate some of these people. Nixon justified such actions as necessary to maintain national security, arguing that those who challenged government policies posed a serious danger to the nation.

Nixon's campaign committee collected millions of dollars. It used some of this money to create a secret group—nicknamed "the plumbers"—to stop leaks of information that might hurt the administration. Some campaign money also went to pay for operations against Nixon's Democratic foes, but that party had many problems of its own.

Landslide Victory

The Democratic Party was split. Candidates competing for the nomination included: former vice president **Hubert Humphrey,** Senators **Edmund Muskie** of Maine and **George McGovern** of South Dakota, and former governor of Alabama **George Wallace.** Muskie and Humphrey could not gain enough support. Wallace's campaign was cut short in May 1972 by a would-be assassin's bullet that left him paralyzed.

McGovern, the most liberal of the four candidates, won the nomination. Many democrats and labor union leaders were cool towards McGovern's candidacy.

The Democrats' lack of unity as well as an upsurge in the economy and the prospect of peace in Vietnam

Nixon button and McGovern tie

led to a landslide victory for Nixon. He won 60.7 percent of the popular vote. The Republican victory in the electoral college was even more lopsided—520 to 17.

The Energy Crisis

During Nixon's second term as president, severe economic problems confronted the nation. One of the most critical problems was the cost of fuel, especially imported oil.

The U.S. economy depended heavily on oil. Much of this oil came from the Middle East. Arab oil-producing countries belonged to **OPEC,** the Organization of Petroleum Exporting Countries. In 1973 these countries placed an embargo on all oil shipments to the United States. At the same time, they raised their prices.

The sharp price increases and the five-month embargo damaged the nation's economy. Many companies had to lay off workers, while others raised their prices. Angry consumers complained about the high prices and the long lines at gas stations.

The president imposed emergency measures to conserve oil. Nixon also urged Americans to conserve energy voluntarily. Congress reduced speed limits on highways because a vehicle burns less fuel at lower speeds.

To deal with the long-range problem of dependence on imported oil, Nixon urged development of domestic oil, especially in **Alaska,** which possessed vast, untapped oil reserves.

✔ **Reading Check** **Evaluating** Why were gasoline prices increasing during this period?

The Watergate Crisis

During Nixon's second term, what seemed like a small scandal turned into a presidential crisis. The scandal began with the president's reelection campaign. In June 1972, his reelection committee had wanted information about the Democrats' campaign plans. Members of the Nixon campaign ordered "the plumbers" to break into the headquarters of the Democratic National Committee to install telephone listening devices—bugs. This break-in set events in motion that would rock the presidency and the nation.

A Third-Rate Burglary

Sometime after midnight on June 17, 1972, Frank Wills, a security guard at the **Watergate** office-apartment complex in Washington, D.C., noticed tape covering the locks on doors leading to an underground parking garage. "I took the tape off," he later recalled, "but I didn't think anything of it." About an hour later, he found that someone had retaped the locks. Wills decided to call the police.

Frank Wills's discovery led to the arrest of five men who had broken into Democratic Committee headquarters in the Watergate complex. The arrests of "plumbers" Gordon Liddy and E. Howard Hunt followed soon afterward. Investigations revealed that Liddy and Hunt were connected to the Nixon campaign and were paid from White House funds.

Temporarily...
10 GALLONS PER CUSTOMER
We appreciate your business & cooperation.

Sign of the times

Picturing **History**

Motorists line up outside a Virginia gas station. **Why did Americans face higher fuel prices and gas shortages?**

MORE ABOUT... The Impact of Watergate

The Watergate scandal had threatened the foundation of American democracy—constitutional law. Yet, the system worked. The legislative and judicial branches reasserted their powers to rein in the executive branch.

"I would say only that if some of my judgments were wrong, and some were wrong, they were made in what I believed at the time to be the best interest of the nation."

—Richard Nixon, August 8, 1974

♦1972   **♦1973**   **♦1974**   **♦1975**

June 1972
Watergate break-in reported

Nov. 1972
Nixon reelected

May 1973
Senate hearings begin

June 1973
John Dean implicates Nixon in cover-up

Oct. 1973
Saturday Night Massacre

April 1974
Nixon releases edited tapes

July 1974
Supreme Court orders surrender of tapes. House committee recommends impeachment.

Aug. 1974
Nixon releases tapes and resigns.

The White House denied any involvement. Nixon's press secretary, Ronald Ziegler, dismissed the break-in as a "third-rate burglary." The president declared that "no one in the White House staff, no one in the administration . . . was involved in this bizarre incident."

Investigation

Meanwhile, two newspaper reporters for the *Washington Post*, **Bob Woodward** and **Carl Bernstein,** began publishing a series of articles that linked the burglary to the Nixon campaign. As the election approached, however, fewer than half of the American people had even heard of the Watergate break-in.

John Sirica, the federal district court judge presiding over the trial of the Watergate burglars, resolved to uncover the truth. Eventually, one of the burglars, James McCord, admitted that White House aides had lied about their involvement and had pressured the burglars "to plead guilty and remain silent."

A Scandal Unravels

Early in 1973 the Senate voted to hold hearings on Watergate. As pressures mounted, Nixon shook up the White House staff. He fired the White House counsel, **John Dean,** and forced aides H.R. Haldeman and John Ehrlichman to resign. He also declared that he would take responsibility for the mistakes of others because "there can be no whitewash at the White House." Nixon also agreed to Senate demands to appoint a special prosecutor—someone independent of the Justice Department—to investigate Watergate. **Archibald Cox** took the job.

The Senate Watergate hearings began in May 1973. Chaired by Senator **Sam Ervin** of North Carolina, the hearings slowly revealed the inner workings of the Nixon White House. The most damaging testimony came from John Dean. Dean testified that there had been a cover-up and that Nixon himself directed it, but he produced no evidence to confirm his account.

Then in July investigators learned that a secret taping system had recorded all conversations in the president's office. Ervin and Cox demanded the tapes. President Nixon refused and claimed **executive privilege,** insisting that release of the tapes would endanger national security.

When Cox requested a court order to get the tapes in October, Nixon ordered his attorney general, Elliot Richardson, to fire Cox. Richardson refused—and then resigned. Deputy Attorney General William Ruckelshaus also refused to carry out the order and resigned. Finally, Nixon found a Justice Department official willing to fire Cox. This **Saturday Night Massacre,** as the resignations and firing became known, resulted in a storm of public protest.

In the middle of this turmoil, another scandal struck the administration. The Justice Department charged Vice President **Spiro Agnew** with taking bribes while governor of Maryland. On October 10, 1973, he resigned. Nixon appointed Representative **Gerald R. Ford** of Michigan, the Republican leader of the House, to succeed Agnew. Congress quickly confirmed the nomination.

The Crisis Deepens

Public outrage over the Saturday Night Massacre forced Nixon to appoint a new special prosecutor, **Leon Jaworski.** Meanwhile, the House of Representatives began considering impeachment—the constitutional provision to remove a president from office. If the House charged Nixon with committing "high crimes and misdemeanors," he would then be tried in the Senate. If a two-thirds majority of senators found him guilty, he would no longer be president.

In April 1974, Nixon decided to release printed copies of some of the tapes. These transcripts, heavily edited and missing significant portions, led to new protests. Nixon refused court orders to hand over the unedited tapes. Appeals reached the Supreme Court, which ruled on July 24 that the president had to surrender the tapes.

At the end of July, after weeks of closed hearings, the House Judiciary Committee adopted three articles of impeachment, charging the president with obstruction of justice, abuse of power, and contempt of Congress. Nixon released the tapes on August 5. A conversation on one tape revealed that the president had ordered a cover-up of the Watergate break-in just a few days after it happened. The conversation provided the crucial piece of evidence that linked Nixon to Watergate.

Nixon Resigns

Public reaction and the prospect of an impeachment trial forced Nixon to resign. On the evening of August 8, 1974, he went on national television to announce his decision.

The next morning a tearful Richard Nixon said good-bye to his staff and then left the White House by helicopter. He was succeeded by Gerald Ford, who became the first U.S. president never elected to the office of president or vice president.

The Watergate crisis revealed that the system of checks and balances could work to remove a president that abused his power and violated the Constitution. Congress passed laws to correct some of the abuses. However, the scandal damaged the public's faith in their political institutions and leaders.

Time *magazine,*
August 19, 1974

✓ Reading Check Identifying
Who succeeded President Nixon?

A Time for Healing

After Nixon's helicopter left the White House, Gerald Ford was sworn in as president. Ford assured Americans, "Our long national nightmare is over." To fill the office of vice president, Ford selected Nelson Rockefeller, a highly respected

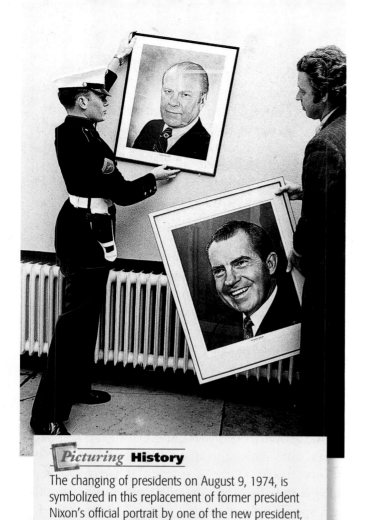

Picturing **History**

The changing of presidents on August 9, 1974, is symbolized in this replacement of former president Nixon's official portrait by one of the new president, Gerald Ford. **What position did Ford hold before becoming president?**

Ford defended his action, the new president never fully regained the trust and popularity he had enjoyed in his first weeks in office.

Spying on American Citizens

In December 1974, Americans were startled to learn that the CIA had spied and kept secret files on some American citizens. A few months later, they discovered that the FBI also had secret files. President Ford appointed special commissions to investigate CIA and FBI misconduct. He and Congress began working on new laws to regulate the activities of the two agencies.

Vietnam Amnesty

Yet another controversy arose when President Ford offered amnesty, or protection from prosecution, to men who had illegally avoided military service during the Vietnam War. Ford promised that these people would not be punished if they pledged loyalty to the United States and performed some type of national service. While many people approved of amnesty, others thought it was too lenient. Supporters of the Vietnam War argued that draft dodgers and deserters should be punished.

Ford and Foreign Affairs

With little experience in foreign affairs, Ford relied on Henry Kissinger, his secretary of state, and continued the policies of the Nixon administration. Ford extended the policy of détente with the Soviet Union. In late 1974, he met with Soviet leader **Leonid Brezhnev** to discuss arms control. The two leaders reached a preliminary agreement on limiting nuclear weapons.

In July 1975, Ford traveled to Helsinki, Finland, where he signed the **Helsinki Accords** with the Soviet Union and various Western nations. The countries pledged to respect the human rights and civil liberties of their citizens.

The Ford administration also worked to improve relations with China. When Chinese Communist chairman **Mao Zedong** died in 1976, a more moderate government came to power. The new Chinese leaders wanted to expand economic and political ties to the United States, and the two nations moved a little closer.

Republican and former governor of New York. Relieved to put the Watergate crisis behind them, most Americans welcomed the new president and a fresh start for the nation.

One of Ford's first acts, however, destroyed much of this confidence. On September 8, 1974, only a month after taking office, Ford granted Richard Nixon a **pardon** for any crimes he may have committed as president.

This meant that the former president could not be prosecuted for his part in the cover-up. Ford hoped that the pardon would help heal the wounds of Watergate. Instead, the pardon stirred controversy. Many Americans questioned why Nixon should escape punishment when others involved in the Watergate scandal went to jail. Some even accused Ford of striking a bargain with Nixon in advance—the promise of a pardon in exchange for Nixon's resignation. Although

A Troubled Economy

The economic problems that the Nixon administration faced continued to plague President Ford. Inflation remained high and unemployment rose.

By the 1970s Europe and Japan challenged America's world economic supremacy. Inexpensive and efficient Japanese cars flooded the American market. European products also provided strong competition to American-made goods.

This foreign competition led to factory closings in the United States and massive layoffs of workers. America began to suffer from underemployment; that is, people worked in jobs for which they were overqualified or that did not fully use their skills. Underemployment resulted, in part, from the loss of jobs to foreign competition.

The actions of OPEC continued to influence the American economy, also. Although the oil shortage caused by the embargo of 1973–1974 had eased, OPEC kept oil prices high, and the high prices contributed to inflation. The American economy seemed to be crumbling and Ford struggled for a solution.

Ford's Response

To fight inflation Ford launched a campaign called Whip Inflation Now (WIN), a voluntary program of wage and price controls. He called on Americans to save their money rather than spend it and to plant their own gardens to counter rising food prices. Although the effort led to a small drop in inflation, the economy declined and the nation headed into recession.

HISTORY Online

Student Web Activity
Visit taj.glencoe.com and click on **Chapter 31— Student Web Activities** for an activity on the Watergate crisis.

Spending Cuts

Another approach Ford urged for controlling inflation was to cut government spending. However, the Democratic-controlled Congress wanted to maintain or increase spending for social programs. Ford vetoed several congressional spending bills in an attempt to control spending, but his actions did not curb inflation.

To stimulate the economy and encourage economic growth, Ford persuaded Congress to pass a tax cut. Although the cut did bring some improvement in the economy, it led to larger budget deficits as government revenue declined and spending remained the same or increased. Despite his efforts, President Ford was unable to solve the nation's economic problems.

✓ **Reading Check** **Evaluating** How did Europe and Japan challenge the U.S. economy?

SECTION 2 ASSESSMENT

Checking for Understanding

1. **Key Terms** Use each of these terms in a sentence that will help explain its meaning: revenue sharing, affirmative action, stagflation, deficit, impeachment, amnesty, underemployment

2. **Reviewing Facts** List two actions that Nixon took to restore law and order.

Reviewing Themes

3. **Continuity and Change** Explain how Gerald Ford came to be president.

Critical Thinking

4. **Synthesizing Information** Explain how the government's checks and balances system worked when Nixon abused his power as president.

5. **Organizing Information** Re-create the diagram below and list reasons each person might have problems being reelected.

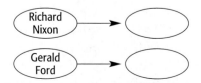

Analyzing Visuals

6. **Political Cartoons** Study the cartoon on page 902. Explain why George Washington is barely visible on the dollar bill. If you were a cartoonist, explain another way to express this idea.

Interdisciplinary Activity

Art Create a bumper sticker that supports or opposes Ford's pardon of President Nixon in the Watergate scandal.

Critical Thinking
SKILLBUILDER

Predicting Consequences

Why Learn This Skill?

Did you ever wish you could see into the future? Predicting future events is very difficult. You can, however, develop skills that will help you identify the logical consequences of decisions or actions.

Learning the Skill

Follow these steps to help you accurately predict consequences.

- Review what you already know about a situation by listing facts, events, and people's responses. The list will help you recall events and how they affected people.
- Analyze patterns. Try to determine what the patterns show. Are some consequences more likely to occur than others?
- Use your knowledge and observations of similar situations. In other words, ask yourself, "What were the consequences of a similar decision or action that occurred in the past?"
- Map out all possible consequences or outcomes.
- Analyze each of the potential consequences by asking, "How likely is it that this will occur?"
- Make a prediction.

Practicing the Skill

Candidates for public office often make campaign promises based on how they think voters will respond. Use the information in the chart below to help you predict what type of candidate would be elected president in 1980. Answer the questions.

❶ Review the facts and events listed on the chart. What patterns do you notice? What do the facts tell you about the 1970s?

❷ Recall similar situations in which voters faced hard times. What kind of president do you think Americans would want?

Applying the Skill

Predicting Consequences Read newspapers for articles about an event that affects your community. Make an educated prediction about what will happen. Explain your reasoning.

 Glencoe's **Skillbuilder Interactive Workbook CD-ROM, Level 1,** provides instruction and practice in key social studies skills.

Events of the 1970s ➡	Results and Reactions
OPEC oil embargo causes a shortage of fuel.	Americans feel helpless and angry.
President Ford vetoes programs in health, housing, and education to reduce government spending.	Many people lose jobs, and the nation suffers the worst recession in 40 years.
Ford pardons Nixon.	Americans feel frustrated.
To conserve energy, Americans buy smaller, imported cars.	American workers suffer unemployment as several automobile plants close.
Americans learn CIA and FBI have secret files on citizens.	Americans become angry at government's abuse of power.

SECTION 3 The Carter Presidency

Guide to Reading

Main Idea
Jimmy Carter approached economic and foreign policy issues differently than Nixon or Ford, but was still unable to win reelection.

Key Terms
trade deficit, human rights, apartheid, fundamentalist

Reading Strategy
Classifying Information As you read the section, re-create the diagram below and list three treaties that the Carter administration negotiated.

Treaties

Read To Learn
• how President Carter emphasized human rights in foreign policy.
• what actions Carter took to improve the economy.

Section Theme
Global Connections Despite some failures, Carter saw success in treaties dealing with the Middle East and arms reductions.

Preview of Events

◆1976	◆1977	◆1978	◆1979
1976 Jimmy Carter wins the presidency	**1977** Panama Canal treaties signed	**1978** Camp David Accords lead toward Arab-Israeli peace	**1979** Iranians take 52 Americans hostage

AN American Story

Jimmy Carter brought a simple lifestyle to the White House. For example, to save money President Carter once planned to visit his hometown of Plains, Georgia, by car instead of by helicopter. He soon discovered that it was much less expensive to go by helicopter. Carter later stated about going by car: "A good portion of the Georgia State Patrol had been marshaled to block every country crossroads for more than 60 miles! It was obvious that I was not simply one of the people anymore."

The Election of 1976

As the 1976 elections approached, President Ford hoped to win the election outright. But Ford's prospects did not look particularly good. Although he had helped to restore confidence in government, Watergate was still fresh in the minds of the American people. In early 1976, **Jimmy Carter** ran as a Democratic candidate in the presidential primary election in New Hampshire. Few voters knew who Carter was. Then Carter began winning key primary elections.

Stressing his integrity, religious faith, and his standing as an outsider, Carter gathered enough delegates to win the Democratic nomination. Senator **Walter Mondale** of Minnesota ran as vice president.

Meanwhile President Ford had struggled to gain the Republican nomination. He faced a strong challenge from the former governor of California, **Ronald Reagan,** who was favored by party conservatives. Ford chose Senator **Bob Dole** of Kansas as his running mate.

During the campaign, Ford tried to stress his achievements as president. Carter promised to clean up the government and ran as much against the memory of Nixon and government corruption as against Ford. Carter won in a very close election, gaining 50.1 percent of the popular vote to Ford's 48 percent. To a great extent, Carter owed his margin of victory to support from African American Southern voters.

☑ **Reading Check** **Explaining** How did Carter represent himself in the 1976 presidential campaign?

An Informal Presidency

Carter, an "outsider" with no experience in national politics, did not fit the image of a typical politician. A former governor of Georgia, Carter liked to say he was just a peanut farmer from a small town called Plains who wanted to serve his country.

From the beginning, Carter set a down-to-earth tone. At his inauguration he wore an ordinary business suit rather than formal clothing. After the ceremony, Carter and his family walked up Pennsylvania Avenue from the Capitol to the White House instead of riding in the traditional limousine. These gestures symbolized Carter's desire to create a more informal presidency. Carter wanted to be seen as an average American.

Struggling With the Economy

When Carter took office, the nation still suffered from high inflation and unemployment. Carter tried to jolt the economy out of recession by increasing federal spending and cutting taxes. Both measures were meant to stimulate economic growth. Unemployment came down, but inflation took off. Carter then reversed course and proposed spending cuts and a delayed tax cut.

Carter's reversals on economic policies made him seem weak and uncertain. As an outsider, the president had trouble gaining support for his programs in Congress. Although Carter needed the backing of congressional Democrats, his administration made little effort to work with them.

Energy Crisis

Carter made energy policy a priority. The high costs of energy added to inflation. In addition, as American money flowed overseas to purchase oil, the nation faced a growing trade deficit—the value of foreign imports exceeded the value of American exports.

In April 1977, Carter presented the **National Energy Plan,** aimed at resolving the energy crisis. To stress the need to reduce energy use, for example, the president turned down the thermostat in the White House.

Picturing **History**

Jimmy Carter and his wife, Rosalynn, worship with African American leaders, including Coretta Scott King, widow of Dr. Martin Luther King, Jr. **Why was Carter viewed as an "outsider" in national politics?**

Carter's plan included the creation of a Department of Energy to coordinate energy policy, research funds to explore alternative sources of energy, and tax policies to encourage domestic oil production and energy conservation. Congress enacted a weakened version of the plan in 1978.

Nuclear Power

In the late 1970s, Americans became more concerned about the threats of nuclear power. In March 1979 a major accident occurred at the **Three Mile Island** nuclear power plant near Harrisburg, Pennsylvania.

An anti-nuclear protest movement soon spread. President Carter, however, was unwilling to halt the nuclear energy program, which provided more than 10 percent of the nation's energy needs. At the same time, supporters of nuclear power argued that, with proper safeguards, nuclear power provided no danger to the environment.

✓ **Reading Check** **Identifying** What economic problems did Carter face when he took office?

Foreign Affairs

Carter based his foreign policy on human rights—a concern that governments around the world grant greater freedom and opportunity without the threat of persecution or violence. He proposed that any nation that violated human rights should not receive aid and support from the United States.

Carter withdrew economic and military aid from such countries as Argentina, Uruguay, and Ethiopia because of human rights violations. He condemned South Africa for its policy of apartheid, racial separation and economic and political discrimination against non-whites.

Carter's human rights diplomacy sometimes caused problems in the United States. In 1980 Cuban dictator Fidel Castro allowed thousands of Cubans, including criminals and political prisoners, to leave Cuba.

Beginning in April, Cuban refugees began leaving from **Mariel Harbor;** most were en route to Florida. The United States, however, had trouble absorbing such large numbers of people. Some of the emigrants were detained in refugee

People In History

Wilma Mankiller 1945–

During the 1960s, Wilma Mankiller lived in California and was active in the women's rights movement and the Native American rights movement. In the 1970s, she took this activism back to her roots in northeast Oklahoma and applied it to the government of her tribe, the Cherokee Nation.

In 1985, Wilma Mankiller became the Cherokee chief, the first woman to ever serve as a chief of a major Native American group. She often faced opposition, but was reelected and held the top position for almost ten years. As chief, she was responsible for 140,000 people and a 75 million-dollar budget.

During her time as the leader of the Cherokee, Mankiller focused on lowering unemployment, increasing educational opportunities, and improving community health care. She also created the Institute for Cherokee Literacy to preserve Cherokee traditions and culture.

camps. In June, President Carter ordered other Cubans be moved to federal prisons to await removal hearings. Then, in September, Castro sealed off the boatlift. About 125,000 Cuban refugees had entered the United States.

Carter had learned that a foreign policy based on a single issue, human rights, had many limitations. Even so, the president continued to speak out on the issue.

The Panama Canal

Carter also acted to end Latin American bitterness over the Panama Canal. Over the years, U.S. ownership of the canal and its control of the Canal Zone had caused friction between the United States and **Panama.** Carter signed two treaties with Panama in 1977. The treaties turned the U.S.-controlled Panama Canal over to Panama by the year 2000 but guaranteed that the canal would remain a neutral waterway open to all shipping. Some Republicans in the Senate tried to block ratification of the treaties, charging that Carter was giving away U.S. property. The Senate approved the treaties in 1978.

The Middle East

President Carter sought to bring peace to the Middle East. When peace talks between Israel and Egypt stalled in 1978, Carter invited Israeli prime minister **Menachem Begin** and Egyptian president **Anwar el-Sadat** to Camp David, Maryland, for a summit meeting.

For two weeks, the three leaders discussed issues dividing Israel and Egypt. In September 1978 they announced an agreement. Known as the **Camp David Accords,** the agreement led to an Egyptian-Israeli peace treaty signed at the White House in March 1979. The treaty marked the first time that Israel and an Arab nation had reached a peace agreement.

The Soviet Union

Carter criticized Soviet human-rights violations, but at the same time, he continued negotiations on arms control. In June 1979, the president signed a second Strategic Arms Limitation Treaty, or **SALT II.** Critics in the Senate charged that the treaty gave the Soviets an advantage, and the Senate delayed ratification.

Picturing **History**

President Carter meets with Egyptian president Anwar el-Sadat (left) and Israeli prime minister Menachem Begin (right). **Why were the Camp David Accords important?**

Any hope of the Senate approving SALT II disappeared in December 1979, when Soviet troops invaded **Afghanistan,** a country in southwestern Asia bordering the Soviet Union. Carter ordered sanctions against the Soviet Union. The United States and other nations refused to take part in the Olympic Games in Moscow. In addition, the United States imposed a grain embargo on the Soviet Union.

Crisis in Iran

In the 1970s, **Iran** was one of the strongest U.S. allies in the Persian Gulf region, an area vital to Western oil needs. Shah Mohammed Reza Pahlavi, the ruler of Iran, used U.S. aid to build up a powerful military force. Many Iranians, however, complained about corruption in the government. Others objected to Western influence in the country, which they felt weakened traditional Muslim values.

In January 1979, Islamic fundamentalists—people who believe in strict obedience to religious laws—forced the shah to flee Iran. The new ruler, Muslim leader **Ayatollah Khomeini,** was hostile to the United States because of its support of the shah.

Iranians present a blindfolded and handcuffed American hostage.

In November 1979, Iranian students, with the support of fundamentalists in the government, stormed the American embassy in **Tehran,** the capital of Iran, and held 52 Americans hostage. The United States was outraged. Attempts to negotiate the release of the hostages failed, and a daring desert rescue attempt ended in tragedy with the death of 8 American soldiers. The hostage crisis dragged on and became a major issue in the presidential election of 1980.

✓ **Reading Check** **Summarizing** Why did the United States boycott the 1980 Olympic Games?

The Election of 1980

The Iranian crisis damaged the president politically. By the time the election campaign began, Carter's popularity among the public had declined dramatically.

The Republicans nominated **Ronald Reagan** for president in 1980. In marked contrast to Carter, Reagan radiated charm and confidence. His conservative message of lower taxes, reduced spending, stronger defense, and a restoration of American pride attracted Americans weary of government and economic problems. When Reagan asked, "Are you better off now than you were four years ago?" most Americans answered, "No!"

Reagan swept to victory, with an electoral vote margin of 489 to 49. Republicans also gained control of the Senate for the first time since 1954. The election resulted in a bitter defeat for Jimmy Carter, who only 4 years earlier had promised a new era in American politics.

A final disappointment for Carter came in January 1981. During the last weeks of his presidency, he worked to obtain the release of the hostages. The Iranians finally did release them—after Ronald Reagan took the oath of office.

✓ **Reading Check** **Evaluating** How was Reagan perceived differently than Carter?

SECTION 3 ASSESSMENT

Checking for Understanding

1. **Key Terms** Use the following terms in a paragraph to help explain their meaning: trade deficit, human rights, apartheid, fundamentalist.
2. **Reviewing Facts** How did Jimmy Carter's manner differ from many other presidents'?

Reviewing Themes

3. **Global Connections** What issue guided Carter's foreign policy? How did the president attempt to implement this policy?

Critical Thinking

4. **Drawing Conclusions** Which of Carter's actions do you think did the greatest damage to his chances for reelection?
5. **Organizing Information** Re-create the diagram below and identify three problems facing the Carter administration and the actions taken in response.

Problems	Actions

Analyzing Visuals

6. **Picturing History** Study the picture at the top of this page. What effect do you think this image on television had on the American people? How do you think this picture and similar images affected Carter's campaign for a second term?

Interdisciplinary Activity

Geography Draw a world map and label the different countries that Carter dealt with during his presidency.

America's LITERATURE

Ernesto Galarza (1905–1984)

Like many immigrants who come to the United States, Ernesto Galarza arrived facing the challenge of adjusting to his adopted country. This excerpt from his autobiography, *Barrio Boy,* tells the story of how Galarza and his mother, Doña Henriqueta traveled from Mexico to California to meet his uncles, Gustavo and José. His story describes experiences common to those arriving in the United States then and now.

READ TO DISCOVER

Unable to speak English and unfamiliar with the customs in the United States, 6-year-old Galarza and his mother embarked on a new life. Their trip was a journey into another world for young Ernesto. As you read, think about what it would be like to move to a new country.

READER'S DICTIONARY

barrio: Spanish word for "neighborhood"

Tucson: a city in southeastern Arizona

Sacramento: the capital of California

Barrio Boy

In the sunny morning of the next day we walked back to the station. Our train was still there, the flats and boxcars and coaches deserted, Mexican and American soldiers walking back and forth. "Look, the American flag," my mother said. It was flying over a building near us. Down the street, beyond the depot, there was a Mexican flag on a staff. "We are in the United States. Mexico is over there." . . .

. . . In **Tucson** we found our way to the address Gustavo had sent. It was a small hotel where the clerk spoke Spanish. He took us down a long, dark hall to a room, where I immediately began to explore the remarkable inventions of the Americans.

. . . Regularly we went to the hotel to ask for mail from Gustavo. Almost always there was a letter with money, but it was many weeks before we received the most important one of all, the one that had the pass and the instructions for the trip. We were to take the train to **Sacramento,** go to the Hotel Español and stay there until Gustavo and José came for us.

. . . And from what I saw in the coach on that long ride, the Americans were indeed different. They ate the repulsive sandwiches with relish. They put their feet, shoes and all, on

the seats in front of them. When the men laughed it seemed more like a roar, and if they were close by it scared me. Doña Henriqueta frowned and admonished me. "Be careful I never hear you braying like that." Many of them kept their hats on as if they didn't know that the inside of a coach was like the inside of a house, and wearing your hat in either a sure sign of being *mal educado* [ill-mannered].

From *Barrio Boy* by Ernesto Galarza. © 1971 by the University of Notre Dame Press. Used by permission of the publisher.

ANALYZING LITERATURE

1. **Recall and Interpret** What observations do Ernesto and his mother make about Americans?

2. **Evaluate and Connect** What parts of Ernesto's story are probably shared by all people coming to a new place?

Interdisciplinary Activity
Descriptive Writing Imagine that you are Ernesto writing a postcard to a friend in Mexico. Describe your impressions of America and of the people you've seen.

915

TIME NOTEBOOK

What were people's lives like in the past?

What might our lives be like in the future? These two pages will give you some clues to everyday life in the U.S. as you step back—and look ahead—with TIME Notebook.

Profile

After getting HIV from a blood-clotting drug when he was just 13, **RYAN WHITE** *was asked to speak before a Presidential Commission on AIDS in 1988:*

"I CAME FACE TO FACE WITH DEATH AT thirteen years old. I was diagnosed with AIDS: a killer. Doctors told me I'm not contagious. Given six months to live and being the fighter that I am, I set high goals for myself. It was my decision to live a normal life, go to school, be with my friends, and enjoy day-to-day activities. It was not going to be easy.

The school I was going to said they had no guidelines for a person with AIDS.... We began a series of court battles for nine months, while I was attending classes by telephone. Eventually, I won the right to attend school, but the prejudice was still there."

Ryan White

HUBBARD–LIAISON

MINI TO THE MAX
Future Medicine

"TAKE 200 TINY ROBOTS and call me in the morning." Don't laugh. Your doctor may be saying that to you sometime during the next few decades.

Nanotechnologists are researchers and makers of microscopic robots. In the future, these germ-sized robots—called nanomachines—will cruise through your body, making sure everything's running in order. They'll report back to a mainframe that's also in your body to report on your condition. Then the tiny robots will scrape away blockages in the arteries, clean up dangerous cancer cells, and blast away blood clots.

Doctors predict that living to be 100 or older won't be any big deal—possibly in this generation. And you may have the nanorobots to thank for it!

FUTURE SHOCK
Population Growth in the United States

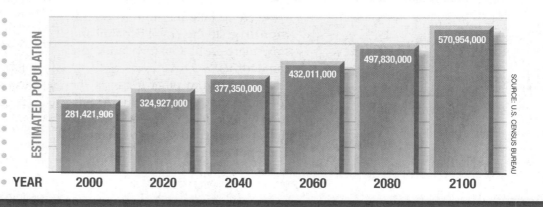

ESTIMATED POPULATION

YEAR	2000	2020	2040	2060	2080	2100
	281,421,906	324,927,000	377,350,000	432,011,000	497,830,000	570,954,000

SOURCE: U.S. CENSUS BUREAU

MILESTONES

EVENTS AND PEOPLE OF THE TIME

Oil-covered sea bird found in Prince William Sound, Alaska.

AL GRILLO/ALASKA STOCK

HARMONIZED. MICHAEL JACKSON with 45 rock stars as they sing the tune Jackson co-wrote with Lionel Ritchie called "We Are the World." On April 5, 1985, about 5,000 radio stations around the world played the song at the same time—all in an effort to raise money for starving people in Africa. After just one year, "We Are the World" made over $44 million.

RELEASED. Fifty-two American **HOSTAGES** after 444 days in captivity in Iran. Held by terrorists who were angry over America's favorable treatment of Iran's former ruler, the group was snatched from the U.S. Embassy in Iran. The fact that the U.S. couldn't negotiate their release was a factor in **PRESIDENT JIMMY CARTER'S** 1980 election loss.

SPILLED. Over 11,000,000 gallons of crude oil in the clean waters of Prince William Sound, Alaska, in March 1989. A huge tanker struck a coral reef, dumping hundreds of thousands of barrels of crude oil into the water, devastating commercial fishing and wiping out precious Alaskan wildlife.

President Carter

BETTMANN/CORBIS

FUTURE SHOCK

What You Do Today Affects Tomorrow's World

In May 2001, there were about 284 million people in the United States. India's population was about 1.03 billion. But Americans use 25 percent of the world's resources and cause 25 to 30 percent of the world's waste. Compared to the typical person in India, the average U.S. citizen uses:

50 times more steel

56 times more energy

170 times more synthetic rubber

170 times more newsprint

250 times more motor fuel

300 times more plastic

NUMBERS

U.S. AT THE TIME

11,600 The number of air traffic controllers who went on strike in 1981, grounding the nation's commercial airlines

70¢ The amount earned by a woman for every dollar earned by a man in 1987

E.T.

PHOTOFEST

$229,000,000 Ticket sales from the movie, *E.T., the Extra-Terrestrial*, released in 1982—one of the highest-grossing films ever

50% The percent of all African American children living in poverty in 1989

1,200,000 Los Angeles children in 1986 who observed a moment of silence in honor of astronaut and teacher Christa McAuliffe who was killed when the space shuttle *Challenger* exploded

Christa McAuliffe

TIME INC. PICTURE COLLECTION

Chapter Summary

Search for Stability

Nixon's Foreign Policy

- Nixon opens relations with China and the Soviet Union
- U.S. backs an overthrow of Communist Chilean government

Nixon and Watergate

- Nixon introduces New Federalism
- Economy suffers under inflation
- White House involvement with Watergate break-in revealed
- Vice President Agnew resigns
- Nixon appoints Gerald Ford as new vice president
- Nixon resigns presidency

Ford and Carter

- Ford grants pardon to Nixon
- Ford continues détente with Soviet Union
- Inflation rises
- Carter makes energy policy a priority
- Carter bases foreign policy on human rights
- Carter works to bring peace in Middle East

- Islamic fundamentalists take 53 Americans hostage in Iran
- Carter loses 1980 election to Ronald Reagan

Reviewing Key Terms

On graph paper, create a word search puzzle using the following terms. Crisscross the terms vertically and horizontally, then fill in the remaining squares with extra letters. Use the terms' definitions as clues to find the words in the puzzle. Share your puzzle with a classmate.

1. détente
2. embargo
3. shuttle diplomacy
4. stagflation
5. deficit
6. impeachment
7. amnesty
8. human rights

Reviewing Key Facts

9. Which two nations were the focus of Nixon's attempt to ease Cold War tensions?
10. What was shuttle diplomacy?
11. Explain why President Nixon was forced to resign.
12. What did Congress do in the aftermath of Watergate?
13. Why did the United States lose its place as a world economic leader in the 1970s?
14. What did President Carter do to resolve the energy crisis?
15. How did Carter bring temporary peace to the Middle East?

Critical Thinking

16. **Analyzing Themes: Global Connections** What was Nixon's main reason for establishing friendly relations with the Soviet Union?
17. **Analyzing Information** What did Nixon do to create a New Federalism?
18. **Analyzing Themes: Global Connections** What did Carter think the United States should do to any nation that violated human rights?
19. **Drawing Conclusions** How did Carter's support of the shah of Iran ignore the interest of Islamic fundamentalists in that country?
20. **Analyzing Themes: Continuity and Change** Re-create the diagram below and describe how the foreign policies of Ford and Nixon were alike.

Nixon — Similarities — Ford

Geography and History Activity

In 1973 Saudi Arabia imposed an embargo, or a restriction of trade, on oil shipped to Israel's allies including the United States. At the same time, other OPEC countries raised their prices. Although the embargo was lifted in 1974, its economic effects continued through the end of the decade. Study the chart below; then answer the questions that follow.

Gasoline Consumption and Prices				
Year	Consumption (Billions of gallons)	Cost per Gallon		
		Reg.	Prem.	No lead
1973	110.5	$ .40	.45	NA
1974	106.3	.53	.57	.55
1975	109.0	.57	.61	.60
1976	115.7	.59	.64	.61
1977	119.6	.62	.67	.66
1978	125.1	.63	.69	.67
1979	122.1	.86	.92	.90
1980	115.0	1.19	1.28	1.25

Source: *Statistical Abstract of the United States*

21. In what year did gasoline consumption first exceed 120 billion gallons?

22. How much more did a gallon of regular gasoline cost in 1980 than in 1973?

23. Based on billions of gallons of gas consumed, in which year shown on the chart was the environment most polluted with automobile fumes?

Practicing Skills Activity

24. **Predicting Consequences** Review the skill on predicting consequences on page 909. Then read the following statements and predict three consequences for each. Rank the three consequences in order of most likely to occur to least likely to occur.
    - If a person in a public office, including the president, commits a crime, he or she should not be pardoned.
    - Engineers develop an effective, efficient electric-powered automobile.
    - The school year is lengthened by 30 days.

Self-Check Quiz
Visit **taj.glencoe.com** and click on **Chapter 31—Self-Check Quizzes** to prepare for the chapter test.

Citizenship Cooperative Activity

25. **Serving on a Jury** Find people from your school or city who have served on a jury. Ask them to recall their impressions of the experience. With a partner, think about what happens if you have received a jury notice in the mail. Write a description of what you would do next and what you would expect to happen. Then note what you plan to tell the judge about your understanding of a juror's responsibilities. Share your writing with the class.

Alternative Assessment

26. **Expository Writing** Review the chapter and make a list of the successes and failures of Presidents Nixon, Ford, and Carter. Based on your list, which of the three would you vote for in a presidential election today? Explain your choice.

Standardized Test Practice

Directions: Choose the *best* answer to the following question.

Which of the following was a key feature of the Carter administration?

A foreign policy based on human rights

B emphasis on formality

C clear economic policies

D close cooperation with Congress

Test-Taking Tip:

Eliminate answers that you know are wrong. For example, Carter was different from his predecessors because he was personally casual. Therefore answer **B** must be wrong.

CHAPTER 32

New Challenges

1981–Present

Why It Matters

The 1980s and 1990s ushered in a period of great change. With the collapse of communism in Europe, relations between East and West changed dramatically. Former foes sought closer ties. At home, new advances in technology, medicine, and industry helped the nation move forward.

The Impact Today

The technological innovation during this period accounts for today's communications revolution and globalized economy.

The American Journey *Video The chapter 32 video, "America Responds to Terrorism," focuses on how Americans united after the events of September 11, 2001.*

1990
• Americans with Disabilities Act passed

1981
• Ronald Reagan becomes president

1983
• U.S. troops invade Grenada

1986
• Space shuttle *Challenger* explodes

1989
• Bush becomes president

United States
PRESIDENTS

Reagan 1981–1989

G.H.W. Bush 1989–1993

1980   *1985*   *1990*

World

1980
• Solidarity trade union formed in Poland

1989
• Students protest in Tiananmen Square
• Fall of communism in Eastern Europe

1990
• Nelson Mandela released from South African prison

FOLDABLES™
Study Organizer

Organizing Information Study Foldable
Make this foldable to help you organize what you learn about the challenges facing the United States today.

Step 1 Fold a sheet of paper into fifths from top to bottom.

This forms five rows.

Step 2 Open the paper and refold it into fourths from side to side.

Fold it in half, then in half again.

This forms four columns.

Step 3 Unfold, turn the paper, and draw lines along the folds.

Step 4 Label your foldable as shown.

	Reagan	Bush	Clinton	G.W. Bush
Political Party				
Foreign Policy				
Domestic Policy				

Reading and Writing As you read the chapter, write information about the presidents, their political parties, and their foreign and domestic policies in the correct spaces of your foldable.

A New President George W. Bush was inaugurated the nation's forty-third president on January 20, 2001.

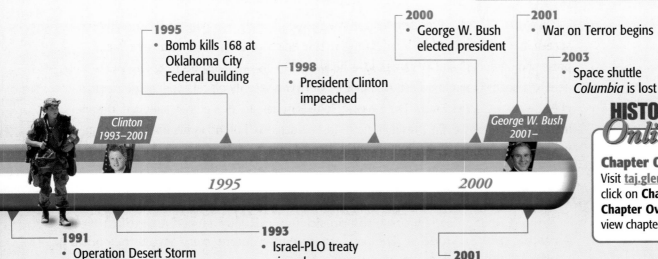

1995
• Bomb kills 168 at Oklahoma City Federal building

1998
• President Clinton impeached

2000
• George W. Bush elected president

2001
• War on Terror begins

2003
• Space shuttle *Columbia* is lost

Clinton 1993–2001

George W. Bush 2001–

1995   *2000*

1991
• Operation Desert Storm
• Breakup of Soviet Union; Apartheid ends in South Africa

1993
• Israel-PLO treaty signed

2001
• Former Yugoslav president Slobodan Milosevic arrested

HISTORY Online

Chapter Overview
Visit taj.glencoe.com and click on **Chapter 32—Chapter Overviews** to preview chapter information.

The Reagan Presidency

Guide to Reading

Main Idea
Ronald Reagan took a conservative approach to both domestic and foreign policy.

Key Terms
deregulation, federal debt, glasnost, perestroika

Reading Strategy
Classifying Information As you read the section, re-create the diagram below and provide three conservative actions taken by Ronald Reagan.

Ronald Reagan's conservatism

Read To Learn
- how Ronald Reagan implemented supply-side economics.
- how Ronald Reagan was active in foreign policy.
- how the Soviet Union changed.

Section Theme
Economic Factors Ronald Reagan was conservative at home and built up the military to counter the Soviet Union.

Preview of Events

1980	1985	1990

1981
Sandra Day O'Connor appointed to Supreme Court

1985
Mikhail Gorbachev becomes leader of Soviet Union

1987
Reagan and Gorbachev sign INF Treaty

AN American Story

On March 30, 1981, President Reagan gave a speech at the Washington Hilton. After the speech, the president left the hotel through a side entrance and passed through a line of press photographers and TV cameras. As he walked to his car, gunshots rang out. The president had been shot in the chest. Also injured were two security officers and the president's press secretary, James Brady. The assassin, John Hinckley, Jr., was quickly subdued. Despite the attempt on his life, the president never lost his sense of humor. In the operating room, he told the surgeons, "Please tell me you're Republicans."

The Reagan Revolution

Ronald Reagan's election to the presidency in 1980 marked a significant conservative shift in America. The conservative movement grew across the country, particularly in the South and Southwest, a region known as the **Sunbelt.** When the Sunbelt's population increased during the 1970s, the conservative movement gained political power.

Many Americans wanted a return to what President Ronald Reagan, a former actor with Illinois small-town roots, called "traditional American values"—an emphasis on family life, hard work, respect for law, and patriotism. They shared the conservative view that the federal government made too many rules, collected too much in taxes, and spent too much money on social programs.

Air Traffic Controllers' Strike

A few months after Ronald Reagan became president, the nation's air traffic controllers went on strike. They refused to go back to work despite the president's orders to do so. President Reagan acted at once, firing the controllers and ordering military staff to oversee air traffic while new controllers were trained to do the work.

President Carter had been criticized for his lack of leadership and indecision. With this action, Ronald Reagan showed that he would stand firm and use his position as president to carry out the policies in which he believed.

Deregulation

As part of his promise to reduce government and "get the government off the backs of the American people," President Reagan pursued a policy of deregulation. This meant cutting the rules and regulations government agencies placed on businesses. Under President Reagan, for example, the Department of Transportation wrote new rules for automobile exhaust systems and safety measures that were easier for car manufacturers to meet.

The Supreme Court

Reagan also put a conservative stamp on the Supreme Court by naming justices to the Court who shared his views. He appointed **Sandra Day O'Connor** in 1981, the first woman ever appointed to the Court. Reagan later appointed **Antonin Scalia** and **Anthony Kennedy.**

Reaganomics

Deregulation and his court appointments showed President Reagan's commitment to a conservative view of government. It was his

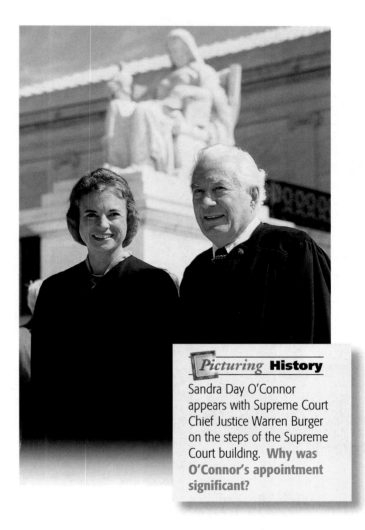

Picturing **History**

Sandra Day O'Connor appears with Supreme Court Chief Justice Warren Burger on the steps of the Supreme Court building. **Why was O'Connor's appointment significant?**

economic policies, however, that formed the core of the "Reagan Revolution." Reagan believed that lower taxes would allow individuals and corporations to invest in new businesses. Because a tax cut would mean less income, Reagan also called for less government spending. Supporters called Reagan's economic policy **supply-side economics** because it proposed to stimulate the economy by increasing the supply of goods and services. The president's critics ridiculed the policy as "Reaganomics."

In 1981 Congress lowered taxes and slashed nearly $40 billion from federal programs such as school lunches, student aid, welfare, low-income housing, and food stamps. Critics charged that these cuts hurt both the working poor and unemployed people. Supporters argued that Reaganomics would boost the economy, helping everybody in the long run.

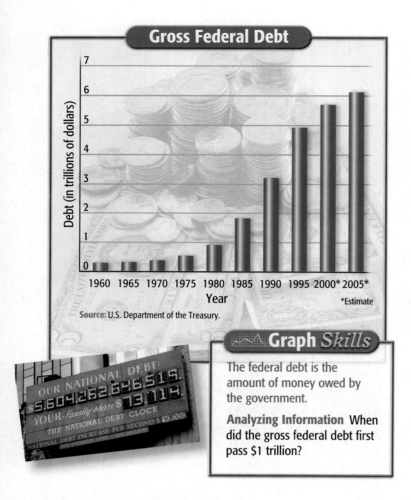

Gross Federal Debt

Debt (in trillions of dollars)

1960 1965 1970 1975 1980 1985 1990 1995 2000* 2005*
Year
*Estimate

Source: U.S. Department of the Treasury.

Graph Skills

The federal debt is the amount of money owed by the government.

Analyzing Information When did the gross federal debt first pass $1 trillion?

While Reagan cut domestic programs, he pushed for sharp increases in military spending. The president declared that the Soviet threat made it necessary to build up the military.

Government Debt

With higher defense spending and lower taxes, the government spent more money than it collected in revenue. It had to borrow money to make up the difference. This borrowing increased the federal debt—the amount of money owed by the government. Between 1970 and 1980, the federal debt had grown from $381 to $909 billion. By 1990 the debt had jumped to $3.2 trillion.

$ Economics
Recession and Recovery

President Reagan's new economic policies seemed to falter when a serious recession began early in his first term. However, the economy recovered a year later and began to boom.

In 1983 the economy began a long, steady rise. Businesses expanded, and the high jobless rate of 1982 declined. Investors showed confidence in the economy with a boom in stock trading.

The federal debt continued to grow as well. In 1985 Congress tried to halt growth of the debt by passing the **Gramm-Rudman-Hollings Act.** The act set a series of targets for eliminating the federal budget deficit by 1991. If Congress and the president could not agree on *voluntary* spending cuts, the law called for *automatic* spending cuts to balance the budget. The provision for automatic cuts did not apply to all areas of the budget, however, so it had limited success.

✓ Reading Check **Explaining** What is the amount of money the government owes called?

Reagan's Foreign Policy

Ronald Reagan pledged in his campaign to wage a tough fight against communism. To carry out his policy, President Reagan launched a massive buildup of the military. He expanded the American arsenal of tanks, ships, aircraft, and nuclear missiles. He defended these actions by quoting George Washington's advice: "To be prepared for war is one of the most effective means of preserving peace."

Reagan also proposed an antimissile defense system, the **Strategic Defense Initiative** (SDI). Nicknamed "Star Wars," the SDI would provide a defensive shield against enemy missiles. However, scientists were unable to develop the technology for the SDI.

Latin America

Besides building up the nation's military strength, Reagan also committed American forces and aid to the fight against communism, especially in nearby Latin America.

Late in the Carter presidency, Communist rebels in **Nicaragua**—called **Sandinistas**—had overthrown the government. After becoming president, Reagan sent aid to the **contras,** a group battling the Sandinistas. The fighting in Nicaragua continued for many years and became a source of disagreement between President Reagan and Congress.

In October 1983, President Reagan took direct military action in the Caribbean. Rebels on the tiny Caribbean island of Grenada staged an uprising. Concerned about the fate of 800 American medical students on the island, Reagan dispatched troops to rescue the Americans and establish a prodemocracy government. Reagan's action won widespread approval at home.

The Middle East

President Reagan was less successful with peace efforts in the Middle East. In 1982, he sent a force of marines to help keep the peace in the war-torn nation of Lebanon. The Americans soon were caught in a web of violence. A car bomb blast killed more than 60 people at the U.S. embassy in Beirut in April 1983. Then in October, 241 Americans and 58 French died in attacks on U.S. and French military headquarters. Rather than become more deeply involved in the struggle, the president withdrew all U.S. forces from Lebanon.

✔Reading Check **Summarizing** What is SDI?

Reagan's Second Term

By 1984 the American economy was booming. In his State of the Union Address, President Reagan declared:

❝America is back—standing tall, looking [toward the future] with courage, confidence and hope.❞

President Reagan and Vice President **George Bush** continued using this optimistic theme in their campaign for reelection. The Democrats chose **Walter Mondale,** vice president under Jimmy Carter, and **Geraldine Ferraro,** a member of Congress from New York. Ferraro became the first woman to run for vice president on a major political party ticket.

Reagan won the electoral votes of 49 out of 50 states. It was one of the most lopsided presidential elections in American history. Spurred on by high employment, a strong economy, and low interest rates, Reagan enjoyed high popularity ratings early in his second term.

Presidents and Labor Unions

President Reagan was once president of a labor union. The former broadcaster, Hollywood screen actor, and governor of California was president of the Screen Actors' Guild. He is the only president to have also been the chief official of a union.

The Iran-Contra Scandal

Despite his popularity, a scandal cast a shadow over part of President Reagan's second term. Terrorists, with ties to the Iranian government, held U.S. citizens hostage in Lebanon. Hoping to secure the release of the hostages, Reagan officials made a deal with Iran.

Marine lieutenant colonel **Oliver North** and Navy vice admiral John Poindexter, both assigned to the White House National Security Council, arranged for the sale of weapons to Iran in return for help in freeing American hostages. North and Poindexter decided to funnel money from this secret arms sale to help the Nicaraguan contras.

News of these deals—which came to be known as the **Iran-Contra scandal**—created an uproar. Critics charged that these deals violated federal laws barring officials from aiding the contras. They also said that the deals violated the Constitution by interfering with Congress's role in making foreign policy. Congress held hearings to determine whether the president took part in breaking the law. But there was never any proof of the president's involvement.

A Changing Soviet Policy

A remarkable shift in Soviet-American relations began to take shape at the beginning of Reagan's second term as president. Changes in Soviet leadership helped trigger the change. In 1985 Communist Party leaders of the Soviet Union chose a new general secretary, or leader—**Mikhail Gorbachev.** To the surprise of people all around the world, Gorbachev was committed to reforming the Soviet government. He called for a policy of glasnost—opening Soviet society to new ideas.

President Reagan and Soviet leader Gorbachev shake hands at their June 1988 summit meeting in Moscow. **What major step did both leaders take earlier toward ending the threat of nuclear war?**

Gorbachev also tried to change the way his country was governed. Moving away from the government's near-total control of the economy, he allowed more democracy and local economic planning. This new policy, perestroika, encouraged the Soviets to seek even greater changes.

With the Soviet economy in trouble, Gorbachev knew that the Soviet Union could not afford to build nuclear weapons. At several meetings he tried to convince President Reagan that he wanted to end the nuclear arms race. These early meetings accomplished little.

In 1987, however, President Reagan and Premier Gorbachev signed an agreement, the **Intermediate-Range Nuclear Forces (INF) Treaty.** The treaty aimed to reduce the number of nuclear missiles in each superpower's arsenal. Reagan explained the agreement by quoting what he said was a Russian proverb: "Trust, but verify." While both nations still held vast nuclear arsenals, they had taken a major step toward reducing the threat of nuclear war.

✔ **Reading Check** **Explaining** What were glasnost and perestroika?

SECTION 1 ASSESSMENT

Checking for Understanding

1. **Key Terms** Use each of these terms in a complete sentence that will help explain its meaning: deregulation, federal debt, glasnost, perestroika
2. **Reviewing Facts** List two of President Reagan's actions that proved he was committed to creating a more conservative government.

Reviewing Themes

3. **Economic Factors** Why did President Reagan believe that lowering taxes would aid the economy?

Critical Thinking

4. **Drawing Conclusions** Do you think Reagan administration officials were justified in violating congressional laws in the Iran-Contra incident? Explain.
5. **Organizing Information** Re-create the diagram below and explain why each of these people was in the news.

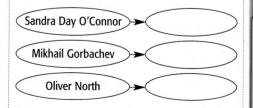

Analyzing Visuals

6. **Graph Skills** Review the graph of the Gross Federal Debt shown on page 924. What years are shown? What was the first year the debt was almost twice the amount it was five years before?

Interdisciplinary Activity

Research Find the literal meaning of the terms *contras* (Spanish) and *perestroika* (Russian). Then find an English word or phrase that has the same meaning. Use the two terms in a complete sentence.

Technology

SKILLBUILDER

Using an Electronic Spreadsheet

Why Learn This Skill?

People use electronic spreadsheets to manage numbers quickly and easily. You can use a spreadsheet any time a problem involves numbers that you can arrange in rows and columns.

Learning the Skill

A spreadsheet is an electronic worksheet. All spreadsheets follow a basic design of rows and columns. Each column (vertical) is assigned a letter or a number. Each row (horizontal) is assigned a number. Each point where a column and row intersect is called a *cell*. The cell's position on the spreadsheet is labeled according to its corresponding column and row—Column A, Row 1 (A1); Column B, Row 2 (B2), etc.

Spreadsheets use *standard formulas* to calculate the numbers. You create a simple mathematical equation that uses these standard formulas and the computer does the calculations for you.

Practicing the Skill

Suppose you want to know how many votes the Republican, Democratic, and Independent candidates received across six states in the 2000 presidential election. Use these steps to create a spreadsheet that will provide this information:

1. In cells B1, C1, and D1 respectively, type a candidate's name or political party. In cell E1, type the term *total*.

2. In cells A2–A7, type the name of a state. In cell A8, type the word *total*.

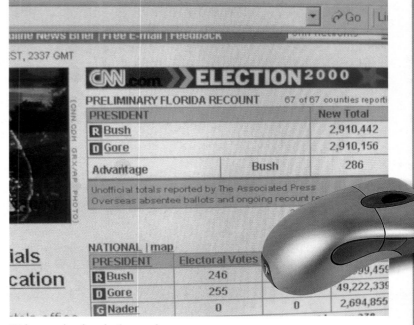

Web page showing election results

3. In row 2, enter the number of votes each candidate received in the state named in cell A2. Repeat this process in rows 3–7.

4. Create a formula to calculate the votes. The formula for the equation tells what cells (B2 + C2 + D2) to add together.

5. Copy the formula down in the cells for the other five states.

6. Use the process in steps 4 and 5 to create and copy a formula to calculate the total number of votes each candidate received.

Applying the Skill

Using a Spreadsheet Use a spreadsheet to enter your test scores and your homework grades. At the end of the grading period, the spreadsheet will calculate your average grade.

SECTION 2 The Bush Presidency

Guide to Reading

Main Idea
George Bush had an active foreign policy and presided over the fall of the Soviet Union and the end of the Cold War.

Key Terms
coup, bankruptcy

Reading Strategy
Organizing Information As you read the section, re-create the time line below and provide three key events leading to the fall of communism.

1980   1989   1990

Read To Learn
- how the Soviet Union collapsed.
- how George Bush used the military overseas.
- how George Bush had difficulty domestically.

Section Theme
Global Connections Great political changes marked the global situation during George Bush's presidency.

Preview of Events

◆1988	◆1990	◆1992

1988
George Bush is elected president

June 1989
Chinese students protest in Tiananmen Square

November 1989
The Berlin Wall is torn down

January 1991
Allies launch Operation Desert Storm

December 1991
The Soviet Union is dismantled

AN American Story

On September 2, 1944, a young pilot took part in a bombing mission against Japanese bases. World War II was raging. His plane—launched from an aircraft carrier—suffered a direct hit from a Japanese anti-aircraft gun. The pilot and his two crew members bailed out into the Pacific Ocean. A U.S. submarine rescued the pilot from a life raft, but the other two men were never found. For his heroism, the pilot—George Bush—was awarded the Distinguished Flying Cross. More than 40 years later, Bush would become the forty-first president of the United States.

A New World Order

As Ronald Reagan's second term drew to a close, the election campaign for his successor heated up. Vice President **George H.W. Bush** swept through the 1988 primaries to win the Republican presidential nomination. Bush chose Indiana senator **Dan Quayle** as his running mate. Many Democrats vied for their party's nomination, but the field quickly narrowed to two candidates—civil rights leader **Jesse Jackson** and Massachusetts governor **Michael Dukakis.** Dukakis, who ran the most effective primary campaign, won the nomination and chose Senator **Lloyd Bentsen** of Texas as his running mate.

On Election Day, Bush carried 40 states, giving him 426 electoral votes to 112 for Dukakis. However, Bush's victory did not extend to Congress. The Democrats retained control of the House and the Senate.

A Changing Soviet Union

With much experience in foreign affairs, newly elected president George Bush was called upon to steer the United States through a time of sweeping change facing the world. Many important changes dealt with the Soviet Union.

In December 1988, Soviet leader Mikhail Gorbachev stood before the United Nations to describe the "new world order" to come. Gorbachev stressed that people throughout the world wanted "independence, democracy, and social justice."

Gorbachev wanted to end the arms race so he could focus on reforms within the Soviet Union. He sought to continue the progress on arms control begun with President Reagan. In 1990 Gorbachev and President Bush agreed with European leaders to destroy tanks and other conventional weapons positioned throughout Europe. In 1991, with the **Strategic Arms Reduction Treaty** (START), they achieved a breakthrough. For the first time, two nuclear powers agreed to destroy existing nuclear weapons.

Unrest in the Soviet Union

Most Soviet citizens, however, were more concerned about their own problems than about arms control. For years they had endured shortages of food and basic items such as shoes and soap because of government mismanagement

Lech Walesa

and heavy defense spending. Gorbachev's policies aimed to solve the economic problems, but changes came slowly. The shortages continued, and people grew impatient with the conditions.

With Gorbachev's policy of glasnost, Soviet citizens began to express their dissatisfaction openly. Thousands of people marched through Moscow in February 1990, demanding an end to Communist rule. Unrest and calls for democracy had also spread throughout the Soviet Union. Many of the republics that made up the Soviet Union demanded independence.

A Rising Tide of Freedom

While events were unfolding in the Soviet Union, the people of Eastern Europe also grew restless. Many people sensing change occurring in the Soviet Union under Gorbachev's leadership felt freer to demand change in their countries as well.

The first democratic moves outside of the Soviet Union occurred in **Poland,** where shipyard workers had won the right to form an independent labor union—called **Solidarity**—in August 1980. **Lech Walesa,** the leader of Solidarity, emerged as a symbol of resistance to Communist rule. He led the Poles in calling for reforms. Although the government cracked down on the democratic movement in the mid-1980s, the movement gained strength and forced the government to hold open elections in June 1989.

The democratic cause spread to neighboring countries. Across Eastern Europe demonstrators filled the streets of major cities. As a result of a relaxation of Soviet control and public pressure, long-sealed national borders were opened and Communist governments toppled. In the last three months of 1989, the iron curtain that had separated Eastern and Western Europe for more than 40 years began to crumble. Throughout 1989 Gorbachev not only refused to intervene, but he encouraged reform.

NATIONAL GEOGRAPHIC

Russia and the Independent Republics

Geography *Skills*

By the early 1990s, all the republics had declared independence from the Soviet Union.
1. **Location** What republics border Belarus?
2. **Location** Which of the republics have the best access to shipping lanes in the Black Sea?

The Wall Comes Tumbling Down

Freedom also came to East Germany—the focus of so much cold war tension. With protests raging and thousands of citizens fleeing to West Germany, the Communist government opened the Berlin Wall on November 9, 1989.

Germans brought hammers and chisels to chop away at the Berlin Wall, long the symbol of the barrier to the West. In 1990 East Germany voted to reunite with West Germany.

Collapse of the Soviet Union

As Europe was changing, Gorbachev faced mounting opposition from political rivals within the Soviet Union. Some reformers demanded that he move more quickly. Hard-line Communists in the military and secret police resisted his changes and feared the collapse of the Soviet empire.

In August 1991, the hard-liners struck back. A group of Communist officials and army generals staged a **coup**, an overthrow of the government. They held Gorbachev captive and ordered soldiers to seize the parliament building.

As the world waited anxiously, about 50,000 Russians surrounded the parliament building to protect it from the soldiers. **Boris Yeltsin,** president of the Russian Republic and a reformer, stood on top of a tank and declared, "Democracy will win!" President Bush telephoned Yeltsin to express America's support. On August 22 the coup collapsed. Freed, Gorbachev returned to Moscow.

The defeat of the coup turned the tide of democracy into a tidal wave. Soon all 15 republics had declared their independence from the Soviet Union. Yeltsin outlawed the Communist Party in Russia. On December 25, 1991, Gorbachev announced the end of the Soviet Union and the Soviet flag that flew over the Kremlin was lowered for the last time.

The End of the Cold War

President Bush responded quickly to the new situation. In the spring of 1992, Bush and other world leaders pledged $24 billion in assistance to the former Soviet republics. President Bush declared:

> ❝For over 40 years, the United States led the West in the struggle against communism and the threat it posed to our most precious values. That confrontation is over.❞

Reading Check **Cause and Effect** How did the fall of communism in Eastern Europe affect Germany?

A New Foreign Policy

With the end of the Cold War came both renewed hope and new challenges to maintaining world peace. While trying to redefine the goals of American foreign policy, President Bush had to deal with crises in Central America, China, the Middle East, and the Balkans.

Panama

President Bush had declared that a "war on drugs" was one of the major goals of his administration. This war played a role in Bush's policy in Central America.

Under the rule of General **Manuel Noriega,** political repression and corruption had become widespread in Panama. In 1988 Noriega was charged with drug trafficking by an American court. Previously, he had refused to yield power to the newly elected president of Panama, Guillermo Endara. In December 1989, Bush ordered U.S. troops to the Central American nation to overthrow Noriega. When the troops gained control of the country, Noriega surrendered. Endara became Panama's new president, and the U.S. troops left Panama. In 1992 Noriega was tried and convicted in the United States.

China

George Bush had served as the first U.S. **envoy**—diplomatic representative—to China, when the two countries reopened relations in 1974. He took a special interest in China, claiming, "I know the Chinese." During the 1980s, China's Communist government began to reform the economy, but it refused to make political reforms. In May 1989, students and workers in China held demonstrations calling for more democracy. As the protests spread, the country seemed on the verge of revolution.

The Chinese government sent troops to crush the uprising. On June 4, 1989, soldiers and tanks killed several hundred protesters gathered in **Tiananmen Square** in the center of Beijing. World leaders condemned the slaughter. Although President Bush disapproved of the Chinese leaders' use of force, he carefully avoided words or actions that might lead the Chinese to break off relations with the United States. He did not believe that international pressure or trade sanctions would result in a change in Chinese policies. Although Bush's policy met opposition, it permitted U.S. trade with China to continue to grow.

The Persian Gulf War

The Bush administration—and the world—faced a serious challenge to stability in 1990. On August 2 Iraq's dictator, **Saddam Hussein** (hoo•SAYN), sent his army into **Kuwait,** a small neighboring country rich in oil. Kuwait was quickly overwhelmed. The fear grew that Iraq would also invade Saudi Arabia.

Vowing to "draw a line in the sand," President Bush persuaded other nations to join what he called **Operation Desert Shield.** Hundreds of thousands of troops moved to Saudi Arabia to prevent an invasion of that country. The coalition forces were under the command of U. S. general **Norman Schwarzkopf.** Hussein was ordered to withdraw his troops from Kuwait—but the Iraqi troops did not leave and tension mounted. The United Nations set a deadline. Iraq must withdraw by January 15, 1991, or the allies would use force to remove them. Congress voted to support military action if Iraq did not withdraw.

Operation Desert Storm

Iraq refused to budge, and on January 16 the allies launched **Operation Desert Storm.** Laser-guided missiles and thousands of tons of bombs

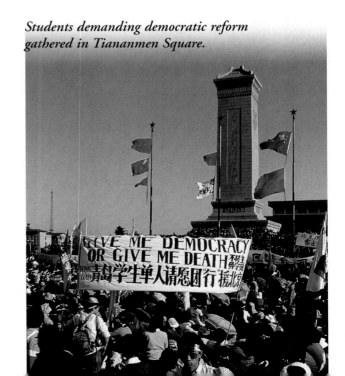

Students demanding democratic reform gathered in Tiananmen Square.

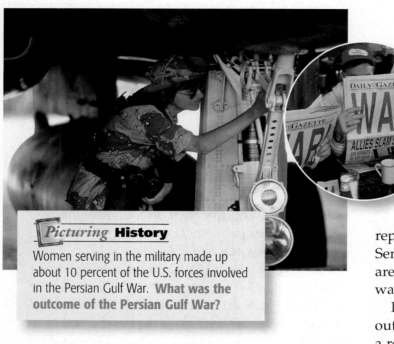

Picturing History

Women serving in the military made up about 10 percent of the U.S. forces involved in the Persian Gulf War. **What was the outcome of the Persian Gulf War?**

fell on Iraq, destroying its air defenses and other military targets and damaging many civilian sites. President Bush explained the attack:

66The world could wait no longer. . . . While the world waited, Saddam Hussein met every overture of peace with open contempt.99

After almost six weeks of round-the-clock bombardment, Hussein's forces still refused to leave Kuwait. In late February the allies opened the second phase of Desert Storm—a ground war in which they attacked Iraqi troops from the side and rear. At the same time, planes bombarded Iraqi positions.

Thousands of Iraqi soldiers died. Thousands more surrendered. Just 100 hours after the ground war began, President Bush suspended military action. "Kuwait is liberated," he announced. "America and the world have kept their word." Iraq accepted the allied cease-fire terms, and Saddam Hussein's troops finally left Kuwait.

Americans celebrated the sudden victory. They hailed the leaders of Desert Storm, Norman Schwarzkopf and General **Colin Powell,** chairman of the Joint Chiefs of Staff, and held parades for the troops. President Bush's approval rating in opinion polls soared above 90 percent. After the war, the United States helped rebuild Kuwait. It took nine months to extinguish the hundreds of oil well fires set by fleeing Iraqi troops.

War in the Balkans

Another challenge to world peace arose in Yugoslavia. Yugoslavia had been composed of several republics. After the collapse of Yugoslavia's government, the republics of **Slovenia, Croatia,** and **Bosnia-Herzegovina** declared independence in 1991. The population of Croatia and Bosnia included many Serbs—people from the Yugoslav republic of Serbia. These Serbs, backed by the Serbian republic, fought to hold on to certain areas of Croatia and Bosnia. In the terrible civil war that followed, thousands died.

Reports of atrocities committed by the Serbs outraged world leaders. In 1992 the UN passed a resolution that placed a boycott on trade with Serbia until the fighting stopped.

✓ Reading Check **Evaluating** How long did Operation Desert Storm last?

Domestic Issues

Early in his presidency, Bush faced a banking crisis. During the 1980s, the Reagan administration had cut regulations in many industries. New laws eased restrictions on savings and loan associations (S&Ls)—financial institutions that specialized in making loans to buy homes.

The new laws allowed managers of S&Ls to become more aggressive in offering attractive returns to savers—and in making far more risky loans. When many borrowers could not repay their loans and real estate values declined, S&Ls began to lose millions of dollars. Many failed completely and closed their doors. Individual deposits in S&Ls were insured by the government, which now had to pay out billions of dollars to the customers of the failed institutions. To prevent the crisis from spreading, the government bailed out other struggling S&Ls. This policy eventually cost taxpayers almost $500 billion.

Economic Downturn

The heavy borrowing of the 1980s loomed as another source of trouble for the economy. As the federal debt continued to reach new highs, business and personal debt grew as well. In 1990, when the economy slowed to a recession, many people and businesses could not meet loan payments. Some had to declare bankruptcy, selling off everything they owned to pay debts. Across the country businesses closed. Cuts in military spending, made possible by the end of the Cold War, led to additional job losses.

Many people called for the government to step in to stimulate the economy. President Bush refused to increase federal spending. He did agree to extend unemployment benefits for people who had lost their jobs, but he opposed further government involvement. The nation had to wait out the recession.

Accomplishments

While the president and Congress disagreed on many issues, they cooperated on some legislation. In 1990, for example, the president signed a law updating the Clean Air Act. The next year he signed a law combating job discrimination.

Bush and Congress agreed on a major civil rights law as well. The Americans with Disabilities Act of 1990 outlawed job discrimination against people with disabilities. It also required institutions to provide disabled people with easier access to workplaces, communications, transportation, and housing.

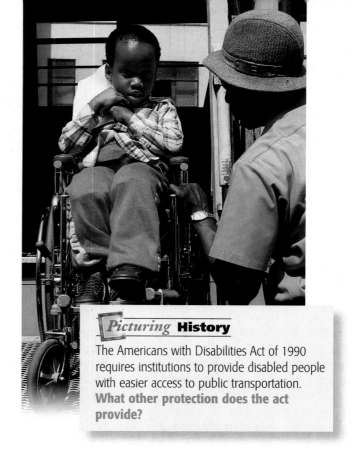

Picturing **History**

The Americans with Disabilities Act of 1990 requires institutions to provide disabled people with easier access to public transportation. **What other protection does the act provide?**

Another important part of the president's domestic agenda was the war on illegal drugs. In 1989 President Bush created the Office of National Drug Control Policy. This department coordinates the activities of more than 50 federal agencies involved in the war on drugs.

✓ **Reading Check** **Identifying** What is an S&L?

SECTION 2 ASSESSMENT

Checking for Understanding

1. **Key Terms** Use each of these terms in a complete sentence that will help explain its meaning: coup, bankruptcy

2. **Reviewing Facts** Explain why the people of Eastern Europe abandoned communism.

Reviewing Themes

3. **Global Connections** Compare President Bush's handling of the Tiananmen Square incident in China to his handling of Iraq's invasion of Kuwait.

Critical Thinking

4. **Determining Cause and Effect** What economic issues reduced Bush's popularity?

5. **Organizing Information** Re-create the diagram below and list what each person did to cause Bush to respond with military power.

Analyzing Visuals

6. **Geography Skills** Examine the map on page 930. Which of the independent states is larger—Georgia or Uzbekistan? What bodies of water does Russia border?

Interdisciplinary Activity

Geography Make a photocopy of your state map. Draw a "wall" that runs down the middle of your state north to south. If you could not cross this wall, which large cities would you be cut off from?

GLOBAL CANDY

THE CHOCOLATE CANDY that you buy at your local store is produced by a vast network of people and businesses all around the world.

The raw ingredients for chocolate are grown all over the world, then are processed into candy in high-tech factories in industrialized nations. Cacao beans, chocolate's primary raw material, are gathered from trees in countries along the Equator. Approximately 40 percent of the world's cacao comes from the West African nation of Côte d'Ivoire.

Sugar to sweeten chocolate is processed from sugarcane and sugar beets. Major exporters of sugar are found in nearly every continent.

Almond trees grow in Morocco, Iran, in southern Europe, and on the west coast of the United States.

Cacao beans are processed into cocoa butter and mixed with other ingredients in factories located mainly in Western Europe and North America. The exact process and the proportions of ingredients are usually closely guarded secrets.

Chocolate is an international product. Before World War II most products were made in a single country. As transportation and communication networks have improved, more and more multinational companies have come to rely on natural resources and manufacturing facilities in many countries. Now roughly one third of all products produced involve several nations. What we decide to buy today affects people and businesses all around the world.

LEARNING from GEOGRAPHY

1. **Why would a nation need to import resources rather than use its own?**

2. **What patterns do you see in the locations of the countries that grow cacao? Almonds?**

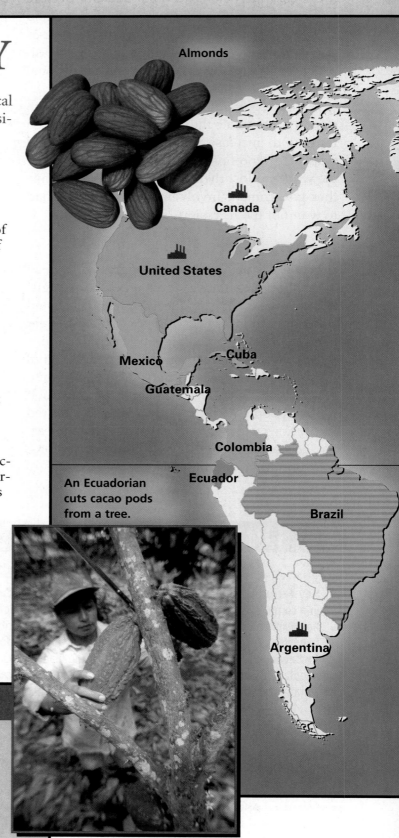

An Ecuadorian cuts cacao pods from a tree.

Almonds

Canada

United States

Mexico

Cuba

Guatemala

Colombia

Ecuador

Brazil

Argentina

Workers pack chocolates at a candy factory in Belgium.

Belgium
United Kingdom
Switzerland
France
Portugal
Spain
Italy
Greece
Morocco
Germany
Poland
Austria
Russia
Turkey
Iran
Japan

Ghana
Côte d'Ivoire
Nigeria
Cameroon

Thailand

Malaysia

EQUATOR

Indonesia

South Africa

Australia

Candy Bar Raw Materials

	Almond growers
	Cacao growers
	Sugar exporters
	Chocolate-producing country

0   1500 miles
0   1500 kilometers

Farmers oversee a sugarcane harvest in South Africa.

N
W   E
S

935

SECTION 3 A New Century

Guide to Reading

Main Idea
During the Clinton and Bush administrations, the nation faced new challenges at home and abroad.

Key Terms
grassroots, budget deficit, line-item veto, gross domestic product, impeach, incumbent, Internet, ozone, global warming, terrorism

Reading Strategy
Classifying Information As you read the section, re-create the diagram below and describe three domestic programs of the 1990s.

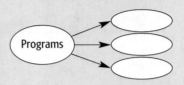

Read to Learn
• why President Clinton was impeached by Congress.
• why the election of 2000 triggered controversy.

Section Theme
Continuity and Change As the nation looked to the future, a changing world created new challenges.

Preview of Events

✦1992	✦1996		✦2000
1992 Bill Clinton elected president	**1996** Clinton wins reelection	**1998** Impeachment trial results in Clinton's acquittal	**2000** George W. Bush elected president

AN American Story

A president appears on MTV. Politicians perform rock music on talk shows. What would George Washington have thought about such events? In 1991, polls showed that voters were turned off by politics. So the 1992 presidential candidates found new ways to reach the public—especially young people. President Bush and challenger Bill Clinton appeared on TV and radio talk shows. Both candidates appeared on MTV.

The Clinton Administration

After the Gulf War victory, President Bush's popularity soared. A troubled economy, however, hurt Bush's reelection chances for 1992 and encouraged challengers to enter the race. The Democrats nominated Arkansas governor **Bill Clinton** to run against President Bush. Clinton chose Tennessee senator **Al Gore** as his running mate. The Clinton campaign focused on the economy and the high unemployment rate.

Unhappy with "politics as usual," many Americans did not want to vote for either Bush or Clinton. A grassroots movement—people organizing at the local level around the nation—put Texas businessman **H. Ross Perot** on the ballot as a third-party candidate. Perot stressed the need to end the government's **deficit spending,** or spending more money than it takes in.

Americans elected Clinton, the first president born after World War II. Clinton received 43 percent of the popular vote, Bush 38 percent, and Perot 19 percent. Clinton received less than a majority of the votes because of Perot's strong showing, the highest percentage of popular votes for any third-party candidate since Theodore Roosevelt in 1912.

Domestic Program

One of the new president's goals was reducing the budget deficit—the amount by which spending exceeds revenue. Clinton proposed cutting government spending, raising taxes for middle- and upper-income Americans, and providing tax credits to the poorest. Most Republicans in Congress opposed this plan, but it narrowly passed.

Clinton faced even stronger opposition to his plan for health-care reform. His goal was to control rising health-care costs and provide adequate health insurance for every American. The president named the First Lady, **Hillary Rodham Clinton,** to head the task force.

Congress rejected the Clinton plan, calling it too expensive and too reliant on government control. Later, Congress did pass a number of measures that provided more health-care protection for workers who changed jobs, the elderly, children, and other groups not covered.

During his first term, President Clinton won some legislative battles. Despite strong opposition, the president succeeded in passing the Brady Bill of 1993. The law imposed a waiting period and background checks for handgun purchases. The 1994 crime bill banned 19 kinds of assault weapons and provided for 100,000 new police officers.

Another Clinton proposal that became law was the Family and Medical Leave Act of 1993. It permitted workers to take time off from their jobs for special family situations.

Contract with America

Before the 1994 congressional elections, a group of Republicans crafted a new plan of action. Led by Representative Newt Gingrich of Georgia, congressional Republicans declared a **Contract with America** to

❝return to the basic values that had built the country: work and family and the recognition of a higher moral authority.❞

In the contract, Republicans promised to reduce the federal government, balance the budget, lower taxes, and reform how Congress operates. They also pledged to pass laws to reduce crime, reform welfare, and strengthen the family.

The result was a strong Republican victory in the 1994 elections. For the first time in 40 years, the Republicans controlled both houses of Congress. In their first hundred days in office, the Republicans passed many parts of the Contract with America.

Congress passed a line-item veto bill. Intended as a way to reduce wasteful spending, the line-item veto allowed the president to cancel any individual items within a spending bill. The Supreme Court later overturned the law. It ruled that such an increase in the president's power could be granted only through a constitutional amendment.

Other parts of the Contract with America were also rejected. Some proposals stalled in the Senate, and President Clinton vetoed several Republican bills on welfare reform and the budget. Clinton argued that budget cuts would hurt elderly people on Medicare, damage the environment, and damage education.

Health Care for America's Families

Picturing **History**

Health-care reform was an important program for both the president and Congress. **Why did Congress reject the Clinton plan?**

Analyzing *Political Cartoons*

Cartoonists often use the elephant to represent the Republican Party and the donkey to represent the Democratic Party. **What statement is the cartoonist making about Congress and the president?**

Budget Problems and Compromise

Disagreement between the president and congressional Republicans continued. A major dispute blocked passage of the 1996 budget, causing the federal government to run out of money. The government shut down nonessential services twice for a total of 27 days. Congress and the president recognized that compromise was needed.

Both the Republicans in Congress and President Clinton proposed plans for a balanced budget. The president also pushed for an increase in the minimum wage and sponsored a welfare reform bill that set a work requirement for people receiving benefits and put a five-year time limit on benefits.

Clinton Wins a Second Term

The Republicans hoped to recapture the White House in 1996. However, passage of the Brady Act and the Crime Act weakened Republican arguments that Clinton was soft on crime. Most important, the economy was healthy and unemployment was at a 30-year low. President Clinton easily won reelection, beating the Republican candidate, former Senate majority leader **Robert Dole.**

The American economy continued to grow. One measure of this growth is the gross domestic product (GDP), which is the value of all the goods and services produced in a nation in a year. In 1996 and 1997, the GDP grew by about 4 percent a year—one of the highest rates of growth since the post-World War II boom.

The economy's growth increased the amount of tax money the government received. At the same time, the president and Congress cut back the size of the federal budget. The federal budget is prepared for a **fiscal year**—a 12-month planning period. The 1998 fiscal year ended with a federal **budget surplus**—the amount of money remaining after all expenditures—of about $80 billion, the first surplus in three decades.

Under Investigation

In 1994 legal questions arose relating to real estate investments Clinton had made while governor of Arkansas. Attorney General **Janet Reno** appointed an independent counsel to investigate the president. **Kenneth Starr,** a former federal judge, led the investigation. As other scandals were exposed, Starr widened the scope of the investigation.

In early 1998 a new scandal emerged involving a personal relationship between the president and a White House intern. Evidence suggested that the president may have committed **perjury,** or lied under oath, about the relationship. In September, Starr sent a report to Congress claiming that President Clinton had committed perjury and obstructed justice in an effort to conceal the personal relationship.

The House of Representatives voted to hold hearings to decide whether to impeach the president, in response to Starr's report. To impeach is to make a formal accusation of wrongdoing against a public official. The House scheduled the hearings for November, following the 1998 congressional elections.

With Clinton in trouble, the Republicans expected to make major gains in the 1998 elections. Instead, the Democrats gained 5 seats in the House, although they still trailed the Republicans 223 to 211. The Senate remained unchanged, with 55 Republicans and 45 Democrats. Incumbents—the current officeholders—did extremely well in the 1998 elections.

Impeachment

Although there was general agreement that the president had lied, Congress was divided over whether his actions justified impeachment. Clinton's supporters argued that his offenses did not qualify as "high crimes and misdemeanors," as stated in the Constitution. Clinton's accusers insisted that the "rule of law" is a fundamental principle of American society, and that the president should be held accountable if his actions were illegal.

On December 19, 1998, the House of Representatives passed two articles of impeachment, one for perjury and one for obstruction of justice. With this action, Bill Clinton became only the second president ever to be impeached. The case moved to the Senate for trial. A two-thirds majority Senate vote is needed to convict and remove a president from office.

On February 12, 1999, the senators cast their votes. The result was 45 guilty to 55 not guilty on the perjury article, and 50 guilty to 50 not guilty on the obstruction of justice article. Acquitted of both charges, Bill Clinton had survived the challenge to his presidency.

✓ **Reading Check** **Describing** What role did Kenneth Starr play?

Foreign Policy

Even as the nation struggled with domestic issues, international matters presented new challenges.

TWO VIEWPOINTS

Should We Convict the President?

In 1998 a political storm brewed in the nation's capital over the future of President Bill Clinton. The House of Representatives accused President Clinton of lying under oath and obstructing justice, and voted to impeach him. Now it was up to the Senate to convict and remove him from office. Passionate voices cried out for and against conviction.

Statement of Senator Paul Sarbanes (D-Md.), 1999

The gravity of what is at stake—the democratic choice of the American people—and the solemnity of the proceedings dictate that a decision to remove the President from office should follow only from the most serious of circumstances. . . .

The Articles of Impeachment that have been exhibited to the Senate fall far short of what the Founding Fathers had in mind when they placed in the hands of Congress the power to impeach and remove a President from office. They fall far short of what the American people demand to be shown and proven before their democratic choice is reversed. . . .

Statement of Senator Pete Domenici (R-N.M.), 1999

The President had a choice to make during this entire, lamentable episode. At a number of critical junctures, he had a choice either to tell the truth or to lie, first in the civil rights case, before the grand jury and on national television. Each time he chose to lie. He made that fateful choice. . . .

The President has committed high crimes and misdemeanors, in violation of his oath of office. He lied under oath. He obstructed justice. His behavior was unworthy of the Presidency of the United States.

President Clinton

Analyzing Primary Sources

1. What reasons does Senator Sarbanes give for his vote to not remove President Clinton from office?
2. Why does Senator Domenici believe that the president should be removed from office?
3. Would you have voted to remove President Clinton from office? Why or why not?

Important decisions faced American policy-makers on defining the nation's role in the post-Cold War world.

In 1993 Clinton persuaded Congress to ratify the **North American Free Trade Agreement,** or NAFTA. Under NAFTA the United States, Canada, and Mexico agreed to eliminate trade barriers among the three nations. NAFTA opponents feared a loss of U.S. jobs. Farmers also feared NAFTA, saying that low-priced Mexican produce would undercut American goods. Supporters argued that the treaty would lower prices for American consumers and expand markets.

Middle East Peace Accords

In September 1993 President Clinton invited Israeli prime minister Yitzhak Rabin and Yassir Arafat, head of the Palestine Liberation Organization (PLO), to the White House for the signing of a historic agreement between the two leaders. Israel recognized the PLO as the representative of the Palestinian people, and the PLO recognized Israel's right to exist. The agreement created a plan for limited Palestinian self-government over certain areas in Israel.

Opposition to the plan emerged on both sides and the violence continued. In 1995 an Israeli extremist assassinated Prime Minister Rabin. In 2001 Ariel Sharon, the new Israeli prime minister, pledged to put Israel's security above the peace process. The region remained as far from peace as ever.

Peacekeeping in the Balkans

As you read earlier, civil war had erupted in the former Yugoslavia. Bitter fighting followed, especially in Bosnia, where Serbs engaged in **ethnic cleansing**—forcibly removing or killing members—of the Muslim population. NATO air strikes on their positions brought Serbs to the bargaining table. The Clinton administration then led peace talks, which produced the Dayton Accords in December 1995.

In 1998 Serbian leader **Slobodan Milosevic** attempted to drive the Muslims out of the Kosovo region. The United States and NATO launched air strikes against Serbia, until Serb troops withdrew from Kosovo and its Muslim population could return.

✓ **Reading Check** **Summarizing**
What did critics say NAFTA would cause?

A New President for a New Century

President Clinton's two terms in office left the country divided. Many Americans were pleased with the economy, but were disappointed with the president's personal behavior. As the 2000 election approached, the major parties looked for candidates who appealed to a broad cross section of voters.

Picturing **History**

The Senate has tried two presidents on impeachment charges: Andrew Johnson and Bill Clinton. Johnson was acquitted by only one vote in 1868. **What was the verdict in Clinton's trial?**

Andrew Johnson and ticket of admission to impeachment trial

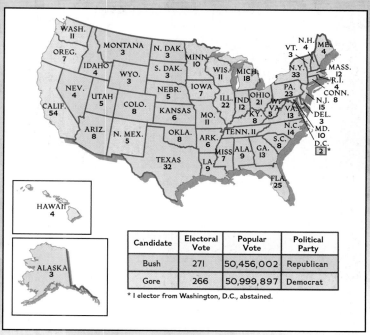

Candidate	Electoral Vote	Popular Vote	Political Party
Bush	271	50,456,002	Republican
Gore	266	50,999,897	Democrat

* I elector from Washington, D.C., abstained.

Geography Skills

The 2000 election marked the first election in 112 years where the candidate who won the popular vote did not win the electoral vote.

1. **Location** What states have more than 20 electoral votes?
2. **Location** What candidate won the electoral votes in each of these states?

The Election of 2000

The Democrats nominated Vice President Al Gore for president, hoping that the popularity of Clinton's policies would convince Americans to vote for Gore. The large Republican field eventually came down to two men: Governor **George W. Bush** of Texas and Senator **John McCain** of Arizona. Ultimately, the Republicans chose Bush, the son of former President Bush, as their nominee.

Gore made history by naming Senator **Joseph Lieberman** as his running mate. This marked the first time in U.S. history that a Jewish American ran on a national ticket. George W. Bush chose **Richard Cheney** as his running mate. Cheney served as chief of staff to President Gerald Ford and defense secretary to former President George Bush in 1989.

A major issue of the campaign of 2000 was what to do with the budget surplus. Gore and Bush agreed that Social Security and Medicare needed reform, but disagreed on the details. Both also supported tax cuts and plans to help seniors pay for prescription drugs. Consumer activist **Ralph Nader** also entered the race. Noting that "too much power in the hands of the few has further weakened our democracy," Nader ran as the nominee of the Green Party.

The 2000 election was extraordinarily close between Bush and Gore. Although Bush had a slim lead in Florida, the results were so close an automatic recount was required by law. Without Florida's 25 electoral votes, neither Bush nor Gore had the 270 electoral votes needed to win.

Gore also asked for manual recounts in several counties, and a battle began over whether and how to conduct them. Lawsuits were filed in state and federal courts. The issue ultimately reached the United States Supreme Court. On December 12, five weeks after the election, the Court issued its decision after a five-to-four vote. In *Bush* v. *Gore,* the Court ruled that a hand recount of selected votes in Florida ordered by the Florida Supreme Court violated the equal protection clause of the Constitution. It further held that there was not enough time to conduct a recount that would pass constitutional standards.

President Bush meets with the cabinet.

In a televised speech the following day, Gore conceded. On January 20, 2001, Bush became the 43rd president of the United States.

The Bush Administration

Protests followed the election. Some groups claimed the Florida counts were unfair. Others criticized the decision of the Supreme Court. In his Inaugural Address, President Bush repeated his campaign message of "inclusion, not division," saying America should be united.

The need for unity and cooperation was important in Congress as well. After the election the Senate was evenly split—50 Republicans and 50 Democrats. This meant that the Republicans held control because Vice President Richard Cheney, as president of the Senate, could cast the deciding vote when there was a tie.

Then Vermont senator James Jeffords left the Republican Party in May 2001 and became an independent. This led to a historic switch in power, transferring control to the Democrats in mid-session.

Cabinet and Advisers

Nominating the members of the cabinet was one of the new president's first responsibilities. President Bush named popular retired General of the Army **Colin Powell** as secretary of state. The Senate quickly approved Powell and most of Bush's other nominees. However, Bush's choice for secretary of labor, Linda Chavez, was forced to withdraw when questions arose over her housing an illegal immigrant. Replacing Chavez was

Elaine Chao, the first Asian American woman to serve in a president's cabinet. Chao had previously served as director of the Peace Corps.

Other women played leading roles in the new administration. **Condoleezza Rice,** the first woman in history to hold the job of national security adviser, was instrumental in shaping foreign policy. First Lady **Laura Bush** promoted education. She organized a series of book festivals to raise money for libraries. She also called attention to the need for recruiting more teachers and improving reading skills.

Tax Cut

During the campaign, Bush promised a tax cut, and he quickly presented his proposal to Congress. The proposal caused much debate. Republicans argued that it was the peoples' money and that they deserved it back. They also claimed that the tax cut would help the slowing economy. Opponents argued that the money could be used more responsibly elsewhere, such as for Social Security or for paying off the national debt.

In June 2001 President Bush signed into law the largest reduction in federal taxes since 1981. Joined by a bipartisan group from the House and Senate, the President signed a 10-year, $1.3 trillion tax-cut bill into law.

International Affairs

The Bush administration proposed a National Missile Defense system, designed to protect the United States from any incoming missiles by shooting them down before they reach American airspace. Supporters viewed the system as a means of protection against an unstable leader who might use nuclear weapons. Critics countered that the system would renew an international arms race.

As President Bush's top military adviser, Colin Powell laid out a blueprint for intervention in international conflict. The **Powell Doctrine** calls for using American troops only when a vital national interest is at stake and there is a clear and realistic goal.

✓ **Reading Check** **Describing** What is Elaine Chao's role in the Bush administration?

Looking to the Future

As Americans entered a new century, they faced many uncertainties—and opportunities. New technologies and a changing society had begun to transform America in new ways.

President Bush said one of his major aims was to stimulate global economic growth. He called for a world trading system that is dramatically more open and more free:

❝We know that nations that open their economies to the benefits of trade are more successful in climbing out of poverty. . . . We also know that free trade encourages the habits of liberty that sustain freedom. . . . ❞

Since 1995 the World Trade Organization (WTO) has administered trade practices between many nations. The WTO has more than 146 members.

Growth of technology industries boosted economic growth. Personal computers were being used in homes, schools, and businesses in greater numbers than ever before. Through the Internet, a worldwide linking of computer networks, American students could communicate with students in countries halfway around the world.

A Changing Society

As America entered the twenty-first century, its population had begun to change significantly.

By 2002, more than 10 percent of the population was foreign-born. Asian Americans made up about 4 percent of the population; Hispanic Americans more than 12 percent. The Hispanic community is now the nation's largest minority community.

Because Americans were living longer than in the past, elderly people formed an increasing portion of the population. The Census Bureau reported that more than 12 percent of the population was over 65 years of age in the year 2000.

An important issue facing the nation was reform of Medicare. Medicare is the federal health care program for the elderly. By the summer of

People In History

Colin Powell 1937–

During the Persian Gulf War, the highest-ranking military officer serving was Colin Powell, the chairman of the Joint Chiefs of Staff. He was the youngest person and the first African American to hold that position. A four-star general, Powell had a very distinguished military career for thirty-five years, serving twice in Vietnam and working for four presidents.

Born to Jamaican immigrants, Powell was raised in Harlem and the South Bronx of New York City. He attended public school and the City College of New York, where he studied geology and began military training.

After the Gulf War, Powell wrote an autobiography and established a charitable organization, America's Promise—the Alliance for Youth, that helps children.

In 2001, Powell went to work for his fifth president, George W. Bush, as the first African American secretary of state.

2002, both the House and the Senate had passed bills that added a benefit for prescription drugs.

Congress also reacted to an increase in corporate scandals. For example, at one large energy trading company, Enron, corporate leaders cost investors and employees billions of dollars before the company went bankrupt. The federal government tightened accounting regulations and toughened penalties for dishonest executives.

Environmental Challenges

For years, scientists noted that the earth's atmosphere was losing ozone. This layer of gas protects life on Earth from cancer-causing rays of the sun. In 1987, the United States and 23 other nations agreed to stop making chemicals that might be weakening the ozone layer.

Scientists continued to debate the effects of global warming. They warned that the steady increase in average world temperatures could bring about major changes in weather patterns, the environment, and crop production.

Threats to Peace and Security

Preserving peace remains the most pressing global issue. In the late 1900s and early 2000s, acts of terror multiplied. New dangers lurked with the development of new kinds of warfare, including chemical weapons and biological weapons, which deliberately spread disease among humans.

Terrorism—the use of violence by groups against civilians to achieve a political goal—threatened the security of the nation. On April 19, 1995, a massive bomb exploded at the Murrah Federal Building in downtown Oklahoma City, leaving 168 dead. The tragedy focused national attention on the violent anti-government feelings of private American militia groups. In January 1998, Theodore Kaczynski pleaded guilty to a string of mail bombings, dating from 1978 to 1995, which killed 3 and injured 29 others. Kaczynski hoped to inspire a rebellion against modern industrial society. These are examples of domestic terrorism. People engage in **domestic terrorism** when they attack people in their own country.

In addition to concern about domestic terrorism, the United States also faced **international terrorism.** As the world's most powerful nation, the United States frequently served as a target for terrorists—either acting independently or with the support of a hostile government. The attack on the World Trade Center and the Pentagon on September 11, 2001, was an example of international terrorism.

HISTORY Online

Student Web Activity
Visit taj.glencoe.com and click on **Chapter 32— Student Web Activities** for an activity on today's technology.

SECTION 3 ASSESSMENT

Checking for Understanding

1. **Key Terms** Use each of these terms in a complete sentence that will help explain its meaning: budget deficit, gross domestic product, impeach, incumbent.

2. **Reviewing Facts** Summarize the events of Clinton's impeachment.

Reviewing Themes

3. **Continuity and Change** How did the 1994 election affect the balance of parties in Congress?

Critical Thinking

4. **Predicting Consequences** How might an aging population affect the nation's workforce?

5. **Determining Cause and Effect** Use a diagram like the one below to list the effects of recent technological advances on your life.

```
            Technological advances
           /          |          \
      [    ]       [    ]       [    ]
```

Analyzing Visuals

6. **Geography Skills** Examine the election map on page 941. What was the difference in the electoral vote count?

Interdisciplinary Activity

Citizenship During the next week, pay attention to the news to find what actions the president has taken on different issues. Write down your findings. Next to each entry, indicate your stand on the issue and whether or not you agree with the president's actions.

The War on Terrorism

Guide to Reading

Main Idea
After suffering the worst terrorist attack in its history, the United States launched an effort to fight international terrorism.

Key Terms
counter-terrorism

Reading Strategy
Organizing Information As you read about America's war on terrorism, complete a diagram like the one below to explain how Americans responded to the events of September 11, 2001.

September 11, 2001

Read to Learn
• how Americans responded to terrorism.
• what actions the government took to fight terrorism.

Section Theme
Global Connections The United States called for a worldwide coalition to fight against terrorism.

Preview of Events

1975 — 1985 — 1995 — 2005

1979
Soviet Union invades Afghanistan

1988
Al-Qaeda is organized

1998
Bombs explode at U.S. embassies in Kenya and Tanzania

2001
Attack on the Pentagon and World Trade Center

AN American Story

The first airliner hit the World Trade Center's north tower in New York City at about 8:45 in the morning. Eighteen minutes later, a second plane hit the south tower. Those who died on the airplanes were the first victims. Fire and falling wreckage from the twin towers of the World Trade Center killed thousands more, and hundreds of rescuers—fire fighters, police officers, and volunteers—themselves became victims. "The smoke was so bad, I was suffocating. When the buildings toppled, it was like a volcano," one survivor noted. "We have a lot of heroes," said one firefighter, "and we lost a lot of good people."

The crash of two passenger airplanes into the World Trade Center was not an accident. Early on the morning of September 11, 2001, terrorist hijackers had seized control of the planes, then deliberately flew them into the buildings. Terrorists took control of a third plane and crashed into the Pentagon, the headquarters of the nation's Department of Defense. Hijackers also seized a fourth airplane, but passengers heroically attacked the hijackers, causing that plane to crash in Pennsylvania. In all, thousands of people died.

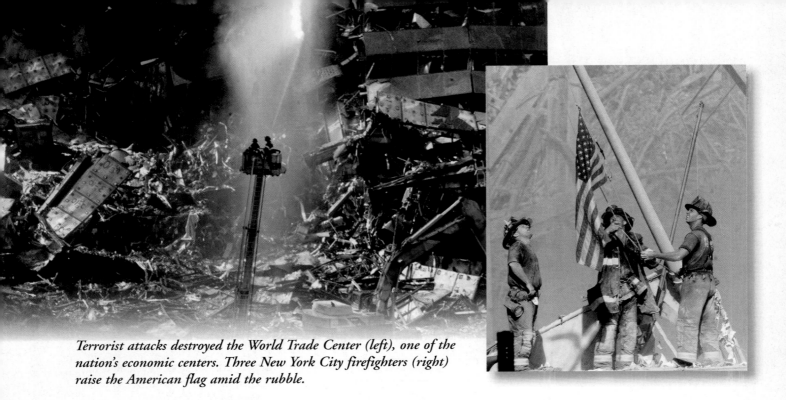

Terrorist attacks destroyed the World Trade Center (left), one of the nation's economic centers. Three New York City firefighters (right) raise the American flag amid the rubble.

Many New York City rescue workers who went to help also lost their lives when the towers collapsed. Hundreds of firefighters, police officers, and volunteers gave their lives in the line of duty trying to save others. Among those who died were Fire Department chaplain Mychal Judge and first deputy commissioner William Feehan, a 42-year veteran of the fire department. The largest number of New York City firefighters to have died in a single disaster before the terrorist attack was 12.

The Terrorist Threat

The attacks on the World Trade Center and the Pentagon were acts of terrorism. Terrorism is the use of violence by groups against civilians to achieve a political goal.

Who Was Responsible?

Intelligence sources and FBI investigators quickly identified **Osama bin Laden** as the prime suspect. Like most people in the Middle East, bin Laden is a **Muslim**—someone who believes in and practices the religion of Islam. Although the vast majority of the 1 billion Muslims worldwide believe Islam rejects terrorism, militant **fundamentalists** like bin Laden do not. They believe that any action is justified to drive American influence out of the Arab world.

Bin Laden believed that Western ideas had harmed Muslim society. His experience in Afghanistan convinced him that superpowers could be beaten.

War in Afghanistan

In 1979 the Soviet Union had invaded the nation of **Afghanistan,** in Southwest Asia, to support that nation's pro-communist government.

Muslims from across the Middle East went to Afghanistan to fight against the Soviets. Among them was bin Laden, who came from one of Saudi Arabia's wealthiest families. In 1988, he founded an organization called **al-Qaeda** (al KY•duh), or "the Base." Al-Qaeda recruited Muslims to fight against the Soviets and bought arms for the Afghanistan soldiers. After Soviet forces withdrew from Afghanistan, bin Laden became a hero to many fundamentalists.

Terrorist Acts

Operating first from Sudan and then from Afghanistan—then under the control of Muslim fundamentalists known as the **Taliban**—bin Laden led al-Qaeda on a mission to drive Americans and other non-Muslims out of the Middle East. In 1998 terrorist truck bombs exploded at the American embassies in the African countries of **Kenya** and **Tanzania.** The bombs killed more than 200 people, including 12 Americans, and injured over 4,500.

In late 1999, terrorists linked to al-Qaeda were arrested trying to smuggle explosives into the United States in an attempt to bomb targets in Seattle, Washington. In October 2000, terrorists backed by al-Qaeda crashed a boat loaded with explosives into the **USS *Cole,*** an American warship, while it was refueling in Yemen.

✓**Reading Check** **Describing** How did Osama bin Laden become so influential in Afghanistan?

A New War Begins

Then on September 11, 2001, terrorists struck on an even greater scale. The shock was felt across the nation, and thousands of people sought a way to help.

The Spirit of America

From coast to coast, thousands attended prayer services and vigils. Across the nation, Americans lined up to donate blood. Others raised money and collected food, blankets, and other supplies for the victims and rescue workers. Firefighters and medical workers from many cities headed to New York to help.

Using a combination of imagination and hard work, young people throughout the nation volunteered to help. Students in Western Springs, a village near Chicago, Illinois, encouraged their entire community to take part in a toys, books, and games garage sale to raise money. Students at a school in Cedar Rapids, Iowa, started a project called Working for America. The students worked by doing chores for family and neighbors

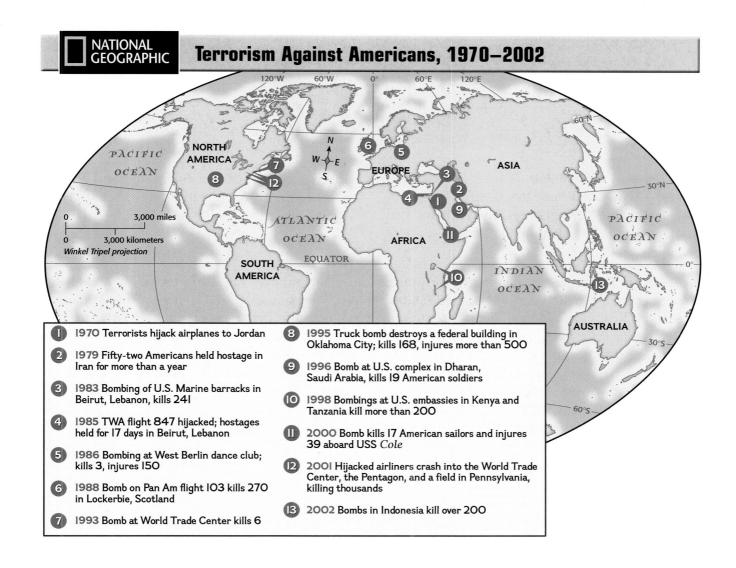

NATIONAL GEOGRAPHIC

Terrorism Against Americans, 1970–2002

1. 1970 Terrorists hijack airplanes to Jordan

2. 1979 Fifty-two Americans held hostage in Iran for more than a year

3. 1983 Bombing of U.S. Marine barracks in Beirut, Lebanon, kills 241

4. 1985 TWA flight 847 hijacked; hostages held for 17 days in Beirut, Lebanon

5. 1986 Bombing at West Berlin dance club; kills 3, injures 150

6. 1988 Bomb on Pan Am flight 103 kills 270 in Lockerbie, Scotland

7. 1993 Bomb at World Trade Center kills 6

8. 1995 Truck bomb destroys a federal building in Oklahoma City; kills 168, injures more than 500

9. 1996 Bomb at U.S. complex in Dharan, Saudi Arabia, kills 19 American soldiers

10. 1998 Bombings at U.S. embassies in Kenya and Tanzania kill more than 200

11. 2000 Bomb kills 17 American sailors and injures 39 aboard USS *Cole*

12. 2001 Hijacked airliners crash into the World Trade Center, the Pentagon, and a field in Pennsylvania, killing thousands

13. 2002 Bombs in Indonesia kill over 200

AMERICA'S HEROES

New York City Fire Department chaplain Mychal Judge, shown here in prayer, was killed while administering last rites to a firefighter.

New York City firefighter Tony James salutes during a funeral service.

Jessica Malone, who comes from a large family of firefighters, went to New York City to help.

and donated money they earned to the Red Cross. The South Bronx Job Corps Center put together canine care packages for search and rescue dogs at the World Trade Center site.

Fair Treatment

Realizing that many people might turn their anger against Muslims in the United States, President Bush visited the Islamic Center in Washington, D.C. There he issued a statement explaining that Islam is a peaceful religion. He urged all Americans to uphold the nation's values and treat Muslim Americans fairly.

President Bush created a special fund to help the children of Afghanistan. Many of the children in Afghanistan are orphans and do not have enough to eat. The president asked the children of the United States to send $1—or whatever they could—to America's Fund for Afghan Children.

New Threats

Concern over the use of biological and chemical weapons grew in the wake of the September 11 tragedy. Letters containing deadly anthrax spores were mailed to several political leaders and the news media. **Anthrax** is an animal disease that has existed for tens of thousands of years.

Law enforcement investigated to determine the identity and the motives of the attackers, but so far, no suspects have been identified. Officials do not think al-Qaeda sent the anthrax.

"In the face of all this evil, we remain strong and united, one nation under God." —President George W. Bush

Protecting America

President Bush and his advisers began planning a response to the terrorist attacks. The president placed the armed forces on high alert. Fighter aircraft began patrolling the skies over major cities. Security at airports was increased, and the FBI began a massive investigation. The president created a new cabinet-level post, **Homeland Security,** to coordinate counter-terrorism efforts. Counter-terrorism involves military or political activities intended to combat terrorism. He named Pennsylvania governor Tom Ridge as head of the department. 📖 *(See pages 978–979 of the Appendix for President Bush's address to Congress after the attacks.)*

The Office of Homeland Security had trouble coordinating counter-terrorism efforts. In June 2002, President Bush asked Congress to combine all of the agencies responsible for the public's safety into a new department to be called the Department of Homeland Security.

In late October 2001, Congress passed and the president signed into law new measures to combat terrorism. The **USA Patriot Act of 2001** gave federal prosecutors and FBI agents new powers to investigate those who plot or carry out acts of terrorism. The law expanded the power of federal agents to tap telephones and track Internet usage in the hunt for terrorists. It also permits agents to conduct secret searches of a suspect's home or office without giving prior notice to the owner of the property.

Attorney General **John Aschroft** promised that government agents would waste no time putting the new tools to use in the hunt for terrorists. Although both houses of Congress passed the bill overwhelmingly, some critics expressed concern that measures could be used not only against suspected terrorists, but people and organizations engaged in lawful activity. To make sure civil liberties were not compromised by the new law, many of its powers will expire in late 2005, unless extended by Congress.

Building a Coalition

The death and devastation caused by the terrorism affected not only Americans, but also people around the world. World leaders responded with statements of sympathy and outrage. NATO members promised to support the United States as did other nations including Pakistan, India, Turkey, and Israel. Some Muslim nations, including Saudi Arabia and Egypt, offered more limited support because they feared widespread protests from their people.

On the Trail of Terrorism

The war against terrorism first concentrated on Afghanistan where bin Laden was reported to be in hiding. The Taliban controlled most of Afghanistan and imposed their religious views on the Afghan people. Taliban leaders had come under criticism for discriminating against women and being intolerant of other religions. Since 1996, when the Taliban captured the Afghan capital, **Kabul,** the main opposition force, the **Northern Alliance,** had battled the Taliban but had made little headway.

President Bush demanded that the Taliban in Afghanistan turn over bin Laden and his supporters. After the Taliban refused, on October 7 the U.S. military attacked Taliban and al-Qaeda forces. Cargo jets also dropped food, medicine, and supplies to the Afghan people.

The air strikes by U.S. warplanes allowed the Northern Alliance to quickly take control of the country. After the Taliban fell from power, the United States and its allies worked with Afghan leaders to create an interim—or temporary—government to run the country. Nations around the world pledged a total of more than four billion dollars to help Afghanistan.

Although the war in Afghanistan was going well, terrorist attacks in South Asia and the Middle East created new problems. In December 2001, terrorists from Kashmir—a region in northern India—attacked India's parliament. India has fought many wars with Pakistan over Kashmir. India's leaders blamed Pakistan for the attack on the parliament, and began mobilizing India's army.

By June 2002, the two nations were ready to go to war. The situation was very dangerous because both sides had nuclear weapons. Although India and Pakistan eventually stepped back from the threat of nuclear war, neither side showed signs of setting aside their arms.

South Asia was not the only region where terrorism created problems. In the Middle East, Palestinian terrorists sent suicide bombers into Israel. These bombers concealed explosives under their

Americans gathered at parks, churches, and fire stations across the nation to express not only their grief but their patriotism.

clothing. They detonated the bombs in Israeli restaurants, shops, and buses, killing dozens of other people. After several suicide bombings took place in Israel, the Israeli army invaded several Palestinian cities where they believed the terrorist groups were based.

In response to the violence in the Middle East, President Bush outlined a plan for ending the Israeli-Palestinian conflict. He announced his support for the creation of a Palestinian state living in peace beside Israel. He asked Israel to stop raiding Palestinian cities. At the same time, he demanded Palestinian leaders stop terrorist attacks and reform their government to make it more democratic and less corrupt.

Continuing the War on Terrorism

President Bush made it clear that while the war on terrorism would start by targeting al-Qaeda, it would not end there. "It will not end," the president announced, "until every terrorist group of global reach has been found, stopped, and defeated." He also warned that the United States would regard "any nation that continues to harbor or support terrorism" as an enemy.

The war against terrorism, President Bush warned Americans, would not end quickly, but it was a war the people of the United States were now called to fight:

> 66Great harm has been done to us. We have suffered great loss. And in our grief and anger we have found our mission and our moment. . . . We will not tire, we will not falter, and we will not fail.99

Widening the War on Terror

The attacks of September 11, 2001, raised fears that al-Qaeda and other terrorist groups might acquire nuclear, chemical, or biological weapons. These **weapons of mass destruction** could kill tens of thousands of people all at once.

In his 2002 State of the Union address, President Bush said his goal was "to prevent regimes that sponsor terror from threatening America or our friends with weapons of mass destruction." He singled out Iraq, Iran, and North Korea, claiming these states "and their terrorist allies constitute an axis of evil arming to threaten the peace of the world."

In October 2002, North Korea, announced that it had restarted its nuclear weapons program. The Bush administration used diplomatic pressure to persuade the North Koreans to stop. However, North Korea warned the U.S. that it would continue to build its nuclear power.

Confronting Iraq

Iraq's dictator Saddam Hussein had already ordered the use of chemical weapons twice, once in Iraq's war against Iran in the 1980s and again against the Kurds, an ethnic minority in northern Iraq who had rebelled against Hussein. After the Gulf War in 1991, UN inspectors found evidence that Iraq had developed biological weapons and was working on a nuclear bomb.

In the summer of 2002, President Bush increased pressure on Iraq. On September 12, he asked the UN to pass a new resolution demanding that Iraq give up its weapons of mass destruction. The president made it clear that the United States would act with or without UN support.

In mid-October, Congress voted to authorize the use of force against Iraq. Then, in early November, the United Nations set a deadline for Iraq to readmit weapons inspectors. It required Iraq to declare all of its weapons of mass destruction, to stop supporting terrorism, and to stop oppressing its people. The resolution threatened Iraq with "serious consequences" if it did not cooperate.

Iraq agreed to allow UN inspectors into the country, but questions arose over whether Iraqi officials were cooperating as they had promised. President Bush argued that the Iraqis were still hiding weapons of mass destruction. The Bush administration asked the UN Security Council to pass a resolution calling for the use of force in Iraq. When Council members France and Russia said they would veto a resolution, the United States prepared for war.

On March 20, the American military, aided by soldiers from Great Britain, attacked. Over the next six weeks, much of Iraq's army fell into disarray. American troops quickly seized control of the country. On May 1, President Bush declared the end of major combat operations. About 140 Americans, and several thousand Iraqis, had died.

The controversy over Iraq and the fighting, though, continued. While many Iraqis welcomed the fall of Saddam Hussein's regime, others did not. U.S. and British troops faced continued attacks. By the fall of 2003, more Americans had died after May 1 than had died in the six weeks of major combat. As American deaths and expenses mounted, President Bush began to seek support from the UN and other countries to rebuild Iraq. Despite the capture of Saddam Hussein in December 2003, the path toward a free and stable Iraq appeared to be long and difficult.

Reading Check **Analyzing** Why did President Bush call for military action against Saddam Hussein's regime?

SECTION 4 ASSESSMENT

Checking for Understanding
1. **Key Terms** Define: counterterrorism.
2. **Reviewing Facts** What happened to the USS *Cole* when it was refueling in Yemen?

Reviewing Themes
3. **Global Connections** Do you think the dangers of terrorism require global cooperation? Explain and support your point of view with reasons.

Critical Thinking
4. **Drawing Conclusions** Why do you think President Bush specifically chose to visit the Islamic Center in Washington, D.C.?
5. **Organizing Information** Use a diagram like the one below to identify what you think are the three major effects of terrorism on Americans.

Effects of terrorism

Analyzing Visuals
6. **Geography Skills** Examine the map on terrorism on page 947. How many Americans were taken hostage in Iran? What events on the map took place in the 1990s?

Interdisciplinary Activity
Expository Writing How will world events affect your future? Write an essay entitled "The World's Future and My Own" identifying important issues and explaining how events could affect your life.

Chapter Summary
New Challenges

The Reagan Presidency
- President Reagan pursues deregulation
- Reagan appoints conservative justices to Supreme Court, including the first woman appointment
- Reagan cuts taxes and spending on domestic programs
- Reagan and Gorbachev sign INF Treaty

The Bush Presidency
- Communist governments fall and democracy spreads in many countries
- Allies launch Desert Storm
- Federal debt and banking crisis require major government funds

The Clinton Presidency
- President Clinton proposes health-care reforms that fail in Congress
- Congress ratifies North American Free Trade Agreement
- Clinton is impeached following a scandal, but is cleared by Senate

George W. Bush wins presidency
- Tax-cut bill signed into law
- The nation begins a fight against terrorism
- Saddam Hussein is deposed as Iraqi leader

Reviewing Key Terms
On a sheet of paper, define the following terms:
1. deregulation
2. federal debt
3. perestroika
4. coup
5. incumbent
6. global warming
7. ozone
8. line-item veto

Reviewing Key Facts
9. What was Reagan's economic policy?
10. How did Mikhail Gorbachev try to reform the Soviet government?
11. How did Poland lead the way in toppling communism in Eastern Europe?
12. What triggered the Persian Gulf War?
13. Why was health care an important issue in the 1990s?
14. What was the significance of the Middle East Peace Accords?
15. What was the outcome of President Clinton's impeachment trial?
16. Who won the presidential election in 2000? Why was the election unusual?

Critical Thinking
17. **Economic Factors** What was the goal of President Reagan's policy of deregulation?
18. **Global Connections** What event marked the end of the Cold War?
19. **Groups and Institutions** Why did the federal government run out of money in the mid-1990s?
20. **Groups and Institutions** What message do you think voters were sending by electing a majority of Republicans to both houses of Congress in 1994?
21. **Evaluating** Re-create the diagram below and rank the four presidents that you studied in this chapter from best to worst. Then explain why you ranked them as you did.

President	Your reasons
1	
2	
3	
4	

Geography and History Activity

Study the map and answer the questions that follow.

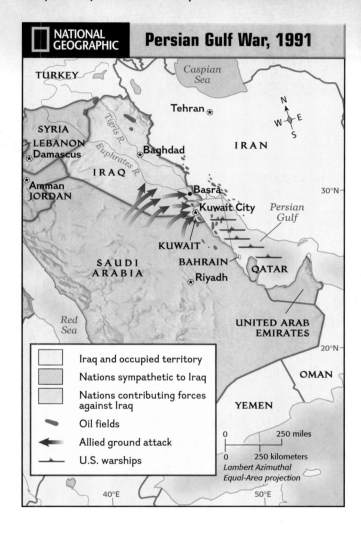

NATIONAL GEOGRAPHIC **Persian Gulf War, 1991**

Iraq and occupied territory
Nations sympathetic to Iraq
Nations contributing forces against Iraq
Oil fields
Allied ground attack
U.S. warships

0 _____ 250 miles
0 _____ 250 kilometers
Lambert Azimuthal Equal-Area projection

22. Region What country borders Iraq to the northeast?

23. Movement The blue lines indicate invasion forces. From what country was the invasion launched?

24. Location In what body of water were warships present?

Practicing Skills

25. Using an Electronic Spreadsheet Use a spreadsheet to enter the daily high, average, and low temperatures for your community for four weeks. At the end of this period, calculate your average local temperature. Then use the spreadsheet to make line graphs showing the monthly high temperatures, average temperatures, and low temperatures for your community.

Self-Check Quiz
Visit **taj.glencoe.com** and click on **Chapter 32— Self-Check Quizzes** to prepare for the chapter test.

 ## Technology Activity

26. Using the Internet Use a search engine to search the Internet for information about Afghanistan. Write a short description of the change in power in that country during the past 20 years.

Citizenship Cooperative Activity

27. Your Community and the World Ask family members and neighbors about ways in which your community is connected to other parts of the world. Prepare a short fact sheet on the international connections of your community and the world. Discuss your view with the other groups.

 ## Alternative Assessment

28. Portfolio Writing Activity Review the chapter for information about how the three presidents in office from 1980 to 2000 viewed the role of the federal government. Record the information in your journal. Use your notes to summarize each president's view in a single sentence.

Standardized Test Practice

Directions: Choose the *best* answer to the following question.

The government had to shut down nonessential services twice in 1996 in response to what situation?

F power outages

G disputes over the budget

H bipartisan agreement

J the "Contract with America"

Test-Taking Tip

Eliminate answers that don't make sense. For example, why would the government shut down because of "bipartisan agreement"? Answer **H** must be wrong.

Appendix

Contents

What Is an Appendix and How Do I Use One?

An appendix is the additional material you often find at the end of books. The following information will help you learn how to use the appendix in **The American Journey.**

Primary Sources Library

The **Primary Sources Library** provides additional first-person accounts of historical events. Primary sources are often narratives by a person who actually experienced what is being described.

Presidents of the United States

The **presidents** have served as our nation's leaders. In this resource you will find information of interest on each of the nation's presidents, including their term in office, political affiliation, and their occupations before they became president.

Documents of American History

This is a collection of some of the most important writings in American history. Each **document** begins with an introduction describing the author and placing the selection within its historical context.

Supreme Court Case Summaries

The **Supreme Court Case Summaries** provide readable discussions of important Supreme Court cases. The summaries are listed in alphabetical order and include a summary of the facts of the case and its impact.

Gazetteer

A **gazetteer** (GA•zuh•TIHR) is a geographical dictionary. It lists some of the largest countries, cities, and several important geographic features. Each entry also includes a page number telling where this place can be found in your textbook.

Glossary

A **glossary** is a list of important or difficult terms found in a textbook. Since words sometimes have other meanings, you may wish to consult a dictionary to find other uses for the term. The glossary gives a definition of each term as it is used in the book. The glossary also includes page numbers telling you where in the textbook the term is used.

Spanish Glossary

A **Spanish glossary** contains everything that an English glossary does, but it is written in Spanish. A Spanish glossary is especially important to bilingual students, or those Spanish-speaking students who are learning the English language.

Index

An **index** is an alphabetical listing that includes the subjects of the book and the page numbers where those subjects can be found. The index in this book also lets you know that certain pages contain maps, graphs, photos, or paintings about the subject.

Acknowledgements and Photo Credits

This section lists photo credits and/or literary credits for the book. You can look at this section to find out where the publisher obtained the permission to use a photograph or to use excerpts from other books.

Test Yourself

Find the answers to these questions by using the Appendix on the following pages.

1. **What does ironclad mean?**
2. **Who was the sixth president of the United States?**
3. **On what page can I find out about William Penn?**
4. **Where exactly is Roanoke located?**
5. **What was the Supreme Court's decision in *Marbury* v. *Madison*?**

Primary Sources Library

Working With Primary Sources

Suppose that you have been asked to write a report on changes in your community over the past 25 years. Where would you get the information you need to begin writing? You would draw upon two types of information—primary sources and secondary sources.

Definitions

Primary sources are often first-person accounts by someone who actually saw or lived through what is being described. In other words, if you see a fire or live through a great storm and then write about your experiences, you are creating a primary source. Diaries, journals, photographs, and eyewitness reports are examples of primary sources. **Secondary sources** are secondhand accounts. For instance, if your friend experiences the fire or storm and tells you about it, or if you read about the fire or storm in the newspaper, and then you write about it, you are creating a secondary source. Textbooks, biographies, and histories are secondary sources.

William Clark's log book

Checking Your Sources

When you read primary or secondary sources, you should analyze them to figure out if they are dependable or reliable. Historians usually prefer primary sources to secondary sources, but both can be reliable or unreliable, depending on the following factors.

Time Span

With primary sources, it is important to consider how long after the event occurred the primary source was written. Chances are the longer the time span between the event and the account, the less reliable the account is. As time passes, people often forget details and fill in gaps with events that never took place. Although we like to think we remember things exactly as they happened, the fact is we often remember them as we wanted them to occur.

Reliability

Another factor to consider when evaluating a primary source is the writer's background and reliability. First, try to determine how this person knows about what he or she is writing. How much does he or she know? Is the writer being truthful? Is the account convincing?

Opinions

When evaluating a primary source, you should also decide whether the account has been influenced by emotion, opinion, or exaggeration. Writers can have reasons to distort the truth to suit their personal purposes. Ask yourself: Why did the person write the account? Do any key words or expressions reveal the author's emotions or opinions? You may wish to compare the account with one written by another witness to the event. If the two accounts differ, ask yourself why they differ and which is more accurate.

Interpreting Primary Sources

To help you analyze a primary source, use the following steps:

- **Examine the origins of the document.**
  You need to determine if it is a primary source.

- **Find the main ideas.**
  Read the document and summarize the main ideas in your own words. These ideas may be fairly easy to identify in newspapers and journals, for example, but are much more difficult to find in poetry.

- **Reread the document.**
  Difficult ideas are not always easily understood on the first reading.

- **Use a variety of resources.**
  Form the habit of using the dictionary, the encyclopedia, and maps. These resources are tools to help you discover new ideas and knowledge and check the validity of sources.

George Washington's compass

Classifying Primary Sources
Primary sources fall into different categories:

 Printed Publications

Printed publications include books such as autobiographies. Printed publications also include newspapers and magazines.

 Songs & Poems

Songs and poems include works that express the personal thoughts and feelings, or political or religious beliefs, of the writer, often using rhyming and rhythmic language.

 Visual Materials

Visual materials include a wide range of forms: original paintings, drawings, sculptures, photographs, film, and maps.

Oral Histories

Oral history collects spoken memories and personal observations through recorded interviews. By contrast, oral tradition involves stories that people have passed along by word of mouth from generation to generation.

Personal Records

Personal records are accounts of events kept by an individual who is a participant in, or witness to, these events. Personal records include diaries, journals, and letters.

 Artifacts

Artifacts are objects such as tools or ornaments. Artifacts present information about a particular culture or a stage of technological development.

Different Worlds Meet

Until the arrival of Christopher Columbus, the lifestyle and culture of Native Americans had endured for centuries. They told stories, sang songs, and recited tales that recounted their past and their close relationship with the natural world. These stories and songs survived through oral tradition. This means that each generation passed down its stories and songs to its young people by word of mouth. As you read, think about how oral history, folklore, and tradition connect us to the past.

Reader's Dictionary

Lakota: a member of the Sioux people of central and eastern North America

prophecy: a prediction about the future

Black Hills: mountains in the western Dakotas and northeast Wyoming

elder: a person who is honored for his or her age and experience

Pinta: one of the three ships under Columbus's command during his first trip to the Americas

White Buffalo Calf Woman Brings the First Pipe

Oral Histories

Joseph Chasing Horse of the Lakota people tells the story of the White Buffalo Calf Woman.

We **Lakota** people have a **prophecy** about the white buffalo calf. How that prophecy originated was that we have a sacred bundle, a sacred pipe, that was brought to us about 2,000 years ago by what we know as the White Buffalo Calf Woman.

The story goes that she appeared to two warriors at that time. These two warriors were out hunting buffalo . . . in the sacred **Black Hills** of South Dakota, and they saw a big body coming toward them. And they saw that it was a white buffalo calf. As it came closer to them, it turned into a beautiful young Indian girl.

[At] that time one of the warriors [had bad thoughts] and so the young girl told him to step forward. And when he did step forward, a black cloud came over his body, and when the black cloud disappeared, the warrior who had bad thoughts was left with no flesh or blood on his bones. The other warrior kneeled and began to pray.

And when he prayed, the white buffalo calf, who was now an Indian girl told him to go back to his people and warn them that in four days she was going to bring a sacred bundle.

So the warrior did as he was told. He went back to his people, and he gathered all the **elders,** and all the

Kiowa animal hide calendar

leaders, and all the people in a circle and told them what she had instructed him to do. And sure enough, just as she said she would, on the fourth day, she came.

They say a cloud came down from the sky, and off of the cloud stepped the white buffalo calf. As it rolled onto the earth, the calf stood up and became this beautiful young woman who was carrying the sacred bundle in her hand.

As she entered into the circle of the nation, she sang a sacred song and took the sacred bundle to the people who were there to take [it from] her.

. . . And she instructed our people that as long as we performed these ceremonies we would always remain caretakers and guardians of sacred land. She told us that as long as we took care of it and respected it that our people would never die and would always live.

The sacred bundle is known as the White Buffalo Calf Pipe because it was brought by the White Buffalo Calf Woman. . . .

When White Buffalo Calf Woman promised to return again, she made some prophecies at that time. One of those prophecies was that the birth of a white buffalo calf would be a sign that it would be near the time when she would return again to purify the world. What she meant by that was that she would bring back [spiritual] harmony. . . .

Astrolabe

Columbus Crosses the Atlantic

 Personal Records

Christopher Columbus reached the new world on October 12, 1492. At sea for over two months, his sailors worried that they would not find land before their food and water ran out. Columbus's entries in his logs show the mood of his crew, and their impressions of the natives.

October 11:

The crew of the **Pinta** spotted some . . . reeds and some other plants; they also saw what looked like a small board or plank. A stick was recovered that looks man-made, perhaps carved with an iron tool . . . but even these few [things] made the crew breathe easier; in fact the men have even become cheerful.

October 12:

The islanders came to the ships' boats, swimming and bringing us parrots and balls of cotton thread . . . which they exchanged for . . . glass beads and hawk bells . . . they took and gave of what they had very willingly, but it seemed to me that they were poor in every way. They bore no weapons, nor were they acquainted with them, because when I showed them swords they seized them by the edge and so cut themselves from ignorance.

Analyzing Primary Sources

1. What did the Indian girl tell the Lakota warriors?
2. What prophecy did the White Buffalo Calf Woman make to the people?
3. What does the use of the animal hide tell you about the people who made the calendar?
4. Why were the members of Columbus's crew cheerful when they spied the objects at sea?

Colonial Settlement

Early America was a nation of people unafraid to experiment. Because colonists often had to learn new ways of obtaining food and shelter in a primitive country, they grew to appreciate ingenuity. Because of the need to cooperate—for companionship, and even for survival—they overlooked the differences in cultures that separated them in the old country. As you read these primary source selections, think about how the necessity to adapt affected the way the colonists approached everyday situations.

Reader's Dictionary

enlightened: informed

haughty: proud, vain

indigence: poverty

habitation: home

phial: small bottle

blunder: mistake

tolerable: satisfactory

What is an American?

Printed Publications

J. Hector St. John Crevecoeur of France traveled widely in the American colonies and farmed in New York. His Letters from an American Farmer *was published in 1782.*

I wish I could be acquainted with the feelings and thoughts which must . . . present themselves to the mind of an **enlightened** Englishman, when he first lands on the continent. . . . If he travels through our rural districts he views not the hostile castle, and the **haughty** mansion, contrasted with the clay-built hut and miserable cabin, where cattle and men help to keep each other warm, and dwell in meanness, smoke, and **indigence.** A pleasing uniformity of decent competence appears throughout our **habitations.** The meanest of our log-houses is dry and comfortable. . . . What then is the American, this new man? He is either a European, or the descendant of a European, hence that strange mixture of blood, which you will find in no other country. I could point out to you a family whose grandfather was an Englishman, whose wife was Dutch, and whose son married a French woman, and whose present four sons have now four wives of different nations. . . . There is room for everybody in America; has he particular talent, or industry? He exerts it in order to produce a livelihood, and it succeeds. . . .

Butter churn

Ben Franklin

We often think of Benjamin Franklin as a successful diplomat and inventor. In 1750, Franklin wrote to a friend about an experiment that did not go as well as he had planned.

I have lately made an experiment in electricity, that I desire never to repeat. Two nights ago, being about to kill a turkey by the shock from two large glass jars, containing as much electrical fire as forty common **phials,** I . . . took the whole [charge] through my own arms and body, by receiving the fire from the united top wires with one hand, while the other held a chain connected with the outsides of both jars. The company present (whose talking to me, and to one another, I supposed occasioned my inattention to what I was about) say, that the flash was very great, and the crack as loud as a pistol; yet, my senses being instantly gone, I neither saw the one nor heard the other. . . . Nothing remains now of this shock, but a soreness in my breast-bone, which feels as if it had been bruised. I did not fall, but suppose I should have been knocked down, if I had received the stroke in my head. The whole was over in less than a minute.

You may communicate this to Mr. Bowdoin, as a caution to him, but do not make it more public, for I am ashamed to have been guilty of so notorious a **blunder;**. . . . I am yours . . .

B. Franklin

P.S. The jars hold six gallons each.

Penn's Colony

In a letter written in 1683, William Penn describes the growth of his colony.

Our capital town is advanced to about 150 very **tolerable** houses for wooden ones; they are chiefly on both the navigable rivers that bound the ends or sides of the town. The farmers have got their winter corn in the ground. I suppose we may be 500 farmers strong. I settle them in villages, dividing 5,000 acres among ten, fifteen, or twenty families, as their ability is to plant it. . . .

Hornbook from colonial school

Analyzing Primary Sources

1. How does de Crevecoeur describe the typical home in the colonies in the late 1700s?
2. What do you think Franklin was trying to learn with his experiment?
3. During what season of the year did Penn write this letter? How can you tell?

For use with the Prologue

Creating a Nation

In settling North America, the colonists developed a sense that they were taking part in the birth of a new society, where people had the opportunity to better themselves. As you read these primary source selections, think about the reasons the colonists began to find fault with Great Britain. What words would you use to describe the American "spirit" that made them determined to fight for independence?

Reader's Dictionary

sovereign: king or leader

destitute: lacking

procure: gain or obtain

gall: to become sore by rubbing

Powderhorn

Common Sense

Printed Publications

In Common Sense, *written in January 1776, patriot Thomas Paine called upon the colonists to break away from Great Britain.*

Every thing that is right begs for separation from [Great] Britain. The Americans who have been killed seem to say, 'TIS TIME TO PART. England and America are located a great distance apart. That is itself strong and natural proof that God never expected one to rule over the other.

The Bold Americans

Songs & Poems

Broadside ballads—emotionally-charged story poems printed on a single sheet of paper—were distributed widely and helped fuel colonists' passion for freedom.

Come all you bold young Bostonians, come
    listen unto me:
I will sing you a song concerning liberty.
Concerning liberty, my boys, the truth I will
    unfold,
Of the bold Americans, who scorn to be
    controlled.
We'll honor George, our **sovereign,** on any
    reasonable terms,
But if he don't grant us liberty, we'll all lay down
    our arms.
        But if he will grant us liberty, so plainly
            shall you see,
        We are the boys that fear no noise!
            Success to liberty!

Surviving at Valley Forge

Below are excerpts from the personal records of two different people who served at Valley Forge. The first selection is by Albigence Waldo, a surgeon who tended the sick and injured.

I am sick—discontented . . . Poor food—hard lodging—cold weather—fatigue—nasty cloathes—nasty cookery. . . . I can't endure it—Why are we sent here to starve and freeze? . . .

In this selection, soldier Joseph Plumb Martin, age 16 at the time, remembers the hardships on the way to Valley Forge.

The army was not only starved but naked. The greatest part were not only shirtless and barefoot, but **destitute** of all other clothing, especially blankets. I **procured** a small piece of rawhide and made myself a pair of moccasins, which

Military drum of the American Revolution

kept my feet (while they lasted) from the frozen ground, although, as I well remember, the hard edges so **galled** my ankles, while on a march, that it was with much difficulty and pain that I could wear them afterwards; but the only alternative I had was to endure this inconvenience or to go barefoot, as hundreds of my companions had to, till they might be tracked by their bloods upon the rough frozen ground.

Immigrant Life in America

A German immigrant wrote this account of his experiences.

But during the voyage there is on board these ships terrible misery, stench, fumes, horror, vomiting, many kinds of sea-sickness, fever . . . all of which comes from old and sharply salted food and meat, also from very bad and foul water, so that many die miserably. . . .

Many parents must sell and trade away their children like so many head of cattle. . . . [I]t often happens that such parents and children, after leaving the ship, do not see each other again for many years, perhaps no more in all their lives.

Analyzing Primary Sources

1. What is the main point that Thomas Paine makes in the excerpt from *Common Sense*?
2. What do the bold Americans scorn?
3. What might have kept the soldiers from leaving Valley Forge, under such horrible conditions?

The New Republic

The Constitution established a completely new framework of government that was meant to be flexible and lasting. Along with the excitement of starting a new nation came challenges and growing pains. Many people, both American-born and foreign-born, wondered: Can this new kind of government last? As you read these primary source selections, think about how well the government served the people as the nation grew.

Reader's Dictionary

gallery: outdoor balcony

proclamation: announcement

agitated: upset and nervous

ungainly: awkward, clumsy

plainest manner: in a simple way

discord: disagreement, conflict

rapture: joy

marsh: soft, wet land

corduroy-road: a road made of logs laid side by side

Washington's First Inaugural

Personal Records

Pennsylvania Senator William Maclay was one of the many witnesses to the nation's first presidential inauguration.

The President was conducted out of the middle window into the **gallery** [overlooking Wall Street], and the oath was administered by the Chancellor [the highest judicial officer in the state of New York]. Notice that the business done was communicated to the crowd by **proclamation** . . . who gave three cheers, and repeated it on the President's bowing to them.

As the company returned into the Senate chamber, the President took the chair and the Senators and Representatives their seats. He rose, and all arose also, and [he] addressed them. This great man was **agitated** and embarrassed more than ever he was by the leveled cannon or pointed musket. He trembled, and several times could scarce make out to read, though it must be supposed he had often read it before. . . . When he came to the words *all the world,* he made a flourish with his right hand, which left rather an **ungainly** impression. I sincerely, for my part, wished all set ceremony in the hands of the dancing-masters, and that this first of men had read off his address in the **plainest manner,** without ever taking his eyes from the paper, for I felt hurt that he was not first in everything.

Copy of letter written by President Washington

Song of Liberty

Songs & Poems

The following song is one of the hundreds of anonymous patriotic songs written, printed, and distributed in little song books during the early 1800s.

The fruits of our country, our flocks and
    our fleeces,
What treasures immense, in our mountains
    that lie,
While **discord** is tearing Old Europe to
    pieces,
Shall amply the wants of the people
    supply;
New roads and canals, on their bosoms
    conveying,
Refinement and wealth through our forests
    shall roam,
And millions of freemen, with **rapture**
    surveying,
Shall shout out "O Liberty! this is thy home!"

Flag flown at Fort McHenry during War of 1812

On the Road

Printed Publications

David Stevenson described a journey by stage-coach along a typical route of the time.

Sometimes our way lay for miles through extensive **marshes,** which we crossed by **corduroy-roads.** . . . At others the coach stuck fast in mud, from which it could be [moved] only by the combined efforts of the coachman and passengers; at one place we traveled . . . through a forest flooded with water, which stood to a height of several feet. . . . The distance of the route from Pittsburgh to Erie is 128 miles, which was accomplished in forty-six hours . . . although the [stagecoach] by which I traveled carried the mail, and stopped only for breakfast, dinner and tea, but there was considerable delay by the coach being once upset and several times "mired."

A woman named Elizabeth Smith Geer wrote about winter travel in her diary:

My children gave out with cold and fatigue and could not travel, and the boys had to unhitch the oxen and bring them and carry the children on to camp. It was so cold and numb I could not tell by feeling that I had any feet at all. . . . I have not told you half we suffered.

Analyzing Primary Sources

1. What was it about Washington's public speaking manner that Maclay criticized?
2. In the song, what does the phrase "treasures immense" mean?
3. How did roads of the early 1800s differ from roads that we travel on today?

The Growing Nation

In the early 1800s, the United States had a firmly established democracy, but the freedoms it guaranteed did not extend to everyone. Native Americans were forced from their lands, while African Americans were enslaved—torn from their homelands and often separated from their families. As you read these primary source selections, think about how long these conditions existed before ideas of reform began to take hold.

Reader's Dictionary

detachment: group or body of people

inclemency: harsh conditions

auction block: site where enslaved people were bought and sold

piteous: sad, distressed

vociferously: loudly

battery: a grouping of weapons

rent: opened or parted

Trail of Tears

Printed Publications

Although recognized as a separate nation by several U.S. treaties, the Cherokee people were forced to leave their lands because white people wanted it for farming. Thousands died before they reached Indian Territory, the present-day state of Oklahoma. This forced journey came to be called the Trail of Tears. A newspaper published this account.

On Tuesday evening we fell in with a **detachment** of the poor Cherokee Indians . . . about eleven hundred Indians— sixty wagons—six hundred horses, and perhaps forty pairs of oxen. We found them in the forest camped for the night by the road side . . . under a severe fall of rain accompanied by heavy wind. With their canvas for a shield from the **inclemency** of the weather, and the cold wet ground for a resting place, after the fatigue of the day, they spent the night . . . many of the aged Indians were suffering extremely from the fatigue of the journey, and the ill health consequent upon it . . . several were then quite ill, and one aged man we were informed was then in the last struggles of death.

Map of Georgia in 1826 showing Cherokee land (left) and seal of Cherokee Nation (right)

Delicia Patterson

Oral Histories

Delicia Patterson provided this look at life under slavery. She was 92 years old when she was interviewed.

I was born in Boonville, Missouri, January 2, 1845. Mother had five children but raised only two of us. I was owned by Charles Mitchell until I was fifteen years old. They were fairly nice to all of their slaves. . . .

When I was fifteen years old, I was brought to the courthouse, put up on the **auction block** to be sold. Old Judge Miller from my county was there. I knew him well because he was one of the wealthiest slave owners in the county, and the meanest one. He was so cruel all the slaves and many owners hated him because of it. He saw me on the block for sale, and he knew I was a good worker. So, when he bid for me, I spoke right out on the auction block and told him:

"Old Judge Miller, don't you bid for me, 'cause if you do, I would not live on your plantation. I will take a knife and cut my own throat from ear to ear before I would be owned by you. . . ."

So he stepped back and let someone else bid for me. . . . So I was sold to a Southern Englishman named Thomas Steele for fifteen hundred dollars. . . .

THE ALMIGHTY HAS NO ATTRIBUTE, THAT CAN TAKE SIDES WITH THE SLAVEHOLDER.

Anti-slavery banner

Religious Camp Meeting

Personal Records

The desire for self-improvement was closely connected to a renewed interest in religion. By the 1830s, the Second Great Awakening, the second great period of religious revival in the United States, was in full swing. The camp meeting was especially important to isolated frontier families. One preacher, James Finley, described a revival meeting:

The noise was like the roar of Niagara. . . . Some of the people were singing, others praying, some crying for mercy in the most **piteous** accents, while others were shouting most **vociferously**. . . . At one time I saw at least five hundred swept down in a moment, as if a **battery** of a thousand guns had been opened upon them, and then immediately followed shrieks and shouts that **rent** the very heavens.

Analyzing Primary Sources

1. Do you think the writer of the newspaper article feels sympathy toward the Cherokee?
2. Why did Delicia, the formerly enslaved woman, not want to serve on Judge Miller's plantation?
3. What scene is James Finley describing?

Civil War and Reconstruction

The American Civil War, or the War Between the States, was a major turning point for the American people. When the fighting ended, 600,000 Americans had lost their lives, slavery had been abolished, and most of the South lay in ruin. Leaders argued over how to reunite the shattered nation. And even though slavery had been abolished, African Americans quickly discovered that freedom did not mean equality. As you read these selections, think about the changes that took place during this era.

Reader's Dictionary

exterminating: destructive

bondage: slavery

suffrage: the right to vote

musket: soldier's rifle

Swing Low, Sweet Chariot

Songs & Poems

Spirituals—songs of salvation—provided the enslaved African Americans who wrote and sang them with not only a measure of comfort in bleak times but with a means for communicating secretly among themselves.

Swing low, sweet chariot,
Coming for to carry me home,
Swing low, sweet chariot,
Coming for to carry me home.

I looked over Jordan and what
   did I see
Coming for to carry me home,
A band of angels coming after me.
Coming for to carry me home.

If you get there before I do,
Coming for to carry me home,
Tell all my friends I'm coming too,
Coming for to carry me home.

I'm sometimes up and sometimes down,
Coming for to carry me home,
But still my soul feels heavenly bound,
Coming for to carry me home.

The Fisk Jubilee Singers

On the Plight of African Americans

Personal Records

In 1867 Frederick Douglass appealed eloquently to Congress on behalf of African Americans.

. . . Yet the Negroes have marvelously survived all the **exterminating** forces of slavery, and have emerged at the end of 250 years of **bondage,** not [sad and hateful], but cheerful, hopeful, and forgiving. They now stand before Congress and the country, not complaining of the past, but simply asking for a better future.

. . . It is true that a strong plea for equal **suffrage** might be addressed to the national sense of honor. Something, too, might be said of national gratitude. A nation might well hesitate before the temptation to betray its allies. There is something . . . mean, to say nothing of the cruelty, in placing the loyal Negroes of the South under the political power of their rebel masters. . . . We asked the Negroes to [support] our cause, to be our friends, to fight for us and against their masters; and now, after they have done all that we asked them to do . . . it is proposed in some quarters to turn them over to the political control of the common enemy of the government and of the Negro. . . .

What, then, is the work before Congress? . . . In a word, it must [allow African Americans to vote], and by means of the loyal Negroes and the loyal white men of the South build up a national party there, and in time bridge the [gap] between North and South, so that our country may have a common liberty and a common civilization. . . .

The Fire of Battle

Personal Records

Union soldier George Sargent served in the area west of Washington, D.C., throughout the Shenandoah Valley. He wrote his impressions of how soldiers react in battle.

Can you imagine a fellow's feelings about that time, to have to face thousands of **muskets** with a prospect of having a bullet put through you? If you can, all right; I can't describe it. I've heard some say that they were not scared going into a fight, but I think it's all nonsense. I don't believe there was ever a man who went into battle but was scared, more or less. Some will turn pale as a sheet, look wild and ferocious, some will be so excited that they don't know what they are about while others will be as cool and collected as on other occasions.

Analyzing Primary Sources

1. What does "Swing Low, Sweet Chariot" show about the condition and faith of the people who sang it?
2. What did Frederick Douglass urge Congress to do?
3. What does George Sargent say happens to all soldiers in battle?

Reshaping the Nation

In the period from the end of the Civil War to 1900, America grew at a remarkable rate. The settlement of the West was filled with tragedy for Native Americans, adventure for the settlers, and hardship for just about everyone. The trend toward large-scale industrial operations led to the Age of Big Business. Immigrants from Europe flocked to America, arriving with the hope of a better life. However, the growth of factories and new ways of working caused problems between workers and owners.

Reader's Dictionary

reservation: land set aside for Native Americans

abide: follow

kosher: approved by Jewish law

Sioux ghost dance shirt

Indian School

Ah-nen-la-de-ni of the Mohawk people describes his first experience in school.

After the almost complete freedom of **reservation** life the cramped quarters and the dull routine of the school were maddening to all us strangers. There were endless rules for us to study and **abide** by, and hardest of all was the rule against speaking to each other in our own language. We must speak English or remain silent, and those who knew no English were forced to be dumb or else break the rules in secret. This last we did quite frequently, and were punished, when detected, by being made to stand in the "public hall" for a long time or to march about the yard while the other boys were at play.

The Sweat Shop

Oral Histories

In factories, people had to work at an inhumane pace. Following is the account of a young woman employed in New York City's garment industry.

At seven o'clock we all sit down to our machines and the boss brings to each one the pile of work that he or she is to finish during the day. . . . This pile is put down beside the machine and as soon as a skirt is done it is laid on the other side of the machine. . . . The machines go like mad all day, because the faster you work, the more money you get. Sometimes in my haste I get

Young coal miners in Kingston, Pennsylvania

my finger caught and the needle goes right through it. . . . We all have accidents like that. . . . Sometimes a finger has to come off. . . . All the time we are working the boss walks about examining the finished garments and making us do them over again if they are not just right. So we have to be careful as well as swift. . . .

An Emigrant's Story

Printed Publications

In her book The Promised Land, *Mary Antin tells of leaving her native country, Poland, to come to America when she was 13 years old.*

What did they not ask, the eager, foolish, friendly people? They wanted to handle the ticket, and mother must read them what is written on it. How much did it cost? Was it all paid for? Were we going to have a foreign passport or did we intend to steal across the border? Were we not going to have new dresses to travel in? Was it sure that we could get **kosher** food on the ship?

[After we boarded the train] when the warning bell rang out, it was drowned in—fragments of blessings, farewells—"Don't forget!"—"Take care of—" "Keep your tickets—" "Moshele—newspapers!—" "Garlick is best!" "Happy journey!" "God help you!" "Good-bye!" "Remember—"

Analyzing Primary Sources

1. How does the boy at the Indian school compare life there with the life on the reservation?
2. Why did the workers in the sweat shop work quickly?
3. What words does Mary Antin use to describe the people of her town who asked the many questions?

Reform, Expansion, and War

As city populations grew, living and working conditions became worse. The Progressive movement worked to protect workers and the poor, while much attention was turned overseas. During the late 1800s and early 1900s, the United States used the Monroe Doctrine to oppose European involvement in Latin America. By enforcing it in a war with Spain, the United States became a colonial power. World War I was a global conflict with unprecedented casualties. This war meant the fall of the old-world empires, and an end to a quieter way of life. As you read these primary source selections, think about how the focus of average citizens changed from the Civil War to World War I.

Reader's Dictionary

bewildered: confused

damages: money

ruefully: regretfully

starboard: the right side of the ship

periscope: a viewing device for submarines to see above the ocean surface

stern: the rear of the ship

score: twenty

Hull House

Printed Publications

Social workers established settlement houses in the slums of the large cities. One of the more famous was Hull House, founded in Chicago by Jane Addams. This excerpt explains how settlement houses helped poor and disadvantaged people living in the city.

We early found ourselves spending many hours in efforts to secure support for deserted women, insurance for **bewildered** widows, **damages** for injured operators, furniture from the clutches of the installment store. The Settlement is valuable as an information and interpretation bureau. It constantly acts between the various institutions of the city and the people for whose benefit these were erected. The hospitals, county agencies, and State asylums are often but vague rumors to the people who need them most. Another function of the Settlement to its neighborhood resembles that of the big brother whose mere presence on the playground protects the little one from bullies.

LEST WE FORGET
The Sinking of the Lusitania, May 7th 1915.
Propaganda poster

Aboard the *Lusitania*

Despite the threat of German submarine attacks, Theodate Pope, an American, boarded the Lusitania *to sail home from Europe. On May 7, 1915, a torpedo sank the British ship. After being rescued, Pope wrote this letter.*

Friday morning we came slowly through fog, blowing our fog horn. It cleared off about an hour before we went below for lunch. A young Englishman at our table had been served with his ice cream, and was waiting for the steward to bring him a spoon to eat it with. He looked **ruefully** at it and said he would hate to have a torpedo get him before he ate it. We all laughed, and then commented on how slowly we were running. We thought the engines had stopped.

Mr. Friend [another passenger] and I went up on deck B on the **starboard** side and leaned over the railing, looking at the sea, which was a marvellous blue and very dazzling in the sunlight. I said, "How could the officers ever see a **periscope** there?" The torpedo was on its way to us at that moment, for we went a short distance farther toward the **stern,** . . . when the ship was struck on the starboard side. The water and timbers flew past the deck. Mr. Friend struck his fist in his hand and said, "By Jove! they've got us." The ship steadied herself a few seconds and then listed [tilted] heavily to starboard, throwing us against the wall of a small corridor. . . .

. . . [The] deck suddenly looked very strange, crowded with people, and I remember that two women were crying in a pitifully weak way. An officer was shouting orders to stop lowering the boats, and we were told to go down to deck B. We first looked over the rail and watched a boat filled with men and women being lowered. The stern was lowered too quickly and half the boatload were spilled backwards into the water. We looked at each other, sickened by the sight. . . .

The United States and Cuba

Sympathy for Cubans under Spanish rule grew as newspapers competed with each other in reporting stories of Spanish atrocities. An editorial in Joseph Pulitzer's New York World *is a case in point:*

How long are the Spaniards to drench Cuba with the blood and tears of her people?

. . . How long shall old men and women and children be murdered by the **score,** the innocent victims of Spanish rage against the patriot armies they cannot conquer?

. . . How long shall the United States sit idle and indifferent . . . ?

Analyzing Primary Sources

1. According to Jane Addams, what is the role of the settlement house?
2. The *Lusitania* passengers were aware that Germany had threatened to attack British ships. From Theodate Pope's account, do you think they took the threat seriously?
3. What action do you think the newspaper editorial wants the United States to take? Explain.

Turbulent Decades

After World War I, Americans enjoyed a decade of relative prosperity. The Great Depression ended that. The terrible economic slump shook the lives of the rich and made life even harder for those who were already poor. In the 1940s, international events became the center of attention, and fighting in World War II became the nation's top priority. As you read these selections, think about the various ways Americans demonstrated personal courage, in the good times and in the bad.

Reader's Dictionary

soup line: outdoor kitchen set up to distribute free food to needy people

contemptuous: scornful

A fruit seller

Standing in the Soup Line

Oral Histories

Peggy Terry came from the hills of Kentucky, but her family spent the hard years of the Depression in Oklahoma City. She describes how the family managed to eat during the tough times.

I first noticed the difference when we'd come home from school in the evening. My mother'd send us to the **soup line**. . . . If you happened to be one of the first ones in line, you didn't get anything but water that was on top. So we'd ask the guy that was ladling out the soup into the buckets—everybody had to bring their own bucket to get the soup—he'd dip the greasy, watery stuff off the top. So we'd ask him to please dip down to get some meat and potatoes from the bottom of the kettle. . . .

Then we'd go across the street. One place had bread, large loaves of bread. Down the road just a little piece was a big shed, and they gave milk. My sister and me would take two buckets each. And that's what we lived off for the longest time.

I can remember one time, the only thing in the house to eat was mustard. My sister and I put so much mustard on biscuits that we got sick. And we can't stand mustard till today. . . .

When they had food to give to people, you'd get a notice and you'd go down. So Daddy went down that day and he took my sister and me. They were giving away potatoes and things like that. But they had a truck of oranges parked in the alley. Somebody asked them who the oranges were for, and they wouldn't tell 'em. So they said, well, we're gonna take those oranges. And they did. My dad was one of the ones that got up on the truck. They called the police, and the police chased us all away. But we got the oranges.

It's different today. People are made to feel ashamed now if they don't have anything. Back then, I'm not sure how the rich felt. I think the rich were as **contemptuous** of the poor then as they are now. But among the people that I knew, we all had an understanding that it wasn't our fault. It was something that had happened to the machinery. . . .

I remember it was fun. It was fun going to the soup line. 'Cause we all went down the road, and we laughed and we played. The only thing we felt is that we were hungry and we were going to get food. Nobody made us feel ashamed. There just wasn't any of that.

On the Home Front

The U.S. government appealed to civilians to support the war effort in many ways. This bulletin was posted in meat markets.

1] THE NEED IS URGENT—War in the Pacific has greatly reduced our supply of vegetable fats from the Far East. It is necessary to find substitutes for them. Fat makes glycerine. And glycerine makes explosives for us and our Allies—explosives to down Axis planes, stop their tanks, and sink their ships. We need millions of pounds of glycerine and you housewives can help supply it.

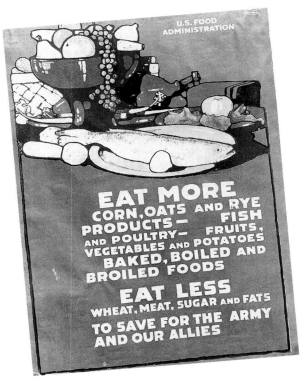

Wartime conservation poster

2] DON'T throw away a single drop of used cooking fat, bacon fat, meat drippings, fry fats—every kind you use. After you've got all the cooking good from them, pour them through a kitchen strainer into a clean, wide-mouthed can. Keep it in a cool dark place. . . .

3] TAKE THEM to your meat dealer when you've saved a pound or more. He is cooperating patriotically. He will pay you for your waste fats and get them started on their way to war industries. . . .

Analyzing Primary Sources

1. What does Peggy Terry mean when she says that the hard times were due to "something that had happened to the machinery"?
2. For what purpose did the government ask people to save their cooking fats and meat drippings?

Turning Points

During the Cold War era, the world lingered on the edge of nuclear disaster as the superpowers—the United States and the Soviet Union—both tried to extend their influence around the world. At home, families tried to prepare for a nuclear attack as best they could. At the same time, African Americans began to demand better treatment from their government. The nation found a voice in protest. Protest against injustice toward African Americans marked the late 1950s. In the 1960s, the youth of America protested involvement in the Vietnam War. Women demanded equal pay for equal work. As you read these selections, think about how the government reacted to the passions of the American citizens. Did their actions make a difference?

Reader's Dictionary

fallout: particles of radioactive material that drift through the atmosphere after a nuclear explosion

Conelrad: (from "Control of Electromagnetic Radiation") a radio broadcasting system that would replace normal broadcasts in an emergency

Fallout Fears

 Printed Publications

By 1961 fears of nuclear war were so great that the government urged people to be prepared for a nuclear attack. LIFE *magazine reminded Americans what to do during such an attack.*

The standard Civil Defense signal for an alert is a steady 3- to 5-minute blast of a siren or whistle. The warning to take cover is a 3-minute period of short blasts or a wailing siren. If an attack should come, however, the first warning you may get could be the flash itself. Your first move should be to close your eyes and bury your head in your arms or clothing to block out the light. The flash may last for several seconds, so keep covered until it begins to dim.

The shockwave will come next. Take cover so you will not be knocked down. If you are in a car, roll down windows to avoid flying glass and lie on the floor. Try to count the seconds between the flash and shockwave. This will help you estimate how far away the bomb has hit and how long you have to find better cover before the **fallout** can reach you. . . .

Wherever you are, try to reach a radio—preferably a battery radio since the electricity may be out—and tune it to 640 or 1240 on your dial, which are the **Conelrad** frequencies for emergency instructions. If you have a shelter, go to it immediately. . . .

If you have no shelter and there is an hour or so left before the fallout is due to reach your area, you can block up the windows of your basement with one foot of earth, and take shelter there under tables on which you have piled books and magazines for extra shielding. You should also get together a supply of food and water and take it to the basement with you. . . .

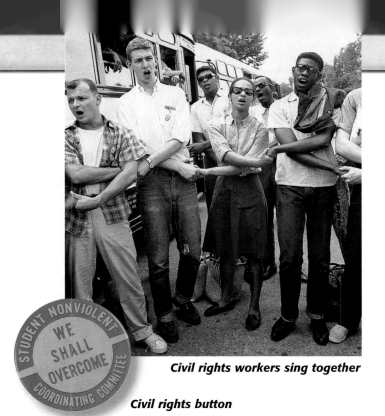

Civil rights workers sing together

Civil rights button

We Shall Overcome

As civil rights supporters marched in protest, they often raised their voices in unison to drown out their fears and bolster their hopes. Many considered this song the civil rights anthem.

We shall overcome, we shall overcome
We shall overcome someday
Oh deep in my heart, I do believe
That we shall overcome someday

We'll walk hand in hand, we'll walk hand
in hand

We'll walk hand in hand someday
Oh deep in my heart, I do believe
We shall overcome someday

We shall live in peace, we shall live in peace
We shall live in peace someday
Oh deep in my heart, I do believe
That we shall overcome someday

Working Women

Oral Histories

During the 1960s and 1970s, women began demanding equal pay for equal work. Women such as Joanne Gus, a warehouse worker, filed lawsuits to get back pay from their employers. In this excerpt, Gus describes the difficulties she and her coworkers faced after receiving a disappointing $500 offer to settle their lawsuit.

. . . I was ready to cry. You can't realize all the aggravation and amount of work that had been done so far. The really sad part about it was that most of the women were willing to settle. They were afraid to take it any further. Well, I can be very stubborn, especially if I know I'm right about an issue. So I refused the offer for them all. Well, the next few days were really [awful] at work. Still, I knew I was worth more.

The case made it to federal court. A settlement of $548,000 in back pay for 246 women was reached.

Analyzing Primary Sources

1. According to the *LIFE* magazine article, in what order would someone probably experience the effects of a nuclear attack some distance away?
2. What things did workers in the civil rights movement want to "overcome" as is implied in the song?
3. How did Joanne Gus's attitude differ from those of her coworkers?

Modern America

World events since the 1970s have moved with breathtaking speed. The Soviet Union collapsed, ending the Cold War. New advances in technology helped the world move forward. Millions of immigrants came to the United States, following the promise of freedom and economic opportunity. At the same time, terrorism threatened the American way of life. As you examine these selections, think of the challenges and opportunities facing the United States today.

Reader's Dictionary

extremism: the holding of unreasonable views

humanitarian: committed to improving the lives of other people

pluralism: society with different ethnic and religious groups

tolerance: acceptance of and fairness toward people who hold different views

Proud to Be an American

"God Bless the USA," by singer Lee Greenwood, topped the country music charts in the 1980s. It was adopted as a theme song for President Reagan's 1984 reelection campaign.

I'm proud to be an American
where at least I know I'm free,
And I won't forget the men who died
who gave that right to me,
And I gladly stand up next to you
and defend her still today,
'Cause there ain't no doubt I love this land
God Bless the U.S.A.

Address to Congress

On September 20, 2001, President George W. Bush addressed Congress, nine days after New York City and Washington, D.C., were shaken by suicide aircraft attacks.

On September the eleventh, enemies of freedom committed an act of war against our country. Americans have known wars—but for the past 136 years, they have been wars on foreign soil, except for one Sunday in 1941 [the attack on Pearl Harbor]. Americans have known the casualties of war—but not at the center of a great city on a peaceful morning. Americans have known surprise attacks—but never before on thousands of civilians. All of this was brought upon us in a single day—and night fell on a different world, a world where freedom itself is under attack. . . .

The terrorists [who carried out the attack] practice a fringe form of Islamic **extremism** that has been rejected by Muslim scholars and the vast majority of Muslim clerics— a fringe movement that perverts the peaceful teachings of Islam. . . .

This group [al-Qaeda] and its leader, a person named Osama bin Laden, are linked to many other organizations in different countries. . . . The leadership of al-Qaeda has great influence in Afghanistan and supports the Taliban regime in controlling most of that country. . . .

The United States respects the people of Afghanistan—after all, we are currently its largest source of **humanitarian** aid—but we condemn the Taliban regime.

[The terrorists] hate what we see right here in this chamber—a democratically elected government. Their leaders are self-appointed. They hate our freedoms—our freedom of religion, our freedom of speech, our freedom to vote and assemble and dis-agree with each other. . . .

This is not, however, just America's fight. And what is at stake is not just America's freedom. This is the world's fight. This is civilization's fight. This is the fight of all who believe in progress and **pluralism, tolerance,** and freedom. . . .

The civilized world is rallying to America's side. They understand that if this terror goes unpunished, their own cities, their own citizens may be next. Terror, unanswered, can not

President Bush thanks rescue workers

only bring down buildings, it can threaten the stability of legitimate governments. And we will not allow it. . . .

I ask you to uphold the values of America, and remember why so many have come here. We are in a fight for our principles, and our first responsibility is to live by them. No one should be singled out for unfair treatment or unkind words because of their ethnic back-ground or religious faith. . . .

Great harm has been done to us. We have suffered great loss. And in our grief and anger we have found our mission and our moment. Freedom and fear are at war. The advance of human freedom—the great achievement of our time, and the great hope of every time— now depends on us. Our Nation—this gener-ation—will lift a dark threat of violence from our people and our future. We will rally the world to this cause, by our efforts and by our courage. We will not tire, we will not falter, and we will not fail.

Analyzing Primary Sources

1. What themes does Lee Greenwood express in his song?
2. To what other tragic event does President Bush compare the events of September 11, 2001?
3. Why does the president believe other nations should help in the fight against terrorism?

Presidents of the United States

In this resource you will find portraits of the individuals who served as presidents of the United States, along with their occupations, political party affiliations, and other interesting facts.

**The Republican Party during this period developed into today's Democratic Party. Today's Republican Party originated in 1854.*

1 George Washington

Presidential term: 1789–1797
Lived: 1732–1799
Born in: Virginia
Elected from: Virginia
Occupations: Soldier, Planter
Party: None
Vice President: John Adams

2 John Adams

Presidential term: 1797–1801
Lived: 1735–1826
Born in: Massachusetts
Elected from: Massachusetts
Occupations: Teacher, Lawyer
Party: Federalist
Vice President: Thomas Jefferson

3 Thomas Jefferson

Presidential term: 1801–1809
Lived: 1743–1826
Born in: Virginia
Elected from: Virginia
Occupations: Planter, Lawyer
Party: Republican**
Vice Presidents: Aaron Burr, George Clinton

4 James Madison

Presidential term: 1809–1817
Lived: 1751–1836
Born in: Virginia
Elected from: Virginia
Occupation: Planter
Party: Republican**
Vice Presidents: George Clinton, Elbridge Gerry

5 James Monroe

Presidential term: 1817–1825
Lived: 1758–1831
Born in: Virginia
Elected from: Virginia
Occupation: Lawyer
Party: Republican**
Vice President: Daniel D. Tompkins

6 John Quincy Adams

Presidential term: 1825–1829
Lived: 1767–1848
Born in: Massachusetts
Elected from: Massachusetts
Occupation: Lawyer
Party: Republican**
Vice President: John C. Calhoun

7 Andrew Jackson

Presidential term: 1829–1837
Lived: 1767–1845
Born in: South Carolina
Elected from: Tennessee
Occupations: Lawyer, Soldier
Party: Democratic
Vice Presidents: John C. Calhoun, Martin Van Buren

8 Martin Van Buren

Presidential term: 1837–1841
Lived: 1782–1862
Born in: New York
Elected from: New York
Occupation: Lawyer
Party: Democratic
Vice President: Richard M. Johnson

9 William H. Harrison

Presidential term: 1841
Lived: 1773–1841
Born in: Virginia
Elected from: Ohio
Occupations: Soldier, Planter
Party: Whig
Vice President: John Tyler

10 John Tyler

Presidential term: 1841–1845
Lived: 1790–1862
Born in: Virginia
Elected as V.P. from: Virginia
Succeeded Harrison
Occupation: Lawyer
Party: Whig
Vice President: None

11 James K. Polk

Presidential term: 1845–1849
Lived: 1795–1849
Born in: North Carolina
Elected from: Tennessee
Occupation: Lawyer
Party: Democratic
Vice President: George M. Dallas

12 Zachary Taylor

Presidential term: 1849–1850
Lived: 1784–1850
Born in: Virginia
Elected from: Louisiana
Occupation: Soldier
Party: Whig
Vice President: Millard Fillmore

13 Millard Fillmore

Presidential term: 1850–1853
Lived: 1800–1874
Born in: New York
Elected as V.P. from: New York
Succeeded Taylor
Occupation: Lawyer
Party: Whig
Vice President: None

14 Franklin Pierce

Presidential term: 1853–1857
Lived: 1804–1869
Born in: New Hampshire
Elected from: New Hampshire
Occupation: Lawyer
Party: Democratic
Vice President: William R. King

15 James Buchanan

Presidential term: 1857–1861
Lived: 1791–1868
Born in: Pennsylvania
Elected from: Pennsylvania
Occupation: Lawyer
Party: Democratic
Vice President: John C. Breckinridge

16 Abraham Lincoln

Presidential term: 1861–1865
Lived: 1809–1865
Born in: Kentucky
Elected from: Illinois
Occupation: Lawyer
Party: Republican
Vice Presidents: Hannibal Hamlin, Andrew Johnson

17 Andrew Johnson

Presidential term: 1865–1869
Lived: 1808–1875
Born in: North Carolina
Elected as V.P. from: Tennessee
Succeeded Lincoln
Occupation: Tailor
Party: Republican
Vice President: None

18 Ulysses S. Grant

Presidential term: 1869–1877
Lived: 1822–1885
Born in: Ohio
Elected from: Illinois
Occupations: Farmer, Soldier
Party: Republican
Vice Presidents: Schuyler Colfax,
Henry Wilson

19 Rutherford B. Hayes

Presidential term: 1877–1881
Lived: 1822–1893
Born in: Ohio
Elected from: Ohio
Occupation: Lawyer
Party: Republican
Vice President: William A.
Wheeler

20 James A. Garfield

Presidential term: 1881
Lived: 1831–1881
Born in: Ohio
Elected from: Ohio
Occupations: Laborer, Professor
Party: Republican
Vice President: Chester A.
Arthur

21 Chester A. Arthur

Presidential term: 1881–1885
Lived: 1830–1886
Born in: Vermont
Elected as V.P. from: New York
Succeeded Garfield
Occupations: Teacher, Lawyer
Party: Republican
Vice President: None

22 Grover Cleveland

Presidential term: 1885–1889
Lived: 1837–1908
Born in: New Jersey
Elected from: New York
Occupation: Lawyer
Party: Democratic
Vice President: Thomas A.
Hendricks

23 Benjamin Harrison

Presidential term: 1889–1893
Lived: 1833–1901
Born in: Ohio
Elected from: Indiana
Occupation: Lawyer
Party: Republican
Vice President: Levi P. Morton

24 Grover Cleveland

Presidential term: 1893–1897
Lived: 1837–1908
Born in: New Jersey
Elected from: New York
Occupation: Lawyer
Party: Democratic
Vice President: Adlai E.
Stevenson

25 William McKinley

Presidential term: 1897–1901
Lived: 1843–1901
Born in: Ohio
Elected from: Ohio
Occupations: Teacher, Lawyer
Party: Republican
Vice Presidents: Garret Hobart,
Theodore Roosevelt

26 Theodore Roosevelt

Presidential term: 1901–1909
Lived: 1858–1919
Born in: New York
Elected as V.P. from: New York
Succeeded McKinley
Occupations: Historian, Rancher
Party: Republican
Vice President: Charles W.
Fairbanks

27 William H. Taft

Presidential term: 1909–1913
Lived: 1857–1930
Born in: Ohio
Elected from: Ohio
Occupation: Lawyer
Party: Republican
Vice President: James S.
Sherman

28 Woodrow Wilson

Presidential term: 1913–1921
Lived: 1856–1924
Born in: Virginia
Elected from: New Jersey
Occupation: College Professor
Party: Democratic
Vice President: Thomas R.
Marshall

29 Warren G. Harding

Presidential term: 1921–1923
Lived: 1865–1923
Born in: Ohio
Elected from: Ohio
Occupations: Newspaper Editor,
Publisher
Party: Republican
Vice President: Calvin Coolidge

30 Calvin Coolidge

Presidential term: 1923–1929
Lived: 1872–1933
Born in: Vermont
Elected as V.P. from:
Massachusetts
Succeeded Harding
Occupation: Lawyer
Party: Republican
Vice President: Charles G. Dawes

31 Herbert C. Hoover

Presidential term: 1929–1933
Lived: 1874–1964
Born in: Iowa
Elected from: California
Occupation: Engineer
Party: Republican
Vice President: Charles Curtis

32 Franklin D. Roosevelt

Presidential term: 1933–1945
Lived: 1882–1945
Born in: New York
Elected from: New York
Occupation: Lawyer
Party: Democratic
Vice Presidents: John N. Garner,
Henry A. Wallace, Harry S
Truman

33 Harry S Truman

Presidential term: 1945–1953
Lived: 1884–1972
Born in: Missouri
Elected as V.P. from: Missouri
Succeeded Roosevelt
Occupations: Clerk, Farmer
Party: Democratic
Vice President: Alben W.
Barkley

34 Dwight D. Eisenhower

Presidential term: 1953–1961
Lived: 1890–1969
Born in: Texas
Elected from: New York
Occupation: Soldier
Party: Republican
Vice President: Richard M.
Nixon

35 John F. Kennedy

Presidential term: 1961–1963
Lived: 1917–1963
Born in: Massachusetts
Elected from: Massachusetts
Occupations: Author, Reporter
Party: Democratic
Vice President: Lyndon B. Johnson

36 Lyndon B. Johnson

Presidential term: 1963–1969
Lived: 1908–1973
Born in: Texas
Elected as V.P. from: Texas
Succeeded Kennedy
Occupation: Teacher
Party: Democratic
Vice President: Hubert H. Humphrey

37 Richard M. Nixon

Presidential term: 1969–1974
Lived: 1913–1994
Born in: California
Elected from: New York
Occupation: Lawyer
Party: Republican
Vice Presidents: Spiro T. Agnew, Gerald R. Ford

38 Gerald R. Ford

Presidential term: 1974–1977
Lived: 1913– 2006
Born in: Nebraska
Appointed as V.P. upon Agnew's resignation; succeeded Nixon
Occupation: Lawyer
Party: Republican
Vice President: Nelson A. Rockefeller

39 James E. Carter, Jr.

Presidential term: 1977–1981
Lived: 1924–
Born in: Georgia
Elected from: Georgia
Occupations: Business, Farmer
Party: Democratic
Vice President: Walter F. Mondale

40 Ronald W. Reagan

Presidential term: 1981–1989
Lived: 1911–2004
Born in: Illinois
Elected from: California
Occupations: Actor, Lecturer
Party: Republican
Vice President: George H.W. Bush

41 George H.W. Bush

Presidential term: 1989–1993
Lived: 1924–
Born in: Massachusetts
Elected from: Texas
Occupation: Business
Party: Republican
Vice President: J. Danforth Quayle

42 William J. Clinton

Presidential term: 1993–2001
Lived: 1946–
Born in: Arkansas
Elected from: Arkansas
Occupation: Lawyer
Party: Democratic
Vice President: Albert Gore, Jr.

43 George W. Bush

Presidential term: 2001–
Lived: 1946–
Born in: Connecticut
Elected from: Texas
Occupation: Business
Party: Republican
Vice President: Richard B. Cheney

The Magna Carta

The Magna Carta, signed by King John in 1215, marked a decisive step forward in the development of constitutional government in England. Later, it became a model for colonists who carried the Magna Carta's guarantees of legal and political rights to America.

1. . . . [T]hat the English Church shall be free, and shall have its rights entire, and its liberties unimpaired. . . . we have also granted for us and our heirs forever, all the liberties written out below, to have and to keep for them and their heirs, of us and our heirs:

39. No free man shall be seized or imprisoned, or stripped of his rights or possessions, or outlawed or exiled, or deprived of his standing in any other way, nor will we proceed with force against him, or send others to do so, except by the lawful judgment of his equals, or by the law of the land.

40. To no one will we sell, to no one deny or delay right or justice.

41. All merchants may enter or leave England unharmed and without fear, and may stay or travel within it, by land or water, for purposes of trade, free from all illegal exactions, in accordance with ancient and lawful customs. This, however, does not apply in time of war to merchants from a country that is at war with us. . . .

42. In future it shall be lawful for any man to leave and return to our kingdom unharmed and without fear, by land or water, preserving his allegiance to us, except in time of war, for some short period, for the common benefit of the realm. . . .

60. All these customs and liberties that we have granted shall be observed in our kingdom in so far as concerns our own relations with our subjects. Let all men of our kingdom, whether clergy or laymen, observe them similarly in their relations with their own men. . . .

63. . . . Both we and the barons have sworn that all this shall be observed in good faith and without deceit. Witness the abovementioned people and many others. Given by our hand in the meadow that is called Runnymede, between Windsor and Staines, on the fifteenth day of June in the seventeenth year of our reign.

Illuminated manuscript, Middle Ages

The Mayflower Compact

On November 21, 1620, 41 colonists aboard the Mayflower drafted this agreement. The Mayflower Compact was the first plan of self-government ever put in force in the English colonies.

In the Name of God, Amen. We, whose names are underwritten, the Loyal Subjects of our dread Sovereign Lord King James, by the Grace of God, of Great Britain, France, and Ireland, King, Defender of the Faith, etc. Having undertaken for the Glory of God, and Advancement of the Christian Faith, and the Honour of our King and Country, a Voyage to plant the first Colony in the northern Parts of Virginia; Do by these Presents, solemnly and mutually, in the Presence of God and one another, covenant and combine ourselves together into a civil Body Politick, for our better Ordering and Preservation, and Furtherance of the Ends aforesaid: And by Virtue hereof do enact, constitute, and frame, such just and equal Laws, Ordinances, Acts, Constitutions, and Officers, from time to time, as shall be thought most meet and convenient for the general Good of the Colony; unto which we promise all due Submission and Obedience. In Witness whereof we have hereunto subscribed our names at Cape-Cod the eleventh of November, in the Reign of our Sovereign Lord King James, of England, France, and Ireland, the eighteenth, and of Scotland, the fifty-fourth, Anno Domini, 1620.

The Federalist, No. 10

James Madison wrote several articles supporting ratification of the Constitution for a New York newspaper. In the excerpt below, Madison argues for the idea of a federal republic.

By a faction, I understand a number of citizens . . . who are united and actuated by some common impulse . . . adverse to the rights of other citizens. . . . The inference to which we are brought is that the causes of faction cannot be removed and that relief is only to be sought in the means of controlling its *effects*. . . .

James Madison

A republic, by which I mean a government in which the scheme of representation takes place . . . promises the cure for which we are seeking. . . .

The two great points of difference between a democracy and a republic are: first, the delegation of the government, in the latter, to a small number of citizens elected by the rest; secondly, the greater number of citizens, and greater sphere of country, over which the latter may be extended.

The effect of the first difference is . . . to refine and enlarge the public views, by passing them through the medium of a chosen body of citizens, whose wisdom may best discern the true interest of their country, and whose patriotism and love of justice will be least likely to sacrifice it to temporary or partial considerations. . . .

Washington's Farewell Address

At the end of his second term as president, George Washington spoke of the dangers facing the young nation. He warned against the dangers of political parties and sectionalism, and he advised the nation against permanent alliances with other nations.

. . . Citizens by birth or choice of a common country, that country has a right to concentrate your affections. The name of American, which belongs to you in your national capacity, must always exalt the just pride of patriotism more than any appellation derived from local discriminations. With slight shades of difference, you have the same religion, manners, habits, and political principles. You have in a common cause fought and triumphed together. . . .

In contemplating the causes which may disturb our union it occurs as matter of serious concern that any ground should have been furnished for characterizing parties by *geographical* discriminations. . . .

No alliances, however strict, between the parts can be an adequate substitute. They must inevitably experience the infractions and interruptions which all alliances in all times have experienced. . . .

George Washington

The great rule of conduct for us in regard to foreign nations is, in extending our commercial relations to have with them as little *political* connection as possible. . . .

. . . I anticipate with pleasing expectation that retreat in which I promise myself to realize . . . the sweet enjoyment of partaking in the midst of my fellow citizens the benign influence of good laws under a free government—the ever-favorite object of my heart, and the happy reward, as I trust, of our mutual cares, labors, and dangers.

The Star-Spangled Banner

During the British bombardment of Fort McHenry during the War of 1812, a young Baltimore lawyer named Francis Scott Key was inspired to write the words to "The Star-Spangled Banner." Although it became popular immediately, it was not until 1931 that Congress officially declared "The Star-Spangled Banner" as our national anthem.

O! say can you see by the dawn's early light,
What so proudly we hailed at the twilight's last gleaming,
Whose broad stripes and bright stars through the perilous fight,
O'er the ramparts we watch'd, were so gallantly streaming?
And the Rockets' red glare, the Bombs bursting in air,
Gave proof through the night that our Flag was still there;
O! say does that star-spangled Banner yet wave,
O'er the Land of the free, and the home of the brave!

The Monroe Doctrine

In an 1823 address to Congress, President James Monroe proclaimed the Monroe Doctrine. Designed to end European influence in the Western Hemisphere, it became a cornerstone of United States foreign policy.

. . . With the existing colonies or dependencies of any European power we have not interfered and shall not interfere. But with the Governments who have declared their independence and maintained it, and whose independence we have, on great consideration and on just principles, acknowledged, we could not view any interposition for the purpose of oppressing them, or controlling in any other manner their destiny, by any European power in any other light than as the manifestation of any unfriendly disposition toward the United States. . . .

Our policy in regard to Europe, which was adopted at an early stage of the wars which have so long agitated that quarter of the globe, nevertheless remains the same, which is, not to interfere in the internal concerns of any of its powers; to consider the government *de facto* as the legitimate government for us; to cultivate friendly relations with it, and to preserve those relations by a frank, firm, and manly policy, meeting in all instances the just claims of every power, submitting to injuries from none. . . .

James Monroe

Memorial of the Cherokee Nation

Beaded shoulder bag, Cherokee people

The Indian Removal Act of 1830 called for the relocation of Native Americans to territory west of the Mississippi River. Cherokee leaders protested the policy.

We are aware that some persons suppose it will be for our advantage to remove beyond the Mississippi. We think otherwise. Our people universally think otherwise. . . .

We wish to remain on the land of our fathers. We have a perfect and original right to remain without interruption or molestation. The treaties with us, and laws of the United States made in pursuance of treaties, guaranty our residence and our privileges, and secure us against intruders. Our only request is, that these treaties may be fulfilled, and these laws executed. . . .

. . . We have been called a poor, ignorant, and degraded people. We certainly are not rich; nor have we ever boasted of our knowledge, or our moral or intellectual elevation. But there is not a man within our limits so ignorant as not to know that he has a right to live on the land of his fathers, in the possession of his immemorial privileges, and that this right has been acknowledged by the United States; nor is there a man so degraded as not to feel a keen sense of injury, on being deprived of his right and driven into exile. . . .

The Seneca Falls Declaration

One of the first documents to express the desire for equal rights for women is the Declaration of Sentiments and Resolutions, issued in 1848 at the Seneca Falls Convention in Seneca Falls, New York. Led by Lucretia Mott and Elizabeth Cady Stanton, the delegates adopted a set of resolutions that called for woman suffrage and opportunities for women in employment and education. Excerpts from the Declaration follow.

When, in the course of human events, it becomes necessary for one portion of the family of man to assume among the people of the earth a position different from that which they have hitherto occupied, but one to which the laws of nature and of nature's God entitle them, a decent respect to the opinions of mankind requires that they should declare the causes that impel them to such a course.

We hold these truths to be self-evident: that all men and women are created equal; that they are endowed by their Creator with certain inalienable rights; that among these are life, liberty, and the pursuit of happiness; that to secure these rights governments are instituted, deriving their just powers from the consent of the governed. Whenever any form of government becomes destructive of these ends, it is the right of those who suffer from it to refuse allegiance to it, and to insist upon the institution of a new government, laying its foundation on such principles, and organizing its powers in such form as to them shall seem most likely to effect their safety and happiness. Prudence, indeed, will dictate that governments long established should not be changed for light and transient causes; . . . But when a long train of abuses and usurpations, pursuing invariably the same object, evinces a design to reduce them under absolute despotism, it is their duty to throw off such government, and to provide new guards for their future security. . . .

The history of mankind is a history of repeated injuries and usurpations on the part of man toward woman, having in direct object the establishment of an absolute tyranny over her. To prove this, let facts be submitted to a candid world. . . .

Now, in view of the entire disfranchisement of one-half the people of this country, their social and religious degradation—in view of the unjust laws above mentioned, and because women do feel themselves aggrieved, oppressed, and fraudulently deprived of their most sacred rights, we insist that they have immediate admission to all the rights and privileges which belong to them as citizens of these United States. . . .

Elizabeth Cady Stanton

The Emancipation Proclamation

On January 1, 1863, President Abraham Lincoln issued the Emancipation Proclamation, which freed all enslaved people in states under Confederate control. The Proclamation was a step toward the Thirteenth Amendment (1865), which ended slavery in all of the United States.

. . . That on the 1st day of January, in the year of our Lord 1863, all persons held as slaves within any state or designated part of a state, the people whereof shall then be in rebellion against the United States, shall be then, thenceforward, and forever free; and the Executive Government of the United States, including the military and naval authority thereof, will recognize and maintain the freedom of such persons, and will do no act or acts to repress such persons, or any of them, in any efforts they may make for their actual freedom.

That the Executive will, on the 1st day of January aforesaid, by proclamation, designate the states and parts of states, if any, in which the people thereof, respectively, shall then be in rebellion against the United States; and the fact that any state, or the people thereof, shall on that day be in good faith represented in the Congress of the United States, by members chosen thereto at elections wherein a majority of the qualified voters of such states shall have participated, shall, in the absence of strong countervailing testimony, be deemed conclusive evidence that such state, and the people thereof, are not then in rebellion against the United States. . . .

And, by virtue of the power and for the purpose aforesaid, I do order and declare that all persons held as slaves within said designated states and parts of states are, and henceforward shall be, free; and that the Executive Government of the United States, including the military and naval authorities thereof, will recognize and maintain the freedom of said persons.

And I hereby enjoin upon the people so declared to be free to abstain from all violence, unless in necessary self-defense; and I recommend to them that, all cases when allowed, they labor faithfully for reasonable wages.

And I further declare and make known that such persons, of suitable condition, will be received into the armed service of the United States. . . .

And upon this act, sincerely believed to be an act of justice, warranted by the Constitution upon military necessity, I invoke the considerate judgement of man-kind and the gracious favor of Almighty God. . . .

Abraham Lincoln

Members of the 4th Infantry

Documents

The Gettysburg Address

On November 19, 1863, President Abraham Lincoln gave a short speech at the dedication of a national cemetery on the battlefield of Gettysburg. His simple yet eloquent words expressed his hopes for a nation divided by civil war.

Four score and seven years ago our fathers brought forth on this continent a new nation, conceived in liberty, and dedicated to the proposition that all men are created equal.

Now we are engaged in a great civil war, testing whether that nation, or any nation so conceived and so dedicated, can long endure. We are met on a great battlefield of that war. We have come to dedicate a portion of that field as a final resting place for those who here gave their lives that that nation might live. It is altogether fitting and proper that we should do this.

But, in a larger sense, we can not dedicate—we can not consecrate—we can not hallow—this ground.

The brave men, living and dead, who struggled here, have consecrated it far above our poor power to add or detract. The world will little note nor long remember what we say here, but it can never forget what they did here. It is for us, the living, rather, to be dedicated here to the unfinished work which they who fought here have thus far so nobly advanced. It is rather for us to be here dedicated to the great task remaining before us—that from these honored dead we take increased devotion to that cause for which they gave the last full measure of devotion; that we here highly resolve that these dead shall not have died in vain; that this nation, under God, shall have a new birth of freedom; and that government of the people, by the people, for the people, shall not perish from the earth.

Soldier's kit, Civil War

Gettysburg Memorial

I Will Fight No More

Shield made of buffalo hide

In 1877 the Nez Perce fought the government's attempt to move them to a smaller reservation. After a remarkable attempt to escape to Canada, Chief Joseph realized that resistance was hopeless and advised his people to surrender.

Tell General Howard I know his heart. What he told me before I have in my heart. I am tired of fighting. . . . The old men are all dead. It is the young men who say yes or no. He who led the young men is dead. It is cold and we have no blankets. The little children are freezing to death. My people, some of them have run away to the hills, and have no blankets, no food; no one knows where they are—perhaps freezing to death. I want to have time to look for my children and see how many of them I can find. Maybe I shall find them among the dead. Hear me, my chiefs. I am tired; my heart is sick and sad. From where the sun now stands I will fight no more forever.

The Pledge of Allegiance

In 1892 the nation celebrated the 400th anniversary of Columbus's landing in America. In connection with this celebration, Francis Bellamy, a magazine editor, wrote and published the Pledge of Allegiance. The words "under God" were added by Congress in 1954 at the urging of President Dwight D. Eisenhower.

I pledge allegiance to the Flag of the United States of America and to the Republic for which it stands, one Nation under God, indivisible, with liberty and justice for all.

Students in a New York City school recite the Pledge of Allegiance

The American's Creed

William Tyler Page of Friendship Heights, Maryland, wrote The American's Creed. This statement of political faith summarizes the true meaning of freedom available to all Americans. The U.S. House of Representatives adopted the creed on behalf of the American people on April 3, 1918.

I believe in the United States of America as a Government of the people, by the people, for the people; whose just powers are derived from the consent of the governed; a democracy in a republic; a sovereign Nation of many sovereign States; a perfect union, one and inseparable; established upon those principles of freedom, equality, justice, and humanity for which American patriots sacrificed their lives and fortunes.

I therefore believe it is my duty to my Country to love it; to support its Constitution; to obey its laws; to respect its flag, and to defend it against all enemies.

The Fourteen Points

On January 8, 1918, President Woodrow Wilson went before Congress to offer a statement of aims called the Fourteen Points. Wilson's plan called for freedom of the seas in peace and war, an end to secret alliances, and equal trading rights for all countries. The excerpt that follows is taken from the President's message.

. . . We entered this war because violations of right had occurred which touched us to the quick and made the life of our own people impossible unless they were corrected and the world secured once for all against their recurrence. What we demand in this war, therefore, is nothing peculiar to ourselves. It is that the world be made fit and safe to live in; and particularly that it be made safe for every peace-loving nation which, like our own, wishes to live its own life, determine its own institutions, be assured of justice and fair dealing by the other peoples of the world as against force and selfish aggression. All the peoples of the world are in effect partners in this interest, and for our own part we see very clearly that unless justice be done to others it will not be done to us. The program of the world's peace, therefore, is our program; and that program, the only possible program, as we see it, is this:

I. Open covenants of peace, openly arrived at, after which there shall be no private international understandings of any kind but diplomacy shall proceed always frankly and in the public view.

II. Absolute freedom of navigation upon the seas, outside territorial waters, alike in peace and in war, except as the seas may be closed in whole or in part by international action for the enforcement of international covenants.

XIV. A general association of nations must be formed under specific covenants for the purpose of affording mutual guarantees of political independence and territorial integrity to great and small states alike. . . .

Brown v. Board of Education

On May 17, 1954, the Supreme Court ruled in **Brown** *v.* **Board of Education of Topeka, Kansas,** *that racial segregation in public schools was unconstitutional. This decision provided the legal basis for court challenges to segregation in every aspect of American life.*

. . . The plaintiffs contend that segregated public schools are not "equal" and cannot be made "equal" and that hence they are deprived of the equal protection of the laws. Because of the obvious importance of the question presented, the Court took jurisdiction. . . .

Our decision, therefore, cannot turn on merely a comparison of these tangible factors in the Negro and white schools involved in each of the cases. We must look instead to the effect of segregation itself on public education.

In approaching this problem, we cannot turn the clock back to 1868 when the Amendment was adopted, or even to 1896 when *Plessy* v. *Ferguson* was written. We must consider public education in the light of its full development and its present place in American life throughout the Nation. Only in this way can it be determined if segregation in public schools deprives these plaintiffs of the equal protection of the laws.

Today, education is perhaps the most important function of state and local governments. Compulsory school attendance laws and the great expenditures for education both demonstrate our recognition of the importance of education to our democratic society. . . . In these days, it is doubtful that any child may reasonably be expected to succeed in life if he is denied the opportunity of an education. Such an opportunity, where the state has undertaken to provide it, is a right which must be made available to all on equal terms.

We come then to the question presented: Does segregation of children in public schools solely on the basis of race, even though the physical facilities and other "tangible" factors may be equal, deprive the children of the minority group of equal educational opportunities? We believe that it does.

. . . We conclude that in the field of public education the doctrine of "separate but equal" has no place. Separate educational facilities are inherently unequal. Therefore, we hold that the plaintiffs and others similarly situated for whom the actions have been brought are, by reason of the segregation complained of, deprived of the equal protection of the laws guaranteed by the Fourteenth Amendment. . . .

Troops escort students to newly integrated school

John F. Kennedy's Inaugural Address

President Kennedy's Inaugural Address on January 20, 1961, set the tone for his administration. In his address Kennedy stirred the nation by calling for "a grand and global alliance" to fight tyranny, poverty, disease, and war.

We observe today not a victory of party but a celebration of freedom—symbolizing an end as well as a beginning—signifying renewal as well as change. For I have sworn before you and Almighty God the same solemn oath our forebears prescribed nearly a century and three-quarters ago.

The world is very different now. For man holds in his mortal hands the power to abolish all forms of human poverty and all forms of human life. And yet the same revolutionary beliefs for which our forebears fought are still at issue around the globe—the belief that the rights of man come not from the generosity of the state but from the hand of God.

We dare not forget today that we are the heirs of that first revolution. Let the word go forth from this time and place, to friend and foe alike, that the torch has been passed to a new generation of Americans—born in this century, tempered by war, disciplined by a hard and bitter peace, proud of our ancient heritage—and unwilling to witness or permit the slow undoing of those human rights to which this nation has always been committed, and to which we are committed today at home and around the world.

Let every nation know, whether it wishes us well or ill, that we shall pay any price, bear any burden, meet any hardship, support any friend, oppose any foe to assure the survival and the success of liberty.

This much we pledge—and more.

To those old allies whose cultural and spiritual origins we share, we pledge the loyalty of faithful friends. United, there is little we cannot do in a host of cooperative ventures. Divided, there is little we can do. . . .

Let us never negotiate out of fear. But let us never fear to negotiate.

Let both sides explore what problems unite us instead of belaboring those problems which divide us. . . .

Let both sides seek to invoke the wonders of science instead of its terrors. Together let us explore the stars, conquer the deserts, eradicate disease, tap the ocean depths, and encourage the arts and commerce. . . .

And so, my fellow Americans: ask not what your country can do for you—ask what you can do for your country.

My fellow citizens of the world: ask not what America will do for you, but what together we can do for the freedom of man. . . .

President Kennedy speaking at his inauguration

I Have a Dream

On August 28, 1963, while Congress debated wide-ranging civil rights legislation, Dr. Martin Luther King, Jr., led more than 200,000 people in a march on Washington, D.C. On the steps of the Lincoln Memorial he gave a stirring speech in which he eloquently spoke of his dreams for African Americans and for the United States. Excerpts of the speech follow.

. . . There are those who are asking the devotees of civil rights, "When will you be satisfied?"

We can never be satisfied as long as the Negro is the victim of the unspeakable horrors of police brutality. . . .

We cannot be satisfied as long as the Negro's basic mobility is from a smaller ghetto to a larger one.

We can never be satisfied as long as a Negro in Mississippi cannot vote and a Negro in New York believes he has nothing for which to vote. . . .

I say to you today, my friends, that in spite of the difficulties and frustrations of the moment I still have a dream. It is a dream deeply rooted in the American dream. I have a dream that one day this nation will rise up and live out the true meaning of its creed: "We hold these truths to be self-evident, that all men are created equal."

Dr. Martin Luther King, Jr.

I have a dream that one day on the red hills of Georgia the sons of former slaves and the sons of former slaveowners will be able to sit down together at the table of brotherhood.

I have a dream that one day even the state of Mississippi, a desert state sweltering with the heat of injustice and oppression, will be transformed into an oasis of freedom and justice.

I have a dream that my four little children will one day live in a nation where they will not be judged by the color of their skin but by the content of their character. . . .

. . . When we let freedom ring, when we let it ring from every village and every hamlet, from every state and every city, we will be able to speed up that day when all of God's children, black men and white men, Jews and Gentiles, Protestants and Catholics, will be able to join hands and sing in the words of the old Negro spiritual: "Free at last! Free at last! Thank God Almighty, we are free at last!"

The March on Washington

Supreme Court Case Summaries

The following summaries give details about important Supreme Court cases.

Brown v. Board of Education (1954)

In *Brown* v. *Board of Education of Topeka, Kansas,* the Supreme Court overruled *Plessy* v. *Ferguson* (1896) [see p. 999] making the separate-but-equal doctrine in public schools unconstitutional. The Supreme Court rejected the idea that truly equal but separate schools for African American and white students would be constitutional. The Court explained that the Fourteenth Amendment's requirement that all persons be guaranteed equal protection of the law is not met simply by ensuring that African American and white schools "have been equalized…with respect to buildings, curricula, qualifications and salaries, and other tangible factors."

The Court then ruled that racial segregation in public schools violates the Equal Protection Clause of the Constitution because it is inherently unequal. In other words, nothing can make racially segregated public schools equal under the Constitution because the very fact of separation marks the separated race as inferior. In practical terms, the Court's decision in this case has been extended beyond public education to virtually all public accommodations and activities.

Dred Scott v. Sandford (1857)

Dred Scott was taken by slaveholder, John Sandford, to the free state of Illinois and to the Wisconsin Territory, which had also banned slavery. Later they returned to Missouri, a slave state. Several years later, Scott sued for his freedom under the Missouri legal principle of "once free, always free." In other words, under Missouri law enslaved people were entitled to freedom if they had lived in a free state at any time. Missouri courts ruled against Scott, but he appealed the case all the way to the United States Supreme Court.

Dred Scott

The Supreme Court decided this case before the Fourteenth Amendment was added to the Constitution. (The Fourteenth Amendment provides that anyone born or naturalized in the United States is a citizen of the nation and of his or her state of residence.) The court held that enslaved African Americans were property, not citizens, and thus had no rights under the Constitution. The decision also declared that it was unconstitutional to prohibit slavery in the territories. Many people in the North were outraged by the decision, which moved the nation closer to civil war.

Furman v. Georgia (1972)

This decision put a halt to the application of the death penalty under state laws then in effect. For the first time, the Supreme Court ruled that the death penalty amounted to cruel and unusual punishment, which is outlawed in the Constitution. The Court explained that existing death penalty laws did not give juries enough guidance in deciding whether or not to impose the death penalty. As a result, the death penalty in many cases was imposed arbitrarily, that is, without a reasonable basis in the facts and circumstances of the offender or the crime.

The Furman decision halted all executions in the 39 states that had death penalty laws at that time. Since the decision, 38 states have rewritten death penalty laws to meet the requirements established in the Furman case.

Gibbons v. Ogden (1824)

Thomas Gibbons had a federal license to operate a steamboat along the coast, but he did not have a license from the state of New York to travel on New York waters. He wanted to run a steamboat line between Manhattan and New Jersey that would compete with Aaron Ogden's company. Ogden had a New York license. Gibbons sued for the freedom to use his federal license to compete against Ogden on New York waters.

Gibbons won the case. The Supreme Court made it clear that the authority of Congress to regulate interstate commerce (among states) includes the authority to regulate intrastate commerce (within a single state) that bears on, or relates to, interstate commerce.

Before this decision, it was thought that the Constitution would permit a state to close its borders to interstate commercial activity—which, in effect, would stop such activity in its tracks. This case says that a state can regulate purely internal commercial activity, but only Congress can regulate commercial activity that has both intrastate and interstate dimensions.

Gideon v. Wainwright (1963)

After being accused of robbery, Clarence Gideon defended himself in a Florida court because the judge in the case refused to appoint a free lawyer. The jury found Gideon guilty. Eventually, Gideon appealed his conviction to the United States Supreme Court, claiming that by failing to appoint a lawyer the lower court had violated his rights under the Sixth and Fourteenth Amendments.

The Supreme Court agreed with Gideon. In *Gideon v. Wainwright* the Supreme Court held for the first time that poor defendants in criminal cases have the right to a state-paid attorney under the Sixth Amendment. The rule announced in this case has been refined to apply whenever the defendant, if convicted, can be sentenced to more than six months in jail or prison.

Korematsu v. United States (1944)

After the Japanese bombing of Pearl Harbor in 1941, thousands of Japanese Americans on the West Coast were forced to abandon their homes and businesses, and they were moved to internment camps in

In 1983 Fred Korematsu (center) won a reversal of his conviction.

California, Idaho, Utah, Arizona, Wyoming, Colorado, and Arkansas. The prison-like camps offered poor food and cramped quarters.

The Supreme Court's decision in *Korematsu v. United States* upheld the authority of the federal government to move Japanese Americans, many of whom were citizens, from designated military areas that included almost the entire West Coast. The government defended the so-called exclusion orders as a necessary response to Japan's attack on Pearl Harbor. Only after his reelection in 1944 did President Franklin Roosevelt rescind the evacuation orders, and by the end of 1945 the camps were closed.

Marbury v. Madison (1803)

During his last days in office, President John Adams commissioned William Marbury and several other men as judges. This action by Federalist president Adams angered the incoming Democratic-Republican president Thomas Jefferson. Jefferson then ordered James Madison, his secretary of state, not to deliver the commissions, thus blocking the appointments. William Marbury sued, asking the Supreme Court to order Madison to deliver the commission that would make him a judge.

The Court ruled against Marbury, but more importantly, the decision in this case established one of the most significant principles of American constitutional law. The Supreme Court held that it is the Court itself that has the final say on what the Constitution means. This is known as judicial review. It is also the Supreme Court that has the final say in whether or not an act of government—legislative or executive at the federal, state, or local level—violates the Constitution.

McCulloch v. Maryland (1819)

Following the War of 1812, the United States experienced years of high inflation and general economic turmoil. In an attempt to stabilize the economy, the United States Congress chartered a Second Bank of the United States in 1816. Maryland and several other states, however, opposed the competition that the new national bank created and passed laws taxing its branches. In 1818, James McCulloch, head of the Baltimore branch of the Second Bank of the United States, refused to pay the tax to the state of Maryland. The case worked its way through the Maryland state courts all the way to the United States Supreme Court.

The Supreme Court declared the Maryland tax unconstitutional and void. More importantly, the decision established the foundation for expanded Congressional authority. The Court held that the necessary and proper clause of the Constitution allows Congress to do more than the Constitution expressly authorizes it to do. The decision allows Congress to enact nearly any law that will help it achieve any of its duties as set forth in the Constitution. For example, Congress has the express authority to regulate interstate commerce. The necessary and proper clause permits Congress to do so in ways not actually specified in the Constitution.

Miranda v. Arizona (1966)

In 1963, police in Arizona arrested Ernesto Miranda for kidnapping. The court found Miranda guilty on the basis of a signed confession. The police admitted that neither before nor during the questioning had Miranda been advised of his right to consult with an attorney before answering any questions or of his right to have an attorney present during the interrogation. Miranda appealed his conviction, claiming that police had violated his right against self-incrimination under the Fifth Amendment by not informing him of his legal rights during questioning.

Miranda won the case. The Supreme Court held that a person in police custody cannot be questioned unless told that he or she has: 1) the right to remain silent, 2) the right to an attorney (at government expense if the accused is unable to pay), and 3) that anything the person says after stating that he or she understands these rights can be used as evidence of guilt at trial. These rights have come to be called the

In 1963, the arrest of Ernesto Miranda (left) led to a landmark decision.

Miranda warning. They are intended to ensure that an accused person in custody will not unknowingly give up the Fifth Amendment's protection against self-incrimination.

New York Times Company v. United States (1971)

In June 1971, the *New York Times* published its first installment of the "Pentagon Papers," a classified document about government actions in the Vietnam War era. The secret document had been leaked to the *Times* by antiwar activist Daniel Ellsberg, who had previously worked in national security for the government. President Richard Nixon went to court to block further publication of the Pentagon Papers. The *New York Times* appealed to the Supreme Court to allow it to continue publishing without government interference.

The Supreme Court's ruling in this case upheld earlier decisions that established the doctrine of prior restraint. This doctrine protects the press (broadly defined to include newspapers, television and radio, filmmakers and distributors, etc.) from government attempts to block publication. Except in extraordinary circumstances, the press must be allowed to publish.

Plessy v. Ferguson (1896)

In the late 1800s railroad companies in Louisiana were required by state law to provide "separate-but-equal" cars for white and African American passengers. In 1890 a group of citizens in New Orleans selected Homer Plessy to challenge that law. In 1892, Plessy boarded a whites-only car and refused to move. He was arrested. Plessy appealed to the Supreme Court, arguing that the Louisiana separate-but-equal law violated his right to equal protection under the Fourteenth Amendment.

Homer Plessy lost the case. The Plessy decision upheld the separate-but-equal doctrine used by Southern states to perpetuate segregation following the Civil War. The court ruled that the Fourteenth Amendment's equal protection clause required only equal public facilities for the two races, not equal access to the same facilities. This decision was overruled in 1954 by *Brown* v. *Board of Education of Topeka, Kansas,* (discussed previously).

Roe v. Wade (1973)

Roe v. *Wade* challenged restrictive abortion laws in both Texas and Georgia. The suit was brought in the name of Jane Roe, an alias used to protect the privacy of the plaintiff.

In this decision, the Supreme Court ruled that females have a constitutional right under various provisions of the Constitution—most notably, the due process clause—to decide whether or not to terminate a pregnancy. The Supreme Court's decision in this case was the most significant in a long line of decisions over a period of 50 years that recognized a constitutional right of privacy, even though the word *privacy* is not found in the Constitution.

Tinker v. Des Moines School District (1969)

During the Vietnam War, some students in Des Moines, Iowa, wore black armbands to school to protest American involvement in the conflict. Two days earlier, school officials had adopted a policy banning the wearing of armbands to school. When the students arrived at school wearing armbands, they were suspended and sent home. The students argued that school officials violated their First Amendment right to free speech.

The Supreme Court sided with the students. In a now-famous statement the court said that "it can hardly be argued that either students or teachers shed their constitutional rights of freedom of speech or expression at the schoolhouse gate." The Supreme Court went on to rule that a public school could not suspend students who wore black armbands to school to symbolize their opposition to the Vietnam War. In so holding, the Court likened the students' conduct to pure speech and decided it on that basis.

United States v. Nixon (1974)

In the early 1970s, President Nixon was named an unindicted co-conspirator in the criminal investigation that arose in the aftermath of a break-in at the offices of the Democratic Party in Washington, D.C. A federal judge had ordered President Nixon to turn over tapes of conversations he had with his advisers about the break-in. Nixon resisted the order, claiming that the conversations were entitled to absolute confidentiality by Article II of the Constitution.

The decision in this case made it clear that the president is not above the law. The Supreme Court held that only those presidential conversations and communications that relate to performing the duties of the office of president are confidential and protected from a judicial order of disclosure. The Court ordered Nixon to give up the tapes, which revealed evidence linking the president to the conspiracy to obstruct justice. He resigned from office shortly thereafter.

Worcester v. Georgia (1832)

State officials in Georgia wanted to remove the Cherokees from land that had been guaranteed to them in earlier treaties. Samuel Worcester was a Congregational missionary who worked with the Cherokee people. He was arrested for failure to have a license that the state required to live in Cherokee country and for refusing to obey an order from the Georgia militia to leave Cherokee lands. Worcester then sued the state of Georgia. He claimed that Georgia had no legal authority on Cherokee land because the United States government recognized the Cherokee in Georgia as a separate nation.

The Supreme Court agreed with Worcester by a vote of 5 to 1. Chief Justice John Marshall wrote the majority opinion which said that Native American nations were a distinct people with the right to have independent political communities and that only the federal government had authority over matters that involved the Cherokee.

President Andrew Jackson supported Georgia's efforts to remove the Cherokee to Indian Territory and refused to enforce the court's ruling. After the ruling Jackson remarked, "John Marshall has made his decision. Now let him enforce it."

Gazetteer

The gazetteer is a geographical dictionary that lists political divisions, natural features, and other places and locations. Following each entry is a description, its latitude and longitude, and a page reference that indicates where each entry may be found in this text.

A

Abilene city in Kansas (39°N/97°W) 535

Afghanistan country in southwestern Asia (33°N/63°E) RA11, 949

Africa continent of the Eastern Hemisphere south of the Mediterranean Sea and adjoining Asia on its northeastern border (10°N/22°E) RA13

Alabama state in the southeastern United States; 22nd state to enter the Union (33°N/87°W) RA3, 82, 95

Alamo Texas mission captured by Mexican forces in 1836 (29°N/98°W)

Alaska state in the United States, located in northwestern North America (64°N/150°W) RA4, 640

Albany capital of New York State located in the Hudson Valley; site where Albany Congress proposed first formal plan to unite the 13 colonies (42°N/74°W) RA3

Allegheny River river in western Pennsylvania uniting with the Monongahela River at Pittsburgh to form the Ohio River (41°N/79°W)

Andes mountain system extending along western coast of South America (13°S/75°W)

Antietam Civil War battle site in western Maryland (40°N/77°W)

Appalachian Mountains chief mountain system in eastern North America extending from Quebec and New Brunswick to central Alabama (37°N/82°W) RA5, 11

Appomattox Court House site in central Virginia where Confederate forces surrendered, ending the Civil War (37°N/78°W)

Arizona state in the southwestern United States; 48th state to enter the Union (34°N/113°W) RA2, 29

Arkansas state in the south central U.S.; acquired as part of Louisiana Purchase (35°N/94°W) RA3, 95

Asia continent of the Eastern Hemisphere forming a single landmass with Europe (50°N/100°E) RA13

Atlanta capital of Georgia located in the northwest central part of the state (34°N/84°W) RA5

Atlantic Ocean ocean separating North and South America from Europe and Africa (5°S/25°W) RA12

Australia continent and country southeast of Asia (25°S/125°E) RA13

Austria-Hungary former monarchy in central Europe (47°N/12°E) 668

B

Baltimore city on the Chesapeake Bay in central Maryland (39°N/77°W) RA3

Barbary Coast north coast of Africa between Morocco and Tunisia (35°N/3°E)

Bay of Pigs site of 1961 invasion of Cuba by U.S.-trained Cuban exiles (22°N/79°W) 868

Beijing capital of China located in the northeastern part of the country (40°N/116°E) 647

Belgium country in northwest Europe (51°N/3°E) RA13, 668

Bering Strait waterway between North America and Asia where a land bridge once existed (65°N/170°W) RA9

Beringia land bridge that linked Asia and North America during the last Ice Age (65°N/170°W)

Berlin city in east central Germany; former capital divided into sectors after World War II (53°N/13°E) 775

Birmingham city in north central Alabama; scene of several civil rights protests (33°N/86°W) 570

Black Hills mountains in southwestern South Dakota; site of conflict between the Sioux and white settlers during 1870s (44°N/104°W) 545

Boston capital of Massachusetts located in the eastern part of the state; founded by English Puritans in 1630 (42°N/71°W) RA3

Brazil country in eastern South America (9°S/53°W) RA12

Breed's Hill site near Boston where the Battle of Bunker Hill took place (42°N/71°W)

Buffalo industrial city and rail center in New York State (43°N/79°W) 318

Bull Run site of two Civil War battles in northern Virginia; also called Manassas (39°N/77°W) 55

C

Cahokia largest settlement of the Mound Builders, built in Illinois after A.D. 900 (39°N/90°W) 6

California state in the western United States; attracted thousands of miners during gold rush of 1849 (38°N/121°W) RA2, 533

Cambodia country in Southeastern Asia bordering Gulf of Siam; official name Democratic Kampuchea (12°N/105°E) RA13, 874

Canada country in northern North America (50°N/100°W) RA9, 7

Cape of Good Hope southern tip of Africa (34°S/18°E)

Caribbean Sea tropical sea in the Western Hemisphere (15°N/75°W) RA8

Central America area of North America between Mexico and South America (11°N/86°W) RA8

Chancellorsville Virginia site of 1863 Confederate victory (38°N/78°W)

Charleston city in South Carolina on the Atlantic coast; original name Charles Town (33°N/80°W) RA3

Chesapeake Bay inlet of the Atlantic Ocean in Virginia and Maryland (38°N/76°W) RA5

Chicago largest city in Illinois; located in northeastern part of the state along Lake Michigan (42°N/88°W) RA5

Chile South American country (35°S/72°W) RA12

China country in eastern Asia; mainland (People's Republic of China) under Communist control since 1949 (37°N/93°E) RA13, 639

Chisholm Trail pioneer cattle trail from Texas to Kansas (34°N/98°W) 535

Cincinnati city in southern Ohio on the Ohio River; grew as a result of increasing steamship traffic during the mid-1800s (39°N/84°W) RA3

Cleveland city in northern Ohio on Lake Erie (41°N/82°W) RA3

Colombia country in South America (4°N/73°W) RA12

Colorado state in the western United States (39°N/107°W) RA3

Colorado River river that flows from the Colorado Rockies to the Gulf of California (36°N/113°W) RA4

Columbia River river flowing through southwest Canada and northwestern United States into the Pacific Ocean (46°N/120°W) RA4

Concord village northwest of Boston, Massachusetts; site of early battle of the American Revolution (42°N/71°W) 23

Connecticut state in the northeastern United States; one of the original 13 states (42°N/73°W) RA3

Cuba country in the West Indies, North America (22°N/79°W) RA8, 8

Czechoslovakia former country in central Europe; now two countries, the

Czech Republic and Slovakia (49°N/16°E) RA13

D

Dallas a leading city in Texas (33°N/97°W) RA3

Delaware state in the northeastern United States; one of the original 13 states (39°N/75°W) RA3

Detroit city in southeastern Michigan; site of significant battles during the French and Indian War and the War of 1812; center of automobile industry (42°N/83°W) RA3

Dien Bien Phu site in northwestern Vietnam where French troops were defeated by Vietminh troops in 1954 (21°N/102°E) 872

Dodge City Kansas cattle town during the 19th century (37°N/100°W) 535

Dominican Republic country in the West Indies on the eastern part of Hispaniola Island (19°N/71°W) RA8

Dust Bowl area of the Great Plains where the drought of the 1930s turned the soil to wind-borne dust (37°N/98°W) 756

E

East Germany country in central Europe; reunified with West Germany in 1990 (52°N/12°E) 792

Egypt country in northeastern Africa (27°N/27°E) RA10, 771

England division of the United Kingdom of Great Britain and Northern Ireland (52°N/2°W) RA12–RA13

Erie Canal the waterway connecting the Hudson River with Lake Erie through New York State (43°N/76°W)

Ethiopia country in eastern Africa, north of Somalia and Kenya (8°N/38°E) RA13, 753

Europe continent of the northern part of the Eastern Hemisphere between Asia and the Atlantic Ocean (50°N/15°E) RA13

F

Florida state in the southeastern United States (30°N/85°W) RA3, 59

Fort McHenry fort in Baltimore harbor; inspired poem that later became "The Star-Spangled Banner" (39°N/76°W)

Fort Necessity Pennsylvania fort built by George Washington's troops in 1754 (40°N/80°W)

Fort Sumter Union fort during the Civil War located on island near Charleston, South Carolina; site of first military engagement of Civil War (33°N/80°W)

Fort Ticonderoga British fort on Lake Champlain (44°N/73°W)

France country in western Europe (50°N/1°E) RA13

Fredericksburg city and Civil War battle site in northeast Virginia (38°N/77°W)

Freeport city in northern Illinois; site of 1858 Lincoln-Douglas campaign debate (42°N/89°W)

G

Gadsden Purchase portion of present-day Arizona and New Mexico; area purchased from Mexico in 1853 (32°N/111°W) RA7

Galveston city on the Gulf of Mexico coast in Texas; created nation's first commission form of city government (29°N/95°W) 611

Gaza Strip narrow coastal strip along the Mediterranean (31°N/34°E) RA10, 899

Georgia state in the southeastern United States (33°N/84°W) RA3

Germany country in central Europe; divided after World War II into East Germany and West Germany; unified in 1990 (50°N/10°E) RA13, 667

Gettysburg city and Civil War battle site in south central Pennsylvania; site where Lincoln delivered the Gettysburg Address (40°N/77°W)

Great Britain commonwealth comprising England, Scotland, and Wales (56°N/2°W) 667

Great Lakes chain of five lakes, Superior, Erie, Michigan, Ontario, and Huron, in central North America (45°N/87°W) RA5

Great Plains flat grassland in the central United States (45°N/104°W) RA4

Great Salt Lake lake in northern Utah with no outlet and strongly saline waters (41°N/113°W) RA3

Greece country in southeastern Europe (39°N/21°E) RA13, 790

Greensboro northern North Carolina city; scene of sit-ins to protest segregation (36°N/80°W) 848

Grenada country in the Caribbean (12°N/61°W) 925

Guadalcanal island in the Solomons east of Australia (10°S/159°E) 779

Guam U.S. possession in the western Pacific Ocean (14°N/143°E) 653

Guatemala country in Central America, south of Mexico (16°N/92°W) RA8

Gulf of Mexico gulf on the southeast coast of North America (25°N/94°W) RA5, 91

Gulf of Tonkin gulf in South China Sea east of northern Vietnam (20°N/108°E) 874

H

Haiti country on Hispaniola Island in the West Indies (19°N/72°W) RA8

Hanoi capital of Vietnam (21°N/106°E) 872

Harlem northern section of Manhattan in New York City; cultural center of African Americans in the early and mid-1900s (41°N/74°W) 700

Harpers Ferry town in northern West Virginia on the Potomac River (39°N/78°W)

Hartford capital of Connecticut located along the Connecticut River (42°N/73°W) RA3

Hawaii state in the United States located in the Pacific Ocean (20°N/157°W) RA5, 644

Hiroshima city in southern Japan; site of first military use of atomic bomb, August 6, 1945 (34°N/132°E) 780

Hispaniola island in the West Indies in North America (17°N/73°W) RA8

Horseshoe Bend Alabama site where Creek-U.S. battled in 1814 (33°N/86°W)

Hudson Bay large bay in northern Canada (60°N/86°W) RA8

Hudson River river flowing through New York State (53°N/74°W) RA5

Hungary country in central Europe (47°N/20°E) RA13, 690

I

Idaho state in the northwestern U.S.; ranks among top states in silver production (44°N/115°W) RA2, 530

Illinois state in the north central United States; one of the states formed in the Northwest Territory (40°N/91°W) RA3

Indian Territory land reserved by the United States government for Native Americans, now the state of Oklahoma (36°N/98°W)

Indiana state in the north central United States; one of the states formed in the Northwest Territory (40°N/87°W) RA3

Indochina region in Southeast Asia (17°N/105°E) 762

Iowa state in the north central U.S. acquired as part of the Louisiana Purchase (42°N/94°W) RA3

Iran country in southwestern Asia (31°N/53°E) RA11, 913

Iraq country in southwestern Asia (32°N/42°E) RA11, 931

Ireland island west of England, occupied by the Republic of Ireland and by Northern Ireland (54°N/8°W) RA12, 771

Israel country of the Middle East in southwestern Asia along the Mediterranean Sea (33°N/34°E) RA10, 794

Italy country in southern Europe along the Mediterranean (44°N/11°E) RA13

Jackson Mississippi capital (32°N/90°W) RA3

Jamestown first permanent English settlement in North America; located in southeastern Virginia (37°N/77°W) 11

Japan island country in eastern Asia (36°N/133°E) RA13, 639

Kansas state in the central United States; fighting over slavery issue in 1850s gave territory the name "Bleeding Kansas" (38°N/99°W) RA3

Kentucky state in the south central United States; border state that sided with the Union during the Civil War (37°N/87°W) RA3

Korea peninsula in eastern Asia between China, Russia, and the Sea of Japan, on which are located the countries North Korea and South Korea (38°N/127°E) RA13, 802

Kuwait country of the Middle East in southwestern Asia between Iraq and Saudi Arabia (29°N/49°E) RA11, 931

Lake Erie one of the five Great Lakes between Canada and the U.S. (42°N/81°W) RA5

Lake Huron one of the five Great Lakes between Canada and the U.S. (45°N/83°W) RA5

Lake Michigan one of the five Great Lakes between Canada and the U.S. (43°N/87°W) RA5

Lake Ontario the smallest of the five Great Lakes (43°N/79°W) RA5

Lake Superior the largest of the five Great Lakes (48°N/89°W) RA5

Laos southeast Asian country, south of China and west of Vietnam (20°N/102°E) RA13, 874

Latin America Central and South America; settled by Spain and Portugal (14°N/90°W) RA12

Lexington Revolutionary War battle site in eastern Massachusetts; site of first clash between colonists and British, April 19, 1775 (42°N/71°W) 23

Leyte island of the east central Philippines, north of Mindanao (10°N/125°E) 779

Little Rock capital of Arkansas located in the center of the state; site of 1957 conflict over public school integration (35°N/92°W) RA3

London capital of United Kingdom located in the southeastern part of England (51°N/0°) RA12

Los Angeles city along Pacific coast in southern California; industrial, financial, and trade center of western United States (34°N/118°W) 531

Louisiana state in the south central United States (31°N/93°W) RA3

Louisiana Territory region of west central United States between the Mississippi River and the Rocky Mountains purchased from France in 1803 (40°N/95°W) RA7

Lowell city in Massachusetts (43°N/83°W)

Maine state in the northeastern United States; 23rd state to enter the Union (45°N/70°W) RA3

Mali country in Western Africa (16°N/0°) RA12

Manchuria region of northeast China; invaded by Japan in 1931 (48°N/125°E) 754

Manila capital and largest city of the Philippines located on southwest Luzon Island and Manila Bay (14°N/121°E) RA13, 651

Maryland state in the eastern United States; one of the original 13 states (39°N/76°W) RA3

Massachusetts state in the northeastern United States; one of the original 13 states (42°N/72°W) RA3

Massachusetts Bay Colony Pilgrim settlements along the Charles River (42°N/71°W)

Mediterranean Sea sea between Europe and Africa (36°N/13°E) RA13

Memphis Tennessee city on the Mississippi River near the Mississippi border (35°N/90°W) RA3

Mexican Cession territory gained by the United States after war with Mexico in 1848 (37°N/111°W) RA7

Mexico country in North America south of the United States (24°N/104°W) RA8

Mexico City capital and most populous city of Mexico (19°N/99°W) RA8

Michigan state in the north central United States; one of the states formed in the Northwest Territory (45°N/85°W) RA3

Midway Islands U.S. possession in the central Pacific Ocean (28°N/179°W) 778

Milwaukee city in eastern Wisconsin (43°N/88°W) 605

Minnesota state in the north central United States; fur trade, good soil, and lumber attracted early settlers (46°N/96°W) RA3

Mississippi state in the southeastern United States; became English territory after French and Indian War (32°N/90°W) RA3

Mississippi River river flowing through the United States from Minnesota to the Gulf of Mexico; explored by French in 1600s (29°N/89°W) RA5

Missouri state in the south central U.S.; petition for statehood resulted in sectional conflict and the Missouri Compromise (41°N/93°W) RA3

Missouri River river flowing through the United States from the Rocky Mountains to the Mississippi River near St. Louis (39°N/90°W) RA5

Montana state in the northwestern United States; cattle industry grew during 1850s (47°N/112°W) RA3, 530

Montgomery capital of Alabama located in the central part of the state; site of 1955 bus boycott to protest segregation (32°N/86°W) RA3

Montreal city along the St. Lawrence River in southern Quebec, Canada (45°N/73°W)

Moscow capital of former Soviet Union and capital of Russia (56°N/37°E) 774

Nagasaki Japanese city; site of the second atom-bombing in 1945, ending World War II (32°N/130°E) 780

Nashville capital of Tennessee located in the north central part of the state (36°N/87°W) RA3

Natchez city in western Mississippi along the Mississippi River (32°N/91°W)

National Road road from Baltimore, Maryland, to Vandalia, Illinois (40°N/81°W)

Nebraska state in the central United States (42°N/101°W) RA3

Netherlands country in northwestern Europe (53°N/4°E) RA13

Nevada state in the western United States (39°N/117°W) RA2

New Amsterdam town founded on Manhattan Island by Dutch settlers in 1625; renamed New York by British settlers (41°N/74°W)

New England region in northeastern United States (42°N/72°W) RA5

New France French land claims stretching from Quebec to Louisiana (39°N/85°W)

New Hampshire state in the northeastern United States; one of the original 13 states (44°N/72°W) RA3

New Jersey state in the northeastern United States; one of the original 13 states (40°N/75°W) RA3

New Mexico state in the southwestern United States; ceded to the United States by Mexico in 1848 (34°N/107°W) RA3

New Netherland Dutch Hudson River colony (42°N/72°W)

New Orleans city in Louisiana in the Mississippi Delta (30°N/90°W) RA5

New Spain part of Spain's empire in the Western Hemisphere (35°N/110°W) RA7

New York state in the northeastern United States; one of the original 13 states (43°N/78°W) RA3

New York City city in southeastern New York State at the mouth of the Hudson River; first capital of nation (41°N/74°W) RA3

Newfoundland province in eastern Canada (48°N/56°W) RA8

Nicaragua country in Central America (13°N/86°W) RA8, 707

Normandy region along French coast and site of D-Day invasion, June 6, 1944 (48°N/2°W) 772

North America continent in the northern part of the Western Hemisphere between the Atlantic and Pacific oceans (45°N/100°W) RA12

North Carolina state in the southeastern United States; one of the original 13 states (36°N/81°W) RA3

North Dakota state in the north central U.S.; Congress created Dakota Territory in 1861 (47°N/102°W) RA3, 530

North Korea Asian country on the northern Korean Peninsula (40°N/127°E) RA13, 802

North Vietnam communist nation in Southeast Asia; unified with South Vietnam in 1976 to form Vietnam (21°N/106°E) RA13, 872

Northwest Territory territory north of the Ohio River and east of the Mississippi River (47°N/87°W) RA6

O

Ohio state in the north central United States; first state in the Northwest Territory (40°N/83°W) RA3

Ohio River river flowing from Allegheny and Monongahela rivers in western Pennsylvania into the Mississippi River (37°N/85°W) RA5

Oklahoma state in the south central United States; Five Civilized Tribes moved to territory in the period 1830–1842 (36°N/98°W) RA3, 539

Oregon state in the northwestern United States; adopted woman suffrage in 1912 (44°N/124°W) RA2, 356

Oregon Trail pioneer trail from Independence, Missouri, to the Oregon Territory (42°N/110°W)

P

Pacific Ocean world's largest ocean, located between Asia and the Americas (0°/175°W) RA12–13

Palestine historical region in southwest Asia between the Mediterranean Sea and the Jordan River; area sometimes called the Holy Land (32°N/35°E) 794

Panama country in the southern part of Central America, occupying the Isthmus of Panama (8°N/81°W) RA8, 656

Panama Canal canal built across the Isthmus of Panama through Panama to connect the Caribbean Sea and the Pacific Ocean (9°N/80°W) 657

Pearl Harbor naval base at Honolulu, Hawaii; site of 1941 Japanese attack, leading to United States entry into World War II (21°N/158°W) 645

Pennsylvania state in the northeastern United States (41°N/78°W) RA3

Persian Gulf gulf in southwestern Asia between Iran and the Arabian Peninsula (28°N/50°E) RA11, 931

Peru country in South America, south of Ecuador and Colombia (10°S/75°W) RA12

Philadelphia city in eastern Pennsylvania on the Delaware River; Declaration of Independence and the Constitution both adopted in city's Independence Hall (40°N/75°W) RA3

Philippines island country in southeast Asia (14°N/125°E) RA13, 651

Pikes Peak mountain in Rocky Mountains in central Colorado (38°N/105°W)

Pittsburgh city in western Pennsylvania; one of the great steelmaking centers of the world (40°N/80°W) RA3

Plymouth town in eastern Massachusetts, first successful English colony in New England (42°N/71°W) 11

Poland country on the Baltic Sea in Eastern Europe (52°N/18°E) RA13, 755

Portugal country in southwestern Europe (38°N/8°W) RA12

Potomac River river flowing from West Virginia into Chesapeake Bay (38°N/77°W)

Providence capital of Rhode Island; site of first English settlement in Rhode Island (42°N/71°W) RA3

Puerto Rico United States commonwealth in the West Indies (18°N/67°W) RA8

Pullman a company town south of Chicago; site of 1897 railroad strike (42°N/87°W) 575

Q

Quebec city in Canada, capital of Quebec Province, on the St. Lawrence River; first settlement in New France (47°N/71°W) RA9

R

Rhode Island state in the northeastern United States; one of the original 13 states (41°N/72°W) RA3

Richmond capital of Virginia located in the central part of the state; capital of the Confederacy during the Civil War (37°N/77°W) RA3

Rio Grande river between the United States and Mexico in North America; forms the boundary between Texas and Mexico (26°N/97°W) RA4

Roanoke island off the coast of present-day North Carolina that was site of early British colonizing efforts (35°N/76°W)

Rocky Mountains mountain range in western United States and Canada in North America (50°N/114°W) RA14

Russia name of republic; former empire of eastern Europe and northern Asia-coinciding with Soviet Union (60°N/64°E) RA13, 640

S

Sacramento capital of California located in the north central part of the state (38°N/121°W) RA2

Saigon present-day Ho Chi Minh City; former capital of South Vietnam (11°N/106°E) 879

Salt Lake City capital of Utah located in the northern part of the state; founded by Mormons in 1847 (41°N/112°W) RA2

San Antonio city in south central Texas (29°N/98°W) RA3

San Diego city in southern California (33°N/117°W) RA2

San Francisco city in northern California on the Pacific coast (38°N/122°W) RA2

Santa Fe capital of New Mexico located in the north central part of the state (36°N/106°W) RA3

Santa Fe Trail cattle trail from Independence, Missouri, to Santa Fe, New Mexico (36°N/106°W)

Saratoga Revolutionary War battle site in the Hudson Valley of eastern New York State (43°N/74°W)

Savannah city in far eastern Georgia (32°N/81°W) RA3

Seattle Washington city bordered by Puget Sound and Lake Washington (47°N/122°W) RA2

Selma Alabama city; site of a 1965 voter-registration drive (32°N/87°W) 852

Seneca Falls town in New York State; site of women's rights convention in 1848 (43°N/77°W)

Shiloh site of 1862 Union victory in Tennessee (35°N/88°W)

Sicily Italian island in the Mediterranean (37°N/13°E) 772

Sierra Nevada mountain range in eastern California (39°N/120°W) RA4

Sinai Peninsula peninsula in the Middle East separating Egypt from Israel (29°N/34°E) 899

South America continent in the southern part of the Western Hemisphere lying between the Atlantic and Pacific oceans (15°S/60°W) RA12

South Carolina state in the southeastern United States; one of the original 13 states (34°N/81°W) RA3

South Dakota state in the north central United States; acquired through the Louisiana Purchase (44°N/102°W) RA3, 530

South Korea country in Asia on the Korean Peninsula (36°N/128°E) RA13, 802

South Vietnam country in Southeast Asia united in 1976 with North Vietnam to form Vietnam (11°N/107°E) RA13, 873

Soviet Union former country in northern Europe and Asia (60°N/64°E) 754

Spain country in southwestern Europe (40°N/4°W) RA12

St. Augustine city in northeastern Florida on the Atlantic coast; oldest permanent existing European settlement in North America, founded in 1565 (30°N/81°W)

St. Lawrence River river flowing from Lake Ontario, between Canada and the United States, through parts of Canada to the Atlantic Ocean (48°N/69°W)

Stalingrad city in the former Soviet Union on the Volga River; present name Volgograd (49°N/42°E) 774

Sudetenland region in northwest Czechoslovakia; taken by Hitler's forces in 1938 (50°N/18°E) 755

Suez Canal canal built between the Mediterranean Sea and the Red Sea through northeastern Egypt (31°N/32°E) 771

Switzerland European country in the Alps (47°N/8°E) RA13

Taiwan island country off the southeast coast of China; seat of the Chinese Nationalist government (24°N/122°E) RA13, 794

Tehran capital of Iran (36°N/52°E) RA11, 914

Tennessee state in the south central United States; first state readmitted to the Union after the Civil War (36°N/88°W) RA3

Tenochtitlán Aztec capital at the site of present-day Mexico City (19°N/99°W)

Texas state in the south central United States; Mexican colony that became a republic before joining the United States (31°N/101°W) RA3

Tokyo capital of Japan located on the eastern coast of Honshu Island (36°N/140°E) 779

Toronto city in Canada on Lake Ontario; capital of the province of Ontario (44°N/79°W) RA12

Trenton capital of New Jersey located on the Delaware River in the central part of the state; site of Revolutionary War battle in December 1776 (40°N/75°W)

Union of Soviet Socialist Republics See Soviet Union.

United Kingdom country in northwestern Europe made up of England, Scotland, Wales, and Northern Ireland (56°N/2°W) RA12, 771

United States country in central North America; fourth largest country in the world in both area and population (38°N/110°W) RA2–3, RA12

Utah state in the western United States; settled by Mormons in 1840s (39°N/113°W) RA2

Valley Forge Revolutionary War winter camp northwest of Philadelphia (40°N/75°W)

Venezuela South American country on the Caribbean Sea (8°N/65°W) RA12, 658

Vermont state in the northeastern United States; 14th state to enter the Union (44°N/73°W) RA3

Vicksburg city and Civil War battle site in western Mississippi on the Mississippi River (42°N/85°W)

Vietnam country in southeastern Asia (16°N/108°E) RA13, 871

Virginia state in the eastern United States; colony of first permanent English settlement in the Americas (37°N/80°W) RA3

Wake Island island in the central Pacific Ocean; annexed by United States in 1898 (19°N/167°E) 777

Washington state in the northwestern United States; territory reached by Lewis and Clark in 1805 (47°N/121°W) RA2, 530

Washington, D.C. capital of the United States located on the Potomac River at its confluence with the Anacostia River, between Maryland and Virginia coinciding with the District of Columbia (39°N/77°W) RA3

West Indies islands in the Caribbean Sea, between North America and South America (19°N/79°W) RA8

West Virginia state in the east central United States (39°N/81°W) RA3

Willamette Valley valley of the Willamette River in western Oregon (45°N/123°W)

Wisconsin state in the north central United States; passed first state unemployment compensation act, 1932 (44°N/91°W) RA3

Wounded Knee site of massacre of Native Americans by soldiers in southern South Dakota in 1890 and of American Indian Movement protest in 1973 (43°N/102°W) 547

Wyoming state in the western United States; territory provided women the right to vote, 1869 (43°N/108°W) RA3, 530

Yalu River river in eastern Asia, between China and North Korea (41°N/126°E) 804

Yorktown town in southeastern Virginia and site of final battle of Revolutionary War (37°N/76°W)

Yugoslavia country in southeast Europe, on the Adriatic Sea (44°N/20°E) RA13, 690

Gazetteer

A

abolitionist a person who strongly favors doing away with slavery (p. 92)

affirmative action an active effort to improve educational and employment opportunities for minority groups and women (p. 902)

affluence the state of having much wealth (p. 822)

airlift a system of transporting food and supplies by aircraft into an area otherwise impossible to reach (p. 792)

allege state as a fact but without proof (p. 808)

alliance system defense agreements among nations (p. 667)

amendment an addition to a formal document such as the Constitution (pp. 27, 39)

amnesty the granting of pardon to a large number of persons; protection from prosecution for an illegal act (p. 907)

anarchist person who believes that there should be no government (p. 701)

anarchy disorder and lawlessness (p. 658)

annex to add a territory to one's own territory (p. 86)

annexation bringing an area under the control of a larger country (p. 645)

anti-Semitism hostility toward or discrimination against Jews (p. 753)

apartheid racial separation and economic and political discrimination against nonwhites, a policy formerly practiced in the Republic of South Africa (p. 912)

appeasement accepting demands in order to avoid conflict (p. 755)

appropriate to set something aside for a particular purpose, especially funds (p. 41)

arbitration settling a dispute by agreeing to accept the decision of an impartial outsider (p. 621)

armistice a temporary peace agreement to end fighting (pp. 652, 680)

arms race the competition between the United States and the Soviet Union to build more and more weapons in an effort to surpass the other's military strength (p. 817)

assembly line a production system with machines and workers arranged so that each person performs an assigned task again and again as the item passes before him or her (p. 565)

assimilate to absorb a group into the culture of a larger population (p. 585)

autocracy government in which one person has unlimited power (p. 675)

automation a system or process that uses mechanical or electronic devices that replace human workers (p. 830)

B

baby boom a marked increase in the birthrate, especially in the United States immediately following World War II (p. 822)

balance of power the distribution of power among nations so that no single nation can dominate or interfere with another (pp. 667, 897)

bankruptcy the condition of being unable to pay one's debts; one's property is managed or sold to pay those to whom one owes money (p. 933)

barrio a Spanish-speaking neighborhood in a city, especially in the southwest U.S. (p. 633)

black codes laws passed in the South just after the Civil War aimed at controlling freedmen and enabling plantation owners to exploit African American workers (p. 98)

blacklist list of persons who are disapproved of and are punished, such as by being refused jobs (p. 807)

blitzkrieg name given to the sudden, violent offensive attacks the Germans used during World War II; "lightning war" (p. 759)

blockade cut off an area by means of troops or warships to stop supplies or people from coming in or going out; to close off a country's ports (p. 869)

border states the states between the North and the South that were divided over whether to stay in the Union or join the Confederacy (p. 96)

boycott to refuse to buy items from a particular country (p. 21); to refuse to use in order to show disapproval or force acceptance of one's terms (p. 841)

brand a symbol burned into an animal's hide to show ownership (p. 534)

budget deficit the amount by which government spending exceeds revenue (p. 937)

C

cabinet a group of advisers to the president (p. 75)

canal an artificial waterway (p. 89)

capitalism an economic system based on private property and free enterprise (p. 701)

casualty a military person killed, wounded, or captured (p. 97)

censure to express formal disapproval of some action (p. 809)

checks and balances the system in which each branch of government has a check on the other two branches so that no one branch becomes too powerful (p. 37)

circumnavigate to sail around the world (p. 9)

citizen a person who owes loyalty to and is entitled to the protection of a state or nation (p. 47)

civil disobedience refusal to obey laws that are considered unjust as a nonviolent way to press for changes (p. 842)

civil service the body of nonelected government workers (p. 612)

closed shop a workplace in which the employer by agreement hires only union members (p. 798)

cold war a struggle over political differences between nations carried on by methods short of war (p. 792)

collective bargaining discussion between an employer and union representatives of workers over wages, hours, and working conditions (p. 574)

concurrent powers powers shared by the states and the federal government (p. 37)

conquistador Spanish explorer in the Americas in the 1500s (p. 9)

conservation the protection and preservation of natural resources (p. 622)

consolidation the practice of combining separate companies into one (p. 557)

constituents people that members of Congress represent (p. 41)

constitution a formal plan of government (p. 51)

containment the policy or process of preventing the expansion of a hostile power (p. 791)

convoy a group that travels with something, such as a ship, to protect it (p. 678)

cooperative store where farmers bought products from each other; an enterprise owned and operated by those who use its services (p. 549)

corporation a business in which investors own shares (p. 568)

cotton gin a machine that removed seeds from cotton fiber (p. 81)

counterculture a social movement whose values go against those of established society (p. 878)

counter-terrorism military or political activities intended to combat terrorism (p. 949)

coup a sudden overthrow of a government by a small group (pp. 873, 930)

credibility gap lack of belief; a term used to describe the lack of trust in the Johnson administration's statements about the Vietnam War (p. 879)

D

D-Day the day on which the Allied forces invaded France during World War II; June 6, 1944 (pp. 772, 774)

default to fail to meet an obligation, especially a financial one (p. 726)

deferment an excuse, issued by the draft board, that lets a person be excused from military service for various reasons (p. 878)

deficit the shortage that occurs when spending is greater than income (p. 903)

demilitarized zone a region where no military forces or weapons are permitted (p. 805)

deport to send out of a country aliens who are considered dangerous (p. 701)

deregulation the act of cutting the restrictions and regulations that government places on business (p. 923)

détente a policy which attempts to relax or ease tensions between nations (p. 897)

dictator a leader who rules with total authority, often in a cruel or brutal manner (p. 753)

disarmament removal of weapons (p. 761)

discrimination unfair treatment of a group; unequal treatment because of a person's race, religion, ethnic background, or place of birth (p. 628)

dissent disagreement with or opposition to an opinion (p. 685)

dividend a stockholder's share of a company's profits, usually as a cash payment (p. 568)

dollar diplomacy a policy of joining the business interests of a country with its diplomatic interests abroad (p. 659)

domestic tranquility maintaining peace within the nation (p. 35)

domino theory the belief that if one nation in Asia fell to the Communists, neighboring countries would follow (pp. 819, 873)

dove a person who opposes war or warlike policies, such as one who opposed the Vietnam War (p. 878)

dry farming a way of farming dry land in which seeds are planted deep in ground where there is some moisture (p. 539)

due process of law idea that the government must follow procedures established by law and guaranteed by the Constitution (p. 46)

Dust Bowl the name given to the area of the southern Great Plains severely damaged by droughts and dust storms during the 1930s (p. 736)

E

---

emancipation freedom from slavery (p. 64)

embargo an order prohibiting trade with another country (p. 899)

emigrate to leave one's homeland to live elsewhere (p. 583)

entente an understanding between nations (p. 667)

enumerated powers powers belonging only to the federal government (p. 37)

escalate to increase or expand (p. 874)

espionage spying (p. 686)

ethnic group a minority that speaks a different language or follows different customs than the majority of people in a country (pp. 583, 667)

Glossary

evolution the scientific theory that humans and other living things have evolved over time (p. 718)

executive order a rule issued by a chief executive that has the force of law (p. 867)

exile a person forced to leave his or her country (p. 868)

expansionism a policy that calls for expanding a nation's boundaries (p. 639)

expatriate a person who gives up his or her home country and chooses to live in another country (p. 716)

fascism a political system, headed by a dictator, that calls for extreme nationalism and racism and no tolerance of opposition (p. 753)

favorite son candidate that receives the backing of his home state rather than of the national party (p. 83)

federal debt the amount of money owed by the government (p. 924)

federalism the sharing of power between federal and state governments (p. 37)

Federalists supporters of the Constitution (p. 27)

federation a type of government that links different groups together (p. 6)

feminist a person who advocates or is active in promoting women's rights (p. 857)

flapper a young woman of the 1920s who defied conventions in her behavior and dress (p. 714)

flexible response a plan that used special military units to fight guerrilla wars (p. 867)

Fourteen Points the peace plan to end World War I and restructure the countries of Europe, proposed by Woodrow Wilson (p. 689)

free silver the unlimited production of silver coins (p. 550)

freedman a person freed from slavery (p. 502)

front a region where warfare is taking place (p. 679)

fugitive runaway or trying to run away (p. 438)

fundamentalist a person who believes in the literal meaning of religious texts and strict obedience to religious laws (p. 913)

genocide the deliberate destruction of a racial, political, or cultural group (p. 775)

ghetto a part of a city in which a minority group lives because of social or economic pressure (p. 830)

ghost town former mining town that became deserted (p. 530)

Gilded Age the name associated with America in the late 1800s, referring to the extravagant wealth of a few and the terrible poverty that lay underneath (p. 592)

glasnost a Soviet policy allowing more open discussion of political and social issues, as well as more widespread news and information (p. 925)

global warming a steady increase in average world temperatures (p. 944)

grassroots society at the local and popular level away from political or cultural centers (p. 936)

gross domestic product the value of all the goods and services produced in a nation during a one-year period (p. 938)

gross national product the total value of all goods and services produced by a nation's residents during a year, regardless of where production takes place (p. 709)

guerrilla warfare a hit-and-run technique used in fighting a war; fighting by small bands of warriors using tactics such as sudden ambushes (p. 25)

hawk a person who advocates war or warlike policies, such as a supporter of the Vietnam War (p. 878)

Hispanic a person from or descended from people who came from the countries of Latin America or Spain (p. 858)

Holocaust the name given to the mass slaughter of Jews and other groups by the Nazis during World War II (p. 776)

homestead to acquire a piece of U.S. public land by living on and cultivating it (p. 537)

horizontal integration the combining of competing firms into one corporation (p. 569)

hot line a direct telephone line for emergency use (p. 870)

human rights rights regarded as belonging to all persons, such as freedom from unlawful imprisonment, torture, and execution (p. 912)

Hundred Days a special session of Congress that dealt with problems of the Depression (p. 732)

impeach to formally charge a public official with misconduct in office (pp. 41, 98, 938)

impeachment charging a public official with misconduct in office; if proven guilty before a designated court, the official is removed from office (pp. 51, 906)

imperialism the actions used by one nation to exercise political or economic control over smaller or weaker nations (p. 640)

implied powers powers not specifically mentioned in the Constitution (pp. 39, 76)

incumbent someone who currently holds an office or position (p. 939)

Industrial Revolution the change from an agrarian society to one based on industry which began in Great Britain and spread to the United States around 1800 (p. 81)

Glossary

inflation a continuous rise in the price of goods and services (p. 796)

initiative the right of citizens to place a measure or issue before the voters or the legislature for approval (p. 614)

injunction a court order to stop an action, such as a strike (p. 575)

installment buying a system of paying for goods in which customers promise to pay small, regular amounts over a period of time (p. 711)

integrate to end separation of different races and bring into equal membership in society (p. 840)

Internet a worldwide linking of computer networks (p. 943)

internment camps the detention centers where Japanese Americans were moved to and confined during World War II (p. 768)

interstate across state lines; connecting or existing between two or more states (p. 849)

iron curtain the political and military barrier that isolated Soviet-controlled countries of Eastern Europe after World War II (p. 790)

ironclad armored naval vessel (p. 97)

island hopping a strategy used during World War II that called for attacking and capturing certain key islands and using these islands as bases to leapfrog to others (p. 779)

isolationism a national policy of avoiding involvement in world affairs (pp. 639, 707)

isthmus a narrow strip of land connecting two larger land areas (p. 657)

J

joint-stock company a company in which investors buy stock in the company in return for a share of its future profits (p. 12)

judicial review the right of the Supreme Court to determine if a law violates the Constitution (pp. 40, 78)

K

kamikaze during World War II, a Japanese suicide pilot whose mission was to crash into his target (p. 779)

L

laissez-faire policy that government should interfere as little as possible in the nation's economy (p. 621)

land-grant college originally, an agricultural college established as a result of the 1862 Morrill Act that gave states large amounts of federal land that could be sold to raise money for education (p. 598)

League of Nations an association of nations to preserve peace and resolve international disputes proposed in Wilson's Fourteen Points (p. 689)

lease to hand over property in return for rent (p. 705)

lend-lease the act passed during World War II allowing the United States to sell, lend, or lease arms or other war supplies to any nation considered "vital to the defense of the United States" (p. 761)

line-item veto the power that allows the president to cancel individual spending items in a budget or bill (p. 937)

lode a mass or strip of ore sandwiched between layers of rock (p. 529)

Loyalists American colonists who remained loyal to Britain and opposed the war for independence (p. 24)

M

maize an early form of corn grown by Native Americans (p. 5)

majority more than half (p. 64)

Manifest Destiny the idea popular in the United States during the 1800s that the country must expand its boundaries to the Pacific (p. 85)

martial law the law applied by military forces in occupied territory or in an emergency (p. 887)

mass media types of communication that reach large numbers of people, such as newspapers, radio, and television (p. 714)

mass production the production of large quantities of goods using machinery and often an assembly line (p. 566)

materialism attaching too much importance to physical possessions and comforts (p. 830)

Mayflower Compact a formal document, written in 1620, that provided law and order to the Plymouth colony (p. 12)

Medicaid a social program that gives the states money to help those who cannot afford to pay for their hospital bills (p. 847)

Medicare a social program that helps pay for medical care for the elderly (p. 847)

mercantilism the theory that a state's or nation's power depended on its wealth (p. 18)

merger the combining of two or more businesses into one (p. 571)

MIAs soldiers classified as missing in action (p. 889)

migrant worker a person who moves from place to place to find work harvesting fruits and vegetables (p. 737)

migration a movement of a large number of people into a new homeland (p. 5)

militarism a buildup of military strength within a country (p. 667)

militia a group of civilians trained to fight in emergencies (p. 23)

mobilization gathering resources and preparing for war (pp. 683, 765)

moderate opposed to major social change or extreme political ideas (p. 815)

monopoly total control of a type of industry by one person or one company (p. 570)

muckraker a journalist who uncovers abuses and corruption in a society (p. 613)

National Grange the first farmers' organization in the United States (p. 549)

nationalism loyalty to a nation and promotion of its interests above all others (p. 667)

nativism the belief that those born in a country are superior to immigrants (p. 717)

naturalization to grant full citizenship to a foreigner (pp. 47, 54)

New Deal the name given to the new laws aimed at relieving the Depression, which were passed by Congress during the Hundred Days and the months that followed (p. 733)

nomadic moving from place to place with no permanent home (p. 543)

nomads people who move from place to place, usually in search of food or grazing land (p. 5)

Northwest Passage water route to Asia through North America sought by European explorers (p. 11)

on margin to buy stock by paying only a fraction of the stock price and borrowing the rest (p. 725)

Open Door policy a policy that allowed each foreign nation in China to trade freely in the other nations' spheres of influence (p. 647)

open range land not fenced or divided into lots (p. 534)

ore a mineral mined for the valuable substance it contains, such as silver (p. 529)

override to overturn or defeat, as a bill proposed in Congress (p. 43)

ozone the layer of gas composed of a form of oxygen that protects the earth and its people from cancer-causing sun rays (p. 944)

pacifist person opposed to the use of war or violence to settle disputes (p. 686)

Patriots American colonists who were determined to fight the British until American independence was won (p. 25)

patronage another name for the spoils system, in which government jobs or favors are given out to political allies and friends (p. 612)

peaceful coexistence agreement between opposing countries that they will compete with one another but will avoid war (p. 820)

pension a sum paid regularly to a person, usually after retirement (p. 743)

perestroika a policy of government and economic reform in the Soviet Union in the mid-1980s (p. 926)

perjury lying when one has sworn an oath to tell the truth (p. 807)

philanthropy charitable acts or gifts of money to benefit the community (p. 570)

political machine an organization linked to a political party that often controlled local government (p. 610)

pool a group sharing in some activity, for example, among railroad barons who made secret agreements and set rates among themselves (p. 559)

popular sovereignty political theory that government is subject to the will of the people (p. 36)

Populist Party U.S. political party formed in 1892 representing mainly farmers, favoring free coinage of silver and government control of railroads and other monopolies (p. 550)

poverty line a level of personal or family income below which one is classified as poor according to government standards (p. 847)

preamble the introduction to a formal document, especially the Constitution (p. 35)

precedent a tradition (p. 75)

primary an election in which voters choose their party's candidate (p. 614)

productivity how much work each worker does (pp. 710, 822)

prohibition the forbidding by law of the making or selling of alcoholic beverages (p. 619)

Prohibition the nationwide ban on the manufacture, sale, and transportation of liquor in the United States that went into effect when the Eighteenth Amendment was ratified in 1919 (p. 717)

propaganda ideas or information designed and spread to influence opinion (p. 672)

proprietary colony colony run by individuals or groups to whom land was granted (p. 12)

protectorate a country that is technically independent, but is actually under the control of another country (p. 653)

public works projects such as highways, parks, and libraries built with public funds for public use (p. 727)

Puritans Protestants who, during the 1600s, wanted to reform the Anglican Church (p. 12)

quota system an arrangement placing a limit on the number of immigrants from each country (p. 718)

R

ragtime a type of music with a strong rhythm and a lively melody with accented notes, which was popular in early 1900s (p. 601)

ration to give out scarce items on a limited basis (p. 766)

realism an approach to literature, art, and theater that shows things as they really are (p. 600)

rebate discount or return of part of a payment (p. 559)

recall the right that enables voters to remove unsatisfactory elected officials from office (p. 614)

recession a downward turn in business activity (p. 709)

Reconstruction the reorganization and rebuilding of the former Confederate states after the Civil War (p. 98)

referendum the practice of letting voters accept or reject measures proposed by the legislature (p. 614)

regionalism in art or literature, the practice of focusing on a particular region of the country (p. 600)

relief aid for the needy; welfare (p. 727)

Renaissance a period of intellectual and artistic creativity, c. 1300–1600 (p. 7)

reparations payment by the losing country in a war to the winner for the damages caused by the war (p. 690)

republic a government in which citizens rule through elected representatives (p. 26)

republicanism favoring a republic, or representative democracy, as the best form of government (p. 36)

reservation an area of public lands set aside for Native Americans (p. 543)

reserved powers powers retained by the states (p. 37)

resolution a formal expression of opinion (p. 54)

revenue incoming money (p. 52)

revenue sharing money raised from federal taxes and given to the states for use at the state and local levels (p. 902)

S

sabotage secret action by enemy agents or sympathizers to damage a nation's war effort (p. 686)

search-and-destroy mission a strategy used in Vietnam in which American forces sought Vietcong and North Vietnamese units to destroy them (p. 875)

secede to leave or withdraw (p. 84)

secession withdrawal from the Union (p. 95)

Second New Deal a new set of programs and reforms launched by Franklin D. Roosevelt in 1935 (p. 744)

sectionalism loyalty to a region (p. 82)

segregation the separation or isolation of a race, class, or group (p. 838)

Separatists Protestants who, during the 1600s, wanted to leave the Anglican Church in order to found their own churches (p. 12)

settlement house institution located in a poor neighborhood that provided numerous community services such as medical care, child care, libraries, and classes in English (p. 593)

shareholder a person who invests in a corporation by buying stock and is a partial owner (p. 568)

shuttle diplomacy negotiations between nations carried on by a person who travels back and forth between them (p. 900)

silent majority the phrase used by Nixon to describe the majority of Americans, those who did not protest or demonstrate (p. 882)

sit-in the act of occupying seats or sitting down on the floor of an establishment as a form of organized protest (p. 849)

slum poor, crowded, and run-down urban neighborhoods (p. 591)

Social Security Act a law requiring workers and employers to pay a tax; the money provides a monthly pension for retired people (p. 744)

socialist person who believes industries should be publicly owned and run by the government rather than by private individuals (p. 686)

sodbuster a name given to the Plains farmer (p. 539)

sphere of influence section of a country where one foreign nation enjoys special rights and powers (p. 647)

square deal Theodore Roosevelt's promise of fair and equal treatment for all (p. 621)

stagflation a combination of rising prices and a sluggish economy with relatively high unemployment (p. 903)

stalemate a situation during a conflict when action stops because both sides are equally powerful and neither will give in (p. 804)

standard gauge the uniform width of 4 feet, 8.5 inches for railroad tracks, adopted during the 1880s (p. 558)

standard of living a measure of people's overall wealth and quality of life; a minimum of necessities and luxuries that a group is accustomed to (p. 822)

steerage cramped quarters on a ship's lower decks for passengers paying the lowest fares (p. 584)

stock shares of ownership a company sells in its business which often carry voting power (p. 568)

stock exchange a place where shares in corporations are bought and sold through an organized system (p. 725)

strikebreaker person hired to replace a striking worker in order to break up a strike (p. 575)

subsidy grant of money from the government to a person or a company for an action intended to benefit the public (pp. 530, 733)

suburbs residential areas that sprang up close to or surrounding cities as a result of improvements in transportation (p. 592)

subversion an attempt to overthrow a government by persons working secretly from within (p. 806)

suffragist a man or woman who fought for a woman's right to vote (p. 616)

summit a meeting of heads of government (p. 820)

surplus excess; amount left over after necessary expenses are paid (p. 815)

sweatshop a shop or factory where workers work long hours at low wages under unhealthy conditions (pp. 573, 585)

tariff a tax on imports or exports (p. 84)

tenant farmer farmer who works land owned by another and pays rent either in cash or crops (p. 91)

tenement a building in which several families rent rooms or apartments, often with little sanitation or safety (p. 591)

terrorism the use of violence by groups against civilians to achieve a political goal (p. 944)

theocracy a form of government in which the society is ruled by religious leaders (p. 5)

total war war on all aspects of the enemy's life (p. 97)

totalitarian a political system in which the government suppresses all opposition and controls most aspects of people's lives (p. 754)

trade deficit the situation when the value of a country's foreign imports exceeds the value of its exports (p. 911)

trade union organization of workers with the same trade or skill (p. 573)

transcontinental extending across a continent (p. 531)

triangular trade a trade route that exchanged goods between the West Indies, the American colonies, and West Africa (p. 17)

trust a combination of firms or corporations formed by a legal agreement, especially to reduce competition (pp. 569, 612)

trustbuster someone who breaks up a trust into smaller companies (p. 621)

underemployment the condition when people work at jobs for which they are overqualified or that do not utilize their skills (p. 908)

Underground Railroad a system that helped enslaved African Americans follow a network of escape routes out of the South to freedom in the North (p. 93)

unemployment insurance payments by the government for a limited period of time to people who have lost their jobs (p. 744)

utopia community based on a vision of a perfect society sought by reformers (p. 91)

vaquero Hispanic ranch hand (p. 536)

vaudeville stage entertainment made up of various acts, such as dancing, singing, comedy, and magic shows (p. 602)

vertical integration the combining of companies that supply equipment and services needed for a particular industry (p. 570)

Vietcong the guerrilla soldiers of the Communist faction in Vietnam, also known as the National Liberation Front (p. 872)

Vietnamization Nixon's policy that called for South Vietnam to take a more active role in fighting the war and for Americans to become less involved (p. 885)

vigilantes people who take the law into their own hands (p. 529)

work relief programs that gave needy people government jobs (p. 733)

writ of assistance legal document that enabled officers to search homes and warehouses for goods that might be smuggled (p. 20)

yellow journalism writing which exaggerates sensational, dramatic, and gruesome events to attract readers, named for stories that were popular during the late 1800s (p. 600); a type of sensational, biased, and often false reporting (p. 650)

yeoman Southern owner of a small farm who did not have enslaved people (p. 91)

Glossary

Spanish Glossary

A

abolitionist/abolicionista una persona que favorece firmemente suprimir la esclavitud (p. 92)

affirmative action/acción afirmativa un esfuerzo activo para mejorar las oportunidades de educación y empleo para grupos de minorías y de la mujer (p. 902)

affluence/afluencia la condición de tener mucha riqueza (p. 822)

airlift/puente aéreo un sistema de transportar comida y abastos por vehículos aéreos hasta un área que no se puede alcanzar de otras maneras (p. 792)

alleged/alegado dicho como un hecho pero sin pruebas (p. 808)

alliance system/sistema de alianza acuerdos de defensa entre naciones (p. 667)

amendment/enmienda una adición a un documento formal tal como la Constitución (pp. 27, 39)

amnesty/amnistía el otorgar perdón a un número grande de personas; la protección del proceso a causa de una acción ilegal (p. 907)

anarchist/anarquista una persona que cree que no debe de haber ningún gobierno (p. 701)

anarchy/anarquía desorden y sin ley (p. 658)

annex/anexar añadir un territorio a su propio territorio (p. 86)

annexation/anexión traer un área bajo el control de un país más grande (p. 645)

anti-Semitism/antisemitismo hostilidad hacia o discriminación en contra de los judíos (p. 753)

apartheid/apartheid la separación racial y discriminación económica y política en contra de la gente no blanca, una política anteriormente practicada en la República de África del Sur (p. 912)

appeasement/apaciguamiento aceptar demandas para evitar conflictos (p. 755)

appropriate/destinar apartar para un propósito en particular, dicho especialmente de fondos (p. 41)

arbitration/arbitraje arreglo de una disputa por medio de un acuerdo para aceptar la decisión de una persona imparcial (p. 621)

armistice/armisticio un acuerdo temporal de paz para suprimir combates (pp. 652, 680)

arms race/carrera de armas la competición entre los Estados Unidos y la Unión Soviética para construir más y más armas, cada uno con el propósito de sobrepasar el poder militar del otro (p. 817)

assembly line/línea de montaje un sistema de producción arreglado con máquinas y trabajadores para que cada persona haga vez tras vez su trabajo designado mientras el artículo pasa por en frente de él (p. 565)

assimilate/asimilar introducir a un grupo dentro de la cultura de una población más grande (p. 585)

autocracy/autocracia gobierno en el cual una persona lleva el poder sin límite (p. 675)

automation/automatización un sistema o proceso que usa aparatos mecánicos o electrónicos para reemplazar a los trabajadores humanos (p. 830)

B

baby boom/auge de nacimientos un aumento marcado de la proporción de nacimientos, como el de los Estados Unidos inmediatamente después de terminar la Segunda Guerra Mundial (p. 822)

balance of power/balance de poder la distribución de poder entre naciones para que ninguna nación en particular pueda dominar o interferir con otra (pp. 667, 897)

bankruptcy/bancarrota la condición de no poder pagar sus deudas; la propiedad de uno es manejada o vendida para pagar a las personas a las cuales uno debe dinero (p. 933)

barrio/barrio una vecindad hispanoparlante de una ciudad, especialmente en el sudoeste de EE.UU. (p. 633)

black codes/códigos negros leyes establecidas en el Sur al terminar la Guerra Civil para controlar a los libertos y permitir a los dueños de plantaciones la explotación de los trabajadores afroamericanos (p. 98)

blacklist/lista negra una lista de personas que son desaprobadas y castigadas, tal como rehusar a darles trabajo (p. 807)

blitzkrieg/*blitzkrieg* nombre dado a los ataques ofensivos súbitos y violentos usados por los alemanes durante la Segunda Guerra Mundial; "guerra relámpago" (p. 759)

blockade/bloqueo el cerrar un área por medio de tropas o de buques de guerra para prohibir el entrar y el salir de abastos y de personas; cerrar los puertos de un país (p. 869)

border states/estados fronterizos los estados entre el Norte y el Sur que fueron divididos sobre el problema de quedarse en la Unión o de unirse a la Confederación (p. 96)

boycott/boicotear rehusar comprar artículos de un país en particular (p. 21); rehusar usar (p. 841)

brand/marca a fuego un símbolo quemado en la piel de un animal para mostrar título de propiedad (p. 534)

budget deficit/déficit del presupuesto la cantidad por la cual los gastos exceden las rentas, especialmente referente al gobierno (p. 937)

C

cabinet/gabinete un grupo de consejeros al presidente (p. 75)

canal/canal vía artificial de agua (p. 89)

capitalism/capitalismo un sistema económico basado en la propiedad particular y la empresa libre (p. 701)

casualty/baja un miliciano muerto, herido, o capturado (p. 97)

censure/censurar expresar desaprobación formal de alguna acción (p. 809)

checks and balances/inspecciones y balances el sistema en el cual cada rama de gobierno refrena las otras dos ramas para que ninguna rama vuelva a ser demasiado poderosa (p. 37)

circumnavigate/circunnavegar navegar alrededor del mundo (p. 9)

citizen/ciudadano una persona que debe ser leal y tiene derecho a la protección de un estado o nación (p. 47)

civil disobedience/desobediencia civil el rehusar obedecer las leyes que uno considera injustas como una manera pacífica para inisistir en cambios (p. 842)

civil service/servicio civil el cuerpo de trabajadores gubernamentales no elegidos (p. 612)

closed shop/taller cerrado un lugar de trabajo en el cual, por acuerdo, el empresario contrata sólo a los miembros del sindicato (p. 798)

cold war/guerra fría una lucha sobre diferencias políticas entre naciones llevada a cabo por métodos fuera de guerra (p. 792)

collective bargaining/negociaciones colectivas discusión entre el empresario y los representantes sindicales de los trabajadores sobre salario, horas, y condiciones del taller (p. 574)

concurrent powers/poderes concurrentes poderes compartidos por los estados y el gobierno federal (p. 37)

conquistador/conquistador explorador español en las Américas en los años 1500 (p. 9)

conservation/conservación la protección y preservación de recursos naturales (p. 622)

consolidation/consolidación la práctica de juntar compañías particulares en una (p. 557)

constituents/constituyentes personas representadas por miembros del Congreso (p. 41)

constitution/constitución un plan formal de gobierno (p. 51)

containment/contención la política o proceso de prohibir la expansión de un poder hostil (p. 791)

convoy/convoy un grupo que viaja con algo, tal como un buque, para protegerlo (p. 678)

cooperative/cooperativa una tienda donde los granjeros compraban productos uno al otro; una empresa poseída y operada por los que usan sus servicios (p. 549)

corporation/sociedad anónima un grupo autorizado por ley a montar una actividad pero con los derechos y deberes de una persona particular (p. 568)

cotton gin/despepitadora de algodón una máquina que sacaba las semillas de las fibras de algodón (p. 81)

counterculture/contracultura un movimiento social cuyos valores están en contra de los de la sociedad establecida (p. 878)

counter-terrorism/*contraterrorismo* actividades militares o políticos con el fin de combatir el terrorismo (p. 949)

coup/golpe derrocamiento súbito de un gobierno por un grupo pequeño (pp. 873, 930)

credibility gap/resquicio de credibilidad falta de creencia; un término usado para describir la falta de confianza en los anuncios de la administración de Johnson referente a la Guerra en Viet Nam (p. 879)

D

D-Day/D-Day el día en el cual las fueras Aliadas invadieron Francia durante la Segunda Guerra Mundial; el 6 de junio de 1944 (pp. 772, 774)

default/incumplimiento de pago fallar en hacer una obligación, especialmente una financiera (p. 726)

deferment/aplazamiento un perdón, aprobado por la junta de reclutamiento, que permite que sea perdonada una persona del servicio militar por varias razones (p. 878)

deficit/déficit escasez que ocurre cuando los gastos son más que los ingresos (p. 903)

demilitarized zone/zona desmilitarizada una región donde no se permite ninguna fuerza militar ni armas (p. 805)

deport/deportar mandar afuera de un país a los extranjeros que se consideran peligrosos (p. 701)

deregulation/deregulación el acto de quitar las limitaciones y reglamentos que el gobierno había puesto en el comercio (p. 923)

détente/*détente* una política que intenta relajar o aliviar tensiones entre naciones (p. 897)

dictator/dictador un líder que manda con plena autoridad, a menudo de una manera cruel o brutal (p. 753)

disarmament/desarme el quitar armas (p. 761)

discrimination/discriminación trato injusto de un grupo; trato parcial a causa de la raza, la religión, los antecedentes étnicos, o lugar de nacimiento de alguién (p. 628)

dissent/disensión desacuerdo con u oposición a una opinión (p. 685)

dividend/dividendo cheque que se paga a los accionistas, por lo general trimestralmente, representa una porción de las ganancias de la corporación (p. 568)

dollar diplomacy/diplomacia del dólar una política de unir los intereses comerciales de un país con sus intereses diplomáticos al extranjero (p. 659)

domestic tranquility/tranquilidad doméstica mantener la paz dentro de la nación (p. 35)

domino theory/teoría dominó la creencia de que si una nación de Asia hubiera caído a los comunistas los países vecinos la habrían seguido (pp. 819, 873)

dove/paloma una persona que se opone a la guerra y las políticas de guerra, tal como una persona que se oponía a la Guerra en Viet Nam (p. 878)

dry farming/agricultura seca una manera de cultivar tierra seca en la cual las semillas se plantan al fondo de la tierra donde hay un poco de humedad (p. 539)

due process of law/proceso justo de ley idea de que el gobierno debe de seguir los procesos establecidos por ley y garantizados por la Constitución (p. 46)

Dust Bowl/Cuenca de Polvo el nombre dado al área del sur de las Grandes Llanuras extensivamente dañada por las sequías y las tempestades del polvo durante los años 1930 (p. 736)

emancipate/emancipar liberar de la esclavitud (p. 64)

embargo/embargo una orden que prohibe el comercio con otro país (p. 899)

emigrate/emigrar dejar su patria para vivir en otras partes (p. 583)

entente/convenio un acuerdo entre naciones (p. 667)

enumerated powers/poderes enumerados poderes que pertenecen solamente al gobierno federal (p. 37)

escalate/intensificar aumentar o extender (p. 874)

espionage/espionaje espiar (p. 686)

ethnic group/grupo étnico una minoría que habla un idioma diferente o que sigue costumbres diferentes que la mayoría de la gente de un país (pp. 583, 667)

evolution/evolución la teoría científica de que los seres humanos y otros seres vivos se han desarrollado tras largos períodos de tiempo (p. 718)

executive order/orden ejecutiva una regla emitida por un jefe ejecutivo que lleva la fuerza de ley (p. 867)

exile/exilio una persona forzada a abandonar su patria (p. 868)

expansionism/expansionismo una política que demanda el extender las fronteras de una nación (p. 639)

expatriate/expatriado una persona que abandona su patria y decide vivir en otro país (p. 716)

fascism/fascismo un sistema político, dirigido por un dictador, que demanda nacionalismo y racismo extremo, y ninguna tolerancia de oposición (p. 753)

favorite son/hijo favorito candidato que recibe el apoyo de su estado natal en lugar del partido nacional (p. 83)

federal debt/deuda federal la cantidad de dinero debido por el gobierno (p. 924)

federalism/federalismo el compartir el poder entre el gobierno federal y los gobiernos estatales (p. 37)

Federalists/federalistas apoyadores de la Constitución (p. 27)

federation/federación una forma de gobierno que une grupos diferentes (p. 6)

feminist/feminista una persona que aboga por o está activa en promulgar los derechos de la mujer (p. 857)

flapper/_flapper_ una jovencita de los años 1920 que retaba las costumbres de comportamiento e indumentaria (p. 714)

flexible response/respuesta flexible un plan que usaba unidades militares especiales para montar guerras al estilo guerrilla (p. 867)

Fourteen Points/Catorce Puntos el plan de paz para suprimir la Primera Guerra Mundial y reestructurar los países de Europa, propuesto por Woodrow Wilson (p. 689)

free silver/plata libre la producción sin límite de monedas de plata (p. 550)

freedman/liberto una persona liberada de la esclavitud (p. 502)

front/frente una región donde la guerra activa se lleva a cabo (p. 679)

fugitive/fugitivo evadido que trata de huir (p. 438)

fundamentalist/fundamentalista una persona que cree en el sentido literal de escrituras religiosas y la obediencia estricta a leyes religiosas (p. 913)

genocide/genocidio el eradicar un grupo racial, político, o cultural (p. 775)

ghetto/_ghetto_ una parte de una ciudad en la cual vive un grupo de minoría a causa de presión económica o social (p. 830)

ghost town/pueblo de espectros pueblo anterior de mineros que se dejó (p. 530)

Gilded Age/la Época Dorada el nombre asociado con América al final de los años 1800, referente a la gran riqueza de los tiempos y la terrible pobreza que estaba debajo (p. 592)

glasnost/_glasnost_ una política soviética que permitía discusión más abierta de cuestiones políticas y sociales, y la promulgación más amplia de noticias e información (p. 925)

global warming/calentamiento mundial un aumento contínuo del promedio de temperaturas mundiales (p. 944)

grassroots/la gente común la sociedad al nivel local y popular afuera de los centros políticos y culturales (p. 936)

gross domestic product/producto interno bruto valor de todos los productos dentro de las fronteras nacionales de un país en un año (p. 938)

gross national product/producto nacional bruto valor total de todos los productos producidos en un año con la mano de obra y la propiedad suplidas por los residentes de un país, sin importar donde toma lugar la producción (p. 709)

guerrilla warfare/contienda a guerrilleros una técnica de tirar y darse a la huída usada en combates de guerra (pp. 25, 867)

hawk/halcón una persona que aboga por la guerra y las políticas de guerra, tal como un apoyador de la Guerra en Viet Nam (p. 878)

Hispanic/hispano una persona o descendiente de la gente que vinieron de los países de Latinoamérica o de España (p. 858)

Holocaust/Holocausto el nombre dado a la matanza extensa de judíos y otros grupos por los nazis durante la Segunda Guerra Mundial (p. 776)

Spanish Glossary

homestead/*homestead* adquirir una pieza de tierra pública de EE.UU. por medio de vivir en ella y cultivarla (p. 537)

horizontal integration/integración horizontal la asociación de firmas competitivas en una sociedad anónima (p. 569)

hot line/línea de emergencia una línea telefónica directa para uso en caso de emergencia (p. 870)

human rights/derechos humanos derechos, tal como la libertad de encarcelamiento ilegal, tortura, y ejecución, considerados como pertenecientes a todas las peronas (p. 912)

Hundred Days/Cien Días una sesión especial del Congreso llamada por Franklin D. Roosevelt para tratar los problemas de la Depresión (p. 732)

I

impeach/acusar acusación formal a un oficial público de mala conducta en la oficina (pp. 41, 98, 938)

impeachment/acusación el acusar a un oficial público de mala conducta en la oficina; si se le prueba culpable ante una corte designada, se le despide de la oficina (pp. 51, 906)

imperialism/imperialismo las acciones usadas por una nación para ejercer control político o económico sobre naciones más pequeñas y débiles (p. 640)

implied powers/poderes implícitos poderes no mencionados específicamente en la Constitución (pp. 39, 76)

incumbent/titular alguién que actualmente tiene un oficio o posición (p. 939)

Industrial Revolution/Revolución Industrial el cambio de una sociedad agraria en una basada en la industria que empezó en la Gran Bretaña y se promulgó a los Estados Unidos alrededor del año 1800 (p. 81)

inflation/inflación aumento contínuo del precio de productos y servicios (p. 796)

initiative/iniciativa el derecho de los ciudadanos de poner una medida o tema ante los votantes o la legislatura para aprobación (p. 614)

injunction/amonestación una orden judicial para terminar una acción, tal como una huelga (p. 575)

installment buying/compra a plazos un sistema de comprar productos en el cual los clientes prometen hacer pagos pequeños y regulares a través de un período de tiempo (p. 711)

integrate/integrar suprimir la segregación de las razas diferentes e introducir a membrecía igual y común en la sociedad (p. 840)

Internet/Internet enlace a través de todo el mundo de redes de computadoras (p. 943)

internment camps/campos de internamiento los centros de detención adonde los americanos japoneses fueron trasladados y allí encerrados durante la Segunda Guerra Mundial (p. 768)

interstate/interestatal a través de fronteras estatales; que conecta o existe entre dos o más estados (p. 849)

iron curtain/cortina de hierro la barrera política y militar para los países de Europa Oriental controlados por los soviéticos que los aislaba después de la Segunda Guerra Mundial (p. 790)

ironclad/acorazado buque armado (p. 97)

island hopping/saltar islas una estrategia usada durante la Segunda Guerra Mundial que demandó el atacar y capturar ciertas islas importantes para usarlas como bases para saltar por encima de otras (p. 779)

isolationism/aislacionismo una política nacional de evitar el involucramiento en asuntos mundiales (pp. 639, 707)

isthmus/istmo una faja estrecha de tierra que conecta dos áreas de tierra más grandes (p. 657)

J

joint-stock company/compañía por acciones una compañía en la cual los inversionistas compran acciones de la compañía a cambio de una porción de las ganancias en el futuro (p. 12)

judicial review/repaso judicial el derecho del Tribunal Supremo para determinar si una ley viola la Constitución (pp. 40, 78)

K

kamikaze/kamikase durante la Segunda Guerra Mundial, un piloto suicida japonés cuya misión era chocar con el blanco (p. 779)

L

laissez-faire/*laissez-faire* la creencia de que el gobierno no debe de involucrarse en los asuntos comerciales y económicos del país (p. 621)

land-grant college/colegio de tierras donadas originalmente, un colegio agrícola establecido como resultado del Decreto Morrill de 1862 que dio a los estados, grandes cantidades de tierras federales que podrían ser vendidas para recaudar dinero para la educación (p. 598)

League of Nations/Liga de Naciones una asociación de naciones para mantener la paz y resolver disputas internacionales propuesta en los Catorce Puntos de Wilson (p. 689)

lease/arrendar entregar propiedad en cambio de renta (p. 705)

lend-lease/prestar-arrendar el decreto aprobado durante la Segunda Guerra Mundial que permitía a los Estados Unidos que vendiera, prestara, o arrendara armas u otros abastos de guerra a cualquier nación considerada "vital para la defensa de los Estados Unidos" (p. 761)

line-item veto/veto de partida el poder que permite al presidente que cancele partidas particulares de gastos de un presupuesto o proyecto de ley (p. 937)

lode/filón una faja o venero de mena intercalada entre estratos de piedra (p. 529)

Loyalists/lealistas colonizadores americanos que quedaron leales a la Bretaña y se opusieron a la guerra para la independencia (p. 24)

M

maize/maíz una forma antigua de elote cultivado por los Nativos Americanos (p. 5)

majority/mayoría más de la mitad (p. 64)

Manifest Destiny/Destino Manifiesto la idea popular en los Estados Unidos durante los años 1800 de que el país debería de extender sus fronteras hasta el Pacífico (p. 85)

martial law/ley marcial ley administrada por las autoridades civiles en una situación de emergencia (p. 887)

mass media/difusoras de información formas de comunicación que alcanzan a grandes números de personas, tal como periódicos, radio, y televisión (p. 714)

mass production/fabricación en serie la producción de grandes cantidades de productos usando máquinas y muchas veces una línea de montaje (p. 566)

materialism/materialismo atribuir demasiada importancia a las posesiones y comodidades físicas (p. 830)

Mayflower Compact/Convenio del Mayflower un documento formal escrito en 1620 que proporcionó leyes para el mantenimiento del orden público en la colonia de Plymouth (p. 12)

Medicaid/Medicaid un programa social que da dinero a los estados para ayudar a las personas que no pueden pagar la factura del hospital (p. 847)

Medicare/Medicare un programa social que ayuda en pagar el esmero médico para los ancianos (p. 847)

mercantilism/mercantilismo idea de que el poder de una nación dependía de ampliar su comercio y aumentar sus reservas de oro (p. 18)

merger/fusión de empresas la asociación de dos o más negocios en uno (p. 571)

MIAs/MIAs soldados clasificados como extraviados en la guerra, inglés *missing in action* (p. 889)

migrant worker/obrero migrante una persona que se mueve de un lugar a otro para buscar trabajo en la cosecha de frutas y vegetales (p. 737)

migration/migración el movimiento de un gran número de personas hacia una nueva patria (p. 5)

militarism/militarismo un desarrollo de poder militar dentro de un país (p. 667)

militia/milicia un grupo de civiles entrenados para luchar durante emergencias (p. 23)

mobilization/mobilización juntar recursos y preparar para la guerra (pp. 683, 765)

moderate/moderado opuesto a gran cambio social o ideas políticas extremas (p. 815)

monopoly/monopolio control total de una industria por una persona o una compañía (p. 570)

muckraker/expositor de corrupción periodista que descubre abusos y corrupción en una sociedad (p. 613)

N

National Grange/Granja Nacional la primera organización de granjeros de los Estados Unidos (p. 549)

nationalism/nacionalismo lealtad a una nación y promoción de sus intereses sobre todos los demás (p. 667)

nativism/nativismo la creencia de que aquellos que nacieron en un país son mejores que los inmigrantes (p. 717)

naturalization/naturalización el otorgar la plena ciudadanía a un extranjero (pp. 47, 54)

New Deal/Nuevo Trato el nombre dado a las leyes nuevas con la meta de aliviar la Depresión que fueron estatuidas por el Congreso durante los Cien Días y los meses siguientes (p. 733)

nomadic/nómada que se mueve de un lugar a otro sin hogar permanente (p. 543)

nomads/nómadas personas que se mueven de lugar a lugar, generalmente en busca de comida o de tierras para pastar (p. 5)

Northwest Passage/Paso Noroeste ruta acuática para Asia por América del Norte buscada por exploradores europeos (p. 11)

O

on margin/al margen comprar acciones por pagar sólo una fracción del precio del valor y el resto del préstamo recibido a un corredor (p. 725)

Open Door policy/política de Puerta Abierta una política que permitía a cada nación extranjera en China que comerciara libremente en las esferas de influencia de las otras naciones (p. 647)

open range/terreno abierto tierra sin cercas ni dividida en solares (p. 534)

ore/mena un mineral minado por la sustancia valorable que contiene, tal como plata (p. 529)

override/vencer rechazar o derrotar, como un proyecto de ley propuesto en el Congreso (p. 43)

ozone/ozono el estrato de gas compuesto de una forma de oxígeno que protege la tierra y a su gente de los rayos del sol que causan el cáncer (p. 944)

P

pacifist/pacifista persona opuesta al uso de guerra o violencia para arreglar disputas (p. 686)

Patriots/patriotas colonizadores americanos que estaban determinados para luchar en contra de los británicos hasta que se ganara la independencia americana (p. 25)

patronage/patronazgo otro nombre del sistema de recompensa política en el cual puestos y favores gubernamentales se dan a aliados políticos y a amigos (p. 612)

peaceful coexistence/coexistencia pacífica acuerdo entre países opuestos de que competirán uno con el otro pero evitarán la guerra (p. 820)

Spanish Glossary

pension/pensión una cantidad pagada a una persona, generalmente después de la jubilación (p. 743)

perestroika/*perestroika* una política de gobierno y economía empezada por Gorbachev en la Unión Soviética a mediados de los años 1980 (p. 926)

perjury/perjurio el mentir después de haber jurado decir la verdad (p. 807)

philanthropy/filantropía acciones caritativas o donaciones de dinero para beneficiar a la comunidad (p. 570)

political machine/máquina política una organización aliada con un partido político que muchas veces controlaba el gobierno local (p. 610)

pool/consorcio un grupo compartiendo de una actividad, por ejemplo, entre barones ferrocarrileros que hacían acuerdos secretos y fijaban tipos entre ellos mismos (p. 559)

popular sovereignty/soberanía popular la teoría política de que el gobierno está sujeto a la voluntad del pueblo (p. 36)

Populist Party/Partido Populista partido político de los EE.UU. formado en 1892 que representaba principalmente a los granjeros, que favorecía la acuñación libre de plata y el control gubernamental de ferrocarriles y otros monopolios (p. 550)

poverty line/línea de pobreza el nivel de ingresos personales o familiares clasificado de pobre según la norma del gobierno (p. 847)

preamble/preámbulo la introducción de un documento formal, especialmente la Constitución (p. 35)

precedent/precedente una tradición (p. 75)

primary/elección preliminar una elección en la cual los votantes escogen al candidato de su partido (p. 614)

productivity/productividad la cantidad de trabajo que hace cada trabajador (pp. 710, 822)

prohibition/prohibición leyes que prohiben el hacer o vender de bebidas alcohólicas (p. 619)

Prohibition/Prohibición entredicho contra la fabricación, transportación, y venta de bebidas alcohólicas por todo los Estados Unidos (p. 717)

propaganda/propaganda ideas o información diseñadas para influenciar la opinión (p. 672)

proprietary colony/colonia propietaria colonia dirigida por personas o grupos a quienes se les había otorgado la tierra (p. 12)

protectorate/protectorado un país que es técnicamente independiente, pero que en realidad está bajo el control de otro país (p. 653)

public works/proyectos públicos proyectos tal como carreteras, parques, y bibliotecas construidos con fondos públicos para el uso del público (p. 727)

Puritans/puritanos protestantes que, durante los años 1600, querían reformar la iglesia anglicana (p. 12)

quota system/sistema de cuotas un arreglo que pone un límite en el número de inmigrantes de cada país (p. 718)

ragtime/*ragtime* una clase de música con un ritmo fuerte y una melodía animada con notas acentuadas que era popular al principio del siglo (p. 601)

ration/racionar distribuir los artículos escasos sobre una base limitada (p. 766)

realism/realismo una perspectiva de literatura, arte, y teatro que representa las cosas tal como son (p. 600)

rebate/rebaja descuento o devolución de una porción de un pago (p. 559)

recall/elección de revocación el derecho que permite a los votantes que despidan de la oficina a los oficiales elegidos que son inadecuados (p. 614)

recession/recesión un deslizamiento en actividades comerciales (p. 709)

Reconstruction/Reconstrucción la reorganización y la reconstrucción de los anteriores estados confederados después de la Guerra Civil (p. 98)

referendum/referéndum la práctica de permitir a los votantes que acepten o rechazen medidas propuestas por la legislatura (p. 614)

regionalism/regionalismo en arte o literatura, la práctica de enfocar en una región en particular del país (p. 600)

relief/ayuda social ayuda para los pobres; asistencia pública (p. 727)

Renaissance/Renacimiento un período de creatividad intelectual y artística, alrededor de los años 1300–1600 (p. 7)

reparations/reparaciones pago por el país que pierde una guerra al país que gana por los daños causados por la guerra (p. 690)

republic/república un gobierno en el cual ciudadanos gobiernan por medio de representantes elegidos (p. 26)

republicanism/republicanismo que favorece una república, o sea una democracia representativa, como la mejor forma de gobierno (p. 36)

reservation/reservación un área de tierra pública apartada para los Nativos Americanos (p. 543)

reserved powers/poderes reservados poderes retenidos por los estados (p. 37)

resolution/resolución una expresión formal de opinión (p. 54)

revenue/ingresos entrada de dinero (p. 52)

revenue sharing/ingreso compartido dinero recaudado de impuestos federales y dado a los estados para uso a los niveles estatales y locales (p. 902)

S

sabotage/sabotaje acción secreta por agentes del enemigo o los que compadecen para dañar el esfuerzo de guerra de una nación (p. 686)

search-and-destroy mission/misión de buscar y destruir una estrategia usada en Viet Nam en la cual las fuerzas americanas buscarían las unidades nortevietnameses y vietconenses para destruirlas (p. 875)

secede/separarse abandonar o retirar (p. 84)

secession/secesión retiro de la Unión (p. 95)

Second New Deal/Segundo Nuevo Trato un nuevo juego de programas y reformas lanzados por Franklin D. Roosevelt en 1935 (p. 744)

sectionalism/regionalismo lealtad a una región (p. 82)

segregation/segregación la separación o aislamiento de una raza, una clase, o un grupo (p. 838)

Separatists/separatistas protestantes que, durante los años 1600, querían dejar la iglesia anglicana para fundar sus propias iglesias (p. 12)

settlement house/casa de beneficencia institución colocada en una vecindad pobre que proveía numerosos servicios a la comunidad tal como cuidado médico, cuidado de niños, bibliotecas, y clases de inglés (p. 593)

shareholder/accionista una persona que invierte en una sociedad anónima por comprar acciones y que es un dueño parcial (p. 568)

shuttle diplomacy/diplomacia de lanzadera negociaciones entre naciones llevada a cabo por una persona que viaja entre ellas yendo y viniendo (p. 900)

silent majority/mayoría callada la frase usada por Nixon para describir la mayoría de los americanos, los que no protestaban ni demostraban (p. 882)

sit-in/plantón el acto de ocupar asientos o de sentarse en el suelo de un establecimiento como una forma de protesta organizada (p. 849)

slum/barrio bajo vecindad pobre, superpoblada, y de de vecindades ruinosas (p. 591)

Social Security Act/Decreto de Seguro Social una ley que exige a los empleados y a los empresarios que paguen un impuesto; el dinero provee una pensión mensual para personas jubiladas (p. 744)

socialist/socialista una persona que cree que las industrias deben de ser poseídas por el público y manejadas por el gobierno en lugar de personas particulares (p. 686)

sodbuster/rompedor de césped nombre dado al granjero de las Llanuras (p. 539)

sphere of influence/esfera de influencia sección de un país donde una nación extranjera tiene derechos y poderes especiales (p. 647)

square deal/trato justo la promesa de Theodore Roosevelt para el trato justo e igual para todos (p. 621)

stagflation/stagflación una combinación del alza de precios y una economía estancada con una tasa alta de desempleo (p. 903)

stalemate/estancamiento una situación durante un conflicto cuando la acción se para debido a que ambos partidos son igualmente poderosos y ningún de los dos lo abandonará (p. 804)

standard gauge/medida normal la anchura uniforme de 4 pies, 8.5 pulgadas de las vías ferroviarias, adoptada durante los años 1880 (p. 558)

standard of living/norma de vivir una medida de calidad comprensiva de vida y riqueza de la gente; el mínimo de las necesidades y lujos a los cuales un grupo está acostumbrado (p. 822)

steerage/entrepuente los cuarteles apretados de las cubiertas bajas de un barco para los pasajeros que pagan los pasajes más bajos (p. 584)

stock/acciones valores de propiedad de comercio que vende una compañía que llevan muchas veces el poder de votar (p. 568)

stock exchange/mercado de acciones un lugar donde acciones de sociedades anónimas se venden y se compran a través de un sistema organizado (p. 725)

strikebreaker/esquirol una persona contratada para reemplazar a un huelguista para suprimir una huelga (p. 575)

subsidy/subsidio donación de dinero del gobierno a una persona o una compañía para una acción con el propósito de beneficiar al público (pp. 530, 733)

suburbs/suburbios áreas residenciales que brotaron cerca de o alrededor de ciudades como resultado de mejoramientos de transportación (p. 592)

subversion/subversión un esfuerzo para derrocar un gobierno montado por personas trabajando secretamente desde adentro (p. 806)

suffragist/sufragista un hombre o mujer que luchaba para el derecho al voto de la mujer (p. 616)

summit/conferencia cumbre una reunión de altos jefes de gobierno (p. 820)

surplus/superávit exceso; la cantidad que sobra después de pagar los gastos necesarios (p. 815)

sweatshop/fábrica-opresora un taller o fábrica donde se explota a los trabajadores, trabajándolos muchas horas por poco pago y en condiciones malsanas (pp. 573, 585)

T

tariff/tarifa impuesto sobre productos importados o exportados (p. 84)

tenant farmer/granjero arrendatario un granjero que labra la tierra de otro dueño y paga renta ya sea con la cosecha o al contado (p. 91)

tenement/casa de vecindad un edificio en el cual varias familias alquilan cuartos o apartamentos, a menudo con pocas medidas sanitarias o seguridad (p. 591)

terrorism/*terrorismo* el uso de la violencia contra ciudadanos para lograr un gol político (p. 944)

theocracy/teocracia una forma de gobierno en la cual la sociedad está gobernada por líderes religiosos (p. 5)

total war/guerra total la guerra en todo aspecto de la vida del enemigo (p. 97)

Spanish Glossary

totalitarian/totalitario un sistema político en el cual el gobierno suprime toda oposición y controla muchos aspectos de la vida de la gente (p. 754)

trade deficit/déficit de cambio la situación cuando el valor de las importaciones de un país excede el valor de las exportaciones (p. 911)

trade union/gremio una organización de artesanos con el mismo oficio o destreza (p. 573)

transcontinental/*transcontinental* que se extiende a través del continente (p. 531)

triangular trade/trato triangular una ruta de comercio para cambiar productos entre las Antillas, las colonias americanas, y África del Oeste (p. 17)

trust/cártel una combinación de firmas o sociedades anónimas formada por un acuerdo legal, especialmente para reducir la competición (pp. 569, 612)

trustbuster/rompedor de cárteles alguién que divide un cártel en compañías más pequeñas (p. 621)

underemployment/empleo insuficiente la condición cuando la gente trabaja en puestos para los cuales están sobrecalificados o que no utilizan sus destrezas (p. 908)

Underground Railroad/Ferrocarril Subterráneo un sistema que ayudó a los afroamericanos esclavizados a seguir una red de rutas de escape afuera del Sur hacia la libertad del Norte (p. 93)

unemployment insurance/seguro de desempleo pagos por el gobierno durante un cierto período limitado de tiempo a las personas que han perdido sus trabajos (p. 744)

utopia/utopía una comunidad basada en una visión de la sociedad perfecta buscada por los reformistas (p. 91)

vaquero/vaquero trabajador ranchero hispánico (p. 536)

vaudeville/teatro de variedades entretenimiento compuesto de varios actos, tal como baile, canción, comedia, y espectáculos de mágica (p. 602)

vertical integration/integración vertical la asociación de compañías que abastecen con equipo y servicios necesarios para una industria particular (p. 570)

Vietcong/*Vietcong* los soldados guerrillistas de la facción comunista en Viet Nam, también conocidos por el Frente Nacional para Liberación (p. 872)

Vietnamization/vietnamización la política de Nixon que demandó que Viet Nam del Sur tomara un papel más activo en luchar la guerra y que los americanos se involucaran menos (p. 885)

vigilantes/vigilantes gente que toman la ley en sus propias manos (p. 529)

work relief/ayuda de trabajo programas que dieron trabajos gubernamentales a los pobres (p. 733)

writ of assistance/escrito de asistencia documento legal que permitía a los oficiales que exploraran las casas y bodegas en busca de productos que tal vez pudieran ser de contrabandeado (p. 20)

yellow journalism/periodismo amarillista escritura que exageraba acontecimientos sensacionales, dramáticos, y repulsivos para atraer a los lectores, citando historias que fueron populares durante los fines de los años 1800 (p. 600); una clase de reportaje sensacional, prejuzgado, y a menudo falso (p. 650)

yeoman/terrateniente menor dueño sureño de una granja pequeña que no tenía esclavos (p. 91)

Spanish Glossary

Abbreviation of Pro is used to indicate Prologue pages. Italicized page numbers refer to illustrations.
The following abbreviations are used in the index: m = map, c = chart, p = photograph or picture,
g = graph, crt = cartoon, ptg = painting, q = quote

A

Abbott, E.C., q534

Abbott, Grace, 587

Abilene, Kansas, 535, 536

abolitionists, Pro92–93: Emancipation Proclamation, Pro97, 990; Underground Railroad and, Pro93

ACLU (American Civil Liberties Union), 718

Acoma, the, Pro6

Act of Toleration, Pro13

Adams, John, Pro24, qPro24, pPro52, Pro76, p980; drafting of Declaration of Independence, Pro24; France and, Pro76; *Marbury* v. *Madison*, 998–99; presidency, Pro76; Second Continental Congress and, Pro24

Adams, John Quincy, Pro84, p980; "corrupt bargain" and, Pro84; elections of 1824 and 1828, Pro84

Adams, Samuel, Pro21, Pro24; founding of the Sons of Liberty, Pro21

Addams, Jane, p593, q593, 616, 617, 972

Adventures of Huckleberry Finn **(Twain),** 600

Adventures of Tom Sawyer **(Twain),** 600

affirmative action, 902

Afghanistan, 913, 946, 948, 950

AFL (American Federation of Labor), 573–74, 745

Africa: Peace Corps, 867

African Americans: after Reconstruction, Pro98; American Revolution and, Pro24; anti-slavery movement, Pro92–93; back-to-Africa movement, 703; civil rights movement, 1950s, 838–42; civil rights movement, 1960s, 848–53, p849, q851; Civil War and, Pro94, Pro97, p990; Congressional members, Pro98; cowhands, 536, p536; discrimination against, Pro89, 629, 630–32, p630, 652, 676, 685–86, 703; education of, Pro89, 599, 631, 994, 997; factory workers, 591; farmers' alliances, 549; free, Pro12, Pro89, Pro91; Great Depression, 737; Great Plains homesteaders, 538; Harlem Renaissance, 715; home front, World War II, 766–67; in industrial jobs, 684; inventors, 564, 599; jazz, 715; in labor unions, 702–03; music of, 601; newspapers owned by, 600; Nobel

Peace Prize, 599; Olympic medal winners, 757; in politics, 550; post-World War II, 800–01, p801; railroad laborers, 531; school integration and, 839–40, m839, p840; scientists, 632; Spanish-American War, 649, p649, 651, 652; urban migration of, 591; violence against, Pro99, 630, 632, 703, 717; voting rights, 550, 852; women leaders of, 632; women's clubs, 616; in World War I, 676; World War II, 767, p767; writers, 601. *See also* slave trade; slavery

Agent Orange, 875

Age of Innocence, The **(Wharton),** 601

Agnew, Spiro, Pro70, 906

Agricultural Adjustment Administration (AAA), c732, 745

agriculture: colonial, Pro12–13, Pro17; expansion of, Pro81; irrigation, Pro6; Middle Colonies, Pro17; Native American, Pro5, Pro6; Plains, 536, 537–39, p537, p538; Southern, Pro13, Pro17, Pro91

Aguinaldo, Emilio, 651, 654

AIDS, 916

airplanes: invention of, p561–62, 576; jet travel, 824, p824; Lindbergh flight, 713–14; World War I, p669, 670; World War II, 760, p760, p761

Alabama, RA15, Pro82, Pro84, Pro95

Alaska, RA15; gold in, 640; National Park System, 626–27; purchase, 640, p640; statehood, RA15, 816

Albany Plan of Union, Pro19

alcohol: Eighteenth Amendment, Pro6, 717; prohibition, Pro68, 716–17; Twenty-first Amendment, Pro68, 717. *See also* prohibition; temperance movement

Alger, Horatio, 601

Alianza Hispano Americo **(Hispanic American Alliance),** 633

Alien and Sedition Act, Pro76

Allied Powers: World War I, 668–69, m668. *See also* World War I

al-Qaeda, 946, 947, 950

amendment, Pro27, Pro39

Amendments, U. S. Constitution, Pro39, Pro62–71. *See also* Constitution of the United States; individual amendments by number

America, Colonial, Pro10–14, 16–21; agriculture, Pro 14, Pro17; causes and effects of Revolutionary War, cPro20, Pro20–21; first English settlements, mPro10, Pro10–14; French and British clashes and, Pro18–19; French settlements, Pro14; government, Pro18, Pro24, Pro26–27; growth and change in, Pro16–21; Jamestown settlement, Pro11–12; mercantilism, Pro18; Middle Colonies, Pro12–13, Pro17; New England Colonies, Pro12, Pro17; population growth in, Pro17; proprietary colonies, Pro12; Puritans, Pro12, Pro17; religion in, Pro12, Pro14, Pro17; royal colonies, Pro12–13; Separatists, Pro12; slavery in, Pro13–14, Pro17; Southern Colonies, Pro13, Pro17; Spanish explorations and, Pro11; Spanish settlements, Pro14; Sugar Act and, Pro20; taxation without representation and, Pro20–21; trade in, Pro17, mPro18; unity against Great Britain, Pro21, Pro22–23; voting rights, Pro18; writs of assistance and, Pro20

America First Committee, 760

American Civil Liberties Union (ACLU), 718

American Colonization Society, Pro92

American Crisis, The, Pro24

American Expeditionary Force (AEF), 679–80

American Federation of Labor (AFL), 573–74, 745

American Indian Movement (AIM), 859–60

American Protective Association (APA), 629

American Revolution, Pro24–25; African American soldiers in, Pro24; British advantages in, Pro24; Continental Army, Pro24–25; Continental Congress and, Pro23; early years of, Pro24–25; guerrilla warfare in, Pro25; Second Continental Congress and, Pro24; support of America by France, Spain, Netherlands, Pro24; surrender of Cornwallis, Pro25; Treaty of Paris, Pro25–26; victory at Saratoga, Pro25; victory at Yorktown, Pro25

American Socialist Party, 613

Index

Index

Index

Index

Index

Index

Index

Index

Index

Index

Index

Index

Index

Index

Teacher, Student & Parent One-Stop Internet Resources

This textbook contains one-stop Internet resources for teachers, students and parents. Log on to taj.glencoe.com for more information. Online study tools include Chapter Overviews, Self-Check Quizzes, an Interactive Tutor, and E-Flashcards. Online research tools include Student Web Activities, Beyond the Textbook Features, Current Events, Web Resources, and State Resources. The interactive online student edition includes the complete Interactive Student Edition along with textbook updates. Especially for teachers, Glencoe offers an online Teacher Forum, Web Activity Lesson Plans, and Literature Connections.

Acknowledgements and Photo Credits

Acknowledgements

769   Reprinted with the permission of Simon & Schuster Books for Young readers, an imprint of Simon & Schuster Children's Publishing Division from *The Invisible Thread* by Yoshiko Uchida. Copyright © 1991 by Yoshiko Uchida.

841, 996   Reprinted by arrangement with the Heirs to the Estate of Martin Luther King, Jr., c/o Writers House, Inc. as agent for the proprietor. Copyright © 1963 by Martin Luther King, Jr., copyright renewed 1991 by Coretta Scott King.

843   From *I Know Why the Caged Bird Sings*, by Maya Angelou. Copyright © 1969 by Maya Angelou. Reprinted with permission of Random House, Inc.

915   From *Barrio Boy* by Ernesto Galarza. Copyright © 1971 by the University of Notre Dame Press. Used by permission of the publisher.

978   "God Bless the USA," words and music by Lee Greenwood. Copyright © 1984 Songs of Universal Inc. and Universal-Songs of Polygram International Inc. (BMI) International Copyright Secured. All Rights Reserved.

Glencoe would like to acknowledge the artists and agencies who participated in illustrating this program: Morgan Cain & Associates; Ortelius Design, Inc.; QA Digital

Photo Credits

Cover (tr)CORBIS, (cr)The Corcoran Gallery of Art/CORBIS, (br)Wally McNamee/CORBIS, (bl,cl)Digital Stock, (c)CORBIS, (background)PhotoDisc; RA16/1 PhotoDisc; 2 (t)Robert W. Madden/National Geographic Society, (b)Rich Buzzelli/Tom Stack & Associates, (others) PhotoDisc; 3 PhotoDisc; 6 CORBIS; 7 (l)The Andrew J. Russell Collection, The Oakland Museum, (r)Library of Congress; 10–11 PhotoDisc; 0 David A. Schorsch; 0–1 Washington University Gallery of Art, St. Louis, Missouri, Gift of Nathaniel Phillips, 1890; 1 Peter Harholdt/SuperStock; 2 Addison Doty/Morning Star Gallery; 3 (t)Bettmann/CORBIS, (c)New York Historical Society, (b)Bettmann/CORBIS; 5 (l)Richard Alexander Cooke III, (r)David Hiser/Getty Images; 13 file photo; 17 (t)courtesy Peabody Essex Museum, Salem, MA, (b) file photo; 20 North Wind Picture Archives; 25 SuperStock; 27 CORBIS; 28 (t)National Portrait Gallery, Smithsonian Institution/Art Resources, NY, (c) Bettmann/CORBIS, (b) Fraunces Tavern Museum; 31 CORBIS; 33 Bettmann/CORBIS; 34 Picture Research Consultants; 36 Doug Martin; 38 CORBIS; 40 AP/Wide World Photos; 42 CORBIS; 43 Mark Burnett; 44, 47 CORBIS; 48 Bob Daemmrich/Getty Images; 50 Wes Thompson/The Stock Market/CORBIS, (inset)Library of Congress; 52 White House Historical Association; 54 CORBIS; 56 Boltin Picture Library; 57 White House Historical Association; 58 file photo; 64 Joseph Sohm, ChromoShom/Corbis; 68 White House Historical Association; 69 file photo; 70 TimePix; 71 Sandy Schaeffer/TimePix; 72 (t)Independence National Historic Park/Joseph Painter, (c)White House Historical Association, (b) Scala/Art Resources, NY; 73 (t)United States Naval Academy Museum, (b)PhotoNetwork; 75 Chicago Historical Society; 76 Private Collection/Picture Research Consultants; 80 Burstein Collection/CORBIS; 81 National Museum of American History, Smithsonian Institution; 83 New York Historical Society; 84, 85, 87 SuperStock; 89 Peabody Essex Museum, Salem, MA/Mark Sexton; 90 (l)The Bay and Harbor of New York c. 1853–1855 Samual B. Waugh (1814–1885) Watercolor on canvas, 99⅓ x 198¼, Gift of Mrs. Robert L. Littlejohn, Museum of the City of New York, 33.169(detail), (r)Courtesy of The Bostonian Society/Old State House; 92 Collection of William Gladstone; 96 (l)The Museum of the Confederacy, Richmond, Virginia/Photography by Katherine Wetzel, (r)Getty Images; 98 The Museum of American Political Life, University of Hartford; 100 (t)Frank & Marie-Therese Wood Print Collection, Alexandria, VA, (c)Picture Research Consultants, (b)David Meunch/CORBIS; 524 National Park Service Collection; 524–525 Peter Harholdt/CORBIS; 525 Brown Brothers; 526 (tl)Library of Congress, (tr)Archive Photos, (b)Stock Montage; 526–527 (b)White House Historical Association; 527 (b)Collection of David J. & Janice L. Frent; 527 From the original painting by Mort Kunstler, The Race, Mort Kunstler, Inc.; 530 Colorado Historical Society; 531 (l)Brown Brothers, (r)L. Berger/SuperStock; 535 Thomas Gilcrease Institute of American Art; 536 Photograph from the book: The Life and Adventures of Nat Love, Better Known in the Cattle Country as "Deadwood Dick" – BY HIMSELF – A True History of Slavery Days, Life on the Great Cattle Ranges and on the Plains of the "Wild and Wooly" West, Based on Facts, and Personal Experiences of the Author/Rare Book and Manuscripts, Special Collections Library, Duke University, Durham, North Carolina; 537 (l)Nebraska State Historical Society, Lincoln, Tulsa, OK, (r)Montana Historical Society, Helena; 538 Kansas Collection/University of Kansas Libraries; 543 (r)Smithsonian Institution, National Museum of American Art, Washington, DC/Art Resource, NY; 545 Denver Public Library, Western History Collection; 546 Smithsonian Institution, National Museum of American Art, Washington, DC/Art Resource, NY; 546 Stock Montage; 550 AP/Wide World Photos; 552 (t)the Oakland Museum, (bl)The Beinecke Rare Book & Manuscript Library, Yale University, (br)The Museum of the American Indian, Hye Foundation, NY; 554 (t)courtesy Rockefeller Archive Center, (c)Stanford University Museum of Art, (b)Michael Freeman; 555 (t)Fine Arts Museum of San Francisco, Gift of Mr. and Mrs. John D. Rockefeller 3rd 1979.7.4, (b)National Air and Space Museum; 562 NASA; 562–563 Brown Brothers; 563 National Air and Space Museum; 564 Stock Montage; 565 (tl)Smithsonian Institution, (tc)Picture Research Consultants, (tr)Lewis Latimer Collection, Queens Borough Public Library/Long Island Division, NY, (bl)Picture Research Consultants, (br)courtesy George Eastman House; 566 courtesy Ford Motor Company; 568 CORBIS; 569 Library of Congress; 570 National Portrait Gallery/Smithsonian Institution/Art Resource, NY; 573 Library of Congress; 576 (t) Library of Congress, (c)National Portrait Gallery/Smithsonian Institution/Art Resource, NY, (b)Westmoreland Museum of Art, Greensburg, PA, (background) Hulton Archive; 578 Michael Freeman; 579 (t,c)Aaron Haupt, (br)Timothy Fuller;

580 (b)Hulton Deutsch/CORBIS, (t)courtesy California History Room, California State Library, Sacramento; 581 (t)Orchard Films, (b)White House Historical Association, Bettman-CORBIS; 583 Library of Congress; 585 Jacob A. Riis Collection, Museum of the City of New York; 586 (t)Rykoff Collection/CORBIS, (b) CORBIS; 588–589 Library Company of Philadelphia; 592 Archive Photo; 593 University of Illinois at Chicago. The University Library, Jane Addams Memorial Collection; 594 Brown Brothers; 596 Rudi von Briel; 598 Library of Congress; 599 (br)Bettman-CORBIS, (others)Library of Congress; 600 Smithsonian Institution; 601 Winslow Homer American, 1836–1910. Girls with Lobster, 1873. Watercolor and gouache over graphite, 24.2 x 32.9 cm. © The Cleveland Museum of Art, 2002. Purchase from the J.H. Wade Foundation, 1943.60; 603 (l)National Portrait Gallery, Smithsonian Institution/Art Resource, NY, (r)from the collection of Paul Urbahn at Steamboats.com; 604 (t)Bettman-CORBIS, (c, chart) Library of Congress, (b)Smithsonian Institution, (background)Edwin Levick/Hulton/Archive; 606 National Archives; 606–607 Ansel Adams Publishing Rights Trust/CORBIS; 607 CORBIS; 608 (t)Collection of David J. & Janice L. Frent, (b)CORBIS; 609 (t)National Gallery of Art, Washington. Chester Dale Collection, (b)White House Historical Association, (l)By permission of the Houghton Library, Harvard University, (br)The Schomberg Center for Research in Black Culture, New York Public Library; 611 Library of Congress; 613 The Ida M. Tarbell Collection, Pelletier Library, Alleghany College; 616 CORBIS; 618 Schlesinger Library, Radcliffe College; 619 (l)CORBIS, (r)Picture Research Consultants; 621 Collection of David J. & Janice L. Frent; 622 David J. & Janice Frent Collection/CORBIS; 623 (t)David J. & Janice L. Frent Collection/CORBIS, (c)Collection of David J. & Janice L. Frent, (cr)file photo, (bl)The Museum of American Political Life, University of Hartford, (br)Library of Congress; 625 Theodore Roosevelt Collection/Harvard College Library/by permission of the Houghton Library/Harvard University; 626 Daniel J. Cox/naturalexposures.com; 627 Robin Brandt; 629 Brown Brothers; 630 (l)Bettman-CORBIS; 630 (r)Private Collection; 631 Culver Pictures; 632 The Schomberg Center for Research in Black Culture, New York Public Library; 633 Oscar B. Willis/The Schomburg Center for Research in Black Culture, New York Public Library; 634 (tl)By permission of the Houghton Library, Harvard University, (tr)Doug Martin, (c)Collection of David J. & Janice L. Frent, (b)file photo; 635 Steve Kelley/Copley News Service; 636 Franklin D. Roosevelt Library; 636–637 (t)Woodfin Camp & Associates, (b)White House Historical Association; 637 (l)United States Military Museum, West Point, (r)Picture Research Consultants; 639 courtesy US Naval Academy Museum; 640 (l)Historic Seward House/James M. Via, (r)Hulton-Deutsch/CORBIS; 645 Bishop Museum; 647 Library of Congress; 649 United States Military Museum, West Point; 650 (l)CORBIS, (c)Library of Congress, (r)Bettman-CORBIS; 653 Library of Congress; 655 Aaron Haupt; 657 (l)Leonard de Selva/CORBIS, (r)Private Collection/courtesy R.H. Love Galleries, Chicago; 658 National Archives; 659 Library of Congress; 660 Courtesy of the Webb County Heritage Foundation; 661 CORBIS; 662 (t)National Postal Museum, (c)Frederic Remington Art Museum, Ogdensburg, NY; (b)Picture Research Consultants; 664 (tl)Bettman-CORBIS, (c,tr)Collection of Colonel Stuart S. Corning/Rob Huntley/Lightstream, (b)Collection of Colonel Stuart S. Corning/Rob Huntley/Lightstream; 664–665 (t)Hulton-Deutsch Collection/CORBIS, (b)White House Historical Association; 665 The National Gallery of Art, Washington DC/Gift of Ethelyn McKinney in memory of her brother, Glenn Ford McKinney; 667 Bettman-CORBIS; 669 US Airforce; 670 UPI/Bettman-CORBIS; 672 (l)Bettman-CORBIS, (c)Bettman-CORBIS, (r)Larry O. Nighswander/National Geographic Society Image Collection; 673 Culver Pictures; 674–675 Hulton-Archive/Getty Images; 675 National Archives; 679 Brown Brothers; 680 (l)Lambert/Archive Photo, (r)Collection of Colonel Stuart S. Corning/Rob Huntley/Lightstream; 681 US Signal Corps/National Archives; 684, 685 Brown Brothers; 686 CORBIS; 687 (t)Archive Photos, (b)Franklin D. Roosevelt Library, (c)Library of Congress; 689 CORBIS; 692 (t)Bettman-CORBIS, (r)Collection of Colonel Stuart S. Corning/Rob Huntley/Lightstream, (background) Scott Swanson/Archive Photos; 694 Hulton/Archive; 695 Timothy Fuller; 696 Private Collection; 696–697 Hulton-Deutsch/CORBIS; 697 file photo; 698 (l)Private Collection, (r)Brown Brothers; 698–699 (t)CORBIS, (b)White House Historical Association; 699 (l)Museum of Modern Art, NY/Gift of Mrs. Nickolas Muray, (r)Bettman-CORBIS; 701 (l)Bettman-CORBIS, (r)AP/Wide World Photos; 702 Bettman-CORBIS; 705 Brown Brothers; 706 Picture Research Consultants; 708 Brown Brothers; 710 courtesy Ford Motor Company; 711 FPG; 714 (t)The Schomburg Center for Research in Black Culture, New York Public Library, (b)Billy Rose Theater Collection/New York Public Library at Lincoln Center; 715 The Beinecke Rare Book & Manuscript Library, Yale University; 716 (l,cr)Frank Driggs Collection, (r)CORBIS; 717 Underwood & Underwood/CORBIS; 718 Culver Pictures; 720 (t)Collection of David J. & Janice L. Frent, (c)Brown Brothers, (b)Picture Research Consultants; 722 Library of Congress; 723 (t)CORBIS, (bl)Collection of David J. & Janice L. Frent, (br)courtesy of the Academy of Motion Picture Arts and Sciences; 725 file photo; 726 Bettman-CORBIS; 727 (l)Berenice Abbot/Federal Arts Project "Changing New York"/Museum of the City of New York, (r)Detroit Publishing Company; 728 Library of Congress; 730 (l)The Franklin D. Roosevelt Library, (r)CORBIS; 731 Margaret Bourke-White/TimePix; 732 (l)Collection of David J. & Janice L. Frent, (r)Library of Congress; 733 Library of Congress; 734 CORBIS; 736 Brown Brothers; 737 Library of Congress; 738 (l)CORBIS, (c)Parkers Brothers/National Geographic Society, (r)Picture Research Consultants; 740 Library of Congress; 741 (t)Photo by Rilla (Hubbard) Wiggins, Friday, June 4, 1937, 6 o'clock p.m., Hugoton, Kansas, copied by National Geographic Photographer Chris Johns, (b)Photo by Dorothea Lange, Library of Congress; 743 (l)AP/World Wide Photos, (r)Collection of David J. & Janice L. Frent; 744 Collection of David J. & Janice L. Frent; 745 Franklin D. Roosevelt Library; 748 (t)UPI/Bettman-CORBIS, (c)Detroit Publishing Company, (b)Collection of David J. & Janice L. Frent; 750 (l)White House Historical Association, (r)The Franklin D. Roosevelt Library; 750–751 courtesy National Guard Heritage; 751 (c)Warren Motts Photographic Center, (l)Warren Motts Photographic Center,

(r)National Geographic Society Image Collection; **753** Manezh, Moscow; **754** National Archives; **759** Imperial War Museum; **760** (l)Jack Novak/SuperStock, (r)Bettman-CORBIS; **761** Imperial War Museum; **762** US Army; **763** National Archives; **765** US Air Force Museum; **766** FDR Library; **767** CORBIS; **768** National Archives; **769** (t)Deborah Storms/Macmillan Publication Co., (b)Los Angeles Daily News Morgue, Department of Special Collections, Research Library, University of California; **772** (t)Department of the Army, (l)Brown Brothers, (r)CORBIS, (bl)Brown Brothers, (br)Woodfin Camp; **774** Brown Brothers; **775** (t)Bettman-CORBIS, (b)AP/Wide World Photos; **778** (t)Carl Mydans, Life Magazine ©Time Inc., (b)Picture Research Consultants; **780** Library of Congress; **781** National Geographic Society Image Collection; **782** (t)Hugo Jaeger, Life Magazine © Time Inc., (tc)National Archives, (l)National Archives, (b)Picture Research Consultants, (bc)US Army; **784** Larry Burrows/Time, Inc.; **784–785** courtesy The Norman Rockwell Museum at Stockbridge/Norman Rockwell Trust; **785** Bettman-CORBIS; **786** (tl)file photo, (tr)George C. Marshall Research Library, Lexington, VA, (b)AP/Wide World Photos; **786–787** (t)CORBIS, (b)White House Historical Association; **787** (l)AP/Wide World Photos, (r)AP/Wide World Photos; **790** Reprinted from the Des Moines Registrar/Jay N. Darling, 1946; **792** (l, background)UPI/Bettman-CORBIS, (r)Walter Sanders/TimePix; **793** UPI/Bettman-CORBIS; **795** (l)Aaron Haupt, (r)Bettman/CORBIS; **797** Chicago Tribune cartoon by Carey Orr; **798** (l)Indiana University Photo Services, (r)Superstock; **799** (l)Margaret Bourke-White/TimePix, (br)Brown Brothers; **800** Bettman-CORBIS; **801** (l)Cornell Capa/Life Magazine ©Time Inc., (r)Collection of David J. & Janice L. Frent; **804** UPI/Bettman-CORBIS; **807** Bettman-CORBIS; **808** CORBIS; **809** Picture Research Consultants; **810** George C. Marshall Research Library, Lexington, VA, (tc)US Army, (b)Nato, (bc)UPI/ Bettman-CORBIS; **812** (l)White House Historical Association, (r)FPG; **812–813** Edenhurst Gallery; **813** (l)Fred DeWitt/TimePix, (r)PictureQuest; **815** (l)Hulton-Deutsch Collection/CORBIS; **817** National Geographic Society Image Collection; **818** file photo; **819** (l)SuperStock, (r)Woodfin Camp and Associates, (background)Brown Brothers; **823** FPG; **824** (l)Museum of Flight/CORBIS; **825** Mark Burnett/Photo Researchers; **826** Robert Reiff/FPG; **827** Bettman-CORBIS; **830** Dan Weiner/courtesy Sandra Weiner; **834** (t)National Geographic Society Image Collection, (c)Picture Research Consultants, (b)AP/Wide World Photos; **836** (l)Artis Lane, (c)Collection of David J. & Janice L. Frent, (r)Picture Research Consultants; **836–837** (t)Flip Schulke/Black Star, (b)White House Historical Association; **837** (l)Ralph J. Brunke, (br)W. Cody/CORBIS; **840** Francis Miller/TimePix; **841** Flip Schulke/CORBIS; **842** SuperStock; **843** (t)Don Perdue/Liaison Agency, (b)The Metropolitan Museum of Art, Arthur Hoppock Hearn Fund, 1950; **845** (l)AP/Wide World Photos, (r)David J. & Janice L. Frent/CORBIS; **846** Bettman-CORBIS; **849** (l)Hulton-Archive/Getty Images, (r)Charles Moore/Black Star; **850** Collection of David J. & Janice L. Frent; **850–851** Bettman-CORBIS; **852** UPI/Bettman-CORBIS; **854** Bettman-CORBIS; **855** (t)Bettman-CORBIS, (b)Paul Schutzer/TimePix; **857** (l)Bettman-CORBIS; **858** Bettmann; **859** (t)AP/Wide World Photos, (b)Collection of David J. & Janice L. Frent; **860** Bruce Kliewe/The Picture Cube; **861** Bob Daemmrich/Stock Boston; **862** (tl)Don Uhrbroch/TimePix, (tr)Collection of David J. & Janice L. Frent, (tc)Arthur Schatz/TimePix, (b)Picture Research Consultants; **863** Collection of David J. & Janice L. Frent; **864** (b)Black Star, (t)Larry Burrows, Life Magazine ©Time Inc.; **864–865** (t)Larry Burrows/TimePix, (b)White House Historical Association; **865** (l)Collection of David J. & Janice L. Frent, (r)courtesy Turner Publishing Inc./Claudio Vazquez; **867** (l)Collection

of David J. & Janice L. Frent, (r)courtesy Archive of the American Illustrator's Gallery, NY; **868** FPG; **870** Collection of David J. & Janice L. Frent; **872** (l)UPI/Bettman-CORBIS, (r)AP/Wide World Photos; **873** US Center For Military History; **874** Ray Cranbourne, Empire/Black Star; **875** Larry Burrows, Life Magazine ©Time Inc.; **876** Private Collection; **878** CORBIS; **879** (l)©Bernie Boston, (r)L. Kalvoord/Image Works; **880** Brown Brothers; **881** Steve Shapiro/Black Star; **883** Black Star; **885** Larry Burrows, Life Magazine ©Time, Inc.; **885** (b)Aaron Haupt; **887** (l)John Filo, (r)copyright TIME Inc.; **888** Christopher Morris/Black Star; **890** John Olson; **892** John Sohm/ChromoSohm/Stock Boston; **892–893** NASA; **893** (t)Joseph Sohm, Chromosohm/CORBIS; **894** (t)Dirck Halstead/Gamma Liaison, (b)Mike Mazzaschi/Stock Boston; **895** (t)Charles E. Rotkin/CORBIS, (b)White House Historical Association, Liaison Agency; **897** (l)Dennis Brack/Black Star, (r)UPI/Bettmann; **898** Pat Oliphant. The Denver Post, 1971; **899** Rueters/Bettman-CORBIS; **900** Magnum/Black Star; **902** Courtesy of the Richmond Times-Dispatch; **903** Collection of David J. & Janice L. Frent; **904** (l)Bettman-CORBIS, (r)Mike Mazzaschi/Stock Boston; **905** Alex Webb/Magnum Photos, Inc.; **906** TimePix; **907** AP/Wide World Photos; **911** Jimmy Carter Library; **912** David & Peter Turnley/CORBIS; **913–914** Liaison Agency; **915** (l)San Jose Mercury News, (r)Karen Tweedy-Holmes/CORBIS; **918** (t)Bettman-CORBIS, (c)AP/Wide World Photos, (b)Liaison Agency; **920** (t)Michael R. Brown/Liaison International, (c)Terry Ashe/Time Magazine, (b)file photo; **920–921** (t)AP/Wide World Photos, (b)White House Historical Association; **921** Sergei Guneyev/Time; **923** Fred Ward/Black Star; **924** (t)Latent Image, (b)Chris Hondros/Liaison Agency; **926** (l)Collection of David J. & Janice L. Frent, (r)David Burnett/Contact Press Images; **927** Aaron Haupt; **929** Collection of David J. & Janice L. Frent; **932** (l)Luc Delahaye/Sipa Press, (r)Steve Liss/Time Magazine; **933** Marion Bernstein; **934** (t)Digital Stock, (c)John A. Rizzo/Photo Disc/Picture Quest, (b)Owen Franken/CORBIS; **935** Dave G. Houser/CORBIS; **937** Dirck Halsted/Liaison International; **938** Heng/Lianhe Zaobao (Singapore); **939** Greg Gibson/AP/Wide World Photos; **940** (tr)CORBIS, (l)CORBIS, (br)file photo; **941** TimePix; **942** CORBIS; **943** AP/Wide World Photos; **946** (l)CORBIS, (r)Thomas E. Franklin/Bergen Record/SABA/CORBIS; **948** (l)CORBIS, (r)Sygma/CORBIS, (c)Joe Raedle/Getty News, (background)AFP/CORBIS; **950** (t)Ethan Miller/Reuters, (b)Steve Liss for Time; **952** Reuters/TimePix; **954** (tc, tlc)file photo, (br)Smithsonian Institution, (bc)Brown Brothers, (others)PhotoDisc; **954–955** PhotoDisc; **956** Missouri Historical Society; **957** Chicago Historical Society; **958** National Anthropological Archives, Smithsonian Institution; **959** Scala/Art Resources, NY; **960** W. Saunders/Time-Life Syndication; **961** Brown Brothers; **962** courtesy American Antiquarian Society; **963** Fort Ticonderoga Museum; **964** CORBIS; **965** Massachusetts Historical Society, Boston; **968** courtesy Fisk University, Nashville, TN; **970** file photo; **971** Brigitte Merle/Stone; **972** Mary Evans Picture Library/Photo Researchers; **974** Smithsonian Institution; **975** Culver Pictures; **977** (t)Steve Shapiro/Black Star, (b)Collection of David J. & Janice L. Frent; **979** Reuters/TimePix; **980–984** White House Historical Association; **985** North Wind Picture Archive; **986, 987, 988** Bettman-CORBIS; **989** National Portrait Gallery/Smithsonian Institution, Art Resource; **990** (t)PhotoDisc, (b)Mark Burnett; **991** (l)file photo, (r)Mark Burnett; **993** (t)The Museum of the American Indian, NY, (b)CORBIS, **993, 994, 995** CORBIS; **996** Flip Schulke/Black Star; **997** Missouri State Historical Society; **998** CORBIS; **999** Bettman-CORBIS.

TIME

PRESIDENT
GEORGE W. BUSH
NOVEMBER 3, 2004

FOUR MORE YEARS

ELECTION ★ NOTEBOOK

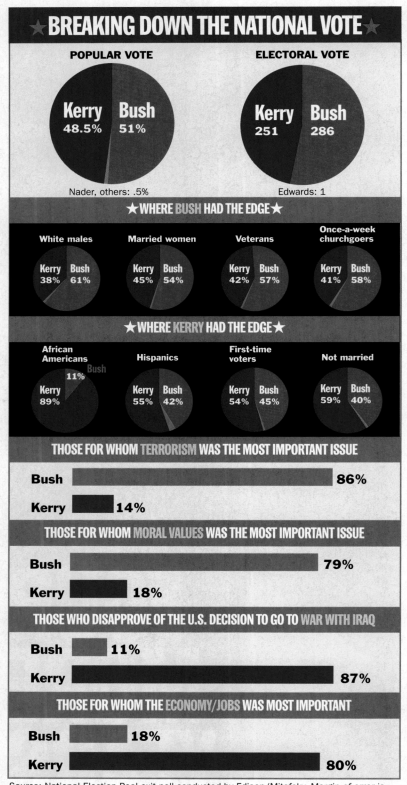

★ BREAKING DOWN THE NATIONAL VOTE ★

POPULAR VOTE

Kerry 48.5%
Bush 51%

Nader, others: .5%

ELECTORAL VOTE

Kerry 251
Bush 286

Edwards: 1

★ WHERE BUSH HAD THE EDGE ★

White males
Kerry 38%
Bush 61%

Married women
Kerry 45%
Bush 54%

Veterans
Kerry 42%
Bush 57%

Once-a-week churchgoers
Kerry 41%
Bush 58%

★ WHERE KERRY HAD THE EDGE ★

African Americans
Bush 11%
Kerry 89%

Hispanics
Kerry 55%
Bush 42%

First-time voters
Kerry 54%
Bush 45%

Not married
Kerry 59%
Bush 40%

THOSE FOR WHOM TERRORISM WAS THE MOST IMPORTANT ISSUE

Bush 86%
Kerry 14%

THOSE FOR WHOM MORAL VALUES WAS THE MOST IMPORTANT ISSUE

Bush 79%
Kerry 18%

THOSE WHO DISAPPROVE OF THE U.S. DECISION TO GO TO WAR WITH IRAQ

Bush 11%
Kerry 87%

THOSE FOR WHOM THE ECONOMY/JOBS WAS MOST IMPORTANT

Bush 18%
Kerry 80%

Source: National Election Pool exit poll conducted by Edison/Mitofsky. Margin of error is ±3 percentage points for national data and ±4 percentage points for state data.

★ NUMBERS ★

34 Number of states visited by George W. Bush during the presidential campaign

41 Number of states visited by Senator John Kerry

36 Number of visits made by Kerry to Ohio, the most by any candidate to one state

630,000 Total number of TV campaign commercials aired this election season

5,480 Number of campaign ads aired in Florida's Miami-Fort Lauderdale market during October

$1.45 billion Total spent at all levels on campaign advertising this year

$140 million Amount raised during the campaign by liberal 527 groups (non-profit organizations whose goal is to influence elections)

$75 million Amount raised by conservative 527 groups

2,256 Number of lawyers the Democrats sent to Ohio to monitor voting

8 Number of U.N. electoral assistance workers in Iraq

Samantha Appleton/Aurora

★ VERBATIM ★

Gregory Heisler/Time Life Pictures/Getty Images

"My fellow Americans, this is the most important election of our lifetime."

JOHN KERRY,
Massachusetts Senator, accepting the Democratic nomination for President

"Trying to challenge the two-party dictatorship is like trying to climb a cliff with a slippery rope."

RALPH NADER,
independent candidate, who won less than 1% of national vote

"Jenna and I aren't very political, but we love our Dad too much to watch from the sidelines."

AP Photo/Susan Walsh

BARBARA BUSH,
23, on why she and her twin sister decided to campaign

"We promised ... that every vote would count and that every vote would be counted."

JOHN EDWARDS,
Democratic vice-presidential candidate, at 2:30 a.m. on Nov. 3, 2004, on why Kerry was holding back his concession

"I'll reach out to everyone who shares our goals."

GEORGE W. BUSH,
at his first post-election press conference, Nov. 5, 2004

★ A LOOK AT VOTER TURNOUT ★

More Americans voted for—and against—George W. Bush than for any other presidential candidate in U.S. history, and turnout was higher than in any election since 1968. Among 18- to 24-year-olds, turnout rose by 5.8 percentage points, with nearly 2 million more members of this age group voting than in 2000.

Turnout of Young Voters in Presidential Elections, 1972–2004

Year	% of 18- to 24-year-olds who voted	% of adults 25 and over who voted
1972	52%	68%
1976	45%	66%
1980	43%	66%
1984	44%	67%
1988	39%	64%
1992	46%	67%
1996	36%	61%
2000	36.5%	64%
2004	42.3%	70%

Source: The Center for Information and Research on Civic Learning and Engagement; 2004 figures are preliminary estimates based on exit polls

★ WHAT HAPPENED IN THE SWING STATES ★

Three of the most intense battles between Kerry and Bush came in Pennsylvania, Ohio, and Florida, key swing states with a total of 68 electoral votes among them. While Kerry won in Pennsylvania, Bush carried Florida and Ohio. A Kerry win in either Florida or Ohio would have given him the White House.

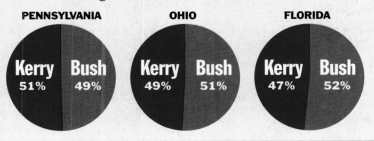

PENNSYLVANIA
Kerry 51% | Bush 49%

OHIO
Kerry 49% | Bush 51%

FLORIDA
Kerry 47% | Bush 52%

ELECTION 2004: THE PRESIDENCY

FOUR MORE YEARS

How the Bush team orchestrated its nail-biting win

By NANCY GIBBS

IN THE END, AN ELECTION that was supposed to be about all the ways the country is divided at least brought Americans together at 193,000 polling places in democracy's messy leap of faith. Turnout was huge even in states where the result was assured. In Ohio the polls closed at 7:30, but the lines were so long that people were still voting at midnight. Some people admitted they just did not want to face their neighbors or their children at the end of the day and say they had not bothered to show up. Others said if you don't vote, you can't complain and did not want to be silent at a time like this.

About 120 million Americans voted, 15 million more than in 2000. When the electoral votes were tallied, Republican George W. Bush had won 286 to Democrat John Kerry's 251. Of the three most hotly contested swing states, Kerry took Pennsylvania, while

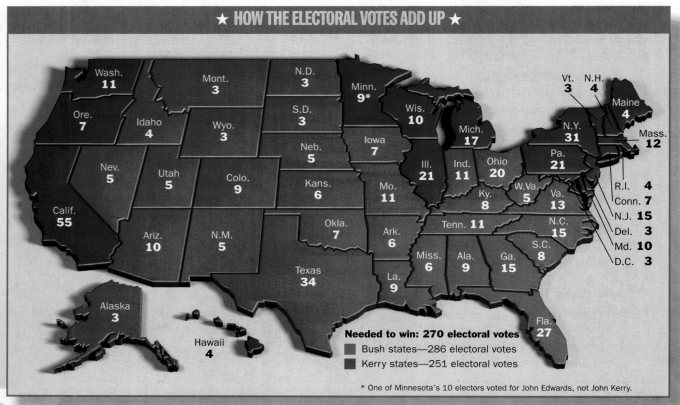

★ HOW THE ELECTORAL VOTES ADD UP ★

Wash. 11 — Mont. 3 — N.D. 3 — Minn. 9* — Vt. 3 — N.H. 4 — Maine 4
Ore. 7 — Idaho 4 — Wyo. 3 — S.D. 3 — Wis. 10 — Mich. 17 — N.Y. 31 — Mass. 12
Nev. 5 — Utah 5 — Colo. 9 — Neb. 5 — Iowa 7 — Ill. 21 — Ind. 11 — Ohio 20 — Pa. 21
Calif. 55 — Ariz. 10 — N.M. 5 — Kans. 6 — Mo. 11 — Ky. 8 — W.Va. 5 — Va. 13 — R.I. 4
Okla. 7 — Ark. 6 — Tenn. 11 — N.C. 15 — Conn. 7
Texas 34 — La. 9 — Miss. 6 — Ala. 9 — Ga. 15 — S.C. 8 — N.J. 15
Alaska 3 — Hawaii 4 — Fla. 27 — Del. 3 — Md. 10 — D.C. 3

Needed to win: 270 electoral votes
Bush states—286 electoral votes
Kerry states—251 electoral votes

* One of Minnesota's 10 electors voted for John Edwards, not John Kerry.

Bush snagged Florida and Ohio. Bush also became the first president since 1988 to win a majority of the popular vote, with about 51% to 48.5% for Kerry.

So consider the obstacles Bush overcame to win the hotly contested election. Since the country previously

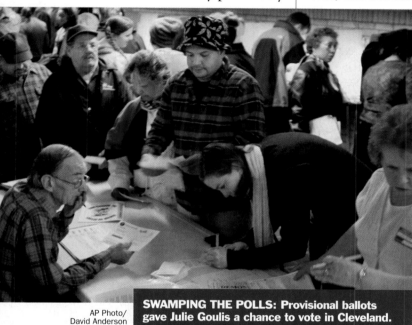

SWAMPING THE POLLS: Provisional ballots gave Julie Goulis a chance to vote in Cleveland.

met at the polls, voters have encountered a record deficit, job losses, airport shoe searches, rising bankruptcies, and bruising battles over stem-cell research and the definition of marriage. On the eve of Election Day, fully 55% of voters said the country was moving in the wrong direction. Only 49% approved of the job the president was doing, and anything below 50% is supposed to be fatal to an incumbent. A war that Bush promised would cost no more than $50 billion a year

is running at nearly three times that. His character and values were attacked by well-organized detractors throughout the campaign. And he faced an opponent with a long record of public service, decorations from his service during the Vietnam War, and a Democratic base that had never been so united.

Bush says the war on terrorism is not a clash of civilizations, but this campaign was, by his careful design. He never really pretended to have much to say to Democrats beyond I will keep you safe. He relied largely instead on inspiring those who agreed with him already, who want to protect marriage as an institution, think stem-cell research has been oversold, and believe abortion is a sin. Even Republicans who disagreed with him on one or more issues—like the civil libertarians who would like the Patriot Act changed or the fiscal conservatives who worry about the massive national debt—are still willing to side with him.

His 97% approval rate within his party surpassed even Ronald Reagan's. Bush plainly understood that his best weapon against Kerry was less what Bush did than who he was. You may disagree with me, he said at every stop, but you know where I stand.

Overall, Bush succeeded in making Kerry appear an elitist defending moderation at a time when nothing less than passion would do. In Boston at their convention, the Democrats held a somber remembrance of 9/11. A month later in New York City, the Republicans unleashed a battle cry, and the contrast was plain: the party of victims vs. the party of warriors.

For Kerry supporters, there is some consolation that Bush will have to take responsibility for finishing what he started in Iraq. For Bush supporters, there is an obligation to recognize that the intense effort of the other side was as much an expression of love of country as any pledge, hymn, or flag. For people on both sides, there is relief that the day affirmed the sustaining virtue of American democracy. However fierce the battle and however high the stakes, on Election Day citizens go to the polls, close a curtain, and cast their vote—and then go home to honor the outcome because we have only one president at a time.

REPUBLICANS EXTEND CONTROL OF CONGRESS

G.O.P. Strengthens Its Decade-Long Grip on the House, Adds Senate Seats

REPUBLICANS PICKED up seats in both chambers of Congress on Election Day, leaving Speaker Dennis Hastert (R-IL) and Majority Leader Tom DeLay (R-TX) in charge of the House and toppling Tom Daschle (D-SD) from his post as Senate Minority Leader. The key to strengthening G.O.P. control of the House lay in Texas, where four incumbent Democrats lost their seats as a result of a controversial redistricting plan backed by DeLay. This is the sixth consecutive election since 1994 in which Republicans have held a majority in the House.

Democrats had hoped to regain control of the Senate this year but wound up losing ground. They were defeated in several pivotal races, including those in Georgia, South Carolina, North Carolina, Alaska, and Florida. Despite these losses, Senate Democrats will retain enough votes to make it hard for Republicans to pass legislation without opposition. That's because it takes 60 votes to end debate on a bill.

Given the makeup of the new Congress, Republicans say they'll push for approval of measures that have been stalled—including oil exploration in the Arctic National Wildlife Refuge and limits on lawsuits.

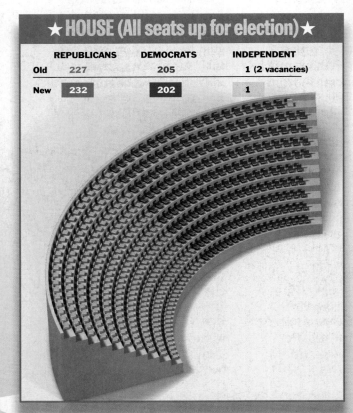

★ HOUSE (All seats up for election) ★

	REPUBLICANS	DEMOCRATS	INDEPENDENT
Old	227	205	1 (2 vacancies)
New	232	202	1

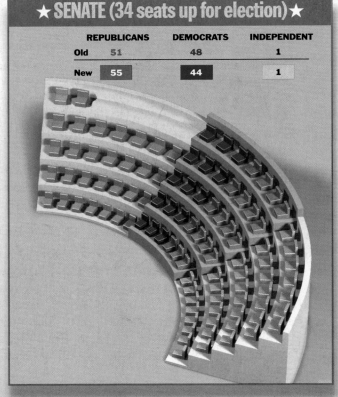

★ SENATE (34 seats up for election) ★

	REPUBLICANS	DEMOCRATS	INDEPENDENT
Old	51	48	1
New	55	44	1

Faces to watch in the 109th Congress

AP Photo/Doug Dreyer

★ SENATOR JOHN THUNE (R-SD)

The Giant Killer

Elections are not just about votes. They're also about symbols. And for Senate Republicans, minority leader Tom Daschle has long been Moby Dick. Here was a Democrat from a solidly Republican state, South Dakota, who not only couldn't be defeated but also seemed to emerge from each electoral and legislative battle bigger and more powerful. So when John Thune arrives in Washington, he will not be just another freshman senator. He will be a conquering hero—the man who fulfilled the G.O.P.'s 18-year quest to unseat Daschle.

Thune, a former congressman, ran a profoundly focused race, taking every opportunity to remind voters that Daschle's positions on gun control and abortion set him at odds with "South Dakota values." But he did not bag his big game alone. Majority leader Bill Frist broke with Senate etiquette by visiting South Dakota to campaign for Daschle's ouster. In fact, the last time a Senate leader visited his opposite's state to rail against him was in 1900.

★ SENATOR BARACK OBAMA (D-IL)

"We're All Connected"

In the past year, Barack Obama, 43, has been compared, in all seriousness, to Abraham Lincoln, Martin Luther King Jr., and Bill Clinton. Democrats debate whether he should run for President in 2012 or 2016. Following a landslide victory on Election Day, Obama became the only African American in the U.S. Senate—and just the third in the past 100 years.

AP Photo/Stephan Savoia

The turning point in Obama's career came in Boston on July 27, 2004, when he delivered one of the best speeches ever heard at a political convention. Facing thousands of Democrats, he spoke of a country not pockmarked by racism or fear—a place in which an African immigrant could marry a Midwestern white woman and their middle-class son could go to Harvard Law School. And he told the cheering crowd that "we're all connected as one people. If there is a child on the South Side of Chicago who can't read, that matters to me . . . If there's an Arab American family being rounded up without benefit of an attorney or due process, that threatens my civil liberties."

★ SENATOR MEL MARTINEZ (R-FL)

The Tough-Talking Cuban

When Cuban parents launched Operation Pedro Pan in 1960, they were trying to get their children safely out of Cuba and into the U.S. Nobody knew then that one of those children—Mel Martinez— would go on to become the first Cuban American elected to the U.S. Senate. Martinez, now 58, served as Secretary of Housing and Urban Development from 2001 to 2003 and received strong support from the White House and Florida Governor Jeb Bush.

AP Photo/Chris Omeara

★ REPRESENTATIVE ALLYSON SCHWARTZ (D-PA)

An Advocate for Children

As a state senator, Allyson Schwartz was called the "Mother of Pennsylvania Children's Health Insurance" for devising an insurance plan that many states later copied. Now she hopes to pass similar legislation on the federal level. Schwartz is one of 65 women who will serve in the House—a gain of five from the 108th Congress. Among the new faces are Melissa Bean (D-IL), who unseated Philip Crane, the longest-serving Republican in the House; and Gwen Moore (D-WI), the first African American to represent Wisconsin.

Courtesy Allyson Schwartz